THE

LIFE AND TIMES

OF

JOHN CALVIN,

THE GREAT REFORMER.

TRANSLATED FROM THE GERMAN OF

PAUL HENRY, D.D.,

MINISTER AND SEMINARY-INSPECTOR IN BERLIN.

BY

HENRY STEBBING, D.D., F.R.S.

AUTHOR OF 'HISTORY OF THE CHURCH AND REFORMATION' IN LARDNER'S CYCLOPÆDIA; HISTORY OF THE CHURCH OF CHRIST FROM THE DIET OF AUGSBURG, LIVES OF THE ITALIAN POETS, ETC

IN TWO VOLUMES.

VOL. II.

WIPF & STOCK · Eugene, Oregon

Wipf and Stock Publishers
199 W 8th Ave, Suite 3
Eugene, OR 97401

The Life and Times of John Calvin, Volume 2
The Great Reformer
By Stebbing, Henry and Henry, Paul
Copyright © 1849 by Stebbing, Henry All rights reserved.
Softcover ISBN-13: 979-8-3852-6518-3
Hardcover ISBN-13: 979-8-3852-6519-0
eBook ISBN-13: 979-8-3852-6520-6
Publication date 04/21/2026
Previously published by Whittaker & Co., 1849

This edition is a scanned facsimile of the original edition published in 1849.

CONTENTS.

PART II.—Continued.

Chapter X.

Page
State of the Church in the years 1544 and 1545 1

Chapter XI.

The German War.—League of Smalcalde.—Defeat of the Protestants.—Calvin writes against the Interim.—The Church of England.—Calvin's literary labours 19

Chapter XII.

Anabaptists.—Spiritual libertines.—The antichristianity of Geneva.—Political libertines opposed to the Refugees 41

Chapter XIII.

Fury of the libertines.—Anger and severity of Calvin.—Ameaux, Perrin, and Gruet 55

Chapter XIV.

Insults heaped on Calvin.—His resolution, inward peace, and consolation in friendship.—Viret.......................... 69

Chapter XV.

Efforts to re-establish peace.—Struggle on behalf of a Great Church Union.—Agreement of the Zurichers on the Lord's Supper.................................... 7

Chapter XVI.

Page

Union of great minds.—A plan to effect unity of doctrine and discipline by a community of spirit.—Harmony between Luther and Calvin in living faith.—Melancthon 84

PART III.

Chapter I.

Introductory remarks.—Characteristics of Calvin 103

Chapter II.

The outward condition of the Church, and Calvin's circumstances at Geneva in the years 1550, 1551, 1552.—His work 'De Scandalis.'—Letters to Cranmer and Melancthon 108

Chapter III.

The first great controversy.—The dispute respecting Predestination.—Bolsec 128

Chapter IV.

Calvin's second great controversy, on the Trinity, 1553.—Dispute with Servetus.—Its consequences 158

Chapter V.

Servetus condemned to death.—His last hours in prison.—His execution.—An inquiry into the circumstances attending it.—Review of his doctrines 214

Chapter VI.

Other teachers of false doctrine respecting the Trinity.—Matthæus Gribaldi.—Blandrata.—Gentilis—his system and history 263

Chapter VII.

Page

Calvin's controversy with Westphal and Hesshus on the doctrine of the Sacrament.—Rise and progress of the dispute.—Parties engaged.—Results 274

Chapter VIII.

Final struggle against the libertines.—Berthelier.—Triumph of discipline.—Failure of Calvin's enemies.—Educational plans .. 306

Chapter IX.

Calvin's activity.—His influence in England and Scotland.—John Knox.—Correspondence with the English exiles in Frankfort .. 326

Chapter X.

Calvin's relation to the Northern churches.—His influence in Poland.—Correspondence with King Sigismund and with the Polish nobles 340

Chapter XI.

Influence of Calvin in France.—Rapid development of the Reformation in the fire of persecution.—Martyrs in the reign of Henry II. at Lyons, Chambery, and other places.—Calvin's distress.—He exhorts the German princes to interfere.—Beginning of the Church in Paris.—Emigration of the Reformed to America.—Heroic courage of the Confessors.—Anne du Bourg.—Sketch of events preceding the Colloquy of Poissy.—Belief and discipline of the French Church.—Unity of the Church under Calvin's influence.—His success at its highest point.—Animating address to all the great personages in France belonging to the Evangelical party 353

Chapter XII.

Beza at the Colloquy of Poissy, 1561.—His account to Calvin.—Occurrences September 9, 1561.—The Reformed Church recognized by the Edict of January 1562 380

CHAPTER XIII.

Page
First religious war.—The Peace.—1562–1563................ 396

CHAPTER XIV.

Calvin's latest controversies.—The false reports published by his enemies.—Struggle against Balduin 410

CHAPTER XV.

Calvin takes leave of the world.—Review of the close of his life. —His outward circumstances and inward state.—His last labours.—Farewell address to the Ministers and to the council. —General mourning.—Beza's character of Calvin.......... 419

APPENDIX 437

INDEX 445

PART II.—(CONTINUED.)

LIFE AND TIMES OF CALVIN.

PART II.—Continued.

CHAPTER X.

STATE OF THE CHURCH IN THE YEARS 1544 AND 1545.

THE beginning of a letter from Calvin to Bullinger contains a notice of the progress of the Gospel in France. He speaks of the descendants of the Waldenses in Provence and Piedmont: "Their piety and the innocence of their lives is such, that their salvation must be precious in the eyes of every believer. Three years ago they presented a copy of their confession to the parliament of Aix: it is pure and simple, and such a one as we ourselves should have delivered. Do not believe that it was a zeal, fair in appearance, but soon to vanish. They have been again and again summoned before the tribunal; have endured the trial with unflinching firmness, and are still exposed to the most cruel persecutions. The king himself proposes to examine and judge their cause. Two commissaries have received command to inquire, both publicly and secretly, into their doctrine and manners. The brethren have no fear of these officers, for they have ever so conducted themselves, that even their enemies bear testimony to their integrity. Now bishops, prefects, and even the parliament, are strenuously labouring to hinder the fulfilment of the king's intentions; and if the old rule be followed, they will rouse up all the lions and wolves they can to rage against them. But even if he be obeyed, they are not freed from danger. They have already introduced the pure worship of God into three cities, and into several villages, and have even established a church purified from all papistical corruption. In that church they celebrate baptism and the Lord's Supper according to our usage.

"Now, the greater the danger on all sides, the more must we strive to be ready to afford help, especially since they exhibit so noble an example of firmness; and we should deserve, did we forsake them, to be overwhelmed with shame. Add to this, that the present matter does not concern them alone, for either the way will be opened by their persecution to the rage of the wicked against the churches, in all parts of the kingdom, or the Gospel will by this means be everywhere diffused. What remains therefore for us but to employ all our strength, lest our pious brethren should perish through our sloth, and the door be long closed to Christ? I have desired to say this to you, in order that, should they seek refuge with you, your government might be prepared to render them assistance. One of two things must be done for them; that is, we must either induce the king to exercise his promised good-will towards them, or soften his anger, should it have been excited to their prejudice."

Thus it appears that the persecution which broke out in the following year already threatened the unfortunate Waldenses. We find Calvin busily occupied at Geneva, in 1545, in receiving the sufferers, and affording them every possible kind of help.

Another storm also was now brooding over the church in Germany. Charles had commenced in 1542 an expedition against France; but this was concluded in 1544 by the peace of Crespy, and in a manner very advantageous to the French. This course was adopted by the emperor, that he might employ his whole activity against the league of Smalcalde. It had been determined by the diet at Speier, that both parties should resolve on certain points of reformation. In the expectation of carrying this into effect, the states assembled in 1545 at Worms. The Wittenberg reformation, as the plan offered by the protestants was called, had been sketched by Melancthon with the greatest moderation. Paul III. opened the council in opposition to these proceedings, and in order to prevent the emperor from interfering with religious affairs: this constrained Charles to support the interests of the reformers.

During the hostilities in France and the disturbances in Germany, the Gospel continued to advance; and Beza shows how the power of faith, exhibited by many Christians in their martyrdom, gave occasion to the further triumphs of the Holy Spirit. It was just now that the violent persecution of the innocent Waldenses was commenced, at the instigation of the cardinal Tournon, and a certain Menyer d'Opede, governor of Provence. They pretended to the king of France, that they would send the unfortunate people to Marseilles, and convert the country into a Swiss canton. The ardent and volatile Francis believed this statement, and the accused were surrendered as a prey to their persecutors, who assailed them with inconceivable cruelty, and even ordered that the little children should be left to die of hunger*. Those who escaped the persecution, and fled to the mountains, obtained at their earnest entreaty a safe-conduct into Germany. A part of these afterwards returned into their valleys, where, after the endurance of many persecutions, their descendants are still existing.

Beza has given in his history of the reformation in France, a transcript of the 'Instruction' which Henry II. issued, at the request of his dying father, who repented of the course which he had pursued, against the persecutors of the Waldenses. We learn from this instrument, and from the acknowledgment of the persecutors themselves, the treacherous and barbarous character of the persecution. Twenty-two villages were reported as burnt, and their inhabitants were murdered without even the form of a trial. Calvin, most deeply afflicted at the sufferings of these unfortunate people, to whom he had formerly sent a minister for their instruction in pure doctrine, so exerted himself on their behalf, that 4000 Waldenses found support in Geneva. He instituted collections for them†. The council allowed them to be employed on the public works, and opened a way for them through Switzerland. In the year 1554 those who still remained in Geneva obtained grants of land. Calvin

* "Les mamelles coupées à plusieurs femmes, auprès desquelles mortes furent vus mourans de faim les petits enfans, ayant fait crier le dit Opede sur peine de la hard, qu'on ne donnât vivres ne soulagement quelconque à aucun d'iceux. Tout fut pillé, brulé, saccagé, et ne furent sauvés que ceux, que Poulin choisit pour ses galères. Les femmes rassemblées et brulées dans une grange; 800 personnes tuées dans le temple." Leger in his account of his country says, that the Eternal, who destined it to be the theatre of his miracles and the asylum of his ark, had naturally and wonderfully fortified it. (T. i. p. 9.)

† Reg. du 8 Juin 1545.—"Collection for the poor, made at the request of Calvin, and which produced 76 florins."

turned especially to the Swiss cantons and the German princes, and pressed them to intercede strongly with France in behalf of the Waldenses. Thus he wrote to Schaffhausen and to Bullinger, July 24, 1545, desiring that an embassy might be sent to the king:—"You must assail their base opponents, and those who are excited against them by false reports. The greater number of these unhappy people are perishing in chains, others are dispersed by flight. None dare venture even to indulge the wish of ever again seeing their families. Continual attacks are made, and that with the knowledge of the king, upon the lordship of Avignon. Prisoners are carried from all sides to Paris, and if some effort be not made to resist these proceedings, you will soon hear that a vast conflagration is raging through the whole kingdom, and which the times will leave no chance of extinguishing. Use all your influence therefore to promote the sending of a respectable embassy, which may earnestly entreat the king to free the prisoners, to restore their goods to those who have fled, and to institute a fair inquiry into the faith and manners of these pious sufferers."

Notwithstanding Calvin's active and zealous exertions, the embassy, if we may judge from a letter to Viret, dated August 17, 1545, seems not to have been sent. In September he despatched two Waldenses to Viret, and wrote, "You will see that Satan is using every means to turn the hearts of all against them; to prevent their receiving any help, and to exasperate the feelings of the king and his courtiers, fierce as they already are, still more to their prejudice. Even the Swiss are greatly distressing me by supposing that I am bringing upon them the anger of the French monarch. But nothing can appear sufficiently important in our eyes to turn us from a duty, which is more than ever indispensable."

It appears that Viret, during these troubles, had undertaken a journey, the means for which had been provided by Geneva. In the following year Calvin encouraged Farel and Viret to travel to Worms, to make exertions in behalf of the sufferers in France:—"It is your business to fulfil my promise, even though it might be given improvidently. This circumstance itself will afford you help, you not being the originators of the affair." His whole life, in fact, was marked by the most diligent endeavours to suppress, by the interference of Germany and Switzerland, which had then a certain degree of political importance, the persecutions in France.

We learn from a letter addressed to Calvin by Myconius*, some of the darkest features of that afflicting season. The writer thanks him for his letter to Charles V., and says of the emperor:—"He is now persecuting the saints in Belgium. Queen Mary, the emperor's sister, has not been able to defend even her own chaplain. This is the case in numberless other instances, and the emperor hopes by these means to obtain his reconciliation with the offended pope. Why does he not much rather endeavour to procure peace with God, whose hand lies now so heavy upon him, weighing him down with grievous sicknesses? I hear from the council that it is suspended. The diet is not proceeding. Up to the present time the bishop of Augsburg, lately made a cardinal, is the only prelate at Worms, and he has been playing a game, which is quite the mode in little cities, and has not wholly gone out of fashion even in Rome. Men in masks force themselves into the houses of the citizens, eat, drink, play, dance, and commit all sorts of follies and debaucheries, which may seem gay and jovial enough, but greatly scandalize the masters of families, though there are none, as I hear, who dare venture to oppose them. This is a worthy preparation, as well for the diet as for the synod! O let us pray that God may arise to uphold his cause and declare his righteousness! The offences of the great continually increase, so that the day of God's wrath seems nearer than men believe. The Lord grant that we may meet Him with joy."

But what was most important for Calvin and Geneva at this period, was the deep impression which evangelical truth was then making in France. This is, we lament to say, one of the most unnoticed portions of church history, which only delights in repeating the great events of an age, instead of exhibiting for admiration the work of the Holy Ghost on the souls which shone like stars in this night of gloom. The history of the martyrs in France has been till now almost totally neglected.

The following scenes afford a fitting contrast to the levity of which Myconius speaks, and to the vanities of the council. The year 1546, so pregnant with events, produced a fearful persecution of the church of Meaux. It had been already once dispersed in the year 1523; but the seed of the divine Word soon after took still deeper root there, so that the Lutherans of Meaux were spoken of proverbially in France. They formed a complete church, according to the model of that which Calvin

* March 1545. Ep. 61.

had established at Strasburg. Having fasted and prayed, they chose for their minister Pierre Leclerc, a wool-comber by trade, but who was deeply versed in the holy Scriptures. His preaching was so blessed, that in a short time between 300 and 400 believers assembled to hear him. On the 3rd of September 1546, St. Mary's day, sixty persons were taken prisoners in the house where he preached, and who, far from attempting to defend themselves, submitted quietly to be bound, praising God for the honour. The Lutherans who were outside immediately joined them in singing the seventy-ninth psalm. Those who were seized (nineteen women and forty-one men) had been selected from the rest, because at the time they were celebrating the Lord's Supper. Having been thrust into wagons, prepared for the purpose, they were conveyed in the most unmerciful manner to Paris. Several of them arrived with broken limbs, but this did not protect them against the infliction of the rack. Fourteen, whose names have been preserved in the history of the church, were condemned to unusual tortures, and afterwards to be publicly burnt. The house in which they had been accustomed to assemble was pulled to the ground, and a chapel built on the spot, in which every Sunday mass was to be performed. All the expenses attending this were furnished by the confiscated property of the sufferers.

Some of the prisoners had been placed in a monastery, that an attempt might be made to convert them. As this experiment did not succeed, they were sent back to Meaux, attended by two Sorbonnists, who continued to press their conversion while seeking their blood. The sentence of death pronounced upon them was executed October 7, in the place before their meeting-house, and in the following manner. The tongue of one of them being torn out, he was still heard to murmur, "The name of God be praised." The several martyrs were then dragged up, that they might be burnt at the fourteen stakes, placed in a circle. Owing to this position of the stakes, they were able to see and encourage each other. This they did; praising God with a loud voice to their last breath, although their words were often interrupted by the priests, who shouted forth like madmen their hymns, "O salutaris hostia," and "Salve Regina." On the following day, in order to complete the triumph, the catholic priest proceeded under a golden canopy to the spot, where the fire was still burning, and preached to the people. Among other things, he said, that "it was necessary for the salvation of souls to believe that the fourteen heretics were now in hell; that if an angel from heaven should say otherwise, he must be rejected; and that God would no longer be God if He did not eternally damn them." This seemed incredible even to the catholics themselves, who had known the pure and simple conversation of the martyrs; and instead of the seed of the Gospel being destroyed by this rage and cruelty, other churches, as Beza relates, were built of the stones of the ruined temple, and there is even to the present day a reformed community at Meaux; that city, in which, at a later period, under Louis XIV., the zealous Bossuet reposed. Calvin said to Farel (1546), "The parliament of Paris continues, I hear, a fiery war with Christ. Certain it is, that a vast number of believers, far and wide, are lying in bonds. Sardanapalus in the meanwhile is dreaming of victory in the midst of his courtesans. May the Lord look down upon his church!"

The new life was now beginning to diffuse itself abroad, when Francis I., oppressed by political cares and terrors, died at Rambouillet in 1547. He has been dignified by some with the title of Great, but Beza says,—"This surname had been much more to his praise, if it could have been truly said of him, that he was as great a warrior and patron of letters as he was a determined adversary to the interests of religion." His only son, Henry II., an enemy to the Gospel and a weak prince, easily allowed himself to be deceived, and became a cruel persecutor. His whole reign exhibits a succession of crimes, and his untimely death was regarded in France as a divine judgement*.

A multitude of exiles, driven from their homes by the persecution, flocked out of various lands, but especially from France, to Geneva. Humanity, religious fellowship, and love for his countrymen, induced Calvin to make the most strenuous exertions to gather them together in that city, and to obtain their support in the establishment of his principles. A great number of letters, in his own handwriting, may be appealed to as showing how anxiously he advised them to leave their country. Many respectable families however had not the resolution to follow his advice. The storm of persecution had led them to adopt the erroneous notion, that they might serve God in secret, while outwardly they appeared to adhere to the old errors. But the reformer was of too resolute a mind to yield in a

* Calvin refers to this subject in a letter to Farel (MS. Gen.), July 19, 1549, and in one to Bullinger, August 15, 1549 (MS. Tig.).

matter like this. The sincerity of his profession would not allow a violation of truth, and the duty of making a good confession of his faith, and of annihilating every temptation to hypocrisy, induced him to write at this period his two useful little works against the Nicodemites.

Calvin's ideas, as expressed in these essays, are regarded as too violent, and he has been accused of speaking with severity in a case in which he himself was free from danger. The writings referred to are now chiefly valuable in an historical point of view, but at the time when they were produced they had a real practical worth, being well-calculated to strengthen timid minds against the terrors of martyrdom, and thus to do good, not only in France, but also in Switzerland and Germany. In these moments of approaching danger, when Luther was already advanced in life, Calvin, his junior, laboured with determined energy. We can now form no conception of the heroism of that Waldensian in Calabria, who, being allowed to choose between kissing the cross and being thrown headlong from a lofty tower, immediately preferred the latter. But the triumph of evangelical truth then depended upon this devoted courage. Hypocrisy, at such a time, would have bowed the church to the dust. "Dissimulation," says Calvin, "makes a man an offender against himself, by hiding what is in his own heart. Hypocrisy however is still worse, for it consists in the endeavour to give us that in appearance of which we are destitute in reality. God is not satisfied with the heart. When Peter assails the vice of uncleanness, he says, 'Are ye not the members of Christ?' &c."

He next examines all the various ceremonies of the catholic church, and shows how we defile ourselves, as protestants, when we take any part in their performance. I will here quote only what he says respecting the funeral service, the Calvinistic simplicity having now almost totally disappeared. "We who have embraced the pure doctrine of the Gospel, all know well enough that the services for the dead, and funeral solemnities generally, are abominations, for they are founded in falsehood, are contrary to Scripture, and do dishonour to the meritorious sufferings and death of our Lord Jesus Christ." Calvin means by this, that Christ having died for souls, it is unlawful to pray for their deliverance from purgatory, for the dead must either have believed or not, and this alone will have determined their fate. He speaks even still more severely against any apparent conformity to the catholic worship, and confutes the argument brought from the example of Naaman, permitted by the prophet Elisha to enter the heathen temple, and bow himself, with the king. The instance of St. Paul, who retained some Jewish customs*, is explained in a similar manner; and he presses upon his readers the sublime example of the martyrdom of the seven brothers, in the time of the Maccabees. But having thus condemned a carnal caution, he pleads with mildness for the weak:—"I protest before God, that, so far am I from lightly blaming my poor brethren who are in such bonds, I would far rather, out of mere pity and mercy, find arguments by which to excuse them. After all I have said on the subject, I sigh over them, and pray God to comfort them. It is far from me to condemn them. God knows that the opinion which I entertain of many in France is, that they are holier in life, and more perfect than I am. I acknowledge, that it is a greater virtue in them to walk in the fear of God, in the midst of such an abyss, than it is for me, who have not so many trials to endure; and that if they fall, I ought to regard it as more deserving of excuse, than would be the case were I to fall. So far also am I from not considering them as brothers, that I praise them in all other respects before God and man, and hold them as more deserving than myself to have a place in the church." In conclusion, he imparts noble counsel and consolation to the weak. So much love and tenderness is expressed in this address, that none of his writings are better calculated to confute the accusation which has been brought against him of hardness or want of feeling.

The following little work, 'His Apology to the Nicodemites,' is written in a stronger tone: this was because he had learnt that people were not satisfied with the former. He here characterises, with considerable humour, the various classes of Nicodemites existing in those times: first were those who imperfectly explained the Gospel, according to human taste; and next those who were glad to seize upon the Gospel as a means of making themselves agreeable in the sight of the ladies, and furnishing amusing topics for conversation; the only drawback to this being, that it would not allow them to live after their own taste.

In the same line with the persons last-mentioned, were the court favourites and the ladies, who had no other wish but that homage should be paid them; and hence it was not to be won-

* Acts xviii. 18–24.

dered at if all such were against him, their common watchword being, "Do not speak to us of Calvin—he is a monster."

There were also the Nicodemites, who understood Christianity philosophically, and the merchants, and other little people, who were happy enough in their homes, and did not wish to be disturbed by the Gospel. He continues with great earnestness:—"If the believers in the primitive church had acted thus, where now would the church have been? The whole theology of the old martyrs consisted in the knowledge of one God, whom we are bound to worship, and in whom alone we must place our trust; and in that of Jesus Christ, beside whom there is no Saviour. Nor had they any such lofty acquaintance with these things, that they would have been able to deduce them, in order, from each other. They held them in all simplicity, but they rushed with rejoicing hearts into the fire to bear testimony to the truth of these doctrines. Nay, even the women readily committed their children to the flames. We, on the other hand,—we, who are such great doctors, scarcely know what is meant by bearing witness to the truth."

This is followed by a defence of his own conduct. He had been accused of giving people advice at a distance, when it would have been better for him to have furnished them with an example in his own person. This was, in fact, a very delicate point. "If Calvin be so very brave," it was said, "why does he not come here, that we may see how he would conduct himself?"

He expresses his indignant feeling against the people who thus vilified him, in a very characteristic passage:—"Because they cannot endure that any one should expose their leprosy, they have recourse to the wretched subterfuge of saying, that their inward affection is towards God; this is as much as to say, that they make a division between God and the devil, and give their soul to the one and their body to the other. Will they however satisfy, in this manner, Him who says, 'To him all knees shall bow,' &c.? It is a miserable, unhappy attempt at escape, to make ourselves blind in order not to see our misfortune. I know not with whom we can better compare them than with some cleaner of sewers, who, having been so long employed in the filth that he has lost all sense of the horrible odour, ridicules those who hold their noses at the stench. And to carry out the comparison: as the scavenger arms himself by strong salves and onions against the poisonous effluvia, and resists one evil smell by another, so these people, that they may not suffer through the odour of their idolatry, fill themselves with wicked excuses, like stinking spices, in such a manner that they may hinder any other impression." This species of irony will be considered as the more pointed, when it is recollected, that it was intended for the multitude in Paris, and for the court, debased by a miserable habit of flattery.

Melancthon, Martin Bucer, and Peter Martyr, also gave their opinion on the same question: they all agreed with Calvin. The latter has further expressed his sentiments on the subject in two letters, written in 1546; and in four sermons preached in 1552. An epistle was addressed to Calvin by the Zurichers in 1549, and from this we learn that the matter had been long under their consideration. Even from France Calvin received communications, calling upon him to obtain Luther's counsel on the subject.

The letter which Calvin wrote to Luther, in conformity with this desire, is interesting as the only one which he addressed to the German reformer. His great reverence for him is clearly shown by this document. He proceeded very cautiously while speaking with the venerable father of the church, who died the next year; and he felt while approaching him almost as a young beginner, scarcely supposing that, in the following century, the common consent of mankind would place him by his side. Zwingli would not have written such a letter to Luther*.

"My honoured father!†—Being assured that many of my fellow-countrymen in France, having turned from the darkness of popery to the pure light of the Gospel, have, notwithstanding, been backward to change their open profession, and therefore continue to pollute themselves with the horrors of popery, as if they had no knowledge of pure doctrine,—being informed of this, I could not refrain from assailing such sloth and indifference with the severity which I think they deserve. For what kind of faith is that which remains buried in the recesses of the soul, and never declares itself by an open confession? What

* MS. Tig.

† Another letter written by Calvin at this time, to some unknown person, expresses his feelings respecting the difficulty of the present design (Ep. 392. Ed. Amst. p. 235). He mentions his own narrow circumstances, the difficulty of meeting the calls upon him even in good times, and the expense attending borrowing money of the merchants or others. It was not the best time, he added, to ask counsel of Luther, whose mind was but just beginning to enjoy repose after his long struggle.

kind of witness is that which shrinks concealed behind a hypocritical respect for catholic idolatry? But I will not here discuss this matter, of which I have treated in two little writings, from which you may easily learn, if you be pleased to look over them, what my opinion is, and upon what grounds it rests. Some of our brethren, aroused by reading these papers, have awaked from the slumber in which they were sunk, and begun to consider what it is their duty to do. But since it is a hard thing either to exercise such self-denial as to expose one's life to danger, or to bring upon ourselves the hatred of the whole world, through opposition to its customs and opinions, and to suffer the loss of country and property by a voluntary exile, so it is that many have found themselves unable to persevere in their resolution. They suggest however other excuses for their conduct, and it is plain that they are only anxious to find a pretext for yielding. While they thus vacillate to and fro, they seem desirous of learning your opinion, which, honouring it as they ought to do, will have great weight with them. They have therefore entreated me to despatch a trusty messenger to inquire your sentiments on the subject. This I have been unwilling to refuse, assured as I am that it is of importance to their best interests to find themselves supported by your judgement, and delivered from their present state of uncertainty; and still further, feeling as I do that the same help will be of great use to myself.

"I therefore beseech you by Christ, my very honoured father in the Lord, out of regard for them and for me, to endure the trouble of reading, in the first place, this letter which is written to you in their name, and my own two little books. This you may do for pass-time, in your leisure hours, or may commission some one to do it for you, and then make you acquainted with the principal points. In the second place, I would beg you to state to us, in few words, your opinion on the subject. It is against my will that I thus disturb you, occupied as you are with so many important and such various affairs; but I am convinced that, according to your wonted kindness, you will pardon me, while I only yield to necessity in laying before you this request. Would to God that I could hasten to you, were it to enjoy but a few hours of your conversation! Much should I prefer it, and far more useful would it be to speak with you personally, not only on this, but on many other affairs. I hope, however, that that which is not allowed us on earth, will soon be granted us in the kingdom of heaven. Farewell, very renowned man, and faithful servant of Jesus Christ, and my, at all times, revered father! May the Lord continue to guide you by his Spirit to the end, for the common good of his church."—Jan. 20, 1545.

Calvin sent with his letter to Luther another to Melancthon*, and it is easy to see that he feared the latter might accuse him of too great severity in his second book against the Nicodemites. This letter is also remarkable as exhibiting Calvin's diligent endeavour to establish a union of opinion with Melancthon, probably in reference to the last statement of the latter on election. On the doctrine of the Lord's Supper they had already long agreed.

Melancthon's answer, which has, perhaps, never been printed till now, affords a striking view of his position at that period. We see how he stood in respect to Luther, seeking peace and finding none; what he thought of his life, how oppressed he felt, and yet full of hope. Much is contained in few words. He had not the courage to lay Calvin's letter before Luther, but he sent Calvin his opinion, as found in the works of the Genevese reformer :—

"To the very renowned doctor John Calvin, distinguished by learning and virtue, minister of the church at Geneva, his pious and true and very dear friend, Melancthon, sends greeting. Thankful should I be, my beloved Calvin, to receive from you, on my own account, some good advice. The strife from which at an earlier period I escaped, is now increasing here. Having ever considered that one must strive to uphold the peace of the church in these wild and terrible lands, and having always expressed myself accordingly in the most temperate language, something more difficult is now demanded of me. Therefore I beseech you to commend me to God in your pious prayers. I have not given your letter to doctor Martin: he looks at things with suspicion, and does not like to have his sentiments on such questions as you ask, published abroad. I have answered them as well as I could, and do not set my judgement higher than your own, or that of other pious men. It is a satisfaction for me to know that I have lived without seeking to indulge in theological disputes, but that I have laboured, not unprofitably, to disentangle and explain many difficult subjects. Notwithstanding this, I now expect banishment and other sorrows. Fare-

* Ep. 60. ed. Amst. p. 31.

well.—The day when, 3846 years ago, Noah entered the ark, and God intended to show us, by his example, that He would never forsake his church, however it might be tossed about on the stormy waves of the world*."

Luther's angry feeling, as alluded to in the above letter, was connected with the dispute between him and the reformers of Zurich. This will lead us to speak of the part taken by Calvin in the sacramentarian controversy, and of the earnest endeavour which he made to restore peace. We must first look back to the origin of those unhappy circumstances which occasioned the long and distressing schism †.

The Swiss had adopted in 1538 the Wittenberg confession, and although even in the time of peace opinions were not altered, people were thoroughly weary of dispute. This was especially proved by the cold silence preserved, when Luther, a few years before his death, began to renew the controversy, and, left by his friends, remained alone in the arena. He had already, in 1543, written to Froschauer, saying, that neither he nor any church of Christ could have communion with the Swiss. Melancthon sought in vain to tranquillize him. In 1544 Luther published new libels, pouring forth his gall in his 'Annotations on Genesis,' and setting forth his last confession on the subject of the Lord's Supper, in which Zwingli and Œcolampadius, with their followers, were called heretics and reprobates. The cause of his wrath, according to Hospinian, who follows Pezel, may be traced to Zwingli's latest production, his 'Exposition of the Christian Faith,' edited and published by Bullinger in 1536 ‡. This work seemed to Luther so contrary to its author's statement at Marburg, that he was convinced that Zwingli must have acted towards them with false heart and mouth. Other reasons for his anger have been found in the injurious reports, that he was no longer esteemed at Zurich; and in the circumstance that a new German translation of the Bible, undertaken by Leo Juda and other reformers, was published in 1543; while, on the other hand, Schwenkfeld accused him of a secret understanding with the Helvetian church, because he had suffered the elevation of the bread to be discontinued. So again, Amsdorf and others in Wittenberg occasioned him much vexation; Melancthon himself not concealing his favourable feelings towards the Swiss.

* Melancthon's opinion is added to Calvin's Excus. ad Nicodemitas.

† Schrockh, Reformationsgeschichte, t. i. p. 363–420.

‡ Hess. Leben Bullingers, t. i. p. 432.

Now, while the traces of advancing age were beginning to appear, he allowed the following words to escape him:—"Let Zwingli not only speak as he will against the sacraments, but let him be a heathen altogether, and place the impious pagans side by side with Christ in the kingdom of heaven. But where then were Christianity and the sacraments? Therefore is all hope gone; nor ought any more prayers to be offered up for those who are soul-consumers and murderers." At the same time it is evident from all this, that the sentiments which may be ascribed to his own personal feelings ought not to be regarded as possessing a dogmatic value, or as justifying the separation of his church from the reformed.

Melancthon, deeply afflicted at this breach, wrote to Bullinger,—"That he would receive a letter from Luther, according to which all hope of reconciliation must be given up; that he himself would retreat quietly into his own soul, and there endeavour to find that freedom of conscience which he could not enjoy under the guardianship of Luther."

The Swiss, though warned on many sides, replied, by Bullinger, in a German and Latin writing, entitled, "A genuine statement of the servants of the church at Zurich, as to what they teach; especially concerning the Lord's Supper, in answer to the slanders, condemnation and jests of Doctor Martin Luther." People were far from satisfied with this production. Calvin said in a letter to Melancthon, "One must write better, or not at all: the work is meagre and puerile*."

Luther refrained from saying anything publicly in answer to this last attack of the Swiss; but he continued to the end hostile to the Zwinglians. After his death, his letter to the provost Jacob, dated January 17, 1546, became commonly known, and in this he says, "Blessed is the man who hath not walked in the counsel of the Sacramentarians; nor stood in the way of the Zwinglians; nor sat in the seat of the Zurichers." He also alludes to the controversy in his work against the theologians of Louvain.

Many of Calvin's writings show how, mindful of his high calling, he sought at this time to quiet men's minds, while he saw with a prophetic glance the approaching schism†. Thus in a

* Hess. Leben Bullingers, t. i. p. 455. Ep. 63. ed. Amst. p. 33.

† He expressed his feelings on this subject in a letter to Farel, dated October 10, 1544, MS. Gen.—"We must now, before all things, pray to the Lord, who alone can avert this evil, which will soon blaze forth like a burning brand. We may now look for the end."

letter to Bullinger, dated November 25, 1544, he adjured him to treat the great man, meaning Luther, with respect:—"I hear," he says, "that Luther assails not only you, but all of us, with horrible abuse. Now I can scarcely ask you to be silent, since it is not right to allow ourselves to be so undeservedly abused, without attempting some defence. It is difficult moreover to believe that such forbearance could do any good. I wish however that the following may be clearly understood:—in the first place, how great a man Luther is; by what extraordinary gifts he is distinguished; and with what energy of soul, with what perseverance, with what ability and success he has continued up to the present day to overthrow the kingdom of antichrist, and to extend at the same time the doctrine of salvation. I have already often said, that were he to call me a devil, I should still continue to venerate him as a chosen servant of God, uniting with extraordinary virtues some great failings. Would to heaven that he had striven more to subdue those tempests of feeling which he has so continually allowed to break forth! Would that he had only employed that violence, so natural to him, against the enemies of the truth, and not against the servants of God! Would that he had exercised more care to discover his own defects! Unhappily there was too great a crowd of flatterers about him, who added still more to the self-confidence peculiar to his nature. It is even our duty to view his failings in such a light, that we may the more properly estimate his extraordinary gifts. I beg you therefore to bear in mind, that we have to do with one of the first servants of Christ; with one to whom we all owe much. I would also have you consider, that you could not possibly gain any advantage by entering into a struggle with him. You would only, by such a course, afford pleasure to the enemy, who would delight not so much in our defeat as in that of the Gospel. People will everywhere willingly believe what is said, when we vilify and condemn each other. You must consider this, rather than what Luther may have deserved on account of his violence; lest that should happen to us of which Paul speaks, namely, that while we bite and devour one another, all may go to the ground. Nay, even should he challenge us to the contest, we must rather turn away than hazard by our twofold fall the injury of the church."

Calvin also comforted Melancthon, who, in the latter years of Luther's life, found himself in a very painful position. Not agreeing with Luther on the subject of the spiritual presence of

Christ in the Lord's Supper, he had entered fully into Calvin's purer views.

The statements of the latter on Luther's great power and influence are also worthy of remark, in connection with the question of discipline*. Shortly before his last journey to Eisleben Luther spoke to Melancthon in a conciliatory tone. This statement is made by Haller, provost of Zurich, in his continuation of the Bullinger Chronicle, but without reference to his authority.

Luther, weary of life and conflict, left the arena at the moment when the approach of a storm was evident. Calvin was then thirty-six years of age, armed for the strife and not fearing it. It is interesting at the present day, when the churches are united, and after we have been so long accustomed to think only of Luther at Wittenberg, to meditate by his grave on Calvin also, and on the united consequences of their labours. The relation existing between these two witnesses of the Lord is seen in the common and the general; what was opposite in them consisted in their appearance; the work of each had its own proper limits; the twofold spirit was still the same, and is one to us: more of living energy was given on this side, more depth of thought on the other. The one sought to clear catholicism of what was antichristian; the other went further, penetrated critically into the Gospel, rejected what did not closely agree with it, and completed the reformation. We may conclude from the contrast in their habits of thought, and accustomed as they were to execute their will with determined resolution, that they could not easily have lived near each other. But as John, Paul and James treated of the same truth, only from various points of view, so did Luther and Calvin believe altogether but the same. Hence, though they never saw each other, they never felt as strangers, but entertained a mutual respect, while each expressed his belief according to his particular character. These men, with some few others, were the greatest of their kind, and humanity owes to them its highest blessings. With the heroism of self-devotion, and continuing the conflict which they began, in the name of God, to their latest breath, they persevered, whatever their individual imperfections, in proclaiming the great truth, that one only is holy, that is the Lord. It is right that Luther's grave should be left without any inscription. All words would have been tame; just as

* Epis. lxiii. Ed. Amst. p. 33, of the year 1545.

it would have been impossible to find a fitting inscription for the tombs of the apostles. While however the entire people of Germany thus honour him by their silence, the words of the other evangelical party are not to be passed over, and might well adorn his chamber in the Augustine monastery.

Calvin says of him:—"We sincerely testify that we regard him as a noble apostle of Christ, by whose labour and ministry the purity of the Gospel has been restored in our times*." Again:—"If any one will carefully consider what was the state of things at the period when Luther arose, he will see that he had to contend with almost all the difficulties which were encountered by the apostles. In one respect indeed his condition was worse and harder than theirs. There was no kingdom, no principality, against which they had to declare war; whereas Luther could not go forth, except by the ruin and destruction of that empire, which was not only the most powerful of all, but regarded all the rest as obnoxious to itself†." Similar sentiments are expressed, we have seen, in the epistle already quoted.

But if we desire to adduce the most honourable testimony to Luther, it is that which the noble, virtuous Zwingli delivers respecting him‡. "Luther," he says, "is in my opinion an admirable soldier of God. He has examined Scripture with as great earnestness as any one has done within the last thousand years. I consider it as deserving not the slightest attention, if the papists should abuse both him and me as heretics. No one can be compared to him for the manly, unflinching courage with which he has assailed the pope of Rome. As long as the papacy has endured, all others have been blameless. What the eternal, unchangeable Word of God contains, that he bears richly forth, and shows the heavenly treasure to poor, wandering Christians, neither caring for what the enemies of God may do against it, nor trembling at their fierce looks or threats. I have designedly read him but little; but what I have read, insofar as it respects the doctrines, meaning and sense of Scripture, is commonly so well considered and grounded, that it is not possible that any one should mistake it. He yields in some things too much to the weak and foolish, and in this I do not agree with him. But Luther preaches Christ. He does it as I do it, although, God be praised, a countless world of people have been converted by

* T. viii. p. 123. † T. viii. p. 119.

‡ Nüscheler's Lebensgeschichte Zwingli's, p. 159.

him more than by me and others, whose limits, however, whether great or small, are divinely appointed*."

CHAPTER XI.

THE GERMAN WAR.—LEAGUE OF SMALCALDE.—DEFEAT OF THE PROTESTANTS.—CALVIN WRITES AGAINST THE INTERIM.—THE CHURCH OF ENGLAND.—CALVIN'S LITERARY LABOURS.

Two other combatants left the arena soon after Luther; that is, Francis I. and Henry VIII. of England. The circumstances of society had received on all sides an extraordinary impulse, as if the spirit of the world were challenging the spirit of God to the fight, for the purpose of deciding their quarrel in open conflict. Whilst the council of Trent was treating things useless and trifling as important, and things most important with levity, still pretending that its object was the peace of the whole church, Charles had already conceived the notion of suppressing the league of Smalcalde by force of arms. Already, in 1546, was the little state of Geneva, lying among the Alps, on the borders of Germany, France and Italy, greatly agitated. It was expected that the emperor would pass through Geneva on his way from Italy. An instant resolution was taken to arm. The whole of Switzerland offered supplies of troops. Bern alone was ready with 2000 men. But such was the feeling then existing in Geneva, that, dreading the loss of its independence, the citizens rejected the offer; and the little state, with a population of only 20,000 souls, prepared itself singly for the struggle. Calvin approved of this, and said in a letter to Farel,—"It is a wretched condition not to be able to accept defenders without putting ourselves in bondage to them." The news however was received that the troops of the emperor had been repulsed. In the state-protocol of the republic Charles is constantly described as the enemy of the Gospel.

The protestants had firmly declared their sentiments at Worms

* Bullinger, Zwingli's successor, speaks of Luther's death in a similar style. Füslin: Epist. Reformat. p. 238.

in opposition to the will of the emperor, had refused to furnish help against the Turks, and were preparing themselves for war. The year 1547, the most eventful, and, at the same time, the saddest year in the whole century, was now at hand. Beza, in his account of Calvin, thus expressed at a later period the pain which he felt:—"That great edifice of the German reformation, raised with so much toil, now seemed ready to perish, and they were accounted happy who had been suddenly snatched away by death." He bears witness to Calvin's having at this time exhibited all the greatness and elevation of his character:—"How must he have suffered, he who, even in times of peace, bore in his heart the remotest even of the churches, and participated in the cares of all, as if their burdens rested upon him alone! How must his pious soul have been tortured through the misery of so many! He beheld at this moment his most intimate friends, Melancthon, Bucer, Peter Martyr, involved in the greatest danger, and nearer death than life. But his writings and letters of that period prove that he overcame all those storms by the energy of his noble soul. His opponents in Geneva persecuted him to the uttermost, but he yielded to them not so much as an inch."

It is evident indeed that Calvin, who speaks of himself as naturally timid, exerted the whole force of his spirit at this time, which may well be regarded as the brightest in his career as a reformer. He was especially useful to the interests of the church: the combatants needed a leader, and he was admirably suited to become the centre-point of their power. His resolution, his firmness, doubtless contributed greatly to prevent the courage of the persecuted from sinking. No sooner did all seem lost in Germany, than people turned their eyes towards Switzerland, which still enjoyed some degree of security under the shield of its ancient renown.

The league of Smalcalde was to be destroyed. It was the object of the emperor to become absolute, and he intended, as soon as he had vanquished the protestants, to make himself the master of both the council and the pope. But both he and the pope were deceived in their reckoning, and the conquered became the conquerors. The league of Smalcalde might certainly have established itself by force of arms, had not John Frederic, firm and constant in the spiritual struggle, but unfitted for outward action, been chosen for its leader. The emperor, secretly united with Maurice of Saxony, very cautiously declared that he would not attack doctrine. Union was wanting among the protestants, and a council of war determined that the whole should be summoned to Ulm. Schärtel unfortunately was no longer at their head; and when Maurice advanced upon Saxony, and sequestered it in the name of the emperor, the elector hastened back from the south of Germany to repossess himself of his dominions. Augsburg fell first, and all the others, with the exception of Magdeburg and Bremen, which remained invincibly faithful, opened their gates to the emperor. The hardest conditions were accepted; so that even the king of France found it wise to raise the spirits of the protestants again by promises, and once more to excite the Turks and the pope against the conqueror.

Calvin however had not lost his courage, and hoped much from the Germans. In a letter to the Sr. de Bourgogne, Feb. 25, 1547, he says, "I hope that our Antiochus (Charles V.), who now oppresses us, will be chained so tightly that he will not remember the marks on his feet and hands, for he will have them over his whole body. May God grant the same in respect to his companion, Sardanapalus (the king of France), for they both deserve one and the same measure." But after the battle of Mühlberg he writes, "If God will chastise us so severely as to give the reins to this tyrant, who meditates nothing but destruction, the lesson for us to learn is, to be prepared to suffer. He who has taken us for his servants is the ruler in the midst of enemies. It becomes us therefore to have patience, and to comfort ourselves with the hope that he will at length bring his enemies to shame. But I trust that He will bear our weakness, convert these distresses to a good end, and bridle the violence of those who triumph before their time, and even against God himself."

A proof was now given of the truth of that which the landgrave Philip said to Bucer,—"It is not the will of God to uphold the interests of the Gospel by the sword, or by force, but by preaching, by knowledge, by suffering, by death and the cross,"—words which clearly indicate the secret cause of the apparent want of activity in the protestants, but which was accounted for their honour. They acted not, because they were convinced that God must contend for his Gospel. Luther even had long hesitated on this subject, and had at last only slowly decided that self-defence was lawful, which in reality gave a false direction to the entire power of protestantism.

On the 24th of April the emperor attacked the elector John at Mühlberg. The latter was attending a sermon at the time, and would not allow himself to be disturbed. He fled when it was too late. Alba pursued him with his cavalry, and took him prisoner without a struggle. The emperor allowed sentence of death to be passed upon him. John renounced his electoral dignity, but declared that he was not subject to the council of Trent. Soon after this, Philip of Hesse, during an entertainment given him by Alba, was treacherously made prisoner, and in the presence of the elector of Brandenburg, who had agreed to be surety for his safety. Granvella and Charles answered disdainfully all representations made to them on the subject. The latter led John Frederic and Philip about with him in triumph, and trampled all Germany in the dust.

Calvin expressed himself well on these unhappy occurrences, and employs the same sentiments as the landgrave Philip. "We have news from Germany (July 14, 1547); affairs are at present in such a state that I know our Lord will take from us the victorious Gospel, in order to compel us to fight under his cross. But He consoles us by the reflection that He intends to uphold his church by the wonderful exercise of his power, and not by the hand of man. The trial, I acknowledge, is severe; but our forefathers have experienced it as well as we, and they remained constant and unshamed. We may now prove the truth of the proverb, 'Let us hope, and then we shall see.' For the rest, we must not be surprised if God proves to us by so hard a method that there is an eternal life. But may those who have not yet been shaken, contemplate themselves in the mirror of these examples, and so be prepared to stand in this manner before the judge."

After the death of Francis I. and Henry VIII. the emperor felt himself at the summit of his power. He was master of Germany, but his thirst for rule was to prove the deliverance of the church. The diet was opened at Augsburg, and he now declared openly that he was resolved to establish unity in religion. But the entire uprooting of protestantism formed no part of his plan: the evangelical church was to be made a barrier to the papal power. The pope, on his side, jealous of the proceedings of the emperor, concluded a treaty with Henry II., and transferred, under pretence of the plague, the council from Trent to Bologna. He thus placed it more under his own immediate control. Charles did not conceal his anger at this proceeding:

the Germans could not send their representatives into Italy; and when the Synod recommenced its sitting in 1548, he protested solemnly against its translation. A plan was at the same time proposed to the Diet of Augsburg for the re-establishment of religious union, and from this arose the celebrated Interim. But both parties were brought into a hostile position by the Interim and the Council. The pope demanded an unconditional subjection to his will: he allowed but the single choice, antichrist or excommunication. His sole object was to raise the spiritual power to its greatest height; while the emperor desired the union of parties, in order to exalt in a similar degree the authority of the state.

At the commencement of this unhappy epoch, Calvin entreated the Geneva council to allow him to visit the Swiss churches, for the purpose of gaining information as to the state of those in Germany; perhaps also to exhort the Swiss themselves to union. He returned on the 10th of February, 1547, and he concludes his address to the council, in which he mentions the capture of Ulm, with these apostolic words: "Seeing that the devil torments those who have a zeal for the Gospel, because of our sins and our forgetfulness of God, let us recommend ourselves to the Lord."

The danger for Switzerland became every day greater by the entrance of the Spaniards into Germany, and their possession of that country. Calvin earnestly exhorted the cantons to rise. Strasburg and Constance were the bulwarks of their church. Thus he wrote to Bullinger in September, 1547: "The people of Strasburg are alarmed because the emperor intends to spend the winter among them: they would shut their gates against him, if they could obtain assistance from other quarters. Let him enter Strasburg, and he will form a camp, from which he will make war upon you. Now, dear Bullinger, were there an opportunity of taking counsel among each other, and you neglected to do so, would you not be, as it were, holding your throats to the knife? But it is useless to speak. I know that your fellow-townsmen are wise enough to wish for some remedy to these disorders. Your neighbours, who have no idea of employing means to bridle the beast, lose their reason. But if they have actually resolved to perish, the Lord will direct his elect by the spirit of his good counsel, that in due time they may be delivered from the danger. Many are the reasons which ought to make you shrink with alarm from forming a league with France. But though it can be of no possible advantage to you to entangle yourselves with that country, yet I do not see why you should refuse all offers of union*."

Calvin's firm, exalted sentiments, in the midst of these troubles, appeared the still more encouraging. In a letter, dated July 24, 1547, he warns the faithful in France that the agitation in Germany could hardly fail to affect them in some degree. "It is impossible for us, if we once find ourselves established on this firm foundation of the church, not to be prepared to breast even the fiercest waves and storms, and to hold out against their assault. Yea, it is even good for us to be exposed to such afflictions as may prove our constancy and the firmness of our faith. In Germany the Lord has so humbled whatever was great and glorious among our brethren, and has so increased the power of him from whom nothing but evil is to be expected, that he seems to be engaged in re-establishing his spiritual kingdom wherever it before existed. According to human appearance, there is the least possible cause for hope; but if we do not cease to commend the unhappy church and the kingdom of Christ in prayer to the Lord, I still hope that He will, beyond our expectation, lend his hand to the work. It is to be feared, that we have hitherto allowed our eyes to be too much dazzled by the expectation of human help. Now that we have been taught to depend upon Him alone, we must recall to our minds the truth, by which He supported the church in former ages, and so do nothing but what may tend to his glory. Often have we had occasion to wonder at that which no one before hoped to see. In the meantime let us continue our warfare as soldiers fighting under the standard of the cross of Christ. This has already gained triumphs surpassing all those of the world."

Turning his eyes from the great disorders existing in Geneva, he says, "It is not worth while to trouble you with these. Moses and the prophets, the earlier leaders of God's people, had other troubles to bear, and such trials are altogether necessary for us. It is your present duty to seek God by prayer, and to entreat Him that we may not become weak, but that, if it be necessary, we may be prepared to give up our lives for his service, and to regard the rage and threats of the impious as

* In a letter to Bullinger, dated May 1549, he shows, by examples from Scripture, that a league might be formed with the wicked, though it was to be feared. The sufferings of the unfortunate brethren in France influenced him, and he adjured Bullinger to think of them.

nothing in comparison with the fear of the Lord. God grant that all tumults may at last be stilled, for they sorely afflict the souls of the weak, and that to me is of all things the most distressing."

Strasburg was obliged to sign a capitulation, April 12, 1547, whereby it agreed to pay 30,000 dollars and surrender twelve pieces of cannon. Even this however could not long protect the city. Switzerland suffered still more. The free imperial city of Constance lost both its spiritual and political liberties. The emperor took advantage of this event to unite it to the dominions of Austria. An army of three thousand Spaniards attacked it, and were repulsed; but a ban was now pronounced against it, and it was compelled not only to receive the Interim, but to give itself up to Ferdinand. Altars and masses were now introduced, and evangelical ministers were forbidden to reside there. Farel says, "As the ruin of Sodom is described, so will that of insensate Constance be related. They celebrate the Interim, like bacchanals, with dancing, gaming and drinking." "You would be astonished," remarks Bullinger, "if you could see the form of oath by which Constance has pledged itself to the king. They have sworn by God and the holy angels to adopt his opinions." The celebrated Ambrosius Blaarer, and all the evangelical party, departed with grief from the state, where Huss, a century before, had suffered for freedom.

Musculus had already fled from Augsburg, and sought refuge in Switzerland. The council of Zurich, though fearing the emperor, allowed Bullinger to receive him. He was afterwards appointed professor at Bern. Calvin wrote thus to Farel, April 30, 1548: "I say nothing respecting the fearful destruction which threatens so many churches: I am too much troubled at it. Such is the state of things, that no one can be reckoned among the servants of Christ who is not ready boldly to venture his head in their defence. If Viret wish it, I will hasten to him with all speed, that we may all three go together to Zurich." Mention is soon after made of the meeting of this triumvirate, to consult for the good of the church. Calvin says: "If our prayer has any weight with the people of Zurich, they will prevent, unless I err, the coming evil by a timely interference. A means will then be found to extend the discussion, till we have adopted some common measure of safety." To Viret he writes, June 1548, "Believe me, the eyes of both the wicked and the good are directed towards you. Each party inquires what kind of spirit animates you. By prudent conduct you will preserve that reputation which is now exposed to such danger, and will soften the rage of the enemy."

But the Swiss remained divided and inflexible. Bullinger speaks only of a bold answer, which they had resolved to give the emperor, who, strange enough, had shown no willingness to unite with them. The catastrophe was accomplished at Strasburg. In 1549 the Interim was fully introduced; those who would not acknowledge it were to be sent to the galleys. The teachers fled; but in the midst of the general apostasy, a feeling of strength and dignity was again awakened in Germany. "Many firmly reject the deceitful, double-meaning *deformation*." The weaker indeed the resistance when the struggle was only for territory, so much the bolder it became when it regarded matters of conscience. Melancthon had disapproved of the Interim in almost all its particulars: Maurice of Saxony opposed and protested openly against it: the captive elector expressed himself in noble language, and still more definitely against it. A host of writings followed. The landgrave Philip yielded, but his clergy did not. Frederick II., of the Palatinate, and Joachim II. adopted it. The margrave of Brandenburg-Kustrin, on the contrary, and all the principal cities, took the part of its opponents. At Augsburg Musculus had preached against it; Osiander also was obliged to flee; Bucer, Fagius and Martyr went to England. The Interim was everywhere ridiculed, especially at Magdeburg, which distinguished itself by its determined opposition. The power of the emperor however at length prevailed; but the fiercest hatred was awakened, and the way prepared for new events.

Calvin comforted all those who had been obliged to flee. Brentius, who hastened to Basil, wrote to the reformer. His courageous answers are filled with the joyful sentiments of the Gospel; and in the whole of this period we meet with opinions and events in France and Germany which recall to mind the first centuries of Christianity, and exhibit a zeal unknown to our mild, free age, in which the persecution of opinion is the only thing visited with anathemas.

It was under the name of the Interim that the emperor, in 1548, published a formulary, which was to serve as a rule for both parties in the church, till a general council should have pronounced definitively on the disputed points of belief. All that the Interim granted to the protestants was the communion in both kinds, and the marriage of the clergy; but it was declared that even this was only conceded for the time. In other respects the decision was wholly against the Lutherans, and under the pretence of impartiality questions of the utmost importance were solved, to the injury of the evangelical cause. Notwithstanding this however the catholics were as little contented with the Interim as the protestants. It already existed in the germ at Ratisbonne, and was wrought out by the politic, but far from conscientious, theologians, Pflug, Helding and Agricola. The first two were catholics, but they were honoured on account of their personal character: the third, Agricola, was a protestant, who, as it was suspected, had been bribed to mislead or betray his party. The emperor had passed a law which rendered it a capital offence to write against the Interim. Still, more than thirty-seven papers appeared against it. Calvin was also called upon by his friends to controvert it. He wrote to Farel, August 10, 1548: "Bullinger has exhorted me to write against the bastard reformation (*adultero-Germanum*, as he named the Interim). I was already prepared for this, before his letters reached me, but I had put the work aside. I have asked Bucer's advice: if he think it right, I will attempt something." In the then state of things it was a proof of great courage to dare to attack the dreaded emperor, who might any day fall upon Switzerland.

Bullinger was rejoiced to see his writing, and mentions that an answer had appeared in Saxony, but that it contained nothing but abuse. He had himself prepared something, but would not let it be printed. Calvin, in the paper referred to, again opposed with minute particularity the Roman Catholic doctrine in all its details, and shows especially how the church might have been reformed, and peace established, had the authors of the Interim really desired to settle the dispute. He proves, on the other hand, the sophistry of the so-named mediators, according to all the various catholic principles. "Not the smallest truth," he says, "must be lost, unless we mean to be guilty of what is indisputably a sacrilege." In the part of the work where he treats of the supremacy of Rome, he asserts, among other things, that Peter never was in that city. He develops his ideas on marriage and divorce, opposes the notion that marriage is a sacrament, and particularly refutes a catholic who had written against the Interim on the ground that it allowed the marriage of priests. He concludes with an admirable exhortation to all his evangelical brethren to die, if necessary, for the faith, and to fix their thoughts on eternal life with God. When Melancthon, at a subsequent period, did not reject the modified Leipzig Interim, Calvin reproached him in the severest manner, and with the most passionate love of truth. "Vacillation in so great a man is not to be tolerated. I would a hundred times rather die with you, than see you survive a doctrine which you had betrayed." Thus he reproved him, but without undervaluing, as others did, his greatness.

To one of the impressions of this work the printer affixed an admonition, stating that he did not agree with an opinion contained in the book, which seemed to affirm that the children of believers are already, before baptism, holy and regenerate, and that baptism therefore is not unconditionally necessary. Calvin opposed the attack of the unknown editor in an especial appendix, which appeared only in 1550.

The distracted state of the church in Germany had occasioned the flight of many of Calvin's friends to England; and the learned and christian Peter Martyr became in Cranmer's hand a chief instrument of the Reformation, which now, notwithstanding great imperfections and abuses, of which Calvin speaks in many of his writings, and especially in his letter to Somerset, went more prosperously forward. The earlier measures of the king, under whom court cabals, passion and the love of women entered into the conduct of church affairs, had given such a bad direction to the operations of the clergy, that even the best teachers could not overcome the difficulties in their way. Hertford, the uncle of the heir apparent, was appointed protector during the minority of Edward VI., and, as duke of Somerset, ruled with kingly power, but with justice and moderation. The disturbed state of the nation as to religious affairs, the variety of parties, rendered the control of a ruler at this time more especially necessary. Sincerely devoted to the Reformation, he looked to Cranmer for the accomplishment of his ends. This prelate sought not only Bucer and Martyr, but Fagius, Ochinus and Musculus as his fellow-labourers. The first four only came to England; with them however was associated John à Lasco, who had been converted to the truth at Zurich by Zwingli. It was at Bucer's suggestion that Calvin undertook to exhort the duke of Somerset to despise all difficulties in the execution of his purpose. Somerset seems to have received this advice favourably, Calvin having subsequently said in a letter to Farel, "Canterbury has told me that I cannot do anything more useful than to write often to the king."

"I hear," he says in his epistle to the protector, "that there are two classes of agitators in your kingdom, the one consisting of fanatics, who, under the pretence of zeal for the Gospel, overturn all social order; the other of those who obstinately desire to retain the whole mass of catholic superstitions. Both deserve to be punished by the sword, which God has given you, for they rise in defiance against the king and against God. The best means however to check the evil is to instruct men in the knowledge that we are created after the image of God, and that Christianity is opposed to all disorder. What I have to say to you therefore may be reduced to three points. First, in what manner the people may be best taught; second, what means may be used to remove the abuses of the church; and third, how the scandals which exist, the vices and luxury of the day, may be overcome."

He wrote at the same time to Bucer in England, encouraging him to promote peace and union there; he also prayed him, with great freedom of expression, to speak more clearly on the doctrine of the Lord's Supper, and begged him to have the honour of the Holy Spirit and of Christ more distinctly before his eyes, that no part of it might be ascribed to the mere minister, or the elements of the sacrament. The letter is well worth reading, and affords an excellent view of the subject. "You must be careful to devote yourself to the church, and to the service of the Lord. You have already run over a long course, and you know not how much still remains to you. I, who left the cradle a little earlier, stand perhaps nearer the goal, but the direction and the end of our lives are in the hand of the Lord." He then speaks of the wretched condition of France, and expresses a hope that England may raise itself up. "I have exhorted the protector, as you wished me, and as the present state of affairs requires. It is now your duty, in all possible ways, if you can but obtain a hearing, to press especially for the abolishing of all ceremonies, which always carry somewhat of superstition with them." It was Somerset's design only to purify the English church and the papacy, not to reconstruct them.

Bucer promised, in order to avoid contention, to speak of the Lord's Supper in the same language as Martyr. In the year 1551 a new strife arose, as to which of the catholic ceremonies should be abolished. Hooper, who, even according to Calvin's opinion, viewed the subject too strictly, was thrown into prison. Calvin immediately entreated the duke of Somerset to protect Hooper, and he was soon after liberated.

Bucer died the same year, and Calvin deplored his death in a letter to Viret:—"I feel as if my heart would break, whenever I think of the manifold loss which the church has suffered in Bucer. May the Lord grant that all the rest whom I might have to weep may survive me, and so let me die joyfully!" But he was still very dissatisfied with the state of the church of England*. "There is yet much to be desired. Among others, it is an incurable evil, that, so long as the king remains under guardianship, all the revenues of the church will be squandered by the great. In the meanwhile, they give a mere pittance to men without merit, but who perform the character of pastors. I will not cease however to rouse the consciences of all on this subject." He developed a grander plan, in a subsequent letter to Cranmer, for a general union of the evangelical churches.

The young king Edward, who ascended the throne in his tenth year, ruled till 1553. His noble dispositions awakened the greatest hope, and Calvin sought to gain him more and more for the Gospel. This is strikingly shown by his sending him a copy of his Commentary on Isaiah. This was followed by a dedication of the Commentary on the Catholic Epistles. In the epistle dedicatory he arms the young prince against the Council of Trent. Lastly, he dedicated to him the Commentary on the eighty-seventh Psalm, with a French letter, dated 1552.

Evident progress was made by the Reformation at this period. The parliament in 1549 appointed a committee of bishops and clergy to undertake the task of forming a new liturgy. They retained only so much of the Mass as was consistent with the principles of the Reformation; thus the invocation of saints was abolished, and Latin was exchanged for English. The marriage of the clergy was allowed. But the evil disposition of Henry VIII. was still at work; even Cranmer knew not of what spirit he was, and became the persecutor of those who differed from his opinions. Bishop Bonner was deprived of his office, because he supported the old doctrine of the real presence. Even some mechanics, who adhered to their extravagant notions, were brought to the scaffold; and Cranmer pressed it upon the young king as a duty to order them to be executed. He yielded, but

* Epis. 123, Ed. Amst. p. 240.

with tears. Violence like this led only to an outward unity, and not to the truth. Thus an altogether different system became necessary.

Calvin's influence in Scotland was not exercised till a later period; but he already took a comprehensive survey of the churches in foreign lands. In the year 1545 he renewed his intercourse with the Austrian reformed communities, to which he dedicated his catechism, with the view of establishing a union of doctrine between them and his own church. He also addressed himself to the Poles, and dedicated his Commentary on the Hebrews, in 1549, to king Sigismund Augustus, whom he exhorted to give himself to the service of Christ, "which places us in the rank of angels," and to walk in the footsteps of his glorious father, Sigismund, who, while persecution raged in so many other countries, never stained his pure hand with blood. The great men of his kingdom, he added, were now expressing their zeal for Christ and the truth; John à Lasco, a descendant of a most renowned family, shining conspicuous before the rest.

The Reformation was established in Denmark as early as 1536, but it was not till 1552 that Calvin had any intercourse with that nation. In that year he dedicated the first half of his Commentary on the Acts of the Apostles, to the excellent king Christian I.; and in 1554 he dedicated the second half to the son of that monarch, Frederic, expressing on both occasions his high esteem for those princes, and his love towards the Danish church. His intercourse with Sweden was of a still later date. Beza says, "He bore all these churches on his shoulders."

It is a characteristic and a joyous sign of the freshness and overflowing living energy in this great man, that at this busy period of his career he published so many works, that it might have been supposed he had nothing else to do. When moreover we consider their solidity, especially in the case of his exegetical writings, we feel that he had an internal, especial existence for himself, as well as his outward being; or, as he expresses it, 'all the conflicts which took place around him, and the consequences of which seemed to oppress him so severely, were but, in his eyes, as skirmishes*.'

If he was by anything more especially characterized, it was by the exegetical element, with which he wrought upon the intellectual world. The clearness and sedateness of his understanding, the tranquillity, the caution against extravagances, in

* Epis. ad Pios Gallos.

a word the higher cultivation in contrast with the rudeness of an earlier period, the simple style, the dogmatic freedom, the tact, the learning and christian sentiment, the practical character of his interpretation,—all characteristic of his genius and writings, have been spoken of in the first part of this work.

It was Bucer who first encouraged him to undertake the labour of a commentator. "The Lord," he said, "has endowed you with an excellent ability to interpret his Gospel. You have again bestowed upon us a noble gift by your commentary on the Epistles to Timothy. May the spirit of God himself guide you!"

The first part of his Commentary on the Epistles to the Corinthians he dedicated, in 1546, to the Sieur de Bourgogne; and ten years later another to Galliazzo Carraccioli. In writing to the former, he gives a proof of pure Christianity and of greatness of soul, and at the same time of his skill in addressing persons of rank. The second Epistle to the Corinthians was dedicated to Melchior Wolmar, to whom Calvin expresses his thankfulness, while he reminds him of the days of his youth, which he spent with him. The Epistles to the Galatians, Ephesians, Philippians, Colossians, were dedicated to Christopher, archduke of Wirtemberg and Mümpelgard, to strengthen him in his christian course. But the first Epistle to the Thessalonians he dedicated, in 1551, to the aged Maturin Cordier, his former teacher, principal of the gymnasium at Lausanne, and to whom he expresses his gratitude that he so carefully instructed him in his early years. In the year 1551 he sent his Commentary on the Second Epistle to the Corinthians to his physician, Textor, whom he thanks for his friendship, and adds, "When I think of my departed wife, I am daily admonished how much I am indebted to you, both because you once before cured her of a heavy sickness, and employed all your art and efforts to afford her help in her last sufferings." In 1548 he dedicated the two Epistles to Timothy to the duke of Somerset, that, as Paul exhorted Timothy, so he might exhort the youthful king, and show him in what the true church consisted. The Epistle to Titus he dedicated to Farel and Viret, as we have already stated. Mention has also been made of the Catholic Epistles, and of that to the Hebrews.

Calvin's methodical unity of thought, which he yet knew how to combine with freedom, was strongly shown in his scientific style of interpretation. He wished to cultivate reverential feelings rather than mere knowledge, but he never unexegetically sacrificed the meaning of Scripture to the desire to establish a particular doctrine. He was therefore naturally averse to all hot-headed people, who rashly rushed onward before their time. This leads us to speak again of his dignified opposition to the celebrated Castellio. His struggle for doctrine and discipline in the church began with the year 1544. We pass over a polemical *intermezzo* which he had with Chaponneau, a minister at Neuchatel, which is only interesting on account of a characteristic letter, addressed to a party in that city, which it drew from Calvin. He met Chaponneau's strife-loving disposition in an indirect way, showing his own disinclination to dispute, and at the same time the little worth of his opponent. So also he stated to the members of the church at Neuchatel his opinion of their rules in respect to discipline and ecclesiastical censures. He touches upon, and explains, all the difficulties which had anything to do with the delicate office of correcting manners. "Let it be universally agreed," he says, "that the erring should be openly exposed; they would otherwise go to other churches, and so all discipline would cease."

This operation of spiritual censures throws some light also upon the affair of Castellio, who was the representative in his age of that free, passionate spirit which has only in later times burst forth and become so fearless.

Calvin became acquainted with Castellio at the university of Strasburg in 1539–40. He lived for some time in the same house with him, and endeavoured to obtain the diligent young man, the ingenious student of antiquity, for Geneva, it always being the wish of the great reformer to secure for his church a scientific cultivation. But Castellio was determined to be a theologian also. Beza described him, according to his own style, by the Greek term ἰδιογνώμων, self-opinionated. His residence at Geneva, as principal tutor in the Gymnasium, lasted about three years. He did not receive any appointment as a preacher, but he now began to put forth some singular exegetical opinions on scriptural subjects. Thus he declared the Canticles to be a mere obscene song, especially the seventh chapter. It was written, he said, by Solomon in his youth, and ought to be struck out of the canon. He never considered the difficulty of setting bounds to such experiments, and to what end they would lead where the catholics were concerned. His perverseness was even still more apparent in his denial of the descent of Christ into hell, in his refusal to receive Calvin's intelligent and cautious exposition of the subject, or to consider the vast importance of a reference to the sentiments of the early believers.

Calvin was obliged to declare aloud his disapprobation of this conduct. He spared him, from the great regard which he entertained for him, as much as he could; but Castellio, deeply offended, wished to enter into an open discussion with him on the point in dispute. The council refused its consent, and thereby evinced its discretion; but for the sake of truth, and not to limit the freedom of opinion, the discussion was allowed to take place in the presence of the assembled preachers. It was continued a long while, but without any good result. Castellio was now so embittered, that he openly abused the ministers in a sort of congregation, in which every one was allowed to bring forward his complaints. He then took his departure, but without being obliged to leave Geneva in a degrading manner, as Beza falsely reports.

This occurrence is worthy of attention, because it was the first time that the council was wholly on Calvin's side; and through him it was that that union of opinion was established upon which the safety of the protestant church entirely depended. It appears indeed, from the whole of Castellio's history, that he was by no means a man of vicious disposition, but an ingenious, bold and earnest theologian, interesting and worthy of esteem, notwithstanding his failings, which mainly arose from inconsiderateness, a want of forbearance and love of strife. He was such a person, in short, as the French call *une mauvaise tête*. His ability was not sufficiently exalted to enable him to understand Calvin's worth and calling as a peace-maker in those times of excitement, and he named that despotism which was really but fidelity to duty. Bayle was as little able to understand Calvin. This is evident when, at the end of his article on Castellio, he observes, that the latter had only failed in not knowing how kings—that is, theologians who hold the rank of authorities—must be managed. Schlosser judges him correctly, when he describes him, Castellio, as "the learned, but unfortunate, proud and restless Sebastian." Beza regarded him as honest; and the testimony given him by Calvin and the ministers of Geneva tends equally to prove his integrity. The first cause of annoyance between these two distinguished men was connected with the printing of Castellio's French translation of the Bible, which Calvin would willingly have corrected, but Castellio would not allow him.

Castellio bore himself so unbecomingly in the whole of this affair, that we may easily account, by his passionate conduct in the one instance, for his rage in other and later occurrences against the reformer. Calvin wrote to Farel, May 30, 1544: "I now again see what it is to live in Geneva. I lie among thorns. There have been terrible quarrels among my colleagues during the last two months. Our Castellio, on the other hand, raves against us with the fury of despair. About sixty hearers were present at the meeting yesterday, when the Scriptures were expounded. The following passage was proposed: 'Let us prove ourselves the servants of God in all long suffering.' Castellio now raised a constant opposition, in order to create between us and Christ's servants the greatest possible dissension. Thus he played with the words in this manner: 'Paul was a servant of God,—we serve only ourselves: he was the most patient of men; —we are impatience itself: he watched the night through for the edifying of the church,—we watch to amuse ourselves: he was modest and temperate,—we have a drunken boldness: he was persecuted by the rebellious,—we excite them: he was chaste,—we are licentious: he was himself cast into prison,—we cast others in, if they but utter a word against us: he looked to the power of God,—we to the strength of others: he was oppressed,—but we oppress, and that the innocent.' What more is necessary? It was in short a cruel, exciting speech throughout. I was silent for the moment, lest a greater dispute might be kindled in the presence of our numerous friends, but I complained to the syndics. Such a conduct marks the beginning of all schismatics. I am induced to oppose myself to his rage, not so much on account of the perverseness of his conduct and the rashness of his abuse, as because of the perfect groundlessness of his accusations*."

At Basel, where it was not felt to be so absolutely a duty to contend for unity, Castellio was appointed to the office of Greek professor. If we again consider the relation in which these two eminent men stood to each other, we shall find that Castellio

* Other letters however exist which show, that, full of indignation as Calvin was on account of Castellio's slanderous abuse, he yet continued to befriend him. Thus he recommended him to his acquaintances, only lamenting his fierce and inconsiderate conduct: 1544 (MS. Gen.). In a letter to Viret, March 26, 1544 (MS. Gen.), he says, "Consider what can be done for him."

continued all his life through the same noble but absurd champion of unlimited toleration; while Calvin, as the supporter of the grand truth which he viewed as the source of life, pursued with enthusiasm to the end of his career the one great object which he had always in view. The strife was soon revived. Castellio published a paper on the doctrine of predestination and justification, as founded on the ninth chapter of the Romans. It was directed against Calvin's principles. The essay on toleration is also generally, and rightly, ascribed to him: it appeared after the trial of Servetus, under the assumed name of Martin Bellius, and with the following title, "Hæretici, an sint persequendi, multor. sententiæ." Calvin answered this work. Beza also wrote a very strong reply to it, at Lausanne, under the title of "De Hæreticis a magistratu gladio puniendis." He supported his views with great talent, painted Servetus in the darkest colours, and undertook the defence of his friend against all assailants. But Castellio was not yet silenced. An anonymous writing, the author of which Calvin and Beza could easily guess, appeared at Paris, under the title of "Extracts from the Latin and French works of Calvin." In this publication the fundamental doctrine of election, that which supplied all deficiencies, was trodden underfoot with the biting wit and the keen logic which might have been looked for from a Voltaire. Beza and Calvin however exhibited far greater ability in the answer, and again trod the adversary in the dust. Worth and dignity were on their side, and it cannot be denied that Castellio would have done better to be silent. It is not so much matter of surprise, therefore, that they should have spoken severely of him in the preface to their translation of the New Testament, and warned every Christian to beware of a man "who had been chosen by Satan to deceive the thoughtless and indifferent." Castellio indeed, in his Apology, published in 1558, complains of Calvin's fierceness against him, and declares that he had never seen the two works which Calvin ascribed to him*. But who can doubt that they were his, when they breathe so entirely his spirit? Still we must praise the moderate tone of this Apology. He accuses the reformer of believing too easily all the evil which was told him of his opponents. Among other things Calvin, deceived by a false report, had accused him of stealing wood to warm his chamber. Castellio spoke very temperately of this slander, and cleared it up in the following manner. He was

* Bayle, art. Castellio.

indeed in very necessitous circumstances, having to bring up a family of four sons and four daughters. In order to finish his translation of the Scriptures, he was obliged to sit up during the night, and to provide fuel he went to the bank of a stream which flows into the Rhine, to pick up the pieces of wood borne down by the current, and which two hundred men had done at the same time. He appealed to all Basel in proof of the truth of this statement. This gives us a glimpse of the state in which this great and accomplished scholar lived. He had not the means of warming his chamber, and such was his poverty or necessity, that he was obliged to cultivate by his own labour a little spot of ground outside the city. He died in want, in the year 1563, and was buried in the grave of Grynæus. But his remains were subsequently disinterred, and some Polish students buried him in the high church at Basel, adorning his tomb with an inscription. Montaigne* devotes to him some expressions of sympathy: "To the great shame of our age, two distinguished scholars, as I hear, have died before our very eyes in a condition in which they had not sufficient to eat,—Lelio Giraldi in Italy, and Castellio in Germany. Thousands, I should think, would have come to their help had they only known their state."

We may close our account of Calvin's present labours by the mention of two works, which had an immediate relation to the common intellectual character of the period. They show how sick the world was, and form a proper introduction to that which we have to say on the anti-christianity of those times. The first is a work against relics: it is written with much humour and irony, and was likely to be useful from its popular tendency. The second was a treatise against astrology. Although a certain degree of light had been diffused, even the most powerful minds were affected by the remains of superstition, and it was Calvin's peculiar characteristic to be able by his own active spirit to penetrate, in that unlearned age, the mists of error and falsehood. Even Beza himself, according to Schlosser, believed at one time in astrological signs, and thought that the appearance of the famous star in Cassiopea betokened the overthrow of all things. It is well known that Melancthon inclined to this weakness. The regions of presentiment and mysticism were equally strange to Calvin, and there are only two cases in which such matters are touched upon. In the very year in which his work against astrology appeared, he wrote to Viret, Septem-

* Essais, lib. i. ch. 34.

ber 23: "In the packet which you lately forwarded to me, were letters from Poland: they contained nothing new, except the account that a lake (in ditione Marcicii) had appeared for two days like blood, and that the people had here and there taken up masses of the gore. A fearful wonder, the meaning of which will soon become clear to us. There being now so many fables abroad, I can scarcely believe it, till our booksellers come back from the fair." In speaking of one of Calvin's sicknesses Beza says, "He was lying in bed; it was Saturday; the north wind had raged terribly for the last two days; Calvin lifted up his voice in the presence of many persons, and said, 'I know not what I ought to think of it, but the whole night through I have seemed to hear a tremendous sound of warlike instruments, and I could not convince myself that it was not so. Let us, I beseech you, pray; for certain it is that some great event is at hand.' And, strange to say, on that very day the great battle of Dreux was fought."

It is not uninteresting to hear the remarks of so clear a mind on the then famous science of the heavenly bodies, especially at a time when the curtain has fallen, and a Chalmers has brought this new branch of knowledge into harmony with the Gospel. Calvin had yet no idea of the system of Copernicus, although the work of that astronomer was written in 1530. "The whole heaven moves itself around the earth," said Calvin, even in the last edition of his Institutes. The writings of Aristarchus of Samos, the only one among the ancients who awoke out of the egoistical dream, had been but lately discovered; and how slowly this knowledge was diffused appears from the case of Galileo, who in 1610 first ventured to proclaim the truth of the new system. Somewhat later Beza shows, in his work on the plague, that he was acquainted with the Copernican system, though he might not understand it.

Astrology is certainly indebted for its origin to the desire of the human spirit to look upwards, and there, above, to seek the solution of all mysteries. Nor is the influence of the heavens on the organisation of man to be despised. The repressed superstition of catholics and protestants had now again concentrated itself in this art, familiar in Calvin's time to all men of learning. Francis I. dismissed his physician because he had shown himself unwilling to prophesy from the stars respecting the future. The celebrated Renata, duchess of Ferrara, the friend of Calvin and a promoter of the pure faith, received instruction from her astrologer, Luc Gauric, in order not to be ignorant of the matter. At the court of king Henry II., Francis II. and Charles IX. the far-famed Michael Nostradamus, doctor and professor of medicine, enjoyed as much distinction as if he had been really endowed with the prophetic spirit. He had, as well as Luc Gauric, foretold the death of the king in a duel, which happened in close agreement with their predictions. The influence indeed of this error arose to such a height in France in the time of Catherine, that both the church and the state found it necessary to check it. Under the old system of astronomy, which regarded the heavens only in relation to the earth, and the latter as the central point of the whole, the notion could be easily justified that the stars were the language of God, seeing that all was appointed for the use of man alone.

Calvin, who opposed himself to this error, did not intend to write a learned work on the subject, but such a one as might be useful to persons of moderate understanding. "God," he simply says, "has given us his word, but men surrender themselves to superstition. The true astrology and astronomy is the knowledge of heaven. We learn from Moses that God appointed the sun and the stars for the day and the night, for months and seasons. But it is not given to every one to understand their courses, their changes, or their oppositions. This belongs to science."—"Astronomy teaches the period of time which each planet requires for its course round the sun, what relations the sun has to the other planets, and how eclipses may be calculated even to a minute. The fact is this: our astrologers start with the correct principle, that all earthly bodies are subject to those above; but they draw a wrong conclusion herefrom. Natural astrology teaches rightly that the moon exercises an influence on bodies; that, for example, when it grows or wanes, the joints are more or less affected; and from this science of astrology physicians derive what insight they possess. We are therefore obliged to confess that there is a certain degree of harmony between the stars and human bodies. But these presumptuous people have invented, under the name of an art, a system of astrology, which is twofold, and consists, 1. in the knowledge of nature and the organisation of man, and 2. in an inquiry into all the occurrences of human life,—into what men have to do and suffer, what will be the issue of their undertakings,—nay, into the minutest affairs of existence." He then shows them, in his peculiar and cutting style, that they are fools who believe in such a system.

We find from this writing, that Calvin despised all such things as presentiments, regarding them in the same light as astrology, and that he recognized no slumbering and re-awakening faculty in man to look into the future. Thus he rejected the predictions of Ascletario, who foretold Domitian his death, and those of Spurinna, who warned Cæsar to beware of the Ides of March. He thus argues:—"I ask you, whether there were not many other persons born at Rome, and in Italy, on the same day and under the same star as Cæsar? Did they all die on the same day, and by a similar death? It is evident then that there is no truth in your art, since, if there were, what happens to one must happen to all. There may be thirty who have the same nativity: one may die when he is thirty, another when he is fifty; one at home, another in battle. Theagenes had foretold Augustus that he would be emperor, having been born under the sign of Capricorn: but how many poor wretches were there not born under the same sign, and who attained to no higher glory than that of being swineherds or cowherds? If the stars had given the kingdom, not only to Augustus, but to all the rest who were born under the same sign, a very little portion of territory would have remained for him."

"Let us allow," he continues, "that some predictions are fulfilled; still, this is only the devil's work. God allows it, in order to punish disbelievers, as he did in the case of Saul." Thus he ascribes the whole of this dark side of human knowledge to the influence of the evil spirit. It appears also that people in his time had gone very far in these practices: he speaks of the secret exorcism of spirits; and in contemporary writings, as for example in the life of Cellini, it is mentioned, that a marvellous necromancer dwelt in the Coliseum at Rome. "Who," he asks, "has made the devils subject to them, that they should serve them? The children of God cannot but regard them as their most cruel enemies, must flee from or repel them, instead of seeking communion with them. They who would make use of their service will at last see that they have played into the hand of their master."

It should be remarked that Calvin has said nothing respecting magnetism and clairvoyance, by which the whole empire of the supernatural is placed under another and higher point of view, unknown to the reformers.

We proceed now to consider the anti-christianity of those times. Having seen how Calvin, by his Institutes, endeavoured to give stability and consistency to the whole church, and then directed his attention to the common necessities of the age, we have at present to examine more particularly the efforts which he made at Geneva to fix the constitution and discipline of his church. In order to do this, we must first describe the character of his opponents. Full of the thought that the Gospel is no speculation, and that it is but a dead letter without a christian life, he could not fail to regard all as antagonists who ridiculed what is spiritual and moral. Yet, as in the middle ages the rude violence of the world, which so long resisted the power of the papacy, was at length compelled to give way, so, in this case, libertinism was in the end subjected to a moral rule.

CHAPTER XII.

ANABAPTISTS.—SPIRITUAL LIBERTINES.—THE ANTICHRISTIANITY OF GENEVA.—POLITICAL LIBERTINES OPPOSED TO THE REFUGEES.

It is evident that the principles which gave birth to the opposition which Calvin had to endure in Geneva, were diffused through the whole church, but had their stronghold in that city; as if, according to Beza's remark, the power of evil was to be manifested in its most satanic forms where it was to meet with the boldest resistance. Popery no longer concealed its worst features: it was unmasked. Far more dangerous was the spirit of malice, which was inwardly consuming the life of the re-awakened church. Under the veil of a pious pantheism, and the form of a new, more perfect doctrine, that spirit was seeking to win away unstable souls. How well it succeeded in this appears from the case of queen Margaret of Navarre, who protected the spiritual libertines at her court, and in consequence quarreled with Calvin. This is sufficient to prove how necessary it was that he should stand forth, and endeavour to quiet the waves which had been raised by the storm of various passions, and of life, now in the progress of its new development. The awakening of a fresh principle must ever be attended with something unusual. When the human spirit is excited by great objects, it goes forward with the same daring feeling which prompted it to the overthrow of idols, and easily yields itself up to the ideas which carry with them the contempt of all rule and order. The anabaptists are an example of this perversion.

It is well known that, when Luther was residing on the Wartburg, great disturbance was created at Wittenberg through a sect of this kind. He left the castle to restore quiet, and delivered, during eight successive days, his famous sermons, so distinguished by practical good sense and discretion, against the spirit of fanaticism. But neither his powerful influence*, nor the death of Thomas Munzer, and the disgraceful defeat of the fanatics at Münster, availed wholly to suppress their errors. The same notions, not long after, took another and more speculative direction,—not so rude, but equally deceptious. The main doctrine of the anabaptists was the necessity of re-baptism in mature years, and the rejection of infant baptism as not apostolical. The libertines went much further: they were pantheists of the worst kind, trampling all morality to the ground, as well as Christianity, against which they raged in the most awful manner.

Calvin, to confute their erring and wretched notions, wrote against both. The work against the libertines appears, in the Amsterdam edition, with the date 1544: that against the anabaptists was of the same year, but is written with so much solidity that it deserves to be read in all times. The two works are closely connected, the notion of an individual inspiration being the fundamental error, and that which required to be combated, in both sects.

In the preface to the second work, Calvin writes to the brethren of Neuchatel, who had begged him to oppose the fanatics, and states, that he dedicated his book to them as a public proof of the friendship which was so dear to him, and that the world might see how they agreed in zeal and doctrine. "Our William Farel, who is endowed by the Holy Spirit with so many excellent gifts, and who, as an old veteran, has ever stood forth against the enemies of God, has already done more than was necessary in that which you have required of me."

The first error, namely that children ought not to be baptized, and that those only ought to be admitted to the rite who are walking in the Lord, is thus refuted: "In the time of the apostles children were baptized: the command of Jesus refers only to unbelievers. Christians who enjoy the promise have

* A.D. 1522.

received it also for their children. These are baptized because they are already in the covenant, and are so born. The circumcision of children was practised among the Jews, and had reference to repentance and conversion."

In respect to excommunication, they supposed that open sin, after a second admonition, rendered the offender ripe for the infliction of the anathema; and further, that even he who sinned through ignorance, though still more he who willingly transgressed, could never receive forgiveness. According to their notions therefore every actual sin is a sin against the Holy Ghost, which is blasphemy.

"To what does this lead?" asks Calvin. "What Christian lives without sin? and where, if such a doctrine be correct, is the consolation for penitents? Actual sin is not always sin against the Holy Ghost, but is only so when the transgressor opposes himself with all his might to divine truth. A man however may actually sin, though he has never declared war against God or blasphemed his word." Some excellent observations follow against every species of separatism. "These people want a perfectly pure church, and insist that no believer ought to remain in a church which does not excommunicate all who are wicked." In opposition to this he says, "A church may exist with imperfections. Every church is stained with sin. The prophets and Christ are members of the church, though it be conjoined with reprobate communities. We ought to improve, not to separate."

Again: "Those who dream of a perfect church are unwilling to recognize any temporal power in the church, or any authority independent of itself, seeing that it is perfect in itself. Excommunication has supplied the place of the sword. Christ, they say, would not judge the adulteress, nor decide between the brethren, nor be a king, nor allow his brethren to exercise authority."

So also he justifies the christian oath, as grounded on the Old Testament, and not abrogated by the New. Lastly, he confutes the doctrinal errors of the fanatics. They spoke of the Lord's having a heavenly body, as the Marcionites contended for his having only an apparent body, whence it would follow that Christ was not really man. So too they reasoned of a sleep after death, which error Calvin had already opposed in his Psychopannychia.

But although he designated these people as dreamers, and

even as swine, who delighted to wallow in the mire, a tone of pity and great gentleness pervades his work, as if it were intended to be addressed to those who had only exalted themselves too much from a well-intended though erroneous design. It appears that the anabaptists, though pursued with fire and sword in catholic countries, instead of being so reckless in his time as they had been at an earlier period in Germany, were now well-disposed. This was not the case with the libertines.

In order to justify a free and licentious life by christian principles, the spiritual had united with the political libertines in exhibiting a false view of christian freedom. They were distinguished from the German fanatics in this, that they grounded immorality on a system. No attempt to characterize them is made in the smaller lives of Calvin, and even Schröckh passes them over in his church history. Calvin's work against them is very original and peculiar.

He describes this sect as "reprobate, and not merely sinful, but horribly corrupt above all others. Its end is licentiousness: it gives a false idea of freedom, and calls itself spiritual. Those who hear these people speak might suppose them to be carried away by their raptures above the skies. Their heresy reminds us of that of Cerdo, who adopted the notion of two principles, and denied the resurrection. This was the case also with Marcian, with the Gnostics and the Manichæans. They took something from all, but rejected the Gospel, and gave nicknames to the apostles. Neither wit nor reason can be found in their speech, no more than it could in what old women might say on astronomy. And I am expected to be silent when the name of Christ is abused, and when it is employed to screen the introduction of such wickedness into the world as has never been heard of, and thus to expose him again to the shame of being accounted worse than a demon. Were I to do this, I should be baser than a dog, which will not allow his master to be attacked without at least barking. I must cry out aloud then with a clear voice, so that if heresy dare boldly utter its wretched and horrible blasphemies, this may be heard above them."

"It would be ridiculous were I to oppose myself to the pope and his coadjutors with all my power (for I cannot edify the church of God if I do not make war with those who would pull it down), and yet should excuse those who are still worse enemies of God, and much greater destroyers of the truth. For the pope does allow a shadow of religion to remain; he takes not away the hope of eternal life; he desires men to fear God; he makes a distinction between good and evil; he acknowledges our Lord Jesus Christ to be true God and true man; he ascribes honour to the Word of God. But the only end which these people have in view is to confound heaven and earth together, and to nullify all religion. All, even the little children, ought to spit at them in sign of horror, as they see them passing along the streets, and thus to heap infamy upon those who, by supporting them, have been the cause of ruin to thousands of souls."

Calvin next complains greatly of their unintelligible, mystical mode of expression, and accuses them of playing the catholic under the pretence of christian freedom. They indulged in an allegorical interpretation of the Bible. Calvin, on the other hand, shows what Paul meant when he said, 'The letter killeth.' On the one side they exalted themselves very high and desired to be called spiritual, and on the other they sank down into the very mire. 'Their main defence was, that there is only one spirit; but it is a very different thing to say with Scripture that all creatures come from God, and that what God has created is God himself. They speak of the devil as identical with the world and sin. The devil and his angels have no proper existence: wickedness is only a negation of good, and the distinction between good and evil vanishes. The human soul is not eternal, since it is of the world. The spirit accomplishes whatever is done in the universe. Man has no freedom, and therefore everything is good to him; or, in other words, God commits sin. Thus both the belief in God and every trace of morality are lost in their system, crimes of every kind, even those pertaining to God, being allowed. The consequences are, first, the blasphemous position, that God is the devil himself, not providence; secondly, that men have no conscience or ability to distinguish right from wrong; thirdly, that all kinds of sin are to be praised, and that none are punishable, all being the work of God.'

These conclusions are assailed in a manner as convincing as it is pious. The Scriptures are the source of the writer's arguments: he shows by the strongest evidence that God performs his own proper work, and man his, without God's either assisting man too much or taking too much from him. Christ, according to the Libertine system, is the spirit which is in the world, and in us all. The death upon the cross was in appearance only. Christ is in his people: they are all Christ, and can no more suffer, all being now accomplished. The new birth consists in the power of suppressing the fear of God and conscience, and in living according to Christian freedom. Men can sin no more in that perfected state of innocence. The freedom thus possessed is boundless; as if Paul, who is cited, had allowed them to steal, to slay and commit every species of licentiousness. Calvin proves, on the contrary, that the law retains its force for Christians, with this distinction only, that it no longer condemns us without recall, grace being provided by the Gospel. "Let every man live according to his inclination." It is thus that they understand what Paul says of the calling of Christians. But Calvin shows that we ought to follow the inward calling of God. If every one were to obey his own inclinations as a call, married people might separate from each other. The new marriage is a spiritual marriage.

And further. They would fain establish a perfect community of goods. Calvin however proves that the first Christians understood thereby nothing more than the greatest degree of liberality and benevolence. The resurrection, they say, is already passed, seeing that the spirit now returns to God*.

We shall shortly find to what extent these principles obtained ground in Geneva: they were not those of the anabaptists, which never revived after they had been opposed and openly confuted by Calvin, but the doctrines of an antichristian pantheism.

It appears that in France the higher ranks were especially infected by this spiritual libertinism. Those who had rejected catholicism in their hearts misused their christian freedom, living according to their will, but preserving an appearance of attachment to catholic forms. The enemies of the faith therefore took advantage of the publication of the work against the libertines to excite the queen of Navarre against Calvin, her favourites Quintin and Poques having been rendered ridiculous by the satirical freedom with which he had treated their names. When he learned at Geneva the change which had taken place in her opinions, he wrote to her, and in a style which combined equal dignity, firmness and prudence†. A perfect understanding was hereby restored between them, and the sect, which had spread

* A letter to the Faithful of Rouen refers to the same subject. It was written "Contre un Franciscain sectateur des erreurs des libertins." Farel also wrote against this wretched sect. Calvin had exhorted him to do all in his power to suppress it. A Franciscan wrote an answer to his work.

† According to Beza, "ingenue et cordate."

itself at various times over France, was for ever suppressed, no trace of it remaining except in Belgium.

The system of the libertines however exhibited itself at Geneva under still darker colours. A perfectly formed antichristianity, a true offspring of hell, sprung forth. We learn from many circumstances that this spiritual libertinism was in close union with the political, but not necessarily so. Among the signs of the evil spirit thus existing we may particularly mention the blasphemies uttered against the truth of the Gospel. These are found in the work of a certain Genevese citizen of the libertine party, and exhibited in the most hideous forms. An utter disregard for all morality is shown, among other instances, in the trial of the wife of the councillor Ameaux. Proofs of superstition and of the grossest egotism are afforded, especially in the compacts formed with the devil, in order to obtain from him a certain degree of power. These appear in the process against the persons who were accused of diffusing the plague. Numberless other things of an equally infamous character, but of a different kind, are grouped together.

Gruet's work is now only known by the sentence pronounced upon him, and by Calvin's extract. As even this however was never generally circulated, Gruet was always confounded with the authors of the "Three Impostors*." But it is certain that he had no hand in that work. He speaks of God and Christ, of Moses, the prophets, and the apostles, but never of Mahomet, which could not have been unobserved by Calvin. The main object of his work seems to have been to show, that the founders of both Judaism and Christianity were deceivers, and that Christ was justly put to death. But the work entitled "De Tribus Impostoribus" is a species of philosophical treatise, in which a disbeliever pretends to show, tranquilly and with regret, but without abuse, that the three revealed religions are founded in fraud, and that the only true religion is that of nature.

The world was for three hundred years mystified respecting this production: it was at length printed. Till it was thus made known, it was dreaded as a kind of monster lurking in secret. People considered that they were affording one of the best proofs of conversion if, just before their death, they burnt the extracts from this work which they had secretly obtained at some exorbitant price. But Gruet's work was still more adapted

* Traité des Trois Imposteurs, 1777. Diss. de la Monnoye, p. 108.

to horrify the world, and we owe a debt of gratitude to those by whom it was destroyed. The present generation is tolerably well hardened against atheistical writings, but the daring blasphemy of this production was so frightful, that no one could read it without terror; for what are all the antichristian writings of the French revolution compared with the hellish laughter which seemed to peal from its pages*?

It was not till a later period that the work to which we allude was discovered, but it was at the present time (1545–6) that it was written, and secretly read at Geneva. The principles of the anti-calvinistic party are sufficiently apparent. The pantheism of the libertines led directly to atheism, and this, among the initiated, to a secret but most decided hatred to Christ. How indeed could such a wicked and blasphemous disposition have developed itself in Gruet, had he not been living in the midst of an infected atmosphere? The book consisted of thirteen sheets, was in Gruet's own handwriting, and was bound in parchment. It was discovered in 1550, under the roof of his own house, where he had probably placed it at the time of his apprehension, and was delivered to the magistrate. Only some single, detached passages were found among his papers, but they seem to have contained the elements out of which the work was composed. They formed the foundation of the charge of blasphemy brought against him, and in pursuance of which he was condemned to death. The work itself was burnt, but Calvin's remarks, and the evidence respecting its general character, are sufficient for the permanent justification of the Genevese magistrates, who, according to their principles and the feeling of their times, believed themselves bound to punish such offenders with the sword, and whom we still deem it right to load with chains.

The corruption of morals in Geneva has been already mentioned. It is evident, even from the numerous trials for witchcraft, that the state of manners in that city was fierce and turbulent. Men, clothed in black and masked, frequently appeared to women, and gave themselves out for the devil, intending no

* Although this work, *De Tribus Impostoribus,* is attributed by many to the emperor Frederic II., or rather to his chancellor *Petrus à Vineis,* it is probably a production of the sixteenth century. It is written in Latin, and bears the title, *De Imposturis religionum breve Compendium.* There have been two editions of the Latin text; the latter with the title, *De Tribus Impostoribus.* A later work, of the same blasphemous character, has appeared in French, which however is nothing more than a copy of the *L'Esprit de Spinoza.* A sect known as that of the Lucianists existed in the latter half of the sixteenth century, and from this proceeded the *De Tribus Impostoribus.*

doubt to fill their minds with terror, and subject them to their will.

But this immorality received a new impulse from the principles of the spiritual libertines; and numberless processes before the tribunals prove that this state of things must have long continued. The account of the wife of the councillor Ameaux belongs to the same period. Her principles, which were identical with those of the libertines, show by their very nature that they were not gathered from the clouds, or created by the wanderings of a sick or phrenzied mind. It was the wish of her friends to make it believed that she was mad: they hoped by that means to secure her escape. But her opinions had a deeper root; and her conduct compromised her husband, whose condemnation followed at a later period. According to the report of her trial, she not only gave herself up to the grossest immorality, but justified this immorality as founded in principle. The process shows, that she was convinced that she might place herself at the disposal of any believer. This was a notion common to the spiritual libertines, as appears from the trial of Gruet, and other acts. "It is in this sense," she said, "we ought to take the communion of saints, spoken of in the Apostles' Creed; for this communion can never be perfect, till all things are common among the faithful, goods, houses, and the body. Believers have then only reached the highest grade of love when they understand this principle. No one ought to forbid this communion even between the nearest relatives. Such a union is holy, if it take place between a protestant and a catholic, since, according to Saint Paul, the believer sanctifies the unbeliever. A union of this kind cannot be forbidden without wickedness, the first command which God gave to man being, 'Increase and multiply'."

The consistory and the council employed themselves earnestly about these matters, and granted the husband the separation which he desired. The woman was committed to prison for life.

At a somewhat later period, the history of Raoul Monnet, a representative of the madness and folly of this sect, affords a further illustration of the prevailing power of Antichrist. Raoul boasted his illicit connection with women of the highest families in Geneva, especially with the wife of the first syndic Perrin. He had a collection of obscene prints, copied from Aretino, and which he insultingly called his New Testament: so too he had spoken disgracefully of his fatherland.

Raoul was beheaded, and his pictures were burnt by the common hangman. He had been long connected with the faction of Perrin, and it was only shortly before his apprehension that he had left it. This party, well-skilled in the arts of intrigue, hastened as much as possible his execution, that he might not have time to address the people, and expose their conspiracies*. It is well-worthy of observation, that Calvin makes no mention in any of his letters of these circumstances. They might occur perhaps too rapidly, or they might seem of too tragical a nature to form the subject of friendly communication.

But still more horrible was the iniquity of the *egoism*, which appeared in the alliance of the so-called *infectionists*. A pestilential disorder had for many years prevailed in Geneva, and the surrounding districts, to such a degree, that the population was in fact decimated, two thousand inhabitants dying out of twenty thousand, the highest estimate of the population of this little city. All the relations of life were disturbed: the courts of justice were closed; and the evil would have become still worse, had not circumstances led to the discovery of a conspiracy, of rare iniquity even in those times, formed by a set of wretches who diffused the infection by means similar to those employed in 1530. Their practice was to mix up the virus drawn from those who were sick of the plague with salve, and then to place it upon the locks and bars of doors, and on the lines in the public streets. The disease was thus spread in the most awful manner. Even some of the inspectors of the hospital were in league with these wretches, whose only object it was to share among each other what belonged to the dead. They had bound themselves by an oath not to cease from this course, till Geneva, as they expressed it, might be fed by a single measure of corn, when it would be possible for them to take possession of the entire city†.

A man named Tallent betrayed the conspirators, and one Lentille was the first brought to trial. He pretended to know nothing of the matter, but said, that care ought to be taken to

* Picot, T. i. p. 426.

† Some suspicion respecting this crime existed at an earlier period. In the registers of April 17, 1543, we read: "J. Goulaz, accusé d'avoir semé la peste, a enduré sept estrapades et le tourment des Bujegnins sans rien avouer; on le gardera encore en prison, puis l'on avisera. June 8: L'on soupçonne que de nuit il y a des empoissonneurs, qui sement la peste par la ville. Ordonné d'en parler à Mr. Henri, portier de la Tartasse. May 16, 1545: On bannit pour trois ans, sous peine de fouet, les maris des femmes executées pour avoir communiqué la peste."

watch those who were engaged in the hospital, if the magistrates wished to stop the pestilence. According to Spon and others, the affair was made a matter of jest among these people: they inquired, when they met each other, how the plague went on, and gave it the name of the *cripple*, as death and fever have been called. Thirty-one of these wretches were apprehended and burnt: Jean Lentille died in consequence of the torture to which he had been subjected: the physician and the two assistants were quartered. Notwithstanding the horrible punishments which the culprits had suffered, the same crime was renewed in 1568. It is impossible to account for the perpetration of such enormities without supposing them to have been connected with others of a still more secret character. We trace, for example, the existence of a fanaticism among the conspirators, which had its origin in superstition and in the most frightful selfishness. They were resolved to destroy all or to gain all, and their confessions show that they believed themselves protected against infection by a league with the devil; being indeed guarded, and allowed to gain possession of the treasures of the world, while they prayed to him, who has promised them to his worshipers.

It may easily be conceived how these horrors afflicted Calvin and all other holy men: he ascended the pulpit, and, deeply moved, spoke with great vehemence against the levity and vice which prevailed in the city. Convinced that the pestilence was a scourge sent by God, he declared aloud that the corruption of manners was the cause of the affliction, and besought the council to inflict severer punishments on those guilty of adultery and harlotry. He seems indeed from this time to have resolved that adultery ought to be punished with death: the offence was connected in his mind with others of a still higher kind; he regarded it as resulting from the anti-christianity of the age, and which he desired to extirpate with fire and sword.

Some writers have sought in later times to throw suspicion on these accounts, and to compare the belief in their truth to the absurd notion which attributed the cholera to certain physicians, and so to establish the position that fanaticism discovered horrors where none existed. They seem however to forget that it was the educated, and not the lower class of people, in Geneva who undertook to punish the accused, that the crime was repeated at three different times, and that a period of twenty years was sufficient to afford ample opportunities for reflection, and for the investigation of evidence. To this it may be added, that two of the culprits were, with Calvin's help, converted, and by the grace of God went tranquilly to their death. We cannot suppose that they did not make a true confession to their spiritual adviser. Calvin therefore may be taken as a witness, in whose testimony we may place entire confidence: he speaks of their fanatical ideas, but without saying anything further. It seems that they were instigated to their hellish work by some fearful kind of influence. Calvin viewed this with grief and awe; but he communicated the fact to his friends very briefly, and without attempting to determine what is true or false in the supposed operations of Satan. This laconic mode of expressing himself led to the suspicion that he did not willingly speak on the subject. His own words are as follows*:—"The Lord is trying us in a wonderful manner. A short time back the discovery was made of a conspiracy of men and women, who for three years past have contrived by some species of witchcraft to circulate the pestilence through the city. Already have fifteen women been burnt: several men, dreadfully tortured, have killed themselves in prison: there are still twenty-five in confinement. But notwithstanding this, the locks on the doors of houses continue to be every day besmeared with the infectious salve. Such are the dangers to which we are exposed. God has hitherto guarded our house, but it stands in the midst of perils. Well it is that we know He careth for us. Farewell, my honoured friend and dear brother!"

To Farel he wrote†:—"Why should I relate to you what has taken place in regard to the infection? Weber (Textor) is with you, and he can explain to you all the circumstances much more clearly than I could in a letter. Renat has filled us with surprise: it is perfectly wonderful that a man who remained firm under torture should be overcome by a supposed promise; that is, by its being told him that I had obtained the promise of a pardon for him from the council. His wife confessed that she had destroyed eighteen men by witchcraft or poisoning, and that he had killed four or five. The power of the Lord was wonderfully shown at the death of this culprit, so perfect was the conversion of his soul. In the morning he evinced no sign of repentance, but still, as it seemed, hurried on by his fanaticism, he complained that he was about to be punished though the Lord had pardoned him. But the Lord, as I have said, has wrought marvellously

* MS. Gen. March 27, 1545. † MS. Gen. April 25, 1545.

and beyond my hope. Both met their death joyfully, with the greatest firmness, with the strongest faith, and with the surest indications of repentance."

About this time also a so-called wizard was apprehended at Peney, but he was dismissed by the magistrates as a madman. This is a proof that some distinction was made among offenders of this kind.

To such an extent did these disorders proceed, that Geneva was suspected by the people of the neighbouring states of being engaged in the sale of poison. Thus in 1565 a simple, ignorant man from the country came to the city for the purpose of purchasing from the *seigneurs*, that is the council, a portion of the well-known salve: he is said to have been in league with the devil, and was burnt alive*.

In conjunction with the spiritual libertines, and as active instruments of the same spirit, were another class to which the name of political libertines was applied. Among these may be ranked those families in Geneva who, not comprehending Calvin's theocratical views, employed all their influence to resist them. This party desired nothing but emancipation from the despotism of Savoy, and the establishment of free institutions. The Reformation offered them the means of attaining their end. They were not necessarily connected with the spiritual libertines: their leader Perrin does not appear to have been imbued with any speculative anti-christian element, but to have simply desired reputation and power. But Calvin was a stumbling-stone to these people: so long as he stood with the thunder of his eloquence, with his iron will, and with the Gospel in his hand, they could not advance a step. Calvin's vocation and zealous spiritual efforts were a riddle to them, and they ascribed his conduct to a boundless ambition, judging his principles by their own passions. Both parties were repeatedly brought into rude collision with each other, and the apple of strife was the spiritual authority of the consistory and the right of excommunication. There was but one celebrated man of the anti-consistorial party, Bonnivard, who though burning with zeal for the freedom and welfare of his fatherland, and daring in his opinions, could yet understand Calvin and humble his libertine opposers.

Calvin's design extended further than to the present establish-

* This horrible transaction did not take place till a year after Calvin's death. The unhappy old man was evidently a lunatic; he had been urged to desire the poisonous salve, so he said, that he might take vengeance on those who had taken away his daughter.

ment of his institutions and principles. That which he was effecting on a small scale, he hoped to accomplish still more gloriously in the great kingdoms of the world, and thus to obtain for his principles a universal victory. To succeed in this object however, it was necessary for him to procure allies, to surround himself with friends, and to form a new Geneva in the old. The persecutions which still raged, especially in France, favoured his plan; fugitives from all parts gathered round his standard; among them were faithful, earnest Christians, some from Italy, others from the Netherlands and Spain, and with whom conscience availed more than fatherland. New churches were established; one of the first was that of the Italians, to whom the *Chapelle des Maccabées* was granted, or, according to others, *La Grand Salle du Collège**. In *Notre Dame la Neuve* the service was performed in English, in *St. Gervais* in Spanish, and in *St. Germain* in Flemish.

Calvin, as we have already seen, proclaimed it to be the bounden duty of the followers of the Gospel to leave their country, to die or become exiles, rather than incur the guilt of hypocrisy. Many of his writings, as those against the Nicomedites, show what were the arguments which he employed for this purpose. In one of his unpublished letters he exhorts a whole family to flee, proves why they ought to do so, tells them what course they should take, and what they had to expect at Geneva. These exiles found in that city the pestilence, hatred, and continual strife; but they willingly bore all this, settling themselves in the neighbourhood of this great man, that they might cheer themselves by the beams of his noble spirit, and listen to his sublime discourse. Thus a hundred youths sat at his feet in the lecture-room and noted down every word which he spoke, that they might publish his interpretation of the Scriptures in foreign lands. This was the state of things on the field of strife. Calvin's present efforts were all directed to obtain the admission of these worthy people to the rank of citizens, that, adopting his principles as they did, they might contend with him in the council for their establishment. The greater their number, the greater his influence: a majority of votes was thereby secured to him in the assemblies; but this led the entire faction of the libertines to persecute these people, or at least to render their lives as miserable as they could; and hence arose numberless disturbances. Nothing was neglected to pre-

* Picot. T. i. p. 391. Regis. Oct. 13, 1542.

vent their acquiring the right of citizenship. They demanded that they should be forbidden to bear arms; and it was at one time feared that they were plotting some murderous design against them. The exiles on the other hand rejoiced in the especial protection of the consistory. Galiffe, and the state-protocol show, that it was not safe for any one to speak insultingly against either the ministers or the refugees; to do so was regarded as an offence against God; and it is known that Calvin, when he had gained a majority in the council, procured the enrolment of three hundred new citizens at one time. They were for the most part Frenchmen, and it was openly declared that the measure was adopted "for the better protection and support of the lesser council." A change was now produced in the spirit of the republic, the state being, according to Calvin's idea, an oligarchy. Nothing more was to be heard of the great assembly of the whole body of the citizens, the central point of primitive freedom; and they who wished to revive it were marked as unquiet spirits and disturbers of the people.

Thus the party which consisted of the old Genevese were brought, though too late, to the conviction that they were overpowered by intruders, and that they had been guilty of a gross oversight in committing the conduct of their spiritual affairs to a stranger. But the new citizens, strong in spirit, retained the upper hand, and vanquished these modern Canaanites. The reformation, after a period of fearful contention, was accomplished, and a new Calvinistic Geneva brought into existence.

CHAPTER XIII.

FURY OF THE LIBERTINES.—ANGER AND SEVERITY OF CALVIN. —AMEAUX, PERRIN, AND GRUET.

It cannot be matter of surprise that the rage of the fanatical libertines was excited to the highest degree against a man who, unarmed, and aided only by the sword of his eloquence, could confound them all. It may be that he occasionally acted with too much of passion, that he allowed himself to be carried away by his indignation. The world can form no proper idea of his zeal, but vast is the debt of gratitude which it owes to Calvin for his having with such stedfastness resisted that torrent of infidelity which, but for him, had to this day invaded and oppressed us. The libertines gnashed their teeth at him, and cried aloud that the state was lost. Calvin did not allow himself to be alarmed; the more they raged the higher rose his courage. He let the law take its free course; and the first councillor, as well as the simplest burgher, felt his severity and his power. But the wicked spirit which prevailed would yield neither to these efforts, nor to the solemn signs of the times; it was rather excited to new outbreaks of violence, and Calvin's stern announcement of the coming vengeance of God was found no false or empty prophecy. The libertines, who knew that they could not resist the continual thunder of his attacks, at length threw off the mask. All were resolved to venture the utmost; and from henceforward they desired to be made accountable for their offences not to the consistory, as the moral tribunal, but to the council of state. The former however was anxious to preserve the discipline of which it was the guardian, and which was sanctified by the Word of God. It appealed therefore to the council for support; this it obtained, and the spiritual principle was victorious. The struggle here alluded to is worthy of note in the history of the church; it shows the difficulties with which such a tribunal, especially in a small state, has to contend; and we cannot sufficiently admire the firmness of the council.

Calvin pours out his heart on this subject in his introduction to the commentary on the Psalms, and thus characterizes the rage of his enemies:—"If I should describe the course of my struggles from this period, it would make a long history. But it affords me no slight consolation, that David preceded me in these conflicts. For as the Philistines vexed this holy king by continual wars, but the wickedness and treachery of the faithless of his own house grieved him still more, so was I on all sides assailed, and had scarcely a moment's rest from outward or inward struggles. But when Satan had made so many efforts to destroy our church, it came at length to this, that I, unwarlike and timid as I am, found myself compelled to oppose my own body to the murderous assault, and so to ward it off. Five years long had we to struggle without ceasing for the upholding of discipline; for these evil-doers were endowed with too great a degree of power to be easily overcome; and a portion of the people, perverted by their means, wished only for an unbridled freedom. To such worthless men, despisers of the holy law, the ruin of the church was a matter of utter indifference, could they but obtain the liberty to do whatever they desired. Many were induced by necessity and hunger, some by ambition or by a shameful desire of gain, to attempt a general overthrow, and to risk their own ruin as well as ours, rather than be subject to the laws. Scarcely a single thing, I believe, was left unattempted by them during this long period which we might not suppose to have been prepared in the workshop of Satan. Their wretched designs could only be attended with a shameful disappointment. A melancholy drama was thus presented to me; for much as they deserved all possible punishment, I should have been rejoiced to see them passing their lives in peace and respectability; which might have been the case, had they not wholly rejected every kind of prudent admonition."

The trial of Ameaux may be especially mentioned as one of those which took place at this period, and as affording a profound view of Calvin's determined conduct. Pierre Ameaux, or Ameaulx, was a member of the council of Two Hundred, whose wife had been already punished for her libertinism. He was now in close alliance with some of its most depraved ministers, and had spoken loudly in a social meeting against both the doctrine and the person of Calvin, whom he called a mean and wicked man*. This was mentioned to the council, which felt itself bound, in remembrance of what Calvin had done for the church and state, to take serious notice of the matter, and having put Ameaux into prison to examine him judicially. It was deemed proper however at the same time to call the council together, that an inquiry might be entered into, whether there was anything in Calvin's conduct deserving of reprehension. Several ministers were summoned on the occasion, and they were desired to state, in the absence of Calvin himself, their candid opinion respecting him. They bore the most honourable testimony to the purity both of his doctrine and his conduct. It was not deemed proper however to inflict on Ameaux any further punishment than that of a fine of sixty dollars. He had retracted his complaints against Calvin, and had declared that he was not in his right senses when he uttered the objectionable words, adding still further, that he would for the future show him all becoming respect. But Calvin now appeared before the council, accompanied by

* Picot, T. ii. p. 410. In the state-protocol of Jan. 27, 1546, it is said, "On met Pierre Ameaulx en jugement pour avoir dit que Mr. Calvin prêchoit une fausse doctrine, étoit un très-méchant homme, et n'étoit qu'un Picard."

all the ministers and elders of the church. He complained of the lenity of the judges, and demanded that the sentence should be set aside. The process was accordingly renewed, and the council condemned Ameaux to the following humiliating punishment: he was to pass through the whole city bare-headed, and with a lighted torch in his hand, and then to kneel down and openly proclaim his repentance, which was called "*faire amende honorable.*" Calvin may appear in this to have acted with fanatical severity; but it ought to be considered of what vast importance it was to him, in one respect at least, to secure a perfect purity of doctrine. In the present case he identified himself with his principles, and he founded his proceedings upon his knowledge of Ameaux and his party, to which Christianity was hateful, and whose aim it was to destroy it. He was fully prepared, the attempt having been made against religion itself, to fall with the respectability of the consistory. If we carefully observe that the extension of God's kingdom was his only desire, we must admire the grandeur and freedom of spirit which he exhibited under these circumstances, and which was sufficient to raise him above every other consideration, even above the painful feeling, that he might be suspected of indulging personal revenge, and thus be in danger of losing many of his followers. It required moreover no slight degree of courage and determination to proceed in such a manner against a man who occupied so high a position as Ameaux. We cannot for a moment impute to him the vulgar desire of triumphing over an opponent: he had proved how readily he could forgive, in other circumstances, and where he was only personally concerned. Could he have been fairly accused of the love of revenge, or of any dishonourable wish, he must have lost for ever the confidence of his party. As this however was far from being the case, we may conclude that it was evident to them that he acted according to higher principles. Could it either be supposed that Ameaux only spoke in jest, we should scarcely be able to account for the earnestness and severity which marked the proceedings of the council.

The sentence passed upon Ameaux gave rise to an outbreak of popular fury in one quarter of the city: but Calvin despised the tumultuous shouts of the multitude. Two preachers who had taken the part of Ameaux were deprived of their office: one of them, Henri de la Mar, was kept some days in prison. All the wine-shops were strictly closed, and the whole council proceeded to the disturbed quarter, and ordered a gallows to be erected in the Place de St. Gervais. This threat produced the desired effect: tranquillity was restored, and the sentence was executed on Ameaux, April 5, 1546.

Calvin's severity increased, and laws of the sternest character were passed against all offences. The consistory summoned a great number of licentious persons to appear before it, and submit to a strict examination of their morals. New edicts were published by the council against luxury*, and the public representation of a play, 'The Acts of the Apostles,' after having been performed ten times with great applause, was forbidden at the request of the clergy. Calvin describes in a letter to Farel† his conflict, under these circumstances, with the tumultuous people. The feeling of popular indignation was still further increased by an order which forbade the naming of children after the Roman catholic saints: among the most favourite names were those of Claudius and Balthazar, with which the people had associated certain superstitious ideas‡. To heap insult on morality and religion was the order of the day.

The principal family in the libertine party was that of Faber: Francis Faber had excited many to struggle for freedom. At the head however of the party was a man, Amied Perrini§, who, without any intellectual endowments, had made himself so conspicuous by his insolence and extravagant ambition, that Calvin was accustomed to call him the stage-emperor: his wife was the daughter of Faber.

A fierce opposer of the strict rule of the church, Perrin stood forth in 1553 with increased force against Calvin, nor was it till two years after that he began to shrink before the reformer. Having been raised by the voice of the people to the chief military station in the republic, he had a great show of worldly distinction to aid him in his struggle with Calvin. The latter had in this respect a more difficult position than Luther, who was protected by the prudent elector, and lived in the midst of a people who understood his heroic daring, and encouraged him by their applause. The laws of the consistory prohibited dancing, the

* Regis. 16 Av. 1543. Ep. lxxvi. Ed. Amst. T. viii. pp. 44–46.

† Epis. lxviii. Ed. Laus. Amst. p. 43.

‡ Picot, T. ii. pp. 413, 414. Regis. 1546, Av. 27. Chapuis was put in prison for having persisted in naming his child Claude, which the minister did not wish, but desired to call him Abraham.

§ Perrin is known under various names. In the old history of Servetus he is called Amadeus Gorrius; and in French, Amy Pierre or Ame Perrin. Calvin gives him the nickname of Cæsar Comicus and Cæsar Tragicus.

use of ornaments and worldly amusements. But some of the principal families had refused to deny themselves these indulgences, and having kept a festival at Bellerive, they were summoned first before the council and then before the consistory*. The answers which they gave at their examination evinced the lively hatred which they all entertained of the church discipline. Faber was condemned to three weeks' imprisonment. He would not however humble himself before the consistory as Perrin did, but went to prison exclaiming "Freedom, freedom!" Calvin's own words give interest to these circumstances, and show to what lengths he was led on the principle of moral government.

In a letter to Farel† he says: "The dance has given us more to do since your departure than I had at first expected. All who were present on the occasion were called before the consistory, and, with two exceptions (Corneus a syndic, and Perrin), blasphemed God and belied us with daring effrontery. I burned with indignation, and spoke with all my strength against this open contempt of God, declaring at the same time that it was in vain for them to mock at the holy pledge which we had taken. They persevered in their scorn. Having thoroughly considered the matter, I could do no otherwise than adjure them by God to repent of such wickedness; at the same time declaring that, at the peril of my life, I would make the truth known, that they might not for a moment imagine they had gained anything by their lies. Francisca Perrin also greatly abused us, because we are hostile to the Fabers. I answered her as I thought fit, and as she deserved, asking her whether her family was sacred and superior to the laws. Her father had been found guilty of one adultery, we were on the point of proving him guilty of another, and there was no little talk of a third: her brother had publicly ridiculed both the council and ourselves. I added lastly that they might if they pleased build a new city, in which they could live as they chose, if they did not like to be governed here by us, as under the yoke of Christ; but that as long as they were in Geneva it was useless for them to strive not to obey the laws. Were there, I further said, as many diadems in the house of Faber as there were phrenzied heads, this would not alter the fact that God is the Lord. Perrin himself had in the meantime fled to Lyons, hoping that the business might be buried in

* Perrin's wife is thus described by Calvin, "*uxor est prodigiosa furia*": and, "*impudenter criminum omnium defensionem suscipit.*" Ep. 70.

† Epis. lxxi. 1546.

silence. It was my opinion that they ought to be obliged to take an oath that they would acknowledge the truth. Corneus warned them respecting the danger of taking a false oath: they however not only declared what we desired, but added that they had danced on the same day at the house of the widow Balthazar. All were thrown into prison. The syndic afforded a remarkable instance of coolness; but having received a severe rebuke on the part of the consistory, he was deprived of his dignity till he should evince sincere repentance. It is reported that Perrin has come back from Lyons: let him do as he may he will not escape punishment. Henri, with our consent, was deposed from his office and committed to prison, but liberated after three days. It is already matter of public observation that the guilty have no hope of escaping punishment; and this, because the highest have not been spared, and my friends have escaped no better than my enemies. Perrin and his wife are raving in prison: the widow is almost mad; the others blush and are silent."

The two parties became more and more enraged against each other. Calvin's eloquence gave him a decided superiority in the little republic. On the 24th of July 1547 he wrote to Viret*:— "I continue to employ my usual severity while labouring to correct the prevailing vices, and especially those of the young. The right-thinking tell me of the dangers by which I am surrounded, but I take no heed of this, lest I should seem too careful for my personal safety. The Lord will provide such means of escape for me as He sees good." The families which belonged to the libertine party took a very formidable position; but Calvin remained master of the field, and never ceased to avail himself of his office as a preacher to attack his opponents. Somewhat later, that is August 21, 1547, he states in a letter to Farel that "letters were daily brought him from Lyons, from which he learnt that he had been killed ten times over." "Amadeus is in France; his wife is with her father, where she plays the Bacchanal according to her usual fashion. We besought the council that, if she showed true repentance, all the past might be forgotten. But this has not occurred, and she is so far gone as to have cut off all hopes of pardon. I will seek Penthesilea, when the season for administering the Lord's Supper arrives."

Still worse signs of confusion appeared soon after, and it became more and more evident that the enemies of Calvin would leave nothing undone to destroy his power. This is shown by

* Epist. lxxx.

an important letter, addressed at this time to Viret, and in which, not unlike Cicero, he boasts of the courage and eloquence, by which he had restrained the excited multitude*.

Calvin entertained originally very friendly feelings towards the captain-general, but this was before they were properly known to each other. Perrin, as a promoter of the reformation, had taken his part in recalling Calvin from Strasburg. At a later period, when they discovered the opposition existing in their principles, their mutual dislike became the fiercer from their former acquaintance. Calvin saw in Perrin only the libertine Genevese citizen, who, rash, active and frivolous, was on the way to become a Catiline†. He tried one means after another, either to win, or at least to bridle, this powerful opponent. Entreaty, admonition, threats, all were employed in vain, and he was compelled to resolve on subduing him by force. Whether Perrin's rashness had led him to form any treacherous design against the state, cannot be sufficiently proved; but it is evident that he was ready to excite a rising to overturn the existing order of things; and his conduct appears in the highest degree suspicious, when we read that Savoy calculated upon his assistance in its plans against Geneva. As an idol of the people, Perrin was all-powerful with the multitude, and the council itself felt that the pretensions of his family must be humbled. The imprisonment of his wife and of his father-in-law inflicted a deep wound on his pride, and he appeared before the lesser council, of which he was a member, with bitter complaints and threats. But his insolent words produced no effect on the council: his imprisonment was the more resolutely enforced, and the people suffered it to take place without opposition. He was accused especially of playing the tyrant, and of entertaining designs

* Ep. lxxxii. Sept. 17, 1547. Calvin here describes the tumultuous character of the assembly about the doors of the building where the council met. "Fearful," he says, "was the sight. I cast myself into the thickest of the crowd. I was pulled to and fro by those who wished to save me from harm. I called God to witness that I was come to offer myself to their swords, if they thirsted for blood." He next speaks of his conflict in the council, but adds, that the people shrunk from harming him, "as they would from the murder of a father."

† Many indications of this appear in his letters. In one addressed to Viret in Jan. 1546, he says, referring to Perrin, "O how I fear that he will at length render himself intolerable to this free city!" In addressing Perrin himself, he speaks to him as to a Judas, and uses the words *Quæ facis, fac citius.* Ed. Amst. p. 53. In a letter to Farel, Nov. 27, 1548, Ep. lxxxviii. MS. Gen., he describes him thus: "Eodem die Cæsar Comicus noster soccos iterum induit. Nunc ferocior aliquanto redditus inter histriones suos se thrasonico suo more jactat."

against the freedom of his fatherland, having formed the intention of introducing a body of two hundred soldiers from France, and quartering them in Geneva*. The whole city busied itself about this trial: many wished his death, others his liberation. The lesser council, after consulting the advocates, acquitted him on the capital charge, but condemned him to lose his offices, and desired that he should pray both God and the state to pardon his treasonable speeches. The office of captain-general was for ever abolished.

Farel and Viret were twice called to Geneva for the purpose of attempting to reconcile the two parties. They appeared before the council, and we hear Farel thus defending his friend:—"How," he exclaimed, "can you fail to honour Calvin? There is not a man in the world who has warred against Antichrist with such vigour as he; there is no one so learned; and if he have not spared you, neither has he shrunk from blaming the greatest men, Luther and Melancthon."

Tranquillity seemed restored, but the ministers were defeated. Perrin recovered his position, and it was said, indeed, by Calvin's recommendation; but the consequence was, that the wicked spirit of his party soon reached the height of iniquity. His followers wore a species of cuirass, that they might be known to each other, and they heaped upon the reformer every species of abuse. Farel and Viret, who were obliged to return, again effected a reconciliation between Calvin and Perrin; but it was only in appearance. A great many of Calvin's enemies had declared aloud, that it was their dislike to him which kept them from the Lord's Supper; but he and his brethren put them all to shame by their bold and resolute preaching of the truth. The council took their part, and on the 18th of December, 1548, an amnesty was proposed and settled†. But the events which succeeded show that Perrin had practised deceit, and had nothing else in view but to obtain for himself the first place in the state, and with it the means of accomplishing his designs. In the following year, 1549, he was first syndic. The old syndics,

* Regis. 25 Juill. 1555. It is said that when the Duke of Alba was told of Perrin's offer of help, he laughed and replied, that if he had two thousand men under the walls of Geneva, and he found any discord in the city, he would take it without any aid from Ami Perrin.

† In a letter to Viret, Nov. 1548 (MS. Gen.), Calvin ascribes the restoration of Perrin, whom he speaks of as *Comicus Cæsar*, to the small number of the members of the council present. This, it is observed, does not agree with what is said by Senebier, who states that Calvin assisted in restoring Perrin, and adds, "Il eut la satisfaction chrétienne de voir son ennemi rehabilité."

contrary to the law, allowed him the highest rank. His power was thus firmly established, and he again stood opposed to Calvin as the champion of the evil principle against the good.

Anticipating the narrative of other events, I will here state that, after another treasonable movement of Perrin's party, the council at length became calvinistic, and suppressed the worst of the agitators by force. A sound policy had taught them that it was impossible to allow two hostile parties to exist together, without the ruin of the republic. It is possible however that the council may have made use of the disturbances as a pretence. The accusations do not appear of sufficient importance; and the council, as was too often the case in those times of excitement, seems to have played with the lives of individuals, and not to have shrunk from shedding blood on the slightest suspicion, for the sake of establishing peace. Perrin himself escaped to France, and was only hung in effigy. Bern especially demanded the annulling of the sentence; and thus some degree of obscurity must ever involve the actual criminality of this notorious personage.

Immediately after the apprehension of Faber and Perrin, which took place on Monday, June 27, 1547, it was discovered that one of the libertines, the before-named citizen Jacobus Gruet, descended from an old and respectable family, had affixed a libel to the pulpit in the high church of St. Peter. This paper contained an expression of hatred against the established discipline, and a threatening intimation that a plan was laid to annihilate the champions of the church party by murder.

The judicial proceeding against Gruet is important as a prelude to that of Servetus. It exhibits the principles of the council, the prevailing laws of the city, and at the same time the connection between the spiritual and the political libertines. The accusation brought against Servetus was purely religious, whereas in that against Gruet the religious was mingled with the political, and presented a more awful specimen of unbelief. We will leave Calvin himself to give an account of this affair.

Addressing Viret*, he says, "We must now contend in earnest." Then having alluded to the wife of the stage hero, and to her rage against the spiritual rule which had bridled her love of dancing, he continues:—"The council committed her to close confinement. She fled. The next day a paper was found affixed to the pulpit, threatening us with death if we did not remain silent. The council, greatly moved by such proceedings, have

* Epis. lxxvii. July 11, 1547.

given command to investigate thoroughly the nature of the conspiracy. As the suspicion of many rests on Gruet, he has been apprehended, but the hand-writing does not agree with his. A search however having been made among his papers, several others were found of a not less guilty character, one of which was an intended address to the people on the day of assembly, and in which he endeavoured to prove that that only ought to be punished by the laws which might appear injurious to the state. There was the danger, he argued, that whilst the city was under the government of a single melancholy man (Calvin), an insurrection might be excited, and the city might thus be deprived of thousands of its inhabitants. Two sides were written in Latin, and in these he made a mock of Scripture altogether, and abused the Saviour. Immortality he called a dream and a fable, and struck at the very root of all religion. I do not believe that he is the author of this paper, but it is in his handwriting, and the process therefore is carried on. It is possible that he may have employed his own wit to reduce to a whole that which he has heard from others." Calvin here recognised the doctrine of that satanic association founded by the spiritual libertines.

Some circumstances may be mentioned which serve to throw light on the origin of Gruet's wrath. In order to make his freedom of opinion publicly known, he had introduced a part of the Bernese costume, the people of Bern being opposed to Calvin and the council*. This luxurious dress was immediately prohibited, and the compulsion thus exercised inspired the great champion of freedom with the most violent indignation. The preachers exhibited little moderation towards their opponents. Cop, a bold energetic minister, had called the Genevese ladies of the libertine party, and who were in the habit of attending theatrical representations, harlots. Thus too Abel Poupin described Faber as a hound, and Calvin, Gruet as "*balaufre.*"

Gruet, who felt his strength, was greatly embittered to see his friends humbled, and obliged to bend the knee before the consistory. The words of the libel were†, "You and yours shall gain little by your measures; if you do not take yourselves away, no one shall save you from destruction; you shall curse the hour when you forsook your monkhood. Warning should have been given before, that the devil and his legions were come

* "Les hauts de chausses chaplés aux genoux."

† Galiffe, Not. Gen. Art. Gruet.

hither to ruin everything. But though we have been patient for a time, revenge will be had at last. Defend yourselves, or you will share the fate of Verle of Freiburg*. We do not wish to have so many masters here. Mark well what I say."

Suspicion must have been already directed towards Gruet; he would not otherwise have been so immediately accused in the present instance. As a rash, enterprising man, occupying a conspicuous place in his party, he must have betrayed his anti-christian sentiments in a thousand ways to the eye of an observer like Calvin. The process was begun, attended as it seems with some agitation. According to established usage, the accuser was to be imprisoned with the accused; but in this case the whole council must have gone to prison, the charge being one of high-treason, and as such could be brought by no other body. Gruet however was subjected to the torture morning and evening during a whole month: he bore his sufferings firmly, and without betraying one of his confederates, of whom he must have had many.

In a letter to P. de Bourg, he says of Calvin, whom he names "Episcopum Asculanensem," "He is a great hypocrite, who would fain be worshiped himself, while he robs our holy father the pope of the honour due to him. His audacity is so great that he declares he will make even kings and emperors tremble." In another letter he accuses him of trifling with holy things. It is worthy of remark, that a copy of the work against the Anabaptists and libertines was found in his house: he had written on the margin "*toutes folies*," which shows plainly that he had employed himself on the subject, and felt that he was aimed at in the passage which he had marked.

On the 9th of July he confessed that he had been guilty of affixing the threatening placard to the pulpit. On the 12th he repeated this confession, with some alterations: he also stated that the writings found in his house were his own composition, and prayed with tears that he might be at once led to execution.

We cannot repress a sigh, that the rude period which we are contemplating would not allow men to discover, that intolerance is as hateful as blasphemy, and the actual infliction of torture as great a crime as uttering a threat of murder. But in the present case the state was a principal actor: it would therefore be unjust to attribute Gruet's death solely to the religious government of Geneva, as if it had been effected simply through

* A gentleman who had been murdered.

the hatred of his spiritual opponents. His condemnation must have taken place, had Calvin not been in Geneva. The latter had no doubt rightly judged his character, although it was not till after his death that his worst crime came to light, and that his punishment appeared proportioned to his offence. But nothing can be more ridiculous than the clamour raised at the mention of Gruet's torture, as if Calvin was the author of its infliction. Not the slightest evidence exists in history that such was the case, while it is well known that no important trial took place in those times, in any part of the world, without the application of the rack. In the proceedings carried on against mere heretics, as in the trials of Servetus and Gentilis, no mention is made of torture; but it would be contrary to all historical principles to judge Calvin and his times by the rule of modern opinion. With equal right, and with the same consequences, it might be objected against him that he did not wear a peruke *à la* Louis XIV., or found his decisions according to the Code Napoleon. Calvin speaks on these things with great simplicity and earnestness in his letters, written about this time, to Bourgogne, and calls the libertines young people whom he must constrain and bridle, and thus do them good against their own will*.

Gruet was brought to the scaffold July 26, 1547. The sentence, which was read aloud to him, purported, that he had insulted religion, and had declared that the laws, both divine and human, were but the invention of man; that he had written blasphemous and obscene verses, and defended the grossest licentiousness; and that he had thereby endeavoured to overturn the institutions of the church, and lessen the authority of the consistory. It was further added, that he had threatened the reformers and the clergy, and had spoken with especial disrespect of Calvin; that he had written letters to excite the French court and the monarch against him; and lastly, that he had threatened even the council itself.

It is to be observed, that his unchristian sentiments and immorality were first noticed, and that then followed his resistance to the consistory, and in the third place his threatening of the council. But in a republic, where religion was so closely bound up with the political government, every attempt against the former must have been viewed as equally directed against the latter, which hence must have incurred the charge of into-

* July 14, 1547.

lerance whenever it inflicted temporal punishment. As Gruet's resistance was directed against the moral institutions of the state, so was that of Servetus against its principal doctrine, which, as the foundation of its religion and its power was of still greater importance, and demanded a sterner sacrifice. With religion must the republic flourish or be overthrown.

It is really inspiriting to hear how Calvin stormed in his sermons against the opposite party, while at the same time he laboured to convert them. "I am ashamed," says he, "to preach the Word here among you, where such horrible disorders are taking place; and were I to follow my inclination, I should pray God to take me from this world. I would not live three days amid the vanities by which I am surrounded. And shall we still boast that we have established a reformation! Not servants of God, our judges might be blind, for they may feel our worthlessness with their hands. I know not indeed whether God may not send the executioner among us, refusing as we do to hear the admonitions of his mouth: yea, there is reason to fear that he is preparing to raise his armed hand. But this is not said to excite resistance against him, but that we may confess our misery, and no longer harden ourselves in sin. He has called us to repentance: let us then embrace both his promises and his threats; let those who serve the state fulfil their duties now with more faithfulness; let the clergy labour more diligently to cleanse the churches of their impurity; let every one look to his own house; from our houses let us look to ourselves, and sanctify ourselves, that when we celebrate the Lord's Supper, we may be more and more established in his grace, and be engrafted into his body, so that we may live in Him and He in us, and that we may be able to boast ourselves the children of God."

Still more striking is the deep religious earnestness which breathes in the statement put forth by him in the year 1550, on the vicious proceedings of Gruet:—"Not only did he oppose himself to our holy religion, but he poured forth such blasphemies that they make the hair stand on end. These things must tend to bring a curse upon the whole land: all therefore whose consciences are awake will feel the necessity of praying God to forgive this abuse of his name amongst us. The council ought again to declare aloud that this blasphemer has been justly condemned, that the wrath of God may be averted from the city which has harboured such wickedness; that the associates of this reprobate and more than devilish sect may have an example of vengeance before their eyes, and that thereby the mouths of those may be shut who would treat these crimes with levity." Gruet's book was cast into the fire by the common hangman, in the name of the Father, the Son, and the Holy Ghost. The Scriptures lay open before the people, and the ceremony took place at the door of the house, in the Bourg de Foux, where he had dwelt.

The Gospel thus gained a victory over its enemies; in the same manner as in Germany freedom triumphed when Luther burnt the pope's bull, and the papal decrees.

CHAPTER XIV.

INSULTS HEAPED ON CALVIN.—HIS RESOLUTION, INWARD PEACE, AND CONSOLATION IN FRIENDSHIP.—VIRET.

THE enemies of Calvin left nothing untried to injure or afflict him: he was exposed to insult, not only in the council, but in the open street. He says, in reference to this period, that he expected to be killed; and had his enemies succeeded, this would in all probability have been the case. Beza observes, among other things, that they gave the name of Calvin to their dogs; others converted it into Cain, the fratricide, in allusion to the execution of Gruet*. But he allowed nothing to rob him of his courage or his peace: he says to Viret, "I awaited tranquilly what my enemies might do; they tried every means to overthrow me; but, on the one side, I would take no notice of their insults; and, on the other, I let them understand that I regarded all their machinations with contempt. Had they discovered a single indication of fear in me, they would have supposed they had conquered. There is certainly nothing better

* To Viret, Feb. 12, 1545. "I must continue as ever to fight in darkness with hypocrisy." And further, Dec. 1547, he says emphatically, "Nunc redeo ex Senatu. Multa dixi, sed canitur surdis fabula: Dominus illis mentem restituat!" In the same month he again said, "that he knew not what he should do, but that he certainly could not much longer endure the conduct of such a people."

calculated to disappoint their aim, or to encourage the good to persevere, than my resolution."

Even the council was in many instances opposed to Calvin, and acted so as to increase his difficulties: as for example in regard to the printing of his works*. The following circumstances however gave rise to a still more serious persecution against him. When the new syndics, and among them his opponent Amadeus Perrin, were chosen in 1545, Calvin wrote to Viret respecting these persons. The letter was lost, and Viret's servant, into whose hands it fell, gave it to the syndics. Troillet translated it into French, and made it public. As the council was at that time unfavourably disposed towards Calvin, it excited complaints against him, and he was accused of having written, that the Genevese desired to be ruled without God, which was to slander the whole council. It might be well enough for him to assail his opponents in the pulpit, but he had no right to abuse them in his private letters. Calvin wrote hereupon to Farel, August 10, 1548, "As far as I can gather from common report, my letters have been given to them. The worst passage in these letters is this:—'Our people here, under the mask of Christians, wish to govern without Christ.' They regard this as an arrow directed against themselves. But I should readily endure any kind of death if it could tend to the defence of the truth. They are ashamed however to show these letters, of which they have gained possession by cunning, and they know well enough that I am in a position to endure many insults unmoved." (August 20, 1548). "Trusting to the testimony of my conscience, I fear no assault, for what can they inflict upon me worse than death?"

His enemies felt confident that they had him now in their power†; and the affair would have been carried to extremities could they have established the accusation against him. But his resolute and prudent conduct gained the victory. Although he supposed that he had sufficiently explained‡ the circumstance to the council, showing that he had only passed judgement on his opponents in a private letter, and as a Christian, without inflicting any public injury upon them, yet the council reproved him, and this was the cause why Farel and Viret came to Geneva to afford him the support of their influence.

It is well for us, after contemplating his struggle with the

* To Farel, 1548, MS. Gen.

† To Viret, Sept. 20, 1548.

‡ Galiffe, Not. Gen. p. 528.

outward world, to penetrate into the soul of this same man, armed as he was by God, and so living as it were with him, to learn to imitate his firmness. In an age characteristically wanting in force, it is elevating and strengthening to associate with noble minds; not only to survey with their eagle-like glance the divine plan, but to share with them the higher impulses of the spirit, grounded upon a holier sense of duty. Calvin's life was not rich in great visible circumstances, but the contrary was the case as to his inner conflicts, thoughts and works. We have not in him the joyous outbreaks and noble instances of proud defiance displayed by Luther, but he ever exhibited the persevering resolution and the truth, even to death, which win the crown of life.

It is important for the display of the fine inner life of Calvin, to read how greatly he was distressed, under present circumstances, at the approach of the season for celebrating the Lord's Supper. He says, "The coming Sunday is the day for administering the sacrament. You can easily imagine with what anxiety I am oppressed. Would that it could be celebrated in my absence, even under the condition that I should come creeping to you on my hands and knees*!" Thus we see Calvin contrasted with men who, according to his conviction, often approached the table of the Lord with hypocrisy; while he only sought it under the influence of deep feeling, and an immoveable faith in the righteousness of God, and in the presence of Christ in the sacrament. He frequently indeed yielded himself to the spirit of the Old Testament, but communion with Christ in the sacrament was the middle-point of his life. None of these struggles could affect him. During the whole of this turbulent period he was supported by a loftier principle, which kept him firm, and imparted to him that wise, determined will which nothing could bow. A more than human strength and confidence in this respect characterized his position. Those who study the lives of men celebrated in the world, will find that such men feel themselves impelled to action in a manner not to be explained by an ordinary understanding. It was so with Calvin, and it is only by this consideration that we can throw any light upon his conduct. He had no self-interest to promote, when he defied those who opposed him, and stood exposed to the hatred of half the world. How gladly would he have retreated and sought repose! What was it which kept him to his post, except the

* Ep. 70. To Farel, Sept. 1, 1546.

feeling that he had to fulfil a higher will than his own? What else could have moved him to employ the severest methods to gain his end, but the consciousness that the interests of truth could only be effectually supported by such means? This conviction gave him confidence, joy, and untiring patience, even when he saw himself mistaken by his friends and exposed to their censures*. It was from his entire resignation to the divine will that he drew consolation and life, and thus he says, "I bring my heart as an offering and gift to the Lord; I subject my bound and vanquished soul to the obedience of God." In the same humble spirit he adds, that his sufferings and conflicts were far less than those of other servants of the Lord,—that his struggles were but a jest.

"It is not worth the trouble," he says, writing to France, "to vex you. Far different were the anxieties endured by Moses and the prophets, the leaders of God's people. Such trials are necessary for us." A little afterwards he expresses the same joyous feeling. Moses rose to his mind, and rightly, for, like the lawgiver, Calvin led a new people to the Lord, triumphing over a thousand dangers. His address to Farel is very noble. "With respect to your exhortation, that I and my brethren should persevere with unbroken resolution, neither dangers nor troubles lessen my courage. But since I know not sometimes in this confusion where to look for counsel, I wish that God would allow me to depart. I can easily understand that you will say this is a foolish wish. But did not Moses, that glorious example of patience, complain of the burden which seemed to lie too heavily upon him? I am indeed assailed to a certain degree by such thoughts, but I do not encourage them." Certain it is, that while all his friends trembled more and more for him, and while the whole city was raging against him, he alone enjoyed profound tranquillity of soul. All that he says gives proof of this. At a moment full of disquietude for many he thus speaks:—"The two hundred are deliberating. I am kept in a state of expectation, that I may look for rest in the Lord alone. If we serve Him with a good conscience, we can never avoid the rage of those who would fain involve everything in ruin. But it will always be to us a strong tower that we hold fast by the Lord." At the same time he also says, "I am con-

* To Farel, Dec. 28, 1547. Ep. 83. "There are some, I know, who complain to Viret of my severity; I am not aware of what Viret himself thinks, but I suspect that he fears I am giving too much room to my zeal."

vinced, in the first place, that God shields us; and in the next, that when it pleases Him to expose us to suffering, to die for Him will be my deliverance. The present time warns us more than ever to be prepared to receive from God whatever He may send us. My apprehensions, as far as they concern my own danger, hinder me not from sleeping tranquilly. While I am pursuing the path which He prescribes me, I learn how to cast the greater part of my cares, if not all, upon Him."

Altogether, in this respect, like Luther, God was his strong tower. Like him he exhibited the courage which had faith for its firm foundation; but he was not so happy as Luther, who, surrounded by powerful friends, could find a refuge in the fortress of Sickingen, Schaumburg and others. Geneva had the Savoy and French territory at its very gates, and was connected only by the lake with the Swiss cantons, but half of which had as yet received the reformation. The little republic lay like a rock in the sea, and this rock was occupied by parties and treachery. How often might the reformer utter the words of the prophet, those words which he so continually repeated when he was dying, "O that I had the wings of the dove!" His eye rested upon the distant Alps, which stretched before him tranquilly, eternally glistering; he remembered the rock of God's strength, and raised his thoughts to Heaven. "I lift up mine eyes towards the hills," he says, "but my help cometh from the Lord."

In contrast to the fierce, hostile commotions of which we have spoken, is the deep affection of Calvin for his friends, and his lively care for them, comforting and active to the uttermost even in the midst of those stormy times. The dedications which he wrote at this period show that he sought consolation in friendship, and gladly reverted in thought to the tranquil days of his childhood and youth. There is a loftiness of expression in the letters which he addressed to John Sturm in Strasburg. They are those of a man who felt himself safe above the ruins of the world. "Let it even be that entire destruction awaits us, or rather that the Lord, overturning the present system, and establishing his heavenly kingdom, has determined to gather together those who are now unhappily dispersed, and are wandering to and fro, still should we preserve with true constancy that friendship whose band is holy."

As Viret was numbered among the friends dearest to his heart, he extended his affection to those who were related to Viret, and he thus expresses the feelings of his soul in a letter addressed to him in March 1545:—"We greet you with your wife, whose health we have commended to God. Be assured that we are as anxious about her as if she were our own wife or daughter. May the Lord uphold and strengthen you with the consolations of his spirit." Again he writes:—"Could you really suppose that I would refuse you anything which you are anxious that I should grant*?"

In respect to vigour of mind and habits of business, Calvin seems to have estimated Viret even more highly than Farel. But the heart of the latter was more closely united to Calvin, and their respect for each other increased with their mutual labours. According to the conviction common to both, each was the *complement*, the completion of the other. Farel was accustomed to compare Calvin to Moses. Although much older than Calvin, he undertook nothing without consulting him; and when he himself took the part of an adviser, he jested, and prayed Calvin to suffer this for friendship's sake†.

When Viret's wife fell sick, Calvin manifested the most affectionate concern, and sent him a physician. After her death he wrote to him, saying, "Come, not only for the sake of lessening your present grief, but to obtain some respite from all other distresses. Do not fear that I should impose any new burden upon you; my only care would be to let you be quiet, according to your own wish. If any one should prove troublesome to you, I will come to your relief. The brethren promise you what I do. I will even obtain from the citizens what you wish. I know not how sufficiently to execrate the wretches who have spread the report of your death. Nothing could be more opportune than your letter. In spite of what was said respecting your death, mention having been made of poison, Textor prepared to set off at once for the place on horseback. A great many of the brethren assembled in my house, all in great anxiety and affliction. As soon however as your letter came to sight, such was the storm of joy which succeeded, that we were scarcely masters of ourselves. It is well that we had not had a night of sorrow. I should not have been able to endure the contrast. But why do I detain you, and not rather urge you to hasten hither with all possible speed? Farewell, my brother and dearest friend!"

* March, 1545, MS. Gen.

† Sept. 7, 1555, Ed. Amst. p. 234, Ep. 211, Ed. Laus. Schmidt, Études sur Farel, p. 57.

When Calvin had to endure the same grief, Viret comforted him in his turn. Bucer, who knew Calvin's wife, and was united with them both in the strictest bonds of friendship, expressed at the beginning of the year 1549, his earnest desire for their happiness. It is evident that they all feared that anxiety, and the death of his wife, might break Calvin's strength*. "I fervently pray to God that He may restore your wife, and this I do rather for the church of Christ than for you, that you may be able still to do for it, and with a lighter and more cheerful heart, what you are now doing. My brethren and my wife unite in praying that you may have all that can be wished for, both in the year just commenced and in all eternity." Calvin's wife was soon after this called to the Lord. He now stood alone in the storm and in the conflict with half the world, but his soul remained firm as ever. Farel and Viret manifested their care for him during his domestic afflictions†.

CHAPTER XV.

EFFORTS TO RE-ESTABLISH PEACE.—STRUGGLE ON BEHALF OF A GREAT CHURCH UNION.—AGREEMENT OF THE ZURICHERS ON THE LORD'S SUPPER.

NOTWITHSTANDING his zeal, and the bursts of ardour which he often exhibited, Calvin lost none of the tranquillity and moderation proper to his character. As far as possible he avoided strife: this is shown by his conduct towards Servetus, when they were now again brought into collision. In the midst of the agitation which we have described, Servetus, who had been living in France as a physician, and had taken part in the most fanatical projects of reformation, was desirous of forming a league with Calvin, from the conviction that the support of so great a mind might enable him to accomplish his designs. Calvin had refused him, and at length, when Servétus continued to reproach him, he remained silent. Servetus now attacked Viret. Calvin, who thoroughly knew the man, was resolved to have no

* Ep. 96, Jan. 9, 1549.
† Ep. 102 (Ed. Amst. p. 52,), April 10, 1549.

further communication with him, and was anxious to avoid him. This appears from a passage in a letter to Viret:—"I think you have already seen the answer which I sent Servetus. I have resolved to have no further contest with this perverse, stiff-necked, heretical man. It is certainly right in this case to follow the precept of the apostle Paul. He now attacks you, and it behoves you to consider how far it will be prudent for you to oppose his folly: for my part he shall force nothing further from me." Calvin sought peace: both the office imposed upon him by God and his own heart led him to desire to reconcile the jarring spirits of his age, and to secure the permanency of that which he had accomplished. Among all these storms raging without, his mind was occupied with a great and extensive plan, to fix the little republic of Geneva on a firm and tranquil basis. His thoughts were constantly directed to a system of general church polity, and to the establishment of the faith by a common confession. I have already spoken of his efforts to accomplish this object, and have remarked the desire expressed in his work on the Lord's Supper, to subdue the violence of hostile parties. His soul contemplated the unity of the entire evangelical church in Christ, its head and centre.

It was in conformity with these feelings that he now promoted, by all the means in his power, the Zurich confederacy, or the union of the French reformed party with that of Switzerland. This was the first step towards the accomplishment of his greater plan. Calvin, agreeing almost entirely with Melancthon, had been recognized even by Luther as a fellow-believer. The last proceeding of the German reformer was a matter of mere private concern, and had no dogmatic importance. Thus even his own immediate followers suffered him to indulge his passion, without mingling in the strife. Calvin could therefore reasonably entertain the hope, after Luther's death, that, with the help of Melancthon, he might mediate successfully in promoting a union between Germany and Switzerland. Had this been really accomplished, the church would have formed one great and harmonious whole, and Calvin would have repaired, by his intervention, what Luther's violence had marred. But as an essential to this union, the Swiss must have confessed the spiritual, real, substantial presence of Christ in the sacrament. Most of them indeed had already adopted this doctrine, but from regard to Zwingli they refrained from openly confessing it, and this, though Zwingli himself had latterly represented the subject with more force and life than he had done in the earlier part of his career.

Great diversity of opinion however prevailed on this subject in the church at Bern. Viret was involved in a dispute with Sulzer; and opinion fluctuated between the old, one-sided, abstract view of the understanding, and the more concrete, living one supported by Calvin. Both he and Viret were accused at Zurich of having, according to report, dissented from the Swiss Confession and inclined to Lutheranism: but the contrary was known to be the case when Farel and Calvin visited Zurich in 1548. The former, greatly beloved there for his zeal and piety, was able to accomplish much. He was still, as ever, a fervent missionary for the things of the Lord, so unwearied that he could even exhort Calvin himself to action. They worked together unceasingly to calm the spirit of controversy which had arisen among individuals*.

The *Consensus Tigurinus*, which, had it not been for the foolish intervention of the Lutheran preacher Westphoal in Hamburg, and that of other, for the most part vain, followers of Luther, would have effected by degrees a general union in the whole protestant church, was completed in 1549†. Calvin had rightly felt that he must unite with Bullinger, the most powerful and influential man in that part of the church, and use every means to remove the old distrust. Hence there was commenced a correspondence, characteristic of both parties. That the undertaking which had already engaged so much of Calvin's attention, as his letters to Bullinger from Strasburg show, could not be an easy one, after all that had taken place, appears evident from a letter written to Viret in April 1548. He there complains that the Zurichers were so perverse, that they were ready to admit the most slanderous reports. His good sense, foresight and integrity, as well as the difficulties which he had to encounter, will be seen by some extracts which we will give from the letters which he wrote at this period, and in which he speaks openly of the matters in hand. Thus he says to Bullinger, March 1, 1548:—"Although I am conscious in myself of a more inward union with Christ in the sacrament than you express in your

* Calvin had shortly before this warned some of the ministers at Bern of the evils which continued strife would produce:—"Malum proculdubio in dies gliscet et crescet, nisi brevi tollatur."

† Salig. Hist. Augs. Confes. T. ii. p. 1076. Plank, Protest. Lehrbegriff, B. vi. p. 24.

words, yet this ought not to prevent our having the same Christ, or our being one in Him. It is only perhaps through this inward *consensus* that we can unite with each other. I have always loved the greatest candour: I cannot endure subtleties, and the praise of clearness is given me by those who object to others on account of their obscurity. Cunning therefore can never be laid to my charge. I have never employed dissimulation to please men, and my mode of teaching is too simple to give rise to suspicion, and too full and explicit to be accused of darkness. If I do not content others by such means, let me be pardoned for honestly seeking to render back, in all simplicity and truth, that which I have received. I therefore felt no little surprise, when I was lately at Basel, to hear it stated by a friend, that you have complained that I have taught differently in my commentaries to what I promised you. I at once answered, and truly, that I spoke no otherwise at Zurich than at Geneva. But I ascribe all this rather to some error; for why should I now, without any necessity for so doing, alter my doctrines or principles? If however I cannot convince men of this, I will remain content with knowing myself that God is witness to the truth of what I say."

Thus also in the following letter he seeks to win Bullinger by his gentleness:—"We are anxious to come to a friendly understanding with you. It is no mere theatrical affair, which would be as disagreeable to you as to me, that we propose. I say nothing about Farel, whose mind, as you well know, shrinks with disgust from every kind of ostentation. That which we wish is to speak with you in a friendly way on the subject about which we so little agree. This is the best mode among brethren, and, if I do not greatly err, that which we should find the most profitable. In respect to the question of the sacraments, we do not confine the grace of God to them, nor do we commit to them the office and power of the Holy Spirit, or ascribe to them the securing of salvation. We plainly acknowledge that God alone works by the sacraments; all which is efficacious belongs to the Holy Spirit, and its efficacy is seen only in the elect. In no other way do we teach that the sacraments can help us, but as they may lead us by the hand to Christ, and that we may seek in Him the fountain of all good things. I do not see indeed what you can wish for more in this doctrine, which shows that salvation is to be sought in Christ alone; that God only perfects and applies the mystery, and that salvation is enjoyed only by the secret working of the Spirit. We teach that the sacraments are the instruments of the grace of God."

This is followed by a remarkably admirable letter, containing a developed view of the Calvinistic doctrine of the Lord's Supper. Calvin took the middle path, avoiding all the excesses of Lutheranism, but at the same time showing the followers of Zwingli that they could receive no other faith. He declares aloud his reverence both for that reformer and for Œcolampadius, but without entering into particulars, there being too great an interval between them and him. Bucer's Apology follows. He subscribed the Confession, and Calvin could easily understand him. To the Swiss he says:—"Christ is present with us under every circumstance. If we seek Him in those earthly elements, it is not permitted us to accuse Him of deception; but this is actually done, if we do not feel that the truth is connected with the sign, it being allowed that the sign by itself is useless. If now, for a brief explanation of the contents of the sacrament, we shortly answer, that we are partakers of Christ, that He may dwell in us and we in Him, and that we may be sharers of all his glory, what is there, I ask, in these words, dark or unreasonable? especially if we distinctly exclude those dreams and fancies which so easily enter the mind. And yet we are censured as if we had fallen from the pure and simple doctrine of the Gospel."

We here see that Calvin was thoroughly occupied with the thought of reconciling the Swiss by a method of his own. They had been violently separated from communion with the German protestants by Luther's rough and intolerant treatment, and were thus driven to a still greater one-sidedness of opinion. Calvin hoped to correct this by the inculcation of higher views, which should not only stretch far above their one-sidedness, but bring into clearer display the truth, held partially by both.

Everything seemed to promise peace when the year 1549 commenced. The Lord mingled joy and sorrow in Calvin's life this year. At Geneva the faction of the libertines, which had caused him so much distress, was for the moment suppressed. The Saxon churches however were disunited on the question, as to what ought to be the conduct of a Christian in matters indifferent, a question which, like many others of a similar kind, had its origin with the Interim. Calvin's opinion was asked, and he gave it freely. Melancthon had been openly accused of having acted with too much gentleness or weakness in this matter. Calvin admonished him, but he said at a later period that he had erred, and that injustice had been done this great man. It was not at that time clearly seen with what an evil spirit the whole multitude of the Flacianer, who subsequently created such commotion in the church, were possessed. Such was their phrenzied conduct, that, as Beza expresses it, they seemed to be bribed by the pope himself. But the deep wounds thus inflicted upon the church in Germany, were healed by the wonderful mercy of the Lord, exhibited towards the churches of Switzerland.

A synod was held at Bern, March 19, 1549. All the German and French ministers of the canton were present on the occasion. The Genevese sent a letter to the meeting. Calvin employed this opportunity to win the Bernese by words of reconciliation, and thus to lay the foundation of union on the question of the sacrament. "That we offer, uncalled for, a statement of our views on the sacraments, requires some brief apology, though no particular preface can be needed in addressing you on so important a subject. Since the venerable council has called you together, for other causes indeed, but also to consult for the peace of the church, whose surest bond of union is agreement in doctrine, it is very probable that mention may be made of the sacraments, a subject long agitated in Bern. Though no exposition therefore of the doctrine has been asked of us, we have yet considered it our duty to state to you what we all with one spirit acknowledge, and with one mouth confess. As it is the same Christ whom we all preach, the same Gospel which we all own, and as we are members of the same body, the church, and exercise the same office, no difference in the temporal rule to which we are subject must either disturb the unity of our faith, or mar the blessings of this holy union, established and sanctified under the auspices of Christ. Nor ought the influence of neighbourhood, which among the children of this world is so powerful a cause of union, to be of less value among us. We are so mixed up together that locality even ought to keep us united: to this may be added the treaty between the two cities: ministers from among us are employed in the territory of Bern, and we again have pastors in the Geneva churches from your canton. It is of vast importance therefore, both for you and for us, that you should know what form of doctrine we follow. To speak of nothing else, we shall at least free ourselves by this proceeding from no slight degree of suspicion."

Twenty articles follow. It was Calvin's main design in these, to show, that the sacraments ought by no means to be regarded as empty signs. He was anxious to give new life to the cold doctrine of the Swiss, and to make them see that they could not properly persevere in holding the early opinion of Zwingli, but ought rather to reconsider it as he himself had done. These articles form the groundwork of the Zurich union, as appears from their twenty-six articles, which exhibit a still fuller development of the same ideas.

At the end of May, after the death of his wife, Calvin suddenly roused himself, proceeded to Neuchatel, took his friend Farel with him, and both hastened in the fine spring weather through the beautiful country to Zurich. Thus, rising superior to earthly sorrow, Calvin felt himself strengthened by the thought, that he might now at length hope to establish a union of opinion on the subject of Christ's presence in the sacrament. To Bullinger, who sent him an invitation, he had written:—"Nothing could be more agreeable to me: it has also contributed to lighten my domestic sorrow, which so greatly bowed me down." The world ought to be taught how closely united Christians are who love the truth. "By prudence and love," Farel had said, "we shall conquer." And he was not deceived. The conference of the ministers continued several days, in the presence of the civic council; and the well-known formulary was drawn up, which all the Helvetic and Rhætian churches, with those of the Grisons, subscribed; and by which Bullinger and Calvin, and the churches of Geneva and Zurich, were united in the strictest alliance. Calvin wrote to Bullinger on the first of August respecting the conference, and sent him the *Consensus* for his signature. He received it back on the thirtieth, and the hope which Beza then expressed, that the union thus effected might be preserved for ever has not been disappointed.

Great was the joy which this event produced. Calvin informed Bullinger that "he had read his writings in company with his brethren, as Viret also had done with his in Lausanne. All were full of delight, and rivalled each other in offering thanksgiving to God." There was therefore some indication of improvement.

The Bernese wished to delay the publication of the proceedings. Calvin however expressed to Viret the joy which he felt at the influence which he knew the Consensus must exercise*. "The hearts of good men will be cheered by that which has taken place; our constancy and resolution will derive new strength from it, and we shall be better able to break the power of the wicked. They who had formed an unworthy opinion of us, will see that we proposed nothing but what is good and right. Many who are still in a state of uncertainty will now know on what they ought to depend; and those in distant lands who differ from us in opinion, will soon, we hope, offer us their hand. Lastly, as it may one day happen, posterity will have a witness to our faith, which it could not have derived from parties in a state of strife; but this we must leave to God." To Farel, whose earnest Christian spirit could not but gain regard, Calvin frequently wrote while these things were in progress. He says indeed, "This unwearied champion of Christ was the originator and leader of the whole."

But Calvin himself had still many minds to tranquillize. Thus he sought to satisfy the minister Sulzer in Bern, and left nothing undone to induce one after the other of his opponents to add their signatures to the new formulary†. "By the formulary proposed in the *Consensus Tigurinus*," says Planck‡, "couched as it was in the strongest language, and intended to reconcile all parties, the union of the Swiss with the Lutheran system, in the first and main point of dispute, was accomplished, or at least declared. It had hitherto been a matter of doubt whether the Swiss, in partaking of the sacrament, recognized the actual presence of the body of Christ, according to the substance. But doubt was rendered impossible by the new formulary, and every kind of suspicion on the subject was accordingly removed. The formulary set forth the idea of a real presence, and of an actual participation of the body of Christ in this sacrament. But it explains, at the same time, the nature and manner of this presence. According to Luther's doctrine, the body of Christ was miraculously present in the sacrament, and brought into such a union with the outward sign of the bread and wine, that it is not only received at the same time with these, but in

* MS. Gen. Sept. 23, 1549.

† In a letter to Farel, Nov. 18, 1549 (MS. Gen.), he shows how powerfully his persuasions had wrought with all, and characteristically adds, "Nostra sinceritate adducti nihil negabunt."

‡ See this author's Remarks on the Separation and Reunion of the Protestant Churches. Tübingen, 1803.

these, and under these, so that it is therefore partaken of by the mouth by every one who receives the sign, even though he be an unbeliever. According to Calvin's opinion, on the contrary, the body of Christ is not brought down into the sacrament, but the soul of him who partakes thereof is raised by faith towards heaven, and is there brought into contact with the body of Christ, and thus made a partaker of the divine life." Simple, but full of profound meaning, is Calvin's whole reasoning on this subject.

The *Consensus* was forwarded through Bullinger to the various confederate churches, and was everywhere received with the greatest respect*. When the Bernese objected to the printing of the document, some dissatisfied individuals being found among them, Bullinger proposed to alter the preface and conclusion. They now however agreed to its publication, giving only their verbal assent to its contents. In October it appeared in its printed form, with a letter, addressed by Calvin to the Zurichers, and the answer. The apostolic language of the latter affords a striking contrast to the vulgar and abusive invectives which were soon after spread abroad. This exalted and tranquil tone of feeling was the more remarkable, as displayed by a people so often irritated, and only so lately reconciled to Calvin, now the object of their grateful regard. It was especially a grand moment for the inner life of the church, which, however outwardly torn, had an inward unity in the Lord, when Melancthon and most of the Lutheran party declared their agreement with Calvin's views, and when the French reformed and the Swiss united themselves anew, and expressed the genuine sentiments of a true and primitive brotherhood. A glorious communion was thus established, such as had never yet been known. The epoch was no less noble in respect to the life of Calvin. As the centre of the reformed churches, he had rendered them the most important service, and had led them, by the knowledge of Scripture and brotherly kindness, to truth and concord.

There were also many admirable and learned men at a distance, says Lavater, who shared the joy of these churches, and were thereby strengthened in the faith. He relates of Melancthon, that he first learnt to understand rightly the doctrine of the Lord's Supper from the *Consensus*, or that he began from this time to incline towards the Zwinglians, not allowing himself to

* See Hess, Leben Bullingers, T. ii. p. 19.

be induced, even by the most violent attempts to irritate him, to speak or write against them. The Swiss sent a copy of the formulary to England, for Bucer, who congratulated the whole church on what had taken place. John à Lasco had also his share in the general delight. Calvin and Farel communicated the intelligence to the faithful in France, who gladly received the good news. There were still some however who expressed their dissatisfaction at the formulary. Melancthon himself seems to have admitted the article on election with some unwillingness. It was objected to the Zurichers that they had falsified Calvin's writing, and to Calvin that he had been guilty of vacillation, and had received the doctrine of Zwingli. But the main attack against the *Consensus* did not take place till some years later, and therefore belongs to another period of our history.

CHAPTER XVI.

UNION OF GREAT MINDS.—A PLAN TO EFFECT UNITY OF DOCTRINE AND DISCIPLINE BY A COMMUNITY OF SPIRIT.—HARMONY BETWEEN LUTHER AND CALVIN IN LIVING FAITH.—MELANCTHON.

WHILE Calvin was occupied with his plan, and with his journey to Zurich, where he hoped also to effect something for his oppressed fellow-countrymen, eight noblemen arrived at Geneva from France, whence they had been driven by the persecution. One of these strangers was distinguished by his noble form and bearing, by his genius, energy and earnestness. But the love of the world was still unconquered in him. When these gentlemen were presented to Calvin, he immediately recognized in the one referred to an old friend of his youthful years. It was Theodore von Beza, of Vezelay in Burgundy. They all asked permission of the council to remain in Geneva, and Calvin employed all his zeal and ardour to induce Beza to unite with him in accomplishing the work of the Lord in Switzerland. He had learnt to admire his talents when he met him, a young man, at the house of Melchior Wolmar; and he saw in him one whom God had sent to share his conflicts, to become, as it were, his right arm, to carry forward the reformation at a later period, and to supply his place in the consistory at Geneva.

Thus a friend was sent to Calvin, just as the loss of his wife had rendered one so especially needed. But Beza, rich, full of talent, and worldly, had first to be freed from the vortex of outward life. His old instructor, Wolmar, had done his part. Beza adopted the reformed faith, married the lady with whom he had lived in France, and associated himself with Crespin in Geneva, in order to establish a learned book-trade, a project which was subsequently productive of great good. Calvin soon after induced him to commence his theological career in Lausanne, to which city he had been invited by the council of Bern, as professor of Greek. He soon after his arrival published a poem on the sacrifice of Abraham, which obtained considerable praise. Not long after, the French refugees earnestly requested him to expound the Epistle to the Romans, and he thus laid the foundation for his learned labours on the New Testament.

With what zeal Calvin had assailed him appears from his own words*. It is delightful to see how he speaks, in his biography of Calvin, of that period, when he first devoted himself to the service of the Lord.

Beza, who united to earnestness and powerful eloquence a fascinating manner, was admirably adapted to uphold, both by his piety and skill, the now flourishing church. From this time Calvin undertook nothing without him, and in the year 1552 Beza had already begun to appear as the champion of the reformer's great design. To all the other arguments advanced by Calvin, he added, that a church divided into sects and opposed to that of Rome, especially in France, could never stand. It is not to be supposed however that he wished to see a single man, acknowledged as the head of the church, and endowed with authority above all the rest. He had even much less affection for the episcopal element than Calvin, and it is grossly unjust to ascribe his zeal for the church to political ambition, as if he had not, as well as Calvin, been urged forward by the Spirit of God. It surely was not from any earthly motive that he defended the doctrine of predestination, nor was it as a contriver of plots that he could have been employed by Calvin in Switzerland. Both the one and the other soared too high to be inspired by motives of this kind; and when they contemplated the miseries of the world, they felt the movements of a mightier will conducting

* To Viret, Oct. 1549 (MS. Gen.), and MS. Goth.

them along the path which they had chosen. Beza's enthusiastic admiration for Calvin was founded on their communion in Christ, whom both had learnt to own as their inner life. There has rarely occurred indeed in the history of mankind so remarkable a period as this. A number of exalted minds, roused by the great events of the age, felt themselves impelled to extend the hand of friendship to each other, and to establish a living union in the Lord. Calvin formed the shining centre of this circle, while other stars, some small and some great, moved around him and gathered light from his rays. The disputatious spirit of a mean and envious faction, which so soon overpowered the voice of faith, and exercised its injurious influence on the age, had not yet been awakened.

If we take a single glance of the others who were united with Calvin in spirit, none will appear more fitted to occupy the place next to Beza than Peter Martyr Vermili, whom Calvin was accustomed to call *miraculum Italiæ.* He was the most learned of the reformers, but was far more beloved and admired for his simplicity, his childlike, pious disposition, his moderation, so free from all ambition, and his pure love of the truth, which rendered him an enemy to every kind of useless controversy. He entertained the highest regard for Calvin. There is a letter of his in which he asked him respecting the mystery of our communion with Christ: the reformer answered him literally according to his fundamental principles. He entertained the most entire love for peace and union. "Can there be anything fairer," he said in a letter to Beza, "than brotherly agreement in the church?" He especially loved all those who hated strife, and thus he cherished the warmest affection for Melancthon. His opinion was in perfect accord with that of Calvin on the subject of the Lord's Supper, and particularly as it was opposed to the doctrine of ubiquity. Christ, he argued, has the two natures united in one person, without any mixture or confusion of their qualities. According to his divine nature, therefore, He is everywhere present; but according to his body, He must have one place, and can therefore neither *realiter* nor *substantialiter* be present in the sacrament. In the affair of Servetus also he thoroughly agreed with Calvin. He defended the doctrine of election with all its awful deductions, induced to adopt these views by the same profound reverence for God as Calvin. When the dispute on the sacrament commenced at Strasburg, he declared himself ready to sign the Augsburg Confession, if it was rightly understood. In this respect also he resembled Calvin, who, although he seemed to have excited an opposition, yet, through his deeper consciousness, the influence of a living faith and his love for union, rose superior to all party considerations.

This mention of Peter Martyr brings to our mind the celebrated Italians of that period, who had found at Ferrara an asylum with the duchess Renata, that noble-hearted protectress of all who were friends of Calvin. The usual tranquil feeling now prevailed in Germany, but the country was still bowed beneath the storms of the Interim, and had little prospect of permanent religious peace. Melancthon, who was ever anxious to promote unity, and habitually overlooked the smaller differences of doctrine, was labouring earnestly to accomplish this object. In this he was supported by Cruciger, and by all who were sincerely devoted to the living doctrines which had been taught by Luther. In Zurich the bold and faithful Bullinger, who kept the churches of Zurich together by his watchfulness, and showed how strongly he was moved by the pure and noble spirit of Zwingli; Pellicanus, and the fervent, deep-feeling Musculus, who, persecuted on account of God's Word, sought consolation in God alone, and found it; and lastly Gualter, the nephew of Zwingli and disciple of Bullinger,—all these lived and laboured with Calvin, in one spirit and with one aim.

If we turn our attention to England, we shall there see Bucer, sometimes indeed vacillating, but always anxious to promote what was good and profitable for the unity of the church; giving a higher place to the faith than to the formularies which express it, and exercising an important influence on the side of the party desiring peace. Nor must Fagius be forgotten; nor the enlightened John à Lasco, who had formed a church of true believers in that country; nor Uttenhoven, who, with the former, was soon to be obliged to flee, on account of his belief; nor the courageous Knox, whose faith also was now to be again proved, that he might become a mightier instrument in the hand of the Lord.

In France, queen Margaret, and her heroic daughter Johanna d'Albret, co-operated nobly with Calvin and Beza: the latter of these ladies had greatly advanced in the knowledge of the truth. On the same side also were Coligni and many other admirable men, all prepared to defend the Gospel. Who could fail to rejoice at this spectacle, or to express delight that this communion in the Lord had been accomplished by the renewed church! Christ ruled spiritually in the regenerated congregation.

Farel had been long anxious to see this living union and peace secured to the church. In 1545 he wrote to Calvin, expressing his wish that all churches would combine together to annihilate strife. The Augsburg Confession might, he considered, be accepted, and he greatly desired that people would make it the ground of union, with this condition, that the Lord's Supper should be viewed according to the doctrine of Melancthon*.

Theological differences and distinctions did not appear to Calvin a sufficient cause for separation: his liberality indeed went so far that, where he did not observe a perverse will, he was ready to admit even freethinkers into his society. We may here mention his treatment of some Italian refugees who joined him at this period, and whom he exhorted with paternal earnestness to submit themselves to the teaching of the Bible. He entertained the highest regard for Bernardin Ochin of Sienna, whom he described as *præclarus vir* and *vir magnus omnibus modis*†. Still more interesting was his connection with Lælius Socinus‡. He discovered in this excellent man some difference of doctrine, and he warned him accordingly; but he never persecuted him, for he saw that he was struggling to find the truth, and was not, like Servetus, engaged in diffusing blasphemous errors for the sake of destroying the church. Calvin's conduct towards him is worthy of especial notice: it throws new light upon his character, and proves that he was not, as has been so commonly believed, a persecutor; but that he was, on the contrary, ready to suffer variety of opinion, if it did not manifestly tend to the ruin of unity. He even recommended Socinus in the strongest manner to prince Radzivil, when the latter was

* His expressions on this subject were very strong:—"Augustanam Confessionem tolerabilem existimo, nec tam abhorrendam reputo ab ea—Quid volumus pro Augustana Confessione novam suscitare tragœdiam? Una est controversia de cœna; si Augustana Confessio de cœna contineat quod sana expositione admitti possit, et secundum mentem autoris, quid prohibet, quin admittamus et sancte conveniamus?"—April, 1558.

† Commending him to Oswald, a minister at Basel, he spoke of him as a man who had gained a great name in Italy, and deserved to be held in honour everywhere.

‡ Lælius Socinus was of Vicenza: he appears to have derived his dogmas from the Grecian philosophy. Having fled into Poland, he there taught antitrinitarianism, explaining allegorically the passages in Scripture which opposed his views. His nephew Faustus inherited his spirit and completed his work. Calvin answered him. Epis. 359. Ed. Amst. p. 197. Ep. 104. Ed. Amst. p. 57. 7 Idus Dec. 1549.

proceeding to Poland, though he was well acquainted with Socinus's peculiar views. Beza in his life of Calvin says, in reference to these times, that Calvin laboured in two very remarkable writings to effect the conversion of this Italian. Socinus however was still hesitating, and put various questions to the reformer, who adhered like a child to Scripture, as the only foundation of a living unity.

Calvin had at length accomplished, by means of the Zurich *Consensus*, that which he had so constantly and resolutely pursued. How gladly would he now have ceased from his restless strife! In the Confession of 1554 he gave full expression to his belief: it was then the same as that of the church in Germany, and could never create any schism among those who were joined together in true communion with the Lord. All who had the genuine spirit and life of religion in their hearts still felt themselves thus united, even when the church exhibited its growth and development, as it sometimes needs must, by means of opposing principles. Calvin, as I have already remarked, was necessarily in contrast with Luther. The peculiarities of his theology, like those of the German reformer, were for a particular purpose; while the separation of the churches arose only from sin and ignorance. They agreed in faith: their opposition lay in the constitution of their minds; this gave a different direction to their course; but instead of contracting their energy, it tended to increase their vigour and activity. Each laboured according to his peculiar character. Calvin sought to establish order, to diffuse knowledge, and reconcile hostile parties. With him the understanding was chief; with Luther, energy and excitement of spirit. But while the latter possessed also the highest intellectual powers, so neither did Calvin fail to exhibit, quickened as he was by the spiritual view which he took of the Lord's Supper, and strengthened by the sublime doctrine of election, energy to fulfil the work which he had commenced. The medium by which the two reformers were brought together was Christian sentiment: this it was which secured the growth of what was evangelical in either party; which lived in the profound mind of Melancthon, and is still even in our own day exercising its general influence. It would not be altogether just to contrast Zwingli with Luther, or to suppose that Calvin occupied the place between them: it was only in respect to the sacrament that this was the case. In regard to the doctrine of predestination, Zwingli appears equally rough and severe.

Nor does he, even as regards the Lord's Supper, stand immediately opposed to Luther. Firmly resisting the catholic doctrine, but with a too narrow-sighted view, he yet did not set aside a pure and rational exposition of the subject: the worst which he did was to deprive his own system of depth and sublimity. Reflection ever prevailed with Calvin; and it was therefore in harmony with the general operations of his mind, that, when the question was put, how Christ was present in the sacrament, he should plainly declare, that, as having a body which was limited, He could be present in one place only, and not in all places and in all times; and consequently, that the believing soul must raise itself in the sacrament to hold communion with Him. But neither the worthy nor the unworthy, he added, could in, with, or under the bread, receive Him bodily, seeing that, where space has ceased to exist, no body can be properly spoken of. At the same time it was equally clear that Luther, who did not investigate the mystery with such careful thought, contemplated the glorified body of our Lord as diffused through all times and in all places, considering no boundary to exist between this world and heaven. Both, in one sense, were right, and both were wrong: for while it is not given to man to comprehend the glorified body of Christ, so each ought to have been contented with simply acknowledging his presence in the sacrament, without attempting to explain the *how*. Luther especially erred in this matter; he insisted on the doctrine of a personal communication, and hence rendered the mystery of the Lord's Supper a subject of long and painful controversy. Calvin, on the other hand, employed his powerful intellect in fathoming, as far as possible, the mighty judgements of God, without feeling the giddiness which seized Luther and Melancthon, when, in the earlier part of their career, they accompanied him on this perilous course. They clearly saw, at a subsequent period, the dangerous nature of the subject; and hence their silence respecting it, and the milder character of the expressions employed by Melancthon, and after him in the *Formula Concordiæ.* Various opinions were not to be avoided, for it is from various points of view that the truth is to be discovered; but it is neither necessary nor becoming that this should be made a cause of separation. The two reformers are in this respect worthy of the highest admiration. Though dogmatic differences became too visible in Luther's lifetime, they felt that there was a bond between them, created by the higher species of unity which they were mutually seeking. Calvin's theology was, as little as Luther's, the mere product of the understanding: he formally protested against such a notion*: it sprung from a living faith in the holy Scriptures. Thus Luther also felt himself as a believer united with Melancthon, notwithstanding the difference of their temper. How otherwise could he have administered the communion to him? But as soon as the pride of reason obscured and chilled belief, and more weight was given to the power of comprehension than to the life of God in the soul, separation was at hand, for the most violent passions gathered about the understanding; the feeling of Christ's presence grew daily less, and the feast of love at length became a source of the bitterest hate. It is necessary therefore, in the history of the church, to place in the clearest light the schismatic conduct of the people, who gave such an undue importance to differences of opinion, annihilating faith in the true communion of Christ, and converting the blessed unity and love of the Gospel into an apple of discord. But even far more culpable are those who, in the present day, when the opposition between the two churches has ceased, strive to give prominence to opposing sentiments, and thus through their wilfulness stifle the principle of communion, instead of acknowledging with Calvin that the mystery of the Lord's Supper far surpasses our comprehension.

The larger portion of the evils of the following century may be traced to the excessive respect which it thus became the habit to render to the decisions of the understanding. Instead of refraining from any interference with the unavoidable difference of opinion existing on the subject of the sacrament, and seeking communion in Christ, each party only hardened itself the more in its one-sidedness, and became fiercer and fiercer against the rest. When we contemplate, in Germany especially, the Flacianer, the followers of Heshusius, Brentius, Westphoal, Marbach and others, treading underfoot the true and living faith, and giving the tone to after times, it is impossible not to feel, that no real reformation had as yet been effected, and that the scourge of the thirty years' war was yet needed to excite, through manifold afflictions, a higher and better spirit. After that event indeed, the unchristian hatred which had so long prevailed be-

* See instances of this, Institutes, lib. i. c. 18, sec. 4. "Let it be understood," he says, "that it is our duty to embrace with gentleness and docility, and without exception, whatever is delivered to us in holy Scripture." So also Institut. lib. iv. c. 17, sec. 24, 25.

came less conspicuous, and the bond of union in the church began to be more distinctly felt. But since the well-being of the next generation depends upon whether we hold fast communion in Christ, or allow the church to be rent and shattered by division, and thus bring forth a blessing or a curse, so it is our bounden duty, in the present day, to take care, that true believers secure a higher stand than those who are quarrelling about nice distinctions; that every one may be able to choose whether he will take his part with the destroyers, or with the benefactors of the church.

Lutherans and reformed stand side by side in the united church. Opposition has entered with union, but the life of Christ is superior to opposition. Calvin, Luther and Melancthon exhibited this principle in their own time, and the union therefore of later days has only expressed their sentiment. It shows little candour, consequently, when the most diligent examination is made of the differences existing in the creed of the reformers, and an utter indifference prevails as to their general agreement. The most marvelous zeal appears in the revival of old disputes, but no effort is employed to give a fresh warmth to languishing faith from the noble example of the reformers.

Let it be supposed that any one should assert, that Calvin had not the right faith, that he did not abide by God's Word, or that the truth, and that through his own fault, was not clearly known to him, it must then follow as a necessary consequence that Luther also was thus deficient, for he recognized Calvin as his fellow-believer. Attempts have been made to fix upon the reformed the old charge of Nestorianism. This has probably been done to give them the right to make a counter-attack upon the Lutherans, and to brand them as Eutychians and Monophysites, as if both parties had torn with their hands the glorified body of the Lord. To-day, when the reformation has reached its object, and the church has been formed, we have to obey a new impulse, and to employ the power of the faith which we have realized in the grand work of converting the people who still lie in the darkness of heathenism. In this respect we are to view the whole reformation as a far-stretching field, from which we are still to press bravely onward. It certainly is not the time to retrace the progress made during three hundred years, for the sake of renewing the controversies of ancient times. Lamentable indeed must be the state of things, if such a profound belief in the mystery of the sacrament as that of Calvin should become the subject of suspicion in a church, where, the former difficulty having been solved, it is now an obvious duty to go forward, and so to consider the still-existing controversy with the catholic church, that sooner or later this also may be settled. It is of importance therefore to state, in this part of our work, all those circumstances which tend to exhibit the harmony of opinion, in matters of actual faith, which existed among the founders of the reformed church. We cannot fail to derive a feeling of security from the unity of living faith discernible in all those of whom we have spoken above, and more particularly in Luther and Calvin.

That the latter did not exhibit in the *Consensus Tigurinus* a mere dry product of the understanding, a so-called parchment-pope, must be evident to all who have the witness of the Holy Spirit, the author of unity, in their hearts. The sacrament was the central point of his spiritual life: he lived only for that. Hence his earnestness in defending it against the approach of the unworthy, or whatever might defile its sanctity; and the profound anxiety which he felt as the seasons came round for its administration. To him it was the medium of a most intimate communion with Jesus: it was associated in his mind with the sublimest ideas,—with faith in the divine sacrifice, and in the present and personal being of Him who alone can give us life. According to Calvin, the faithful enjoy the glorified Christ,—the unworthy and the wicked receive Him not. This depends not on the words of consecration: such a notion is contrary to the spirit of Christ: he imparts not himself to the unholy. Thus also Calvin connected with this doctrine the communion of believers, it being in communion only that the sacrament can be properly enjoyed. Even in his catechism for children he speaks of a real and actual union*. The mystical element therefore existed in Calvin in its highest form and energy: he was convinced that the flesh and blood of Christ are partaken of in the sacrament, and his doctrine was in perfect agreement with that of Luther, except that his expressions were more spiritual, and he rejected from his view of the mystery what is sensual and local. His sound understanding could never comprehend how that which is divine can be eaten and swallowed in earthly elements; nor how that which is local can be regarded as available for the spirit. The godly and glorified Christ is that

* Bossuet found the expressions here referred to so Lutheran that he remarked it in his Hist. des Variat. t. ii. p. 16.

alone which penetrates the believer's soul and becomes one with him.

The doctrine of predestination was a fruitful cause of opposition, but it did not separate Calvin from all those who formed a somewhat different opinion on the subject. He practically agreed with Luther in this matter; and in his last Confession, drawn up in 1562, he speaks more decidedly than ever against those who trusted to predestination, rather than to that which immediately concerned their state*. It is worthy of observation, that his nearest friends, as Farel for example, regarded his teaching in respect to this doctrine, and as he imparted it to them, not as repulsive, but full of consolation†. Calvin and Melancthon did not, it must be owned, agree in this doctrine at a subsequent period. The latter, according to Calvin, viewed it too philosophically; but this did not hinder Calvin from editing Melancthon's principal work, or from showing the world that he did not view this difference of opinion as of any great importance. In our times it would probably be regarded as a sufficient excuse for separation.

It is well known that both by his system of faith, as seen in the period extending from 1541 to 1554, and by the party consolidated through the second *Consensus*, he stood in open opposition to Lutheranism: but nothing was said about division. The churches could not but persevere in those principles, which were subsequently more strongly set forth in the *Formula Concordiæ*, and in the Confession of the Synod of Dort. But neither Calvin nor Luther, had he lived in those days, would have allowed a separation to arise from such a cause. A deeper feeling would have told them both, that the exaltation of the soul to Christ, or the descent of Christ into the bread in the sacrament, can be as little understood as the consistency of election with the free and the moral nature of man: but both are stated in Scripture, and both are realities for the Christian. Many proofs also exist that Melancthon never swerved from the Wittenberg Concordate, but lived, by the influence of a genuine faith, in constant friendship with both parties in the church. When he found himself seized with a dangerous sickness, in

* "We are not of the number of those fanatics who, under the shade of God's eternal predestination, think not of attaining to the life which is promised us by the right way. But regarding ourselves as children of God, we know that it is necessary to believe in Jesus Christ, and that in Him alone we can properly seek salvation."

† Schmidt: Etudes sur Farel, p. 45.

1541, he declared his assent to the established faith. His letters to Dietrich, a minister at Nuremberg, show that he recognized a sacramental presence of Christ, though no inclosing of the body in the bread; that is, that Christ is actually present when we rightly receive the symbols or signs of grace. He thus expressed himself at Ratisbonne in 1541. In 1542 and 1543 he remarked in his letters to Dietrich, that they ought to be severely censured who pretend that the body of the Lord is inclosed in the bread, as by a sort of magic, at the pronouncing of certain words. He is far however from representing the sacrament as a simple supper: on the contrary, he expresses his conviction, that by the use of the outward signs of grace, Christ makes us members of his body, and works mightily in us. It is thus that he represents the doctrine in his *Locis* as published in 1543. He had even resolved to leave Wittenberg, when Luther renewed the controversy, rather than swerve from the Concordat.

That Melancthon agreed in this respect with Calvin, appears from a letter written by the latter to Farel in 1539. Calvin also appealed to his example in his second Apology against Westphal in 1556. "Philip will state in a single word if I be not of his opinion, for I will spend no more words on the subject:" and in 1557 he says, "If I be found guilty of rashly using the name of Melancthon, I will submit to any degree of infamy. I have said it a hundred times, that Philip can no more be torn from me in this cause than from his own bowels." And this agreement continued from 1539 onwards, through a period, that is, of seventeen years. Both also were associated with Caspar Cruciger, whom Luther always loved and distinguished. Melancthon was far from denying this his agreement with Calvin*.

But still more surprising, and in our times more important to the evangelical church, is the perfect harmony between Calvin and Luther in belief. This can be shown by various facts, sufficiently striking to convince any unprejudiced mind. These two great men were never in actual strife; and had Luther lived longer, they would probably have learnt to entertain for each other the strictest regard. With respect to the Lord's Supper, it is well known that Calvin's treatise against Pighius *De Libero Arbitrio* appeared in 1543, that is, before the death of Luther,

* See also Melancthon's letters to Calvin in the years 1552, 1554, 1555. Ed. Amst. p. 66. Ed. Laus. Ep. 137, &c.

and was dedicated to Melancthon. In this work he defended Luther with the greatest zeal, and this was not likely to remain unknown to the German reformer. The argument prefixed to the paper indicates the agreement between them. "That which is the main point in this question, and on account of which all the rest is said, we now defend, as it was originally proposed by Luther and others." Calvin quotes his Institutions several times on this occasion. To this may be added the important fact, that Luther never uttered the least word of disrespect against Calvin, although the latter, eleven years before Luther's death, exhibited in his celebrated catechism, without any alteration, his whole system of doctrine, and especially that on the sacrament. Luther had read his earlier writings, and particularly his Institutes, in the first and second editions, "*cum singulari voluptate*" as he said. He sent him his greeting in his well-known letter to Bucer, in 1539. "*Saluta mihi reverenter J. Sturmium et J. Calvinum,* whose books I have read with especial pleasure." But in the works referred to the whole doctrine of the Lord's Supper was as clearly set forth as at any future period. It is also probable that Luther had in his mind Calvin's little treatises, *De Fugiendis impiorum illicitis sacris,* and *De Papisticis Sacerdotiis,* in which he expressly declares his opinion respecting the sacrifice of the altar. It was against the Zwinglians only that Luther raged so fiercely, and his indignation was excited in their case because he regarded them as annihilating the very essence of the sacrament. His last attack upon the Zurichers is of no dogmatic importance to the church. It was occasioned by the publication of Zwingli's last and somewhat too freely expressed treatise, and by that of the new translation of the Bible into German. Nor must it be forgotten, that Calvin was sent during Luther's lifetime to the Colloquy at Frankfort, and to the Diets of Worms and Ratisbonne, in the character of a deputy, to support the Augsburg Confession, and that he was received there, and treated with marked confidence, by the most celebrated of the Lutheran theologians. If these distinguished men had found him opposed to the doctrine of Luther, Luther himself would not have been long in evincing his resentment. Sleidan numbers him among the friends of the Confession, and to these Luther wrote without exception in the following words:—"Nolite timere, estote fortes et læti, nihil solliciti." But he knew that Calvin was there with the rest.

Had he regarded him as a man who held dangerous or erroneous opinions, he would quickly have warned the princes and others who were present against his discourse.

But still further: it is related, that when Luther, in 1540, according to the command of the Elector, visited Melancthon in Weimar, Dr. Cruciger read to him, as they travelled, Calvin's answer to Sadolet's address to the Genevese. Luther on this occasion bore the following remarkable testimony to Calvin's worth:—"This writing has hands and feet, and I rejoice that God has called up such people, who, if it be his will, may give the final blow to the papacy, and finish by his help what I have commenced against antichrist*."

There is something especially refreshing in the relation, which, bearing all the internal signs of truth, is wanting in none of the outer, and from which it appears evident that Luther agreed with Calvin on the subject of the Lord's Supper, and felt altogether united with him in faith. This narrative carries us to old Wittenberg, and shows us Luther as he used to come from his lecture, surrounded by students, and stood at the door of a famous bookseller's shop. Here are the old and remarkable words, so little known, but which must be very precious to all evangelical christians:—"Calvin's book, thus far translated into Latin by Galasius, appeared again in 1545, and was brought to Wittenberg†. On the Monday after *Quasimodogeniti,* when Dr. Luther had finished his lecture on Genesis, upon which he was still engaged, he proceeded to the shop of the bookseller Maurice Goltschen, who had just returned from the great Easter fair. Luther welcomed him home, and continued in these words: 'Well, Maurice, what good news is there at Frankfort? Do they wish to burn the arch-heretic Luther?' Thereupon Maurice replied, 'I have heard nothing thereof, honoured sir; but I have brought with me a little book, which John Calvin wrote some time ago in French, on the Lord's Supper, and which has been lately republished in Latin. It is said of Calvin, that he is a young but a pious and learned man. In this little book he seems to have shown in what respect your reverence, and both

* A clear and candid account of the Sacramentarian Controversy was written by Christopher Petzel, doctor and professor at Bremen, where he died in 1604. His greatest works were, Examen Theologiæ Melancthonis cum Explicationibus, 1589; Argumenta et Objectiones de Articulis Christianæ Doctrinæ cum Responsionibus, 1788; and De Predestinatione, 1604.

† Calvin's work first appeared in 1540, and in January 1545 it was printed in Latin by Nicolaus Galasius.

Zwinglius and Œcolampadius, have gone too far in your controversy on this subject.' As Maurice Goltschen did not express himself very well, Luther answered quickly, 'Give me the book, friend!' The bookseller immediately gave him an octavo copy, stitched up. Having taken it in his hands, Dr. Luther sat down and read the first three leaves after the title, and then the last four and a half to the end. These he read with particular attention, and at last said, 'Maurice, this is certainly a learned and pious man, and I might well have entrusted the whole affair of this controversy to him from the beginning. I confess my part. If my opponents had done the like, we should soon have been reconciled, since it only needed that Œcolampadius and Zwinglius should have thus explained themselves, to prevent the controversy from proceeding to such lengths.' This was heard by Matthias Stoius, who was one of the numerous students by whom Dr. Luther was then surrounded. He was at that time a boarder in his house, but subsequently became a doctor of medicine, and was appointed private physician to the old duke of Prussia. The story was repeated in the presence of many of the nobility of the archduke Albrecht."

The testimony of Dr. Alesius Scotus, a professor at Leipzig, and the friend of Luther and Melancthon, is well known, and has been often printed. In his answer to Ruard Tapper's defence of the Louvain articles, he says, "They do as if they were ignorant of what Luther said to Philip, ere he set out for his native province, where he died. Philip related it to many, and in various ways, that Luther, unasked, said, 'I own that too much has been done respecting the sacrament:' and when Philip answered, 'Let us then, my good doctor, for the sake of the churches, publish some pacific treatise, in which we may clearly unfold our views'—Luther replied, 'My Philip, I have thought anxiously on this matter; but as I might throw suspicion upon the whole doctrine, I will only commend it to the good care of God. Do you do something after my death.' These words were written down from Melancthon's own mouth." It was the wish of the latter to mention the subject in his testament, but he died too soon. The witness of Dr. Alesius, who had the account from Melancthon himself, is therefore valuable. It seems certain, that as Zwingli had a deeper insight into the sacrament in the latter years of his life, Luther also, a year before his death, was of one faith and of one mind with Calvin.

He regarded him as a brother, and viewed his doctrine as fitted to restore union to the distracted church. And as Luther inclined to Calvin, so did Calvin to Luther. He twice declared his assent to the Augsburg Confession, and stated that, in his opinion, the formulary of the Zurich Union contained whatever was found in the Confession.

We may here, in conclusion, quote some of the most remarkable expressions which he employed to show his agreement with that formulary. Thus, in a letter to Martin Schaling, a minister at Ratisbonne, he says, "I am so far from repudiating the Augsburg Confession, that I have willingly and gladly subscribed it, interpreting it as I am authorized to do*." To Marbach, a minister at Strasburg†, he wrote, "If that excellent servant of the Lord, and faithful doctor of the church, Martin Luther, were still alive, he would not be so severe and implacable as to refuse his ready assent to this Confession, namely, that that is truly afforded us which the sacraments figure, and that we are therefore partakers of the body and blood of Christ. How often did Luther say, that he contended for nothing but that it might be clearly understood, that the Lord does not mock us with empty signs, but that He fulfils inwardly that which is represented to the eye, and that thus the substance is connected with the sign! Hence, if I do not greatly err, we are agreed, that the Supper of the Lord is no vain, dramatic representation of a spiritual feast, but that it truly imparts to us what it presents, and that holy hearts are nourished therein by the body and blood of Christ. Greatly would it trouble me if a doctrine should now be rejected, which I so many years ago taught freely and openly at Strasburg, both in the schools and in the churches."

Thus Calvin, in the second epoch of his career, had firmly established his evangelical system by institutions of corresponding character. It only remained for him to extend his system, and to combat opposing errors. The *Consensus Tigurinus*, which became blended with the Helvetic Confession, should, according to Calvin's plan, have passed into the Augsburg Confession. There would then have been no mention of Lutherans and Calvinists, and the whole evangelical church would have presented one glorious and imposing mass.

* Ed. Laus. Ep. 236. Ed. Amst. p. 112 (1557).
† Ed. Laus. Ep. 177. Ed. Amst. p. 84 (1554).

PART III.

CHAPTER I.

INTRODUCTORY REMARKS.—CHARACTERISTICS OF CALVIN.

A SURVEY of the last period of Calvin's labours will help us to resolve the question, why has not a milder judgement been passed upon him? Why have his merits not been more generally recognized? or how is it that, in some church histories, he has been even passed over with contempt? We here see him involved in difficulties of such a peculiar kind, that it is easy to understand how he might be wrongly judged. Appearances were in some respects against him: his judge must be a Christian, an evangelical Christian: he ought to be also an intelligent, unprejudiced theologian, and one well-acquainted with the state of affairs; otherwise his decision will be faulty. Calvin's life is not popular. The hatred against him is a natural consequence of his resolute effort to establish his doctrine, and with his doctrine the unity of the church. That which concerns the peculiarity of his mind I have shown in the first part of this work, and in the introduction to the second. It will be sufficient therefore here to remark, that if an outward splendour be wanting to the circumstances of his life, his spiritual comprehension was of a sublimer kind than that of other reformers. What place then will he occupy, when his course has been fairly surveyed, in the estimation of mankind? Will he appear in their eyes as one of those unbending, resolute and ambitious men, who have shaken the world with their plans? or will he be ranked with those heroic natures who sought nothing for themselves, and whose labours, resigning as they did all for the good of mankind, bear on them the stamp of godliness, and the fame of which, like a mighty wind, passes on from age to age, and acquires at length the character of greatness? or will he be placed on a still higher eminence? Christians are not called great in the common sense of the expression. Shall he be styled then an apostolic champion of the truth?

A degree of mystery has long hovered over the grave of this celebrated man. It may properly be said of him, "Calvin's greatness was his fate:" or it may be asserted that the world mistook him because of the vastness of the task given him to perform, while before the eternal judgement-seat he will be accounted as a faithful soldier of the Lord. That which displeases in him arose from the nature of his duty. There was a certain fiery excess, a daringness in his nature, which many could not forgive. It mingled itself with his southern blood; and the zeal of a prophet of the old covenant is hardly to be understood in conjunction with Christianity.

But the intelligent observer will not fail to perceive, that the duty imposed upon Calvin to confirm the reformation, was attended with peculiar difficulties. His whole strength was exerted to overcome them, and it was only on some rare occasions that he allowed a doubt as to the final result to enter his mind. At first, indeed, he trembled at the obligation which he was called upon to encounter. The wonderful ways by which God led him were only opened by degrees; but on his death-bed he could say, "that light shone upon him in all his struggles, and that the blessing of God was with him." He sometimes indeed rose to a height whence it was difficult for him to take a distinct view of his actual circumstances. Unconscious of it himself, he was urged onward by an inward fire, by a burning conviction, that he was destined before all others to proclaim certain doctrines, to awaken a new feeling of devotion to God, and to lead men to ascribe to Him alone the work of redemption, independent of all human merit. It would have seemed to him as if all had been lost, had he not hoped to see this doctrine planted in the religious conscience of mankind. Hence he was little understood in his age, and sometimes not even by his friends. But here was the mystery of his vocation, and the world could not tell why he proceeded to such lengths in his desire to fulfil it.

Calvin's designs, as seen at this period of his life, were retrospective; they were formed for the purpose of restraint, for the security of that which had been won. Manifold were the disgusts which hence arose. It is difficult to find the right measure in such cases; and the multitude which readily renders its aid to change and overthrow, is little disposed to assist in building up and securing. To act retrospectively, is never so animating as to advance boldly forward against the vice and oppression which may have been long endured. Thus Luther enjoyed sympathy and gratitude, while Calvin had to encounter blame and criticism: the latter felt himself under the control of a spirit which desired unity: hence his struggles against heresy. But the mass of the people cannot understand why this unity is necessary; they suppose that things would go on well enough without it; and when Calvin employed severe measures to accomplish his purpose, they called him a persecutor; and if he sought to secure the rights of the church at any price, they exclaimed, "he wants to rule like the pope." Even to this day he is regarded by some as a clever politician, a Richelieu, a wise man who sought his own aggrandisement. But further: Calvin was moved in some respects by that grand spirit, the working of which it is so difficult for us to understand, its power being now almost expended, the spirit of the middle ages. The voice of a new life spoke within him: he existed in the season of transition to another period of cultivation, which he partially comprehended, and partially assisted to effect. If we be conscious of some discordant tones in his life, we must not neglect to consider, that after the course of some centuries, when the world is animated by another spirit, history in our present mode of existence will utter more than one discordant note, and that because we are more or less in bondage to the spirit of our age, which can never be absolutely pure. But the individual is not responsible for the spirit of his times. The stern discourses of Calvin on Predestination, as well as his treatises against heretics, may be regarded as having their origin in the necessities of the age. The world was not yet worthy of the milder apostolic spirit. As in the second part of this biography, anti-christianity has shown itself in its gloomiest form, on the path of moral existence, so in the present epoch we have to contemplate the advance of a heresy, which exerted its whole force to mar, or blot out, the first great truth, the very foundation-principle, of the church. And how is it that they, who assume to themselves the right of passing judgement on the history of heroic souls, do not perceive that the mission of such spirits is necessary at certain periods to the salvation of the world? This great man occupied a far different position to that which is ordinarily supposed. It is a melancholy thing when any one receives a commission from God to proclaim his wrath, and teach a doctrine most humbling to the human will. Calvin, on this account, could not but be misunderstood and hated by the world. He himself clearly saw it; and it is very evident even to the present day, that whenever an inclination exists to honour Calvin, Servetus appears as a pale spectre, to snatch the crown of honour from his head. Exposed to the wrathful condemnation of the papists; decried by the Lutherans, as if he were little better than a child of Satan; often mistaken and censured in his own church, he has endured more injustice than any other religious leader of modern times. So was he oppressed at the period of which we are speaking, that he wished for death. "If I had the choice," he said, "I would far rather submit myself at once to be burnt by the papists, than to be thus lacerated, without ceasing, by my neighbours. They envy my great prosperity, and will not let me enjoy a moment's rest, and yet they see me almost overpowered by the weight of my occupations, tormented by the saddest anxieties, and bowed down by insufferable claims. My only consolation is, that death will soon afford me deliverance from this oppressive struggle."

Such indeed has been the indignation often expressed against his zeal, that since Beza, he has found no friend, during a space of three hundred years, ready to exhibit to the world a fitting representation of his faithful and untiring activity. The unbelieving world regarded him as a troublesome zealot, of whom it was better to speak as little as possible. There is something puerile in the judgement which many have formed of his character, and it is full time that justice should be done to Calvin as well as to Servetus.

That which has chiefly tended to the erroneous view of his conduct, may perhaps be found in the circumstance, that however prosperous he was in the accomplishment of his work, his church was never well established in France. It continued oppressed and persecuted, so that the papists have continued to the present day to load it with falsehoods and insult. Their cunning and superior skill in such attacks have rendered them more successful than we have been in the defence. We depend upon the goodness of our cause, and are silent. It became usual in Calvin's father-land to hate him: apparently he obtained not his purpose; and in Germany it was suspected that he was the enemy of peace, though his whole strength was employed to preserve it. All, in short, took the part of the idle world against him. The French have latterly bestowed some attention upon his character, but they have not yet found the key to his inner spiritual life. Hence, in their review of his genius, they speak only of his influence on the French language; of his understanding and logical ability. They even term his whole life a syllogism. In the same manner they describe his subtle policy, his egoism, and especially his feeling of duty, but they rarely allude to his convictions. It is thus that critics may be expected to do, whose heads are possessed with the prejudice, that the manifestation of Calvinism is necessarily connected with something wrong.

It may be hoped therefore that this work is published at a right period. The hostility to Calvin has been re-awakened with disgusting violence. Galiffe, in Geneva, has supplied all his opponents with plausible arguments against him. We can appeal only to the facts of his work. His judgements are palpably false, and he loses all claim to respect or credit when we find him undertaking the defence of Bolsec. The Life of Calvin by Audin, which appeared in France, and has since been translated into German, is a wretched party affair. A critique in the 'Literarische Zeitung' (1841, n. 34) affords a correct view of this work:—"It is altogether unworthy of serious notice, being in fact a sort of caricature of Dr. Henry's book, the contents of which it has perfidiously pirated." The spirit indeed which animates the little production here alluded to, shows that the Romish church has made no step towards improvement since the Reformation. But so long as that church thus avoids the truth, and forms a league with shameless falsehood, it inflicts upon itself the deepest wound, and stands irrevocably separated from the evangelical church, which would so gladly form with it but one body and one communion.

A later author*, who has employed himself much about the old times, and is familiar with all the documents necessary to the task, opposes the false judgements of others by his own well-founded and earnest criticism. Agreeing with me, he says,—"This man (Calvin)—descended from an ancient family, learned and profound as few are, superior to the fear of man, seeking nothing for himself, and hoping nothing, but full of ardour for the glory of God,—became more and more the soul of the protestant cause, the instrument in the hand of the Lord to give firmness, durability, and a steady direction to the new church, and to settle its doctrine on the surest principles of good sense and reason." "People have often supposed that they were insulting Calvin's memory by calling him the pope of protestantism. He was so, but in the noblest sense of the expression, through the spiritual and moral superiority with which the Lord of the church had endowed him for its deliverance; through his unwearied, universal zeal for God's honour; through his wise

* Trechsel: Die Protestantischen Antitrinitarier, 1839, s. 177.

care for the edifying of the kingdom of Christ; in a word, through all which can be comprehended in the idea of the papacy of truth and honour. He had indeed his faults, but they were either those of his time, or sprung from the peculiarities of his character, the greatness, force and elevation of which our weak degenerate race is unable to comprehend in the whole; and which, instead of contemplating it on the bright side, it can only judge of by the few dark spots on the surface."

CHAPTER II.

THE OUTWARD CONDITION OF THE CHURCH, AND CALVIN'S CIRCUMSTANCES AT GENEVA IN THE YEARS 1550, 1551, 1552.—HIS WORK 'DE SCANDALIS.'—LETTERS TO CRANMER AND MELANCTHON.

On the 10th of November 1549, Paul III., then in the eighty-third year of his age, was called to render a final account of his wicked deeds before God. The papal chair remained vacant till the 7th of February 1550, when the choice of the conclave fell on cardinal John Maria del Monte, the legate at Trent and bishop of Palestrina. He ascended the pontifical throne by the title of Julius III., and one of his first acts was to bestow the cardinal's hat on a boy of sixteen, the keeper of his apes. This occurrence furnished Calvin with a reason for writing in the following manner to Farel*:—"The pope whom they have made and consecrated with so much care must be an extraordinary monster, and in truth nothing could be better contrived than to give such a moderator to a Tridentine council."

Charles lost no time in compelling the new pontiff to reassemble the synod, while he himself prepared to assail the protestants more violently than ever. A bitter edict appeared against them in the Netherlands on the 19th of April; and in the diet, held at Augsburg in July, the emperor directed all the princes of Germany to proceed to Trent. This command was expressly repeated on the 13th of February 1551, and on the 1st of May

* MS. Gen. 4 Non. Mart. 1550.

in that year, the assembly recommenced its sittings. The pope had ordered that the Swiss cantons should be courteously requested to send deputies to the council; but the divines of Zurich, who were charged with the answer, sternly declared*, "That they had ceased for thirty years to acknowledge the authority of the pope; that they would persevere in the profession of their evangelical creed till convinced of error by the Bible itself; and that the reformed church could not submit to the council, though desired to do so by the pope, the emperor, the princes, and the catholic cantons." The catholic cantons were, in fact, disunited among themselves, and the king of France declared his intention of protesting against the council, on the ground of its want of catholicity.

We learn, but from a somewhat doubtful source of information†, that Calvin was proposed by the town of Strasburg as its representative at the Council of Trent. It was now that he published his Commentary on the Epistles; and we read with satisfaction the remarks which he made on the council in his dedication to the youthful king of England, Edward VI.:—

"Our Saviour was not more insulted by the servants of antichrist, when they gave Him a reed for a sceptre, and placed a crown of thorns upon his head, than He was in the Council of Trent. The assembly is but a vain shadow; but it is regarded by the pope as a sort of Hercules' club, wherewith he may overthrow the Son of God, and destroy the rest of the church. And if that teacher of impiety so shamelessly attacks the honour of God and the strength of our salvation, is it meet that we should betray our religion by our neglect? No! rather ought we to suffer a hundred deaths than allow so barbarous an oppression of piety to remain unexposed." Then follows an examination of the several members of the synod:—"Among thousands there may perhaps be found some who are partially on the side of truth, as Peter Vergerius. But what is the result? They are thrown into prison until they recant, or drink of that cup which closes their mouths for ever. We do not wish to avoid a legitimate council, but in this what sort of audience could we expect? With what patience would they, who cannot bear a gentle admonition, hear the thunders of the truth? They summon us indeed, but will they allow us to take even the lowest seats? In sooth there is no seat at all for any who pos-

* Ruchat, t. v. of the new ed. s. 426, 427.

† Pezel: Ausführliche Erzählung vom Sakramentstreit, s. 163.

sess not the mitre. But let them sit, if we while standing be only suffered to speak the truth. They will say that they give free hearing to all; and so they do, but it is only that we may deliver our petitions, be immediately removed, and after a fierce outcry for a few days, be called once more to hear our condemnation."

Calvin next examines the doctrine proposed, and shows what was to be expected from "the blood-thirsty pope." "If they raise the war-cry we must preserve our courage, and, armed with his never-failing weapons, follow the standard of our great leader. Every one, unless he obstinately close his eyes to the truth, must acknowledge that the papacy is a detestable monstrosity, a mass of errors and wiles concocted by Satan."

A general movement was now about to take place throughout Germany, and the "Dispersit superbos" was to receive a glorious fulfilment. Whilst the emperor, in his arrogance, trod the professors of the evangelical faith underfoot, those mighty plans unfolded themselves in the breast of prince Maurice, by which he was about to establish the freedom of the truth. Though of too ambitious a spirit, he was a stanch Lutheran, and was now greatly irritated and embittered against the emperor on account of his treacherous conduct towards the unfortunate landgrave. To deceive his old and experienced adversary, he well knew that he must proceed with the utmost caution. He accordingly took up his residence for the time in Saxony.

Melancthon had lately betrayed some degree of weakness. For this he was severely reproached; and Calvin wrote a severe letter to Valentine Pacäus, a doctor at Leipzig, in which he protested against the indiscretion of which his friend had been guilty*.

The course which Calvin took in German politics may be gathered from his letter to Melancthon in 1551†. He there speaks of the conflict carried on with the town of Magdeburg, at that time besieged by Maurice: it subsequently accepted the Interim. Melancthon had declared himself in favour of the adoption of all things that might be regarded as indifferent. He cared only for the fundamentals of Christianity: for this he

* Ed. Laus. Ep. 115. Ed. Amstel. p. 54, a.

† Ed. Laus. Ep. 117. Ed. Amstel. p. 54, b. Among other strong sentences in this epistle occur the following:—"If I know anything of religion, so much ought not to have been conceded by you to the papists;" and, "I would rather die with you a thousand times than see you survive the doctrine which you have taught."

was somewhat severely rebuked by Calvin; but it is delightful to see with what truth and candour, earnestness and confidence, these great men wrote, each fully alive to the merits of the other. Calvin was far from being of the number of those who have mistaken Melancthon's character. He acknowledged the greatness of his mind; he knew that he would have willingly laid down his life a thousand times for the truth's sake; but he was vexed at the pliancy of his disposition.

Maurice had besieged Magdeburg for the sole purpose of lulling the suspicions of the emperor. The divines considered him an enemy to protestantism; and he, to regain their respect, protested against the Tridentine synod, declared his wish that all its decrees should be once more examined, that the protestants should possess a direct voice therein, and that the pope should himself submit to its decisions. The emperor, on the other hand, became every day more excited against the protestants, and prohibited the preachers at Augsburg from touching on the disputed points. Those who offended against this order were to be banished the city within three days.

By these proceedings protestantism was almost suppressed in Suabia. But it soon became evident that Charles was as anxious to dissolve the old constitution of Germany as he was to secure the overthrow of the evangelical church. In pursuance of these designs he set out for Inspruck, whence he hoped to control the movements of the council: he little expected the *exaltavit humiles* which was in store for the reformers.

After the submission of Magdeburg, Maurice was appointed its burggrave: his troops were in the highest spirits, and having concluded a secret alliance with Henry II. of France, against the emperor, he now hoped to free the landgrave of Hesse. It was a favourite saying however of the acute politician Granvella, that nothing very refined could proceed from the heads of the drunken Germans.

Calvin carefully observed all these events. In the March of 1551 Bullinger* received from him a letter in which he says, "The proceedings of the emperor cause much anxiety to many here, who are justly suspicious of his troops which are now passing the Alps. If he takes possession of this country, I shall have nothing left to comfort me but the hope that the Lord will remove me from this miserable world, and not forsake that flock for whose safety I feel so much solicitude." He at this time

* Ed. Laus. Ep. 120. Ed. Amstel. p. 59, b.

continually turned his thoughts to England, and wrote to Somerset on behalf of Hooper. In a letter* to Farel he says, "There is no real union between the pope and the Tridentine council. With the former the French king has a secret understanding. It is thought that the flame of war will again burst forth in Italy. A Turkish ambassador is at this moment at the court of the king of France, for the purpose of exciting him to hostilities. A great fleet threatens Italy or Spain. Thus the Lord will leave them no time to work evil to the church."

Calvin's wish to die was not fulfilled. It was destined that he should see a great number of his fellow-labourers go before him: as Joachim von Watt and Vadian in St. Gallen, well-known as a philosopher, theologian and magistrate; and the minister Oswald Myconius. The famous Sebastian Münster at Basel, and Caspar Hedio at Strasburg, had already died of the plague. In the spring of this year Martin Bucer also departed this life in England. Calvin speaks of him in the following words†:—"When I think how great a loss the church has suffered in this man, I am torn with grief. He would have been of much service to England; and I had hoped even better things yet from his writings. I daily see the church stripped of her true servants. Vadian's character was in high repute among the Swiss; him also has the Lord taken from us." And in another letter he writes‡:—"May God grant that the rest, whom I should so deeply lament, may survive me! I shall then die in peace." And now the news reached him that Beza was seized by the plague. On this occasion he exclaims in his grief, and in his peculiar style§:—"Truly I should be unworthy of the name of a man if I did not love him, who loves me as a brother and honours me as a father;—but the loss to the church distresses me still more, for I saw in him, who is thus in the midst of his course threatened by so sudden a death, a man, whose amiable disposition, fine and noble spirit, and sincerity of mind, have rendered him worthy of the love of all the faithful. I hope however that he may even yet be restored to our prayers." Again ||, "Let us strengthen our souls until we shall have completed our course. Once I feared that, though among those who are hasten-

* Ed. Laus. Ep. 121. Ed. Amstel. p. 60, a.

† Letter to Farel, July 15, 1551. Ed. Laus. Ep. 123. Ed. Amstel. p. 240, b.

‡ To Viret, May 1551. Ed. Laus. Ep. 122. Ed. Amstel. p. 60, b.

§ Ed. Laus. Ep. 124. Ed. Amst. p. 60, b. Prid. Cal. Jul. 1551.

|| Calv. Farello, 15 Jun. 1551. Ed. Laus. p. 123. Ed. Amstel. p. 240, b.

ing on, I should have to atone for the delay of others. Above all things it comforts me, that you, whose zeal has overcome all, have forgiven me and pardoned so much. Let it suffice, if we, avoiding the extravagant errors of others, walk in the right path, satisfied with knowing that if many are in advance, there are still many behind us."

The dawn of the year 1552 beheld in Germany the beginning of a new and eventful career; while Switzerland and Geneva were disturbed by fresh causes of uneasiness, and by a controversy on some of the most abstruse points of Christian doctrine. In the manifesto now issued by the elector Maurice, three things were demanded; namely, "protection for the evangelical church, the integrity of the German constitution, and the liberation of the landgrave." Maurice rushed like a thunderbolt against the old emperor, who, utterly unprepared for such an attack, fled precipitately from Inspruck, and passed over the Alps. The Tridentine council was dispersed with equal haste, the worthy fathers flying in all directions. Thus the plans against Germany were defeated, and the safety of the church was secured on the basis of a general treaty. The king of France, who oppressed his own evangelical subjects, was compelled, much against his will, to assist, as the ally of the elector, in giving durability to the German church.

But disquiet still universally prevailed. The true position of the evangelical church may be learnt from a letter written to Calvin by Melancthon, and in which he exhibits both his natural disposition and the regard which he entertained for our reformer. The satisfaction which the latter experienced when the letter here referred to arrived from Wittenberg may be easily imagined.

"Honoured and dearest brother,—I am anxious to communicate with you on matters of great moment, and this because I hold in the highest esteem your judgement, and the candour and purity of your soul*. I am now living like the ὄνος ἐν σφηκίαις; but shall probably soon leave this world to join the glorious company in heaven. If however my life be prolonged, I may expect banishment; and should I be exiled, I have resolved to see and converse with you. I have pursued my theological studies with some success in this country, but they are now interrupted by the plague and the war. I often lament the phrenzy which exists among our rulers. May the Son of God alleviate our misery and remove its cause! If you would kindly

* Oct. 1, 1552. Ed. Laus. Ep. 137. Ed. Amstel. p. 66.

write to me often, you might send your letters to Dryander. You will find in the inclosed that I have given a brief history of this autumn. Farewell!—I have already answered Osiander. There are now three Turkish pachas in Pannonia, accompanied by two armies, which a short time since took several important towns, and routed the forces of king Ferdinand. Maurice of Saxony has marched towards Austria, against the Turks, plundering in the meantime the margrave Albrecht, laying waste Nuremberg, and levying contributions on Frankfort, towns in the dioceses of Mainz and Triers. The army of the French king is approaching the diocese of Liege, while the emperor Charles assembles his army at Spiers, to restrain the margrave and the French. The son of the earl of Mansfield, who is collecting an army at Bremen in Saxony, is near at hand, and threatens to invade the land of his birth, throwing the whole country into disorder. Desolation hovers over all Germany; the churches weep together in affliction; theological studies are at a standstill; the tumultuous cry of insurrection increases on all sides. I esteem you fortunate in your tranquillity, and pray God to remove our afflictions." It was easy for Calvin to conclude, from the first part of this letter, that Melancthon's feelings were not too deeply wounded by the freedom of his reproaches.

In May, Maurice had accomplished his enterprise against the emperor. Negotiations were opened at Passau on the 26th of that month, and on the 2nd of August a treaty of peace was completed and signed. According to these arrangements it was settled that an edict should be issued by a diet within six months, in favour of religious liberty; that until that time the party attached to the Confession of Augsburg should, on no pretence whatever, be exposed to molestation; and that the imperial court of judicature should act towards both parties with equal justice. This was the first germ of order in the midst of those tumults which Melancthon describes.

The moments of peace, so envied by his friend, Calvin employed in making regulations for the conduct of the church, in literary labours, and in efforts to establish unity. It was in the year 1550 that the arrangement, already alluded to, was made for the more effectual pastoral superintendence of the people. Mere preaching had been found insufficient. It was therefore determined that the ministers should severally visit their parishioners at home: they were to be accompanied by an elder, and after giving instruction, were to require of each individual a statement of his faith. According to the testimony of his fellow-labourer, nothing could exceed the benefit derived from this private and domestic catechising. The great importance which was attributed to it by Calvin may be learnt from a somewhat remarkable occurrence, related by himself. An Englishman at Geneva had come to the conclusion in his own mind, that he himself was Moses, and Calvin Aaron. The latter having preached and greatly exerted himself one Christmas-day, in a certain quarter of the city, where he was anxious to maintain the system of particular inspection, was returning home oppressed with weariness. The Englishman however seized him, and insisted that he should wait and listen to his wondrous revelations. Calvin only escaped from the consequences of the veneration which he had inspired, by humbly entreating to be permitted first to go home and refresh himself.

Calvin passed a portion of this summer in the country, and affectionately invited his friend Viret to visit him there.

An unexpected occurrence happened at Geneva about this time (1550). The event alluded to affords striking evidence of the disturbed state of affairs, and forcibly proves that the church, in opposition to Calvin's principles, was completely subjected to the state. One day, while sitting in his study, his thoughts engaged on very different matters, information was brought him that the Council of Two Hundred had suddenly abolished all the festivals of the church, directing that even the Lord's nativity should only be celebrated on the succeeding Sunday. This affair, concerning which the consistory was not even consulted, was the work of the laity alone, and was closely connected with national feeling. The Bernese, after accomplishing the expulsion of the ministers, had re-established in Geneva the following festivals:—the circumcision, the annunciation, the ascension, and Christmas-day. These the Genevese now at once abolished, and by so doing highly incensed their allies. Calvin, to whom this movement was generally attributed, did not think it necessary to take any steps against it, recollecting probably that the observance of holy days is nowhere expressly enjoined in Scripture. He justified himself to Haller, the pastor at Bern*, and fully proved that this change, though far from being at variance with his own opinions, was nevertheless accomplished without his knowledge. It was rumoured however that, had he had his wish, he would even have abolished the

* 4 Non. Jan. Ed. Laus. p. 118. Ed. Amstel. p. 62, a.

observance of the Sabbath. On this subject he wrote as follows to a minister in the Bernese territory*:—"Before my arrival all festivals, Sunday alone excepted, had been abolished by Farel and Viret. When we were banished, four festivals, together with other observances, were again introduced. Although at my return it would have been easy for me to have suppressed, and that too with applause, all that had been done in my absence, I allowed things to remain as they were. I could, nevertheless, scarcely contain myself when I saw with how great perverseness the day of Christ's circumcision was celebrated at the beginning of the year, whilst the day of the crucifixion was almost totally neglected. The day of the annunciation also has been kept holy by the people, and I have opposed this superstition with all the influence and energy I can command. Notwithstanding this, I by no means wish to be classed with those who would willingly see such festivals entirely disregarded. The earliest of the evangelical Christians here were so opposed to the innovations which were afterwards introduced, that I experienced no mercy at their hands: to them, my moderation had the appearance of lukewarmness. This dispute indeed was at one time carried so far, that recourse was had to the sword; and as each side carried its opinions to an immoderate length, that appeared to me the most advisable course which lay at an equal distance from either, namely, that all shops should be shut, and labour discontinued until mid-day, when the people might resume their customary occupations;—a regulation similar to that which was introduced nine years ago.

"The controversy however was not yet settled. Some of the shops in the town were open and some shut, and perpetual disputes existed between their respective owners. As no remedy could be found for this, I appealed, at the beginning of the year, to the council, and besought it to use its influence with the people. But I said not a word respecting the suppression of the festival. I was far more inclined to praise the moderation which had led to the adoption of the Bernese practice. When I heard of the measure passed by the council, in obedience to the popular wish, I was astonished at so unexpected a proceeding. Certain it is, that if any one had asked my opinion, I should not have ventured to express it in such a manner. Nothing new however has been introduced: we have only returned to the old and better custom. Our church moreover is not the

* Ed. Laus. Ep. 128. Ed. Amstel. p. 62, b.

only one in which Sunday is the only festival observed. This was the practice at Strasburg; but I did not think it right to interfere, on my return, with the existing order."

Bullinger* praises at Zurich the apostolic freedom, by means of which the people of Geneva had succeeded in abolishing the observance of Christmas. The church at Zurich, he says, had, twelve years since, many festivals, but now observed only Sunday, and those of the nativity, the circumcision and the ascension of our Lord. They add Whitsunday to these merely on account of the sacrament. The Genevese continued to observe the regulations which they had introduced, with such tenacity, that, in the year 1555 they subjected some persons who celebrated Christmas to twenty-four hours' imprisonment.

In 1551 a report was circulated that Calvin was dead, and the papists proceeded, as they had done in the case of Luther, to show their hatred of his name by proclaiming a day of thanksgiving. A solemn procession of the canons of the cathedral took place in his native town of Noyon. Calvin speaks of this in a letter to Farel†, dated December 2, 1552:—"You have no doubt heard," he says, "that I survive my birth-place‡. I cannot but weep for this ruined city, although last year, on the report of my death, it offered up solemn thanksgivings, as if it could triumph over Christ." Beza has incorrectly stated that this occurrence took place in 1556. A similar course had been pursued, some time before, when Luther was falsely reported to be dead. The reformer has given an account of this affair, with his own remarks§.

Calvin was busily employed at this time with his work *De Scandalis.* Beza connects this undertaking with the movement at Geneva respecting the festivals, which had occasioned offence to many, and hindered the advancement of God's kingdom. But Calvin only took advantage of these circumstances as affording a good opportunity for publishing his book. We see from the preface that it had been for some time expected, and was the result of his anxious desire to establish unity, so injured by the existence of scandals. He enumerates them in this work, and shows that the church was disturbed by them from the be-

* Calv. Epp. Ed. Laus. Ep. 129. Ed. Amstel. p. 63, a.

† Ed. Laus. Ep. 140, towards the end. Ed. Amstel. p. 67.

‡ Noyon had been lately destroyed by fire.

§ Marheineke, Reform. Gesch. t. iv. s. 325.

ginning. Of the comprehensive plan of this work he had already spoken to Farel, August 19, 1550.

The preface to the treatise *De Scandalis* is well worth reading. Calvin dedicated the work to Laurence de Normandie (lieutenant du roi à Noyon), and suggested to him many topics of consolation. Laurence had resigned country, honours and the world for the sake of the Gospel; and had left Noyon at the same time as Calvin's family. He had lost within a brief space of time, his father, his wife, and his little daughter; and he was almost tempted to believe that the curse of God attended his change of religion. Calvin consoled him with the recollection of what his wife had said on her death-bed*.

Calvin published this work in both Latin and French. A scandal is whatever hinders us from pursuing the right path, or causes us to stumble. Now Christ himself is a rock of offence, because men stumble at him. There are three species of scandals:—1. The first are derived from doctrine. To the wise of this world the Gospel is itself foolishness, and this is the case with its fundamental article, namely predestination. 2. When the Gospel is preached, sects arise, and controversies among the teachers. 3. Another class of scandals spring from moral depravity, hypocrisy, the ingratitude and vanity of worldly professors.

Against the first of these three species of scandals Calvin argued with great force, showing the folly of those who take offence at the Gospel because of the simplicity of its language. He next speaks of the doctrines which commonly create most disgust, as that of the two natures in Christ; of the salvation which we obtain through his sufferings alone; of the blessing enjoyed by his becoming a curse for us; and of our righteousness as existing in God only, and not in ourselves. He also speaks of the cross of Christ, of self-denial, and of constancy in times of persecution. We quote the following admirable passage:—" Let us meditate on this, that however low the outward state of the church may be, it still shines in inward beauty. Though shaken upon earth, it stands fast before God and the

* " I can wish for no better medicine than those excellent words which she spake when rendering up her spirit. She held me by the hand, and thanked God that He had led her from a place where she would not have been suffered to die in peace. 'O how happy I am that I have been delivered from that cursed slavery of Babylon, and am now about to be delivered from my last bondage! How would it be with me now were I still in Noyon, and dare not open my lips to declare my belief?'......I know not which was greater, her faith or her humility."

angels; wretched after the flesh, it is rich in spiritual blessedness. Even so we see that Christ lay in the manger, in the greatest poverty, while angels were singing his praise in the heavens. The star gave notice of his glory, and the wise men from distant lands felt his power. When Satan tempted Him, hungering in the wilderness, and when the bloody sweat dropped from his forehead, angels were at hand ready to minister unto Him. At the moment when He was about to be taken prisoner, his voice cast down the foremost of his enemies; and while He was hanging upon the cross, the darkened sun proclaimed that He was the Lord of the universe. The graves opening, declared that He was the Lord of life and death. In this day, when we behold Him suffering in his body (the church) through the pride and insults of the wicked; oppressed by their tyranny; exposed to their abuse; driven to and fro by their rage, none of these wonders can move us. We ought therefore to do our utmost to keep in mind, that the church is appointed to struggle continually under the cross, as long as we remain in this present world."

Another cause of offence is the poverty of the church, and the conflicts to which it is perpetually exposed. Calvin, in reply, describes the sufferings and oppressions which the people of Christ have had to endure from the beginning. All these things proceed from the disobedience of mankind, the great hindrance to the grace of God, as shown by history. Still, in the end, grace is always mighty and victorious, and that even in the times of antichrist. It is necessary that the church should suffer affliction, in order that our pride may be humbled. Hence the melancholy termination of the religious war in Germany.

"At the time when the knowledge of the Gospel was most widely diffused in Germany, and when those who most zealously upheld it, seemed to stand firm; when that war was undertaken which had so lamentable a termination, and I saw that all our friends were inspired by the most lively hope of success; I often said in my sermons, that the victory which we seemed on the point of gaining would be more perilous to us than anything which the enemy could do against us; for, certainly, no affliction, however heavy, could injure us so much as a too-triumphant Gospel. It would have been disproportioned to our strength. I do not repent having spoken thus."

After expressing his feelings on the fall of many who had

renounced their faith, he thus speaks of the elector John:—"There are others who have shown how invincible is the power of faith when strengthened by the Spirit of God. We could never have supposed, had not the cross been laid upon him, that there was such an heroic feeling in the duke of Saxony as that with which God has inspired him, in order that he might become an example to all times."

Calvin next speaks of the scandals which pertain to those who ascribe their sins to God, or who stumble at the doctrine of predestination. He says well:—"As we offend God when we endeavour to penetrate secrets which He is pleased to hide from us, so is it our duty to hearken with all humility to what it is his will to tell us, and to refrain from any deeper scrutiny of the mystery. True christian prudence consists in this, so to beware of vain curiosity, that we may never wish to know more than that which Scripture reveals. Certain it is, that God has hidden nothing from us but what it would be useless or superfluous for us to know, or what might surpass our power of comprehension."

The scandals next described are those occasioned by the public preaching of the Gospel. Men are offended because the Gospel often gives rise to strife and war. Calvin here speaks in defence of war, when it is carried on for the interest of souls. He does not however seem to be quite consistent with himself on this point:—"I willingly allow," he says, "that if the slavery of the body only were in question, it were better to endure it than cause any great disturbance or bloodshed; but when the everlasting fate of our souls is concerned, we must never regard peace as sufficiently precious to induce us to preserve it at such a sacrifice. Still worse is it to endanger the Gospel, to sacrifice the honour of God's Son, and of his kingdom, in order to keep well with the world. It were far better that heaven and earth should be cast into the abyss, than that the glory given Him by his Father should be lessened. Shall we, to save life, forsake the Author of existence? To have peace with men, shall we make war with God? To save ourselves from the assaults of the wicked, shall we separate ourselves from Christ, who has reconciled men and angels to God the Father? This would be a very unwise proceeding."

Christ foretold that there would be wars. Hence the justification of his religion, when it has been the occasion of wars and commotions, in opposing the papacy. "Must pure and genuine religion be less esteemed because it has dragged this horrible serpent out of its hole?" Calvin speaks in this passage of certain enemies of the Gospel under the name of Agrippa, Villeneuve* and Dolet. He mentions Rabelais also among others. God warns us through such men, and heresies therefore can be no proper cause of offence. They are all blinded by their pride and haughtiness. This was the case with Michael Servetus, who, as well as his doctrine, is here characterized. Thus the libertines also gave cause of scandal by their converting christian freedom into licentiousness.

And further, he speaks of the scandal occasioned by the wicked who live among the good, and more especially against wicked, carnal ministers. The Gospel however is not chargeable with their guilt. Offences appear throughout the entire history of the Gospel. But the wicked must ever be mingled with the good, that the faith of the latter may be proved.

Offences are also created by those who allow themselves to be easily enticed from the profession of the truth. The example of such persons must be opposed by that of those who were willing, at the same time, to become martyrs for the Gospel. God has granted strength for this purpose not to men only, but also to women, who sometimes even surpass men in fortitude. "We learn from church history," he observes, "that no better examples of courage can be found than those afforded by the women in Artois and in the Netherlands."

Another fruitful source of scandals exists in the controversies between the various teachers of the church. Calvin particularly instances the unhappy sacramentarian dispute. "I can say with truth, that I have found to my grief what a contrivance of the devil this was to keep afflicted consciences in a state of perplexity. But as I have since learnt, that I was held back rather through my own weakness than by any actual obstacle, I shall not hesitate to assert the same of others."

"The papists contend daily on all the points of their religion, and their books show that they as constantly support different views. They assert, on the other hand, that we are not in agree-

* Villanovanus was probably not Servetus. Several learned men of this name lived at the time of Servetus, in Spain, France and Italy. Rabelais speaks of a Villeneuve (Pantagruel, liv. iii. c. 13), and calls him 'Le docte Villanovanus, François.' Postell also wrote a book in which he endeavoured to show that the Mohammedans and Lutherans agree, and that Villanovanus wrote the book 'De Tribus Prophetis;' but this same author defended Servetus. The author of the Dialogue between the Vatican and Calvin names Villanovanus, as Calvin himself does, with Agrippa and Doletus.

ment among ourselves. The dispute, however, between Luther and Zwingli shall not keep us from the Gospel, for we see that Paul and Barnabas, and Paul and Peter could fall into sharp contention with each other. I dare indeed assert, that when men's hearts are not too much heated by dispute, or are not befooled by evil suspicions, means may readily be found to reconcile them." Calvin adds, that all the evangelical parties in the church had reverted to his views of the Lord's Supper, and differed from each other only in expression.

Another class of scandals is derived from the slanders of the wicked; and Calvin here enters into a justification of the protestants against the catholic teachers, frequently expressing himself in a very original and characteristic style. Thus, for example, in his observations on the Romish fasts: "They here follow their usual practice, drinking right well the day before, that their hearts may not sink too low on the fast-day. So also, being obliged to fast, they first eat till they are ready to burst from fear of hunger in the evening. The following day they eat double to cool their revenge. Having thus sported with God, as with a child, they are bold enough to accuse us of having abolished fasting and mortification." "The papists wish to make us believe that the dispute which we carry on with them is nothing but a conflict, through which we seek to possess ourselves of women." Here follows Calvin's justification of his own marriage: "Even while I lived in subjection to the pope, I was never bound not to marry. But when God freed me from that bondage, I remained for a long time without taking a wife. At length I found so excellent a one, that I had reason to praise God for his giving her to me; but when she was taken away, I was far from hastening to marry again. And with what do these good champions of chastity charge us? That Luther, inspired by lust, cast himself into marriage, and led the whole swarm of priests, monks and nuns after him, involving them in the same offence! Can anything be more ridiculous than to argue that Romanism must be forsaken unless we can live in chastity?"

The work concludes with an admonition to unity. It is especially rich in thought, and must have possessed great practical utility for the times in which it appeared.

We must here pause for a while, to consider the ruling ideas of this particular epoch. As we saw Calvin in the first period of his course striving for doctrine, and in the second for such a system of church discipline as might give stability to his reformation, so now we are to contemplate him in eager pursuit of the third great object of his labours.

Who desires not unity in the church? The Lord himself prayed for unity, and his prayer must, sooner or later, be fulfilled. Numberless efforts have been made to this end. But what are the right means? That is the difficult question. Ideally, the church of Rome might be supposed to exhibit the unity desired; but its unity is a falsehood, and the means by which it has been sought are antichristian. There can be no grander idea than that of a theocracy, as held by the popes,—of a kingdom ruling by the Spirit, and the design of which is to establish peace and faith among the nations. Sublime was the end which the church seemed to have reached when the rude strength of the people was opposed by its firm barrier; when there was a union of all, even of the most distant churches, supported, quickened and governed by Rome, and when no change was to be looked for in their doctrine. Hence it was that the whole of Christendom seemed inspired by one spirit; hence its power to undertake such mighty enterprises against the Mohammedans; and hence the establishment of monasteries as asylums for science and misfortune.

But what were the means employed to secure this unity? It was necessary that the civil power should be crippled; that consciences should be enslaved, and their most secret movements paralysed by the medium of confession. The servants of the church, separated from the world and brought up for the church alone, were compelled to a celibacy which opposed the rights of nature, not forgetful to avenge itself. But while free from and independent of the state, responsible only to the head of the church, secured from poverty, and living even in princely splendour, they might cherish the hope of rising to the highest stations in the world, and could thus combine ambition with an apparent apostolic humility.

The Inquisition pursued its revengeful course without any regard to the rights of states or the duties of charity; and although it succeeded in effecting an outward unity, whilst the war was still raging within, the wrong means employed, and the schism which resulted therefrom, produced the most distressing consequences to the visible church. Its unity had been broken, and it was already divided into fragments, as Calvin showed in his defence against Sadolet, who accused him of disturbing the communion of the saints, and in his reply to those who summoned him before the judgement-seat of God as a betrayer of the papacy.

But the question so difficult for the protestants to answer was now asked, namely, how they could preserve the holy unity of which they spoke? for it was evident that neither a church nor communion could exist without unity. But for this, each party would have its own church, and the body would be torn into numberless fragments. That both Luther and Calvin were convinced of this fact, appears from the care with which they unceasingly opposed the authors of those false notions which every day brought forth. In that remarkable period, upon which we are now entering, when the churches are more than ever divided, and when principles are contrasted with each other in the rudest antagonism, this subject of the unity of the church possesses a continually increasing interest.

Calvin entered upon the discussion with a holy earnestness peculiar to himself. He not only strove for unity in his contest against error, but, as far as it was practicable, he promoted it by the settlement of the controversy on the Lord's Supper; through the formularies and conventions, which deserved so much respect; and especially by means of the synodal intercourse with France, the first great and apostolic source of all church communion. This was peculiarly the case internally, because the general synod settled the disputes which existed on particular dogmas, and had authority to interpret the Scriptures; and, externally, because it had the control of worldly affairs; in the larger states the episcopal element being combined with the synodal.

But Calvin's thoughts were now occupied with a still wider plan, that, namely, of uniting the several reformed churches, as those of France, Scotland and Germany, in one body. This appears from a letter which he addressed to Cranmer. Beza would fain have pursued the path thus opened to him; and if the divines who formed the assembly at Dort, the last of the reformed synods, peculiarly so called, or if protestantism even would not consent to this unity and entireness, yet does the praise properly belong to Calvin of having shown the way by which it might have been attained. Unity in the Holy Ghost was the cherished object of Calvin's will. It was not the offspring of private intellectual inquiry, the principle falsely ingrafted upon protestantism. The Calvinistic rule is the rightful medium between papal tyranny and protestant anarchy. "Evangelical truth," says Calvin to Sadolet, "is the bond. May God grant that you and yours may see that there is no other bond of union but this, that Jesus Christ may deliver us from the present evil world, and bind us together in his love, so that we may grow up by his word and Spirit as having one heart and one soul!" This principle of a mystic-spiritual union with the Lord is finely embodied in Calvin's doctrinal teaching, but less manifestly so in its practical development.

In the August of 1555 Calvin received a letter from Peter Martyr*, in which he states his wish to have Calvin's opinion on the union of the faithful in Christ. Calvin in his answer very distinctly asserted the existence of this communion. He was not however, as has been intimated, always in agreement with himself on this subject, in so far as phraseology is concerned; and the expressions which he sometimes used excited against him a more than ordinary degree of hatred.

It appears that in the midst of all the differences about doctrine which prevailed, this idea of a visible unity always employed his thoughts. The work of which we have been speaking, *De Scandalis*, had its origin in this feeling; and Calvin now looked to the greatest men of the time, hoping that by arousing their attention to the distracted state of the church, a communion might be effected which would still further diffuse the principles involved in the *Consensus Tigurinus*. We shall hereafter see how constantly Bullinger strove for the same object; while in the year 1561 Beza, at the conference held at St. Germain, urged, in the name of the reformed, the necessity of a general council, in which not the pope but the Scriptures might decide the questions discussed†.

In the work *De Scandalis*, Calvin shows that the catholics accused the reformed as the authors of schism, whereas they themselves were not united, and failed to employ the proper means to establish concord. Calvin was convinced, in his own mind, that he had discovered the means for accomplishing this great end. The tone of his letters both to Cranmer and Melancthon clearly indicates that he felt himself called, by an inward witness, to the highest place in the future conduct of the Reformation. His words to the two distinguished men above-named are well-worthy of attention. To Cranmer he writes‡,—

"In the present distracted state of the church, you suppose

* Ed. Laus. Ep. 208. Ed. Amstel. p. 100, a.
† Hist. Eccles. iv. pp. 716, 717.
‡ Ed. Laus. Ep. 126. Ed. Amstel. p. 61, a.

that no better means can be employed than that pious, sensible men, brought up in the school of God, should unite in setting forth a common confession of christian doctrine. Satan seeks by manifold wiles to extinguish the light of the Gospel. The dogs in the pay of the pope cease not to bark, that they may drown the voices of those who preach the word of truth. Such is the madness, such the impiety which everywhere prevails, that religion can hardly any longer be protected from daring mockery. Even those who have not declared themselves as its open enemies are yet so bold and rash, that, if they be not chastised, they will soon involve everything in horrible confusion. Nor is this state of feeling (the result, in one respect, of immoderate conceit, and in another of extravagant curiosity) confined to the people alone. Still more lamentable to say, it is extending among the clergy. But the Lord will himself communicate to us the unity of a true faith, and that in some wonderful manner, and by means altogether unknown to us; even as He has done from the beginning of the world, so that it may not be destroyed by the strife of men. He will not however suffer those whom He has placed as watchmen to slumber. They are his servants, and by their means the pure doctrine of his Word ought to be preserved from all unholy mixtures, and so handed down to posterity."

Calvin expressed a wish that Cranmer would appoint some place in England where the heads of all the protestant churches might meet, and having settled the main articles of belief, might lay the foundation of a permanent union. "One of the greatest evils of our time," he says, "is that the churches are so widely separated from each other, that there is not even a temporal or human intercourse carried on between them; we may well, therefore, be silent as to a holy communion of the members of Christ, which is in everybody's mouth, but no sign of which exists in the heart. This is partly the fault of the princes. The body of Christ is torn asunder because the members are separated. As far as I am concerned, if I can be of any use, I will readily pass over ten seas to effect the object in view. If the welfare of England alone were concerned, I should regard it as a sufficient reason to act thus. But at present, when our purpose is to unite the sentiments of all good and learned men, and so, according to the rule of Scripture, to bring the separated churches into one, neither labour nor trouble of any kind ought to be spared*."

Cranmer, it seems, fully comprehended Calvin's idea, and was

* Ed. Laus. Ep. 127. Ed. Amstel. p. 61, b.

anxious to establish, at least in England, the proposed plan. Calvin rejoiced at this, and reminded the prelate of the power which his dignity afforded him to excite his zeal:—“ Beware that you may not have to charge yourself with many grievous accusations, if, through negligence or delay, you leave the world in its present distracted state. Besides the waste of church property, which is wicked enough, there is a still more unpardonable crime committed. The public income of the church is employed to fill the bellies of a multitude of idle fellows, engaged to sing vespers in a foreign language. I will say nothing more than that, if you allow yourself to appear as a supporter of such an abuse, at open variance with the true order of the church, nothing can be more absurd. Although I doubt not but that this must appear so to yourself, and must have been so represented by the excellent Peter Martyr, yet the difficulties with which you have to contend are so numerous, that it may not be useless on my part to excite your resolution.”

A letter from Cranmer, dated March 20, 1552, shows that he had adopted Calvin's views, and was anxious to secure unity of opinion on the doctrine of the Lord's Supper. He imparted his wish to Melancthon and Bullinger. The whole plan was destroyed, it seems, by the death of Edward VI.

Calvin now also directed the attention of Melancthon to the necessity of some effort for securing unity of doctrine. The letter* which he wrote on this occasion expressed the feelings of his innermost heart and conscience. He knew well what position he occupied, and that their friendship could not be interrupted without injury to the church. Hence he reproved him in gentle terms for his vacillation in respect to the doctrine of election, which at this time greatly occupied his thoughts, and because his opponents appealed to the doubtful sentiments of Melancthon, who even refused to admit the cautious expressions of the *Consensus Tigurinus.*

It has been already stated how Calvin, in the year 1543, controverted the opinions of Pighius, and dedicated his work to Melancthon. A Benedictine monk in Italy, Georg Siculus, had undertaken to confute Calvin; but no sooner, as we are about to relate, had the controversy on election broken out in Geneva, than the people of that city united to uphold the doctrine, and obtained Calvin's consent to their views. But Melancthon refused to adopt either the Zurich or the Genevese

* Nov. 29, 1552. Ed. Laus. Ep. 141. Ed. Amstel. p. 66, b.

system*. On the 26th of August, 1554, Calvin again wrote to him to obtain his consent to the doctrine, and thus to establish unity†.

CHAPTER III.

THE FIRST GREAT CONTROVERSY.—THE DISPUTE RESPECTING PREDESTINATION.—BOLSEC.

THE letter to Melancthon clearly shows what the zeal of the reformer for unity, in regard to this important controversy, was likely to effect. Calvin, through his love for the doctrine of election, has been almost wholly misunderstood by church historians. We must either indeed view him as an unimpassioned controversialist, or distinctly recognize the part which he took in this matter as pointed out to him by a higher Spirit. This doctrine, in fact, exhibiting as it does the peculiarity of the evangelical in opposition to the catholic church,—namely that man is saved not by his works, but by the grace of God,—necessarily exercises a very extensive influence in the former. It was therefore the bounden duty of its advocate to defend it against all opponents, and to insist upon its introduction into the confession of the several churches, as was done, at a subsequent period, in France, Scotland and Holland, and still later in the case of one-half of the Methodist community.

A dispute on this subject was begun at the commencement of the year 1551. One of the Bernese ministers, indignant at finding that three French refugees, who resided in his village, went on the Sunday to hear Calvin, declared‡, that they were objects of suspicion, for that they worshiped the inventor of a new, false and impious doctrine as an idol. "He attacks me," said Calvin, "like a raging papist," and the circumstance was brought, at his instance, before the Bernese council. "How sincere and

* Beza v. Calv. "Quin etiam his de rebus ita scribere cœperat Phil. Melancthon, ut quamvis antea Calvini adversus Pighium libro diserte subscripsisset, tamen Genevenses quasi Stoicum fatum invehentes notare quibusdam videretur."

† Ed. Laus. Ep. 179. Ed. Amstel. p. 82, a. "Although I grieve that no reply has been received from you to my last letter."

‡ MS. Tigur. 1551.

faithful I have been," he said, "in the declaration of the truth, will our excellent father Musculus readily testify. How earnestly I have sought to establish peace and union, will right-minded men generally acknowledge. That unsavoury monster has endeavoured to pervert the *Consensus* between the Zurichers and Bernese, in order to prove that I am the author of an impious doctrine; and that he, who is but a mole, is alone endued with the power of seeing right."

Calvin appealed to the Bernese, in the name of Christ, and called upon the pious exiles to defend him against his barbarous accuser, the monk, George Siculus,—his opposers being now so numerous, and his time fully occupied with his work against Pighius*. The mysterious subject of election was at present debated in all circles at Geneva. Exiles flocked to that city from every quarter; and our attention is called to two men, of very different intellectual character, who were thus brought together.

The one was a distinguished Neapolitan, Galeazzo Caraccioli, Marquis of Vico, whose history affords us an instance of the most wonderful triumph of grace over nature†. The other was Bolsec, who exhibits, on the contrary, the victory of our common nature over truth and honesty. Vico was descended from the ancient race of the Caraccioli of Capua. His mother, a Caraffa, was sister of Pope Paul IV. Vico heard Peter Martyr at Naples, and from that time his mind had no rest. He was brought up in the court of the emperor, and his parents married him to a woman of great worth, hoping thereby still to keep him in the fashionable world. But Vico resisted their tears and persuasions, overcame all temptations, and firmly resolved within himself, after a severe struggle, to leave father, mother, wife, children, the honours and riches of this world, for the Lord's sake. He met Peter Martyr once again, when he had become professor at Strasburg. Martyr again proved to him that he must cease altogether from attending the mass. Vico revered his aged father. His wife, who was united with him in the tenderest affection, could not resolve to change her faith. Grace triumphed, but it cost the heart of Vico indescribable anguish to separate himself from his children. To accomplish his purpose, it was necessary that he should leave his beautiful country, his lordly palace, the court and its attractions, to be-

* MSS. Gen. Calvin to Viret, August 17, 1551.

† Ruchat, Hist. de la Réform. Suisse. Nouv. Ed. T. V. p. 449.

come an exile, to endure poverty and want, and to become an object of aversion even to his friends. But grace was sufficient for him. "I can now for love of Thee, O Lord, deny myself!" he at length exclaimed: "blessed be banishment and the cross, which tear me away from the vanities, and the sins of the world!"

It was only to some few friends that he dare trust his safety: they left him on the borders of Italy. His family had been led to suppose that he was going to the emperor. He arrived at Geneva in April 1551: Calvin received him with open arms, and continued throughout his life to regard him with the greatest esteem. He expressed this feeling for him in the dedication prefixed to his commentary on the Epistles to the Corinthians, and the historians of Geneva bear witness that he was an example of the sincerest piety. In Naples the agitation produced by the announcement of his departure was universal: nothing was left untried to bring him back. He answered that his conscience would not allow him to live in the midst of Catholic superstition, and that he had sacrificed the glory of this world, that he might not lose the glory which is eternal. At length the emperor proclaimed him guilty of high-treason, confiscated his possessions, and degraded his children. His aged father threw himself in despair at the feet of the emperor, and desired Caraccioli to come to him at Venice. He obeyed, commending himself to the prayers of the whole church at Geneva. His father received him lovingly, and did all in his power to win him back; but he answered firmly, that not even a father could oblige him to prefer the honours and possessions of this world to the glory of God. They separated for ever: Vico returned to Geneva: grace had finally conquered.

In direct contrast with this remarkable man stood Jerome Bolsec. He was born in Paris, and became a Carmelite monk. Having cast aside his cowl, he was obliged to flee into Italy, dreading the consequence of having spoken too freely respecting the catholic church. The duchess of Ferrara had received him, with her accustomed kindness, as a clergyman. But he became a physician, married, and went to Geneva. There he became acquainted with many persons of distinction, among others with De Bourgogne, who had settled in that city at the earnest entreaty of Calvin. Bolsec was, to all appearance, a good Christian, and there are reasons to believe that he employed himself at one time in compiling materials for the life of Calvin; traces of such a collection being found at the beginning of his libel, published at a later period. Not by any means vicious or despicable at first, this man sank by degrees to the lowest depths of error, and became the declared enemy of truth. He commenced by discussing vehemently, in the different circles at Geneva, the abstruse doctrine of election. Calvin admitted him to a conference, and explained to him the nature of the subject, so difficult and profound, but without effect. Bolsec was called before the consistory, and he was desired to consider the inconsistency of his opinion; but he refused to listen. But such an opposition could not be tolerated in the midst of the reformation. It was the well-known custom at Geneva for a minister, whether of the city or country, to preach every Friday, according to his turn, in the cathedral; the other ministers examining and deciding upon the merits of the discourse. Any individual also might at that time go up to the preacher, even in the church, and make such observations as he pleased. This was allowed in order to accustom the people to contend firmly for all points connected with the reformation.

On the 16th of October the minister of St. Andrew's preached to a crowded congregation, on St. John, chap. viii. ver. 47. "He that is of God heareth God's words: ye therefore hear them not, because ye are not of God." All those who are not of God, resist him to the end, because God affords the grace of obedience to his elect alone. As the preacher uttered this remark, a man suddenly started up from the midst of the congregation, and combated with unbecoming vehemence the doctrine which had been thus advanced. All were silent. "How," he said, "can you believe that God has determined the lot of a man before his birth, destining this one to sin and punishment, and that one to virtue and eternal reward? It is a false and impious notion, which Laurentius Valla has started, namely, that the will of God is the cause of all things, and that therefore the origin of all the evils and all the sins which exist must be ascribed to him, as the old poets feign with regard to Jupiter. Would you make of God, the eternal and righteous one, a senseless tyrant? Would you rob virtue of its glory, free vice from its disgrace, and the wicked from the terrors of conscience?"

He who spoke thus was the physician Bolsec. The fathers of the church were cited in his speech, and he concluded by exhorting the people, in the most seditious and abusive language, not to allow themselves to be deceived by the clergy. He was probably induced to adopt this course by some of Calvin's enemies.

A curious scene now took place. Bolsec had ventured to act as he had done, because Calvin was not then present; but just as he was in the midst of his speech, the reformer entered the church. He was concealed by the mass of the people, and listened, in secret, but with astonishment, to the attack made upon his grand doctrine. Scarcely had Bolsec ended, when he pressed through the crowd, hastened up to his opponent, and without preparation proved at once his prodigious powers of argument. He thundered against the antagonist with so many and such apposite quotations from Scripture, and with so many passages from Augustine,—he so assailed him with arguments, that all who were present, it is said, blushed for the defeated monk. He himself however appears to have felt no shame.

Among the hearers was the prefect of police: this officer immediately apprehended Bolsec, as a seditious disturber of the peace, and, the congregation having separated, led him off to prison. Farel was also present, and admonished the people with pious words. How great was Calvin's zeal! On the same evening the clergy assembled, and drew up seventeen questions, to which the prisoner was to give an answer. A long and fruitless dispute was carried on with him, both by word of mouth and by writing. The affair was brought before the council. Bolsec adhered firmly to his opinion, and seems to have believed that many of the Swiss clergy had adopted his views. No judgement therefore was pronounced, but the Swiss ministers were to be asked their sentiments. Bolsec did not venture to oppose himself to this proceeding, but he thought the clergy of the chief city far too united with Calvin to be impartial. He censured Zwingli above all, and declared that Bullinger, Melancthon, and Brenz were of his opinion. From the answer which Bolsec gave in prison, it would appear that he was sincerely anxious to discover the truth, and prayed God to enable him so to do. This also appears from a poem which he wrote at that time.

In the fifth of the questions proposed to him he was asked, "Whether he acknowledged that faith proceeded from the divine election, and that the illuminated received such grace because God had chosen them?" Bolsec answered, "Faith depends not upon election, but election and faith go together. A man cannot be considered as elect before he is beloved of God; and before he is beloved, we must know for whose sake we are beloved, that is, Jesus Christ. There are in God, who knows not past or future, the three following truths ever present,—the union of man with the Son through faith; God's love to him, the love which comes from faith; and election, which rests on faith in Christ. Many of the old doctors agree in this; and so also the three worthy men, Melancthon, Bullinger, Brenz."

Calvin speaks in the eleventh article of the wonderful counsel of God, whose primal reason is not known to us; and of the doctrine of predestination, as not opposed to a sound human understanding; there being still left to the mind, looking behind the veil, the possible deliverance of the reprobate. Bolsec however answered, that he would not on any account pretend to look into these wonderful decrees of God. He proposed, on the contrary, certain questions to Calvin, which are in some degree interesting to all ages. They were such as represent the views taken by a sound, natural understanding, with which the church, which must go deeper if it would annihilate Pelagianism, cannot agree. The questions thus proposed formed, it is probable, the groundwork of Calvin's work on election, which appeared soon after.

The Genevese council now addressed itself to the churches of Zurich, Bern and Basel, and sent them a summary of the errors of Bolsec, the chief of which were, that faith does not come from election, but that election proceeds from faith. The ministers of Geneva also wrote to the ministers of those cities. It is interesting to see how all opposed the severer view of the doctrine alluded to, and how Calvin in his turn attacked them all. The remarks of the Basel theologians deserve notice: they say that "God elected us in Christ before all time; that he who believes in Him is redeemed; but that the Father draws not all; that some will not be drawn, and are therefore left in a state of condemnation; that this fact is clear, but that how it is so must be left with God." "You see therefore," it is added, "our agreement on this subject." Sulzer and Myconius subscribed the document.

A different feeling was expressed by the Bernese: they spoke in a high tone, and preached a toleration to the Genevese not then known to the world. The writing was subscribed by Musculus, whom Calvin greatly loved, but who in this case agreed with the rest in opposing him. The Bernese commenced the letter very cautiously, spoke of the necessity of concord, but not to the sacrifice of charity. We quote the following: "The Genevese ought to treat Bolsec with gentleness, and never lose sight of the love of Christ. For He loves not only the souls of the faithful, but those even of the erring, of whom He takes more especial note. It commonly happens that, when we undertake the defence of a doctrine with peculiar zeal, we forget the claims of Christian love, and fail to keep in sight the conduct which becomes the disciples of Christ, as if the spirit of charity could not consort with zeal for the truth."

To this is added an expression of praise for the earnestness of the Genevese; but they are besought "to consider how easily the mind of man can fall into error, how unwillingly it submits to control, and how much more likely kindness than severity is to gain its object." In reference to Bolsec it is said, "You are well aware how much distress this controversy has occasioned many religious people, who, when they find in Scripture the mention of a common pardon and grace, have not sufficient penetration to understand the mysteries of predestination, and the blindness and wickedness of the human heart, and therefore suppose that the hardening of the sinner cannot be ascribed to God without blasphemy."

These remarks are followed by a reference to those passages of Scripture in which mention is made of a common grace. Great importance is ascribed to them, and it is added, that the doctrine of predestination ought to be spoken of with much caution: it is not the milk for children, but the strong meat for men. "And Jerome plainly shows that even he, in this respect, pertained to the weak; for he says, that he dared not press into the secret counsels of God. Bolsec's answers indicate that he is not a bad man. Were there no strife existing, he might, it is probable, be led to embrace higher views."

This was a strong sermon for Calvin. The Bernese, it seems, were fearful that the matter might be carried too far, Bolsec being still in prison. Even Musculus had remarked, in one of his letters, "that people should be brought back to the truth with gentleness, not with severity or with bonds and imprisonment." The latter words were, for some reason, crossed out.

Such language was novel for that period. But two years afterwards these parties agreed in the condemnation of Servetus; and at a later period the Bernese themselves condemned Gentilis. Haller thus expressed himself to Bullinger, in reference to Calvin*: "We have tried to pray, that God may have mercy upon

* MS. T g. Dec. 5, 1551.

us, and silence these disputes; for I see no article of faith on which it is more perilous to strive than this."

The Zurich ministers answered the council of Geneva more definitely than those of Basel. Their reply is well worthy of notice, it being in the character of an official statement, as a sort of renewed *Consensus Tigurinus*, in which light it has been frequently viewed. The letter is in Bullinger's handwriting, and will be again referred to. Those in whose name he wrote say, "The Genevese council may perhaps not know" (this expression is curious—the council must have known it, as well as Bullinger) "that they are agreed on the subject of the Lord's Supper. Their confession on the doctrine of election follows. The terms used are cautious*, the main point in the dispute—the reprobation of the wicked by God's decree—being avoided. Bullinger's allusion to Zwingli is interesting. "Bolsec errs in supposing that Zwingli believed in the necessity of sin. People should read all his works†", &c.

Bullinger's private letters were equally mild: thus he warned Calvin: "Believe me, many persons are distressed at what you have said in your Institutions on predestination, and connect it with what Bolsec says on Providence from Zwingli's book." To this he adds, "According to the meaning of the apostle, God wills the happiness of all men‡."

Calvin was still less content with the Zurich ministers than with those of Basel§. "My dear Farel," said he, alluding to the Bernese, "I cannot tell you how this barbarity distresses me. There is no more humanity among us than among wild beasts. Edicts have been sent forth (that is, from Bern) which forbid the refugees to have anything with us in common."

We here see Calvin standing alone on the field of conflict, with characteristic firmness and unshaken conviction. Opposed to him were all his old friends, Bullinger, Haller, Melancthon. It is evident, as Bolsec said, that they adhered to the weaker party. Impelled by an irresistible inward feeling, Calvin declared, "that the honour of his God, and the salvation of the world, depended upon this doctrine, and that they who opposed

* "Constituimus enim electionem, qua Deus peccatores in Christo elegit, omnino esse gratuitam. Elegit nos in Christo, antequam jacerentur fundamenta mundi."

† And further: "There are many of us still living, who heard him preach on this subject, and we know that he always spoke of it with great piety."

‡ MS. Tig. 1st Dec. 1551. "Deum bene velle omnibus hominibus."

§ MS. Bern. 8th Dec. 1551.

it assailed God: that unity on this subject must be established, cost what it would." These expressions remind us of what Mathesius said on Luther's extraordinary nature:—"Great men have great thoughts. The One Spirit has many operations; and we who are destined to pursue the highway and the common foot-path, should not pretend to follow those who take their course over field and flood, mountains and valleys. Much less should we venture to judge lightly the fervour, earnestness, zeal and courage of great characters*."

The Bernese council also addressed an epistle, of a very pacific character, to the Genevese; but it contained the explanation which led to so much bitterness when, at a subsequent period, the Genevese were influenced by such different feelings. The warning now given was well meant. It was feared that the business might turn out ill for Bolsec; this was possible according to the ideas then prevailing. Calvin however defended himself against the suspicion thus entertained, as against something which could have no proper foundation. But the Genevese council found it necessary to pronounce sentence of banishment upon Bolsec, December 23, 1551, because he had obstinately resisted the judgement of the church, to which he had promised to submit.

Bolsec returned to Thonon†, where he began again to dogmatise. He was then silent for a time: he soon however recommenced the strife, and was at last banished as an insufferable disputant, even by the Bernese, who would fain have kept him quiet. The worst part of his character now showed itself: he proceeded to Paris, and spoke of repentance, in the hope of obtaining a position as a reformed pastor. A conference with the ministers was allowed him. They represented to him his errors and wicked course, and referred his case to the synod, which was to meet at Orleans, that he might there solemnly renounce his errors. He appeared, exhibited the signs of deep contrition, promised to subscribe the orthodox confession, and to give satisfaction to the churches of Bern and Geneva. But when he saw the reformed church in more danger than ever of a fearful persecution, he fell back into his old state of wretched doubt, and sank deeper and deeper. He again sought Switzerland. We find him some time

* Hess, Leben Bullingers, T. II. s. 56. This author appears to have no idea of Calvin's higher calling: he accuses him of seeking honour in the present controversy.

† Ruchat, Nouv. Ed. t. v. p. 466, t. vi. p. 475.

after in Lausanne, practising as a physician. He was admitted to the rights of a citizen, under the condition that he should adopt the Bernese confession of faith. But he did not remain long there. Beza wrote against him to the faithful of Lausanne. He was once more received by the Bernese, but Haller being full of zeal for purity of doctrine, he was told to remove. His next place of abode was Mömpelgard: he there found Tossanus, who was opposed to Calvin, and in the end rejoined the catholics. Such was the hatred of this man against the reformer, that twelve years after the death of the latter he wrote a libel upon him, which has been the source of all the detestable slanders current in later times.

The Bolsec controversy had caused considerable uneasiness at Geneva, and the ministers feared that the differences of opinion on this abstract doctrine might give rise to new agitation. It was the season for the administration of the Lord's Supper, and a preparatory congregation was held on the 18th of December. Calvin explained the whole matter, and the collective body of ministers, both of the city and country, declared that they were fully agreed with him on the subject. A large number of the congregation subscribed their names to this statement after the clergy. The instrument thus signed was printed, and Calvin compiled and published a work, which he dedicated to the council, January 1, 1552, as a new-year's gift. The progress and termination of this affair proves what influence Calvin had gained, how united the council was become, and what power the convictions which were the result of his labours exercised. To establish unity, Calvin meditated the renewal and enlargement of the 'Zurich Consensus.' This was effected at a later period. The importance which he attached to this formulary appears from his communications to Farel.

Calvin's incredible zeal in the midst of all these disputes was to most people a riddle: his enemies raved on all sides. "It is almost impossible," said Beza, "to describe the agitation in and out of the city: it is as if the devil himself were sounding the trumpet. Calvin, they say, makes God the author of sin."

In Basel, Castellio, and in Neuchatel, Christopher Fabri, though a friend of Calvin, declared his discontent. Melancthon's views are well known: notwithstanding the manner in which Calvin had expressed himself in his work against Pighius, Melancthon conceived that the Genevese entertained the ancient doctrine of fate, or destiny. The papists clamoured loudly against the reformers in this respect; and even in Geneva itself Calvin had to contend with an *eremite* from Burgundy, who had passed over to the evangelical church.

The name of the man to whom we here refer was Troillet, an advocate, and a leader of the malcontents, and who, like Bolsec, a weak man, was ignorant of the real purport of the theological question, and, still more, of the necessity of union and of the force of Calvin's mind. By birth a Genevese, he no sooner found himself weary of an ascetic life than he desired to return to Geneva as a minister. This was against the law. Calvin, who fully understood his pretensions to piety, and saw through his hypocrisy, repelled his advances. The council however directed the consistory to admit Troillet to the situation left vacant by a deceased minister. But Calvin had sufficient influence with the council to procure the reversal of this decree: he even proved that two members of the body had received presents from Troillet: this created great disgust. Troillet gave up his pretensions to the ministerial office, but passed over to the opposite party. He was at this time a member of the chief council. In the hotel where the Libertines held their meetings he declaimed against Calvin, as guilty of the grossest pride, and as contradicting his own opinions, as exhibited in the 'Institutions.' Calvin cited him before the council. Troillet defended himself, and endeavoured to prove that Calvin made God the author of sin. On the first of September, an order was passed prohibiting the reformer from preaching on the doctrine of predestination. Agitation and disorder universally prevailed. The council invited Farel and Viret to Geneva, to undertake the restoration of tranquillity. The discussion between Calvin and Troillet was concluded on the ninth of November, and the book of the 'Institutions' was recognized by the Genevese as "good and Christian," and Calvin as "a true minister of the Word of God." It was forbidden to speak against Calvin's work; but six days after, his opponent received an apology from the council*.

Calvin gave an account of this controversy to a friend. "It grieves me chiefly that Troillet found the means of dragging Philip with him into the quarrel. I shrunk from this, for I could safely declare that I had always spoken of that great man with sentiments of honour." He expresses a suspicion that Falais had sent Troillet from his wretched abode. Of himself he says, that

* MS. Gen. Vol. conten. Mémoires sur Caroli et Troillet.

it was difficult for him to exercise moderation under such circumstances.

But how encouraging was it for Calvin that his writings were spoken of as pious and orthodox, even by the opposite party! It happened after some years that he was called to visit a sick man: he hastened to see him: Troillet lay on his death-bed: disquietude and deep repentance moved his soul: he declared that he could not feel peace unless he was assured, before his end, that Calvin was reconciled to him. With his peculiar earnestness and tenderness, Calvin consoled the dying man, and supported him to the last moment*. Thus the power of his doctrine triumphed, however and on whatever side opposed.

Still Calvin could not easily bear the coldness and indifference of his friends. He appealed to Bullinger with mingled severity and pathos. "Bolsec," he said, "has disturbed by his clamours the peace of the church: he complains that we describe God as possessed of a tyrannical power, and that we set up a poetical Jupiter in his place: and yet you defend this man,—a thing to be most vehemently lamented†."

Not long after he justified himself, in a letter to the same, on his mode of teaching the doctrine of election. "You say that my manner offends many excellent persons. But, between ourselves, Zwingli's little book is filled with so many hard passages, that it far surpasses my weak comprehension‡." This observation confirms what has been said in a former part of this book respecting Calvin's opinion of Zwingli. With regard to Fabri, he complains of the coldness of the Basel people, and of Myconius and Sulzer§. To the Bernese he expresses himself still more strongly: he thus addresses Farel‖: "You might expect them to renounce altogether the doctrine of election, and the wonderful providence of God." He hoped to have exhibited a feeling of tranquillity in his letters, but he had much to do to quiet his agitation. Fearing that he might not meet with a brotherly welcome, he would not go to Bern. Such however was the multitude of evils which prevailed, that it was necessary something should be done. The Consensus itself was endangered; and if the union failed in this point all would be lost. His public writings were characterized by moderation. He lamented that

* Beza, Vie de Calv. † MS. Gen. Jan. 21, 1552. ‡ MS. Gen.

§ "Experti sumus quam parum in iis sit auxilii. Myconius frigide nescio quid attingit, rem nullo modo expendit."

‖ MS. Gen. Jan. 27, 1552.

Bolsec had not expressed himself as the Swiss did in their confession. The latter, though not sufficiently clear, were orthodox in their sentiments*.

But consolation and sympathy were not wanting to him at this period. Calvin ever found in Farel's friendship a great source of support. In March 1551 he wrote to him†: "I cannot say how much I thank you. May Christ, who is both my treasure, and my chief treasure too, repay you!" At the end of December in the same year Viret addressed Calvin in these encouraging words: "The devil persecutes you and Farel, because you defend the interests of Christ. Do you therefore receive his attacks as a sacrament, through which you may become more and more confirmed in the holy struggle to which you are called. Think of the faith by which David was strengthened, when he was going against Goliath; and how he remembered the victory which he had gained over the bear and the lion. He who has hitherto rendered you and your brethren invincible, will perfect the work which he has begun, through you."

During these untoward events, afflicting news arrived from France, respecting the persecution of the evangelical party in that country. But Bullinger thus addressed him‡: "The God who delivered his people out of Egypt lives for ever. He lives who led them back from captivity. He lives, who has given freedom to his church, emperors, kings and princes lying prostrate before him. But we must enter into heaven through much tribulation. Woe however be to them who harm the apple of God's eye! Let us continue to preach the pure word, and to proclaim the Gospel of Christ, and, with all saints, to fix our eyes on heaven. Then He who has said 'I will be with you to the end of the world,' will never forsake us."

Calvin stood in the nearest relation to Jacques de Bourgogne, Sieur de Falais and Bredam. His friendship for this excellent man shows us how strictly he viewed life itself, with all its associations, from the central point of truth and the church. Jacques de Bourgogne had sought in Geneva that peace which he found it impossible to obtain in France. Calvin rejoiced to receive him, and he and his wife resided for some time in the reformer's house. The latter wrote an apology for him, which was laid before the emperor; and he dedicated to him his commentary on

* Ed. Laus. Ep. 134; Ed. Amstel. p. 64. b.
† Kirchhofer, in Farel's Leben.; Farel and Calvin, March 1551.
‡ Ed. Laus. Ep. 139.

the First Epistle to the Corinthians. A reference to the correspondence which they carried on for many years will prove how tender a regard united Calvin and this noble family. It is remarkable, however, that great as was the friendship which the Sieur de Bourgogne entertained for Calvin, he long resisted his persuasion to settle in Geneva. He at first preferred Basel, and Calvin described in vain the beauties of Geneva, adding even that he had bought on his account a cask of old wine. It seems indeed as if the lord of Falais suspected that it was easier to honour a great man at a certain distance than when too near. He was of a somewhat gay temper, and the tone of society at Basel, where the elegant Erasmus had formerly, and where the liberal Castellio now, lived, was not so stern as at Geneva. The ministers of that place were also of a quieter temper, and they saw clearly that it was not every one who could imitate Calvin's eagle flight. At length however Bourgogne yielded, and proceeded to Geneva, where Bolsec became his physician. Now begins the catastrophe. The good Falais and his excellent wife had no suspicion of what was going on, and they understood nothing of the controversy respecting predestination. They could not comprehend the mystery of eternal decrees, and they beheld with astonishment their intimate friend rousing himself like a lion robbed of its young,—his benevolent countenance full of fire, his forehead expressive of the sternest indignation, and the accomplished Calvin raging against all the world. The peace-loving Bourgogne had formerly entreated Bullinger to unite with Calvin in restoring peace to the church; "for two such spirits as yours," he said, "could not easily be found, to perform this work of reconciling that which other pious people may have disturbed." Now he said to Bullinger, with a sorrowful heart, "It is not without tears that I am compelled to see and hear this tragedy of Calvin and his friends. May God ever vouchsafe to grant us the truth!" Bourgogne adopted from benevolence the part of his imprisoned physician; and when the latter was banished, he left for ever the city where a feeling prevailed so contrary to his taste, and where it was considered a violation of propriety to speak of the freedom of the will. He used his influence with the Swiss to protect Bolsec, and he subsequently declared that he agreed with him in his views. Hence Calvin's anger. "Let Falais, if he please, regard Bolsec as a good man; and whilst he defends an unknown babbler, expose his own calling to hazard. But this is the end of the matter. That deceiver shall not be received in the Bernese territory. I am so ashamed when I think of Falais, that I can scarcely bear to see the face of any one who reminds me of his levity*."

It is difficult for us now to understand how so excellent a man as Bourgogne could become the friend of so unworthy a one as Bolsec. But the latter was to him as the protector of his earthly existence. Calvin has let fall some few words on this subject: he even retracted the honour which had bestowed upon his friend a kind of immortality—the dedication, that is, to the Commentary, mentioned above; as a king might take from an unfaithful servant the decorations granted him at a former period. In the year 1556 he dedicated this work, as we have also stated, to the excellent Galeazzo Caraccioli, whose life appeared to him in complete contrast to that of Bolsec. "Would to God," he said, "that when this my commentary first saw the light, he had been unknown to me, whose name I am now compelled to obliterate, or at least that I had known his true character!"

The friendship between Calvin and Bullinger was not for a moment weakened through this controversy with Bolsec. He remained equally united with Haller and Musculus. Bullinger warned him affectionately to be cautious on the doctrine of predestination, when he published the second defence against Westphal, and Calvin did not reject his counsel.

At length, that is at the beginning of the year 1552, Calvin was informed that a courier from Saxony, passing hastily through Geneva, was anxious to see him. This was the son of Justus Jonas, from Wittenberg, sent by the counts of Mansfeld to the king of France. Calvin anxiously asked him the state of the church in Saxony†. "The wrath of God," he exclaimed after this conversation, "is turning the world upside down, because it refuses to rest under his dominion. I dare not say more in a letter. As our conversation referred to the Saxon church, the stranger told me, among other things, that Melancthon was publicly censured, because he had not openly stated his agreement with us on the subject of the Lord's Supper. He himself spoke so prudently, and with so much knowledge of the whole matter, that I could discover nothing whatever injudicious in his conversation, though I took pains to observe him with the greatest attention."

* MS. Gen. Dec. 1551.

† From the year 1552. Ed. Laus. Ep. 140. Ed. Amstel. p. 67.

Melancthon however was now somewhat perplexed: he had viewed the doctrine of predestination with considerable uneasiness, and could not follow the lofty progress of Calvin's ideas. We learn this from his letter to Camerarius*, in which he exclaims, "See the madness of the age! the Allobrogian (the Genevese) controversy on the stoical doctrine of Fate, rages to such a degree, that people are cast into prison if they do not hold the same views on the subject as Zeno." Socinus had written to him, and Calvin replied to him in these noble words: "Nothing shall hinder me from stating openly what I have learnt from the holy Scriptures. The reception of this simple doctrine is, and will ever continue to be, to me, the only rule of wisdom."

The long-existing quarrel between Geneva and Bern had arrived during this controversy at its greatest height. Many historians have well described the internal state of Switzerland at this time†. That however which chiefly concerns the purposes of our biography is the inward, divine impulse which governed Calvin, and convinced him that he must gain the victory for his doctrine. He stood alone against all. We may rightly compare him with the great pontiffs of the middle ages, who, whilst they were often oppressed and insulted by the inferior nobility at Rome, swayed at a distance the destiny of rulers, made nations tremble, and solved the most important of historical problems. This remark will tend to explain how Calvin continued exposed year after year to numberless petty annoyances and persecutions, whilst his influence was so powerfully felt in all directions. It has been said, that the Bernese prohibited all discussion and preaching on the subject of predestination in their territory. There were however many whose zeal prompted them still to rave against Calvin and Geneva. It was a distressing period for him. He now wrote the Defence of the Consensus. Agitation prevailed in the city‡, and in Bern the people were excited to the most bitter feeling of hostility. This arose indeed to such a height that they openly insulted Calvin, and loaded the Genevese with curses from the pulpit. "It is reported throughout the country that we have been con-

* Corpus Reform. Ed. Br. T. vii. p. 390. Cal. Feb. 1552.

† See Trechsel's Antitrinitarier, s. 194; Hess, Leben Bullingers, t. ii. s. 237; and especially Hundeshagen, Conflicte des Zwinglianismus, Lutheranismus und Calvinismus in der Berner Kirche, s. 253.

‡ MS. Gen. Calvinus Bullingero, Sept. 18, 1554. His language is very strong:—"Interim a vicinis nostris *plus quam atrociter proscindor.*"

demned by the Bernese ministers as heretics." This sentence occurs in the epistle of the Genevese to the Bernese ministers, October 6th, 1554; and further, "Zebedæus, babbling on the subject of foreknowledge, exclaimed aloud at a dinner-table, that we are worse than papists. Encouraged by these things, that monster (Bolsec) who lives at Thonon, cries that Calvin is a heretic and an antichrist. On the opposite side of the lake dwells another, not very unlike the former: his name is Sebastian, a banished Genevese. Think now what sport is created for the papists by these occurrences, and what scandal is thereby heaped upon the holy name of Christ." The Genevese demanded satisfaction; but Haller and Musculus had not the courage to lay their letter before the council.

The Bernese again prohibited the discussion of this mysterious doctrine, and still more expressly the subject of discipline, as connected with excommunication.

At the repeated instance however of the Genevese, Bolsec and the more violent of the preachers were brought before the council at Bern. It exhibited great firmness, and desired nothing but peace. The popular dislike to Geneva was only the more remarkable. On this occasion the conduct of the Bernese ministers in general was highly becoming: they warned their superiors with great faithfulness; but none appeared to understand the ground of Calvin's zeal. They answered the Genevese council with implied reproaches, and exhorted all to cultivate peace. A mandate was issued from Bern, in which people were strictly forbidden to go to Geneva, or to receive the sacrament according to the Calvinistic form. This mandate, read by the preachers from the pulpit, and posted up by the order of the magistrates, was unfortunately regarded by the people as an excommunication of the Genevese, and Calvin's name was loaded with execrations. He poured out his griefs to Bullinger*: "Having attained some degree of tranquillity here in Geneva, the Bernese council has not only absolved those who denounce me as a heretic, but they have sent forth against me and this church a host of raging adversaries. We are accused as criminals, and we have shown that we are ready at any moment to give an account of ourselves. With our own free consent we have allowed them to be our judges; but they will not hear us. In the meantime the people are forbidden, by a public edict, to

* MS. Tig. Feb. 24, 1555.

partake of the sacrament with us. Cease then to feel any astonishment at the barbarity of the Saxons; since hatred against a man, who has a hundred times been ready to peril his neck for the sake of peace, can thus be made a cause for rending the churches asunder. Nothing disturbs me more than the feeling that God is hereby manifesting his wrath. But if so it must be, let them satisfy their hunger by driving me into a wearisome exile. I pour out these complaints into your bosom, that you may support me by your holy prayers."

All this tended to the entire destruction of union among the churches of Switzerland. A deputation therefore was sent from Geneva. It consisted of a syndic, a member of the council, Calvin, and another minister, and proceeded to its task in March 1555. Viret in the meantime came from Lausanne, and Fabri from Neuchatel, with two others, to make their complaints on the subject in dispute. Geneva had placed in the hands of its representatives an "Instruction," written by Calvin himself, and containing a firm statement of evangelical faith*. It was required that an inquiry should be instituted into the slanders against Calvin's doctrine, and into those against the Genevese themselves, who were accused of despitefully rejecting the Bernese rites and ceremonies. The firmness of the Genevese in this respect is well-deserving of notice, considering their position in respect to Bern, their political difficulties, their anxious desire to renew their treaty with the Bernese, which the present movement was so ill calculated to promote, and the perils with which their little state was threatened on the side of France and Savoy. The energy of Calvin's faith was their ruling principle through this whole period.

Calvin now stood before the council at Bern†, and stated his complaints. The examination was deferred to a later day, to enable the opposite party to appear. The deputies accordingly repeated their statements, April 2, 1555. Calvin addressed the assembly with his usual eloquence, in a speech of which the following is an abstract:—"No other doctrine is preached at Geneva than that which is preached at Bern; the doctrine, that is, of predestination; and, therefore, we pray you to take means to instruct your subjects thereon, and thereby silence the slanders with which we are assailed. We also beg that these calumnies

* MS.

† Compare Hess, Leben Bullingers, t. ii. s. 246, and the complete account in Trechsel, s. 200. Ruchat, t. vi. p. 127.

may not go unpunished; and that the mandate by which your people are forbidden to partake of the sacrament at Geneva may be otherwise and better worded, seeing that some ill-disposed persons have taken occasion therefrom to assert that you condemn our doctrine."

But the opposition to Calvin was universal; and his adversaries either denied what they had said, or escaped by subterfuge. The Genevese, however, would not be satisfied by such excuses. Calvin boldly brought forth his great doctrine, that to which he had devoted his life, and declared "that he was not contending for himself, but for the truth, and that a synod therefore must decide the question." He would have gone again before the council, but his friends prevented him. Haller, who now seemed to begin to understand him, took a lively interest in his cause. Calvin spoke again the next day; but his ardent zeal only occasioned offence. The preacher L'Ange quoted a passage from his works, said to be heretical. Calvin had somewhere written, that "Christ was despairing on the cross." Calvin in reply declared, "that this was an error of the press." But the council was of opinion that he was answerable for it, and remained inflexible. With a rude angry tone the Bernese admonished the Genevese to preserve peace, and to see that their ministers preached so as to offend no one, nor even in their books to investigate the deep secrets of God, which was not necessary, nor likely to conduce to edification. As for Calvin's doctrine, they would not inquire into it, nor pronounce either for or against it. There should be no controversy on the subject in their territory. They added, that they were aware that Calvin rejected the doctrine of Zwingli on the Sacrament as false and dangerous; and that he directed this censure against themselves, to whom the doctrine pertained as a part of their reformation. They had therefore just cause of offence against him; but they would now pass this over, in order to give him an example of moderation. They notwithstanding warned him, that if they should hereafter find in their territory books, or other writings of his, directed against the doctrine of their church, they would order them to be burnt; and would severely punish any one who should in any wise write or speak against their reformation.

This was the unity after which Calvin panted! The man who could write to à-Lasco:—"Fain would I that all the churches of Christ were so united, that the angels might look down from heaven, and add to our glory with their harmony." The waves which cast him on the strand bore him back. He returned to Geneva with his mighty convictions in his heart, which no one would share with him, but which he was assured would finally conquer. The deputies protested, with all their force, against the resolution of the Bernese. Those of Lausanne and others also remonstrated against them. "Zwingli and Œcolampadius," they said, "would have agreed with Calvin in this matter: quiet would soon be restored if people would but be guided by Scripture." The council however would yield nothing, and Calvin on his side remained if possible still more immoveable. But Bolsec, as a disturber of the public tranquillity, with two others who had affronted the honour of Geneva, were expelled the Bernese territory. The friends of Calvin also now stepped forward, offering their sympathy and encouragements. Farel said to him:—"I must be made of wood and stone, if I do not regard you with the tenderest affection. Christ has worked for us above all our hope, and will accomplish still greater things. Surely we ought to stand unterrified; for the conflict is not ours, nor are we the leaders."

Calvin, as a truly great man, was wholly occupied with the desire of working out his general historic principle. It is easy to perceive what was the spirit which operated on his mind in the remonstrance against the Bernese decree*. "As great hatred had been exhibited against him there," he said, "he wished to appear in Bern as a private person. But it was not he alone who had been condemned: the whole church of Geneva and the Bernese ministers, who agreed with him, were included in the sentence of the late decree." "You think that no books ought to be written on the mysteries of God: but to what does this tend? Many in your territory speak more insultingly of the holy doctrine of predestination than would be suffered even in popish countries. I know well enough that we ought to be humble and modest in the treatment of this profound, incomprehensible mystery; but if you had looked into my much-misrepresented book, your excellencies would have discovered that its only object is to subdue the pride of the human spirit, and to teach it to reverence in all fear and humility the majesty of God, without in any wise giving the reins to an idle curiosity. But if people will indiscreetly abuse this doctrine, and attempt to correct the Holy Spirit, we must strike out of the Scriptures what is openly revealed to us in their pages. I cannot but

* MS. Gen. et Bern., May 4, 1555.

wonder that I alone am attacked; for if what I have said be compared with what has been set forth by the most learned men in Germany, who have seen the light of the Gospel in these our days, it will be found that my language is far more cautious than theirs. I therefore adjure you, according to the precept of our Lord Jesus Christ, that you show no respect for persons; since though my name and books should perish, what the prophets and apostles have said would endure for ever; and it is from them that I have derived the doctrine which man condemns."

At the end of May, Calvin was again sent to Bern, in order if possible to establish some better ground of agreement*. But this experiment led to no useful result. Political rivalries divided the two states, and the libertine party, which had been dispersed, now found a shelter in Bern. But if the enmity against Calvin increased, his sense of duty became still greater†. We learn this from his own expressions. Addressing the Bernese ministers with profound earnestness, he prayed for counsel, protection, and sympathy‡. "Shall I not," he says, "defend a doctrine by my words, for which the holy martyrs doubted not a moment to pour out their blood?" "That they who speak of God's election shall be punished,—consider well whether this ought to be endured. I would rather that my tongue should be cut out, than that such an enormity should be allowed in a church entrusted to my care and fidelity."

It was a circumstance favourable to the cause, that the council of Bern did not declare in his favour. Had it done so, it would no doubt have been believed that Calvin had effected by his influence what was afterwards accomplished by the mere force of truth. All the slanders which had been uttered then vanished as smoke. After Calvin's death, his accuser, Andreas Zebedæus, the man who persecuted him so virulently, confessed, on his death-bed at Nyon, in the presence of many witnesses, the truth of the doctrine which he had assailed; and in order to testify his repentance, desired that all the papers referring to the controversy should be burnt before his eyes. This was more important for the cause of the reformer than all the decisions at Bern§.

The world deals in contraries: Calvin was called to raise one side of this doctrine, that the other might sink into shade. This was not understood till the conscience of his dying opponents

* Bretschn. Epp. Calv. p. 60. † MS. Gen. Calv. Bullingero Jun. 5, 1555.
‡ MS. Gen. 3 Non. Mai. 1555. § Beza, Vie de Calv.

admonished them, that it was the Holy Spirit alone who impelled Calvin to the course which he had adopted. The true historian will take due notice of this important fact.

Beza, Calvin's energetic friend, and who seemed to have one heart and one soul with him, could not remain silent under the circumstances above described: Calvin's belief was his. With the convictions derived therefrom were intimately combined whatever was most excellent in his character, or most useful in his labours. Calvin willingly allowed him the first place in the eyes of the world. In this, the third epoch of the reformer's life, they both pursued the same end; and Beza was thoroughly impressed with the idea, that the evangelical church could only be delivered by the establishment of unity. Hence, in the controversy with Bolsec, he espoused with the utmost zeal the party of Calvin; and undertook to quiet the minds of the Swiss, and to suppress the agitation which existed, by setting the doctrine of his friend in a fair and correct point of view. With this object he lectured at Lausanne, in French, on the Epistle to the Romans. He had already acquired fame by his poem on "Abraham Sacrificing," and was altogether fitted for the office which he undertook*.

But on the other hand, he openly expressed his opinions: "Calvin knows well enough from Bullinger's letter, that people are not pleased with his old treatment of the doctrine of predestination. He ought for the sake of the weak to have spoken with less severity and distinctness." And further: "As Pighius is dead, he had no reason to employ abuse as if he were still alive, for he thereby offended many." Though a confutation of Pighius, his work was not, he observed, a confutation of all opponents. Beza, therefore, suggested to him a plan, according to which the whole would appear much simpler. He could not however write for him to Bern, because it was well known there that he and Viret were on intimate terms with him. Still he was an active and zealous labourer in Calvin's cause. When the ministers in the Lausanne district were most violently excited against the doctrine of reprobation, Beza induced them to hold an assembly, in which they subscribed a formulary, declaring that God has elected to happiness a number of human beings from eternity; not on account of their faith, but to bring them to faith. But the word 'reprobation' was not introduced; and Beza declared to his friend, "that he had acted as a prudent

* Compare Schlosser's Life of Beza, here chiefly referred to.

creditor with an honourable debtor, accepting what was offered him at the time, and looking for the rest at a future and more prosperous period." Beza also undertook the difficult task of reconciling the Swiss; and he prayed Calvin to induce Bullinger and Blaarer especially to write to the Bernese council. They in vain sought to move Melancthon to declare himself. He seemed not to understand Calvin's zeal or love*. But how truly was Beza Calvin's friend! How well did he understand his position! Speaking of him to Bullinger, in terms of the tenderest eulogy, he says:—"I testify before God, that Calvin has not been too earnest in this affair. I admire, on the contrary, his patience and moderation in contending with so many bad spirits†." This witness as given by Beza, who saw Calvin's labours, is worth much to those who would form a fair judgement of the man.

The Zurichers compelled Bolsec, as we have seen, to keep for a time silent. When however he had found a protector in the lord of Falais, Beza sought in several journeys, which he made on foot, to obtain for Calvin the aid of many influential men against Bolsec. So full of zeal was he in this respect, that he brought upon himself the charge of neglecting the proper duties of his office‡, for the sake of labouring to promote unity. This was a cause of great offence to the Bernese.

We have seen that Bolsec again appealed to the council at Bern against Calvin; and that the latter poured out his feelings in a second epistle, addressed to the Bernese ministers, in 1555. The image of his character is deeply impressed upon this writing. Inspired by holy zeal, he displayed his doctrine to the hearts of his opponents as a thing of God. But what he was unable to accomplish by the stormy power of his convictions, Beza effected by the devotion of his friendship. He sought witnesses against Bolsec in order to compel him to an answer. The Bernese could now no longer protect him. By means therefore of Beza, who makes no mention whatever of the circumstance in his Life of Calvin, the latter overcame his most dangerous adversary. Hence also we see the influence of the reformer. Hated though he was, he found friends sufficiently enthusiastic in his cause to expose themselves for his sake to a host of the bitterest enemies. Great as were the trouble and annoyance which Beza

* Beza says (MS. Goth.), "Philip has disappointed my hopes." "O miserum hominem! Hi sunt nimirum fructus eorum, qui non a Deo, sed a cœlo pendent."

† MS. Goth.

‡ Schlosser, Leben Bezas, s. 43, 62.

encountered throughout the proceedings, he exhibited a resolution and self-denial characteristic of the noblest mind. He undertook and endured all in the power of faith, and feared not the banishment, with which he was threatened, from the Bernese territory: "If the earth itself rejected him," he said, "still heaven was open*." And the sacrifice which he made for Calvin must be regarded as of yet higher value, when it is recollected, that he was at this very period occupied with his annotations on the edition of the Testament published by Henry Stephens.

Beza and Viret protested violently against the Bernese edict, issued in 1555, and which forbad in severe terms any participation in the controversy on the side of the ministers. After many arguments, Beza says†, "As far as we are concerned, let it not be supposed that we would impose anything upon ourselves with regard to our faith as Christians, through reverence for Calvin, or any other human being. We confess, however, that having become acquainted with his teaching, with his work on Predestination, and his various expositions of Scripture, we acknowledge, according to our consciences, that his doctrine is agreeable to the Bible." Bolsec was hereupon banished; but the threatened penalties were still inflicted. Beza issued, in 1557, another writing respecting the repeal of the offensive edict, and the Bernese now began seriously to consider the matter. He and Viret, however, at length left the territory. They declared that, though their fellow-labourers yielded their assent, they could not in their conscience adopt the resolutions of the Bernese.

Beza's work against Castellio concludes with the wish, that the authorities of Basel would expel the latter from their land. We shall consider Castellio's reply, after we have reviewed Calvin's "Consensus Pastorum."

He dedicated this work, in the name of the assembled ministers, to the council of Geneva, as a new-year's gift, January 1, 1552. In his address he thanks the members of this body for their untiring defence of pure doctrine; exhorts them to persevere, and to protect all who sought safety in their city, that it might thereby become, in those troubled times, a secure sanctuary, a city of refuge, for the dispersed members of Christ. Bolsec himself is not mentioned, and this because he seemed to have merely wished to gain a name by burning the temple of God. The work is therefore directed against Pighius and Georg. Siculus

* MS. Goth. "Si nos terra non ceperit, at certe cœlum nobis patet." Schlosser, s. 63.

† Schlosser, s. 60, from Beza's Tractat. Theol.

only, it being Calvin's object to treat Bolsec with marked contempt.

Milton, in his description of the world below, shows us the wicked spirits, disputing on the subject of freedom and necessity; on fate and providence; on good and evil; happiness and eternal woe. This was founded on a deep consideration of the human mind, which is too weak to solve the great problem in which such questions are involved, and the discussion of which is described as proper to the damned. The subject indeed is one which cannot but confound the understanding and arouse the fiercest passions, whenever it is treated of without humility, faith and devotion. If grace alone produces all our actions, it is not man who acts, but the eternal law, and many men are of necessity led to salvation, and others to destruction. If, on the other hand, man be left free, he is responsible for his sins, but cannot comprehend why God should have given him a free-will which urges him to eternal ruin. Freedom brings with itself the terrible alternative of eternal life and eternal death. But why was this possibility of sin allowed, when God must have foreseen the consequences? Now if two disputants, both equally convinced of the truth of their views, and inspired with like zeal, stand resolved to force, each upon the other, his own particular notion; they are like those spirits which, as described by Milton, rest solely upon intelligence, and neglect the aid of humble prayer to guide them in their inquiry.

It was not thus with Calvin: prayer and the grace of the Spirit were his support. His work shows that if free-will be incomprehensible, yet the grandeur of the attempt to grasp it is not to be despised; and that we may easily be tempted in our perplexity to look into the great mystery of God's own being. There is at least something striking in the view, which says that all is good before God,—the world with its errors and its crimes; that all sins have happened in agreement with his will, because He turns them to the best purposes; and that there is no evil but in the man,—in the individual. The writer however who could venture to exhibit this daring theory in its boldest form, cherished the profoundest trust in the God in whom he believed. The ground of the whole argument is as follows:—God, before the creation of the world, freely elected a certain number of men, and consigned another portion to eternal reprobation; we being altogether incapable of knowing or understanding why He did so. Predestination embraces three chief points:—1. The eternal decree, through which God determined, before the sin of Adam, what should take place with regard to the whole human race, and to each individual; 2. The principle, that man is condemned to death on account of his own sin and wickedness; and 3. That after Adam fell, the entire human stock was so corrupted and debased in him, that God could not consider one better than another; and that, therefore, those whom He saves, He saves only through his own free grace.

The whole development of this doctrine is, as Calvin himself says, a repetition of that which is found in the Institutions. He proves his theory by Augustin and the Scriptures, referring chiefly to the apostle Paul. Whenever he finds himself compelled to acknowledge the difficulties of his system, he plainly declares that he could not comprehend so great a mystery; and that we ought to be content to receive that which God has been pleased to reveal to us, and to teach in his Holy Word. The intensely sublime idea of the Godhead, which penetrated Calvin's soul, impelled his understanding to place all upon that one point, and thus to bow unceasingly before the solemn thought of God. The tract on Providence, appended to the work, is useful and edifying. Calvin speaks, first, of the general providence which upholds the world at large; secondly, of the particular providence by which God watches over every individual creature; thirdly, he shows the care of God for kingdoms; and lastly, the watchfulness and fatherly goodness which He exercises on behalf of his church.

In the next place, he answers the common objections to the doctrine, and shows that God, whose will governs all, cannot be the author of sin. He does not agree with Augustin in the notion, that sin in itself is merely corruption; but he insists upon the principle, that all wicked actions, and whatever is done by men with a wicked design, are, notwithstanding, good and righteous works of God. "Nothing happens by chance, nothing by necessity. For us there may be contingences, but not for God, who has determined all things beforehand by his own counsel. For example, the bones of Christ might have been broken upon the cross, but not one was broken, because it was so determined by God. Providence works by second causes. We cannot say, 'All is determined, and therefore it is indifferent what we do; for God has commanded us to act thus, and no otherwise.' But the Lord rules over the free-will of men: He it is who excites good in their hearts. He also hardens the heart, and yet the sin which is committed in its hardness comes from man alone. To will and to do is the result of his working; and He bows the human heart to his will. We accordingly cannot say that God merely allows sin: it happens actually by his will. The wicked deeds which are done certainly do not please God, but He has them in his power, and He makes them issue in good. Augustin says, that the will of God is the necessity of things."

Calvin interprets this proposition as signifying that, whatever happens, happens by God's almighty will; not simply in nature, through existing laws, but through his hidden counsel and his grace. This omnipotent God, however, always acts according to law and righteousness. It would be easier to deprive the sun of its warmth than God of his righteousness; and he doubtless sins not in the act which he recognises as sin in the offender. Robbers took away the goods of Job; but he says, "The Lord gave, and the Lord hath taken away;" but assuredly he imputes not to God the crime committed by the robbers. We must judge of everything according to the design and object of him who does it. For example, the judge who condemns a murderer to death, and causes his blood to be shed, deserves praise. And should not God be viewed in the same light? So also a king is commended, who, with the good design of upholding his country, leads an army to battle. While he does this, individuals commit many evil deeds, robbery and murder, but these things are never laid to the charge of the monarch. He is not accounted guilty of blood-shedding. How then should God be unjust, and why should the glory of his righteousness be darkened because He acts by wicked angels and by men? The sun is ever shining in its splendour, though sometimes hidden from us by the black vapours of the earth. And thus it is with the righteousness of God. It is the wish of blasphemers only to involve all in the like condemnation, because the human and the divine will appear in collision.

"But though men's wicked actions come from God, and not without good cause, although this be not known to us, and though his will is the first source of all things, yet I (Calvin) say that God is not the cause of sin. Men act, impelled by the force of passion; but God who acts through them, by means of his righteous judgement, which is wholly incomprehensible to us, cannot sin. What is it which works sin in man, but a wicked disposition, cruelty, pride, envy, evil desires? But there is nothing of all this in God. It was thus that Shimei sinned against David; but David knew that it was the will of God, and that his will is just. So also did the wickedness of the Arabians who robbed Job appear sufficiently evident, for they were wrought upon by sinful desires, but God made use of them in a righteous way to prove the patience of Job. It often seems as if man and God agreed in will; but they do not any more than fire and water; for while the one desires the absolute good, the other desires the absolute wrong. Let us ever return to Augustin, who says, 'The works of God are precious, according to his will, but they are often incomprehensible to us. So that that which happens against his will, happens not without his will. For nothing would take place did not he allow it; and he does not allow it against his will, but according to and with his will.'"

Calvin was well-aware that the banishment of Bolsec would not terminate the struggle. Though little satisfied with their conduct, he had addressed a friendly letter to the ministers of Basel, and proved to them how far removed Bolsec was from their opinions, and how little right he had to expect their support. He foresaw evils to come. There was one great doctrine for which he had to struggle to the end of his life. In Geneva, the libertine party hoped that Calvin would be driven out of the city through these occurrences. The opposition was as fierce in Basel as in Bern. There, where Erasmus so long laboured, a freer opposition against the doctrine of Luther was encouraged; and there less severity was exhibited against the heresy of Servetus. Hence we may understand why the free-thinking people of Basel so readily received the learned Castellio, who stood in direct opposition to Calvin. Castellio, with no remarkable theological acuteness, rather inclined to natural religion. He openly taught his Pelagian doctrines: nor did he possess the capacity to comprehend the profound ideas of the thinking and devout Calvin, and still less the character of his times. According to the writing which appeared under the name of Martin Bellius, abusive anonymous papers were addressed to the Geneva council, against the doctrine of the reformer (1554). Calvin recognized his opponent at Basel in them, and complained to Sulzer. Castellio was accused before the council at Basel; but he denied having any share in the matter. Another later pamphlet, which must also be mentioned as referring to this period, contained an extract from Calvin's exposition of the doctrine of predestination. It was sent by the Swiss to Paris, in order to be printed. A copy came into Beza's hands, and he forwarded it to Calvin. Both wrote answers to these tracts. Schlosser's judgement on the two men is altogether faulty, and as he is the representative of a party, he must be answered. "Castellio," he says, "who had been already called a knave on the title-page of Calvin's work, (he probably had not read Castellio's miserable production), could naturally not remain silent. He spoke, however, discreetly; but Beza replied with much gall, and called him a devil and so forth: '*Quid est diabolum agere, si hoc non est?*' I answer, that a satanic-ironical attack of such a doctrine of Scripture well deserves such an answer as Beza's." The jest, *à la Voltaire,* on sacred things could not fail to excite the zeal of these men for the honour of God. Had they not responded to the call, they would themselves have been guilty. Both acted from inward conviction, not from enmity. Beza's biographer forgets this. Schlosser supposes that "Beza sacrificed his honour to friendship, and Calvin rewarded him with the place of rector of the academy in Geneva, that all Europe might see that he regarded him as a man of learning." There is here a fundamental error. It proceeds on the supposition that Calvin bribed his friend; that he who strove for divine truth alone was impelled merely by the love of learning or the desire of fame. But both these great men were far superior to ambition, or the wish for human honour. No reformation would have been effected had they been subject to the little feelings here ascribed to them. It is also false that Calvin called his opponent a knave. In the French copy he translates the word *nebulo* by *un brouillon,* an idle-talker or babbler, which is but a mild expression.

Calvin himself was not contented with his second work. It merely repeated what had been often said before, and he despised the abuse heaped on him by his opponent. We will therefore give Beza's sharp dialectics in certain passages of the confutation, especially where he cites Calvin, and strives with his argument. It is interesting to see with what truthfulness and affection he defends him. Calvin's object was not to enter into a particular reply, but simply to show that he was no blasphemer. It is worthy of observation, however, that he establishes the innate will on the firm foundation of practical utility. This he does, although in appearance and in theory he seems to oppose it. The whole force of Castellio's argument was derived from the notion that such was the case, and that morality was altogether annihilated by the system of the reformer. Calvin was more distressed at this accusation than at any other. It made it appear that he was guilty of a foolish inconsequence. But he now proved how the doctrine of predestination had grown up with his whole being, and complains that it was despised on his account, and that to God's dishonour. To all the insults uttered by Castellio, he continually replies that his doctrine was that of the Holy Scriptures. "Bark," he says, "as much as you like, you will no more bow God's glory to the dust, than you could darken the light of the sun by spitting at it*." And that Calvin spoke the truth appeared as clear as the sun.

Castellio kept back his name, and played the character of a well-meaning man (though his conduct at Geneva shows that he could act in a very different spirit), and of one who desired to promote the unity of the church. He humbly besought Calvin to explain to him some difficulties in the doctrine of predestination, which seemed to resemble that of the ancient *Fate*, that he might be able to answer the objections of opponents.

Calvin was much more excited than Beza. This is apparent from his work written at the period of which we are speaking†. The well-known expressions, in reference to Castellio, are found in its pages:—"Verily," he says, "would I a thousand times rather that the earth should swallow me up, than that I should fail to listen to that which the Spirit of God reveals to me by the mouth of the prophet, or refuse to bear the insult through which the majesty of God is abased. If there be but a spark of piety in us, such shameful conduct must needs kindle in us the fire of the highest indignation. As far as I am concerned, I will rather rave than not be angry."

When the news soon after arrived that Castellio was dead, Beza expressed himself to Bullinger in the following terms: "I was too true a prophet, I find, to Castellio, when I told him that the Lord would quickly revenge his blasphemies, little willing as I am to judge of the dead."

We must here remark, in conclusion, that the great doctrine of predestination, after it had gained a complete victory in the reformed church, reached its end, and annihilated the Catholic Pelagianism, again sunk from the firmament. It still lives in Scotland, and among the Methodists. No stronger opponent, however, was found to it than the first leader of the Methodists,

* Opus. p. 642, ad Art. X. "Latra quantum voles: non magis tuis maledictis obrues Dei gloriam, quam solis fulgorem spuendo obscurabis."

† Ed. Laus. Ep. 393. Ed. Amst. p. 237.

Wesley, who on this account separated from Whitfield, the constant and powerful advocate of the divine decrees. Wesley employed the same arguments as Castellio, but with the greatest dignity; and nothing in modern times of a stronger character, I might say of a more terrible one, has been advanced against Calvin's doctrine, than the reasoning of Wesley, the founder of the Methodists.

Calvin felt to the last that it was his duty to contend for his doctrine. He again, in later years, expressed his indignation, that men hated the system out of hatred to him. "God's honour," he exclaims, "is trodden under foot, truth is falsified, the unity of the faith torn asunder, the concord of the church destroyed, and its peace ruined;—and would you have me slumber*?" At the end of the work against Castellio he says, "I would fain know why you accuse me of cruelty, except on account of your teacher Servetus, for whom, notwithstanding, I prayed that the judges would allow him a milder death."

These words will lead us to the consideration of the following memorable occurrences.

CHAPTER IV.

CALVIN'S SECOND GREAT CONTROVERSY, ON THE TRINITY, 1553.—DISPUTE WITH SERVETUS.—ITS CONSEQUENCES.

A DARK cloud appears at this epoch to be sinking upon the path of the reformer. Calvin entered upon the new year with Beza's blessing. "I adjure thee, beloved father," he said, "to persevere in thy work, and be sure that, as thou hast often found it to be the case, our united prayers will be a thousand fold mightier in thy behalf, than all the efforts of the servants of Satan against thee."

But at present everything was adverse to him in the little republic. His influence sank to so low an ebb, that he broke forth into loud complaints, in a letter addressed to Bullinger, in the September of the year above-mentioned. The senate was against him; his enemies were at the head of the dominant party. The libertines were rejoiced at the prospect of being at length able to overpower him. To accomplish this object they must deprive

* MS. Bern. Jul. 4, 1558.

the clergy of all share in the management of the state. In this they succeeded. Amied Perrini was chief of the senate, as first syndic. He and his party ventured on the 6th of February to assert, with loud clamours, in the Council of Two Hundred, when that body was engaged in the election of the lesser council, that they were treated with great severity, and were even cast into prison, which was a punishment proper only for murderers, thieves and traitors.

A violent tumult followed this assertion, and it was immediately proposed, without a dissentient voice, that all the ministers should be expressly excluded from the general council; for why, it was asked, should preachers be members of that body, when the priests had formerly been denied a place there? Calvin, who was present, immediately answered, "That the preachers believed themselves bound by their duty as citizens to take part in the council. The comparison which had been made was not a just one, for the priests did not recognise the temporal power."

But on the 16th of March it was resolved, that the attendance of ministers should be dispensed with. Their children, however, were not excluded. At the end of the year the opposite party endeavoured to overturn the entire constitution of the church, by insisting upon the administration of the sacrament to every one, without regard to his moral character. Their plan was one of great extent, as appeared from the sequel. On the 11th of April it was declared that the refugees, of whom many were citizens, were disarmed, and might only wear a sword, the use even of this being restricted to their own houses, or when they were on a journey. They were also prohibited from forming part of the guard, but were to aid in its support by money.

The influence of the first syndic, and the general triumph of Calvin's enemies, tended greatly to depress the power of the consistory.

Calvin's old and faithful friend Farel had fallen ill in March, and all hope of his recovery was given up. Calvin hastened to him at Neuchatel, attended by several of the refugees. Farel exhibited his noble testament, and Calvin subscribed it. To the great joy, however, of all, Farel recovered, and Calvin, who had prayed that his friend might survive him, saw his wish fulfilled, when he was preparing himself for a long separation*. Calvin still desired for himself ten years of active labour in the cause of the church, and they were allowed him. "Let us," he said to

* Ed. Laus. Ep. 145. Ed. Amstel. p. 69, a. Calv. Farello, 6 Cal. Apr. 1553.

Farel, "so live to Christ, that we may every day be prepared to die to Him." It was a year of persecution for many. The glorious strength of true martyrdom, and the weakness of that which was only pretended, now showed itself in the most conspicuous manner. Six weeks before the trial of Servetus, the catholics had burnt three protestants at Lyons. Calvin described to Farel the resolution of a merchant*, who went to execution with wonderful tranquillity. His relations and friends had employed every means to induce him to recant. At the moment when they were using their last endeavours, a woman was seen to approach the scaffold: she threw herself three times at his feet; but he quietly repelled her entreaties†. It was his mother. The execution of the three young students at Lyons, before alluded to, took place this year.

Many of Calvin's friends would fain have seen this period of his history wholly obliterated; and there are others who could conceive the idea of writing his life, without entering into any particular account of the affair of Servetus. I do not agree with them. It is here that Calvin appears in his real character; and a nearer consideration of the proceeding,—examined, that is, from the point of view furnished by the age when it took place,—will completely exonerate him from blame. His conduct was not determined by personal feeling: it was the consequence of a struggle which this great man had carried on for years against tendencies to a corruption of doctrine which threatened the church with ruin. Every age must be judged according to its prevailing laws; and Calvin cannot be fairly accused of any greater offence than that with which we may be charged for punishing certain crimes with death. It has been rightly said, that both the legal and theological feeling of the age, expressed as we find it in a variety of striking forms, allows not a shadow of suspicion to fall upon Calvin's integrity for demanding a judgement which was, in every respect, justified by the laws of the state. Papistical pamphleteers, swallowing the entire history of the Inquisition, and straining at this one execution for heresy, present a ludicrous instance of hypocrisy, as they come forth, with pious mien, to declaim and rave against the cruelty of Calvin.

At the burning pile, where Servetus suffered, the whole Christian church may adduce, through all ages, the fundamental truths which it is its duty to uphold, and prove its faith far better than

* Ed. Laus. Ep. 156. Ed. Amstel. p. 70.
† Beza, Hist. Eccles. t. i. p. 88.

in sight of the numberless iniquities perpetrated, from century to century, in catholic lands, by the blind rage or ferocity of inquisitors. According to Calvin's system every human action comes within the scope of God's providence. This appears in the last controversy; and it is a fact that the misfortunes of Servetus became eventually, through the inquiries which they occasioned, a source of good. Light has been thrown on many opinions, and Servetus by his death, strangely enough, aided in one respect, though in a way very different to that which he sought, the object which he proposed to himself,—the reformation of the world. His burning pile will ever remain a conspicuous point in history. The great question respecting the defence of the church, of its purity and unity, against daring blasphemers, will be repeatedly renewed. That flaming pile however stands as the boundary between the barbarous middle ages and modern times, in which new principles are in operation, and by which we are to learn how far tolerance is possible.

We are here to contemplate two men, meeting in the dark ways of life, the contrast between whom is such as has rarely been witnessed. On the one side was the zeal of Elias, on the other a blind fanaticism; the one a true reformer, the other a would-be reformist. Both were sincere in their intentions, and the one overthrew the other for the honour of the Lord. It is interesting for us, in these tranquil times, to behold the struggle of two such inquirers, the one striving for pure evangelical doctrine, the other for a fantastical-philosophic Bible-system. The picture becomes still more striking when we see in the one the representative of the sacred doctrines of the church in all ages, and in the other a precursor of the champions of philosophic religion in later times. Of these, some have not unfrequently meant the good of Christianity. Servetus, we may remark, did not thoroughly understand himself. There was much in him which was still chaotic, but which in later times has come forth in the light of pure thought. In Calvin, on the contrary, all was already clear and complete.

Mention has been made, in the first part of this work, of his proceedings against Servetus, and the question was suggested, whether he repented of his conduct. But to expect that he would feel as we now do, or to make him responsible, as is the practice of his enemies, for all the coarse severity of his times, is manifestly an absurdity. That he should regret the death of Servetus is to look for too much from him, and utterly to mistake the character of the age. The only glimmering of anything of this kind which we can see is in those moments when he seemed to breathe the new spirit of the period which was just commencing. But in Servetus a bold and restless nature ruled unconcealed. With nothing actually opposed to Christianity in his will, he cherished in his thoughts an unpardonably rash and blasphemous notion. To this sin he adhered to the last; for this he suffered death. We see in the whole the germ of a new, free-thinking age. An obscure presentiment of this coming time wrought on the mind of Servetus; and amidst all the folly and all the sin thus exhibited, there is still something to interest. We would gladly not regard him as an enemy. It is natural for us to defend those who have atoned for their crimes. But I must ask of all the opponents of Calvin, whether, when they find Servetus perpetually pouring out his blasphemies, they would become responsible for these devilries before God? or whether they would not rather join with Calvin and his age in taking up the stone against him? I take it up.

I will here quote a passage which has never yet been brought against him, but which tends to throw new light upon his extraordinary character. In order to make the doctrine of the incarnation appear ridiculous, he insultingly exclaims, "If the Word had become flesh, as woman, then they would have called the Word itself the Son of God, and the woman herself the daughter of man. Hence the Son of God would have been of two sexes." And further, "If the angels, in like manner, were to take asses' bodies, you must allow that then they would be asses, and they would die in their asses'-skins: they would be four-footed animals, and would have long ears. So too you must allow, that were you right, God himself might be an ass; the Holy Spirit a mule; and that He would die if the mule died. O the wondrously altered animal! Can we be surprised if the Turks think us more ridiculous than asses and mules?" It is with grief that we copy this; but it is necessary to show the blasphemous sport which Servetus made of holy things.

That man must indeed have been remarkable whom catholics and protestants equally hate; whom both parties condemn with horror; and who, when found guilty by the whole world, could venture to call upon God and Christ with fervent supplications, and in words which had an edifying sound, as if, indeed, the Spirit of truth dwelt with the culprit. The smoke which arose from Champel long darkened the pure gladsome air of the Geneva

Lake. But now, after three centuries, when we only desire the truth, independent of party interests, the history of Calvin lies clear before us. Public opinion has fixed a brand upon his name. The world has done this because it has no proper understanding either of Servetus or of the character of his age. I shall relate the events of which we are speaking as fully, and yet as succinctly, as possible, and adduce all that can be advanced for Servetus, filling up what may still appear wanting in the evidence on his behalf. The remarkable life of this man; his genial nature; the rareness of his works; his end; his system, so imperfectly comprehended even by himself, and which Calvin examined only from the point of view which the church afforded,—these have all tended infinitely to increase the difficulty of the subject*.

While Servetus presented a singular contrast to Calvin, both in his inner and in his general spiritual character, the contrast was scarcely less remarkable in the circumstances of their lives. The reformer was distinguished by his clear and logical intelligence. Servetus was no less so for his fantastic imaginativeness, and for his defective argumentation. With Calvin there was the profound religious feeling, which proves true faith; with Servetus, on the contrary, there was no acknowledgment of sin, but a mere philosophical element, altogether deficient in clearness. In the one, christian firmness and determination were conspicuous; in the other, indecision, the result of inward excitement, as if the spirit of Ahasuerus dwelt in him, was the main characteristic. The one would have been named by the Saviour, a son of thunder; whilst he would have regarded the other with melancholy; Ser-

* The documents before me are, 'The Writings of Servetus;' Calvin's work referring especially to him; and, besides the labours of Mosheim and Trechsel, the last publication of Nilliet (Relation du Procès Criminel intenté à Genève à Michel Servet. 1844). An abstract of the reports of the trial have also been preserved at Bern; they agree with those which Mosheim had before him. The discovery of the original, however, is still of importance, as proving the fidelity of Mosheim's report. Some additional details are very precious. This is especially the case in regard to the proof which the author produces, that Calvin enjoyed so little favour with the council that he could employ no influence on the trial. The fact however that Servetus was condemned, not as a blasphemer, but for political offences, is not clearly proved. M. de la Roche, the editor of the 'Bibliothèque Anglaise,' who wrote a short history of Servetus, published in 1717 extracts from the reports of the trial. Mosheim's learned work appeared at Helmstädt in 1748. I have also referred to the important work of the same author, 'Neue Nachrichten von dem berühmten Spanischen Artzte Mich. Servet. 1750,' and to the Abbé d'Artigny's 'Nouv. Mémoires de Critique et de Littérateur,' 1749, t. ii. art. 11. The latter author had the acts of the process against Servetus at Vienne before him, and he proves convincingly that Mosheim was not to be depended upon.

vetus receiving the reproach with disdain, till in his last hour a better spirit seemed to take possession of his soul.

And as the inner characters of these men differed, so was the outward course of their lives various. Servetus represented himself, from the beginning, as a new prophet; as one appointed to regenerate Christendom, and as raised above both catholics and protestants. But notwithstanding this boast, he was doubtful and perplexed. We may properly compare him to Hamlet, whose judgement, in reference to his goodwill, was too weak for the great part which he had undertaken, and who therefore had an appearance of insanity. In a similar manner Servetus had not ability corresponding to his extensive design, but yet was skilful enough to disturb the reformation in the south. He was deficient in understanding, and therefore indulged in vain and wanton blasphemies. In one point, however, both these opponents agreed: they were alike in the outburst of feeling, except that Calvin exhibited more of anger; the Spaniard more of haughtiness and heat.

Mosheim estimates the mental qualities of Servetus at a high degree, and places them on a level with Calvin's*. A later writer says of him, "He had a certain penetrating acuteness of mind, which was subsequently increased by his study of the law,—a powerful fancy, which held the understanding in abeyance. He was skilled in analysing, and could annihilate by his critical acumen the notions of others, but he could not bridle his own imagination, or reduce his thoughts to a tranquil and logical development. By his natural wit he could everywhere discover types, similes, analogies, allegories, but could not perceive the eccentricity and perverseness of his own opinions†." I place his natural gifts very high; his moral culture very low. He failed altogether in practical virtue, and consequently in the knowledge of his times, and in a proper feeling for the unity of the church.

Calvin was at this time deeply impressed, as we have shown, with the necessity of preserving this unity: he was anxiously desirous to prevent the existence of any doubt respecting his agreement with Melancthon. But the fearful disturbance excited by the controversy with Servetus threatened to destroy not only the unity of the church, but the church itself. He grasped at not one principle merely, but at the very heart of truth. Thus

* Mosheim, Gesch. Servet's, s. 254. † Trechsel, Antitrinitarier, s. 62.

he assailed the triune Deity and the person of the Redeemer, not in reverent language, but in that of blasphemy; not as a scholar for scholars, but as a reformer who wished to introduce a new christianity, and deprive the people of the old. In this character he opposed himself to Calvin, summoned him forth, and sought to place him on a new and dizzy height, in the hope of making him renounce his doctrine. We feel how great must have been the indignation of the watchman of Israel at these attempts, which he beheld from far. The ardour of his character and his sense of duty must indeed have been roused to the utmost, when, in the progress of events, he knew that all must be saved or all be lost.

The history of Servetus may be divided into three periods: 1. That during which he was developing his system, and when he first appeared, a period extending to the year 1532, when he left Basel and Strasburg. 2. That from 1532 to 1553, during which he lived in various parts of France, and printed his great work. And 3. The period of his trial and death.

In the first of these periods he was known as well by the name of Reves as by that of Serveto. Reves is probably an anagram of Serveto. In the second period he bore the name of Villanovanus; and in the third he took sometimes the one and sometimes the other. During the first of these periods his mind was still comparatively sober; but there was, notwithstanding, no slight degree of irreverence in his view of the opinion held by the church on God. The period closed with the publication of his work on the errors regarding this doctrine. In the second period his mind rose to the highest degree of exaltation: he felt himself called upon to contend in the host of Michael. In the third he stood before the two tribunals. There were now struggling in him the good and the evil principle, fear, confidence, despondency, pride, truth and falsehood. In the end faith conquered, as far as he was capable of its impressions, and he died in anguish and terror, obtaining the sympathy which is allowed to a bowed and hesitating soul. That which he wrote to Œcolampadius at the beginning of his career deserves to be cited as highly characteristic of his nature: "God knows," he says, "that my conscience is clear in all that I have written."

The difficulty which we find in giving any account of his life arises especially from this, that we can learn it only from his own mouth; from the information which he gave to the judges at Vienne, and which contradicts that given before those of Geneva.

The declaration made at Vienne, and which Artigny has adopted, can only be followed with the greatest caution. Servetus on that occasion wove a web of falsehoods, to deliver himself from the danger with which he was threatened, and to prove that he was not Servetus, but Villeneuve. In Geneva, on the contrary, he appeared as Servetus: believing that it would then avail him nothing to conceal his history, he spoke with much freedom.

The christian name of Servetus was Michael: he was born of christian parents at Villanueva, a city of Arragon, in the same year (1509) as Calvin: his father was a jurist and advocate, not of Jewish descent, as the judges supposed in their desire to account for the supposed hatred of Servetus to Christianity by tracing it to his birth. It reported that he was brought up in a Dominican convent. His frame was weak; he himself speaks of a double injury which he had received, and of his unfitness for marriage: but his appearance was agreeable; and in the engraving which Mosheim gives, from an excellent portrait of him, the expression of his eye is free and somewhat wandering. At Vienne he stated that in his fourteenth year he entered the service of Quintana, the confessor of Charles V., and in the year 1529 was present, as one of his train, at the famous meeting which terminated with the coronation of the emperor. The passage occurs in the 'Restitutio,' where he exclaims, "These mine eyes beheld the pope, exalted with vast pomp above the greatest personages, and worshiped by crowds, which knelt before him in the street; those considering themselves the happiest of people who could kiss his feet or his slippers." Then exciting himself to the highest degree of indignation, he continued, "O thou beast, of all beasts the most wicked; of all harlots the most shameless!"

He subsequently went into Germany, in the train of the emperor, and after the death of Quintana he proceeded to Paris. Quintana stated that he knew him by sight (which certainly does not prove that he was familiar with him), and he expressed the greatest anger and vexation that this Spaniard was the author of the work against the Trinity. He had already probably become connected with the free-thinkers in Italy.

At Geneva he stated that his father sent him to Toulouse to study the law. This is worthy of credit, although D'Artigny here contradicts Mosheim. It is probable that he had left Quintana after the journey into Italy, in his nineteenth year, and before he went to Paris. He had no reason for inventing the statement referred to at Geneva, and his writings afford many indications of legal study. At the university he formed the new idea of a further reformation, and then, for the first time, read the Bible, and, as it seems, in the original language. His first work proves that he had been long acquainted with plans of reformation. Like Calvin, he began his career with the study of the law; but we at once discover the different character of their minds, the Spaniard early devoting a portion of his time to astrology, while he despised the philosophy of Aristotle.

But the impulse which he felt to promote the salvation of mankind left him no rest. He read most of the fathers of the church, especially all who lived before Arius. In Tertullian and Irenæus was found, he thought, the true christian doctrine: he also carefully studied the catholic doctors of the middle ages; and lastly, he read such of the writings of the German reformers as were circulated in France. He had undoubtedly by this time renounced Romanism; but he appears to have thought that the reformers had accomplished only half a work. Proclaiming himself even then in the most perfect opposition to the age, he declared that it was not lawful for a christian to punish his fellow-man with death*; and desired to reveal to the world, as an instrument of the Holy Ghost, the being of God and of the Saviour.

This was the groundwork of the seven books on the 'Errors in the Doctrine of the Trinity.' But he could not remain safe at Toulouse; the parliament there had always proved itself sanguinary: he accordingly left France and went to Basel, where Zwingli's reformation was established, in order to make his views known to Œcolampadius, as the foundation of a further improvement in the church.

Of the spiritual state of Servetus, and of the nature of the mysterious thoughts which urged him on, and possessed him even in his early years, we learn somewhat from his work on Justification†: "I agree," he exclaims, "neither with protestants nor catholics in all things, neither am I opposed to them. Each seems to me to have a portion of truth and also of error: the one looks down upon the error of the other and forgets his own: God grant that we may discover our mistakes, and without pride or obstinacy. How easy would it be to separate truth from error, if it were allowed to all to speak their minds in peace; to strive to instruct themselves; and if the spirits of the old prophets were

* Serv. Œcolampadio, Mosheim, p. 393.

† De Justificat. c. 4, de Charit.

subjected to the new, and became silent, according to the commandment of Paul, when the latter, as often as somewhat is revealed to them, speak. But those of our times are only struggling for honour. May the Lord destroy all tyrants of the church*!" In another place he expresses the hope that the catholic church might be converted: "God will, sooner or later, open the minds of the monks, that they may understand the mystery of Christ and the power of his faith, which alone can purge their consciences from a gloomy superstition, and free it of its fetters: then will they bitterly lament the great relapse of Christianity into Judaism, the consequence of doubt and ignorance, and of their not distinguishing between the Law and the Gospel†." He speaks exceedingly well on the power of faith: "Such was the high degree of excellency to which Luther attained in faith, that no danger could appal him: he overcame all the powers of hell, of death and the devil. Through this secure strength of faith he could command the powers of heaven and earth, with such success, that he could bring the angels from heaven to serve him in the wilderness, where he was left forsaken. I doubt not but that this might take place, for hell has no force against believers, any more than it has against Christ: they are made partakers of his kingdom and of his power, and all which He has done shall they also do, if they have faith in Him‡."

The novelty of his notions excited surprise and alarm: he ruined his cause with the gentle Œcolampadius by his rash expressions. The principal point in dispute between them referred to the person of Christ. Servetus denied the union of the two natures: Christ, he said, can only be eternal in the sense in which the world is eternal, the idea thereof being eternal in God. This controversy, Ruchat states§, was carried on quietly between the two disputants by letter. Servetus, as so often happens in such cases, to satisfy Œcolampadius, concealed his philosophical errors under a seemingly orthodox confession; but Œcolampadius was not to be deceived, and in a conference with Zwingli and Bullinger he proved the danger of the opinions which Servetus had advanced. The latter now printed his work 'De Trinitatis Erroribus' at Hagenau, to which place he went himself to speak with the printer, John Sarcerius.

* By the old prophets were meant the protestant and catholic teachers. Servetus wished to represent himself as the one prophet now enjoying revelation.

† Mosheim, s. 53. ‡ Mosheim, s. 53. De Justificat. c. 3, 4.

§ Mosheim contradicts this, s. 16 and 389–92.

The plan of the work consists mainly in an endeavour to prove the great mystery of the Trinity through the man, the historical Christ. Thus the author seeks, in the first place, to show that this man is Jesus Christ; that He is the Son of God; and lastly, that He is God himself*.

No sooner had the work made its appearance than the clamour against it became universal. It was felt that the seeming belief of the writer did, in reality, tread the holy creed of true christians in the dust. People could scarcely understand how Servetus had dared to conceive such extraordinary errors in respect to a doctrine which had been so long free from attack. It was even fabled that he had made a journey into Africa, and had gathered his notions from the Koran: this idea seemed justified by the fact, that he had employed arguments from that book to illustrate his reasoning.

Servetus exhibited in this his first work the pride and bitterness which never left him. His principles are very apparent, and it naturally excites surprise, that in the one-and-twentieth year of his age he could undertake to attempt the reformation of religion and philosophy with such a show of knowledge. His doctrine was original. The antitrinitarians before him were of little account. He professed that the Holy Scriptures were the source of all his knowledge: in the same manner he asserted that they had both a literal and a mystical, or spiritual signification; the former depended upon history, the latter upon Christ. True Christianity, according to him, had been darkened through the Aristotelian philosophy, and a want of the knowledge of Hebrew. Paul of Samosata, he said, who represented Christ as man, had originally a perception of the truth. The doctrine of the Trinity was framed in opposition to the heretics who existed at the time when the pope assumed the sovereignty of the church†. It was then that we lost Christ. The two principles on which Servetus founds his reasonings are the incommunicability of the divine essence; for God is one, and therefore the modifications in God can only be variations or forms, and not persons. God is incomprehensible without a revelation. To make himself known He has sent forth two forms or manifestations, the Son and Spirit. He desires therefore the Father, Son and Holy Ghost to be ac-

* See the abstract of the work in Trechsel, Antitrinitarier, s. 68.

† De Trin. Error. lib. 7. fol. 3, 6. "Puto fuisse divinæ punitionis judicium ut eodem tempore Papa efficeretur rex, quo est Trinitas orta, et tunc Christum perdidimus."

knowledged; but only in the sense in which the Latins use the word *persona*, as representing an outward form. The operation, which is called "the Word," became flesh: God, that is, united himself in this manner with man: Christ therefore is God, and must be adored. The Holy Ghost is a divine energy; an angel. This Trinity is not eternal, but, like the world, is eternal according to the divine idea: *ideal as Logos*: real only in the world.

This new system of ideas would have had even an attractive appearance, had not Servetus heaped terrific abuse upon the ancient faith of the church, calling the persons of the Godhead inventions of the devil, and the triune Deity a hell-hound. So much that was new was here thrust upon the world that catholics and protestants agreed in their expression of indignation. Quintana, offended beyond measure that a Spaniard was the author of such a work, obtained immediately an imperial order, that the book should be everywhere suppressed. The protestants were in still greater excitement. Servetus was in communion with them, and they might be accused of agreeing with him in opinion. It happened that about this time Melancthon wrote in the strongest terms respecting him to Camerarius: "Good God! what tragedies will not the questions, whether the Logos and the Holy Ghost be persons, create for future times?" To Brentius he complains especially, that the Logos should be represented only as the thinking Father, or as his Voice. He calls Servetus a fanatic*.

Zwingli, eminently discreet, spoke, a year before his death, in the most marked manner in regard to Servetus. In the last month of 1530, when Servetus visited Œcolampadius, Zwingli was one day in company with Capito, Bucer and Bullinger; they conversed together on the great phænomena of the times; and Bullinger reports to us the earnest words of the reformer, words which indicate the attention paid at that period to this comet-like, meteoric apparition†: "This year‡," he says, "I was present at a conversation between the pious and beloved servant of God, John Œcolampadius, with Capito and Bucer, in which they discussed how the pure, genuine, evangelical truth and doctrine might be further promoted and upheld in the midst of the present difficulties and opposition. And Œcolampadius greatly complained that he had with him at Basel a rash and obstinate Spaniard, Michael Servetus, who was perpetually annoying him with

* Epist. Mel. ed. Peuc. p. 97–106.

† Mosheim, s. 17, 18.

‡ 1530.

troublesome questions, and talking and acting in a way which proved that he was an Arian. And it was plain that he did not confine his wickedness to Œcolampadius, but poured it out among others. Thereupon Zwingli said, 'Brother Œcolampadius, you must beware and watch, and take good heed; for the false and evil doctrine of that rash Spaniard will otherwise ruin the whole system of our religion: since, if Christ be not truly the eternal God, so neither is He, nor can be, our Saviour; and thus all will be false which the holy prophets, the apostles and the churches have taught, and of this we are more than certain. God forbid that such wickedness should ever appear among us, either now or at any future period. Lose no time then, but employ all diligence. Let him state fully his argument, and try whether you cannot turn and win him to the truth by good and clear reasoning.' Œcolampadius answered, 'I have already attempted this; but he is so proud, presumptuous and quarrelsome, that it has been all to no purpose.' Zwingli said, 'This must not be endured in the church of God, therefore do what you can to prevent the blasphemy from getting abroad, to the injury of Christianity.'" This incident shows that Zwingli thought that Servetus should, at all events, be removed, for the safety of the church.

It is probable that Servetus, having found a publisher for his work in Alsace, removed in the year 1531 from Basel to Strasburg. He was afterwards in Germany; and it is reported that he even heard Luther and Melancthon; but this is involved in doubt*, as is also the question whether he was in Germany after the appearance of his first work, and why he left that country. Supposing that he did visit Germany before the year 1530, and his work appeared a year later, the old mistake is settled, namely, that the first article of the Augsburg Confession was directed against his sect. It is certain however that he again visited Basel, and lived for some time, in the middle of the year 1531, with his friend Marinus. Œcolampadius gave him an ungracious reception, and informed the council of his arrival; but he was induced to speak of him, with some degree of gentleness, in a judgement which he was required to give by that assembly. Such was his anger however at the work of Servetus, that he aroused Bucer against him, and both he and Capito became his determined antagonists. Servetus had visited them while his book was in the press, and explained his system. Both felt more and more con-

* Mosheim, s. 393. Füsslini Centuria I. Epp. Reform. Helv. p. 77.

vinced of the dangerous character of the man, and Bucer began to preach openly against him. It required some boldness to enter upon such a discussion; and the Spaniard exhibited at the same time rashness, versatility, and a glowing imagination. The representations of the Strasburgers were of no avail: he put his name to the work, and set the Inquisition at defiance. The publisher and printer were more cautious, and were silent as to the place where it was printed. When the work began to make a noise, Bucer was again ready to assail Servetus, and such was his indignation that he exclaimed in the pulpit, "Servetus deserves to have his entrails torn from his body*."

We see from the general feeling respecting him, how conspicuous the man had made himself, and how much he was dreaded, long before the controversy between him and Calvin. It is not unreasonably conjectured that he was required in Basel, before he was allowed to leave the city, to make a retractation of his errors, a statement to this effect appearing at the beginning of a little work printed after his stay at Basel†. In this document he humbly prays to be pardoned the offence which he had given; he accuses his own understanding, and calls his writing perplexed and obscure. With this perhaps may be conjoined his Essay on Justification, Œcolampadius having objected to him, that he had insulted the faith of the Lutherans in regard to this doctrine.

But even this retractation bears with it marks of his characteristic insolence. He unsays all that he had stated; but as childish and imperfect, not as false. An advance, however, is visible in the new work; the Logos is more noticed, and the Father retreats: man and God penetrate Christ, but without confusion. In justification, the writer takes a middle course between the Catholic and Lutheran doctrine. The consciousness of sin is obscure, according to his representation, and the idea of justification is proportionably uncertain. Works have a reward, and both Jews and heathen will receive it. The will is free to perform good works, though grace alone conducts to the kingdom of God. He here takes occasion to ridicule the doctrine of the reformers, that good works proceed necessarily from faith.

* Ed. Laus. Ep. 126. Ed. Amstel. p. 70. "Bucerus, cum alioqui mansuetus esset ingenio, pro suggestu pronuntiavit, dignum esse, qui avulsis visceribus discerperetur."

† He wrote two discourses on the Trinity, with a little essay on the Righteousness of Christ's Kingdom. Dialogorum de Trinitate libri duo, de Justitia Regni Christi capp. iv.

Servetus discovered, after his first ill-judged experiment, that it was no easy matter to accomplish a reformation; nor was there, full of ardour as he was, a single trace of the heroism of a martyr in his disposition. Leaving Germany, he proposed to take up his abode in France; and in order to avoid being tried as a heretic, he rejected the name of Serveto and Reves, and called himself Michael of Villanueva.

Here begins the second epoch of his unsettled career, 1532–1553. He tells us that in the year 1534 he studied mathematics and medicine at Paris, in the 'Collège de Calvi,' and subsequently in the 'Collège de Lombards.' He lived securely under the name which he had assumed, till he was condemned at Vienne, as Villeneuve, to the flames. It was not till he went to Geneva that his true name was known. He was probably first at Lyons, for the purpose of circulating his books.

We have seen that in the year 1534, Calvin, still young, but already celebrated, was at Paris, endeavouring to fortify the evangelical church against the dangers by which it was threatened. Servetus resolved upon making his acquaintance, and imparting to him his convictions. The time and place were settled for their meetings: Calvin kept his appointment, but Servetus did not carry out his design: he returned to Lyons, and employed himself about an edition of Ptolemæus. On leaving Paris he went to Orleans. Joh. Wier relates, that it was while he was there the disgraceful spectre-tricks were played by the Franciscans; that he had several not undistinguished friends, and that among them was Michael Villanovanus. Joh. Sturm and Sleidan were also there at that time, as licentiates of law: the latter has described the scene got up by the conspirators.

Subsequently to this, Servetus spent a year in Italy. Mosheim speaks of this journey in connection with his first work; it is not impossible that he was in Italy at that time also: he may have made two journeys to that country, or the former one may have been invented, to afford him, through his connection with Quintana, a reputation for orthodoxy. The earlier cited of his writings on the pope may be referred to this season. The account of his journey is taken from the preface to his edition of Ptolemæus, which appeared in 1535. That he then began to obtain disciples is shown by one of his apologists, Postellus. It is evident that his opinions were received favourably at Venice, from the fact that Melancthon was called upon to address the senate of that city against his errors. "He is circulating," it was said, "the accursed doctrine of Paul of Samosata, and opposes the doctrine of the two persons in Christ. The understanding cannot indeed comprehend how the Word is one person; but we must rest, in faith, on the doctrine of the early church and of the apostles, and thus put Servetus to shame."

In Paris Servetus saw Francis I. touch persons, according to the old custom, to cure them of the king's-evil: he speaks of this in his Ptolemæus, and expresses his doubts on the subject, not seeing the people healed. It appears that he did not ascribe the healing power to faith, as we find was the case at that time in England, where the monarch was supposed to cure the ague and epilepsy by the touch. Lyons, to which Servetus afterwards returned, was a polished city: the book-trade flourished there to a considerable extent, and Servetus became corrector of the press to the brothers Trechsel, who were celebrated for their excellent printing. In the year 1537, with what he had gained in this employment, he went again to Paris, where he obtained the degree of master, and gave lectures on mathematics and astronomy.

With what extraordinary capacity he was endowed appears from the fact, that having hitherto devoted himself to the study of theology, he now pursued with equal ardour the several branches of natural science, and with such success that in a short time he was qualified to lecture upon them. We even find him numbered among the most skilful physicians in France, and it is said, that it was he who gave the first intimation of the circulation of the blood*. Nor did he neglect his theological pursuits: he was still employed about an edition of the Bible. This period indeed might be accounted the happiest of his life: science was his proper field; but dazzled by the unhappy notion that God would make special use of him for the enlightening of the world, he was again impelled into fanaticism. How different was this spiritual darkness to the timidity of which Calvin complains at the beginning of his course!

Servetus gave lectures at Paris, in his character of master, on Ptolemæus, astronomy and mathematics. A numerous auditory assembled around him. In the science of medicine he agreed with the Greek physicians, in opposition to the Arabian. The controversy between these two parties was one of the topics of the day. Champier, a physician, and the friend of Servetus, at Lyons, attributed, in a writing for Leonh. Fuchs, false views to

* Christianismi Restitutio, de Trin. lib. v. pp. 169, 170.

the former, and accused him of inclining rather to the Arabian system. This produced an answer from Servetus, and as whatever he did he did with talent, a very excellent work, on the use of Syrups, with a review of the Galenists and Averroists, appeared, from his pen, at Paris in 1537. This work, as well as the notes on Ptolemæus, was written in Latin, and so excellently, that Mosheim ventures the conjecture, that he intentionally employed a negligent style in his theological writings, it being a principle with him that, in matters of religion, language should always be humble.

But such was the pride of the man, that it prevented his retaining his present honourable position. The university and the faculty rose against him. This was the result partly of envy, and partly because he had accused many learned men of ignorance, especially in astronomy. They attacked him in their lectures. He defended himself by an answer, in which he called them, among other things, the plague of the world. The dispute at last reached such a height, that, to get red of him, his enemies employed, as a pretence, his love of astrology, and he was forbidden to continue his astronomical lectures. He had even had the boldness, trusting to the anonymous appearance of his theological works, every page of which exposed him to the flames, to submit himself to the judge of heresy at Paris, and was acquitted.

It is incredible how a man who wished to look upon himself as a chosen servant of God, appointed to restore Christianity, could devote a part of his life to such follies, and live as a hypocrite among his bitterest enemies. He obtained the degree of doctor of medicine, but it is characteristic of his temper that he never employed this distinction. On leaving Paris he went to Avignon, and then again to Lyons. We at length find him in 1538 at Charlieu, a little town not far from Lyons, where he supported himself as a physician; but here again his arrogance destroyed his repose*. He was now thirty years old, and he thought that he ought to be baptized, at this time, according to the example of Jesus Christ. So strongly was he convinced on this point that he even exhorted Calvin himself to take the same course, that he might receive the Holy Ghost†. Faith, according to his belief, justifies, but baptism saves. Man thereby becomes greater than the angels, and is actually born again. It is not

* "On account of that which he there stupidly and insolently attempted," says Bolsec, if we may cite his pamphlet.

† Christian. Restitut. p. 615, ep. 15. "Vera Christi fide ad Baptismum accede ut accipias donum Spir. S. tibi ita promissi."

erroneously conjectured that Servetus secretly received baptism about this time from some anabaptist in Switzerland or elsewhere, perhaps even in Charlieu, from a person of this persuasion. Of this however Calvin expresses a doubt, being inclined to regard him as a despiser of all religion*. According to a passage in the 'Restitutio†,' he appears to have belonged to some secret sect, in which the Lord's Supper was administered in a different manner to that practised among catholics and protestants.

He now removed to Vienne in Dauphiné: he there found a patron in the archbishop, Peter Palmier, who had attended his lectures at Paris, and was distinguished for his patronage of science. This exalted personage received him into his palace, and thus protected he lived in perfect tranquillity, but as a hypocrite, for he submitted himself to all the practices of the church. He thought of this shortly before his death, and expressed his shame in the presence of the magistrate.

The leisure which he now enjoyed enabled him to prepare a new edition of Ptolemæus, in which, to avoid offending his patron, he left out the passage respecting the unfruitfulness of Canaan, which was afterwards, as we shall see, adduced against him. This second edition he regarded as his own, and dedicated it to the archbishop.

As a convincing proof that he never entirely lost sight of a higher life, he published at this time the translation of the Bible, made by a learned monk, Xantes Pagninus: he altered it very little, but appended his own ideas respecting the translation of the Scriptures: his chief object was to show that the prophecies which occur in the Old Testament were fulfilled before the coming of Christ, and refer only in a spiritual sense to his appearance. There is no levity in this book. According to him, the second and twenty-second psalms speak of David; the forty-fifth of Solomon; but they also prophesy of Christ, because David and Solomon were types of Him. Thus also, Isaiah meant by the virgin, Abi, who was to bring King Hezekiah into the world. In the same manner that prophet mourned the death of Cyrus, when he spoke of the sufferings and death of the Redeemer. The preface, in which he criticises the genius of the Hebrew language, shows the great talent of the writer: he remarks that no translation can reach the beauty of the original.

This edition of the Bible did not please the catholics. At

* The baptism of Servetus is denied by Füsslin.

† Apolog. p. 710.

Louvain it was placed in the list of forbidden books. It was also received very ungraciously in Spain. But Servetus lived twelve years in peace, and was the regularly appointed physician of the city; his zeal however would not suffer him to enjoy any actual quiet; he was still anxious to play the reformer, and for this purpose he must issue a new work.

We approach the third period of his history, and the world has now to become acquainted with his true name. He determined to issue a manifesto against the prevailing antichristianity: the Revelation of John and the signs of the times convinced him that the fall of antichrist was at hand. But we are still interested in the man: his soul had wings. In the introduction to his last work, that which brought him to the flames, he says, "We intend to make manifest the divine revelation from the earliest times—the great mystery of faith, which is superior to all controversy. The God who in former ages was not seen, and whom we shall now see, because the veil is removed from his face, Him shall we see shining in ourselves*." He then thus apostrophizes the Son of God: "O Christ Jesus, Son of God! reveal thyself to thy servant, that this great revelation may be clear to us in its truth. Give me now thy good spirit and thy mighty word; guide my pen and my soul, that I may be able to describe the glory of thy godhead, and to confess to Thee the true faith! This is thy work, which an inward impulse teaches me to attempt, being anxious for thy truth. I undertook the same in time past, and now again I feel myself urged thereto, for the appointed season is fulfilled. Thou hast taught us that thy light must not remain hidden, and woe to me if I do not proclaim thy Gospel†." Servetus may have deeply felt, in the ardour of his imagination, the great mystery of the being of God. The glowing fancy with which he was inspired bore him so away that he spoke of himself as if he had been an apostle of the Lord: he thought that he was appointed to reveal the all-important truth which had been kept concealed for centuries. The right faith, according to him, had been lost in the course of 1260 years, and it was God's will that he should revive it. Thus speaks the book of Revelation, c. xii. v. 1. Greater than the disciples of the Lord, he thus stood upon an equality with the *Theosophers*, who have taught the hidden truths of God's being; with those who went out from among the first teachers; and also with the philosophers, who reveal the secret

* Procem. lib. de Trinit. † Ibid.

things of God through the might of the Spirit, and who are therefore exalted far above the revelations of the apostles.

His doctrine of the Trinity was then not at all known. Man could be saved, he said, through a simple belief in the Messias*. The great mystery seems to have been partly known at the time of the apostles. John was deeply moved to declare it fully: "At the beginning was the Word." The mass of mankind are justified by mere faith in Christ, without a right understanding of his godhead; and as this doctrine was known but by few, and there were but few writers, metaphysical sophists invaded Christianity and its injured God.

Calvin found the Apocalypse so unintelligible, that he could not be persuaded to undertake its interpretation. Servetus, his opponent, on the contrary, commenced with this book. It abounded, as he conceived, with astrological prophecies; but this notion Calvin strongly combated in a separate treatise. He points out especially the vision in the twelfth chapter: "The dragon which would destroy the woman and her offspring is the pope; the woman is the church; her son, whom God delivers, is the faith of Christians. For 1260 prophetic days or years must the church remain under antichrist. Then commences the conflict with the dragon. Michael and his angels conquer, after that the dragon has murdered many, and the good and wicked fight upon the earth. This contest is now at an end. The hosts of Michael are true witnesses of the church. In the time of Constantine the Great, the dragon began to drive the true church into the wilderness: Christ ceased to rule from the moment when the true doctrine respecting him was corrupted, and the divine essence divided into three persons†."

Servetus was one of those who delight in controversy from the notion that they are favoured with a particular revelation, and that God will restore the lost faith in answer to their prayer. It was well that he retained enough of discretion to avoid supposing himself, according to his name, the angel Michael. He wrote to Calvin: "I labour incessantly for the requickening of the church, and you are indignant with me because I take a part in this conflict of Michael, and wish all pious men to follow my example. Consider well this passage, and you will see that there are men thus struggling who are ready to sacrifice their lives, in the

* Mosheim, s. 95. "Hac sola fiducia rudis plebs justificabatur, quamvis Christi divinitatem non plene cognosceret."

† Christ. Restit. l. i. de orbis perditione, p. 396.

blood and in the testimony of Christ. That they are called angels is according to the usage of Scripture. The new-birth from above makes us like the angels. See you not, that the subject here spoken of is the revivifying of the ruined church?"

The manuscript of the 'Restitutio' was sent by Servetus to Calvin through the bookseller Frellon. He was anxious to see what the reformer would say respecting it. Some time after he desired that the manuscript might be returned to enable him to correct it. Calvin, however, did not send it: it was now in the hands of Viret at Lausanne. The correspondence extends, with several intervals, between 1540 and 1548*. It was necessary for Servetus, as a reformer, to measure his strength with the most powerful spirit of the protestant party. Calvin was the greatest obstacle to his plans. His impatience, and the proposed meeting in the early part of his career at Paris, are sufficient indications of his jealousy towards the reformer. He was anxious to obtain his answer to the three following questions†: they will serve to show the materials of which his system consisted:—"Is the crucified man, Jesus, the Son of God, and on what account is He so?" There was, therefore, still a doubt on his mind, although, in the first work, he had professed this faith. "Is the kingdom of God in men, when they go into this kingdom,—when they are born again?"—"Must the baptism of Christ take place in faith, as the Lord's Supper; and why did He institute baptism and the Supper?"

The most remarkable point in Calvin's answer, which exhibits the main principles of his theology, is found in the statement, that faith is necessary to baptism, and is as strength to children. It is sad to think that Servetus was not satisfied with the solid answer which Calvin gave. He replied to him with warmth, and desired an explanation in his second writing, more modest in the conclusion: "I beseech you, by God," he says, "that as you promised to add somewhat to your former statement, so you will now teach me, in the first place, what true faith is." Subsequently he spoke of his opponent as a knave; but his attack on the Calvinistic view of baptism was not wrongly conceived. He was unwilling to regard it as distinct from the Lord's Supper. When he sent several other questions to Calvin, which indicated

* Calvin, in his Tract, p. 517, says, "When he was at Lyons he sent me three questions to answer. He thought to entrap me. That my answer did not satisfy him I am not surprised."

† Calv. Refut. Error. Serveti, Ed. Amstel. p. 517. Ed. Gen. p. 600.

an awakened spirit, the reformer, who would rest on nothing but Scripture, answered him in a friendly manner, but with earnest remonstrances*.

On the baptism of children, which Calvin defended, we have the following excellent remark:—"Should God take them out of the world before they could be spiritually circumcised, we must leave them to the secret dispensation of divine grace;" and this may be regarded as an antidote to all the severity of his system. To the new questions put by Servetus, he returned no answer. He needed time, and it sufficed to refer to his 'Institutes.' The proud Spaniard was so offended at this treatment that he sent a great number of letters to the reformer, one after the other, containing almost countless accusations and offensive expressions, which, however, were very patiently endured. Mosheim throws some doubt on the progress of the affair, as related by Calvin; but he regards as genuine the thirty letters, written in a very calm tone, which Servetus appended to his last work, and supposes that they were really sent to the reformer.

The study of Calvin's character, in respect to these occurrences, shows him to have been a man of extraordinary observation, even in little things. In the correspondence of which we have spoken, he was the slave neither of imagination nor of a cold mechanical memory. Servetus, on the other hand, was continually guilty of a want of candour; was always under the influence of his imagination. He was capable of printing letters never sent to Calvin, and he may have omitted what Calvin calls scurrilous words and curses, if, as is probable, the letters which were sent to Vienne are the same as those appended to the 'Restitutio.' Only two ordinary letters are known, as directed by Calvin to Servetus. The style of the latter displeased him from the beginning; but he was willing to continue the controversy, either in the hope that he might at length convince him of his error, or because he sought a suitable antagonist. Certain it is, however, that several smaller papers were addressed by him to Servetus. Calvin's letter to Frellon, with his answer to Servetus inclosed, is very characteristic of both opponents. We give the following extract:—

"Herr Johann! I would fain satisfy your wish; not that I have much hope to effect anything with such a man, but because I am anxious to try whether any means exist to bring him to a

* "I neither hate you nor despise you, nor do I wish to persecute you; but I would be hard as iron when I behold you insulting sound doctrine with such audacity."—Refut. Error. Serv. Ed. Amstel. p. 521. Ed. Genev. p. 605.

right understanding, or whether God may have wrought in him any change. He has written to me in a very haughty spirit, and I have desired to humble him a little; hence I have spoken to him rather more severely than is my wont. This is all I could do; and I assure you, that nothing is more necessary for him than a lecture on humility. True it is, he can only acquire that grace through the Spirit of God; but we must lend him what help we can. If God be so gracious to him and us as to render this answer profitable to him, I shall have cause to rejoice; but if, on the other hand, he continue to pursue his present course, you will lose your time in urging me to labour for him. I have other occupations of a more pressing nature, and I shall make it a matter of conscience not to concern myself any longer about him, for I have little doubt that he is a Satan, whose end it is to divert me from other and profitable studies. I entreat you, therefore, remain content with what has been already done, if there be no change*."

Calvin entertained a hope that the Holy Spirit might still effect the conversion of Servetus. He was not yet a castaway in his eyes, and this shows that the expressions which he used respecting him to Farel are not to be taken literally.

Frellon's letter to Servetus, sent to him by a trusty messenger, characterizes his impatience, and his desire to stand on an intimate footing with Calvin. When the latter referred him to his 'Institutions,' he sent the work back to him, accompanied with some bitter remarks. Calvin's well-known letter to Farel, who was then at Metz, was dated February 13, 1546. Servetus had sent him a great mass of his heretical writings. He even expressed his wish to come to Geneva; but he required a safe-conduct and an invitation. Calvin, however, would lend him no aid. "Servetus," he says, "wrote to me a short time ago, and sent a huge volume of his dreamings and pompous triflings with his letter. I was to find among them wonderful things, and such as I had never before seen, and if I wished he would himself come. But I am by no means inclined to be responsible for him; and if he come I will never allow him, supposing my influence worth anything, to depart alive†."

This, among a thousand other matters, was but an outbreak of anger, a threat uttered in passion; the letter, which was

* Mosheim, s. 89.

† "Sed nolo fidem meam interponere. Nam si venerit, modo valeat mea authoritas, vivum exire nunquam patiar."—MS. Gen.

sent the same day to Frellon, containing an expression of hope that Servetus might still be converted. Calvin had probably answered his communication, and now spoke of the circumstance to Farel. His enemies have made the sentence referred to of vast importance, because they can find no worse cause of accusation against him. They do not perceive that their complaint is unreasonable, for had Calvin desired the death of Servetus, he would have encouraged his coming to Geneva. It is incredible how many fables have been founded on this expression; to what ravings even it has given occasion, and that up to the present day. For us it is a matter of no importance whatever, since Calvin subsequently acknowledged with all simplicity, that he considered the death of Servetus necessary.

That the correspondence between Calvin and Servetus had wholly ceased in the year 1548 appears from the words of the former to Viret. Not being able to effect anything with Calvin, Servetus had attacked that minister. Calvin says respecting this: "I suppose you have read the answer which I sent Servetus; it was my wish to have nothing more to do with this incurably hard-necked, heretical man, and certainly it was well to follow in this case the precept of the apostle. But now he assails you: it will be right for you to consider how far it is prudent to oppose his folly: he will extort nothing farther from me."

Finding that Calvin would not answer him, Servetus wrote several times to the minister Pepin at Geneva, to obtain the return of his manuscript. He had another in hand, which he sent with certain alterations to the press. The third letter to Pepin is preserved: it is a remarkable document, and was adduced against him, with his other manuscripts, on his trial at Geneva. "Although," he says, "my letter to Calvin shows plainly that the force of the law is taken away, I will quote a passage which will prove to you, still better, how a new order of things has been introduced through the coming of Christ. That the law has lost its authority, you will clearly see, if you read the passage to which I refer. Thus the Prophet Jeremiah, chap. xxxi., teaches, that the covenant with the fathers, when they went out of Egypt, was abolished. So also Ezekiel, chap. xvi., and Paul, Heb. viii. It is not under the influence of this covenant, therefore, that God now receives us as his people; but through faith in Jesus Christ, his beloved Son. Consider well, then, what kind of a Gospel you have, confounded as it altogether is with the law. Your

Gospel is without the One God, without the true faith, without good works. In the place of the One God, you have a three-headed Cerberus; instead of the true faith, you have a set of unhappy dreamings; and good works you regard as nothing better than idle fancies. Your belief in Christ is a mere pretence, and without any reality. According to your system, man is a mere clod, and God a monster with a fettered will. Divine regeneràtion by water is unknown to you, or is a mere fable. You shut man out from the kingdom of God, by making it appear as a mere invention. Woe, woe, woe to you! I would fain have warned you by this last letter, and brought you to a better state of mind; but my warnings are ended. It is, perhaps, a vexation to you that I engage in this struggle on the part of Michael, and wish you would do the same. Read carefully the passage in the book of Revelation, and you will see that the discourse therein is of men, ready to contend, placing their lives in jeopardy, in the blood, and for the testimony of the Lord. That they are called angels, is according to the usage of Scripture. See you not also that allusion is here made to the church of Christ, so long oppressed in the wilderness? Is there not reference made, according to what John himself says, to some future event? Who is that accuser, who complained of our transgressing the law and the ordinances? Before the conflict, he says, there will be accusations and the seducing of the world. Then shall the conflict follow, and the time is near. And who are they who shall gain the victory over the beast, and who bear not his marks? I know it assuredly, that I must die for this thing; but I am not on that account troubled in my soul, or because that I, a disciple, shall be like my Master. I am distressed that, through you, I cannot correct many passages of my writings, which are now in the hands of Calvin. Farewell, and do not expect any more letters from me. I shall stand upon my watch-tower, and see what He will say unto me; for He will come, and will not tarry." The date of this letter is not known, but it appears to have been written when his fanaticism was at the height.

We are now approaching the third epoch of his unquiet course, that in which his passions became engaged in the terrible struggle with the feeling of truth which still lived within him. He had acquired some little knowledge of his great weakness: the castles in the air, which he had created for himself in the magic light of his fanatical pride, had sadly vanished, and nothing was left for him but a fearful reality; the actual struggle of martyrdom, conducting him through imprisonment, dishonour, anguish and the flames. He had nourished the hope that his first work would make an impression on the reformers. When they neglected to notice him, he remembered that the early prophets were taught to listen in silence to what the Spirit should reveal to those who came after. But when he found all opposing him, his feelings were embittered, and then followed his last work, as a hostile manifesto. He had for a long time been an object of suspicion to the Roman Catholics, but it was his own unquiet temper only which first exposed him to trouble.

In order to bring his work before the world, he endeavoured, in the first instance, to have it printed at Basel: in this he failed. The archbishop himself had brought some printers to Vienne. William Queroult, the overseer of the press, could be easily won; he had been driven out of Geneva, and was Calvin's enemy. Balthasar Arnoullet, the director, was not very willing to allow a book to be printed without the license of the clergy; but he was influenced by a bribe, and two presses were set to work in secret. Servetus corrected the proofs. The printing continued from the Michaelmas of the former year to the January of 1553. Five bales of copies were sent to Lyons; as many to Chatillon; still more to Frankfort; and others to Geneva. One of the copies fell into the hands of Calvin.

M. d'Artigny has falsified, in a most unpardonable degree, the history of the detection of Servetus. He has been convincingly answered and properly censured by Mosheim. Calvin can have had no premeditated intention of accusing Servetus. The following statement may be regarded as historically correct.

There lived at Geneva, at the time when the work of which we are speaking was published, a noble Frenchman of Lyons, who had left his native country on account of religion. This was William Trie; and he had a relation at Lyons named Arneys, who, as a zealous catholic, was perpetually persuading him to return to the Romish church. Trie, on the other hand, as anxiously entreated him to come to Geneva. He was well known to Calvin, and it is probable that the latter, greatly excited at reading the work of Servetus, allowed the expression of his indignation to escape him in conversation with Trie, and others of his friends.

On the 26th of February, Trie wrote to Arneys: "I cannot but wonder at your objecting to me, that we have no church discipline and order. I see, God be praised, that crimes are better punished among us than by all your boasted spiritual tribunals. And, as regards doctrine, although we have more freedom here, yet we never suffer the name of God to be blasphemed, or errors to be diffused without opposing them. I can give you an example, which, to say the truth, is greatly to your shame. A heretic is protected among you, who well deserves to be burnt, wherever he is found. When I speak of heretics, I here refer to a man whom the Papists, as well as we, condemn; for although we differ in many things, we have yet this in common, that we acknowledge three persons in one God, and believe that the Son, who is the eternal Logos, was begotten of the Father before all worlds; that He has in himself eternal life, his Holy Spirit. Suppose now, that a man should declare that the Trinity, in which we believe, is a Cerberus, a hellish monster, and should heap upon it all imaginable abuse, and make a mock at all which the ancient fathers have said thereon; suppose that this were the case, I ask you in what light would such a man appear among you? How base a thing it is, that they should be led to death who acknowledge that there is one only God, and that prayer must be offered to Him in the name of Jesus Christ*, while such a man as this, who regards Christ as an idol, who tramples on all the principles of faith, revives all the absurdities of the old heretics, condemns the baptism of children, calling it a devilish invention,—should be held in esteem among you, and treated as if he had done nothing amiss! The man to whom I refer is a Spaniard or Portuguese, Michael Servetus by name. This is his proper name; but he is known by that of Villeneuve, plays the physician, and has just had a work printed at Arnoullet's office in Vienne. You say, that the books, the sole object of which is to persuade men to abide by the simple doctrine of Scripture, corrupt the world; and yet you protect under your wings a venomous creature sufficient to destroy the entire volume of Scripture, and all even which you regard as Christianity." Trie inclosed in his letter the title, the register, and the first four leaves of the 'Restitutio.'

It is easy to perceive that Trie was embittered by his knowledge of the horrible sufferings endured by his evangelical brethren in France; but it was unreasonable in him to accuse the catholics of allowing a heretic to live among them, when, through his assumption of a strange name, he must have been

* The writer here describes the faith of the evangelical reformers.

unknown. It appears surprising to some that he should have sent the title of the work, whereas it is certain that, at this time, at Geneva, nothing was less likely to be talked of among the faithful of that city than the work of Servetus. Calvin's opponents wish it to be supposed, that Trie begged the title of the book of him, as if there had been but one copy in Geneva. People however could have obtained as many copies as they pleased from Stephanus, for Servetus had glutted the world with them. Calvin sent a copy to Bullinger. It ought also to silence opponents, when it is known, that Calvin definitely stated in the 'Refutatio,' that he was ready to say, that had he accused him at that time, it would not have been a thing to deny. He believed indeed that if he had driven him from Geneva by fire from heaven, he would but have done his duty, for he was the reformer of the church, not of the congregation of a single city. It is evident that Servetus, who had managed the affair at Vienne so secretly, had, notwithstanding, a false friend, through whom the whole was made known to the Genevese. How otherwise could Trie have discovered that the work was printed at Vienne, and by Arnoullet? Neither the city nor the printer was named on the title-page, although Calvin immediately recognized the work as written by Servetus. It is now however understood that Frellon, a catholic at Lyons, was acquainted with both Calvin and Servetus, and it is probable that when he found the latter going too far, he joined the rest against him.

The fate of Servetus was now determined. Arneys, a zealous catholic, lost no time in placing Trie's letter before Ory, the judge of heresy at Lyons, where the bloodthirsty cardinal Tournon, who had brought the skilful inquisitor above-named out of Italy, was ready to give ear to any suspicion. Servetus was instantly summoned before the tribunal at Vienne, and underwent an examination before Montgiron, the general-lieutenant of Dauphiné. He had found means however in the two hours whilst he was still at liberty to put aside as many papers as seemed necessary. Presenting himself without any appearance of concern before the magistrate, he declared that he was quite willing to open his house to any one who chose to search it, for that it had always been his wish to be free from every suspicion of heresy. The magistrates did in fact thoroughly search the house, but nothing heretical could be discovered. A man influenced by the Spirit of God would have spoken differently from the beginning.

Queroult was subjected on the 17th of March to a long examination, but being a man of ability he betrayed himself in nothing. All the people employed in the office were examined, and asked whether they knew the handwriting of the work, some leaves of which were placed before them. They all answered in the negative. A catalogue of the books printed at the office for the preceding two years was required: no octavo was found mentioned. All the assistants and servants in Arnoullet's house, with their families, were brought before the tribunal, and they were forbidden, under pain of being punished as heretics, to make public any of these proceedings. On the following day, Arnoullet himself, who had been on a journey, returned; he was immediately summoned before the tribunal. There was nothing against him, and the magistrates were obliged to declare that the Spanish physician could not be imprisoned on the evidence before them.

Ory was called to Vienne: he considered that it was necessary to refer to the original source of the report, and therefore summoned Arneys to his aid. At the same time he himself wrote to Trie, and begged him for an entire copy of the work, of which at present they had only the first pages: among other things he said, "If sufficient proof could be had, people at Geneva should soon see that the honour of God and of the faith was cherished in France, and that they were not so negligent as was imagined." The book now could have done no good, for Servetus denied that he was the author. An answer to the above arrived on the 26th of March.

Trie says to his relation, "When I wrote you the letter which you have given to those whom I accused of negligence, I did not suppose that the affair would go so far; my only design was to make it apparent to you what a fine zeal they must have who call themselves pillars of the church, whilst they could suffer such a wretch among them, and yet persecute so fiercely the poor Christians, whose whole desire it is to worship God in all simplicity. But as my private letters have been made public, God grant that they may at least tend to free Christianity from such filth, yea, from such a deadly pestilence! I cannot send the book itself, but I can furnish you with a better means of proving the guilt of this man, consisting of two dozen written leaves, in which are portions of his heresy. If his printed work be shown to him, he can deny that he is the author, but not so with his own handwriting. I must however plainly confess to you, that I have had great trouble in obtaining from Mr. Calvin what I now send you; not that he wishes such a cursed blasphemer to remain unpunished, but because it seems to him that it is the duty of one, who bears not the sword of justice, to oppose heresies by doctrine rather than by such means. But I so wore him with my importunities, showing that the charge of levity would be cast upon me if I had not his help, that he at last yielded, and gave me what you see." Calvin therefore had a right feeling of his duty, but his consent in this matter is an instance of his wavering between the principle of the old and that of the new covenant.

Notwithstanding the care with which these proofs were collected, they were not sufficient for the purpose intended. Servetus at Vienne was called Villeneuve, and the handwriting of a person was not allowed as decisive evidence in a trial for heresy: it could also be set aside by an oath. The law required that Villeneuve should be proved to be the author of the 'Restitutio,' and further, that Arnoullet had printed the book at Vienne. Arneys begged Trie a second time to furnish him with better evidence. The messenger who brought the letter arrived very late on the last day of March. Trie answered during the night, the questions put to him, stating that Servetus apologized in the last of the letters sent for having taken a strange name; that his identity was therefore proved; and that the manuscript of the work was at Lausanne, and consequently could not be sent: "But that you may know that this is not the first time that that monster has endeavoured to disturb the church, I can inform you, that twenty-four years ago he was expelled from the first of the German churches, and if he had been in this place, he would never have gone out." The writer could not tell how it had become known that Arnoullet was the printer.

Although no clear proofs of their guilt existed, the judges determined that Villeneuve and Arnoullet should be kept in confinement, to afford an opportunity for their more formal trial: they were accordingly both thrown into prison, and in separate places. Servetus was confined in the royal palace, and treated with respect. Palmier conducted the whole affair; he sent a messenger immediately to the chateau Roussillon, about fourteen miles from Vienne, and where the cardinal Tournon was then residing. Ory mounted his horse and was speedily at Vienne; his zeal was extraordinary. In the afternoon, the magistrates assembled in the Palace of Justice, and in the chamber where causes of life and death were decided. The accused appeared: he was required, according to custom, to take an oath that he would speak only the truth: he spoke, alas! scarcely anything but falsehoods. Thus he deprived himself of his only proper consolation and genuine strength. Not as a prophet; not as a servant of the truth; not surely as a soldier in the host of Michael, did he now stand before the tribunal. At every new examination there was a fresh oath, and another instance of perjury: his weakness shows the courage and tranquil spirit of the martyrs at Lyons in a still fairer light.

D'Artigny here relates, from Quintana, the history of Servetus, according to the report of the trial. In the course of his examination two leaves of a printed work were placed before him, with marginal notes, and the superscription "De Baptismo, c. 17*." This was a chapter of Calvin's 'Institutes;' not of the 'Restitutio,' as Artigny absurdly supposed, that work not being divided into chapters. Servetus had, in fact, sent to Calvin a copy of his own work, accompanied by abusive remarks: to this book the leaves of which we are speaking had belonged, and infant baptism is one of the subjects rashly treated of in the marginal annotations. This appears from Calvin's refutation of the errors of Servetus, in the course of which he accuses him of having vilified several of his books.

The judges only wished for some explanation of these notes. Servetus was so imprudent as to give it, and thus to show that he was the author; after however having done so he expressed a doubt whether it was his writing. With regard to the doctrine of baptism, he retracted his opinion, spoke in the most orthodox manner, and submitted himself in all things to the church, as his holy mother†. It is easy to see that his only object was to save his life.

When, at his second examination, he observed that all his letters to Calvin were in the hands of the judges, his courage entirely forsook him; he saw that the affair must terminate badly, and, in this necessity, he could invent no means of deliverance but an insipid lie. "My lords," he said, his eyes streaming with tears, "I will confess the truth. Twenty-five years ago, when I was in Germany, a book by one Servetus, a Spaniard, was printed at Aganon (Hagenau); I know not whence he came; but at that time I was in correspondence with Calvin, and he

* These leaves were out of Calvin's 'Institutes.' Mosheim (Neue Nachr. s. 50, 65) has not clearly represented this matter.

† D'Artigny, t. ii. p. 105.

addressed me as Servetus, for there was a similarity in our appearance, and I assumed his character." For ten years however, he added, he had ceased to write; and he declared, before God and the judges, that he had never desired to do aught against the church, or to dogmatize, in any way, against the Christian religion*.

There must have been something very comical in such a lame and absurd account as this, when addressed to a tribunal for the examination of heretics, and at the head of which was the Italian Ory. In his confusion, he stated, that the letters were written to Calvin in Germany twenty-five years back; while a little after he asserted that they were sent when he was in France. Several letters were shown to him, in which he distinctly expressed his heretical notions: he did not deny that the letters were his; but he argued that they only contained the opinions which he held in former times, and which he had by no means permanently embraced. When the examination was continued, in the afternoon, fourteen other letters were laid before him: he still gave the same answer, stating, "that he did not profess what was heretical in those letters, but only what his judges and the church believed to be right."

Servetus had been allowed considerable freedom, and he employed the present opportunity of getting together some money, and preparing all things for his flight. It is evident that he had friends in the place. The archbishop himself was not yet acquainted with his dangerous book, and his blasphemies. He had been permitted to retain in the prison a gold chain worth twenty ducats, which he wore about his neck, and six gold rings on his fingers. At Geneva ninety-seven gold pieces were still found in his purse. Happily for him, a garden extended up to the room of the prison in which he was placed: it was possible to get from this up the roof of a neighbouring house, and thence along a wall, down which a man could let himself into the court of the palace. When once there, it was no difficult matter to reach the city gate, and the bridge over the Rhone.

The prisoners were allowed to walk about the garden, and to enter it at any time they found necessary. Early in the morning of the 7th of April Servetus dressed himself completely, but threw a large night-gown over his other clothes, put a silk handkerchief about his head, and asked the keeper of the prison for the key of the garden. The man having no fear of his escaping

* D'Artigny, t. ii. p. 108. See also Mosheim, Neue Nachrichten, s. 96–100.

in such a dress, immediately gave him the key, and went unconcerned with his people to tend some vines. Servetus, who had beforehand carefully examined the place, reached the court of the palace without interruption, and passed the bridge. It was not till after many hours that the absence of the prisoner was discovered. A terrible tumult followed. The gates were closed, and all the houses were searched, but the fortunate Servetus was free. After three days, a countrywoman confessed she had seen him go.

This was a rare event in the history of trials for heresy. The process was continued as if Servetus had been present: at length the judge discovered that the 'Restitutio' had been secretly printed at Vienne: he exposed all the errors which it contained. The civil magistrate pronounced judgement before the end of the examination: the ecclesiastical judges did not finish their proceedings till after six months had elapsed, and when Servetus had already been long condemned at Geneva: they declared him to be an arch-heretic*. Independent of his blasphemy, the expressions which he employs in his works against the catholic church, are as powerful as those of Luther and Calvin†.

The temporal power condemned Servetus to be burnt to death, and he was to be burnt in effigy in the interval between his sentence and apprehension. Arnoullet, who proved his innocence, as having been deceived, was set free. Queroult had assured him that the 'Restitutio' was altogether a harmless book. The latter probably fled, and succeeded in making his escape. The copies of the 'Restitutio' were to be destroyed‡.

It was on the 17th of June that the sentence of death was pronounced, and on the same day the executioner conveyed the effigy of Servetus, with five bales of books, on a cart, from the palace to the market-place, and thence to the "Place Charneve:" there he hung the effigy on a gallows, and afterwards threw it into the fire, in which it was slowly consumed. The property

* Mosheim, Neue Nachrichten, s. 100, 101.

† For example, "O Christe Jesu, Fili Dei, liberator clementissime, qui toties populum ab angustiis liberasti, libera nos miseros ab hac Babylonica Antichristi captivitate, ab hypocrisi ejus, tyrannide et idolatria!"

‡ The impression consisted of a thousand copies. Of these, a part had been sent to Lyons, another to Chatillon, and a third direct to Frankfort. Arnoullet took care that the copies sent to Chatillon, for the fair, should be burnt. Calvin wrote to the ministers at Frankfort not to spare a copy (Epis. 153). Of those which came to Geneva, one was tied to the body of Servetus when he was burnt: the others were also destroyed. Mosheim shows that only six copies escaped. Robert Stephanus was the man *pius et integer* of whom Calvin speaks in his letter, and who destroyed the copies at Geneva.

which Servetus had acquired was so considerable, that a nobleman purchased it of the king for his son.

Servetus had determined upon going to Naples, and there practising as a physician: his way led him through Switzerland, fear of pursuers preventing him from passing over Piedmont. He wandered for about a month in France*, and then went quietly to Geneva. A homeless man, impelled by a peculiar fate, he had no sooner escaped from the fire than he rushed into new danger. An extraordinary delight in running hazards was one of his characteristics. He knew that Trie had sent his letters to Vienne; that Calvin could give him no safe-conduct; that he was, on the contrary, his accuser; but notwithstanding all this, a strange irresistible power drove him to Geneva. He had many years before been led, in the same manner, to seek Calvin in Paris; subsequently he forced him into a correspondence, and now at last he came himself, in order to observe in secret this man whom he at the same time both sought and shunned. Calvin had reason to remark, "I know not what to say of him, except that he was seized by a fatal madness to precipitate himself upon destruction."

In the middle of the month of July, a man was seen, on foot, entering the gate of the old city; he turned into a little inn used by strangers, called the *Auberge de la Rose*, and situated on the lake. The night before he had slept in the village of Le Louyset, where he arrived on horseback. It was easy to recognize in the traveller a man of education; in the southern expression of his eye, there was deep thought and dreaming phantasy, and somewhat of passionate excitement: he indulged in some light expressions. The people of the inn wishing to learn more about him, asked if he was married; he answered, that a man could find women enough without marrying. Some one observed him going to the church where Calvin preached.

After remaining about a month at Geneva, he resolved on making a journey to Zurich. For this purpose he engaged a boat to carry him across the lake; but just as he was on the point of departing an officer appeared, and took him prisoner in the name of the council†. This event occurred August 13, 1553.

* According to Calvin's letter to Sulzer, for four months (Ep. 156); but this is not correct. His sentence was pronounced at Vienne June 17th, and Calvin learnt, August 13th, that he was in Geneva.

† See Beza's preface to Calvin's Commentary on Joshua, Bibl. Raisonn. Angl. t. ii. pt. 1. p. 95. Mosheim, s. 152.

Calvin assumed to himself great credit for having rendered such service to God, to the church, and to mankind, by depriving a blasphemer like Servetus of his power to do harm, and exciting him to recant: he often spoke on this subject*, and repeated, that it was his duty to inform the council that Servetus was living in the republic.

Servetus appears to have kept himself quiet at Geneva: he had probably friends or acquaintances in that city; it would otherwise be inconceivable how his presence there should have become known. Some persons relate that he was recognized in the church; at his examination he stated that no one could have a right to apprehend him in Geneva; he had not attempted to promote his reformation in that city, nor was it his intention to remain there. Musculus however said, in a letter to Bullinger, that Servetus was only wishing to make use of the bad feelings of some great men at Geneva against Calvin, in order to obtain a position whence he might be able to agitate other churches†. This may have entered into the plan of the libertine party.

Servetus was conveyed to prison,—the old prison near the church of St. Peter: he complained bitterly of this in his letter to the council. Nicolas de la Fontaine‡, a student, and Calvin's secretary, allowed himself to be named the accuser of the prisoner, and with a full knowledge of the rule established at Geneva, that if the accused was found innocent, the accuser should suffer the punishment which would otherwise have fallen on the criminal. The council was at this period altogether opposed to Calvin, but it regarded his accusation of Servetus with great approbation §. The latter had been long considered as an outlaw.

Calvin had no intention to expose Servetus to capital punishment; he only wished to render him harmless, to make him recant his blasphemy, and so preserve Christianity from injury; but we shall see how the Spaniard opposed himself by his mischievous, obstinate spirit to all the representations of reason, and

* To Sulzer, Sept. 9, Ep. 156. Ed. Amst. p. 70.

† Grotius is altogether wrong in his statement that Servetus went to Geneva to consult Calvin.

‡ Born at St. Gervais: he fled to Geneva, where Calvin protected him, and made him cook to the Sieur de Bourgogne, when that nobleman lived in his house. He next became Calvin's secretary, and manifested great aptitude for the sciences: he had already lived six years with Calvin at the time when Servetus was apprehended, and had advanced far in theological knowledge; thus he was no longer a menial, nor was he unworthy, as enemies pretend, of the part which he undertook. He is called by Spon *étudiant en théologie*. He styles himself *proposant*, and Calvin his *pastor*.

§ "*Magno assensu piorum*," says Beza, in writing to Bullinger, Aug. 27, 1553.

thereby excited most men of Christian feeling against him. Calvin's well-known expression to Farel, hastily uttered, as has been remarked, was but an outbreak of anger: it purported, that if Servetus persevered in his blasphemy he must certainly die, if Calvin's authority had any weight in Geneva. This view is supported by the words, "Add, that no danger of any great punishment hung over him, if he could possibly have been brought to his senses*." All that Calvin required was a recantation. Thus he sorrowfully exclaimed, at a later period, "Would that we could have obtained a recantation from Servetus, as we did from Gentilis!"

But notwithstanding this, he still firmly asserted the principle, that obstinate heretics, who throw all things into confusion, must be punished with death. The conduct of the council towards Servetus is easily understood, when it is recollected, what was the then state of affairs, and how involved the very existence of the civil polity was with that of the church. If the latter sunk, so must the former; if the evangelical faith ceased to prevail, the catholic must be restored, and with it the bishop. It was for this the catholics were looking, and hence the state could never be indifferent to the propagation of heresy. Nor should it be passed over, that the old ordinances of the emperors against heretics, those particularly of Frederic II., were still in force in Geneva, as in the rest of the Christian world. According to these, heretics were placed in the same rank, with regard to guilt and punishment, as traitors.

Nicolas de la Fontaine was required to state to the council the points of accusation, as drawn up by Calvin: he appeared the next day before the tribunal, and formally denounced Servetus as a heretic. Calvin relates the circumstance in his letters†, and mentions, that he had selected forty points of accusation (there are only thirty-eight‡), adding characteristically, and as if freeing himself from the heat of his passion, "that he thought Servetus would be punished with death;" that is, if nothing could be done with him. But still he was unwilling to think for a moment of his dying in the flames.

In reference to the first thirty-six articles, which regarded his doctrine, Servetus answered with candour and serenity, that he

* Refut. p. 517. Opusc. Fr. p. 1532.

† Ed. Laus. Ep. 152. Ed. Amstel. p. 70, a. "Nicolaus meus ad capitale judicium, pœnæ talionis se offerens, ipsum vocavit."

‡ See Trechsel.

acknowledged himself the author of the works named, spoke of his desire to be instructed, and then defended himself with great simplicity, asserting that he had not intended to blaspheme, and that he was ready to recant*. It was immediately objected to him, that he had said, in the seventh article, "Such a division in the being of God makes him into a tripartite God; that is, into a devil with three heads, like Cerberus, which the old poets have called a hell-hound, a monster." There were other blasphemies of a similar kind.

He did not deny this, but declared that he believed in the Trinity; only that by the term *person* he understood something different from what was meant by modern teachers. Since however he practically adhered to the blasphemy involved in the expression, the whole weight of the accusation continued to rest upon him. To the complaint, that he had defamed by means of his book, and through the person of Calvin, the religion of the city, casting all possible insults upon it, he replied, that "Calvin having formerly abused him in many of his books, he had answered him, and shown that he erred in many respects, and was inebriated in his opinions." When his book was placed before him, he observed that that manuscript had been sent six years before to Calvin, for his consideration; that it had not been printed, and still needed a thorough revision. The work 'De Trinitatis Erroribus' was not brought forward, there being no copy of it in Geneva: this appears from a letter written by Viret to Calvin†.

In the second and subsequent examinations, when it was well seen that Fontaine was in nowise equal to the task of confronting such a man, all the ministers were requested to appear. The enemies of Calvin, the leaders of the libertine party, Perrini and Wandel, were also present. Fontaine desired to be excused. Calvin now at length stood face to face with his adversary: all the points of accusation were again brought forward, and Calvin argued so powerfully and correctly, that he led Servetus to conclusions which sounded like madness, but of which, as deductions from his principles, there could be no doubt. The pantheistic tendency of his ideas led necessarily to such consequences.

In his letter to Farel, August 20th‡, Calvin says, "I will not

* Trechsel, p. 285. † Trechsel, p. 228.

‡ Ep. 152. Ed. Amstel. p. 70, 1553. The following expression occurs in this epistle: "Spero capitale saltem fore judicium, pœnæ vero atrocitatem

speak of the rashness of the man; but his frenzy was such that he did not hesitate to say, that the divinity dwells even in devils; that there are actually many gods in each, because the godhead is essentially communicated to them, as it is to wood and to stones." He speaks also of the same subject, and more fully, in the 'Refutatio*': "When he asserted that all creatures were produced from the proper essence of God, and that therefore all were filled with gods, when he blushed not to express his thoughts both in writing and by word of mouth, I was so hurt by this wretched absurdity, that I assailed him with these words: 'What, unhappy man! if any one treading upon this floor should say to you, that he was treading your God under his feet, would you not be scandalized at such an assertion?' He answered, 'I, on the contrary, do not doubt but that this footstool, or anything else which you may point out, is the substance of God.' When it was again objected to him, 'Then will the devil actually be God?' he answered, with a peal of laughter, 'And can you doubt it? This however is my general principle, that out of the substance of God all things have arisen, and that the nature of things is actually the Spirit of God†.'" These words are not in the original account of the trial: it is possible that the reporter may have omitted them from a feeling of piety; all who were present heard them.

These men, both powerful in their way, no longer exercised moderation. Servetus believed Calvin to be his personal enemy, which he in reality was not, and he consequently resigned himself to the force of his southern temperament; whereupon Calvin, according to his own confession, answered him as he deserved. Irrational heat, abuse and blasphemy, so disgusted the people, that at the end of the second examination, the judges decided that Servetus appeared to them well-deserving of punishment. It may be added, that reports were daily brought of the murder of holy confessors in France, Italy and Spain; so that it might seem ridiculous to let such a man as Servetus live. In times of wild excitement like those described, we have rather to wonder at the sedateness of his judges.

Calvin was right when, in his strong argumentation with Servetus, he said, that he threatened to overthrow all religion; for while, in his fanatical notions, he thought to restore Christianity to

remitti cupio,"—I hope that the sentence will at least be a capital one, but I wish that the severity of the punishment may be remitted.

* P. 522. † Refut. Error. p. 522.

its apostolic form, it was very evident that his doctrine was altogether opposed to the primitive belief. So also, whether the received doctrines were true or not, he ought never to have spoken of them as he did, to render them ridiculous in the eyes of the people. It could not be denied that he was endeavouring to introduce something entirely novel, but which he desired both catholics and protestants to receive as the only truth. To treat them with insult because they would not do so was the part of a rash and obstinate man, intolerant against all the world. But his love of blasphemy was the most deserving of condemnation; and if his ridicule of holy things, from which, as if it belonged to his system, he never ceased, even to the last, be excused by some as the mere result of humour, this may be taken as a sign that they are themselves indifferent to all religion. If, in the present day, a teacher should heap similar abuse on the faith of the people in the sacrament, a similar expression of indignation would be the consequence: he would be restrained, according to the laws now existing, and would lose his freedom. From the same principle, in past times, Servetus could not fail to lose his life. The Old Testament commanded that the blasphemer should be punished with death, as we still punish murder, and Servetus found his peculiar delight in laughing at that which is holy.

Fontaine was let out of prison, and Anton, Calvin's brother, became bail for him. Servetus was kept under stricter guard: Calvin assailed him with great severity from the pulpit. It was necessary to make the people acquainted with the real opinions of the Spaniard, and to resist the operations of the libertine party, who were busy with their plans. But it is laughable to hear the enemies of Calvin assert, that he increased the severity of the prisoner's treatment. In the first place, it was not his business to superintend the prison; and in the next, Servetus had pens, ink and paper, and Calvin lent him, out of his own library, whatever books he desired.

The libertine party now began to mix themselves up with the affair: they inspired the prisoner with false hopes, and advised him to attack Calvin with all the power he could. This only rendered the judges more indignant against him. Calvin, on his own part, remained unmoved by passion, although it was he, in fact, who had to bear the whole burden of the proceeding: he expressed himself, in his correspondence, in the most tranquil manner respecting Servetus. Letters, both of an earlier and later date, exist, which show that other things moved him far more than this process.

Servetus was again frequently examined. The sentence passed upon him by Œcolampadius, twenty years before, was cited. Passages were quoted from the 'Common Places' of Melancthon, in which that writer complains of his sporting with the idea of *person*, and calls him a fanatic, a deceitful and godless man. Servetus replied, that the judgements thus passed upon him were not the sentence of a magistrate. According to Calvin, he answered, that Capito and Œcolampadius had been of his opinion, and that he wondered at their having changed. Another accusation was urged, and one which shows the spirit of the age; namely, that he had vilified Moses by asserting that his account of the fruitfulness of the promised land was false. The passage indicates that in the older times certain free-thinkers endeavoured to introduce a different interpretation to that acknowledged by the church. But here there does not appear to have been any blasphemy intended. God is not mentioned; and if it be said, that the beauty of the promised land was extravagantly and falsely praised, it is a matter of wonder how a writer could be so foolish as not to see, that Palestine might formerly have been very lovely, while in later times it might be unfruitful. But as Servetus persisted in defending his position, and accused Moses of employing a vain boast, an insult seemed directed against Scripture. The remark which had been made was not scientifically critical; and if due weight be given to the known rashness of its author's character, it will be evident that he delighted in throwing ridicule on the inspiration and credibility of Moses. Thus to the accusation, founded on the above circumstance, he replied at first, with perfect confidence, "that he had not written the words imputed to him." When Calvin pressed him hard upon the point he said, "that it was not honest indeed to publish the work of another under his name." He was too petulant to prove the truth step by step, and he asserted that, even were he the author of the passage referred to, there was nothing wicked therein. Wiping his mouth, he added, "Let us proceed." Calvin answered him by the most weighty arguments*.

It appears that the proceedings were carried on partially in public. Calvin observes, in regard to the circumstance above

* Op. Fr. p. 1550.

mentioned, "That which I relate would seem incredible, if our gracious senators, and many men of importance, had not been present."

Servetus found himself in a still more perilous condition when his exposition of the Bible was brought forward: this afforded fresh evidence of his impiety. The passages chiefly objected to were selected from the 7th, 8th, and 53rd chapters of Isaiah. His principles of interpretation have been already alluded to: he insisted that these portions of the Old Testament had both an historical and a mystic-prophetic sense. The 53rd chapter ought to be understood, he said, of Cyrus in the first instance, but as also containing a prophecy of Christ. Calvin however proved, with impressive eloquence, without assailing the principle advanced by Servetus, that he was endeavouring, by the false interpretation of this chapter, to shake the foundation of Christian faith. Servetus, in fact, did not understand the doctrine of the Atonement, or how it was related to his system, and he may possibly have intended to tread this grand principle in the dust. Calvin accused him of such a wish*. "Possessed by a mad and devilish lust, he would rather overwhelm himself, shameless as he is, with guilt, than not destroy all." Servetus replied, that Nicolaus of Lyra interpreted these places of Scripture as he did. Calvin desired that the commentary of Lyra might be referred to. This being done, he convinced him that he was altogether wrong. "But," says Calvin, "he manifested no shame at this; for it was his common custom to cite authors whom he had never read."

This afforded a ready introduction to the attack upon his heresy, in respect to fundamental points, and in reference to infant baptism, which he disallowed,—a great offence at that time; the anabaptists having combined many other errors with this part of their system, and being in all countries punished with death.

When the subject of the Trinity was introduced, he called it a dream of St. Augustine, and those who believed in the doctrine, *Tritheists*. The judges treated the other matters as of comparatively little importance, but insisted strongly on the two of which they had now to speak. Servetus declared that he was only anxious to revive the original doctrine with respect to God; that he himself believed in the Trinity (this was not honestly said), and that he only called those Tritheists and Atheists who parted the unity of God. The term *person*, he added, signifies a visible manifestation of God; and he did not condemn those who adopt

* Refut. Error. p 522, b.

a certain distinction of persons, but those only who make a real distinction in the being of God. In the same manner, he stated that he had not called the real Trinity a hell-hound, but the false only. Thus also he defended himself against the complaint that he had spoken wickedly of the Son of God, and had stated that he was only so called because he consisted of the three elements of the Father, fire, air, and water. On the contrary, he asserted "that he believed in the eternal godhead of Jesus Christ, who was begotten from eternity, but conceived in time, by the Holy Ghost, in the womb of the virgin."

That he here threw a cloak over his real doctrine is certain. Pantheistic and Platonic notions lay at the root of his system: Calvin endeavoured to prove this to him. It was also deduced from his principles, that he denied the immortality of man: on this point he defended himself with more success than on the others, in regard to which he depended only upon subterfuges.

When all the several articles of accusation had been summed up, he was desired to state his belief on the peculiar being of God, and on the origin of things. This was very hard for him to do; for, according to his notion, all things were not created, but flowed from the being of God, so that He is everywhere present. He had already asserted that God's essence is in all things, but now he wished to modify his statement, and said that "God is necessarily present by his attribute of omnipresence: things are not parts of God; but the original images, the ideas or forms of all things, are in Him."

The dangerous question respecting infant baptism was next considered. This was more likely to be a source of destruction to him than any of the others on which he was examined. The Genevese council viewed him, in respect to this subject, not only as an enemy of the faith, but as the enemy of all social order. It was thus that the anabaptists were everywhere regarded.

Striking and vehement were the declarations of Servetus. "Infant baptism," he asserted, "was nowhere commanded; it was an invention of the devil. No one could commit mortal sin before his twentieth year, and it was not till then that he required redemption. Till children could understand the mystery of redemption, their sins could not be imputed to them, and an early baptism was therefore useless. He was willing however to be taught, if he was wrong."

But Calvin could not convince him of his error. This was a proof of the earnestness with which he adhered to his opinions, and how superior he now was to the weakness which he had exhibited at Vienne. The last accusation against him was, that he had vilified Calvin, and, in him, the Genevese church. This was founded on the letter in which he denounced woe to those who preached so evil a doctrine.

At the end of the examination he stated, that he had sent a part of the edition of the 'Restitutio,' through Arnoullet, to Frankfort. It was on the information thus received that Calvin wrote so earnestly to the ministers of that city*.

The judges announced, on the fourteenth day, that the accusations brought against Servetus were proved, Colladon declaring, that the evidence had been found sufficient for that purpose. According to custom, the whole affair was now to be referred to the chief procurator, whose office it was to continue the prosecution of the accused, in conformity with the law.

I now proceed to the account of another examination, which took place four days after the last, because Servetus had expressed his belief, that he had stated in his work the doctrine of the primitive church. During the intervening four days Calvin prepared himself for the approaching struggle. On the 21st of August, Servetus again stood before the council with his accusers. Calvin had not arrived: the vacant time was employed in showing Servetus a letter in which Arnoullet directed the bookseller Vertet, at Chatillon, to burn all the books of the Spaniard found in Frankfort. He had been deceived, he said, through Queroult, who proposed to translate the work into French, and he had no knowledge whatever of the heretical nature of its contents.

Calvin now entered, with the ministers. The dispute which was to be decided, and by such opponents, could not fail to be interesting in the highest degree to theologians. A little misunderstanding occurred at the beginning. Calvin sought to prove that the holy *Trias* was acknowledged by Ignatius, Polycarp, Irenæus, and Tertullian, before the Nicene council, in the same sense as by the later fathers. When Justin was mentioned, and Calvin, holding the book in his hand, illustrated his argument from its pages, Servetus requested a Latin translation. Calvin answered that there was none. Servetus, the editor of several learned works, made no apology for this, his insufficient knowledge of Greek, strange as the circumstance must have seemed.

In the argument which ensued, it was Calvin's object to show, that the word ὑπόστασις is to be found in the ancient writers, as

* Ed. Laus. Ep. 153, Amst. p. 71 : August 27, 1553.

in Tertullian: they therefore acknowledged an actual distinction in the divine essence. Servetus, on the other hand, sought to prove, that these writers only intended to speak of a visible manifestation of Deity. The war of words here became so fierce, that the reformer, whom Servetus loaded with unmeasured abuse, mindful of his dignity, considered it prudent to leave his seat. He retired, with all the ministers.

Servetus remained alone on the arena. He expressed his wish to buy several books; many even of those which Calvin had brought with him into the hall: this was readily allowed him. He took Irenæus, Tertullian, Ignatius, and a fourth book, in order to draw up his defence.

A petition, which he presented on the 24th of August, remained unnoticed. He prayed therein to be allowed to go free. According to the practice, he said, of the primitive church, heresies were never judged by the civil power, but by the church itself, which banished the offender. Nor could he, he added, be lawfully punished, seeing that he had committed no offence in the territory of Geneva, and was altogether opposed to the course taken by the anabaptists. Lastly, he desired the aid of legal advisers. But, in the meantime, the examination commenced on the 23rd of August was continued. The chief procurator had laid thirty questions before the accused. Servetus, who now discovered the great danger of his position, prayed imploringly to be liberated. His answers however were given quietly, because perhaps his chief antagonist was not present. He excused the publication of his works on the plea of his good intentions. By the restoration of Christianity, he meant the establishment of true doctrine. He did not believe, he now said, that the churches of Geneva and Germany were on the way to destruction: his strong expressions had reference only to scholastic disputes. If he had erred on the subject of infant baptism, he was ready to recant. To the accusation that he had used the Koran, he answered, that this book had been printed at Basel*, and with the letters of the Zurich ministers. He had only desired to tread in the paths of the ancient doctors of the church.

At the examination held on the 28th of August, the business was well nigh brought to a close†. The judge-advocate proved, that the grounds on which Servetus had founded his petition

* He referred to Bibliander's edition of the old version by Peter, abbot of Clugny. See Trechsel, p. 235.

† See Trechsel, p. 303.

could not be allowed. He adduced the laws of the church, which required that heretics should be punished, wherever they might be found; and he was sure, he added, that the prisoner's own conscience would condemn him to death, if he honestly consulted it. There was no doubt of his agreement with the anabaptists, and justice forbad that an advocate should be accorded to such deceivers*.

For the rest, Servetus had gained in fortitude and prudence. Though he still sought some subterfuge by which to escape, it was now that the grace of God began to move his heart, and to prepare him for death. It is probable that he found support in prayer. At this examination, in which sentence was pronounced upon him, he no longer asked for mercy, but declared that he would abide by his convictions. He continued, in all his speeches, to express himself with fearful violence against Calvin†, and the chief-procurator was now the most active in the business. Calvin however was intimately associated with Colladon, and was himself a lawyer. The judicial sentence, as has been remarked, is also in the hand of one of Calvin's amanuenses; so that it might be imagined, that this last document was even drawn up by Calvin. But a nearer examination of the instrument will show the improbability of this notion: it is full of confusion, and is altogether deficient in argument. The writer passes from doctrine to law, and refers again and again to the life of Servetus, a method altogether contrary to the clear style of Calvin. He appears therefore at most to have been only aware that the document was being drawn up.

The three points advanced by the accused in his petition were rejected, and it was announced to him that the law, with which he was well acquainted, condemned him as a heretic‡. Thirty-eight new questions were now proposed. In an additional examination, at which Calvin was present, Servetus defended his assertion, that the ancient church did not punish heretics. He also apologized for what he had said against the ministers of the reformed doctrine, and justified the statement which he had made as to his agreement with Capito and Œcolampadius. Further, he declared that he was ready to alter his opinions, if he could be shown by Scripture that they were wrong. He therefore desired that opportunity might be allowed him, either

* Bibl. Angl. ii. p. 142.

† Thus he called him, "Simo Magus, impostor, sycophanta, ridiculus mus, cacodæmon, homicida."

‡ Trechsel, p. 236, 237. Processacten, p. 307.

to prove the truth of his doctrine, or to recant. This would have been to repeat the whole process from the beginning.

In the midst of these proceedings, that is, on the 31st of August, the superintendent of the Palace of Justice at Vienne, in which Servetus had been confined, presented himself, with a petition, that the escaped heretic might be delivered again into his hands, so that they might execute the sentence passed upon him at Vienne. Servetus was led forth, and the superintendent having been called in, the former was asked if he knew him. He answered in the affirmative, adding, that he was two days under his guard, and had been twice examined. The council wisely decided that it must be left to the choice of Servetus himself to which tribunal he would submit. He now threw himself upon his knees, and prayed, with a flood of tears, the magistrates of Geneva to continue his judges, and to do with him what they would. He again ascribed his sufferings to the personal hatred of Calvin. But he made, on this occasion, a noble, penitent confession. Lamenting his hypocrisy, he acknowledged that he had written fiercely against the Mass, whilst he continued to partake of it among the catholics. "I sinned," he said, "but the dread of death urged me to it." The superintendent departed, after obtaining from Servetus a declaration, that the gaoler was not privy to his escape. All this took place in the month of August. On the 1st of September another messenger arrived. He brought a letter from the Sieur de Maugiron, to whose son the king had sold the property of the prisoner. This gentleman requested Servetus to name all the persons indebted to him; but Servetus was unwilling to do this, lest he might thereby throw several poor persons into difficulty. The council approved of his conduct in this respect. On the same day Calvin, accompanied by the ministers, appeared again before the council, and Servetus was especially admonished to honour the truth. When Calvin, who had collected all the objectionable passages in the writings of the accused, began to make the experiment of inducing him to recant, he answered, that inward care prevented him now from considering these things; and he laid it down as a principle, that matters of faith were not to be debated before a civil tribunal, but only before one appointed for that purpose. Nor was it very convenient, he added, to handle questions of this kind in a prison.

Calvin declared, in reply, that he should very willingly carry on the dispute in the church, and before the people, for he defended that which was right; but it was not contrary to the law to discuss such things before a civil tribunal. According to the code of the emperor Justinian, which was still in force, heretics were to be treated as malefactors. Servetus therefore, he asserted, suffered no injustice in being brought before the present court, in which also the church was represented by its ministers, engaged to convert him.

Servetus answered, that, in the time of Justinian, the church had already lost its original innocence and purity; and further, that the church of Geneva could not rightly judge him, Calvin, his enemy, being its very life and soul. He submitted himself solemnly to the churches abroad. But he could not make this appeal with any degree of consistency: he had claimed superiority to both catholics and protestants. Had he retained his lofty pretensions, therefore, he must have insisted on being tried by a council of all the various churches of Christendom. Calvin was quite ready to consent, that the opinions of other churches should be collected, as in early times; but he and Servetus could not agree on the starting-point. They were therefore obliged to separate; and the council, which was influenced by a spirit of moderation, determined that, to avoid excitement, Calvin and Servetus should carry on their dispute in writing. The former was to make extracts, in Latin, from the writings of Servetus, for the use of the Swiss; and Servetus was to answer in Latin, and by writing. An indefinite time was allowed him, so that he might retract what he found wrong, and could rectify any perversion of his meaning. The papers, on both sides, should afterwards be forwarded to the Swiss churches, and await their judgement.

The magistrates now expressed their wish, with marked thoughtfulness and caution, that the business might be submitted to the decision of a spiritual tribunal. Calvin spent fourteen days on his new labour. He probably did not require so long a period; a single evening would have been sufficient for the work; but he wished to give Servetus time to collect and tranquillize himself. But whatever was attempted for his good, served only to injure him. He lost all patience. In a petition which he addressed to the council, he stated that he had been now five months in prison, that he still desired the aid of an advocate, and that he wished his cause to be brought before the Council of

Two Hundred, to which he would submit himself. He added, that he would bring a counter-accusation against Calvin.

In this useless and unmeaning petition, he very distinctly retracted his appeal to a spiritual tribunal, because the civil power was incompetent to determine matters of faith. He fell at once from his lofty height into the dust. His present course could have been dictated by no prudent counsellor; he must have adopted it from the suggestion of the party opposed to Calvin. Amied Perrini, the soul of that party, had a majority in the Council of Two Hundred, and made use of Servetus to overcome Calvin, whose position at that time was very uncertain. Servetus knew nothing of the constitution of the Genevese republic, but his appeal indicated a thorough knowledge of its institutions on the part of his adviser. The council rejected his petition, but ordered that he should be better treated in prison. That he was urged forward by the enemies of Calvin appears evident from a letter of the reformer to Farel, in which he relates, that Perrini had appeared in the council for Servetus, and demanded that the business should be brought before the "Two Hundred." Advice was also given the accused to ingratiate himself with the libertine party, and to heap abuse on Calvin*. It was at this period that the attempts of that faction were made to set aside the right of excommunication and the rules of discipline.

Two letters were interchanged between them. Calvin produced thirty-eight points, distinctly heretical, without any addition or remark; they were derived exclusively from the last work of Servetus. The objections therefore to the inspiration of the Mosaic Scriptures, and those which respected the interpretation of the Bible, were no longer the question; but there were the most horrible blasphemies against the fundamental principles of divine truth, against the person of Christ, the Holy Spirit, immortality, and infant baptism.

Servetus replied to Calvin's accusation: "He had assumed to himself a species of Sorbonne authority, without understanding what was meant. His simple object was to show, that when Christ is called in Scripture the Son of God, this is always as the man Christ. The second person in the godhead is called a person, because a personal exhibition of the man Jesus had already taken place, hypostatically, in God, and this might be proved by numberless passages from the old fathers."

* Bibl. Angl. ii. p. 161. Ruchat, vi. p. 36.

This statement is followed by an expression of immoderate hatred against Calvin. The writer reminded him, that the rashness of a man was deserving of all wonder, who dare assert himself to be a true believer, when he was in reality a disciple of Simon Magus, as he, Servetus, had manifestly shown in his Apology*. "Who will say," he asked, "that a criminal accuser and a murderer can be a servant of the church?" He now repeated, in few words, haughtily, and with intense contempt of his antagonist, "Thou art a pitiful wretch, if thou continuest to condemn things which thou understandest not. Art thou not ashamed to assert so much and without reason? Thinkest thou to deceive the ears of the judges, simply and solely through thy howling? Thou hast a dull perception, and canst not comprehend the truth. Wretch! thou knowest not the reason of things. Wretch! disciple of Simon Magus! thou art altogether ignorant, and desirest to make us wood and stone by thy notion of fate. Thou art only dreaming with the sorcerer."

The accusations brought against himself, Servetus treated with the greatest indifference, as if it did not really concern him to attempt a justification of his conduct, or as if he had no idea of the good intentions of the council, of the rights and sanctity of the church, of the state of affairs in general, or of his own.

It was only as a reply to the clergy that this hateful document was received. The council, weary of the matter, gave the ministers but two days in which to consider it. Servetus sent their answer back with great contempt, and accompanied by malicious and wrathful marginal notes. It was like the raving of a madman. To the first accusation, Calvin fairly answered, that it was simply in obedience to the command of the council, against which Servetus made no complaint, that he had selected the passages exhibiting his principal errors. He had performed this task with all honesty†.

Calvin shows, in the next place, that it was the object of Servetus to prove, that Christ, the Word, was not in God, and begotten from eternity; and that he had loaded those who receive this truth with every species of abuse. He then assails the error of Servetus, and shows that he fully comprehended his meaning, and that Christ is not simply ideally, but really in God.

This development of Calvin's doctrine is accompanied with many reproaches against his antagonist. The passages adduced

* Apologia, 674, 701.

† Refut. Error. p. 528, b.

by Servetus in defence of his system are employed in confuting it. He is called a heretic and a monster. "The Clemens," it is said, "whom he quotes, was written by a foolish monk. He avoids those places which prove the contrary of what he asserts. Thus he has altogether forgotten to cite Ignatius, because that father would testify against him. Proceeding with his abuse, he has called Calvin a murderer, to show probably how skilled he is in this species of insult*. He repeats a hundred times such expressions as these in his marginal notes: "Thou dreamest: thou liest." Here we read: "Well, well, thou disciple of Simon Magus, if thou deny that thou art an assassin, I will prove it to thee by thine own conduct. Thou darest not deny that thou art Simon the magician, whoever may believe and think that thou art a good tree. I adhere to this righteous cause, and fear not death†." This is followed by a full confutation of the errors advanced by Servetus, with the just remark, that, whereas he had continually spoken of the doctrine of the Trinity with contempt, he now pretended to acknowledge a distinction of persons, and to view it as threefold. The observation made by Mosheim on this subject will excite surprise: he considers that Calvin must have opposed Servetus on new grounds, in order to win him to his opinion. But the reformer saw well enough that he could do little with this perverse man, who had already heard so often that which he had to say. Calvin was justified in observing, when speaking on the subject of infant baptism, that it did not become any one who pretended to the slightest degree of gentleness or candour to rave as Servetus did, and call infant baptism a scandal, "a detestable abomination." "We do not doubt," Calvin had observed, "but that God upholds all things by his power; but it does not follow from this position, that there is an essential Deity in all things: still less can it be argued, that the floor on which we tread is a part of the godhead, and that all the devils are full of the divine essence, as Servetus asserted at his examination."

In answer to this, the latter remarked, "That is all one. Thou hast heard from Irenæus and others, that 'being,' or 'substance,' is that which supports us. But moving thy foot, thou deniest that it is moved in God. Thus thou wouldst move in Satan. We on the contrary assert, that we move in God, in whom we live; and thou, though a devil, must also move in him."

* Refut. Error. p. 527, b.

† Refut. Error. p. 528, a. b. and p. 533, a. Opusc. Fr. pp. 1567 and 1582.

And further: "I would fain make a list of thine errors. He who is not Simon Magus is, according to Calvin, a Pelagian. The whole body of Christians, consequently, are condemned by him; even the apostles, and the disciples of the apostles, and the doctors of the church; for none of them rejected free-will, as this sorcerer has done. Thou liest, thou liest, thou liest, thou most wicked, wretched monster!"

Servetus also objected to Calvin, that he condemned astrology, while he was ignorant of its nature: "So great is thy impudence that thou judgest of things of which thou knowest nothing, for thy science extendeth not beyond thy grammar*. I am not confuted by Scripture: I stand alone; but Christ is my defender†."

To this document Servetus added a letter to the council, in which he apologized for his marginal notes; and another to Calvin, as if it had been the proper time to accuse him of not being acquainted with philosophy and the natural sciences. "All action takes place through contact; God, consequently, must be in everything in order to give it movement." And further: "No one dare now assert that the law of Moses is still in force."

The frantic passion which Servetus thus exhibited estranged all parties, and wholly deprived him of their respect. They had expected a sensible answer to the accusations of his opponents. No further reply was given to what he had written. The clearest proofs now existed that his obstinate spirit was wrought upon by malicious feeling. He might have been left to the enjoyment of his own convictions, but he was bound to respect and suffer the belief of his antagonists; and he ought, at least, to have expressed regret at having so unreasonably troubled and scandalized worthy and simple Christians, yea, even the entire church.

Calvin says, in reference to what took place before the council, and when freedom was given him to dispute: "I stood before him humbly and patiently, as if I myself had been the prisoner. I was present to bear testimony to the truth of my doctrine. He took every opportunity to abuse me roundly; so much so, that the judges were shocked at his conduct; but I restrained myself from repaying him as he deserved. He would not, indeed, have been in danger of any severe punishment, if he had only conducted himself with moderation, and had afforded any hope of his repenting. But so far was he from this, that,

* Refut. Error. ed. Amst. p. 537. Op. Fr. 1595. † Mosheim, s. 199.

full of wrath and boasting, he utterly rejected all sound and useful admonition. Let it not be said that it was a laudable firmness which induced him to persevere in his confession; for at Vienne he was ready to deny it all, merely to save his life."

It is certainly remarkable, that Servetus now exhibited such an unbending firmness; nor can we say whether it was the consequence of his hatred to Calvin, a fanatical love of his own errors, or of a false security, nourished by the encouragement of the libertine party.

On the 21st of September the interchanged papers were sent with the 'Restitutio' to the churches of Zurich, Bern, Basel, and Schaffhausen. The council requested their opinion on the affair. Calvin had already, on the 7th of the same month, made Bullinger acquainted with the whole of the proceedings*.

That eminent man was the chief promoter of the pacific sentiments, which led to the good understanding existing between the churches of Switzerland, and that of Geneva. At his entreaty, Haller wrote from Bern to Sulzer in Basel. As an illustration of the feeling with which the best men in the country regarded the punishment of heretics, it must be remarked, that Farel opposed Calvin, and advocated putting them to death by fire. In this he agreed with the otherwise benevolent Bullinger, and both exhorted Calvin to be firm and severe. Thus Farel says to him: "It will be a wonder if that man suffering death, should, at the time, earnestly turn to the Lord, dying only one death, whereas he has deserved to die many thousand times; and a wonder it will be, if he should endeavour to edify those present, —he who has sought to destroy so many of those who are already gone, of those who now live, or are still to be born. Adversaries of Christ, and true enemies of the church, will the judges be, if they do not show themselves moved by the horrible blasphemies of this godless heretic, who has so assailed the divine majesty, and laboured to undermine the Word of God, and to destroy the churches. But I do hope that the Lord will so order it, that they who are praised for their righteous sentences on robbers, and on those guilty of sacrilege, will so act, that they will, in this case also, obtain a good report, by putting to death a man who has so long persevered in his heresy, and has involved so many others in misery. If it be thy wish to lighten the horror of the punishment due to such an offender, then wilt thou be acting as a friend towards thy bitterest enemy. But I beseech thee not

* MS. Gen. 7 Idus Sept. 1553. i. p. 95.

to act so as to encourage others to introduce new doctrines among the people, and to hope that they may pursue, uninterruptedly, the same course as Servetus."

Bullinger wrote: "The Lord has given this Spaniard into the hands of your senate. If the council, therefore, assign to this wretch the punishment due to his crimes, the whole world will see that the Genevese hate blasphemers; that they will pursue obstinate heretics with the sword of righteousness, and will avenge the honour of the divine majesty. If, on the contrary, they delay to do this, thou must not neglect the congregation: were you to do so many other evils would arise. Pursue thy course then, unterrified. Trust in God, through Christ. Beseech Him to give thee counsel and help, that He may deliver thee from this peril. We will aid thee with our prayers."

Calvin had written, in the mean time, to the minister Sulzer, at Basel, where the Genevese had many enemies, Castellio among the rest, in order to make him acquainted with the whole business*.

During the progress of this correspondence, the affair at Geneva was quietly drawing towards its conclusion. Servetus, as we have stated, had allowed himself to be tempted, by the enemies of Calvin, to assail the reformer as a mortal enemy; as a false accuser, an unworthy servant of God; as a foe to Christ, and a heretic. He even desired to see him banished the land; the proper punishment, according to his view, of heretics. This was the anxious wish of the libertines; and could it have been effected, Servetus would then have taken his place as a reformer in Geneva, and have destroyed its church.

The accusation which Servetus brought against Calvin may appear an absurdity; but it must be observed, that the party by which he was led, was now ready to venture all to accomplish some important purpose. The most senseless part of the complaint is that which accuses Calvin of sorcery, and the proposal to deprive him of his property, it being well known that he possessed none.

Servetus could certainly not effect his purpose by means so ridiculous as these. The council, which was firm and prudent, refused to receive the complaint, and transferred it to the ordinary "Acts." Servetus then besought an audience; but this was also refused. He now sent a brief letter of remonstrance, complaining of his painful position. This was on the 10th of

* Calv. Epist. 156. Ed. Amst. p. 70. Sept. 9, 1553.

P 2

October. Calvin in the mean time informed his friends, that the hostile party was earnestly engaged in its tumultuous opposition to the church; and that he wished that Farel and Viret were with him at so important a juncture. His position had never been more dangerous. It is characteristic of his nature, that, at a period like this, he could take part in the minutest affairs which were interesting to others. Thus he communicated to his friend the news of the marriage of one of their acquaintances*. That the affair of Servetus would have a very serious termination he states as a thing evident of itself. The Swiss clergy had already, that is, at the beginning of October, come to a decision on the subject. It was soon commonly reported that their sentence was adverse to Servetus. Some voices were immediately raised in his favour. An anabaptist, David Georgii, or Joris†, who, under the name of Johann von Brück, had found refuge at Basel, and was beloved and honoured in the reformed church, seems to have regarded Servetus as a brother, because of his views on baptism. Excited by personal considerations against intolerance, he wrote, but without naming himself, to the Swiss communities, exhorting them to oppose the clergy. "It is an incredible blindness," he said, "that the servants of Christ, who are sent to give life to the dead through the knowledge of the truth, should condemn the erring to death, and through temporal death expose their souls to eternal ruin. The right to pass such a sentence belongs to Him alone who gave life, and suffered death for our redemption. Were it lawful to put heretics to death, there would be a general slaughter, for all religious parties regard their opponents as guilty of heresy. If Servetus (whom he calls good and pious) be a heretic, he ought to be admonished in a friendly manner, and then banished the state. The Lord himself will slay all false teachers with the breath of his mouth, and not with the sword. The tares must be left to grow up with the wheat, and await the judgement which will take place at the end of the world."

An Italian lawyer, Gribaldo‡, at Geneva, also made a similar appeal for Servetus; but it came too late.

The authorities at Zurich did not take long to consider the subject. They received the writings from Geneva on the 28th of September, and on the 2nd of October they replied, that,

* MS. Gen. Oct. 14, 1553. † See Mosheim.

‡ The error of Servetus respecting Christ, as the Son of God, in his human nature only, greatly pleased Gribaldo. (Trechsel, p. 254.)

"According to the advice of their ministers, they now admonished the Genevese to exercise such severity, that the wicked and deceitful intentions of their prisoner might not be accomplished, for that his doctrines were totally contrary to the Christian religion, and gave great scandal and offence*." The ministers of Zurich agreed with Calvin throughout; and though they would not determine respecting the punishment to be inflicted on the prisoner, they readily united in exhorting the Genevese to exercise great severity, and added a prayer, that the Lord might give them wisdom.

From Schaffhausen the council wrote, that it had consulted with the clergy, and now forwarded their letter to Geneva. These ministers went farther than those of Zurich. "We doubt not," they say, "that you will frustrate, according to your great wisdom, the designs of Servetus, and prevent his blasphemies from feeding, like a scorpion, on the members of Christ. But if you were only to resist his mad inventions with long argumentation, this would be merely to rave with the raving†." This is one of the strongest expressions used on the occasion.

The senate at Basel still recollected the controversy which Servetus carried on with Œcolampadius: they laid the papers before the clergy. "All the old heresies," said the latter, "are revived by Servetus. With regard to himself, you must employ all diligence to convert him: it is by this means only that you can allay the agitation which he has excited. If however he be incurable, and continue hardened in his wickedness, he must be chastised according to the power given you by the Lord, and as it will be your duty to proceed, so that he may be prevented from bringing further shame upon the church, lest the last state should be worse than the first‡."

In a letter to Farel§, Calvin, having briefly announced the end of the process, characterizes the brethren of Zurich as *omnium vehementissimi*, because they expressed themselves so sternly on the atrocity of the Spaniard's impiety; and those of Basel as *cordati*. The letter from the Bernese (on whom he passes no judgement) and that of their council also arrived: "Our friends," says Calvin, "were greatly moved thereby."

The Bernese ministers, although they condemned Servetus,

* Bibl. Angl. 1717, Art. 7, p. 163.
† Ep. 158. Ed. Amst. p. 74.
‡ Ed. Laus. Ep. 160. Ed. Amst. p. 72.
§ Ep. 161.

expressed themselves in conclusion as follows*: "We pray the Lord that He may lend you the spirit of wisdom and power, that you may thereby drive this pest from your church and from other communities, and at the same time may do nothing which can seem unworthy of Christian magistrates." But the general language of the document was strong and severe, and the council of Geneva felt itself confirmed in the zeal which it had displayed. On a former occasion, the Bernese had advocated tolerance. In one of Haller's letters to Bullinger† it is said, that the Bernese magistrates, when they learnt the opinion of the ministers on Servetus, were so excited, that they would have burnt him on the spot. The blasphemies which he had uttered terrified them, and they feared for the peace of the land. "We must swallow," they said, "what the Genevese have prepared for us in the way of agitation." In the letter of the Bernese council to the Genevese it is said, "We pray you, doubting not that such is your desire, to use a firm hand, that sects and heresies, whether those now spoken of, or others like them, may not be planted in the church of Christ, our only Saviour; and that so you may avoid trouble and adversity, and effectually advance his glory‡."

CHAPTER V.

SERVETUS CONDEMNED TO DEATH.—HIS LAST HOURS IN PRISON.—HIS EXECUTION.—AN INQUIRY INTO THE CIRCUMSTANCES ATTENDING IT.—REVIEW OF HIS DOCTRINES.

Although the Swiss had not distinctly stated their opinion as to the death which Servetus ought to suffer, it is evident that they wished his death. The ministers of Zurich and Basel prayed that the Genevese might be endowed with wisdom. What they meant by this is very clear, when we recollect the condemnation of Gentilis at Bern, and the burning of the bones

* Ep. 163. Ed. Amst. p. 73.

† See Mosheim in Neue Nachr.

‡ See Schellhorn, who, in Actis Historico-Ecclesiasticis Sæculi xv. et xvi. p. 217, has given a document, which the Bernese ministers laid before the council, on the subject of Servetus.

of Joris at Basel. All expressed their desire that Servetus might no longer be allowed to disturb either the Genevese, or any other community. This was in fact to pronounce his doom. Banishment would merely have transferred the heretic to some other church. They seem to have been only prevented by Christian horror from writing down what they meant. No idea was likely to be entertained of perpetual imprisonment, when capital punishment was the order of the day. Still, that by fire is not mentioned. Calvin says, "All, with one mouth, declared, that Servetus has renewed those impious errors by which Satan, in early times, disturbed the church; and that he is a monster not to be endured."

However, therefore, the clergy might hesitate, they yet generally inclined to severity*. It is also to be borne in mind, that the Swiss Confessions imposed it as a duty on the civil magistrate to punish blasphemers with the sword†.

The proceedings had now reached their last stage. It was not lawful for the lesser council to pronounce sentence of death, without having previously conferred with that of "The Sixty," and obtained a majority of votes‡. The discussions of the council lasted three days. Opinions were greatly divided. Some of the members advocated perpetual banishment; others perpetual imprisonment; but the greater number were in favour of capital punishment. But of what kind? The majority determined upon that by fire, according to the old law, unless the prisoner should recant.

It may have been owing to the difficulty of coming to any conclusion, in the agitated assembly of a republic, that the council would not, or could not, afterwards alter the decision at which it had once arrived. It was now that Perrini represented himself, for four days, sick. He, and other enemies of the church party, weakly retreated, when they ought to have come most boldly forward. In a letter of Calvin to Bullinger§ he says, "What will become of the man I know not: as far as I can understand, sentence will be pronounced tomorrow, and executed the day after." It was not till the last day, that the council resolved upon condemning the prisoner to die by fire.

* We must, on this point, agree with Armand de la Chapelle against Mosheim.

† "Magistratus stringat Dei gladium in omnes blasphemos." Conf. Helv. cap. xxx.

‡ Bibl. Raisonné, t. ii. pt. i. p. 105.

§ Ed. Laus. Ep. 162. Ed. Amst. p. 78, Oct. 25.

Perrini now appeared; but it was too late: he made an attempt, but it was fruitless. "Our play-house Cæsar," says Calvin *, "after pretending a three-days' sickness, presented himself at length in the council, to save this malefactor from punishment. He did not blush to express his wish that the whole business should be transferred to the 'Two Hundred.' But Servetus has been condemned, without dispute; and will, to-morrow, be led to execution." The lesser council, it appears, was unanimous.

As soon as Calvin heard that the assembly, in its zeal, had gone too far, he called the ministers together; and they, with one voice, besought the council to soften the mode of execution. Another colour, in fact, had been given to the whole proceeding, by dooming the culprit to the flames. Calvin had already said to Farel, "I think he will be condemned to die; but I wish that what is horrible in the punishment may be spared him†." We have seen the answer of Farel, who was altogether of another opinion. Calvin now wrote to him, "We have endeavoured to change the mode of execution, but without avail: I will tell you, by word of mouth, why we could do nothing‡." Farel received no more information by letter: he had come suddenly to Geneva.

The last hours of Servetus were the best in his life: his improvement began with his misfortunes; as if the Spirit of the Lord had found the way to his heart, through sorrow and the expectation of death, and had thus rapidly developed his capability of good. He was now about forty-four years of age; but during the short period of his imprisonment at Vienne, his mind had advanced more rapidly than during the whole of his earlier career. This was most conspicuously the case at the last. It is certain, however, that he still failed in acquiring a thorough knowledge of himself.

We find that it was his blasphemy, his rash jesting with holy things,—the insult with which he had treated the majesty of God, which weighed heaviest upon him§. The judges passed over everything else; such as his supposed pantheism, his rejecting the prophecies of Isaiah, and his doubts respecting the spirituality of the soul. Instead of insisting on these things, they confined their attention to that which he had said on the person of Christ, without plunging into the depths of speculation. That

* Ed. Laus. Ep. 161. Ed. Amst. p. 71, to Farel, Oct. 26.

† Ed. Laus. Ep. 152, Aug. 20. Ed. Amst. p. 70.

‡ Ed. Laus. Ep. 161. Ed. Amst. p. 71.

§ Beza, Vita Calv.

however which all regarded with the greatest horror was his blasphemy: his insult of the majesty of God was viewed alike by all. Calvin in his last admonition, and Farel in his address, at the place of execution, and also in his letter to Blaarer, insist on this; and here the offender still remained unbending as iron. He could not be induced to ask for forgiveness, or to retract his infamous expressions. Hence it was that he could not die tranquilly; and that all future generations will lift up the stone against him.

We would fain pass with him these last two days of his unhappy life. He regarded it as a matter of conscience not to think, for a moment, of retracting: and this creates a certain degree of interest in his favour. The gaoler opened the door of the prison; the officers of justice entered, and read to him the sentence, "that he was on the following morning to be burnt alive, and his body consumed to ashes." He remained dumb for a moment, as if a thunderbolt had struck him. Then, after deep sighs which resounded through the hall in which he was seated, groans and howlings followed, like those of a madman*. At last he cried, "Have mercy, have mercy!" A true martyr would now have found strength to praise God for giving him so glorious an opportunity of bearing testimony to the faith. How differently did the five confessors at Lyons, like numberless others of the same spirit, walk to the place of execution, singing as they went the ninth Psalm! The only appearance of dignity which Servetus manifested was when, ceasing to rave, he suddenly mastered himself, and expressed a general repentance.

We have no record how he spent the night, but the next day he was calmer. It was the 27th of October, an autumnal day in that beautiful country, where the neighbouring hills are often seen covered with snow, while the valley still glows with the richest tints of the season, the glaciers of Savoy rising majestically in their glittering vest above all. The words of Servetus indicated, on this day, a mingling of Christian feeling with his depraved notions, and a sentiment which, in relation to his enemy, had something in it noble. When the heart bears such fruit, as reconciliation with enemies, an earnest desire to pray for forgiveness, and a certain trust in God, there appears to be some truth in its sentiments, even though its convictions may want the clearness given by the Spirit.

The excellent Farel was with the prisoner by seven o'clock in

* Op. Fr. p. 1552. Calv. Refut. Error. Serv. p. 523.

the morning: this was in conformity with the express wish of Calvin, who desired him to accompany the wretched man to the place of execution. The Genevese ministers who had borne witness against him could not well perform this duty. Farel has left us an account of the proceedings*. This holy man easily inspired confidence, and Servetus could have desired no better companion on his last journey, to him so terrible. Even to us it seems as if a heavy weight were about our feet. We feel with what different eyes the unhappy Servetus must have surveyed the heavens, and the surrounding landscape as he approached the place of execution, and as he prepared to leave a world which he had been accustomed to look at in the splendour of his imaginary reformation.

Farel, who was intent upon leading his soul to the true faith, began again to speak of his errors, and then passed to the subject of Christian love. He besought him "to repent of his sins, and to confess the God who had thrice revealed himself." But the unhappy man persevered in his original statement, and required that it should be proved to him from Scripture, that Christ was called the Son of God before he became man. Farel answered him, but he could not be convinced of his error: he had nothing to reply, but remained impenetrable and obstinate. The struggle was long-continued, and the hour of execution drew near. Farel, therefore, and some ministers from the country who were then present, warned him, that if he would die as a Christian, he must be reconciled to Calvin, whom he had treated so unjustly. Servetus consented. Calvin was sent for, and appeared accompanied by two members of the council, probably on the supposition that the prisoner might still retract.

Servetus received Calvin tranquilly. The solemnity of the hour of death had sharpened his conscience, and tamed his pride and wrath. Calvin himself has described these last moments: "When one of the members of the council asked him what he wished with me, he answered, that he desired to ask my forgiveness. I readily answered, and it was strictly the truth, that I had never sought to resent any personal affront received from him. I also tenderly reminded him, that sixteen years before, I had diligently sought, at the hourly peril of my own life, to win him to the Lord; that it was not my fault that all pious people had

* In a letter to Blaarer (Blaurer). An extract only of this letter is given in Hottinger, s. 803; and in Ruchat, t. vi. p. 51. The document was communicated literally, to the author, by Orelli, the librarian at Zurich.

not extended the hand of friendship towards him, and that this would have been the case, had he but shown some degree of judgement; that although he had taken to flight, I had still continued to correspond peaceably with him; that, in a word, no duty of kindness had been neglected on my part, till, embittered by my free and candid warnings, he had resigned himself not merely to a feeling of anger, but to absolute wrath against me. Turning however from that which concerned myself, I prayed him to implore the forgiveness of God, whom he had so awfully blasphemed, seeking to annihilate the threefold personality, and calling it a three-headed hell-hound, whenever mention was made of a distinction between Father, Son, and Holy Ghost. I besought him to seek the pardon of the Son of God, whom he had dishonoured by his heresies, denying that Christ, by the human nature which He had taken, had become like us; and thus destroying the band of brotherly union between us and the Saviour, and our only hope of deliverance." But Servetus gave him no answer. Calvin continues: "When I found that I could effect nothing by my arguments and persuasions, I would not attempt to be wiser than the precept of the Master. I withdrew from the presence of a man who had sinned as a heretic, and was condemned of himself. Titus, iii. 10, 11*." And thus Calvin and Servetus parted.

As soon as Calvin was gone, Servetus continued his preparation, with prayer and supplication. He said once, in confidence, to Farel, that he had learnt much from a man who had no little name. "But I know," says Farel, "that he both thought and wrote in after-times very differently. I do not doubt, however, but that he had been not a little harmed by the Rabbinical writings; of which Erasmus somewhere says, that such impious productions ought to be avoided, or read with great caution, to prevent their poisonous influence." Farel says further: "A few hours before his execution he struck his breast, and cried aloud to God, aloud to Christ, praying for forgiveness, and acknowledging Jesus as his Reedemer." But Farel adds, that when he had declared the necessity of punishment for heresy, "the unhappy man could not be brought to confess, in truth, that Christ was the eternal Son of God, but only that He was the Son of God, because God had miraculously created

* Calvin describes the scene in the prison. Refut. Error. Serv. p. 511. They spoke in French, and the very words are reported in the Opusc. Fr. p. 1508.

Him in the womb of the Virgin." Farel calls him, repeatedly, *miser* and *infelix*, a proof that his impressions respecting him were very distressing.

The council continued assembled throughout the morning, either in the hope that he might retract, or to pronounce its final judgement upon him. Servetus was led before it, and the staff was broken over him. The sentence was next read. The unhappy prisoner cast himself at the feet of the magistrate*, and this at the moment when a martyr would have raised victoriously his eyes to heaven. He prayed that they might put him to death with the sword, lest by great pain he might be driven to despair, and so lose his soul. If he had sinned, he said, he had done so through want of knowledge, for it had been his will and his aim to promote the glory of God.

Servetus did not seem to feel the humiliating nature of his entreaty. Farel however interrupted him, and said, that he must first acknowledge his wickedness; and that then he might ask for mercy. Servetus answered, "that he suffered innocently; that he was led to death as a sacrifice; but that he prayed God to forgive his accusers."

Farel regarded these words as insulting in the mouth of so wretched a criminal, thus pretending to play the martyr. He addressed him, therefore, with severity; threatened to leave him to the judgement of God, if he continued thus to speak; said that he had hoped that he would edify the people, and would entreat them to pray for him. It was only with this thought that he had been induced to accompany him to the last. Servetus was silent, and made no further appeal.

But Farel, who had a tender heart, was deeply moved, and, addressing the council, he earnestly implored it to soften the punishment, although originally, as we have seen, he was in favour of the burning. The members of the council, however, were so horrified at the wickedness of Servetus, that they remained inflexible, and answered, that a sentence so passed could not be altered.

We now behold Servetus feebly descending the steps of the senate-house; not passing out by the present door, but by the old gate, the modern fortifications not then existing. We follow his last steps to the *Place Champel*, where already so many malefactors had breathed their last in the flames. He prayed as he went along, both with Farel and with the others, who

* This is stated in the old history, de Morte Serveti.

walked not far from him. Many times he cried aloud, "God, deliver my soul! Jesus, Son of the eternal God, have mercy upon me!" In vain was he entreated to call upon the Saviour as the eternal Son of God.

They were now arrived at the place, where all was prepared for the execution, and a large multitude of people assembled. A wide-stretching eminence about two miles from the city, and originally belonging to the bishops, is still known by the name of Champel, or Champey. The road to it lies through the present *Porte Neuve*, and the friendly, shady path, called the *Tour des Philosophes*, lies to the right. From the top of Champel the view extends, on the one side along the valley, surrounded by vineyards, and to the woody amphitheatre of the Jura mountains; on the other, the eye traces the course of the Arve, rushing along with many windings, and pouring at last its snow-grey waters into the clear bright stream of the Rhone. In the distance may be seen the Fort de l'Ecluse, where the Rhone disappears; and on the Savoy side, the two Salèves, the Mole, and the Voirons, which here cover the glaciers of Savoy. On the opposite side of the Arve lies the little town of Carouge. A pleasant villa, surrounded by gardens, now crowns the summit of Champel; but in the lower part of the eminence, where the old place of execution was, an excavation is still found, effected by the removal of the gravel, called "Le Creux du Bourreau*."

Servetus beheld, as he approached this place, a stake, with a huge heap of oak-wood and leaves in a circle. At the sight of these preparations he cast himself on the ground, and prayed awhile in silence. During this interval, Farel addressed the surrounding multitude. "You see," he said, "what power Satan has at command, when he once gets possession of a man. Here is one, learned above most others, and who, perhaps, believed that he was acting right. He is now, however, possessed by the devil; which might happen also to any of you."

Servetus rose, and Farel encouraged him to speak some few words; but he sighed deeply from his wounded, struggling soul, "O God! O God!" Farel asked, "Hast thou nothing else to say?" "What can I do else," was the answer, "but speak of God?" Farel, who did not know what relations he might have, inquired if he had a wife, or children, and added, that if he wished to make any will, a lawyer was present. He made no answer. When Farel, however, asked whether he would not

* Keyssler's Reisen, b. i. s. 149.

desire the people to pray for him, he yielded to the suggestion, and begged the bystanders to remember him in their prayers. Farel now repeated his former entreaties, and besought him to call upon Christ as the Son of God. This he would not do; but he made no more mention of his doctrine; and Farel regarded this as providential. "Satan," he says, "was hindered from again spitting out his blasphemies."

When Servetus was now led to the pile, Farel exhorted the people to pray for the wretched man; and to entreat the Lord to have mercy on his lost soul, and to turn him from his cursed errors to sound doctrine*.

The executioner employed by the Genevese was not so well-skilled in his work as others. The wood which had been piled up was fresh oak, still in leaf. There was a stake, and before it a block, upon which Servetus was to seat himself. His feet hung to the ground; his body was fastened by an iron chain to the stake, and his neck by a strong rope twisted several times round it. On his head was a wreath, woven of straw and leaves, sprinkled with brimstone, through which suffocation might be speedily effected. The book, which had occasioned all his misery, was, according to the sentence, tied to his body, both the manuscript sent to Calvin for his opinion, and the printed work. He now prayed the executioner to put an end to his sufferings as speedily as possible. The officer brought the fire and kindled the wood, so that he was surrounded by the circling flames. At this sight he cried out so terribly that the whole people shrunk back. As the pile continued to burn but slowly, a great many of the people ran and cast additional bundles of wood into the flames. Servetus cried continually to God for mercy. It is possible, as one report states, that a strong wind prevented, for a considerable time, the action of the fire. The torture, to which the papal tribunals had so long doomed believers in the Gospel, was prolonged in the case of Servetus, if we may believe the account addressed to the Genevese, for half an hour. Farel says nothing on the subject. At last Servetus cried aloud, and this may be regarded as a sure sign that he persevered in his belief, "Jesus, Thou Son of the eternal God, have mercy upon me!"—protesting, in the midst of the flames, and in defiance of the whole Christian world, against the doctrine of the Trinity.

When the sun stood at the highest, in the autumnal sky, and

* Opusc. Fr. p. 1553.

the clock in St. Peter's tower struck twelve, Servetus had ended his sufferings, and the people dispersed in silence.

In the evening of this hot day, and when Calvin was sitting retired in his study, Farel, who had soon to set out on his journey home, most probably came to him to rest awhile, and to describe what had taken place. To realize the image of this hour, I imagine to myself the evening sun colouring the distant glaciers, while Calvin is seated at work, by the light of a lamp, at his library table. On Champel there is a black spot, marked by the signs of fire, and where the ashes of the heretic are still lying, and will be found for many days. It is related that Bernardin Ochino, who arrived from England the day after the execution, entered Geneva and immediately departed*.

And now we inquire, what were the feelings of the reformer at the close of this affair? From a letter which he wrote to Bullinger, and by the statement of Farel, who described his sentiments at this time in a letter to Blaarer, we may form some opinion of the state of his mind. It seems that he had written to inform Farel, who did not receive his last letter, acquainting him with the trouble which he felt at the severity of the senate, which rejected his application to allow Servetus a milder death. The reasons which induced the senate thus to act, he would explain to him by word of mouth. Farel too, it is probable, related what efforts he had made to support Servetus by his prayers. Their conversation will then have turned upon the punishment of heretics, as apart from the crime of blasphemy, Farel having observed, at the beginning of his letter, how necessary such punishments were. He mentions that Calvin had undertaken to confute the errors of the heretic, and to describe his unhappy death. This was done, in quiet, on the same evening, and Farel communicated the necessary information. As he calls Servetus "the wretched and unhappy one" and "the dishonest heretic," this was, no doubt, the general tone in which they spoke of him. The tranquil feeling with which Calvin viewed all the proceedings of this period, serves also to indicate the temper in which he and Farel discoursed. But the effort of the libertines to destroy the discipline established in the church, of which Calvin had shortly before spoken to Bullinger, and on which the conservation of the church in Geneva so mainly depended, must, in all probability, have engaged their attention, far more than the death of an outlaw, whom all the world con-

* In the Vatican Manuscript. Mosheim, s. 292.

demned. In whatever light we view the present period, a great crisis had occurred in Calvin's life: his energy was roused to its highest pitch, but altogether unconsciously to himself.

Contemplating as we are the execution of Servetus, the delicate and interesting question may be asked, whether Calvin ever really thought much about the death of that unhappy man? If he did not absolutely promote it, he certainly considered it just and necessary. But the inquiry has no peculiar value if we confine our attention to the times in which Calvin himself lived. It is for our own age, for that which he helped to introduce, that it is mainly important; and we cannot but wish that his mighty intellect had more clearly perceived the new principles which lay undeveloped in him. And indeed, when some few bold and earnest minds assailed him, affording more striking indications of the Christian spirit unfolding itself with Protestantism, this made a deep impression upon him, although he continued, according to Bullinger's advice, resolutely to defend the old system. At a time when believers were on all sides mowed down in troops, the evangelical church had already reached so high a point in its principles, that it strongly censured, on its own part, and never afterwards pardoned, the few severe acts of which its members were guilty in imitation of the old papal rule. That Calvin was startled hereby does honour to his awakened spirit. Melancthon experienced nothing similar. The Genevese reformer, like Beza, had often silently felt, when the might of apostolic sentiment was victorious over that of the old covenant, that his convictions had carried him too far. That such was the case appears from the fact, that in his last discourses he let not a word fall indicative of the great and serious injustice done him, when his opponents found fault with him for a conduct which was good, and necessary to the upholding of the church. The mention of Servetus is dropped, as if he had never existed. Beza, who was Calvin's second self, seems to have had Servetus in view when he finally judges of Calvin's character, at the conclusion of his biography: "He rarely yielded himself," he says, "to any passionate emotion, except when he had to deal with religious errors and obstinate dispositions."

That Calvin gave the most earnest attention to matters about which any doubt existed, or which appeared to him sometimes holy, and sometimes the contrary, because of the transition-point at which he himself stood, is evident from this: he, who had passed a life pure and holy as few men's have been; a life devoted to the highest interests of humanity, makes repeated and especial mention in his last will of the sins which he had committed. Beza takes particular note of this; and the circumstances referred to can be only such as they had both learnt to view otherwise, under the light of the Gospel, than formerly. Indications of this kind speak strongly in favour of Calvin's tenderness of disposition. It has been already said, that in one of his letters he speaks with a sigh of Servetus and Gentilis: "Ah! if we could but have obtained from Servetus a recantation like that of Gentilis!" His sole wish was to give security to the church. I find another indication of the same sort in his Preface to the Psalms. Here he so surrenders himself to the prevailing sentiment, that he speaks not a word of Servetus; and it is interesting for the student of human character, to find that, while he seems to take pleasure in comparing himself with David, he ventures not to institute the most distant comparison between himself and a prophet or apostle. But David, the man after God's heart, had committed great offences, had to endure many inward struggles, and was surrounded by a host of outward enemies. He might easily indeed understand the sins to which his evil passions had given birth; but Calvin could only by great susceptibility of conscience discover the transgressions of which he had been guilty through his zeal. They sprung from a holy principle, and the prevailing error of his times; so that he could never clearly perceive their nature. At the first he even defended them against his antagonists, and that with a good conscience.

We also see that he did not persevere in his views respecting the punishment of death, even in the case of revilers. Had he retained his original convictions, he would have again stated to the council, in the strongest terms, when he addressed that body, and the clergy, in his last speech, the right which he had against his enemies, and the necessity of retaining such principles for the support of the church. But the world was not yet ripe for a change in these things; and it is well known, that the laws against heretics and blasphemers remained in force another century and a half, even in countries enlightened by the reformation.

In reflecting therefore upon the execution of Servetus, we are concerned with a period very different to that which serves as a point of view for apostolic times. But we must here pause awhile. Servetus deserved his punishment as a blasphemer; but his execution has another aspect for our age. We are here concerned with the toleration of error in its reference to that of blasphemy. The spot where Servetus died marked, as it were, the boundary between the barbarity of the middle ages, and the refinement which has been effected by the light of the reformation. Here it was that those powerful voices, which grew mightier every day, were first lifted up in behalf of freedom of conscience. We stand upon Champel: before us lies a Christian city, but just freed from the trammels of superstition; that city is the abode of a reformer, well-versed in holy writ; at his feet sit hundreds of hearers. It is not however with him we have now to do: he had some perception of approaching changes, and helped to effect them. The Genevese council, the papal church, and the people of the age, claim our present notice.

A burning pile in the midst of evangelical Christendom! What a theme for the lamentation of all future times! More murders were committed at this period by the papal church, according to judicial form, than were ever perpetrated by wretches who lived by crime. But the execution of Servetus made so deep an impression on men's minds, because, forgetting the blasphemy of which he had been guilty, they fixed their attention on the freedom of thought which the reformation advocated, and a course altogether different to that pursued by the papists might naturally be looked for on the side of evangelical Christians. Few genuine martyrs therefore have gained so much notice as this fanatic. A great principle, and the peace of the world, seemed involved in the proceedings against him; since, if intolerance be allowed, one vast series of murders may be looked for, extending even to the last man, who shall hold firm to his convictions. Thus Champel is a melancholy monument of the past, but one on which spirits may be discerned and proved.

Romanists rejoice, even to the present day, at the memorial of this event, and remind protestants of it with bitter scorn. Bossuet, a wicked enemy of the truth, because well-acquainted with Christianity, and an early witness of the persecutions in France, speaks on this subject with diplomatic cunning. "We must remind," he says, "the protestants, of the execution of heretics at Geneva, if they complain so bitterly at being persecuted." And the last wretched pamphleteering antagonist of Calvin raves against him, as if he had been responsible for all the sins of the middle ages, and the inventor of all the instruments of torture employed by the papists. This writer, in fact, sets aside the entire history of the Inquisition, and especially the condemnation of Servetus at Vienne, as if these people could be justified in persecuting us because we committed an error, for the principle of which we have to thank themselves.

Christians weep over their sins when aware of them: the Genevese lamented their early severity. "Would to God," said one of them in the last century, "that we could extinguish this burning pile with our tears!" This is the common sentiment. But the Romanists have imitated the heathen, and burnt numberless of their brethren, confessing their Saviour, to ashes. For ten centuries have the flames raged upon the altar of their Moloch. They could not inflict a greater penalty; but had it been in their power, gladly would they have destroyed the souls of the faithful with their bodies. The death which they inflicted was a symbol of their hatred to the truth. In their imbecile wrath they burnt the body to ashes, or buried it alive, while the spirit escaped their rage unharmed. Nor has the catholic church ever renounced her old principle of persecution, or condemned it as Satanic; on the contrary, she still boldly defends it by her recognized organs. Not one of her teachers has allowed it was the spirit of Antichrist which then blinded them. It was her own principle therefore which triumphed in the Genevese council; her sons are answerable for this deed; the blood that was shed cries out against her; and till Rome pronounce aloud her condemnation of the spirit of persecution, the death even of Servetus will remain as a fearful witness against her. Calvin and the members of the Genevese council, nurtured in these principles, and surrounded by the *auto-da-fees* of the Inquisition, were not answerable for the results. The whole protestant church is on one side, and expresses its sorrow for the injustice perpetrated against Servetus, Krell, and some others. And yet will the papists venture, up to the present day, with insane rashness or childish folly, as the latest publication on their side against the reformer shows, to represent him as one of the worst characters in history, because he desired the death of Servetus: they see not that they are inflicting the deepest wound upon themselves, by thus imputing their own guilt to us. It was they who condemned Servetus to the flames, long before he was judged by the Genevese: they were anxious to become the privileged executioners of the world, and they only regarded such a sin as impossible among the reformers, because their conscience represented it to them as a simple type of their own.

But, whatever may be said, Christians will ever look with

astonishment at the execution of Servetus, and will wonder how Christians, who differed from each other on so many points, could be of one mind in this, that the erring should be punished with death; nay, that all the great intellects of the day should be agreed upon the point, and pronounce their Amen! to the sentence. In contemplating the event therefore of which we have been speaking, we look in fact into the deep abyss of the sins of the middle ages, which paid no regard to the rights of conscience.

Servetus, who insulted the holy and unchangeable faith of the entire Christian world, ought certainly to have been condemned to perpetual silence. But suppose that he had only strange perceptions of Christianity,—perceptions which disturb when they do not spring from a right faith,—still the burning pile which shed its light into the future proclaimed the dawn of better times. Yes, Servetus became a reformer by his freely protesting, even unto death: he has aroused the indignation of evangelical Christians in all ages against the sin of the papacy, which passed, at the beginning, into our own church,—the sin, that is, of punishing error with death. And the attention of mankind has now been fixed on the idea, that there is a development of faith superior to that which is merely protestant or catholic,—a problem for the coming age. Servetus was altogether a different man to Gentilis, who retracted his opinions without a word; and to Joris, who lived in luxury at Basel, under a strange name, and, as a false prophet, predicted his own speedy resurrection. Some even regarded Servetus as a man of piety.

I imagine to myself, now that three hundred years have passed away, a jury of impartial men, gathered from all the various Christian churches, and assembled on the summit of Champel, to pass a final judgement in this remarkable cause. If, aided by all the necessary documents, they could transport themselves to the period when the event took place, and examine those who were eye-witnesses of the proceedings, they would in all probability free Calvin from the charge against him, and pronounce him not guilty. Servetus, on the other hand, they would declare guilty, but with extenuating circumstances. An impartial jury would thus oppose the common judgement, which treads sometimes the one and sometimes the other of these men in the dust, and does justice to neither. Both excite our lively interest. We cannot but shrink from adopting the opinion of Mosheim, expressed with as much harshness as coldness :—" The one searches after lost truth, and becomes a dreamer; the other contends for truth abused, and becomes a homicide." A jury, such as we have described, would especially recognize it as Calvin's duty to punish such an offender, at a time when the preservation of the truth was necessary to the safety of the world; and they would think of Moses, who punished the people at Sinai for their idolatry. It was the spirit of the age to do so; and it would make a strong impression upon the mind of every judge, that the laws which then existed, and the sentiments of mankind, were in accordance with the proceeding. Calvin's zeal was founded upon his conscientiousness: this is the key to his whole being: it was his guide in the development of his system of doctrine, in his moral judgements, and in his struggle for unity. Both he and the council acted from so deep a sense of duty, that it had a powerful influence on every one, as if, in the pressure of the times, thus it was willed by the Spirit of God. All felt that indifference to the schisms which tore the church would ruin the reformation in the south, as was subsequently the case in Poland, through the errors which there prevailed. It is not only unjust, therefore, but a mark of ignorance, to blame Calvin for having nobly done that which he believed it was his duty to perform.

Nor will impartial judges be blind to the real character of Servetus; they will bear in mind that he not only adhered firmly to his convictions, but that, lively, fantastic, and comet-like as he was, he approached at length the spirit of Christianity. His last moments indicate the germ of a genuine sense of freedom, notwithstanding the power which a vicious disposition exercised over him to the end. But Calvin, with his profound religious feeling, with his simple Scriptural faith, rose higher than any step which could be reached by all the philosophical knowledge of God, belonging to that or any future age. The words of Thomas à Kempis will here occur to mind: "What can it help thee to be able to dispute learnedly on the doctrine of the Trinity, if thou be wanting in the humility, without which thou canst never please the Trinity?"

Not revenge, but a holy indignation, would the judges say, must excite every one against the folly-perplexed Servetus. Calvin, as the affair then presented itself, had the right to assert, that the accused wished to overthrow all religion. Had he indeed been left free to exercise his extraordinary endowments, and still for years to come, he being now only forty-four, to spread his unbelief on all sides, and to strengthen his union with the dangerous sects of the libertines and anabaptists, to which he held out both his hands, there is little doubt but that the reformation in the south would have been easily suppressed. A conscientious jury therefore would answer the objection, that Calvin opposed Servetus when not in the territory of Geneva, and hastily acquainted the magistrates with his arrival in that city, by the remark, that he had undertaken to labour, in the name of God, for the spiritual good of all mankind, and not for a small, individual church. This is rather for than against him. His friends have never found fault with him on this account, and his enemies only provoke ridicule, when they adduce the well-known letter to Farel as evidence against him. Calvin considered it as an honour to have deprived Servetus of the power of injuring mankind.

Mosheim asserts that Servetus was himself impetuous, and would have punished Calvin as a heretic had he had him in his power. Here the impartial judge is of a different opinion. Servetus speaks indeed as if heretics might be punished with death*, and denounces Calvin as worthy of its infliction: but this proves nothing; his whole career, and the tendency of his mind, are opposed to it: he was characteristically liberal; it was his grand effort to realize the plan of the apostolic church, and, as a true image of a free-thinker in the protestant community, he did not shrink from comparing himself to the apostles of the Lord†. This was the effect of his gross self-delusion.

A conscientious jury, again, would no doubt earnestly inquire, whether the present age, any more than the past, would allow itself to be judged according to the principles of another, far remote, and of the feelings of which it could form no opinion,—whether, under such circumstances, we might not be charged, as well as the reformers, with all the follies of legislation, and with the hundreds of executions which take place every year,—with the executions, that is, which send so many unconverted souls into eternity, for the purpose of securing the safety of the state, and while it would be possible to proceed according to the principles of a milder age, readily disposed to abolish the punishment of death, as a remnant of barbarous times.

But posterity will never fail to behold the death of Servetus as affording a striking instance of the powerlessness of disbelief, of the curse which rests upon blasphemy; nor will it contem-

* Restit. p. 656. "Hoc crimen est morte simpliciter dignum."

† "Et maximi apostolorum fuerunt aliquando in errore." Ep. ad Œcolamp. Ep. Ref. Helv. p. 78.

plate without admiration the spirit of that mighty man who sought to defend the truth, as it ought ever to be defended, and who at the same time esteemed the methods proper to the age in which he lived as the best adapted to its support. We ourselves should then have acted as he did, and should now restrain such an offender as Servetus, who poured contempt on God, and all that is holy, with the punishments known to our times. Had he died in prison, as Campanus did, no complaint would have been raised against Calvin. And how different was his conduct to that of a Philip of Spain, a Mary of England, an Alba, a Richelieu, and others, all of whom, blinded by a political, fanatical and savage spirit, only desired to accomplish their own selfish purposes! Calvin, on the contrary, was inspired by an earnest, holy zeal for the honour of God. We here behold the peculiar sublimity and keenness of his intellect; and we answer the question, whether there can be times and circumstances in which we may dare, as Christians, to call fire from heaven. We will not say with Grotius, that the spirit of Antichrist was as active on the shores of Lake Leman as on the banks of the Tiber; but we appeal to all the clergy of our age, both catholic and protestant, and ask, who will venture to utter a word against Calvin, or to cast a stone at him,—who there, with Melancthon, Zwingli, Bullinger, Farel, Bucer, and Peter Martyr, raises his countenance in prayer to heaven?

How quickly vanishes the scene which we have described in the grandeur of nature! The smoke of the burning pile darkens not the hills, which shine in perpetual beauty: those other times have come, which were then but about to dawn; and the Alps, in their deep tranquillity, an image of the rock upon which our faith is built, will testify in the day of promise, when the glad message will resound from all quarters of the world, that the pure Gospel has conquered, that the heathen have come in, and that catholic and protestant are known no more in the apostolic community, because the truth has loosened all the fetters of the mind. But here, on the spot where Servetus died, must the disciples of Christ vow to each other never again to mar the reconstructed edifice of Christianity through their prejudices; and if these pure evangelical sentiments find a place in their hearts, the citizens of Geneva will assemble on the 27th of October, 1853, when three hundred years shall have passed away, and will ascend the summit of Champel, and there erect a pillar, with this inscription: "To all defenders of the faith, of freedom of mind, and of conscience!"

But we cannot yet leave this spot. It is but right that we should hear the judgement of contemporary witnesses. Of these, the most worthy are all on the side of Calvin. Christians of that age beheld in Servetus a manifestation of Satan. The Swiss churches feared that they might be regarded by the whole world as his associates in the guilt of heresy, if they did not loudly pronounce his condemnation. They were willing to exercise toleration in the case of a Lælius Socinus. He reasoned only as a scholar, and kept his errors to himself. Servetus, on the contrary, had declared that he would dissolve the protestant as well as the catholic church. This difficult subject has always been eagerly debated: it became at length matter of public controversy between Mosheim and Armand de la Chapelle*. But it is not the judgement of modern times—it is that of Calvin's contemporaries,—which really decides the case. He was the man of the age: the best minds therefore were for him. It has been already stated how Bucer expressed himself in the pulpit, declaring that Servetus deserved to be torn in pieces†. But the most remarkable testimony remains still to be mentioned; it is that of the mild and amiable Melancthon, who, advanced in years and free from passion, judged calmly and thoughtfully. "Honoured man, and most beloved brother," he writes to Calvin, "I have read your letter, in which you excellently confute the horrible blasphemy of Servetus; and I thank the Son of God, who has been the umpire and the director of your conflict. The church of Christ will also, both now and in all future times, own its gratitude to you. I am wholly of your opinion, and declare also that your magistrates, the entire proceedings having been conducted according to law, acted quite justly in condemning the blasphemer to death‡."

Melancthon, whose opinion represented that of the times, judged Servetus even more severely than Calvin, and undertook the defence of the council when the offender suffered in the flames. It is therefore a gross error still to complain of Calvin, when, if he be viewed according to the sentiments of the age, his proceedings were marked by moderation.

* Mosheim, pp. 2, 14, 270–6. Arm. de la Chapelle: in Biblioth. Rais. t. ii. pt. i. p. 169.

† Ep. ad Sulcer.

‡ Ed. Laus. Ep. 187. Ed. Amst. p. 92. Oct. 14, 1554.

Again, Melancthon, speaking to Bullinger on the same subject, says*, "I have read what you have written respecting Servetus, and applaud your piety and your conclusions. I agree with you, that the Genevese council was right in getting rid of so hardened a man, who would never have ceased to blaspheme. It has often been cause of surprise to me, that there are men who can find fault with the severity which has been exercised. I send you a few leaves in which I have stated my opinion." He also gave his judgement still more distinctly, in writing, on the sentence of Servetus, when it had been put in execution†. No one could be more decided as to the punishment of heretics: thus he was especially indignant against the rationalist, Theobald Thamer‡.

In the year 1557 there appeared at Wittenberg a pamphlet, warning people particularly against the errors of this man. It appears to have been written by Melancthon. The author calls upon the magistrates to prevent the spread of blasphemous opinions, and represents the proceeding against Servetus as well deserving imitation. He says of his execution, "that it afforded a pious and memorable example for all posterity." Calvin was therefore justified in appealing, at a subsequent period, to the opinion of Melancthon.

The sentiments of Zwingli, and those also of Œcolampadius, have been already given. Bullinger distinctly called upon Calvin to punish Servetus as a heretic. When Calvin wrote to him to say, that the report of the trial was to be sent to Zurich, Bullinger answered, on the 14th of September§, in the letter already quoted, "If your council would but proceed against this wretched man according to his deserts, the whole world would then see that blasphemers are hated in Geneva, and that people know there how to punish obstinate heretics with the sword of righteousness, to the honour of the divine majesty." Bullinger also expressed at a later period, in a letter to the Poles‖, his horror of Servetus:—"My soul shudders whenever I think of his heresies and blasphemies; I am convinced that, if Satan were to come from hell, and were to proclaim his doctrines, according to his own taste, he would use many of the expressions employed by the Spaniard Servetus." Subsequently to this also, and when Calvin was beset by opponents, he says¶, alluding to his work

* Ed. L. Ep. 214. Ed. Amst. p, 108. Aug. 20, 1555.

† See Christ. Pezel. Concilia, &c., Melancthon, 2, p. 223.

‡ Neander. Theob. Thamer, p. 50–52.

§ Ed. Laus. Ep. 162. Ed. Amst. p. 78.

‖ Epist. Ref. Helvet. p. 371.

¶ Epist. 173. Hess. t. ii. s. 85.

on the punishment of heretics, "I know that many have wished that you had not defended this principle; but many also thank you, and among others our church. Urbanus Regius has long ago proved, in a work of his own, and all the ministers of Luneberg agree with him, that heretics, when they are blasphemers, ought to be punished. There are also many other pious men who think the same, and consider that such offenders ought not only to be silenced, but to be put to death. Do not repent therefore of what you have done: the Lord will uphold your righteous efforts. I know that your disposition is not cruel, and that you will favour no barbarity. Who knows not, that a boundary must be set to things of this kind? But how it could be possible to spare such a man as Servetus, that serpent of all heresies, that most obdurate of men, I see not."

Nothing need be said of Beza and Viret. Martin Chemnits is equally severe against Servetus. The benevolent Musculus uses these characteristic words: "I am horrified at such infamous and godless principles! May the Lord chastise this devil, and keep his church for us in safety and purity of doctrine*."

Three years after the death of Servetus, we read the following judgement, given by Peter Martyr†: "I have nothing to say of him, except that he was the very son of the devil, whose pestilential and frightful doctrine should be everywhere hunted down; and that the magistrate who condemned him to death is not to be blamed, seeing that he gave no sign of improvement, and that his blasphemies were beyond endurance."

We have seen how sternly Farel decided the question‡. He adds, that all who favoured the anabaptists wished heretics to be allowed to escape. "Having read how Paul expressed his willingness to die, if he deserved it, I have often myself felt prepared to die, if I could be charged with having taught false doctrine, and have owned, that I should be worthy of every punishment if I enticed any one from the faith and knowledge of Jesus Christ; and I cannot pass on others a different sentence to that which I should pass upon myself." Supported by such testimony, Calvin might properly, in his controversy with Bern, declare, "that the severity exercised against Servetus was universally approved§."

* Hess. Leb. Bull. t. ii. s. 83, 95.

† Ep. ad Dominos Polonos Evangelium profitentes et Eccles. Ministros. Argent. Feb. 14, 1556. After his Loci, Com. Tigur. 1587.

‡ Calv. Sept. 8, 1553.

§ MS. Gen. Mai. 4, 1555.

How strong the impression was respecting the blasphemy of Servetus, and how great a detestation of his name prevailed long after his death, appears from the judicial proceedings instituted against those who spoke in favour of his doctrine.

All the witnesses, to which we have thus appealed, give a clear and open testimony. There are others who take part against Calvin, but not fairly and openly*; against these it is a duty to protest. Among modern writers, Trechsel, to whose sound judgement we have before alluded, and Leo†, expressly declare themselves in favour of Calvin's conduct. Hase, in his Church History‡, still speaks of "a dark deed."

After this hearing of witnesses, we turn our attention for awhile to the spirit which now animated the Lutheran church; and we shall show, that the "Reformed" were not more intolerant than the Lutherans. The anabaptists were the only people at this period who denied to the magistrate the right of using the sword. We have still to mourn over two executions, those of Krell and Günther.

Protestant churches in later times have vied with each other in the defence of toleration§. The reformers themselves varied in their views on the subject. Luther, like Calvin, spoke sometimes for and sometimes against the principle of toleration; till at length the old spirit of stern severity prevailed in them, and the churches adopted their views. Noble are the expressions of Luther in favour of toleration, in his work on the power of the civil magistrate, written in 1523, when his translation of the New Testament was proscribed. "God will suffer no one to rule over souls, but himself alone." And in his treatise against the anabaptists (1528), he says, "It is not right that such wretched people should be murdered, burnt, and barbarously destroyed. Far better it would be to let every one believe what he will; let the Scriptures, let God's word be appealed to; little can be done by the flames; were it otherwise, hangmen would be the most learned of doctors." The same good feeling is expressed in the Concordian-formularies. But notwithstanding, we see by what an intolerant disposition Luther was governed in his conduct towards the Sacramentarians. The consequence to his church was, that the Reformed regarded it as their bitterest foe.

It is an error to suppose, that Calvin was opposed to all free-

* The author here particularly alludes to Herr Galiffe of Geneva.

† Allgem. Gesch. t. iii. s. 219.

‡ S. 461.

§ Bibl. Angl. t. ii. p. 78.

dom of opinion: he was intolerant only against blasphemy, and what was wilfully designed for the destruction of the faith. In his treatise against the Council of Trent, he insists upon freedom of opinion against the pretensions of the catholic church; but, on the other hand, he speaks against toleration in that part of his work in which he justifies the punishment of heretics, and particularizes the doctrines, the preaching of which ought to be punished with death. Still there are fine passages in all the editions of the Institutes in behalf of this virtue. Even his conduct toward Servetus proves, that he was not intolerant against those who merely differed in opinion from himself: he only desired that they should not openly oppose the recognized doctrines as reformers. Bullinger spoke in this manner respecting Socinus: "I repressed his petulant curiosity as much as possible;" but when Socinus became the assailant, Bullinger used strong words, and in the same sense as Calvin*. Luther considered it very dangerous to allow the principle of intolerance to become general, but still he wished obstinate heretics to be punished†. He was not true therefore to his early sentiments. The anabaptists were put to death in Saxony, as everywhere else. Luther also stated it as his opinion to Philip of Hesse, that it was lawful to inflict capital punishment on heretics; and this opinion was subscribed by Melancthon, Bugenhagen and Cruciger. He urges them to pursue this course in the case of such as deny that Christ is God‡.

It seems evident therefore that Luther would have formed the same judgement on the case of Servetus as Calvin. To an inquiry of the Wittenberg theologians, "whether it was lawful to punish anabaptists with the sword," we find his assent written in his own hand, "*placet mihi Luthero*"§. So we also read, "Whereever they are found to be the authors, or receivers, and have forbidden articles, they may be capitally punished, as those who have instituted conventicles, against the mandates which have been publicly issued."

This variation in Luther's views, and his intolerant conduct toward the Sacramentarians, had so injurious an effect, that immediately after his death, a bitter hostility was excited against the "Reformed." About seven years after his decease, the mem-

* Hess. Leben Bullingers, t. ii. s. 86.

† De Wette, t. iii. s. 347; and for the other view, see Comm. Luth. in Ps. 71.

‡ Luther's Werke: Altenburg, t. v. s. 286, and a longer passage in the German exposition of Psalm 82, v. 4.

§ Heidelberger Universitätsbibliothek, cod. 435, bl. 33.

bers of the English reformed church in London, consisting mostly of Germans and Netherlanders, sought refuge in Hamburgh and Denmark. Their flight had taken place in the winter, but they were forcibly driven from the shelter which they besought, because they differed from the Lutheran church on the subject of Christ's presence in the sacrament. It is universally known, that the clamour against the Crypto-Calvinists was continued into the seventeenth century. Not less generally known are the proceedings against Nicolaus Krell, a doctor, and chancellor to the elector Christian I. of Saxony. On the death of this prince, Krell was apprehended as a criminal, under the pretence that he had endeavoured to introduce Calvinism into Saxony. This event occurred on the 23rd of October, 1591, and after ten years' imprisonment the unfortunate ex-chancellor was beheaded in the Jüdenhof at Dresden*.

This melancholy occurrence, though less known, is far more lamentable, considering all the circumstances of the case, than the affair of Servetus at Geneva. Krell was merely accused of having diffused the so-named Calvinistic errors, and certainly not of having desired to overthrow the church. Other communities were not asked to state their views on the question of his guilt, and nothing was proved against him. Not a word was said of his having blasphemed: on the contrary, he died as a pious Christian; and it would be difficult to explain, why he was not kept as a prisoner at Königstein, if he was really feared. The elector Christian was very favourable to the doctrines of the "Reformed," took the part of the king of Navarre, and sent troops to France. Krell was so greatly esteemed by his master, that the latter entrusted to him the guardianship of his children: but he was hated by the nobility. Both he and the elector were anxious to soften the spirit of Lutheranism; the first ministers of the country agreed with them, and in 1591 the practice of exorcism at baptism was suppressed. The elector's confessor published a Bible, with annotations, which was ascribed to Krell. The hostility against him increased more and more: immediately after Christian's death it broke forth. Four weeks only had elapsed when he was apprehended, and four clergymen with him. The country was placed under a regent, duke Frederic. At his command, and by the consent of the states, the trial was commenced, and Krell was unrighteously accused of numerous offences. It is evident from his history, that he was condemned

* Leben, Schicksal, Ende des Dr. N. Krell. Leipzig, 1798.

illegally and unheard. He admitted not a single point of the accusation, but the judges were expressly instructed not to hear his defence. On the 5th of October, 1601, he was brought from Königstein to Dresden, as strictly guarded as if he had been one of the most dreaded of criminals. Having partaken of the sacrament, he was carried, on account of his weakness, to the court of justice on a chair. The sentence purported, "that he had employed body and life against the peace of the land, and to the ruin of its tranquillity and union; that he must therefore die."

During the reading of the sentence, Krell exclaimed to the judge: "Cease, and hear my answer: listen, whether I acknowledge these crimes, before you execute me!" But the judge broke the staff before the sentence was half-finished. "I confess not one point of that which is laid to my charge," continued Krell. "Where are my accusers? Where are the witnesses? Shall the contrary proof of my innocence avail nothing?" It was answered, that that was not the time for disputation. "I can testify," rejoined Krell, "before God and my conscience, that I am innocent of all these things." The judges rose, expressed their indignation, and were joined by the people. Krell now saw that they had resolved on his death; and bowing his head, with his hands raised to heaven, he said, "Well then, in the name of God, let the will of the elector of Saxony be done! May God have mercy! I perish innocently. I am indeed a poor sinner, but I have never committed the evil deeds here laid to my charge: my accusers must answer it at the last day."

It was eleven o'clock when he was carried forth, still resting on a chair, to the place of execution, the Jüdenhof. He prayed, in the meantime, devoutly and with a loud voice. A large multitude followed him and bewailed his fate. The widow of the elector Christian had taken her position, with some ladies of the court, in the gallery of the new mews, whence the execution might be conveniently seen. That she might be near the spot where the drama was to be performed, the scaffold which, some days before, had been erected at a little distance from the mews, was, by her command, broken up, and reconstructed close to the gallery.

Krell was now brought to the place where he was to end his life. At the sight of the scaffold, his ordinary resolution forsook him, and he fell into a swoon, from which he was only recovered by the use of stimulants. As soon as he revived, he was taken from the chair on which he had been brought, and was placed on another without a back. The Christianity of the man was now well-exhibited: he prayed all those whom he had in any way injured to forgive him; he prayed also for the emperor, the elector, and for his enemies, concluding with these words: "Lord God, Thou who hast created me; Lord, Son of God, who hast redeemed me; Lord, Holy Ghost, who hast sanctified me! today I render back the pledge wherewith Thou hast entrusted me!" While he was thus praying, the executioner stripped the upper part of his body, and asked him if he had prepared himself for death. Krell answered nobly in the affirmative. His hands were then bound, his arms having been drawn behind him and fastened with straps and buckles. He was now allowed to sit for a little while. Expecting the stroke, he made a strong effort, and raised his head: an attendant pressed it down again. The executioner now coming behind him tore away some braids which hindered his operations, and levelled his weapon at the martyr. The moment after he took up the head, and showing it to the people, exclaimed jestingly, "Krell, how liked you the Calvinistic stroke? O how many strange things there were in this head! There are many more such in this crowd. I think some of these people must still fall into my grasp."

On the following day the dead body was carried, accompanied by a procession of the clergy and schools, and with singing, to the Frauenkirche. There the confessor Blume delivered a funeral discourse, which appears to have been harsh and severe. The body was then buried in the churchyard. The sword by which he was beheaded is still shown in the armoury at Dresden. On one side is the following inscription: "Conradin Pols;" and "Cave Calvinianæ. D. N. C." (Dominus Nicolaus Crell). The latter was the name of this martyr of Calvinistic doctrine; the former, that of the executioner.

There is still another occurrence of a similar, but yet more striking, character to be mentioned, as connected with the later history of the Lutheran church. We refer to the execution of Günther, who, like Servetus, opposed the doctrine of the Trinity, and whose last words sounded like those of the Spaniard. Krell's fate might, in some degree, be connected with political motives; but such could not be the case with that of the man whose execution took place in October, 1687, and which was purely the result of fanaticism and the dread of schism. The superintendent Petersen, in Lüneberg, has given an account of this event*.

It is refreshing and encouraging to see how, in many parts of Italy and France, the minds of men were awaking out of slumber, and preparing to declare themselves on the side of freedom and inquiry; some indeed with an intelligence which we could not wish to see excelled even in the present age. It was the dawn of a new civilization. An actual revolt against the council at Geneva appeared in the writings and poems of the day. People declared that a new inquisition was established; that if Christ himself came to Geneva, he would be crucified; and that there was now a pope in that city as well as at Rome. Bolsec published in the Pays de Vaud the most insulting slanders†. The preachers at Geneva in the meantime raged against the name of Servetus, and again condemned him. Thus it was natural that the question should be anxiously asked, whether heretics, and if any, what class of heretics, ought to be punished with loss of life? It is plain, as Luther strongly intimated, that if the principle of intolerance was once allowed, the catholics would want no pretence to annihilate the protestants. But while some insisted upon the necessity of bridling the teachers of false doctrine, others were equally anxious for entire freedom. Beza, in his Life of Calvin, expressed it as his opinion, that Castellio and Socinus were the first among those who contended for liberty of conscience. Castellio uttered bold sentiments on the subject, in the preface to his translation of the Scriptures, which concealed others. Many persons declared themselves scholars of Servetus, without the least knowledge of his doctrines.

Calvin would probably have despised this noisy abuse, as he did so many other attacks; but it so increased, that Bullinger advised him to defend the opinion, that it is the duty of magistrates to punish false teachers‡. This was a remarkable step. Calvin found himself indeed in a perplexing situation. The principle was not yet settled as to the means which should be employed to secure the unity of the church; and the case of

* See Leben Wilhelm Petersens, doctor und superintendant zu Hannover und Lüneberg, s. 66. Also Arnold's Ketser-historie, t. ii. s. 434.

† He sung, as he went about, a song full of infamous expressions against Calvin. Trechsel has given a poem against him, written by Camillus Renatus Rhetus. There were some however in his favour. Mosheim, s. 276.

‡ Responsio ad Bald. Convitia.

Servetus was used against him. Calvin composed accordingly, in the same year, the often-cited work, written in French, against Servetus,—a defence, which only served to excite a still larger number of antagonists. When Calvin was silent, Beza entered upon the controversy, and produced a well and carefully written treatise.

Calvin began by showing, that the civil power ought to bear with the erring, but to restrain incorrigible heretics and blasphemers with the sword. He supported his assertion by an appeal to the law of God*. It is worthy of remark, that Servetus, so passionately in love with liberty, entirely assented to the principle thus asserted by Calvin. Even according to his own views, obstinate heretics ought to be punished with loss of life, and not merely with banishment†. In the second place follows the proof, that Servetus was really the heretic stated, and deserving of the punishment which he received. The argument to this effect is drawn from his own history, from his whole correspondence with Calvin, from his trial and examination, and lastly from his works, the errors contained in which are confuted. This was no private undertaking; it was subscribed by all the Genevese preachers, fifteen in number.

On the whole, this work obtained considerable praise. Some however, and Musculus among others, were not satisfied with the design, and Bullinger considered it too short for the depth and obscurity of the subject‡. How Calvin himself judged of the work appears from the following expressions: "This little book is very brief, and stormily written, but it is better than nothing§." So also, in an answer to Bullinger's criticism, he says||, "I have particularly endeavoured to prevent the brevity of this work from increasing the obscurity of the subject, but I have not been able altogether to avoid it. My plan of itself

* See this remarkable passage. Ed. Amst. Opusc. p. 516. a. Ed. Gen. p. 599. a.

† Christ. Restit. p. 656, Ep. 28. "Illud verum est, quod correctione non expectata Ananiam et Sapp. occidit Petrus; quia Spiritus Sanctus tunc maxime vigens, quem spreverant, docebat esse incorrigibiles, in malitia obstinatos. Hoc crimen est morte simpliciter dignum, et apud Deum et apud hominem. In aliis autem criminibus, ubi Spiritus Sanctus speciale quid non docet, ibi non est inveterata malitia aut obstinatio certa non apparet, aut atrocitas magna, correctionem per alias castigationes sperare potius debemus, quam mortem inferre. Inter correctiones exilium laudamus Christo ita probatum, ut excommunicatio probatur in ecclesia."

‡ Hess, Leben Bullingers, t. ii. s. 95.

§ Ed. Laus. p. 171. Ed. Amst. p. 241.

|| April 29, 1554. The autograph is at Zurich.

constrained me, from various causes, to write with as much simplicity as possible. It was my whole object to make plain and unlearned people easily understand the contemptible character of the Spaniard. I shall be well-satisfied however with the reward of my labour, if it be only allowed that I have, with true faith and honest zeal, defended the right doctrine. You will, I doubt not, from love to me, and from your own just and pure spirit, judge of me with kindness. Others pursue me with harshness, as if I were a teacher of the most horrible cruelty; and as if I still wished, by means of my writings, to tear a dead man to pieces, a man who perished by my hands. But there are some, who have no evil will against me, and who yet wish that I had not written this book on the punishment of heretics. They think that others have been silent simply to avoid being hated*. But it is my good luck to have you for a partner in my offence, if an offence it be; for you in fact are the instigator and author of the undertaking. Be prepared therefore for the strife."

Three voices were now distinctly, in three different works, raised in behalf of freedom of conscience. The productions alluded to were, that of the pseudo Martinus Bellius; the 'Dialogi inter Calvinum et Vaticanum;' and the noble work of Minus Celsus, a reformed Italian nobleman, whose milder tone breathes entirely of the pure spirit of the Gospel†. He had been obliged to flee his native land, and was very much shocked to find at Graubünden, the common rendezvous of the dissenters of that period, instead of the hoped-for harmony, nothing but strife and division, and even the hated rule of persecution. As soon as he was made acquainted with the death of Servetus, and had heard many eye-witnesses speak of his fortitude, and express their conviction that a man could not die as he did without the spirit of God,—when he found that these people regarded the heretic as a martyr, and fell from their orthodox professions, because they were thus led to look on heresy as truth,—he resumed a treatise, which he had begun some time before, and translated it into Latin, just as Calvin's own work made its appearance. Celsus died, and it was not till after twenty years that his excellent work was printed. It is conceived in a true Christian

* This may possibly refer to Bullinger himself, who urged Calvin to undertake the task, instead of doing it on his own responsibility.

† Celsus was a native of Sienna, and was probably first instructed by his countryman Ochino.

spirit, and evinces great love for truth. The toleration which it displays is a lesson for all ages, and its author was no disciple of Servetus. Heretics, according to him, should be restrained, but not condemned. This was the purest testimony in favour of freedom of conscience known in those unsettled times. The principle of toleration exercised no prevailing influence in Germany till after the thirty years' war; and although the mighty voice of De Thou was raised in France against the demon of persecution, especially in his celebrated preface to his history, it re-echoed for the time to no purpose.

A voice in favour of freedom was also raised in Bern: it was that of a distinguished man, Zur Kinden*, the state-secretary at Bern, and a friend of Calvin. He candidly expressed his displeasure, as did others, and considered, that the first part of Calvin's work ought to have appeared in the name of the council, and that he should not have undertaken individually to support a view which was hateful to all. A characteristic letter, written by Calvin to this correspondent at a somewhat later period, still exists: he pours out to him his afflicted heart, and declares, that although people regarded him as implacable, there was no man upon earth less revengeful than himself in any private cause. As for his severity against the wicked, there was this to justify him: he had prophets and apostles for his example. That he was excitable, he did not deny; and he endeavoured to correct the fault, lamenting that he did not make so much progress in the effort as he could wish. If however any one expected him to be rendered gentle and humane by the hasty condemnation of his zeal, which was pious and righteous, as God was his best witness, he would find it difficult to discover others inclined to adopt the same idea.

Many of the Italian refugees now came forth, and with ribaldrous songs threatened that the spirit of Servetus was about to re-appear. The hatred against Calvin continually increased: his name was almost become a word of reproach. Two years later Hotoman wrote†, "People speak of him here, in Basel, as contemptuously as in Paris." But the friends of the reformer supported him in his troubles. Zanchi wrote a tract on the Coercion of Heretics, in 1554: it was in defence of Calvin. The latter himself thus expressed his own present and inward hope:—"It is well that we have a pilot, under whose protection

* He wrote to Calvin, Feb. 10, 1554, on the subject referred to. Bibl. Gen. cod. 114. Trechsel, s. 269.

† To Bullinger, Sept. 27, 1555.

we may be secure against shipwreck, and that we are not far from our haven*." He had even prepared to leave Geneva. Bullinger wrote to him on the subject during the trial of Servetus†. "Forsake not, I beseech you, the flock which contains so many excellent men. Think on Him, who aforetime said to Paul, 'Be not afraid, but speak, and hold not thy peace: for I am with thee, and no man shall set on thee to hurt thee: for I have much people in this city.' You may well suppose how the enemies of the Gospel would rejoice, and to what perils you would leave the pious refugees from France, were you to depart. Remain therefore, and endure what God appoints you." And in another letter of the 12th of January, 1554, he again exhorted him to continue his labour in the same spirit as before, for that God would bless his work and his earnestness.

Calvin had not attacked Servetus in the first edition of his Institutes: the Spaniard had not then become dangerous: it is only in the last edition that mention is made of him; but even here the notice taken of him is but cursory. We may properly however close the history of Servetus with a compressed but systematic account of his doctrine. The chief difficulty in this undertaking arises from the circumstance, that Servetus remained to the last immature in spirit, which at the time of the principal controversy had acquired no degree of firmness or self-confidence. If Calvin had quietly proved him, and learnt to understand his nature, he would probably have accused him on very different grounds. His conscience cried against him, but he neglected to consider the volatile disposition of the man. He regarded him only in an ecclesiastical point of view, and was not aware that, amidst all his failings, there was something lofty and even interesting in his being. Calvin did not comprehend his main disposition, the philosophical element which predominated in him, but without entirely suppressing the religious principle. He neglected to point out to him the contradictions and obscurity which must necessarily spring from such a source, and when again the religious element is subjected to the power of a fantastic imagination.

But herein lies the secret of the mysticism which characterized Servetus: he rejected philosophical reflection, protested against it in the severest terms when the doctrine of the Trinity was concerned, and insisted that people ought to give them-

* Ed. Laus. Ep. 171. Calv. Bullingero. Feb. 22, 1554.

† Ed. Laus. Ep. 157. Ed. Amst. p. 78. Sept. 14, 1553.

selves wholly up to the child-like, living faith of the first apostolic age. But when the doctrine respecting God, in his own system, became the subject of debate, he then sought to comprehend Deity, gave the reins to his fancy, raised a pantheistic structure, and objected to Calvin that he was no philosopher. Knowledge indeed, he said, ought to be kept subordinate to the religious principle, but still the latter is not the all-prevailing fundamental element. Thus his dogmatic propositions are not absolutely bound up, or blended, with his main philosophical ideas.

If Servetus had clearly comprehended his own system of reasoning, or had he fully wrought out his pantheistic notion of Deity, conscious in all things, Christ would probably have become to him the personal, self-revealing God, and God the common substance. It is to this that his system, fairly followed up, would lead; but his religious feeling would not allow him to go so far. He rejected the doctrine of the Trinity, as established by the early councils, the distinctions of persons, the union of the divine and human natures in Jesus, the eternal generation of Christ, and the procession of the Holy Ghost, without perceiving that the apostolic church distinctly recognized these doctrines, and that the Nicene, and the so-called Athanasian Creed, had their gradual and necessary origin in the struggle against heretics, who understood not the revelation of God.

According to Servetus, redemption and justification, in the sense of the church, are not at all necessary. God created his Son to reveal the mystery of the divine nature; He contemplates himself in this his perfect image; and man contemplates God in order to raise and conform himself to that image, and again in God to live, or personally to cease. But this is obscure, God being in Himself incomprehensible. A living knowledge of God can only proceed, according to Servetus, from the historical Christ, independent of whom truth is but an abstraction. Thus the doctrine of Christ is, with him, the fundamental, and the only proper, article of faith belonging to the apostolic church. The distinction of persons in the Godhead was to him altogether unintelligible; but he asserted that God was actually in Christ upon earth, and that Christ must be honoured as God. We would fain view this principle as the groundwork of his system; but here we are met with another difficulty. Servetus had no idea of original sin: thus the doctrine of Christ as a Redeemer was wanting in his creed. Hence also he rejected infant-baptism; and man, in the being of Christ, falls into the background.

It has been commonly supposed that Servetus revived the heresies of Paul of Samosata, Sabellius and Photinus. But that he was far apart from these three ancient heretics, and that his peculiarly constituted mind led him into much greater errors, if it did not indeed embrace those of all the three, is sufficiently evident. He began with placing himself above all other teachers: he rejected Lutherans, Calvinists, Catholics, and confined himself to no one system whatever. "I believe," he said, "that both parties (Protestants and Catholics) have a portion of truth and a portion of error*." True Christianity, according to him, must finally triumph upon earth, and is superior to all earlier systems. Thus the fervours of a living faith, to which his fancy gave wings, are not to be despised†. Servetus in one respect agreed with the present times, in which catholicism and protestantism are often viewed as only two sides of Christianity, while a higher expression of its doctrine is felt to be still needed. How little Servetus thought himself a heretic, appears from the fact, that he placed Paul of Samosata at the head of all who deserve that name‡.

It may be gathered from what has been said, that the relation between knowledge and faith was necessarily left obscure in the system of Servetus. The understanding, and not the Scriptures, was to him the fountain of knowledge. The understanding defines the being of God, and the holy Scriptures must establish it. He set little value on tradition. In philosophy he agreed with Plato, against Aristotle. Plato, he thought, derived his knowledge from the East, and from Anaxagoras, Parmenides, &c. He hoped however to stand higher himself, and, weary of the philosophy of his times, he sought to lay the foundations of a better wisdom. Against the Aristotelian method of reasoning he protested, as against a common evil: the Aristotelian logic, and ignorance of Hebrew, he regarded as the cause of all the errors which existed. Philosophy however was necessary, and he made it the subject of rebuke to his opponent that he was unphilosophical. "I have said it with the best intentions, you

* De Justificat. c. iv. De Charitate.

† His prayer, at the end of his preface to the 'Restitutio,' may be referred to as an illustration of this remark.

‡ De Trinit. Error. lib. vii. fol. 111, b.

are ignorant of the principles of things, you dream of imaginary qualities." He lays down, in a letter to Calvin, a maxim respecting the being of God, which he had derived solely from reflection: it is, that God must be everywhere present. But still, he allowed himself to be guided by Scripture, and he even declares, that all is false which is not derived from that source. In the second development of his system he indulged in a far more speculative course. His knowledge consequently of saving faith must, according to these premises, have been very unsatisfactory. In the work 'De Fide et Justitia,' he expresses himself more clearly than in his early writings. The essence of faith, with him, is a certain confidence, a free movement of the will, and not a habit of the heart, through which we receive Christ, and thus become quickened by his spirit. This faith is the source of every good. "You cannot," he says, "believe that Christ is in truth the Son of God, that he died for the pardon of your sins, without hating the sin for which He suffered so much." Again, "This living faith has, of necessity, hope and charity for its companions." So too, all is made to rest upon the knowledge of Christ. "I have always said, I say it now, and will continue to say, that all Scripture refers to this doctrine, that Christ is the Son of God—Christ acquires a form in us."

But this confession of faith was only seemingly true. No actual acknowledgment of sin, and of condemnation, was connected with it. The law was taken away through Christ, and faith is represented as wonderfully bestowed by Him on men, but without being grounded on the principle of inward conviction. The idea and knowledge of Christ form the starting-point of the system. Thus, according to Servetus, the bright form of Christ is impressed upon us, and it is only when this takes place that we become conscious of our wretchedness.

Here we have a direct perversion of the doctrine of the Gospel. To understand Servetus, we must recur to the principle, that it is possible for us to realize the idea of the divine and human, and to impress it upon our souls as a substantial, luminous form. Thus the form of Christ within us, as the result of the operation of the spirit of Christ, maturing our faith, and impressing upon us the idea of Christ, is to be regarded as the grand object of our inward contemplation. In this manner also, God becomes inwardly visible to the eye of faith; and believers, through the image of the Son of God in their souls, are made partakers of the Lord, to which, in the sacrament, are added his body, flesh and bones, for the nourishment of the new man.

If we now review the doctrine of the being of God, Servetus, who pretended to solve the problem by thought alone, will furnish us with less infallible rules, according to which we may comprehend the nature of the Most High. In the first place, the divine essence is indivisible; and, in the second, that which appears in nature is but a disposition of deity.* Three persons are inconceivable to the understanding. To form however such a notion of persons, we must look to the dispositions of the indivisible God.

At his first appearance, Servetus opposed Œcolampadius with these fundamental principles of his system. He asserted, that Christ had not existed from eternity, except as the idea of Christ. Like Sabellius, he did not absolutely object to the doctrine of three persons; but he would not acknowledge their independent self-existence; he admitted it only as so many relations, under which the divine essence appeared. The perfections of God could not be here spoken of; since his essence, like pure light, disperses not itself in various hues. God, in his entire fulness and strength, is everywhere present, and it is not lawful for human reason to divide God's power, in order to form various powers, seeing that the ray of pure light, broken into various colours, is no longer the light itself. It is inconceivable how the personality of God should be eternally preserved, after it has been displayed in various characters.

We here discover the source of his fierce opposition to the reformers and the catholics, whose fundamental principle is a holy belief in the Most High, in that eternal and personal essence, which, altogether distinct from the world, created it free and separate; which includes all perfections within itself; before which all created beings feel bowed in the sense of their misery and sin; and in which there is a necessary Trinity and Unity.

In the last part of the 'Restitutio' we have the paper written by Servetus against Melancthon, who had powerfully assailed his doctrine in his 'Common Places.' Servetus thought that he was bound to treat Melancthon like Calvin: he spoke of him indeed as somewhat more reasonable than Luther and Calvin, but only in regard to the doctrine of free-will: in other respects he was as senseless as the rest. The devil must have inspired him with his notion of personality. As Melancthon called him

* De Trinit. Error. lib. vii. f. 118, a.

a disciple of Paul of Samosata, so he in return styled Melancthon and Calvin scholars of Simon Magus; Augustin and Athanasius were, according to him, servants of Antichrist. He asserted that the true doctrine of the Gospel was to be found in Irenæus only, and in some few others of the ancient fathers. On the other hand, the church had ceased, he believed, to exist since the council of Nicæa, and the publication of the doctrine of the Trinity. He remained true to the notion advanced in his first work, that there are no persons in God, but dispositions only,—manifestations, that is, of the divine essence. But what such manifestations or dispositions are, or how the one is separated from the other, or the Word from the Spirit, is not stated. The Word, according to him, is not the voice of God, but an oracle, an expression of God, which appeared in the angels, whereby God answered Moses. At the beginning was an expression of God with God, and this oracle was God himself. He subsequently gave a fuller statement of the doctrine thus advanced, as may be seen in his account of the creation, and of Christ. The doctrine of the Trinity was to him Tritheism; and he described the eternal generation of the Son as a vain and unholy philosophy, and the disfiguring of God by a division into persons as the greatest of blasphemies. This is the necessary consequence of his philosophy, God being represented as a simple being, in whom Christ was not personally existing. To avoid all difficulties, therefore, Servetus proceeds from the principle, that God, as an almighty being, can adopt all forms to make Himself manifest. This revelation however is not connected with any inward necessity pertaining to the being of God. Servetus merely supposed, that the Deity could not be comprehended without this manifestation or revelation. In this respect his views were very different to those of later theorists, who assert, that we may apprehend God by pure thought, or by the understanding. God freely closed the two revelations, by which we should feel and perceive Him. These forms pertain only to Deity. The expressions which Servetus employs are, 'disposition,' 'œconomy,' 'form,' 'personal representation,' and 'a kind of revelation,' 'a species of divine relation,' 'a manifestation.' He would own nothing like an emanation of Deity. If the word person, however, were to be taken in the sense in which the Latins used it—that is, as describing the outward form or appearance of a man—a Trinity, he said, might be admitted, and it would not be an error to speak of three persons in one God.

In the Old Testament these persons were shadows and types. They who heard the Word, saw and perceived only an outward appearance; they, on the contrary, who received the Spirit, felt his power. These were, so to say, experiments for bringing forth the personality of Christ, and of the Holy Ghost, as, according to the later philosophy of religion, the eternal law of the universe tends to exhibit the personality of God, in subordinate manifestations, and through a circle of unconscious substances, till at last it produces Christ, the actual personality of God.

And this manifestation of the Trinity, says Servetus, will again disappear, as not of necessity existing. God might also have created worlds altogether different to those now in being. So too He might have adopted other forms; and thus there might have been, instead of a threefold, a fourfold or a fivefold personality;—a bold idea, and one which shows how high a notion he had formed to himself of the divine essence. The unity might have broken itself, by various means, into visible rays; for example, for the sake of beings differently constituted to ourselves.

An interesting passage occurs in the 'Dialogues on the Trinity,' respecting the cause why God created the universe. The invisible God, he says, resolved by his own free will to create the world, and to reveal Himself to us; for the creation would have been without use if God had remained unknown. The Almighty said, "Let it become," and by his word He created the Logos, or Elohim, or Christ. And as He spake, He imposed upon himself a certain rule, and wrought somewhat in himself, when He became a Creator. He now acts otherwise than originally: He reveals himself; whereas before, dwelling in eternal silence, He was known to no one. By the word, 'Let there be light,' He transferred himself from eternal darkness into light, and became comprehensible by a bright-shining form, which John called 'The Word,' and Moses, 'Elohim.' This light remained hidden under the image of angels, till it shone forth in the face of Christ. Then also God the Spirit began to be, for there was no spirit before God breathed.

Servetus afterwards expressed these notions in a more extended form. In the fourth book of the 'Restitutio,' he undertook, as the title intimates, to explain the name of God, the nature of God, and the principle of all things. Having spoken of the names Jehovah and Elohim, he unfolds his platonic idea of God. The original images, or ideas, of all things are in the Almighty. The forms of all things, which were afterwards to exist, were present to his wisdom from eternity. Wise men of all ages have taught this truth, and the holy Scripture itself, according to its design. Plato, who seems to have studied Moses, and who was familiar with the wise men of earlier times, and therefore stood higher than Aristotle, expounded it. He regarded ideas not as mere notions in God, but as the actual images of the things, to which God gave life, according to his good pleasure, and through the light of his being. Thus it is conceivable, how a resplendent image of the future Christ, without any change of his own being, might originate in God from eternity. In this last development of Deity, Servetus proceeds from a pantheistic point of view, which is not the doctrine of Plato. According to that philosopher, matter, or chaos, was separated from God. In the eternal being of God, which, it is probable, had ceased to be contemplated in its personality, there are numberless forms, and the ideas of all things. God himself is the essence and the source of all: unnumbered beings rest in Him. This essence of God takes all forms; and Servetus speaks of an *omniformis Dei essentia.* But with all this manifoldness, there is in God but one *modus*, the principle of all life, of all light, of all spirit,—a divine *modus* of the fulness of the substance, without limit, in the spirit and body of Jesus Christ. The *modus* in him is twofold. Hence the discourse is of two persons; the appearance in the Word, and the communication in the Spirit; other things, both spiritual and corporeal, being created thereby. This is the eternal thought of God concerning things, and their representation, by form and matter. From this root all things arise. There are similar divine *modes* in the angels and in men, and even in individual things. The Godhead dwells in all, but all spring from Christ. This doctrine is represented as that of Scripture, but it is much more that of the Greeks and Orientals, and after them of the Rabbins, in their theory of the soul of the world. Thus the archetype of the world is described as in God, and the wisdom of God is the Logos. The archetypes spoken of are not merely images, but substantial forms.

Hence we find that Servetus was a realist, and he represents knowledge according to the Platonic theory. Thus objects formed according to the original patterns, re-awaken in the soul its innate ideas. The fountain of all light is in the Logos; his light is the formative principle of all things. In his doctrine of God, Servetus firmly asserts the principle, that God is incomprehensible to the creature, except as He reveals himself in the

Word and in the Spirit. The Logos is *Ideal* in God, and no *Person*. The Word is God himself, the whole God. In the representation of the Logos, Servetus employed no settled or definite language. Logos, with him, is the divine thought and speech, identical with the divine will. The eternal thought and will of the person of Christ are the organ of divine revelation. So far as all other divine thoughts are gathered together in the one divine thought, the Logos appears as the Ideal world, which may be represented as the divine understanding. Lastly, Servetus advocates, in his concluding work, the ideality of the divine understanding itself. The revelation of God in Christ fills the intermediate space between God and the creature. In the man Christ the Logos is hypostatically present. The union with God is also become possible to the angels. Of the Holy Ghost, it is said, that He is the communication of the divine essence, which proceeds from Christ after the resurrection.

In all this we recognize a philosophical system in embryo, which never probably would have been brought to maturity; for, on the one side, Servetus stumbled on dialectic difficulties, and on the other, the free course of his speculations was hindered by the element of Christian piety. If he had understood himself, as a philosopher, and had kept his aim steadily in view, he would have described Christ, in relation to God, as God reducing himself within the limits of personality, which was what in reality he always meant. But his system appears as a mass of defective Christian notions on the work of redemption, mixed up with a certain measure of Platonism. Since Christ however, according to him, is a person, God cannot properly be so; for a twofold personality would as little agree with his theory as a threefold.

In the fourth book on the Trinity, in the 'Restitutio,' Servetus proceeds from the original forms, to the origin, of all things. We shall speak briefly of his doctrine of creation. He combines religion and natural theology, and illustrates the one from the other. Light is the ground of all things. God is light; and in this light of the Godhead did Christ appear, as the sun in the midst of created light. He was therefore the first creation of God. The various characteristics of different bodies arise from the light, which mingles itself with them. Heat and cold rule in nature; but both the one and the other derive their essence and power from light. The light of the sun warms, and the watery rays, which are collected in some of the planets, in the moon, in Saturn, and other parts of the heavens, diffuse cold. All this has the Architect of the world, the resplendent character of the divine essence, that is, Christ, accomplished by means of light. All exists by him: he created the elements, and afterwards imparted to each a portion of the light which is in himself. All which takes place in nature, as well as in the kingdom of grace and in the conversion of mankind, is wrought by light.

God, at the beginning, created, out of nothing, two heavens, the earth, and the light. Hence all other things arose: the water first, from the water of heaven, and the air. The air and the light generated fire. The doctrine of Thales is said to be correct; the earth was prior to the heavens. God created air and a watery heaven. Further: there is an uncreated heaven, a heaven of air in God and Christ. This is the third heaven, of which Paul speaks. There is air in the water and in the fire, a heavenly as well as an earthly material, a principle hitherto unknown to all the philosophers of the world. There are four fundamental principles of all things; two material and two formal:—1. Water and earth: 2. The sun-light, which warms, and the watery ray, which creates cold.

The ancients taught rightly, that all things are one, since all exist in God. God is everywhere, because the light of God is in all things: God is in all beings, even in wicked spirits: all things are an effluence of the divine essence, but all things are not a certain species of the Godhead, or parts of God; since, except in regard to the matter of heavenly light, they are earthly, and altogether separate from God.

Servetus, on account of his pantheistic expressions, has been characterized as a forerunner of Spinoza. This is very unjust; his Christian feeling raised him far above Spinoza, while he was singularly unlike him in the obscurity of his reasoning. Spirit and matter, according to him, are not necessarily opposed. He acknowledged a creation out of nothing, by the free-will of God, and he pronounced a curse upon those who assert an unchangeable destiny or law. Man he represents as perfectly free, which alone would be sufficient to exonerate him from partaking in the errors of Spinoza. But since he allows not the creation of the world, as separate from God, the world being imperfect, he is in this respect altogether opposed to Christianity. The natural philosophy of Servetus, and his belief, go always hand in hand, and he availed himself of his experience as a physician to illustrate the operation of grace, and the divine government. He admits of the existence of angels, but only as a breath of God. Of the evil spirit, as a personal being, he frequently speaks, but without especial definition.

This leads us to the notion of Servetus on the fall of man. In the two dialogues on the Trinity, and in the 3rd, 6th and 7th books of the 'Restitutio,' mention is made of the fall, of angels, of punishment in hell, and of salvation. He here expresses the fine idea, which occurs also in Calvin, that through the sin of the first man all the world sunk, and even the stars became unclean. Nowhere however does he speak of the ruin of mankind, and of their condemnation, as grounded, according to the Christian doctrine, on the knowledge of sin. Man, he asserts, can be prepared for good works without being born again of the spirit. This was the first cause of his errors, of his haughty intractable character, and of his perverse conduct. Here and there however expressions occur, respecting the corruption of the human race, which have a pious and orthodox sound. The devil is spoken of as sin dwelling in us, as sickness and death. In a similar manner also he speaks of the tree of knowledge. But these passages are contradicted by others. Original sin is represented as a mere sickness, and as unconnected with guilt. Man is subjected to bodily death, not to spiritual, for he is without guilt; he is not condemned to hell, but, so to speak, is left in school, or the place of the dead, till he arrive at the age of knowledge, that is, his twentieth year. He who sins after this exposes himself to both bodily and spiritual death. Thus Servetus necessarily rejected infant-baptism.

The view which he took of redemption is evident from his doctrine of the nature of Christ: much is said on this subject in his two dialogues on the Trinity, which form the sixth and seventh books of the 'Restitutio,' and in which Michael and Peter are introduced conversing with each other. In the second dialogue he seeks to show, as he states, in what manner Christ was begotten of God. Christ is no creature (these words must be understood in his own sense: He is eternal as thought): his power has no end: He is worthy of worship, and is the true God. Such expressions even as these occur: "The soul of Christ is God; the flesh of Christ is God; the spirit of Christ is God." But the human nature is disregarded, and that he erred in this respect was viewed as his greatest offence. Thus Calvin, while he was in prison, made this a cause of accusation against him; and in his sentence it is stated, "that he wickedly destroyed

Christ's humanity, the main source of consolation to poor, perishing mankind."

It has been already shown, how he despised and blasphemed the doctrine of the church respecting the incarnation, or the union of the divine with the human principle. On the other hand, he speaks in the following manner on the human nature of Christ, and on his generation. The Logos was the paternal seed: a part of the spirit of God, and a part of light, which is Deity itself, passed into the holy Virgin, and a part of her blood mingled therewith. This earthly part of the mother became visible: therefore the blood of Christ, the flesh of Christ, the soul of Christ, is God himself. This Christ is no creature: God himself and the fulness of God dwell in Him. As Servetus would not acknowledge the eternity of the Son of God, but yet confessed his divinity according to the Scriptures, he was obliged to view the union of the divine nature with the manhood of Christ, in such a sense, that the man Christ might be called God, thus setting aside the personality of God. Three light-elements of the Father were combined with the blood of the mother in the generation of the son. Thus in Christ the primal light of God is mingled with the earthly nature of the mother, the divine with the human: he is partaker of both natures, consubstantial with God, ὁμοούσιος.

In the second book of the 'Restitutio' he interprets the first verse of the first chapter of John, and more at length than in his earlier work. He also expounds the passage, in the first chapter of the Epistle to the Colossians, in which Christ is described as the first-born of every creature. The flesh of Christ, the earthly portion of his being, is older than our flesh; his body is derived from the first pure matter, as it existed before sin; whereas our bodies are of the impure matter, as it has existed since the fall. Thus he deified the man in Christ. Calvin remarked this. He combined the Godhead with the flesh of Christ, mingling the two natures; while he separated the flesh of Christ from ours, as far as heaven from earth. Again, he says, that as, through the incarnation, the Word became flesh for all creatures, so, through the resurrection, the flesh ceased to be a creature. The Word from heaven is now the flesh of Christ: the human nature of Christ is the same as the divine.

"But what," says Calvin, "will become of our communion with Christ, and of our salvation, if we thus tear the band asunder which unites us in brotherly communion with Christ, the only pledge of our adoption? Christ, according to the apostle, is our brother; for He was made in all things like unto us, sin only except. Servetus understands this expression as merely intimating that he had a similar life to ours; whereas the apostle speaks of a like nature: and it is evident indeed, that the Son of God could not have reconciled us to the Father, without atoning for sins in that which was truly human flesh, not divine, so that the satisfaction might be accomplished in our own nature. Christ paid the price of our redemption in his flesh. If his flesh had been divine, what should we have had to do with the payment? There is a union indeed of both natures, but no mingling or confusion of the two."

According however to the system of Servetus, this divine Christ is a transient Deity. He had already spoken, in his controversy with Œcolampadius, of this his notion of Christ, and he persevered in defending it, asserting that Christ can be called eternal in no other way than the world is, the idea of which had existed from eternity in the mind of God. He thus expresses himself also respecting the end of the world, and with it, of its Trinity. The person of Christ, consequently, when its work is finished, will cease to be; and thus he not only looses the band which binds us to Him for eternity, but sets aside redemption itself.

The doctrine of the Holy Ghost is equally defective in the system of Servetus. He describes the spirit of God as an energy. In the air which we breathe there is the power of God: He moves nature thereby. The Holy Ghost however works inwardly, enlightens and sanctifies man. Spirit, wind, breath, indicate the outward living energy; the "Holy Ghost" the inward. When God spake, He became God the Spirit: before He thus breathed, there was no Spirit, and He breathed not till He spake. Thus Moses says, that the Spirit of God moved the water. This Spirit, in the Old Testament, was only a shade, a type; but in the New Testament He became a certain power of God, which works in the souls of men; and hence He is no longer called the Spirit of the Lord, but the Spirit of God, the Holy Ghost. He is a movement, which God excites in men; and when it is imparted to men through the ministry of angels, which are only a breath of God, then it is itself also in Scripture called an angel. The Holy Ghost is a person of the Godhead; while, as an angel, He directs the work of God. This Spirit is a "disposition" in God; and in this sense we may speak of three persons in God. At the beginning, however, of this very article Servetus had indulged himself in his usual ridicule and abuse of the church doctrine of the Trinity.

This second revelation of God is not distinct from God himself, and from the Logos, but only in the form of the manifestation.

According to the last development of his system, Servetus represents the Spirit, like everything else in the world, as originally contained in the Word, that is, in idea and substance, as the idea and archetype of all other spirits. The universal Spirit of God, which fills creation, is properly the soul of the world. He first appeared perfect in Christ: He assumed the human nature with the Logos, and formed the soul of Christ. We receive through regeneration and in the sacrament, the Holy Spirit, and that by means of the breath of Christ.

If we look now at the church, which the Spirit of God founded, we shall find that Servetus claimed for it a vast power, which, although it be hidden, is mightier than all powers, so that angels and devils must be subject unto it.

To this part of his system belongs his doctrine of justification by faith, by works, and by Christ. Melancthon wrote to Camerarius, "He is manifestly mad on the subject of justification." The principal exposition of his doctrine respecting the method of salvation is found in the second part of the 'Restitutio.' 1. In the three books on Faith, and on the righteousness of the kingdom of Christ, which surpasses the righteousness of the law. 2. In that which treats of the law and the Gospel. 3. In the description of charity, in its relation to faith and good works. This is a repetition of his earlier work on Justification. He shows here especially, that he sought a higher species of faith than that of either Catholics or Protestants. Lamenting the depression of Christianity, he says, "No one knows what the faith of Christ is, or what charity is." His creed was simple enough:—"The man Christ Jesus is the Son of God, who died for our salvation." The account which he gives of the manner in which we arrive at faith is as follows. The understanding first apprehends all the truths of the Gospel; the heart applies these truths to itself by the drawing of the Father, or the movement of the Holy Ghost. The mind accordingly receives the faith, and freely embraces it: it still retains the ability to choose what is good, and has somewhat of the Godhead: but God must come to its aid, that it may be able to take advantage of its freedom. Faith is a fruit of this freedom.

Justification, he says, is the forgiveness of sins: when a man recognizes Christ as the Son of God and Saviour of the world, he becomes righteous and is saved. The Gospel stands far higher than the law: in the Old Testament we have the righteousness of works, and in the New the righteousness of faith; but he contends against the so-called extravagance of the Protestant doctrine, which will allow of no reward for works. This is discussed in the third book of the second part, *De Mercede et Gloriæ Differentia*, "concerning rewards and the distinction of glory." He shows that in the New Testament a certain species of righteousness becomes available through works, and that the first justification by faith is followed by a second justification, which proceeds from the diligence with which a man performs good works, which God actually rewards. To some interesting reflections, he adds, that salvation comes from faith, but that the materials of it are good works, for love and good works increase blessedness: they clothe faith and preserve it alive.

This leads us to the consideration of his views of free-will: it is characteristic of his peculiar notions, that he felt that, in his time, the freedom of man was not yet comprehended in its proper mystery. Hence he opposed himself with all his force to the main doctrine of Calvin, which he designated as that of fate, or a universal necessity. In the same manner he spoke of the bondage of the will as a sign of Calvin's stupidity. The reformer exhorted men to do what he knew they could not do. "You say a vast deal about *free-doings*, and say that there is no *free-doing*."

In his earlier work on Justification he says, "It is better to perform good works than to inquire into the causes of good works; but as there are many who have little skill in philosophizing, I will here dispense with my philosophy. I believe that good works have their peculiar origin in free-will, which is as distinct from faith as it is from charity. There is an operating Spirit which is higher than any will, or any inward quality, and which freely brings forth good works. The outward action is effected by the movement of the heart, which sends its spirits into the members; and this action of the free-will is something more than the resolution of the will, there being more difficulty in accomplishing than in willing. The meaning of this is: faith excites charity; charity the will; but the higher energy is needed for this. The energy thus spoken of is superior to the will to do good. For of what avail would the pious will be, if there were no power to accomplish its object? It is this power which brings with it a reward from God."

Thus Servetus endeavoured to penetrate the depths of free-will, Calvin and the other reformers being content to comprehend it in an antithesis. Servetus placed freedom in a certain power of the heart to effect the conclusions of the will. Sin excites in the natural man evil desires: faith awakens love and holy desires. There is an ability, however, in the free-will of man to determine whether he will accomplish his good or evil resolves: good or evil works, consequently, may be set to his account; and thus we may look for hell or a sublime blessedness.

In the little work on Justification, in which Servetus seeks a middle path between the old and the new doctrine, he concedes to Luther, that faith justifies without merit or works; and to the Catholic church, that charity and good works may deserve somewhat with God and expect a reward. He contends however with great severity against the dead works of the monks, and speaks of faith with as much fervour as Luther, disagreeing with him only when the discourse refers to free-will and the source of good works. In the times of the old covenant grace was not bestowed on men: he who fulfilled the law as well as he could was righteous: even the holiest men were only righteous in a natural sense; they had earthly desires and feared earthly chastisements. This carnal justification was abolished by Christ. In the new covenant the spirit is justified by faith: to attain it we must hear Christ, repent, deny and sacrifice ourselves, and place our whole trust in this, that man has been redeemed by the blood of Christ, and that by his mercy alone, without any desert on our own part, we may obtain forgiveness of sin, and recover our lost spiritual life. Works avail nothing for salvation. Faith produces charity, and through it we receive the Holy Ghost. But although faith alone, and without works, justifies us, yet Christians who act well may expect their reward both in time and in eternity.

Above all, he says, is obedience acceptable to God; the subjection, that is, of our understanding to the rule of Christ as the Son of God. This one command of faith in Christ has God put in the place of all the law. Through this faith we become children of God.

The distinction between justification, as viewed by Servetus and the Reformers, consists in this, that with Servetus it was not faith in the merits of Christ, without works, which justifies, but the faith in the Son of God which incites us to good works. Hence, according to him, the Lutherans could never understand justification: he wished to give it a practical character.

With this subject is connected the view which Servetus takes of the means of grace. According to him, the christian church has three:—the preaching of the Gospel; baptism; and the Lord's Supper. The power of the keys is the power of preaching,—of the exposition of the truth; while the pope holds the keys of the abyss. In the doctrine of the sacrament, he separates from the Lutherans, whom he designates *Impanatores*; from the Zwinglians and Reformed, whom he calls *Tropisten*; and from the Catholics, whom he reviles as *Transubstantiatores*. He rejects the opinions of each and all of these parties, and adopts a view similar to the Calvinistic doctrine, the idea, that is, of a spiritual eating. In the order to be remarked in the several parts of the work of salvation, baptism, with him, is not the beginning, but the middle point of the course. He would acknowledge but two sacraments, properly so-called. It appears remarkable that he should have assailed the use of infant baptism with such peculiar violence. He even calls it a murdering of the Holy Ghost; a desolating of the kingdom of God; a ruining of Christianity. This is unintelligible, unless we suppose him to have altogether rejected the doctrine of original sin, as received by the church. Servetus however was not properly an anabaptist: he admitted the power of the civil magistrate; the duty of obedience, and the lawfulness of oaths: but, on the other hand, he described adult baptism as alone making men Christians, and as exalting them above the angels. Prior to this baptism faith is imperfect: faith justifies, but baptism saves. In the first instance, the preaching of the word must awaken and enlighten the heart; repentance must then follow; and this will prepare the man for entering into the kingdom of heaven. There must be faith in the Son of God, to induce him to come to baptism; and for this purpose he is to undergo the proper instruction of a catechumen. With respect to those who fall after baptism, no further baptism or reconciliation is possible. This is another reason why children should not be baptized. There is a wonderful efficacy in this sacrament, as in that also of the Lord's Supper: they cannot be separated from each other. Baptism may properly take place in the thirtieth year of a man's life*.

Unbaptized children, nay, even the most excellent men among the heathens and Jews, cannot enter the kingdom of heaven. There are habitations prepared for them where they enjoy the happiness proper to their condition. This leads us to consider his views of the future state.

Servetus adopts without questioning the doctrine of the immortality of the soul. This is evident from the declaration which he made at his trial, and from his behaviour at the stake. It is not so apparent from his works.

In his Defence, written against Melancthon, he advocates the notion of a purgatory, through which all Christians must pass. This he calls the baptism by fire. In the end, souls pass away into the divine vision or idea. This subject is treated of in the seventeenth letter, in the 'Restitutio.' Again: Servetus contended against Calvin, that the visible body of Christ has no place in heaven. Calvin answered, that "if the body of the Lord is in no certain place, the bodies of the saints, after the resurrection, which are visible like his, can have no certain place." Servetus expressed no surprise at this objection, but readily admitted Calvin's assertion; adding, "When heaven and earth shall have passed away, there will be neither time nor place, neither movement nor being. We shall be inclosed by no space, but shall exist in the idea or understanding of God." *Sola idea divina nos post resurrectionem continebimur.* Christ himself will be embraced in the highest idea or understanding of God, and will thus, without any change of place, be everywhere present. *Sola principe idea divina, ipse princeps continetur, et per eam est ubique vult, sine locali motu.* Everything is derived from the idea of God, and to that will everything return. There are ideas and original forms; they have sprung into life, and will again become essential.

Servetus admits the doctrine of infernal punishment and future blessedness. "God himself is the purgatory, Christ the holy fire." The doctrine of the restoration of all things is stated in the third part of the 'Restitutio,' where the kingdom of Antichrist is also spoken of. The sixty signs of Antichrist are described in the fifth part.

The whole world is fallen through sin, and Christ renews it. Satan ruined the natural world by Eve, and the spiritual by

* De Regeneratione, *passim*.

the Romish whore, the pope. Servetus here speaks continually with as great severity against Rome as the Reformers had done. But he speaks with no less rage against the Protestants, and especially against Melancthon, whom he addresses, in his 'Apology,' in words which show the entire disorder of his mind. "You say that the Jews and the Turks do not worship God aright. But what is the notion you yourself have formed of the hell-hound? To what a monster do you not pray! Calvin is drunk when he teaches that man has no power of free action, and yet expects him to act as if he had. You too are drunk, when you exhort to the true love of God, and at the same time say that it nowhere exists. But most of all do you show your error and drunkenness in your belief in the Trinity, in your false conclusions respecting the two natures, which so drive you into a corner, that you are compelled to allow that the Holy Ghost might die in a mule, since you have asserted that your invisible Son of God died in a man."

The system of Servetus, taken as a whole, gives signs of an awakened mind, of ability and lofty views; but it was not the fruit of a renewed heart. The Holy Spirit speaks a different language. The power which inspired Servetus taught him not the wretchedness of sin; hence his pride in opposing what he did not understand, and his shameless language, unparalleled in the history of the church, of either ancient or modern times. The principles, moreover, which he advances, are far more unintelligible as speculations than all the deep things of our faith. Had he developed these creations of his brain scientifically, or merely for himself, as had been done in other times, he might have been pardoned; but when he undertook to establish his system in the place of that which is evangelical and catholic, and when the libertines and the Anabaptists were found to take his part, in order to oppose the Reformation, it was necessary that his fanaticism should be suppressed. Had this not been done, the reformation in the South, which, in the midst of the convulsions which now prevailed, was only supported by the strongest efforts, must have shared the fate of that of Poland; an event which would have been as injurious to the general progress of the world as to the interests of Lutheranism. It was Calvin's task to defend the Reformation with the weapons furnished by the age in which he lived.

CHAPTER VI.

OTHER TEACHERS OF FALSE DOCTRINE RESPECTING THE TRINITY.—MATTHÆUS GRIBALDI.—BLANDRATA.—GENTILIS—HIS SYSTEM AND HISTORY.

As we are only concerned with those teachers of error who stood in special opposition to Calvin, we may pass over the well-known anabaptist Joris or Georg, who died in 1556, after having lived unknown twelve years in Basel. According to his dogma he was the true Christ, and could forgive sin and condemn the world. He had the Spirit, against which no one should dare to sin. It was one of the principles of his sect, that the marriage-vow need not be kept unbroken*.

We must not however neglect to notice the disturbances which prevailed at this time in the Italian church at Geneva, and which threatened to prove dangerous to unity of doctrine. Among the members of the congregation alluded to was the lawyer, Matthæus Gribaldi†. Without understanding Servetus, he declared that one side of his error appeared to him like truth; that Christ, according to his human nature, was properly and truly the Son of God. Thus his views were in reality Socinian. He supposed that the Father alone was the eternal God; the Son being a subordinate God, the first-born among many. Calvin describes this controversy in an interesting letter to Georg of Würtemberg, May 2, 1557‡. It shows that the reformer merely desired the banishment of heretics, when their errors were unaccompanied by blasphemy. Gribaldi was exiled.

But the excitement which he had occasioned at Geneva was not terminated by his removal; other restless spirits were at work. At length the elders and ministers of the Italian church besought the Council that a confession might be drawn up,

* Buchat, t. vi. p. 293, gives his history at length.

† Gribaldi had been a professor at Padua, and witnessed, in 1548, the horrible despair of the conscience-stricken apostate, Franz Spiera. Not being safe at Padua, he obtained, through the recommendation of Vergerio, the appointment to a law-professorship at Tubingen, from the Duke of Würtemberg. He travelled much about, and on coming to Geneva bought the estate of Farges in Gex. Calvin warned Wolmar in Tübingen against him.

‡ Ed. Amst. p. 113, b. Laus. Ep. 238.

which every member of the congregation should be required to subscribe. Calvin employed his influence to effect this object: the several councils favoured the establishment of the rule, and it became the law *. The Italian church was assembled; those who entertained doubts had a conference with Calvin, which lasted three hours: he convinced them all, and all, with the exception of five members of the congregation, subscribed the formulary. Among those who refused was Valentine Gentilis. Both he and his companions soon after, from fear, left the city. These circumstances took place in May 1558. The duke of Würtemberg subsequently learnt that Gribaldi was engaged in spreading his heretical opinions on the Trinity in his territories: he accordingly assembled the divines of Tübingen, to examine Gribaldi respecting his doctrine. Gribaldi requested time to prepare his confession; but he retired secretly from the city, and withdrew to his country-seat at Farges, in the canton of Bern. The duke acquainted the authorities at Bern with all which had taken place: they accordingly summoned Gribaldi before them, and cast him into prison. The clergy of Bern were desired to examine his writings: they replied that Gribaldi taught, "that there are three unequal Gods," &c. He had however a conference with them, and subscribed a confession, in which he acknowledged his errors. Banished from Bern, he was, notwithstanding, permitted to return to Farges, where he remained to the end of his days. He died of the plague.

Another heretic, who went to Poland, there to play his part, and whom Calvin pursued thither with the sword of the Spirit, was the physician Blandrata. This Italian, having exhibited his character in Geneva, and been pronounced a heretic by his countryman Peter Martyr, went, as we have stated, to Poland, and there acquired an honourable position. "I am not surprised," said Calvin †, "that this abandoned man has tried to effect among you, who indulge in more license than we, what he attempted among us. But I am deeply affected at learning from your statement, that many persons among you have been carried away by this fury. A short time ago a writing was brought to me, in which Christ is represented as a sort of strange God; and I wrote an admonition, which I hope has already reached you. I am now induced, by your pious encouragement, again to consider how I may best oppose this continually spreading evil."

* MS. Tig. Oct. 9, 1561.

† MS. Paris. Calv. Stanislao.

With regard to Blandrata, we learn his history from a notice sent by the Genevese ministers to the Wilnaer church, and which was written by Calvin *. The latter, it seems, imagined that he could see wickedness in the countenance of the man: "Your very look," he once publicly said to him, "indicates the monster which you cherish in your heart †." But he warned him against the secret circulation of his errors, and endeavoured by frequent conferences to bring him to a better state of mind. All however was in vain; Blandrata persevered in his fanaticism, and threw the Italian congregation at Geneva into fresh excitement. The elders were anxious for quiet. A discussion took place at which two members of the Council were present. Calvin explained the circumstances. Blandrata had the rashness to accuse him of falsehood, but was convinced of his slander. He stated to an intimate friend, Paul Alciat, that the Genevese worshiped three devils, worse than all the idols of the papists, because they regarded them as three persons. He left the city with this companion.

Blandrata was cited before the consistory. Calvin endeavoured to tranquillize him; a scene however took place, which was sufficiently comical to provoke even the stern Genevese to laughter. While Calvin was once holding a discourse, and Blandrata was present, one of the syndics entered the hall. Blandrata, terrified by his wicked conscience, believed that the syndic was come to try him; putting therefore his handkerchief to his nose as if it were bleeding, he ran out, and immediately hastened through the gate of the city, to which he never returned. No thought of harming him had been entertained. He fled to Zurich, where he was opposed by Peter Martyr, and thence to Poland. Calvin wrote a little treatise against him ‡. Like Gentilis, he separated the person of Christ from the Father; but he agreed with Gribaldus in acknowledging the Godhead of Christ, and hence had many Gods.

We have still to mention some characteristic circumstances respecting Blandrata. In the introduction to the account of this man, before quoted, Calvin declares himself ready to be reconciled to him. He treats the matter somewhat ironically; adding, in his epistle to the church at Wilnaer, which had assembled a synod,—"Blandrata has received no slight recompense for his

* Ed. Laus. Ep. 322. Ed. Amst. p. 161, an. 1561.

† MS. Bern. 13 Cal. Dec. 1558.

‡ Responsum ad Quæstiones J. Blandratæ, 1559.

troublesome journey, having gained so great a name. He seemed worth nothing among other people; but you admire him, as if he were an angel fallen from heaven. I do not envy your good luck. If you distrust my authority in this affair, yet surely the respectability of the elders of the Italian church, and of that excellent servant of Jesus Christ, Peter Martyr, will have some influence with you." This appeal to other authorities we should certainly not find in Luther in his later years.

It appears, indeed, that Blandrata had met with striking encouragement. Calvin praises the Polish Stanislaus, that he was not hurried away like others, who were ignorantly praising the heretic. "Know," he says, "that Valentin Gentilis, whose fanaticism I shortly ago exposed, is of the same party." Felix Cruciger was at that time in Poland. Stancarus had circulated accounts in Geneva, accusing even the Polish believers of inclining to the errors of Arius and Servetus. A synod therefore was assembled, and a confession of faith was sent to Geneva in order to clear them of this slander. Calvin highly praised it. They declare, that they desired always to remain in connexion with the church at Geneva. "May a holy union ever prevail between us!" was Calvin's answer. But how little the volatile Italians understood the deep mystery of the being of God, and how fiercely they disputed on the subject, appears from Calvin's 'Admonition' to the brethren in Poland (1563) and from the following narrative.

Valentin Gentilis was a person of some distinction: he was a native of Consenza; and sought that peace at Geneva which he could not find in his own heart. His history, characteristic of the times, is given partly by Calvin himself, and partly by Benoit Aretius, a theologian of Bern. Calvin relates to the Marquis Caraccioli, before-mentioned, and who so wisely separated himself from the frivolous spirits by which he was surrounded, the excitement which had been caused in the Italian church, and adds, that Valentin had persevered in diffusing his poison, but was now in prison. He describes him "as deceitful and disloyal," and says "he kept a school for secretly disseminating his errors, which are in one respect as detestable as those of Servetus; they are, in fact, thé same. I know not what will be the issue; but the beginning greatly distresses me."

Gentilis asserted, that all power ought to be ascribed to God the Father, who communicated his might to the other two persons; so that he admitted three persons and essences, and consequently three Gods, eternal, almighty, and infinite. He openly acknowledged this doctrine, and declared that his conscience compelled him to teach it. But notwithstanding this, he had subscribed the Confession of the Italian church, which concludes in the following terms: "We approve, receive, and confirm all these articles, asserting that he who does otherwise is perjured and perfidious." While in prison, Gentilis drew up a short account of his belief. The Council desired that it should be stated more at full. He then confessed, that "if the Father, Son, and Holy Ghost were to be acknowledged as equal in the divine essence, a fourfold personality ought to be admitted; since the divine essence was in itself, without any consideration of persons, the true God." The Father alone, he said, expresses the divine essence. The Word is 'the brightness of his glory' and 'the express image of his being,' distinct from the Father, He alone being the true God. Again, "The Word is the Son, and therefore truly God; and yet they are not two Gods, but one and the same."

The clergy frequently visited him, with the desire of inducing him to explain his views; but in vain. He wished to answer them in writing. He accordingly composed an apology, complaining that after he had come so far to see Calvin, of whom he had heard so much, he should be subjected to persecution. Endeavouring to support his opinions by scholastic reasoning, he concluded with a quotation from Melancthon's "Loci," and with several from Irenæus and Tertullian. Calvin answered him, in the name of the ministers, confuting every point in his argument. Valentin requested the assistance of an advocate, "that his innocence might not be oppressed by the power of the man and the volubility of his tongue;" because "I openly acknowledge that I cannot, with a good conscience, adopt his fourfold personality in God." In other respects he expressed himself prudently, avoiding whatever was blasphemous. His trial therefore exhibited a great contrast to that of Servetus, whose shameless blasphemy alone was the cause of his condemnation. Gentilis declared, "that he desired to submit himself altogether to the consistory; and that, as so many agreed in pronouncing him wrong, he would rather believe them, even though they dreamed, than himself, though awake." He entreated the favour of the Council; praised Calvin, and acknowledged his deserts.

But there was something strange in this retractation for the judges. They felt that he was jesting with them, and that they understood little of his real meaning. Five jurisconsults were therefore called to their aid, and they were asked what punishment was due to him according to the law. The lawyers answered, that, according to the imperial law, he ought to be condemned to the flames. Upon hearing this, the members of the council, on the 15th of August 1558, sentenced him to be beheaded. But the affair now took another direction. The lawyers soon felt regret that they had spoken so strongly, and prayed the Council to defer the execution of the sentence till the state of the man's soul could be more clearly determined. The Council was well-content to receive this application, and the milder sentiments which prevailed plainly indicate the transition to better times. Gentilis was re-examined, and he stated his belief in more cautious terms. "I must acknowledge," he said, "that when I made my first confession, my zeal so carried me away, that I would willingly have endured any punishment for the sake of establishing my doctrine. But after I had many times carefully perused the answer given me by the consistory, and which appeals so distinctly to fundamental principles, it pleased the Father of mercies, who allowed me to wander for a time in doubt, to bring me to the knowledge of my error, which rests upon three false supports. In the first place, I was wrong in not observing that, while I asserted that the one only God of Israel is the Father of our Lord, the Godhead of the Son, of the Father, and of Jesus Christ, was excluded by this contrast of one peculiar God. Secondly, when I viewed the being of God, independently of the persons, I insisted upon a fourfold personality; which was erroneous; since the essence can be seen only in the three persons, each of which has the whole essence in himself. My third error consisted in the assertion, that the person of the Father is sophistical; which is false, as has been proved to me. Upon these three rotten foundations I built many false consequences, which I now condemn." He expressed, moreover, his grief that he had caused any trouble to the church, and that he had answered Calvin, that great theologian, so thoughtlessly. So also he stated his hope that the ministers would receive him, the lost sheep, into the bosom of the church again; and he prayed that, as they had mercy on his soul, so they would also consider his bodily necessities, for that he had now been six months in prison, and was poor and sick. He appended a formal renunciation of his errors, and a pure confession of the truth.

Calvin declared, that, although he saw full well that as soon as Gentilis was free he would return to his errors, and that nothing was to be expected of so deceitful a man, they had no wish to resist the mercy of the judges, but would silently acquiesce in their decision.

In the report of the trial it is stated, "that Gentilis had been apprehended on account of his heresy; that although he had subscribed the confession of the Italian church, he had fallen back into error; that while in prison he had resisted all admonitions, remaining hardened in his impiety and in his blasphemous assertion, that we have four Gods, two Fathers, and a Turkish God; but that at length he had manifested repentance." The sentence is remarkable for the time. "Although," it says, "thou didst well deserve, for thy wickedness, to be destroyed from among men, we desire, having regard to thy repentance and conversion, to act towards thee with mercy rather than severity. We therefore sentence thee, Valentin Gentilis, to be stripped to the shirt, and, with naked feet and bare head, and with a lighted torch in thy hand, to kneel before us, and beseech the judges to pardon thee, acknowledging that thou hast wickedly diffused a false, heretical doctrine, and expressing thine abhorrence of the writings in which thou hast taught it. And we command thee to cast with thine own hand these thy writings into the fire here kindled, that, being full of dangerous lies, they may be burnt to ashes. And in order to prove thy repentance more fully, we command that thou be led through the streets of the city, with the sound of trumpets, and we forbid thee to depart the city. We desire that this may be an example to those who might attempt things like to thine."

The sentence thus passed upon Gentilis was executed September 2, 1558. He burned his writings, and exhibited profound humility and grief. All present were astonished; and he besought the Council, with many prayers, to allow him to leave the prison without his being obliged to find security, which his poverty, living as he did upon alms, might render impossible. The council graciously acceded to his request; and he declared with an oath, that he would not depart the city.

But all this was done in mockery. Gentilis no sooner found himself at liberty than he set out, and took the nearest road to his friend Gribaldi, now at his country-seat at Farges. Two other Italians followed him,—Paul Alciat and the physician Blandrata. We may easily conceive how these four Italians discussed, in their retirement, the doctrine of the Trinity, and Calvin's vocation. Gentilis became more confirmed in his error than ever, and went to France for the purpose of spreading it. While with Gribaldi he had drawn up a confession of faith, introducing many abusive expressions against Athanasius and his creed, and also against Calvin. He had the folly to dedicate this work to Simon Wurstenberger, landvogt (bailiff) of Gex, as if he entertained the same sentiments. Having done this, he went to Lyons to give the document to the printer. He was apprehended, but liberated the moment it was known that he had written something against Calvin. The report of his trial was now published, and with it an address to the Lyonnese. Gentilis went to Poland. Driven from thence, with other Antitrinitarians, he visited Siebenbürgen, Hungary and Moravia. He fell into the mistake of supposing that it was Calvin only, and not the principles of the age which were opposed to his system. Returning to Switzerland, he knocked at the door of his friend in Farges, to repose awhile under his roof; but Gribaldi had died a short time before of the plague.

The rash and foolish man now ventured to address himself to the bailiff of Gex, and expressed his desire to hold a disputation at which all the clergy of the neighbourhood might be present. The notice which was issued purported, that "if any one wished to defend the doctrine of Calvin, he should present himself in eight days to dispute with him (Gentilis), under the condition that he who could not support his opinions by God's word should be beheaded as a deceiver; and that if there were none to accept this challenge, the landvogt and the council of the city should solemnly declare, that the doctrine of Gentilis respecting God, the Father, Son and Holy Ghost, was the orthodox doctrine." The landvogt, who had been already greatly offended with Gentilis for having dedicated his confession of faith to him, which had created injurious suspicions at Bern, gave directions for his apprehension. The magistrates of Bern ordered that he should be forthwith brought to the city; and a process was commenced against him, which lasted through a month. He confessed his belief with the greatest firmness. The ministers of Bern, and Beza, who was present, endeavoured to bring him back to the truth; but he obstinately persisted in his heresy and in his insufferable abuse of the Trinity. Some books were found in his possession which he had written on the subject, and dedicated to the King of Poland; and as he had broken his oath at

Geneva, he was sentenced to be beheaded, that he might cause no further trouble to the church. He continued to reiterate his blasphemies to the last. The sentence was executed at Bern, in the year 1566, that is, two years after the death of Calvin.

The system of Gentilis, whose chief error is stated on the title-page of the work which Calvin published against him*, can only here be glanced at. To avoid repetitions, we shall merely mention that he could not comprehend the relation of the Son to the Father. Thus he sometimes separated the Son from the Godhead, so that he was no longer the true God; and sometimes, again, he divided the essence of God from the persons, and converted the Trinity into a quaternity, rendering the whole subject contemptible. At length he admitted three eternal Almighty Godheads, because he could not comprehend the inward and outward relations of the persons. Calvin concluded his work against him, and his argument for the faith in the true God, with the sublime expressions of Gregory of Nazianzum:—"I cannot think of the One without being dazzled with the splendour of the Three: nor can I acknowledge the Three without feeling my soul at the instant beaming back upon the Unity."

John Paul Alciat de la Motte, a Piedmontese nobleman, was summoned in the course of this agitation before the tribunal at Geneva†. He left the city, and wrote to the Council, "that he thanked them for the right of citizenship which they had bestowed upon him, and which he now resigned back into their hands; that there was some one among them whom he would for his own sake take care not to name, who persecuted, and laid snares for him. He besought the pious magistrates to judge between them."

This letter was very unfavourably received. The Council satisfied itself however with pronouncing Alciat's perpetual banishment as a schismatic, heretic, and companion of the devil. When he heard that he had been summoned by sound of trumpet to appear in the city and undergo his trial, he sent in a confession of faith, in which he owned Christ as the true God, and rejected the notion of a plurality of gods as impious.

As the error of which we have been speaking was now, through the instrumentality of Blandrata, Gentilis, Alciat and others, established in Poland, Calvin despatched two brief addresses

* "L'Impiété de Valentin Gentil apertement descouverte et descripte, lequel enseigne ce blasphème plein de sacrilège que Jésus Christ est un Dieu qui a prins son essence d'ailleurs."

† Archives de la République.

to be circulated in that country*. This leads us to mention the heresy of Stancarus, who was involved in the chief errors of the time, and formed a striking contrast to Osiander, of whom he had been the colleague. His principal dogma referred to the mediatorship of Christ, but it was closely connected with the doctrine of the Trinity, the relation of the Father to the Son being in neither case comprehended. Since Christ as Mediator is subordinate to the Father, Stancarus sought to represent Him as less than the Father: being Mediator only in so far as He is man, many came to view the Father only as God.

It appears from several letters† that Calvin's admonition was for some time, either through negligence or treachery, suppressed; and when the Poles wished for other writings, he refused to grant their request. This is said also of his little work against Stancarus, in which he especially attacks his error on the character of Christ as Mediator. "I praise your zeal," he says in a letter to Trecius, "but it is my duty to remark, that I do not cast my writings to the wind for sport. Nay, the less I am endued with foresight, the more timid am I, and the more watchful must I be of my safety." Christopher Trecius, who was returning from Heidelberg to Poland, wished Calvin to give him letters for those who had been led astray by Stancarus. But he also refused to write to the Hospodar of Wallachia and Moldavia. It was in the year 1563, and he alleged his bodily weakness as an apology. In a letter to Stanislaus Sarnicius‡, written the same year, a threat is expressed against Gregorius Paulus, a preacher at Cracow, who had become involved in the Antitrinitarian controversy.

Francis Stancarus, a well-known disputant of those times, was a native of Mantua. He had been invited to Cracow as a teacher of Hebrew§; but he was obliged to leave that city, and joining Felix Cruciger, he went to diffuse his notions in other parts of Poland. Calvin's writings had at that time exercised the most happy influence in the country. Stancarus, who had advanced the erroneous opinion that Christ is our Mediator, not in his divine but only in his human nature, was condemned by the sentence of a synod in 1554. He still however ventured to visit Poland. Lismannius accused him of Sabellianism. He now travelled into Hungary and Siebenbürgen, where, at Clausenburg, a confes-

* These addresses were, first, the Admonition "ad Fratres Polonos," and secondly, an Epistle to the Polish Nobles of Cracow.

† MS. Paris. Calv. Jacobo Silvio. Ibid. Calv. Christoph. Trecio.

‡ MS. Gen. Sept. 13, 1563.

§ Salig. Gesch. der Augsburg Confession. Thl. ii. s. 572.

sion was drawn up in opposition to his doctrine of Christ's Mediatorship; and, as he belonged to the Reformed, the confusion was hereby rendered greater than before. After a colloquy with the Lutheran ministers, and much excitement, he withdrew. At last this wrangler went to Königsberg, where he became professor of theology and Hebrew. The controversy between Osiander, Mörlin and Staphylus, on justification, was then at its height. Stancarus could not long retain his position in Königsberg, and on his departure he described Osiander, in a rash farewell address to the duke, as an Antichrist and a blood-hound. He now assumed the office of a teacher at Frankfort, where he created such disturbance, that Melancthon was obliged to be summoned to restore order. Stancarus had assailed him among the rest, and accused him of Arianism*. The Genevese church declared itself especially opposed to the errors which this Italian taught. Calvin has described this controversy in a little treatise on the subject†.

With regard to justification, Stancarus, from the desire to suppress every idea of communion with Christ, founds the whole work of our reconciliation to God on the sufferings of our Lord's human nature. We find the opposite error in Osiander, who separated justification from the forgiveness of sins, denied the satisfaction effected by the sufferings of Christ, and insisted that we are justified and sanctified through the living apprehension of Christ himself‡.

Melancthon and Calvin expressed themselves strongly against these views. Osiander complained that people contented themselves with an imputed righteousness, and that, though the death of Christ might indeed be our redemption, it was not our justification. His doctrine, he believed, would triumphantly exalt the practical element of Christianity. The visible Christ, his works, his sufferings, are not sufficient of themselves to make us righteous: the inward, the actual essential Christ, alone avails for this. He denies the influence of the satisfaction, and argues that the life, which is in the actual Christ, accomplishes the most. Christ is the righteousness or holiness of God himself; and consequently we are inwardly justified by Him, and outwardly also by his love, which is the fulfilling of God's law. But it is not faith

* MS. Paris, without date.

† Responsum ad Fratres Polonos, quomodo Mediator sit Christus ad refutandum errorem Stancari. 1560.

‡ Planck describes his system, l. c. s. 267.

which justifies: it is the righteousness of Christ, which we apprehend through Christ himself. Calvin thus expresses himself against Osiander in a letter to Melancthon*: "I have always numbered him among our disgraces." He speaks equally strongly on the subject of his doctrine. Having accused him of ambition, he says, "He exalts to the highest degree the shadowy notion of an actual righteousness, allowing nothing to the free acceptance on the side of God, as if that were a subordinate consequence."

Osiander confounded regeneration with justification. He says that we are not so justified by the obedience of Christ, and the satisfaction which He rendered, as we are through his divine and eternal righteousness. Altogether different is the statement of the Apostle, who simply declares that we are made righteous by the obedience of one man.

Having thus described the two obstinate controversies on predestination and on the doctrine of the Trinity, it still remains for us to consider that which originated in the theories advanced respecting the Lord's Supper. Calvin here displayed his earnest zeal for the unity of the church; and this controversy, through the direction which it received from circumstances, became the most important of all others in reference to the church's progress and development.

CHAPTER VII.

CALVIN'S CONTROVERSY WITH WESTPHAL AND HESSHUSS ON THE DOCTRINE OF THE SACRAMENT.—RISE AND PROGRESS OF THE DISPUTE.—PARTIES ENGAGED.—RESULTS.

THE agreement in doctrine established between the Swiss and the Genevese extended their influence to France, England, Scotland, and Holland. In the same manner, the union between Melancthon and Calvin on the subject of the sacrament secured the peace of the Protestant church; and there was every reason to expect its continuance, till Westphal, Hesshuss, and some others, designedly created a breach, and thus aroused the holy indignation of Calvin. This old controversy acquires a fresh interest

* Ep. 141, 1552.

through the circumstance that voices even in the present day are again raised, and with fiery zeal, in favour of the original Lutheran doctrine of the sacrament. This may produce a schism, eventually destructive to the church.

That which was so calculated to excite Calvin's anxiety was evidently the prospect of the indescribable evils which threatened the church through these proceedings in Germany. In the case of a man like Luther, he could forgive anything, even when he most fiercely assailed the doctrine of Zwingli, and rent the church. But Westphal manifestly awakened the strife from an ignorant love of disputation; and Calvin, in order to bridle him, threatened him with the fire, but of a kind altogether different from that which consumed Servetus. Calvin's main effort had ever been to establish concord between the two great parties in the church: he had placed himself in the midst that he might bind them together*.

The Lutherans since the year 1536, when the Wittenberg Concordia was established, had remained satisfied with the fundamental idea of the true bodily presence of Christ in the sacrament. They regarded particular definitions of the manner in which He is present as unnecessary. Melancthon himself had in some degree relinquished the notion of a local presence, to give more force to the spiritual. Luther, indeed, had again begun to rage against the Swiss, but the silence of his party only tends to show more remarkably the existence of a union of belief between the churches themselves. The Zurich "Consensus" seemed finally to adjust the matter. In the apprehension of the mystery involved in the sacrament, of which he said that it exceeded the powers of his understanding, Calvin showed that he possessed as profound a sense as Luther.

In the new formulary, which Calvin persuaded the Swiss to adopt, it was expressly stated, "that there is an actual partaking of the body of Christ in the sacrament; that a perceptible strength is imparted to the soul of the communicant, from the substance of the body of Christ; and that its operation is incomprehensible,—a miracle." But this was followed by a most wicked love of strife; and when the main question was settled, there still remained the collateral inquiry, so difficult to be settled, as to how Christ is present in the sacrament, and which it was

* See Planck, On the Separation and Reunion of Parties in the Christian Church, s. 127; and his work Ueber den Protestantischen Lehrbegriff, Bd. v. Thl. ii.

only necessary to urge, to destroy the peace of the church. Westphal endeavoured to prove that this inquiry was of the utmost importance; and he evinced thereby how little he cared about Christianity itself, and how much was necessary to satisfy his own ambition. As a vain disputant on the mysteries incomprehensible to Calvin, he exposed himself to be branded with the mark of his true character, and to the anathemas of the church.

Calvin never exhibited his prudence more conspicuously perhaps than in this controversy. He stood between two parties, each violently excited against the other, ready to pervert every expression which was uttered, and one of which was utterly averse to peace. He engaged his whole ability in the struggle; and most people will probably be inclined rather to admire his moderation at the commencement of the controversy, than to accuse him of bitterness.

The expressions used by Calvin and Peter Martyr had long since aroused the attention of the sterner Lutherans. Westphal commenced the attack with a little pamphlet in the year 1552: in this work he summoned the Lutherans to the field, and it is evident that he had no other object but that of embroiling both parties in a conflict. He enumerates twenty-eight different interpretations of the consecrating words in the Lord's Supper, and on which the Sacramentarians were opposed to each other. This was a striking evidence, he said, of error; but the Lutherans, he added, had always persevered in asserting one meaning. In conclusion he declared, and with great violence of expression, that the blasphemies of the Sacramentarians ought to be resisted by the power of the magistrate rather than by the pen.

When the Swiss were now silent from regard to Christian feeling, and the Lutherans, Flaccius, Amsdorf, Wigand, and Mörlin, were otherwise occupied, Westphal appeared again with a new pamphlet written against the Sacramentarians at Magdeburg. In this production he summoned the Lutherans to unite to defend their doctrine, everywhere oppressed by Zwinglianism, now spreading on all sides. Bullinger delivered two discourses, in which he treated this subject with the greatest earnestness. Viret also this year translated into Latin a very comprehensive work, written some time before in French: he soon after wrote two other works on the Lord's Supper*. It was at this juncture that Mary ascended the throne of England, and commenced the persecution

* Ruchat, vi. 6, 7, 8. Hospinian, p. 383.

of the Protestants. A reformed congregation in London, whose minister was John a Lasco, was obliged instantly to disperse, its members seeking safety by flight. Laski, a native of Poland, who enjoyed Calvin's profoundest respect, and was a truly noble and enlightened man, had been originally nominated to the richest bishoprics in his own country and in Hungary; but he had resigned all to become a minister of the reformed congregation at Emden, and to teach the simple truth of the Gospel. To avoid signing the Interim, he had proceeded in the reign of Edward VI. to London, and there established a congregation which had now four ministers.

Laski, when the persecution commenced, embarked in September 1553 with 175 persons. The ship was wrecked in a storm. Laski ran into the harbour of Elsinore. It was winter, but the exiles received command immediately to re-embark, and to proceed to the German coast*. Even the women, with children at their breasts, were not allowed to wait for calmer weather. Force was quickly employed to drive them into the ship, or beyond the boundary-line, and this in spite of all their prayers to be allowed to remain to the end of winter†. Even in Germany they were treated as enemies of the country and of the church. Westphal called the members of Laski's exiled community, the devil's martyrs. Bugenhagen refused to acknowledge them as Christians, and they were told that papists could be better endured than they. Laski's children only were allowed to remain in Hamburg till the spring.

The hatred of the Lutherans pursued the wanderers not only in that city, but also in Lübeck and Rostock. At length they found refuge in Danzig; and Laski himself was honourably entertained at Emden, through the influence of the Countess Anna of Oldenburg. Gustavus Vasa also invited him to Sweden.

We learn from these circumstances that the Lutherans had but half escaped from the trammels of the Catholic spirit; and that the feeling still prevailed among them, that their own church was the sole source of salvation;—a fanatical error which still exhibits its force in the new Lutheran communities.

A great number of frantic Lutheran preachers branded the exiles with the name of heretics, and thus excited the populace against them. They were also decried as anabaptists by the

* Krasinski, Geschichte der Reformation in Polen. London, 1841.

† Uttenhoven gave an account of the sufferings of these exiles. The narrative was preceded by a preface from the pen of a Lasco. See also Pontoppidan's Annalen, Thl. iii. s. 317. 24.

clergy; and the magistrates were therefore compelled to deny them a place of shelter. This angry zeal exhibited itself in a manner which proved clearly that it had been nourished in secret before it actually broke forth.

Calvin first received the melancholy tidings through Peter Martyr, in a letter from Strasburg, May 9, 1554. He could now no longer remain silent, and he at once hurled his lightnings against the false protestant ministers*. Disposed originally to use gentle means, he wrote to Caspar Liser, in August 1554,—"I rejoice to see that you approve of my efforts to heal the schism, which has, alas! attended the revival of the Gospel; but we must meet this rebellious spirit with mildness, and thus prevent the fire from spreading far and wide around." He expresses himself with similar moderation in an answer to Sulzer at Basel†; and with the same object in view, he dedicated his Commentary on Genesis to the sons of the Duke, John Frederic, of Saxony, hoping to convince them of the necessity of opposing the Catholics by a union established on the true principles of peace and concord.

At the end of March he wrote to Bullinger, stating that the brethren from France were flocking into Geneva, with the intention of keeping Easter there; as if they knew nothing of the prevailing agitation, or of the guard posted at all the barriers. He also expressed his thanks for the sermons published by Bullinger, and for the honourable mention of himself, inquiring at the same time, whether Bullinger would oppose Westphal? Beza drew his attention to this man; and added, that he might be put down in three days‡.

The condition of Laski greatly affected Calvin. Addressing him, he says, "The cruel conduct of Denmark affects me bitterly. Great God! what an instance of barbarity among a Christian people! It surpassed even the fury of the waves." He praised a Lasco's moderation and firmness. Some strong expressions respecting the king of Denmark follow:—"The more I have celebrated his zeal and friendship, the more distressed do I feel at discovering that this was a false and useless display of mildness. But I see that a devilish frenzy has seized the whole of that coast. Saxony too rages against us without shame or measure. A gay and pleasant exhibition this for the papists! Although I doubt not that this species of fury must be detestable to learned and thoughtful men, yet I feel that I ought not to re-

* Opuscules, p. 1808. † Ep. 176.
‡ MS. Goth. in Bretschneider, p. 41, 5 Cal. Apr. 1554.

main any longer silent; and certainly as far as we are concerned the disposition was to offer resistance from the first. But our most excellent father Bullinger thought otherwise, and made the victory depend upon silence and forbearance. Subsequently however he altered his opinion; and of his own accord urged me to write some little book to confute these infamous slanders."

Calvin in the writing referred to manifestly mistook at first the rude importance of his opponent, and his work shows the profoundest contempt of Westphal, whom he will not once name. He wished to believe that as all the other Lutheran divines had remained silent, he had only to deal with this one. He listened however to Bullinger's advice, made him acquainted with his work, and was guided by his remarks. That he did this with regard both to the past and the future, appears from the writing itself*. It was regarded, in fact, as a repetition of the "Consensus," and was subscribed by all the Swiss †. Bullinger wished Calvin to reject the doctrine of Luther with the strongest expressions of dislike‡: "It has not perhaps yet occurred to you how gross," &c. Calvin had not read Luther's German writings. They sent him some specimens; still Bullinger blamed Calvin's severity, and the latter answered the Zurich ministers that he had struck out the harsh passages in his work according to their suggestion. His apologies are very comical. He says among other things, that what he meant by the Latin word *nebulo* (a scoundrel or paltry knave) was merely 'a good-for-nothing fellow,' 'a man of wind,' 'a darkling §.' The word 'beast' he had struck out. He could not understand, he said, why they wished the name of Westphal to be inserted. To this he was, as before, wholly opposed; the work was more respectable without it. He had but one word to say about Luther, for the sake of peace. They also should take care not to awaken any angry feeling in the heart.

Calvin here relates a circumstance worthy of notice. "When Melancthon," he says, "had occasion to go to Worms, to alter a passage in the Augsburg Confession, the papists exclaimed that both we and the Zwinglians were falsifiers. The elector of Brandenburg, who was then seeking the chief command in the Turkish war, secretly sent a prince of Anhalt to Luther, who was to

* MS. Tigur. Calv. Bullingero, Prid. Non. Oct. 1554.

† MS. Gen. Calv. Molinæo Jurisconsulto, Jan. 1555.

‡ Hess, Leben Bullingers, Thl. ii. s. 217.

§ MS. Tigur. Nov. 13, 1554.

irritate Luther against us, and persuade him to abandon our party. But Luther afforded this proof of his moderation, that he dismissed the traitor, and gave us, of his own accord, an account of the wickedness practised against us."

The milder expressions were adopted by general consent. Calvin learned from private sources that the work had proved displeasing to Melancthon. He had not, he informed the Zurich ministers, followed all their suggestions. The expressions which he employs in calling their attention to what is mysterious in the sacrament are striking and beautiful*. The same may be said of the manner in which he declares his confidence in Luther†.

But the affair was not to be so quickly settled. From a letter to Farel‡ we learn, that the Zurich ministers were well-satisfied with the corrected paper, but still hesitated to adopt it, alleging that it was somewhat confused. Calvin was on the point of burning it in anger, the Council having resolved to submit it to the censors.

This first work however against Westphal was published in French, November 28, 1554, that the people might be made acquainted with the nature of the controversy. In the preliminary address to the Swiss ministers, Calvin expresses his utter unwillingness to engage in controversy with a set of men indulging in absurdities. He would write against one of them only; and to show his contempt even for him, he would not mention his name. In his last epistle however to Westphal, he intimates that it was from tenderness to him that he refrained from naming him.

"This vain and foolish doctor," he says in the French dedication, "who has published a wretched work against the Sacramentarians, although we know better than he how to defend the sacraments, speaks also against our 'Consensus,' as if we contemplated in that document, not the sacrament, but an empty sign." The Latin text is the more correct. We meet with the following reproachful expressions:—"This calf afterwards cites our own words, in which we openly confess, that the body of Christ is actually communicated to the faithful. He answers, that we speak only of a spiritual eating. What then? He would

* "We readily agree that you are right, if it be in your mind to reject the miracles imagined by superstitious men; but to refuse to acknowledge any mystery in the sacrament, that is to dissent too much from the secret power of the Spirit, which we so often celebrate."

† Ep. 177. Ed. Amst. p. 84.

‡ MS. Gen. Calv. Farello, Dec. 26, 1554.

like, I suppose, to make it appear that the flesh of Jesus Christ may be eaten like the flesh of the oxen on his farm*. Christ has a real natural body, as it was once offered upon the cross: and this is daily presented to us in the sacrament."

Calvin complains that Westphal had perverted the expressions employed in the "Consensus." "Is he not like a foolish dog, which bites at every stone that lies in his way? This confusion-counsellor pretends that we are guilty of trickery; that we deceive the simple, by speaking of a spiritual eating. In the same manner this fine champion of the faith shows, that we are all at variance with each other in our views. He has thereby done us a service; for nothing can more plainly prove that we are agreed, since all our views tend to the same end, namely that the mystery is figuratively exhibited. Even the Apostles differ in their words, but this man supposes that we differ in sense. Some may indeed seem to contradict each other; but the church-fathers and the Apostles express themselves in various ways on the mystery of the sacrament."

"You see," he continues, "what grounds this brainless man has for fabricating thunderbolts in his chamber to set, if possible, all Europe in a blaze. In one place he asserts, that the words of Christ are perfectly clear and need no commentary, when he says that the bread is his body; but that he said this figuratively, which yet does not lessen the truth, that the bread is indeed the body of Christ."

Lastly, Calvin objects to him his unholy desire to involve the church in schism, whereas Zwingli, Œcolampadius, and especially Bucer, had agreed to the "Consensus." "I will confine my answer to three words. It is the property of Satan to slander, to darken the light; and as the father of contention, to destroy peace, and break the unity of the faith. Such being the characteristics of this babbler, nothing remains for us but to designate him a child of the devil."

This address is followed by the work itself, which is founded on the second "Consensus" with the Zurichers. Planck remarks the great difficulty of the undertaking, and shows how much acuteness and prudence Calvin combined with his zeal†. This renders it so much the more remarkable that such a work should have been so little regarded‡.

* Ed. Amst. p. 651.

† Geschichte des Protestant Lehrbegriffs, Bd. v. Thl. ii. s. 50.

‡ Opusc. Franç. p. 1821.

Calvin could not deny that the view taken by the Swiss churches was actually different to that of the Lutherans, although in principle the same. He had to show that the greatest Lutheran theologian did in reality, without daring to acknowledge it, vary in some measure from the belief of Luther himself; and to prove, on the other hand, that the doctrine of the Swiss, in regard to the Lord's Supper, which was acknowledged to be different from the Lutheran, might yet have been approved by Luther; in other words, that he gave the true view of the subject, and that the most intelligent theologians recognised it as such*. Calvin therefore started with the fundamental conviction, that Luther in his controversy had protested only against empty signs and symbols. In what degree Luther was right, he would not inquire. The Lutheran divines had been somewhat quieted, at the time of the Wittenberg Concordia, by the declarations of their opponents; but they were not fully satisfied, and therefore he had laboured to establish the "Consensus Tigurinus." This being the case, all he had to do was to prove that in reality the signs of the bread and wine were not to be viewed as empty signs and symbols. Here was the point between him and Westphal; and on this alone it really was that Luther, whatever other differences prevailed between them, separated from the Swiss.

Calvin's first object is to prove that his party never intended to convert the sacrament of the Lord's Supper into a mere ceremony. He asserts, that with the signs there are also actually united the body and blood of Christ, and that they are given us spiritually with the signs. According to the Lutheran doctrine, there were no more signs, but the flesh and blood of Christ; although the bread always remained bread. Calvin, as well as Luther, established his doctrine on the force of Christ's words in the consecration. Luther however insisted that the body of Christ was given bodily with the bread; Calvin, that it was truly given. Luther allowed a manducation with the mouth; Calvin, only a spiritual manducation. But Luther also referred it all to the soul.

In the next place, Calvin shows what he understood by a spiritual eating. Thus he described faith as the organ; and speaks of a quickening power, which proceeds immediately from the flesh of Christ, and exercises its vital energy on the soul. The sacrament has not a mere moral force, but is an incomprehensible my-

* See Planck, Gesch. der Protest. Lehrb. s. 51.

stery to us. As soon as the sign is received, an actual influence, derived from the flesh of Christ and out of his substance, flows into the soul. But still we must not imagine a local presence, or one extended over all space. The expression 'real presence and communication' he would willingly have used, if people would have been content to employ it in a spiritual sense. On the other hand, he stated why he could not admit the Lutheran notion respecting a local presence and eating the flesh of Christ. He candidly confessed that the idea appeared to him altogether irrational. The understanding, he acknowledged, must be silent when the Scriptures speak; but in this case they do not. Christ cannot be corporeally present in many places at once, because that is contrary to the nature of bodies.

But a short time had elapsed after the appearance of Calvin's work, when Westphal's miserable answer was published at Frankfort. He soon renewed also his attack upon Laski and the other exiles, and even called upon the Frankfort ministers to persecute them. It is characteristic of his temper, that when Laski, in a letter written with true Christian feeling, reprehended his conduct, and showed that he had treated them as if they had been thieves, murderers, and poisoners, he had the letter printed, appending an answer to it, in which he senselessly repeated, that they were not only thieves, murderers, and poisoners, but much more infamous, for that by their false doctrine they were murderers of souls.

Luther had never thus forgotten himself; often therefore did Calvin sigh, "Ah! would that Luther were still alive! These people have none of his virtues, but they think to prove themselves his disciples by their clamours *." Westphal gathered together a great number of confessions from the towns of Saxony, which solemnly declared themselves in favour of the Lutheran, and opposed to the Calvinistic, doctrine. Calvin was now assailed on all sides. Brentius appeared in Würtemberg with his homilies, in which he supported the most violent views on the subject of the real presence. Jacob Andrea advocated the same doctrine, at first with more moderation, but he subsequently became one of its fiercest champions: he sent his writing to Calvin, and the latter answered him, praising his moderation †. In the year 1557 Schnepf and others followed in the same track. Westphal himself answered Calvin's second writing; so that the reformer com-

* MS. Goth. ed. Br. p. 43, Calv. Sidemanno, Mar. 1555.

† Ed. Laus. Ep. 240. Ed. Amstel. p. 114, b. Calvin to Dr. Jacob Andrea.

plained to Bullinger that there seemed to be a conspiracy against him*.

Calvin made a second and third experiment to extinguish Westphal's fire by his own; but he only increased the fury of the flames thereby. Westphal answered him with such an excess of zeal, that Calvin, always ardent in the defence of his dignity, though not without discretion, as was apparent in his terrible conflict with Servetus before the Council, drew himself back, and was silent, leaving the field to Beza, fresh and well-armed for the conflict, and ready to take his friend's place in this instance, as he had in the controversy on predestination.

A glance at the writings thus produced, and at the spirit by which they were dictated, will show how wise Melancthon was not to meddle with the controversy; but he should have strongly protested against the wicked temper which now prevailed, and have pointed out the path which Christians ought to tread.

Calvin's second work against Westphal was written with incredible rapidity, and sent to the press without revisal; it is the only work of Calvin's of which this is said. But it exhibits great skill in reconciling and winning hostile minds. Calvin's chief difficulty, with regard to most of the questions before him, arose from his desire to adopt a middle course, and which it is so much less easy to pursue than that which is extreme. This was especially the case in his view of the efficacy of baptism, of the spiritual eating in the Lord's Supper, and of the punishment of heretics. It was in the article of predestination only that he carried his doctrine to the farthest limits of the subject.

Before the work appeared, he wrote to Bullinger as follows: "When I said that Westphal desired nothing more than to bring a countless host of antagonists into the field against us, I felt anxious to say as little as possible that might be offensive to his party. If time allowed, I should have been glad to let you read this work before it was published: I might perhaps have altered some things on your suggestion. But the haste was so great, that I only dictated it, another person read it through, and I then immediately sent it to the press."

Calvin's friends at Geneva did not think the style of this work too violent; and he allowed himself to be easily persuaded that they were right. But soon after its appearance, January 5, 1556, he confessed to Bullinger that he had been too severe,

* MS. Tigur. That is, to crush him under a mountain of books. "Lutheranos conspirasse video, ut librorum mole nos obruant."

adding however a jest to this acknowledgement. It is somewhat strange indeed to find a work on so important a subject sent so suddenly into the world, and with a sort of petulant gaiety, the author himself afterwards doubting whether he had done right. The treatise in fact is the production of a genius which could venture on an arrogant employment of its powers. Bullinger also entered at this time into controversy with Westphal.

But it was Calvin's object, as appeared from the very title-page of the book, to invite to peace; the work being dedicated to all true servants of the Lord in Saxony and Lower Germany. In the preface he called them to witness, that he had been constrained to send his earlier productions into the world by the furious spirits which were raging abroad, and whose conduct was even worse than the barbarity of the papists. He only wrote for the purpose of promoting unity. Expressing himself very properly respecting the hatred manifested by Westphal, he apologises for the heat which he had himself displayed:—"If I have treated him harshly, and used strong expressions in some passages, you must consider, according to your wisdom, how he has goaded me to this. His book appears written with no other object but that of casting us down to hell, and overwhelming us with curses. What could I do otherwise than act according to the proverb, 'The bad ass must have a bad driver,' to prevent his wrath having too much its own way?"

While there was any hope of procuring peace for the church, Calvin could humbly solicit it; but we see the aim of his opponents, and God himself gave him an example to justify his stern treatment of the obstinately wicked:—"Thou wilt save the afflicted people, but wilt bring down high looks." (Ps. xviii. 27.) "Westphal," he says, "allows that I have written correctly on the dignity and operation of the sacraments. Whether I have actually done so, I do not inquire; it is enough if I have done it with a pious feeling." There remained but three points to discuss. Westphal insisted—1. That the substantial bread was the body of Christ. 2. That his body was infinite, and everywhere present. 3. That there was nothing figurative in the words of Christ.

"We assert," says Calvin, "that the body and blood of Christ are actually given to us in the sacrament, that our souls may receive life therefrom; and that they may be nourished by this spiritual food, as our bodies are by earthly bread. We acknowledge therefore that a real communication of the body and blood of Christ takes place in the sacrament. If any one, for the sake of disputing, attaches importance to the word 'substance,' we assert that Christ gives life to our souls through the 'substance' of his flesh."

Westphal says, in the first place, that the substantial bread is the body of Christ. Whence it follows that a wicked man swallows the body of Christ with the bread. Judas therefore received the body of Christ as well as Peter. Westphal and his party in fact had formed a notion of substance which did not agree with the words of Christ. The unbelief of a man cannot indeed alter the virtue of the sacrament, but it will not act upon the unbeliever, because the organ, faith, which is necessary to our receiving Christ, is wanting to such a person.

The second point relates to the mode and manner of the communication, which, according to Westphal, cannot take place if the body of Christ be not infinite. "He insists that the body must appear before our eyes, and that, were this not the case, it could not be communicated to us. We, on the contrary, believe that the separation of place is here of no concern, because it is the energy of the Holy Ghost which derives life for us out of the flesh of Christ. Hence the manifest wickedness of those who, to make us hateful in the eyes of the people, exclaim that we deny the presence of Christ in the sacrament, and measure the power of God by our senses. As if this were not a mystery, the depths of which surpass all understanding, when we say that Christ, although now glorified in the body, yet comes down to us through the secret grace of his Holy Spirit, that we may be partakers of his life,—as if he, who teaches that life flows into us from the flesh of Christ, does not exalt the power of God as highly as he who says, that this flesh comes down from heaven to work life in us."

In the third place, Westphal asserts, that no inquiry need be instituted as to the meaning of the words of consecration, which were plain enough. "We, on the contrary," says Calvin, "appeal to the common usage which gives to the sign the name of the thing signified. But with us, when the discourse regards the sacrament, it is not of an empty sign that we speak; for we declare, plainly and intelligibly, that the Lord fulfils in reality that which he testifies. What we desire is, that people should distinguish the things, and that they should thereby be led from the visible sign to that which is invisible; for to what end does

Christ give us the earthly element unless thus to elevate us? If it be granted as a help to our unbelief, no one must expect to attain to the thing itself without the use of this means; and thus, step by step, ascending from earth to heaven."

Hereupon Calvin exhorts his opponents to the cultivation of peace. "I beseech you, by the most holy name of Christ, and by the bonds of righteousness, which we have in Him, afford your help to accomplish this object. Whatever door you open to us whereby we may effect a reconciliation so greatly to be desired, I solemnly declare to you that I am not only inclined to take advantage of it, but shall seize the opportunity with joy and with all my heart." And yet Westphal persevered in asserting, that Calvin was guilty of tearing the churches asunder, which, under God's guidance, agreed so nobly together in all points of doctrine.

The several ideas here alluded to having been developed with great force and logical precision, there follow some passages full of power and eloquence, and which, while they display the exalted spirit of Calvin, place in an equally clear light the unworthy character of Westphal. Calvin offered to hold a disputation with him; but he would not listen to the proposal. The controversy was not likely to be determined by writing; but Westphal depended upon the number of his associates.

He objected to the "Reformed," that they had abolished all ceremonies. Calvin replied that they (Westphal and his party) retained certain vain observances in the celebration of the sacrament, such as lighting wax-candles in the day-time, and against which practices Luther had for the most part protested, although it was necessary for awhile to allow them. Westphal condemned all the churches of southern Germany and of Switzerland, and then boasts of his humility. Calvin breaks forth into these exclamations:—"O Ishmael, thou whose hand is against us all, may the hands of all be against thee! For as Luther's magnanimity deserved so much the greater praise, because he stood alone, and did not hesitate to attack the whole papacy, so art thou the more contemptible in thy cowardice when thou seekest in light and trivial things for the means of sowing dissension among the people of God."

We now arrive at the objections which Westphal urged against the reformed churches in general, and in respect to which Calvin defended them. It is said, for example, that children were allowed to die without baptism, because women were prohibited from affording it in case of necessity, which was against the commandment of Christ. But "children are not thereby lost, for God has said, 'I will be your God, and you shall be my seed.' The grace which is given to the parents is derived to the offspring." Again: "He accuses us of not giving the sacrament to the sick; but we refuse it to avoid superstition, for it has been the custom to parade the bread about as if it were on a stage, and because moreover the Lord's Supper ought to be partaken of in society." And further: "We have no absolution, it is said, before the sacrament. We answer, that there may be errors among us; but absolution is papistical. It is not my design however to assert that particular absolution may not have something useful in it; I have even recommended its adoption in several parts of my writings, if it be free and without superstition; but it is neither wise nor allowable to make it the law, and so binding upon the conscience."

In the next place Westphal accuses Calvin of retaining the second commandment against images. "We shall show," says the reformer, "on good grounds, that the ten commandments are correctly divided by us: we have ancient testimony on our side. Westphal, in order to darken the commandment which forbids idolatry, tears the last commandment into two pieces." And, finally, Westphal was indignant at the manner in which the Reformed had modified the calendar of the church. Calvin replies: "Mary's day and other saint days are not of primitive origin; but Westphal believes that all is lost if we do not follow the Hamburg calendar." With regard to the arrangement of the lessons from Scripture, Calvin says: "Formerly the whole of the gospel was read to the people; but now only portions, as time allows; and one knows well, and it is only necessary to read the extracts to see, that these little fragments of the Bible have been selected without judgement. Certainly, if it be good to extract certain portions for Sunday reading, the choice ought to have been different to what it is: and assuredly, whoever he may be who made this selection, he has not only incorrectly divided every passage, but has sometimes, through ignorance or negligence, broken off in the very middle of a statement." Westphal spoke also with great indignation respecting the "Postils." "We may pardon Luther," he says; "he accommodated himself to the prevailing custom, all things being then in disorder; and he deserves to be praised for having endeavoured to teach the Gospel in the shortest way."—"Thus Westphal celebrates

St. Martin's day with the papists, and chants with them the gospels and epistles according to the fine sing-song of the mass-book; as if the Gospel would be lost if it were not thus torn into fragments. Is there any one now that can doubt that this man has too much leisure in his corner, when he can venture to annoy people, who have enough to do, with trifles of this sort?" Westphal accused Calvin of pride. Calvin answered: "If I have received a measure of grace from God, I endeavour to use it, without pride or boasting, for the edification of the church. My books bear witness that there is a great deal wanting to make me ambitious of gaining advantage over others, or of appearing in the light of a scholar or a genius. There is nothing which I avoid more than boasting." Westphal having asserted that his church might be compared to the angels in heaven, Calvin exclaims, "O Luther, how few hast thou left behind possessed of the glorious gifts which were in thee! But how many hast thou left who imitate, like apes, thy peculiarities! We wonder not that Luther had frequently such lofty words in his mouth. He could not have warred so bravely under the banner of the Lord, had he not despised the world with all its greatness; but it is insufferable when such a drone as this, whose unintelligible din only throws the bees into confusion, dares to speak so high."

Calvin, referring to himself, says, "If I assert that I am faithful in my endeavour to make the whole world feel that it depends upon the word of Christ alone, I can adduce not only my books and my daily discourses to prove the truth of this, but all those persons who witness my daily labour; and so gloriously does God seal my efforts with his blessing, that were there ten Westphals, the fruits and the profitableness of my toil could not be made to appear contemptible. If, indeed, I speak of the blessing of my calling, I do this in common with the Apostle Paul."—"I should wish," says Westphal, "ignorant as I am, to know what notion this writer forms of learned men."—"As if, in order to find a learned man besides Westphal, we should have recourse to the Platonic theory of ideas."—"It is not in the school of Archimedes that we have learnt that the body of Christ, which was taken up into heaven, is far from the earth. We believe that it is authentically stated in the Holy Scriptures. I dare not, in the weakness of my understanding, pretend to guess from what system of philosophy Westphal has learnt that Christ, when he first celebrated the sacrament, had a twofold body; one mortal, visible, confined to one place; and one invisible, of infinite extension."—"Westphal is proud, and applies to himself what is said in the Psalms. I understand, he says, more than all those who have taught you. And what rank then will Luther have, if he who stands on the lowest step be thus above him?"

"In conclusion, he says, 'That if he were not learned, there would be no ground to fear him.' And truly it requires but little to make me grant what he so much desires."—"As if he were taking the part of Jupiter in a play, and bore a Minerva in his head, he makes no difficulty of clothing all his sentiments in the language of God's word. If it had not been the custom, from remote times, for all false prophets, the farther they are from God, to exhibit the greater audacity, and shield themselves with his name, he might perhaps have gained something by his deceit, and by thus terrifying the people."

This work is not only interesting from its being written in the old, naïve French, in which Calvin delighted to express his powerful humour, but it is also valuable for the force of its crushing argumentation, for the life and sublimity of its style, and the occasional expression of profound indignation by which it is characterized. Calvin has been sometimes accused of too much violence in this controversy; but he everywhere proves the unworthiness and folly of his adversary, and is always considerate.

At the end of the second defence Calvin reviewed the entire subject, and again states his opinion respecting the sacrament of baptism, observing that it is profitable as introducing us into the church, but not indispensably necessary to salvation. He concludes the work with another attack upon his noisy antagonist.

The third work against Westphal crowned the argument. Calvin's indignation here displayed itself in the highest degree; and this though he had been warned by Farel; for he could not, he said, moderate himself in contending with Westphal*. It was impossible, he added, to view this man and his associates any longer as brethren. They themselves had execrated the name. He was willing however to bear blame from Farel, and he did not conceal from himself that he was likely to become an object of general hatred. "But God will be well-pleased if, boldly and joyfully, I do not shrink from awakening against myself the wrath of these wild beasts."

After an introduction, in which he defends, and partly excuses himself, he first answers the accusation advanced by Westphal,

* MS. Gen. Calv. Farello, August 1, 1557.

namely, that he overthrew the Augsburg Confession, and that Melancthon was against him. Secondly, he shows that the primitive church was represented by Augustin, as stated by Westphal; and thirdly, he combats the various doctrines of the Saxon church, and defends his own view of the Lord's Supper. With regard to Melancthon he speaks thus strongly: "It would be as easy for a man to separate Melancthon from me in this thing, as to separate him from himself. He has feared, it is true, the thunder of some people in his neighbourhood (this will be understood by those who know that Luther was excited against him), nor has he always spoken so distinctly as I could wish; but Westphal must not be allowed maliciously to assert, that he only waited for Luther's death to join our party. We discussed this subject together seventeen years ago, and the first words which we interchanged showed that we agreed so well, that we had not to speak of altering a syllable, either on the one side or the other."—"Thus Caspar Cruciger, who, next to Melancthon, was most beloved by Luther, so clearly apprehended the doctrine which Westphal now assails, that nothing could better agree than our expressions*."

Calvin now describes, and refutes, Westphal's last production, in which he called upon the princes and magistrates to punish heretics. Calvin, who in all difficult questions took a middle course, asserts, on the other hand, "that punishment ought only to be inflicted when a trial had been regularly instituted, and the heresy was well-defined, and not according to the course pursued by the papists, who murder the innocent. He speaks, in this case, very strongly in favour of toleration. Westphal called every one a heretic who differed from him in opinion, without any inquiry into the several views which people may adopt; and he insisted that punishment ought to be immediately inflicted. Many churches agreed with him. But how was it that a much greater number of his own party, than of our churches, condemned him? He speaks of the union of the princes at Smalcalde: but it was not the design of these princes to condemn us. Bucer and Melancthon were both present. At Marburg we were regarded as the brethren of Luther, although the question at issue was not then so distinctly stated as it now is. Westphal is so unreasonable that he objects to us, that our doctrine has condemned the popes, Nicholas and Gregory VII., which we, on the contrary, regard as an honour."

* Planck, s. 74, 104.

The accusation brought against Calvin, that he had never read Augustin, is refuted by Calvin's appeal to that author. "Why," says Augustin, "make the teeth and the body ready?—believe, and thou hast eaten." Westphal quotes a great many of Augustin's expressions, in which that father calls the bread the body of Christ. "And we do the same," says Calvin, "in the sense in which he does it;" and he then again patiently states the real point disputed. "Is the sense of Christ's words figurative or not figurative?" This Westphal would never distinctly answer. Hereupon follows the proof, that Augustin also admitted a metonyme. "He says that when Christ distributed the sacrament, he bore, *so to say*, his body. But Westphal leaves out this *so to say*, which is the main part of the sentence. According to Augustin, the good and the wicked receive the sacrament alike. We say the same; for Christ is always therein present; but the wicked receive the sign only, they being destitute of the faith, which is necessary to our partaking of the power of the sacrament."

This is followed by a *résumé* of the argument. "1. Augustin takes the words of Christ figuratively, which Westphal denies. 2. We adopt the doctrine of a spiritual eating, but in such a sense that the sacramental only remains. True piety abhors the gross imagination, that we can swallow what is divine. Westphal, by making the spiritual effect the consequence of the eating, limits the salvation accomplished for us by the death of Christ. 3. Westphal objects to us, that we believe only such a presence of Christ in the sacrament as leaves his human nature altogether disregarded." Hereupon follows the well-known reasoning against ubiquity and consubstantiation. We must not, it is argued, assert things in theology which are altogether impossible according to the laws of the understanding. The statement, "God is not bound by natural laws, because He himself made them," is absurd, or rather proves the contrary. Much necessarily remains incomprehensible to us in the Lord's Supper. With regard to the eating of the sacrament by unbelievers, the Swiss had granted the point in the Concordia, allowing that the signs only were received. In the Zurich 'Consensus' Calvin declared, that he did not agree with the Lutheran doctrine. In opposition to Westphal, who thence argued that Calvin did not acknowledge the real presence of the Lord in the sacrament, the reformer drew up another conclusion.

Calvin refers, in the next place, to the followers of Westphal in the Saxon academies. "They hate Melancthon," he says, "and join with Westphal, because the sharpness of my language displeases them. This is the case with Flacius Illyricus and Erasmus Sarcerus." He shows Westphal how his own party only in some respects agreed with him, while they in others dissented from his views. This leads him to examine the Magdeburg Confession, in reviewing which he very patiently refutes the errors exhibited in twenty-eight articles of that formulary; and also the answer of his opponents to the fifty-nine arguments which he had employed in the present discussion, and had examined anew and defended. The whole is summed up in this, that they wished people to adhere to the Word alone, without any interpretation. "This much is certain, that we have penetrated an insurmountable wall; that the Lord has established a sacrament; and that, according to the common usage of Scripture, these words must be interpreted in a sacramental sense, in the usual style and manner, that is, of the sacrament, namely, that the sign receives the name of the thing which it betokens." Lastly, he controverts the dogmas of several other Saxon churches, as those of Bremen, Hildesheim, &c., which were especially indignant at Calvin's dedicating his second treatise to them.

We see, from what has been stated, that it was Calvin's rule to answer every objection, and to let nothing pass unnoticed. The repetition of so many points is often wearisome, and it was in direct contrast with the plan pursued by Melancthon, who hoped to subdue his enemies by silence. Calvin concludes with a proposal of peace. "Unwilling should I be," he says, "notwithstanding these things, to be a hindrance to the establishment of a solid friendship between us, and the fulfilment of the hope that we may still enjoy peace. With regard to myself, I have been called forth in a very unworthy manner, and circumstances have excited me to speak more vehemently than I wished in this writing; but if anyone will appoint the place and time, and agree to discuss this matter in a friendly spirit with me, I promise to be prepared to meet him immediately, and with such good feeling, that everything shall be done, on my side, which can lead to a true and holy agreement, an event which every one must desire."

Calvin indeed, throughout the controversy, anxiously endeavoured to effect a reconciliation, and challenged his opponents to adduce one word in his statement which did not agree with the 'Confession' drawn up at Ratisbone in 1541. He made the noblest efforts to accomplish a union, and even in the midst of the controversy stretched out the hand of a brother to his adversary. "I call Christ," he says, "and all the angels to witness, that the moment Westphal will abandon his obstinacy, it shall not be my fault if there do not reign between us friendship and brotherly love. Even now, if he will show a brother's heart towards me, I am ready to love him as a brother in return."

Calvin, in fact, always proved himself anxious to seize upon the points which might secure a reunion of the churches; while Westphal, on the contrary, was as disposed to magnify differences. With the one, the spiritual eating in the sacrament was sufficient, because Christ was believed to be actually present; the other held to the words, "This is my body," without understanding them; and Calvin, had he refrained from all personalities, and written with more moderation, would have gained one of the best and fairest of victories. In many instances indeed he did thus triumph, and Calvinism itself has since made the greatest progress in Germany, and has now the common voice of the church on its side.

A letter written by Calvin to Martin Schaling, a minister at Ratisbone, affords a good illustration of his fine and earnest love of unity*. The same desire of peace induced him at last to despise Westphal's wrath, and to let it expend itself in noise†. He once again assailed the Lutheran zealots with admirable force, when he found them renouncing every overture to peace‡. Such were the lengths to which the foolish Saxon ministers allowed themselves to be carried, that they were constantly ready with their anathemas; they excommunicated each other, and it was now a serious question among them, whether they ought not to pronounce the ban upon Calvin. The reformer felt however that if they should indulge their wrath to this ridiculous extent, he had only to meet the attack with silence§.

Melancthon's behaviour in this controversy still remains a riddle. Calvin complained, in the severest terms, of his 'drowsiness.' He adjured him, in the name of God, to come forth and declare his opinions, and prevent the separation of the churches; but he summoned him in vain. Planck supposes|| that Me-

* Ed. Laus. Ep. 236. Ed. Amstel. p. 112, March 25, 1557.
† MS. Tigur. Calv. Bullingero; Nov. 19, 1558.
‡ Ed. Laus. Ep. 292. Ed. Amst. p. 140, April 22, 1560.
§ MS. Gen. Calv. Farello.
|| Bd. v. Thl. 2, s. 416.

lancthon was inclined to adopt a more refined policy; that he meant to let the fire burn itself out; to preserve the appearance of abiding by Luther's doctrine, and yet by his influence to prevent the faith of the church on the points in question from being so exactly defined, as to enable either party to use it for the condemnation of the other. But if this were the case, it is difficult to understand why he did not communicate his design to Calvin, and exhort him also to preserve silence. I think however that Melancthon took a higher stand, and that he held his peace from Christian conviction. He adhered to the expression regarding the actual presence of Christ in the sacrament, agreed altogether with Calvin, and believed that the truth would conquer.

The correspondence between Calvin and Melancthon, the long powerful letters of the former, and the short answers of the latter, are in the highest degree striking. Melancthon was anxious to communicate personally with Calvin before he died. He constantly designated the error of the Lutherans 'bread-worship,' ἀρτολατρεία. Calvin wished to induce him to subscribe the renewed 'Consensus' with the Zurichers. Melancthon, in the year 1555, promised to state his sentiments openly. Calvin hereupon wrote him a letter expressive of the liveliest satisfaction*. Their correspondence now ceased for two years; not three, as is commonly supposed.

Calvin, through this whole period, was occupied with the thought of a Convention, in which certain right-minded representatives of the churches might come to an understanding respecting the points at issue. He communicated this idea to Melancthon, and prayed that he "might yet once more enjoy the glad sight of his countenance in this world, and be somewhat refreshed by him, whilst they wept together over the evils which they could not prevent."

Others, as Blaarer and Martyr (1558), complained, in the strongest language, of Melancthon's weakness (*imbecillitas*). They all considered that if he had but openly declared himself in favour of the views adopted by the Reformed, the separation of the church would never have taken place. But Calvin would not grieve the now aged man, and was silent.

In the year 1559 the Lutheran zealots had forced the condemnation of Calvinism. Melancthon however declared, that no one had a right to make the orthodoxy of the whole church depend upon the private opinions of Luther. He felt himself

* Ed. Laus. Ep. 210 Ed. Amstel. p. 100, Sept. 1555.

also compelled to declare openly against Brentius, who, in the Würtemberg 'Concordia,' had attacked him as 'a neutral theologian,' and had asserted the ubiquity of the human body of Christ as a fundamental doctrine. But this was his last effort. Peucer states, that he defended, as well as the short time before his death allowed him, the doctrine of the union of the two natures in his lectures. This had an important relation to the question at issue. A vast number of his young followers, it is also added, were rightly instructed by him on this subject.

Such was the state of the controversy when Melancthon was called to his eternal rest. It happened at the moment when he was summoned, nay almost compelled, by Brentius, openly to declare his opinions. The melancholy tidings were conveyed to Geneva. Calvin inquired the day when he died: it was the 19th of April, 1560. Melancthon left Calvin alone on the field of strife. They were both destined to be cruelly persecuted in the last days of their life by their own party. The one submitted, and lamented the wickedness of mankind; the other fought bravely on to his end, awakening respect by his courage. We cannot better characterize the feeling of these two men, than by the words which rose from the depth of Calvin's soul, as he meditated on Melancthon:—"O Philip Melancthon, I appeal to thee as my witness! Thou now livest with Christ in the presence of God, and waitest for us to share with thee that blessed rest. Wearied with labour, oppressed with many cares, a hundred times didst thou express thy wish to live and die with me. I too a thousand times wished that we could live together. Assuredly thou wouldst then have been stronger to begin the fight; to despise the hate, and to treat with contempt all the slanders of thine enemies; and thus would the designs of the wicked, rendered bold by what they called your sleepiness, have been disappointed."

When Westphal again answered Calvin, the latter remained silent; his reasons for doing so may be learnt from what is stated at the end of Beza's work: "Westphal uses expressions which are proper only to the lowest class of women." But Beza, like Calvin, preferred friendship, and carried on the controversy so happily, that Westphal was brought to silence. Melancthon had formerly said, that the strife would continue after his death. In January 1561 another controversial writing by Calvin was printed at Geneva, and soon circulated through Germany. Tileman Hesshus, one of the zealots of that period, affords us, in his life, an image of those unquiet times: he had so rude and untamed a heart, that he was seven times deposed from his office, and expelled. This wrangler was now anxious to fasten upon Calvin. The reformer took the pains to confute him fundamentally. Beza also answered him. How Calvin regarded the work directed against him appears from two letters, the one of which, wherein he expresses his contempt for the man, is addressed to Olevianus, and the other to a prince, whose name is unknown. The latter was written for the object of defeating the unheard-of plans of the Lutherans, now proposing to excommunicate the whole of the reformed churches in a mass. Calvin declares himself ready to accept the Augsburg Confession in all its articles, but not the expressions of the new *Stoa* of theologians. He thus criticises Hesshus: "I have read the book written by Hesshus; he inserts the disputed points in the definition; passes over the exposition of the apostle Paul; gives his own, which is new and unheard of, instead, and thus quietly sets it aside. He adduces authorities which have nothing to do with his argument, but rather support the contrary. In fact he writes, not to teach, but to judge and to condemn."

Calvin next declares explicitly his own opinions, and asks, whether any one would personally anathematize him as a heretic? He further proves the absurdities of his opponents, especially those involved in the ubiquity of the body, and the worship of the host. This is followed by a severe expression against those who, in their mad folly, were anxious to assemble a synod for the purpose of condemning the French and Swiss churches. Calvin also shows how the reformed of all countries were excited, and how the queen of England, although inclined to the Augsburg Confession, could not be induced to adopt the carnal form of the words. It was not, he said, the pure or actual doctrine of Luther which these people adopted, but an hyperbole thereof. He next confutes their false and perverted views of Melancthon, whom they described as a weak old man, and shows his agreement with him and Martyr. The whole affair, he reminded them, would serve as a jubilee for the Catholics. The reformer, on the other hand, earnestly desired a national council of the three people, of Germany, France and England,—a council at which some prince should preside, and in which the ambassadors of other princes might take a part. Before the assembling of such a council, the heads of the other parties, as Martyr, Bullinger, Calvin, Beza, should be invited to attend, and the questions at issue might then be fairly discussed. The tyrannical synod which the others proposed to assemble could only tend to create a schism, the flames of which posterity might not be able to extinguish.

Calvin proves, in his writing against Hesshus, how opposed the latter was to Westphal, who boldly asserted that the body of Christ is masticated with the teeth. Hesshus, on the contrary, insisted, that it may be eaten with the mouth, but not touched with the teeth, and is altogether opposed to the grosser idea. Calvin now states how he understood and used the word 'substantial.' Thus Christ, he says, through the secret power of his Spirit, applies to us the life of his own Spirit, so that He lives in us, and his life becomes ours. He now again reviews the whole subject, and expresses his hearty good-will to promote peace and unity, giving at the same time a brief abstract of the points in which the two parties agreed or disagreed, and thus placing the whole subject in the clearest point of view.

But no effort availed to soften the passions which had been excited, and after sixteen years of violent strife, and when Calvin was dead, it belonged to the Lutherans to perpetuate the schism by the Concordate-formulary (1580), in which all the points opposed by Calvin, in regard both to the sacrament and predestination, were adopted as symbolic. The fiery zeal of the Lutherans excited a general movement. The churches of Bremen, Hesse, and the Palatinate; Anhalt, and the house of Brandenburg, passed over to the Reformed. The schism was rendered still greater by the Synod of Dort, which took a political character; and the fanaticism of the Particularists rendered a reunion hopeless. It is impossible to tell the consequences of this unhappy separation. During the thirty years' war, the Elector Palatine was placed on the throne of Bohemia. From the same cause, the Huguenots of France were forsaken by their brethren; and the German schism transferred the judicial power at Münster to the hands of the former country. Alsace was now snatched from enfeebled Germany. The lower Palatinate was overrun with troops; and thus the separation between Luther and Zwingli, and the rage of the zealots, became the curse of our fatherland.

Numberless efforts were made by the Reformed church to restore peace, and thus to repair the ills inflicted by Luther's error. These experiments were indications of the existence of a noble, inward life, it being a principle interwoven with the very consciousness of a Christian to contemplate the church as one. It was Christ's prayer to his Father that his disciples might "be one, as they are one." The Holy Spirit still urges us to the same end.

Calvin hoped much from an assembly of theologians. A meeting took place at Worms, in conformity with the orders of the Emperor Ferdinand. It was an experiment to bring the Lutherans and Catholics nearer to each other, but it only served to render their separation more evident. Representatives from Geneva were present. Calvin sought thereby to accomplish the object which he had in view, and to awaken the sympathy of the German princes and divines in behalf of the poor persecuted believers in France. This could only be rendered possible by inducing the German Evangelical party to acknowledge the Reformed as their brethren : hitherto they had spoken against them rather than in their behalf, although they both received in common the Augsburg Confession.

Farel and Beza had already been sent, at an earlier period, to the Reformed Swiss cantons, to persuade them to employ their influence with the king of France in behalf of the persecuted Waldenses. Having accomplished their purpose in this case, they next hastened to the Elector Palatine, who received them graciously, and sent them to the Duke of Würtemberg. The latter however, to avoid interfering for the Waldenses, pretended that they were Sacramentarians. Thus Farel and Beza found themselves obliged to place in his hands a new and strongly expressed confession respecting the presence of Christ in the sacrament. When the Zurichers were informed of this proceeding, they expressed great anger, and insisted that the confession referred to was not in accordance with their doctrine. They severely reproved Beza, and the latter promised to give them on the first occasion a full explanation of the matter, and to act in constant union with them. Farel heard of this misunderstanding when he came to Beza at Lausanne, and apologized in a letter, in which he says that neither Viret, nor Andreä, nor Calvin, saw anything worthy to blame in what had been done. He was astonished, he says, now that the other party was reconciled, that the Zurichers should still be inclined to wrath, and he speaks very excellently on the sacrament and the unity of the church. "I thank God that this holy union of the churches has now been proclaimed before God, the angels and men. I would willingly have shed my blood for this. Far rather would I that any one should take my life, than that I should separate from this holy union. Tell me therefore if I have offended you in the slightest point, and I will hasten to seek your pardon." Beza also justified himself. But when Calvin asserted that the confession spoken of was the true expression of their belief, Bullinger sharply assailed him, and imputed to him the doubtful language employed by Bucer. Hence it appears, that although the Swiss cantons were desirous of peace, the Zurichers, who adhered with painful anxiety to their opinions, still presented an obstacle to the union of the churches.

Bullinger remained inflexible in his belief that a convention would be of no avail. The assurance that Melancthon was in favour of the meeting was wholly disregarded. Calvin however, who recollected the diet of Ratisbone, hoped much from an oral discussion, if Brentius, that is, were prevented from taking the chief part in the assembly. Such was the state of affairs, when the church of Geneva sent Farel and Beza, for the second time, with John Bude and Caspar Carmel, in order to summon the Protestant powers to interest themselves earnestly with Henri II. of France, in behalf of their brethren in his kingdom. Calvin would not go to Worms, as Farel wished: he wrote however to Melancthon three times in the course of six weeks, to urge him to unceasing exertion. Having spoken strongly against Andreä, he says, "The issue of the meeting at Worms will only be that the papists will invent delays, according to their old fashion, and will have the princes, the defenders of the true faith, for the most part on their side." It was the violent Lutherans however, the followers, that is, of Flacius, who mainly contributed to destroy the fruit of this assembly.

In the meantime, the Genevese deputies, who had been before in Zurich, commenced their duties at Worms; but they created another cause of offence to the Zurichers. Melancthon expressed a hope that something would be done for their afflicted brethren. Another persecution of the Waldenses, among the Alps of Turin and Grenoble, had been begun in October 1557. Three of these unfortunate people were burnt in Paris to spread terror among the rest. The Protestants wished to have a short confession of faith drawn up, that they might be the better able to commend the deputies to the princes. Calvin's Catechism was not fitted for the purpose. The Augsburg Confession was spoken of, and Beza declared himself altogether in favour of its adoption, with the exception of the article on the Lord's Supper; and even this he was ready to admit, according to the interpretation given by Melancthon.

This was sufficient: letters of introduction were given him to the Elector Palatine, to the Landgrave Philip, to the Count-Palatine Wolfgang, and the Duke Christopher, at Würtemberg. These princes promised to intercede for the persecuted brethren. The desired object was therefore attained. But although the confession above-mentioned was given in the name of the French church only, the Zurichers still found cause for quarrel. The Lutherans had certainly the good intention of leading the Reformed to the Augsburg Confession; and Calvin perhaps, having a higher end in view, would not have refused to yield in this respect. He had ever in his thoughts the infinite evil of schism. But Bullinger adhered to his extreme views, and would not go to Worms. Calvin, not unfairly, found fault with this conduct. By being present at Worms, Bullinger might have prevented the condemnation of the Zwinglians. Melancthon, though earnestly admonished by Bullinger, was so perplexed, after refusing to condemn the Zwinglians, the followers of Osiander, and the Majorists, that he subsequently published a statement, in which he declared that he rejected the Zwinglian system, and condemned all teachers who opposed the Augsburg Confession.

This unfortunate issue of the convention at Worms, which tended to fix Bullinger more firmly in his views, did not dishearten Calvin. He desired that a Colloquy might be held for the purpose of uniting parties against the views of the Zurichers. Bullinger, on the contrary, opposed the interests of union; but the brethren of Basel were, in the end, induced to join with Calvin. Sulzer was wholly in favour of union, in opposition to the narrow views of the Zwinglians. Thus a secret antipathy was created between Zurich and Basel, which displayed itself conspicuously on the publication of the Helvetic Confession. Hence it is probable that Calvin would have done better for the interests of the church at large, had he, together with the French Reformed congregations, allied himself with Germany, and subscribed the Augsburg Confession, without demanding any explanation of the tenth article. Their fundamental principles were the same. Calvin was himself a Lutheran, in the same way as the thoughtful Lutherans are Calvinists; and had the union of which we have spoken taken place, the development of the church would have had another direction. Bullinger, in this case, exhibited a despotic anxiety, as Luther had before a stormy despotism. But Calvin's truthfulness, which was not recognised as it ought to have been, held him back*. "You have nothing to fear as to my doing anything injurious to our close alliance. If we should be summoned to a Colloquy, I will attend, as I have already said, not for the purpose of seeking new friends, and leaving you, my old ones, to yourselves, but to win new opponents for us both. Whether I go or not, it will be my care not only not to concede anything which is contrary to my faith, but to adhere to our 'Consensus' with all possible resolution. Threats affect me not; for nothing can be more agreeable to me than the thought of leaving this world, to say nothing of this city, as soon as possible."

The Protestant princes having discovered at Worms how little union existed among their theologians, had reassembled them at Frankfort (1558) in order to effect a reconciliation. The Wittenbergers, guided by Melancthon, were more moderate on this occasion; and Melancthon and some others entered into a correspondence with Bullinger and Calvin. The Reformed expressed themselves again, at Frankfort, in the strongest manner on the presence of the Lord in the sacrament. The followers of Flacius, on the other hand, still raved, asserting that it was Zwingli's and Calvin's, and not Luther's doctrine, which was asserted. Deputies from the French churches also appeared there again with Beza: the latter had only just risen from a bed of sickness. They earnestly implored help for the persecuted, and warned their hearers not to allow themselves to be deceived by the Cardinal Guise of Loraine, who pretended that the embassy would avail nothing with the king of France, and that he would, without its interference, suppress the persecutions, which were then at the height. Beza gained his end. They also begged to be allowed to hold a friendly conference on the disputed points with the German theologians. All seemed to promise tranquillity, when it was heard that the Duke of Würtemberg had published an edict, banishing all who adhered to the Zwinglian doctrine from his dominions. This intelligence excited the greatest astonishment.

Somewhat later, that is in May 1560, Calvin again expressed his profound agreement with Bullinger, remarking that there was nothing to hope from the mimickers of Luther†.

At the same time (1560), two deputies from the Waldensian churches in Bohemia arrived at Geneva: they were also anxious to establish some point of union. Calvin, to whom they brought

* Calvin to Bullinger, May 22, 1558. Hess, s. 395. Buchat, t. vi. p. 239.
† MS. Gen. De Lutheri Simiis.

a letter, dated May 11, from the chief presbyter of the brotherhood at Carmel, received them with open arms*.

Some years before (1557), a misunderstanding had arisen between the Waldenses and the other Protestants in Poland. Calvin had admonished both parties to cultivate peace; there being at the time three sections disputing with each other on the subject of the sacrament; the one Lutheran, the other Waldensian, and the third taking a middle course. It is said, in a letter to Bullinger, that John a Lasco was too violent against these Waldenses. Calvin thought it right to warn him not to separate them from communion.

He now answered the brethren in a friendly, heartfelt letter, abounding in admirable thoughts on the communion of Christians in Christ. This epistle indeed affords a noble proof of the joy which he felt in union, and at the same time throws considerable light on the relations existing between the churches of the north.

It was Calvin's opinion that these Waldenses might be very useful in aiding the diffusion of the Gospel, and he was anxious therefore to retain them in communion with the church; but they had now separated themselves from the Polish Reformed, because they saw that they were continually engaged in theological strife. "If Satan has flung Stancarus and Blandrata among them, is it not your duty to hasten to the succour of the brethren in Poland? If you neglect them, they will, sooner or later, forsake you. The cause of this controversy and of your separation is the dispute existing respecting the communication of the flesh and blood of Christ. Two things have distressed you: the first, that we wrote complaining that your confession was, on account of its brevity, obscure, and likely to excite doubt; and, secondly, that the apology which you set forth was much too violent against those who wish for the light of a sound exposition, in the words where you say, 'The bread is the body of Christ.' You are well-aware of what Melancthon thinks on this point; but honouring as we do his memory, we would not employ the respect due to his name to overthrow our opponents; we only desire to show how unfairly they act who appeal to the Augsburg Confession, when they differ altogether from its author. Your formulary can only be adopted with danger; it would give occasion to great disturbance among the Poles. If your deputy answer, that I have also exhibited great heat in my writings, I do not deny this in the whole; but it is not the right

* Ed. Laus. Ep. 294. Ed. Amst. p. 145.

time to bring such an accusation. I may indeed have attacked some unclean dogs rather severely; but your apology has had a very different aim. It has confused and condemned, without distinction, many pious and learned men, with the most abandoned." Calvin concludes his epistle in a quiet and friendly style, praying those to whom it was addressed not to take what he had said amiss, and hoping that the Genevese would receive a warning if they failed.

In the summer of 1554, Calvin heard that the Reformed church at Strasburg was in danger: his affection for the old congregation, which he himself had established, was awakened anew; and of little importance as this circumstance may seem, we must speak of it, since even what was in itself trifling in his life had a peculiar character. He wrote to Marbach in Strasburg, saying, that his anxiety would no longer allow him to remain silent*. He spoke in the same manner to Farel†. Some people at Strasburg had interested themselves for Servetus, and had spoken against both the punishment of heretics and the doctrine of election. Calvin had therefore addressed a letter to one of the resident ministers in Strasburg: his language is strong, patient but energetic, as it was likely to be when he believed himself unjustly assailed‡.

Peter Martyr spoke with similar severity against Zwingli, the son of the Swiss reformer, from Strasburg; stating that false opinions were preached in that city on the subject of election, and on the capital punishment of heretics. He agreed on both points with Calvin; but the schism was mainly caused by disputes on the subject of the sacrament. The second minister had attacked both the stated doctrine and his associate Garnier, who defended it. Five of the congregation had dissented, and accused the first pastor: they were protected by the Lutherans. It was intended to depose the obnoxious pastor from his office. Calvin prayed for him and for the peace of the church. The council succeeded in restoring tranquillity. At the time of the Interim, which was adopted in Strasburg, the congregation had exhibited considerable firmness. The accused pastor was at length obliged to yield, and in the year 1555 Calvin wrote to Martyr—"The breaking up of the little French congregation afflicts me in no slight degree." He exhorts him to reinstate

* Ed. Laus. Ep. 177. Ed. Amst. p. 84, b Cal. Sept. 1554.

† MS. Gen. Nov. 1, 1554.

‡ Ed. Laus. Ep. 189. Ed. Amst. p. 85.

the church, and remarks that he would find faithful supporters in Sturmius and Sleidan. Sleidan, the well-known historian of this period, was one of the chief men in the congregation; Calvin carried on a confidential correspondence with him, and their letters express a very rash and startling judgement on Melancthon*.

Peter Martyr soon after left Strasburg, went to Zurich, and the Lutheran party was victorious. In 1563, Zanchius, tormented by Marbach, laid down his office and removed to Graubünden, where he became minister. In the same year the 'Formula Concordiæ,' or 'Consensus Argentinensis,' for the settlement of doctrine, was drawn up at Strasburg and subscribed by all the churches. But on the 19th of August, the French reformed church, as not agreeing with the confession thus established, was dispersed: it subsequently however revived.

The dissent of Tossanus, minister in Mümpelgard, was also treated by Calvin as one of the sad consequences of this quarrel. He suspected him of being imbued with the errors of Servetus, and some time after spoke of his follies to Philip of Hesse. It appears from the letter which he wrote on this occasion, that Tossanus invited preachers from Geneva, prepared of his own accord the 'Consensus Pastorum,' and exercised a control over ministers inconsistent with christian brotherhood. The prince was exhorted "not to let one by violence appropriate to himself the command over others†."

We ask now, What had Calvin gained for unity at this period by his zealous, noble struggles? It was the general establishment of the church, as far as it was then possible, and the triumph of the Wittenberg 'Concordia' in Switzerland, effected by the renewal of the 'Consensus' in the years 1551 (?) and 1554. We cannot indeed better conclude the account of the three controversies above-described than by again quoting the noble sentiments which Calvin addressed to Laski:—"Fain would I that such a harmony reigned among all the churches of Christ in this world, that the angels might sing to us from heaven‡!"

* In a letter from Calvin to Sleidan, Aug. 1554, Ed. Amst. p. 85, we read the following: "In summis capitibus philosophis se venditans sanam doctrinam oppugnat,—vel ne in se quorundam excitet odia, sensum suum astute, saltem parum ingenue tegit. Dominus eum fortiore spiritu instruat, ne gravem ex ejus timiditate jacturam sentiat posteritas."

† MS. Gen. Calv. Farello, May 18, 1556.

‡ Ruchat, vi. 558.

CHAPTER VIII.

FINAL STRUGGLE AGAINST THE LIBERTINES.—BERTHELIER. —TRIUMPH OF DISCIPLINE.—FAILURE OF CALVIN'S ENEMIES.—EDUCATIONAL PLANS.

HAVING given a connected view of the disputes concerning doctrine, we now enter upon a period rich in all respects in evangelical operations. Calvin had reached by his perseverance the grand end of his activity, which never, as was the case with Luther in his latter years, declined, his spirit growing no weaker by the conflicts in which it was engaged. His fundamental principles ever urged him to seek the unity of the church. In the first period of his career he laboured to exhibit a correct system of doctrine, and in the second he employed his energies in effecting the security of that which he had thus accomplished by means of church discipline, and the 'Consensus Tigurinus.'

But this reference to the concluding æra of his labours brings him before us engaged in a new conflict with his opponents at Geneva. They were at length however subdued; so that the reformer gained time to nourish his church at home, and yet to extend his influence to Scotland and Poland, and to keep the evangelical church in France on a firm foundation, till he was called away to his rest, in the midst of the storm caused by the wars of the Huguenots.

It is necessary to take a brief review of the troublous year 1553. Calvin was so firmly fixed in the feeling of duty that he watched carefully the course of public events. It was in this year that he published his Commentary on St. John, and dedicated the work to the council. In the preface he extols the members for having so hospitably entertained the persecuted strangers who had found refuge in Geneva, and exhorts them to remain superior to all barkings and tumults.

But fresh clouds were gathering about his head. Since the affair with Bolsec, Bern had been at constant strife with Geneva. The revolutionary party raised its head; the ministers were excluded from the council*; and the French refugees were forbidden to carry weapons†. Perrini had resolved to overthrow

* February 4, 1553.

† April 11, 1553.

the newly-established system of church-discipline, and with it the power of Calvin. Servetus was at this time in prison; Calvin was occupied with the process against him; and now it was that Philip Berthelier, the son of the Berthelier who lost his head in the cause of freedom in 1518, made his appearance. He was very much beloved by the people on account of his father's memory; but in 1552 his disorderly life occasioned his expulsion from the number of communicants, and the magistrates ordered him to be cast into prison. In the month of August he made an appeal to the council, and desired it to reverse the sentence of the consistory. The state protocol shows that he entertained no friendly feeling towards Calvin. If his reasonings had been admitted, all excommunicated persons would have pursued the same course, the council would have assumed the entire government of the church, and Calvin's work would have been abortive. Berthelier had many adherents in the council. They proposed that a minister should be summoned to the assembly and absolve the offenders in its presence. Calvin, greatly excited, proved by the most powerful arguments that the council ought to be the defender, and not the disturber of the sacred laws of the church. He even assembled all the ministers both of the city and country, and proceeded with them on a subsequent day to the council, before which each of them solemnly protested against the contemplated injury; and all declared that, rather than suffer it, they would lay down their office and leave their churches. But the party of the libertines rose tumultuously and gained the victory. "The consistory," they exclaimed, "wished to assume to itself the authority which belonged to the civil magistrates."

This affair was now brought before the "Council of Two Hundred," and it was decided that the council had in reality the right to hear complaints like those referred to, and to absolve. Berthelier was acquitted, and received a document accordingly, sealed with the seal of the republic. Perrini believed that he had now triumphed; that Calvin would either not obey the decree, and so would be judged as a rebel, or that he would yield, and that in such case the power of the consistory would be for ever gone: but he had to do with a man whose energy was of a very different kind to his. In such moments Calvin exhibited the entire greatness of his mind, and the shallow critics who describe him as a mere cold reasoner merit supreme contempt.

It was on the Friday before the first Sunday in September, when the whole reformed church celebrates the Lord's Supper, that Calvin received information of the plan against him. He instantly requested the syndics to summon a meeting of the council. He hastened thither himself, and in an earnest address endeavoured to convince those who were present, that it was their duty to revoke the decree. He concluded with protesting that he was resolved to die rather than disgrace the celebration of the Lord's Supper in so unworthy a manner: "For nothing," he said, "can be worse than your proposing to let this man sport with the church, and thus excite others, by the impunity which he enjoys, to the same insolence." The council however answered that it would change nothing in its decree. Calvin accordingly formed in his heart the resolution to leave the city, or rather he saw himself exposed to a second banishment. The important Sunday now arrived, September 3rd: the reformer ascended the pulpit; his ardent eloquence was employed on the holy mysteries, and on those who despised them. At the end of his discourse he raised his voice, and admonished the congregation to receive the sacrament with holy earnestness. He spoke with great force against those who despised the sacred rite, and, imitating the example of Chrysostom, declared that he would give the sacrament to none of those who were excommunicated; and that, if any one among them should attempt to seize the bread of the Lord by force, he would do so at his peril. Then lifting up his hand, he exclaimed, "I will lose my life rather than let this hand give the holy things to those who have been pronounced despisers of God." These words sounded like a thunder-clap, striking the excommunicated and his associates to the earth. Wonderfully affected himself, Perrini secretly advised Berthelier not to approach the Lord's table; and the holy supper, Beza relates, was celebrated in the profoundest silence, and with a holy awe, as if God himself had been visibly present in the assembly.

In the afternoon of the same day Calvin preached another sermon, and in pursuing the text on which he was discoursing, the twentieth chapter of the Acts of the Apostles lay before him. In referring to the admirable address in which Paul took leave of the church at Ephesus, Calvin appealed to his congregation with the words, "'Watch, and remember, that by the space of three years I ceased not to warn every one night and day with tears; and now, brethren, I commend you to God, and to the word of his grace.'" "I am not," he continued, "the man either to contend against authority myself, or to excite others to do so." He then exhorted the congregation to persevere in the doctrine which he had preached to them, declaring that he was always ready to serve the church, and every individual member of it. "But," added he, in conclusion, "affairs here are now in such a state that I know not whether this may not be the last time that I shall proclaim to you the word of God; for those who have the power in their hands wish to compel me to do a thing which is not lawful before God; therefore must I say to you, as Paul said to the elders at Ephesus, 'I commend you, dear brethren, to the grace of God*.'" These words made a deep impression on the assembly; they terrified the enemies of Calvin and confirmed his friends. The next day he appeared with all the ministers and the other members of the consistory before the lesser council, and before that of the "Two Hundred," in order to ask permission to be heard by the great council: the question concerned a law which that body had sanctioned.

Calvin's request was not granted; but a very different feeling had arisen, and resort was had for the moment to the practice allowed by the "Council of Two Hundred," of adjourning the meeting. It was announced in the mean time that the opinion of the cantons, on the laws of discipline, should be collected, and that, till this was done, things should remain as they were.

All these proceedings took place during the trial of Servetus. Calvin acquainted Bullinger with them in a letter, dated October 25; shortly, that is, before the execution of Servetus, but to whom there is only a cursory allusion. He had already said to Gualter, who was there, that he was prepared to die rather than cast the holy bread to dogs, who, in despite of the Gospel, had audaciously resolved upon treading underfoot the order of the churches†.

The storm passed over, but it gathered again about the head of Farel: he accompanied Servetus, as we have seen, to the place of execution. Soon after this he hastened again to Geneva, in order to bridle by his influence, by his powerful discourse, and

* Ed. Laus. Ep. 162. Ed. Amst. p. 78. An allusion is made to the above discourse in a letter which Calvin wrote to Bullinger, and from which it appears that it was written by a short-hand writer as he delivered it. The manuscript probably exists at Zurich; since Calvin referred Bullinger to the sermon itself, *quam Beza noster vertendam curavit.*

† He spoke somewhat later on the same subject, expressing his inward convictions of duty, and saying that he would remain, out of pity to his church, which would otherwise be ruined. MS. Tig. Feb. 11, 1554.

the respect due to his age, the fury of Calvin's opponents. He ascended the pulpit: all hastened to hear him: he assailed them with the mighty eloquence which he had always ready at command, exhibited the antagonist party in its true light, and then departed. His discourse however was skilfully represented by the disaffected as a gross injustice against them, and they constrained the council to furnish them with a letter for Neuchatel, to compel Farel to answer their complaint in his own person. Calvin considered it advisable for him to yield to their demand. The old man accordingly set out on foot, alone and in the roughest autumnal weather, on his way to Geneva. Calvin dare not let him preach. There was a general excitement. The tumult in the senate-house was so great when the accusation was formally made, that the hostile party exclaimed, that Farel must be flung into the Rhone. A young and courageous man now stepped forth, and warned Perrini to take care that the father of the city suffered no harm. Another young man soon joined him; and when the people began to collect about the council-chamber, the ministers appeared in a body, and admonished the council to defend the honour of God and his word. Justice demanded a loud protest in behalf of Farel.

A general tumult pervaded the place: the citizens and work-people left their homes to defend their ministers. The accusers became alarmed, and were obliged to submit to terms. Calvin, Viret and others, now explained the wicked designs of their enemies. Farel defended himself in a lengthened address, and upheld the truth. In the registers of the republic it is stated, that Farel declared that he had no intention to blame the city, but that, on the contrary, he cherished a sincere love for Geneva. This speech deeply affected the auditory. Among those who had forced their way into the presence of the council, were many who had taken part against Farel; but all now proclaimed that they believed him to be a true servant of the Gospel, and their spiritual father. Upon this the council commanded that every one should give him his hand, and that a feast should be held in token of the general reconciliation. The first syndic was now obliged to declare, with trembling, that Farel's sermon was holy; that nothing could be fairly said against him; that his opponents must be reconciled to him, and that every one must live according to the word of God. The libertines hereby discovered that they had not the mass of the people with them, and Perrini humbled himself before Farel.

Thus this troublous year, in which the church had also to lament the death of King Edward of England, ended prosperously for Geneva. The question respecting discipline was still debated; but the agitation thereby created was only the forerunner of much greater evils. On the eve of the year 1554, Calvin expressed to Bullinger his sorrowful feelings: his position was almost unbearable. The days had arrived when he felt indeed that it was not without cause that he had trembled, when Farel pressed it upon him as a duty to return to Geneva, and when he exclaimed, *Cor meum velut mactatum Deo in sacrificium offero*, "I offer my bleeding heart as a sacrifice to God." On the 1st of January another great feast was celebrated: Calvin was present: the magistrates and the members of the lesser council also attended. "If any one disturbs the peace," it was then said, "let all rise against him." On the 2nd of February, 1554, the people took an oath, with upraised hands, that they would live for the future according to the teaching of the reformers; that they would refrain from all malice, forget the past, and invoke the vengeance of God upon the houses, persons, wives and children of those who should violate this holy vow. On the 23rd of the same month Calvin wrote to Bullinger: "The good citizens have not had sufficient courage to bring the affairs of the church into order, the want of which was the first cause of this agitation. They have satisfied themselves with shaking hands in token of reconciliation, and with proclaiming on oath that they will no longer support injustice. Thus under the pretence of promoting peace, they have set aside church order, the only sure foundation of peace. I was called to the council-chamber, and there declared that I forgave all who felt true repentance; that I, however, was not the consistory; and that I would rather die a hundred times than claim for myself an authority which belonged to the whole church, the right, that is, of establishing rules of discipline. The enemy has made at present but little uproar; it will soon be necessary however to renew the conflict."

Calvin was not mistaken: the evil became greater than he had feared. Complaints were again made to the council respecting the determination of the consistory, and the elders were obliged to appear before the former to defend themselves. Justice was so little regarded*, that the first syndic this year, who required satisfaction for an injury done him, could obtain none

* Ruchat, t. v. p. 116.

from the council, and he openly declared that he would seek justice of the citizens themselves, from door to door. Calvin was now attacked in his own person. It has been already mentioned, that the council, in August 1554, had received a long letter under a strange name, containing fearful accusations against Calvin. It was communicated to him, and he believed that it came from Castellio. We have spoken of the numerous insults heaped upon him; but no mention has yet been made of the circumstance, that as he was once returning from St. Gervais, where he had been preaching, a number of miscreants attacked him on the bridge over the Rhone. He answered their threats by quietly remarking, that the bridge was broad enough for them all. They then directed their rage against a French refugee, whom they pursued to his own shop, and wounded him. The people assembled; swords were drawn and blood flowed. Many cried aloud, "Murder, murder the foreigner!" Similar occurrences took place day after day. Another time, when Calvin was going to give his lecture he was publicly insulted, and his servant was beaten in the open street.

The admonitions of the consistory were utterly despised, and the magistrates were slow to punish offences. They indulged themselves, on the other hand, in the language of threat, when engaged in public business, as if they were the lords of the state. Efforts were made to abolish the moral judicature, and blasphemy and adultery triumphed. The endeavours made to resist this state of things proved fruitless. One of its licentious opponents dared to say to the consistory, that it was more savage than Satan himself, but that it would soon cease to be so. "See," said some other libertines, "how we are governed by the French edicts and by Calvin!" Often at night some fresh attack was made upon the foreigners, and they were cruelly beaten. Calvin reproved the offenders with the whole might of his pulpit eloquence; but the council, which considered his vehemence unseasonable, called him into its presence, and besought him to moderate his zeal. The old Genevese citizens united in opposing the admission of the strangers to equal civil rights; and had obtained a law, by which it was ordained, that no foreigner should be eligible for election into the great council, till he had been resident twenty-five years.

It was at this period that the refugees, who had settled in Wesel, Emden and Frankfort, occasioned Calvin so much anxiety

About the same time also he received a letter from Peter Martyr, at Strasburg, May 9, 1554, stating that Philip of Spain had been acknowledged as king in England; that popery was re-established in that country, and that holy men and believers were obliged on all sides to seek safety by flight. "I write this," says Martyr, "that you and your church may, in these unhappy circumstances, afford help by your prayers." And further, "I do not wish it to be hidden from you, that I and many pious people are in the highest degree troubled, that so many perverse and false reports should have sprung up, both against the truth and against your name, in reference to God's eternal election, and the punishment of heretics."

Nothing indeed but the invincible strength of this man, who had no worldly object of desire, could have resisted the stream of corruption now flowing, or have upheld the rights of the church against it. Beza states that the revolutionary party made obscene songs on the word of God. It was during 1553, and the two following years, that this rebellious feeling reached its height. One night in January 1555, the streets were illuminated, and a mock procession took place, in which the hymns of the church were ridiculed in vulgar parodies*. At this time also it was reported by Beza, that the king of France had commanded the duke of Guise to make himself master of Geneva. The fortifications were accordingly carefully repaired, and the Waldensian refugees were employed in the work. But this gave rise to new disturbances. Perrini, as general of the forces of the little republic, employed himself in circulating a statement, that the Genevese French were in league with the enemy, and that if they agreed with him, the king would admit them to his favour; they ought therefore, he said, to be watched and examined, and to be subjected to an annual tax. The position was one of difficulty for a small city. There was an enemy at the gates, and there were factions within the walls. Calvin rightly said, that if the church was everywhere disturbed, in the case of Geneva it was tossed to and fro like the ark in the deluge. But he observed to Viret, "that he bore all this in silence." If he was now engaged in forming plans against the libertines, as some writers suppose, he would certainly have quietly intimated it to his friends; but he speaks only of his troubles. Before the commencement of the decisive year 1555, we hear him pouring out his deep sighs, and ex-

* An account of these proceedings is given in the registers of the republic, Jan. 9, 1555.

pressing, like Melancthon, his wish to die*: he uttered the same feelings at a somewhat later period†.

But in the year above-mentioned, this fierce struggle respecting discipline was brought to a happy close. The libertines themselves contributed by their turbulence to this result‡. On January 24th, a few days after the procession to which we have alluded, the "Council of Two Hundred" being assembled, the ministers were summoned to attend for the purpose of stating, as they had desired, their views on the important question of discipline. The inquiry was not about excommunication itself, but the tribunal by which it was to be pronounced. The edicts which had been confirmed by the great council, the chief authority in the state, on the return of Calvin, had placed the right of inflicting excommunication in the hands of the consistory alone. That body accordingly pronounced sentence upon incorrigible offenders without appeal. The council had endeavoured to appropriate this right to itself, because it was inconceivably inconsistent, it said, that the government of a state should be without the power of revising whatever decrees were passed. The consistory pretended to the rank of a sovereign tribunal in the state; but sound reason demanded, that for the safe guardianship of freedom, the entire power and rule should be in the hands of the civil magistrate. It was well known what tyranny the popes exercised under the pretence of this spiritual jurisdiction.

To these insinuations the clergy answered by Calvin, "that it was the duty of men to submit themselves to the authority of Christ and his Apostles, to whom He had given the power to loose and to bind, and to administer the sacraments." It was also added, "that the magistrate had no more right to oppose himself to spiritual discipline, than the clergy had to intermeddle with the determinations of a temporal judge. It was their duty therefore to see that the sacraments suffered no dishonour; that since the clergy, as subjects, yielded entire obedience to the magistrates, all persons of rank and authority ought to bow themselves implicitly to the word of God; that pious princes have ever made this distinction; that at the very founding of the church, Aaron received the high-priesthood; David did not sacrifice; the Lord severely punished those who despised his law in this respect; Uzzah died because he laid his hand upon the ark; and King Hoseah was covered with leprosy; that the

* Calvin to Wolf, 7 Cal. Jan. 1555. † Ed. Laus. Ep. 216, Oct. 10, 1555.
‡ Ruchat, vi. p. 133.

laws were a sufficient defence against any abuse of authority on the part of the consistory; and that freedom, if Christ was banished, would be but a lamentable servitude." This reasoning made an impression upon the minds of people, and it was determined by a majority of votes, that all the edicts passed by the great council must have the authority of law; whence it followed, that church discipline must remain solely in the hands of the consistory.

While all the friends of peace were rejoicing that this victory had been gained for religion and morality, the rabble, weakened and restrained by the ministers and their powerful discourses, were loud in exclaiming that preaching ought to be suppressed, and the number of ministers reduced to two; that these should be confined to the reading of Scripture, without interpretation; that the people should be taught the "Credo," the "Lord's Prayer," and the "Ten Commandments;" that it was not only useless but dangerous to allow so much expounding; and taking advantage of the Bernese remonstrance on the doctrine of predestination, they added, that it was unnecessary to print so many books and commentaries.

A still greater feeling of indignation was expressed, when the council at one sitting admitted fifty foreigners, known for their respectability, to the rights of citizenship. It was necessary to make a bold experiment. Amy Perrini and Peter Vandel, members of the council, directed the chief of the police to appear before the lesser council, that a complaint might be made to him, in the name of the people, respecting the admission of these foreigners to the rank of citizens; a measure which disquieted the city, and rendered it necessary to bring the subject before the "Council of Two Hundred." The council, however, would not allow such a proceeding. Perrini returned the next day with a larger number of his tumultuous followers: he was sent away, with the charge to keep himself quiet. The people now spread themselves about in the low drinking-houses, and gave free expression to their wrath. This happened on a Sunday, May 14. Calvin, expecting some great event, commended himself to the prayers of Farel. On the following Tuesday, May 16, the malcontents returned in still greater numbers to the council-house; they were accompanied by fishermen and sailors, and were armed with huge double-handed swords. Their demands were the same as before, and they were again sent back. They continued to perambulate the whole city, and fresh crowds of the lower class were induced to join them. To secure their aid, they distributed food to the work-people and the poor, and commended the city to their care, lest it should fall into strange hands. The more moderate among them desired an assembly of the great council, but they were overpowered by the violence of the rest, who seem to have formed the design of killing the refugees, and those who espoused their cause. The following Sunday was the time appointed for this deed; but the violence of some of the party, and their too great haste to accomplish their design, happily defeated the plan. On the following night, a member of the council named Baudichon, accompanied by two young burghers, made the circuit of the city: they were greatly hated, as well-known champions of the persecuted refugees. In the course of their rounds they were met by a crowd of the disaffected, who, on perceiving Baudichon, instantly shouted, "Down with the traitor," and drew their swords. Hearing the cry, the syndic Aubert hastened to the spot with his staff of office, and ordered one of the leaders to be arrested; but his staff was wrenched from his hand, he was surrounded by the rabble, and the cry became general, "Treason,—the French,—kill, slay,—the French are seizing the city!" But not one of the refugees was to be seen. "The Lord," says Calvin, "had poured a deep sleep upon them." The whole city was soon under arms, without knowing why. Vandel's wife ran about the Bourg de Four, exclaiming, "The French are taking the city: up, and murder them all." When Baudichon reached his house, the crowd assembled around it, and shouted, "The French are there, all armed." But the tumult passed over without bloodshed; and Perrini's plan was defeated. Still, the malcontents hoped to effect their grand design of bringing about a revolution.

Aubert the syndic lost no time in summoning the council: it met that very night; the syndics proceeded, at its command, from street to street, and ordered the people to retire to their homes. In many places this command was disregarded. Vandel, seeing that his orders were useless, appeared in person to quiet the excited multitude. The next day an order was issued by the council prohibiting the people from meeting in crowds. In the following week the "Two Hundred" met, in order to communicate with the council on the subject of these occurrences. When Amied Perrini saw that he was exposed to the danger of a judicial investigation, and that exemplary punishments would be inflicted on the guilty, without respect to persons, he withdrew to his country-seat, in the canton of Bern, whither he was followed by Vandel, Philibert Berthelier, and many others. They were publicly summoned before the magistrates; some of the party appeared, and were slightly punished. Four however of the worst of the malcontents were beheaded. They protested that they did not die as traitors; that they had had no thought of treason; and that their sole object had been to prevent the admission of the new burghers, hoping thereby to defend the city against foreigners. But this policy of the libertines appeared to the government, as Ruchat remarks, highly dangerous. The practice of recruiting itself by the admission of new citizens was necessary to Geneva, as to all little states. Geneva, moreover, was so circumstanced, that the strangers would soon have become more powerful than the old burghers, if they had not been thus incorporated with them. Bern interested itself in the case of the fugitives, but in vain. On the 3rd of June they were pronounced rebels and traitors, and condemned to lose their heads; the sentence was executed in effigy. It was now determined that the existence of a captain-general was dangerous to the little republic, and the office was abolished.

Three letters from Calvin to Bullinger throw additional light on these occurrences. One, which is printed, gives a striking account of the whole affair; another, unprinted, begins with his defence against the accusation that he was present at the torture of one of the criminals. Hence it appears that Calvin did not busy himself, as his vilifiers wish it to be supposed, in proceedings of this kind; it was only as a minister that he visited the prison, and when called by the malefactors themselves. He was accustomed to speak with the utmost confidence to Bullinger, but not a word occurs in his letters to justify the accusations of his enemies. Instead of pronouncing anathemas upon the criminals, as it was wickedly said he did, these unfortunate people placed their full trust in him as their spiritual adviser. The letters show what the accused confessed, and what they retracted. Calvin questioned some of them at the moment when they were being led to execution*.

The friends of Bolsec, at Bern, gladly seized this opportunity

* This was especially the case with regard to two brothers. Having questioned one of them particularly, he concluded by asking him, whether he had ever attempted to force anything from him by threats or promises; to which the young man replied that nothing of this kind had been done. Speaking of the criminals generally, he says that there was not one of them who did not, by his silence, confess the greater part of his guilt.

of slandering Calvin. The libertines now also came to their support: to such an extent did their rancour proceed, that Calvin exclaimed, "I see that the hatred of some against me is so great, that they will never cease to rave till I have fallen a victim to their malice." Speaking of Geneva, he says, "But little was wanting to involve this city in one night, and all of us with it, in destruction*."

But this struggle was followed by tranquillity: Calvin's spirit prevailed, and ruled the church. Discipline was confirmed by the common consent of the cantons. We have the testimony of a noble eye-witness to the events of this period. Knox, who was at Geneva in 1556, writes to his friend Locke †, "I always wished in my heart, nor could I ever cease to wish, that it might please God to bring me to this place, where, I can say, without fear or shame, the best Christian school exists, since the time of the Apostles. I allow that Christ is truly preached in other places also, but in no other have I seen the Reformation so well wrought out, both morally and religiously, as in Geneva." Thus Farel also expressed his astonishment at the grace enjoyed by the church of Geneva, which now, after such perils, flourished as an example for other churches ‡. "I was lately at Geneva," he says, "and so delighted was I, that I could scarcely tear myself away. I would rather be last in Geneva than first in any other place: were I not prevented by the Lord, and by my love for my congregation, nothing should hinder me from ending my days there." Drelincourt expressed the same admiration a hundred years after.

But high now as Calvin stood, there were not wanting things to humble him, both inwardly and outwardly. He was subject to frequent and severe attacks of fever: they sometimes came upon him while in the pulpit; and he once wrote to a friend, saying that it was only with great trouble, and by sitting down, that he could get through his sermon §. But he had a heavier trial to bear: the wife of his brother Anton disgraced the family by her infidelity. Farel observes on this, that it was good for Calvin to encounter these humbling circumstances, "lest his mind might be too exalted by the greatness of the revelations vouchsafed him." The conflict with the libertines was

* MS. Gen. Calv. Bullingero.

† Knox, Leben von M'Crie bearbeitet von Planck, s. 235.

‡ Kirchhofer, ii. s. 124.

§ He speaks of this to Haller, May 9, 1556, and to Blaarer, April 13, 1557.

not yet ended. Bern again exhibited a disposition to tyranny, and took their part; they stood in crowds on the Arve-bridge, and uttered abuse of every kind against the Genevese. On one occasion they violently attacked Viret. The efforts of the council to induce them to depart were of no avail; the people would have rushed out against them, but were held back. According to the declaration of the Bernese, the malcontents had committed no crime. The Genevese however proceeded to expel the wives of the fugitives from the city, confiscated their possessions, and prohibited their return on pain of death. Thus at the moment when the little state was left to itself, it displayed the noblest energy. The refugees were again permitted to bear arms: Calvin and the city-secretary were to acquaint the cantons with this circumstance. To induce the Bernese to consent to the proceeding, the procurator-general of Geneva wished to lay the judicial documents respecting the fugitives before the tribunal at Bern, and there to appear against them*; with this proviso, however, that Geneva did not thereby in anywise subject itself to the Bernese judicature. But Bern resumed the process of its own accord; freed the culprits from the sentence of the Genevese; and condemned the syndics, the council, and the city of Geneva to afford satisfaction to the fugitives, to ask their pardon, and to pay the costs of the trial.

It was thus that Bern treated the little republic, which seemed destined to destruction. The fugitives proposed to assert their right by force, and such of the Genevese as possessed any property in the territory of Bern were exposed to daily attacks. At length the day arrived for Geneva to plead its cause: it besought the Bernese to act with greater moderation, and to renew the old treaty, which terminated in 1556.

Calvin had continued to be hated by the Bernese since the dispute on predestination. Bullinger wrote to him: "People say that you wish to play the part of sole ruler in Geneva by means of your French, and that it is you who hinder an agreement with Bern." He then consoles him by citing the early sufferings of Chrysostom and Ambrose, and gives him excellent advice in respect to moderation, the fatherly care of Geneva, and of the numerous refugees in the city†:—"Watch, I beseech you, dear friend, for all: counsel all: take care of all, that nothing

* Ruchat, vi. 190.

† Hess, Leben Bullingers, t. ii. s. 259, 262, note. Oct. 1559.

may be neglected which can minister to peace and general edification. The days are evil; God give you grace to be wise."

Calvin answered Bullinger in an apologetic letter. Bullinger again promised the interference of the Zurichers; but the whole year 1557 passed away without anything being done. During this period Calvin was often full of anxiety for Geneva, and laboured much in secret to win back the minds of the people to tranquillity. At the end of the year 1556, when the Bernese again rudely repulsed the Genevese, Calvin once more begged Bullinger to engage Zurich in effecting a reconciliation. This circumstance however was kept secret, and the letter to Bullinger is interesting, as connected with the history of Geneva.

The Bernese appear to have intended to weary-out Geneva by petty agitations, till, in the hour of danger, it should throw itself into their arms, and thus give the disaffected the means of indulging in still greater insolence. It is evident indeed, from a letter to Bullinger, that they had made a formal complaint against Geneva. Calvin was anxious to learn from him, confidentially, whether they had any hope, and he wished a letter to be addressed to the city of Geneva. The state of affairs did not improve. In the August of the following year Calvin complains to Bullinger*, that their good neighbours, who, in the pulpit, spoke of the communion of saints, utterly disregarded the present divisions, and were equally indifferent to the fate of Geneva. At the end of the year 1557 the discussion was brought to a close, but it was not till the next year that the business was finally concluded†. After the victory of St. Quentin, Emanuel Philibert returned from Savoy, at the head of his victorious band, to his own country, and might easily have attacked Geneva. The danger thus to be apprehended may have warned the Bernese that Savoy might still be able to strengthen itself against them by means of Geneva. New anxieties arose in the following year. At the end of every letter Calvin entreats his friends to pray for Geneva‡. The dispute was still prolonged; and the Genevese, on their side, acted with characteristic violence. One of the libertine party, whom they caught in a village, lost his head§. Their adversaries, on the other hand, confiscated the possessions of the council, by bringing them within the Bernese territory. But an invisible arm

* MS. Tig. 7 Idus Aug. 1557.

† MS. Par. Calv. Hotomanno, Jan. 10, 1558.

‡ MS. Bern. to Bullinger, Nov. 19, 1558.

§ Ruchat, vi. 232.

was upraised amid all these dangers, and in the year 1560 Calvin could say to Uttenhoven, "that they had been wonderfully delivered*." His feeling was one of joy; and he encouraged another combatant by the suggestion, that all beginnings in the kingdom of God are little, insignificant, and proportionally difficult†. He was again attacked by the quartan ague: the weakness continued for a long time, and his patience was greatly tried‡.

It was at this juncture that the startling intelligence reached Geneva, that Farel, now sixty-nine years of age, was just married, and to a very young person. The astonishment expressed at this event was great. People had been so accustomed to contemplate the old missionary daring all the dangers and difficulties of his position alone, that it was difficult to view him in the light of the father of a family. But when we consider Farel's bold, stormy, romantic character, there is, in reality, nothing discordant in this episode. Calvin expressed himself earnestly and characteristically in his letter on the subject to the Neuchatel clergy§: he besought them to pardon him, in consideration of his thirty-six years' service.

In the midst of all these disquietudes, troubles and dangers, Calvin was intently engaged in promoting the educational advancement of Geneva. He now also published a new edition of the 'Institutes.' This was the third and last revision, and the crowning labour of his life.

Calvin had regularly, since his return from Strasburg, delivered three weekly theological lectures. A school was established at Geneva from the commencement of the Reformation, and we have already mentioned that Castellio and Cordier were early numbered among its teachers. It was Calvin's design to establish an extensive gymnasium, and an academy especially devoted to the study of theology. The means to effect this object were promised, but the little republic was too poor to fulfil its promise, and years passed away, leaving the plan still unaccomplished. At length, after the treaty with Bern, the council began

* MS. Bern, May 15, 1560. "Et mirantur qui nos exitio addixerant non centies periisse."

† Ed. Laus. Ep. 267. Ed. Amst. p. 129.

‡ MS. Calvin speaks of this to a French correspondent in Feb. 1559; he had alluded to an earlier attack in a letter to Bullinger, Nov. 19, 1558, MS. Tig.

§ MS. Gen. Sept. 26, 1558. Kirchhofer, ii. s. 152. This author errs greatly in supposing that Calvin favoured the marriage. "I am dumb with astonishment," he says, speaking of the subject, and he alludes to Farel as his "poor brother."

to turn its attention to the internal affairs of the city. The noble Bonnivard gave his whole fortune to forward the design*. In the year 1558 the gymnasium was founded, and in the following year the academy. A favourable circumstance promoted the success of the undertaking. Several ministers from the Grisons, during the dispute with Bern on the subject of excommunication, had, after many contentions, been either banished or deprived of their office. Among these were Peter Viret, Beza, the excellent Augustus Marlorat, who was destined to win the martyr's crown†, Jacobus Valier, and twenty others. They retired to Geneva, and appealed to the council, in a body, for permission to take up their permanent abode in that city‡. Viret was made one of the ministers of the place, as he had formerly been; but he retained the office only two years. He was invited to France; many of the refugees followed, those only remaining who were invited to assist in the formation of the academy. Calvin would fain have engaged doctors for all the various faculties, but he was obliged to content himself with that which was absolutely necessary. Beza was given him for a colleague, both as professor and minister. The academy, as well as the school, was placed under the government of the clergy, who elected the rector, the professors, and teachers, but submitted their choice to the approbation of the council. Calvin drew up the rules for the management of the academy, and a confession of faith, which all students at their matriculation were to subscribe. The plan which he sketched out for the conduct of the professors, master, and scholars, is altogether stamped with the character of the middle ages. The students were to attend divine service once every Wednesday, and three times every Sunday. In summer they were to attend class at six in the morning; in winter at seven: they were to breakfast in class, and at ten o'clock the teachers were to conduct them to their homes. After dinner, that is, at eleven o'clock, they were to return to school, and practise psalm-singing for an hour: from one to two they were to take their little afternoon refreshment in class. The lessons were to cease at four o'clock, and then the scholars were to assemble in the hall, where the rector was to be present, and dismiss them with kindly counsel, openly censuring those who had merited the reprehension of their teachers. Besides divinity, and the Latin and

* Senebier, Hist. lit. t. i. p. 48.

† He suffered at Rouen in 1562.

‡ Ruchat, t. vi. p. 306.

Greek languages, logic was to form a part of the studies in the first class. This was necessary according to the practice of the age, and as an introduction to the Aristotelian philosophy*.

On the 5th of June, 1559, the doors of St. Peter's church were opened; the magistrates entered; the clergy assembled in a body; all the learned men of Geneva, all the best families of the place, and six hundred scholars, were present. Calvin arose, and in a speech which he delivered in French, he advocated the usefulness of educational institutions, and exhorted all who heard him to pray to God for the success of theirs. Roset, the state-secretary, then read the laws of the new institution, and proclaimed the rector. This being done, Theodore Beza delivered a Latin oration, and Calvin concluded the solemnity with a prayer. The classes were opened the following day. A grand school-festival is still yearly solemnized in the same church at Geneva, and at which one of the scholars pronounces a commemorative oration.

This foundation of an academy affords sufficient proof of Calvin's anxiety to unite the sciences with the church, and to sanctify knowledge by faith: he was anxious also to have his young friend Beza chosen rector of the new institution; and he thus showed how little desire he had for outward fame or power. Many distinguished men have been mentioned in a former part of this work as connected with the academy; but the emoluments attending the office were very slight, amounting only to 280 Geneva florins and a residence: so poor indeed was the city, that in the interval between 1580–90 the institution was supported by a collection made in England, Beza having for a long time performed the duties of all the professors, who had necessarily been discharged.

It is worthy of remark, that as early as the year 1576 it was found expedient to dispense with the subscription to the formulary of faith, originally required of the students. This measure was adopted, that no one who sought the light might be repulsed. According to the former rule, papists and Lutherans must have for ever been deprived of sharing in the studies of the academy.

We learn from Calvin's correspondence with what anxiety he sought to bring learned men to Geneva. It was his early wish to obtain the celebrated Peter Martyr for the Italian congregation, but no sufficient means existed to pay him. He however described the place to him in the most inviting language. "That

* Picot, ii. 91.

church," he says, "is the very flower of Italy*." He thought, probably, of Carracioli.

When the academy was properly established, he wrote to Tremellius, who was then teaching at Heidelberg, and whom he would gladly have brought to Geneva, stating that he proposed founding professorships for the three learned languages, but that the stipends would be very small†. He had wished also to obtain Mercerus as professor of Hebrew‡, but he failed in accomplishing his object. He renewed the invitation October 17, 1563, and begged him to leave Paris, where he then was, for Geneva§. Martyr refused the offer of an appointment to the ministry of the Italian congregation in 1557. Calvin said to him, that he could forgive him, but that his countrymen were not likely to pardon him so easily‖.

It is not necessary to repeat how great an impulse Calvin gave, by these undertakings, to the literary advancement of the reformed church. Certain it is, that he was indebted to the academy, which soon became greatly frequented, for the rapid diffusion of his doctrines in Germany, Holland, France and England. His unclassical adversaries may also be reminded, that previous to the Reformation scarcely a distinguished man was known at Geneva. The human mind was utterly bowed down; while now, on the contrary, beams of light flowed freely upon all. Some difficulties necessarily arose, from the position of the city; it lay between Italy, France and Germany, and a defence was needed against the national vices peculiar to each. The high character of Calvin impressed upon the little republic its own peculiar features. It is curious to observe how mean a spirit will often prevail in states, even when they have attained to great rank and influence. Calvin's humorous remark may be cited in illustration of this fact. Laughing at the want of influence exercised by the sciences on social life, he described the general state of manners in his time by the significant term *barbaries*. The contrast between the present state of the elegant city and this description of its manners in a past age, is sufficiently striking.

We must here briefly state the circumstances which led to the banishment of Viret and Beza, and which are not unimportant in their relation to the history of church discipline. Bern went back to the original Zwinglian principle, and rejected the Cal-

* MS. Gen. Jan. 18, 1555. † 4 Cal. Sept. 1558.
‡ MS. Gen. Mart. 16, 1558. Calv. Mercerio.
§ MS. Bern. Calv. Mercerio. ‖ MS. Par. Oct. 13, 1557.

vinistic: it resolved to order ecclesiastical matters according to the simple rule of civil policy; it would recognize no church authority, and it lost, in consequence, forty distinguished ministers. Geneva, though destined to become a European city, was treated with contempt. The little French community in the Grisons appears to have been weak and changeable. The consistory of Lausanne, therefore, addressed itself to the council of Bern, and besought it to introduce a strong system of church discipline, similar to that established at Geneva. This desire was expressed in the most energetic language (1543). The gentle Viret proved himself in this case endowed with great force of character. The Bernese discouraged the design, and would hear nothing of excommunication. Thus Farel in 1546 could not settle in Lausanne. Some years passed away: the clergy of Lausanne then addressed themselves to the council of the city, to direct its attention to the disorders daily occurring. Certain laws were accordingly proposed; but Bern was greatly displeased at the movement, and sent a copy of its own rule, according to which it desired Lausanne to be guided. The agitation created by the great question concerning excommunication still continued. Some ministers, in the belief that this law, and especially the rules of discipline, were of divine institution, now gave free course to their zeal, and hastened on the storm. The ministers of Lausanne, Payerne and Thonon, were strongly Calvinistic. Bern had commanded that the doctrine of predestination should be treated with great moderation. Four ministers of Thonon preached in the rudest style against the orders of the council. Being deprived of their office, they went to Geneva, and the ministers of Lausanne continued to make every effort to establish a system of discipline. The council however would give no heed to their representations. Viret threatened to refuse the further administration of the sacrament: he was entreated to yield, for he was greatly beloved, and he consented. At length the Bernese consistory established certain rules of discipline, but it utterly repudiated the practice of excommunication, and of testing the faith of dissentients: it saw in things of this kind a hateful inquisition. It still however desired to receive the opinion of the ministers respecting the anathemas of the church. This they regarded as a sign of success. They expressed themselves freely on the subject, and even added the threat, that if their wish was not granted, they would take their departure. The council was enraged, and twelve of the ministers were summoned to answer for their conduct at Bern. The magistrates resolutely opposed them, and it was ordered that no mention should ever be made of anathemas. Viret now again declared to those of Lausanne, that he could no longer administer the communion in that city, his people being distracted as they were by so many vexations. The council answered, that anathemas were not the right means for quieting agitation, and that an entirely pure state of the church was not to be looked for. But Viret remained firm: the other ministers did the same. The council, on the other hand, was settled in the conviction, that the ministers must resign their appointments, and that if the church suffered harm therefrom, the guilt would be theirs.

Viret paused for awhile, but he determined not to administer the sacrament at Christmas 1557, or rather to defer it. Valier and he were accordingly banished. Many other ministers left about the same time (1558 and 1559). The agitation in the Grisons respecting discipline was thus prolonged. Ministers continued to leave the district, and it is probable that many disorders existed in this part of the country not known to the German cantons. A synod was ultimately assembled to consider the matter. The quarrel was an affair of the people. Lausanne remained for a time without ministers. At length a severe rule of discipline and morals was introduced: women of loose character were thrown into prison, and offences named to the magistrates by the consistory were severely punished. No mention however was made of excommunication.

CHAPTER IX.

CALVIN'S ACTIVITY.—HIS INFLUENCE IN ENGLAND AND SCOTLAND.—JOHN KNOX.—CORRESPONDENCE WITH THE ENGLISH EXILES IN FRANKFORT.

We have already spoken of Calvin's influence in England (1553): he had proposed to Cranmer the plan of a great church union. On the death of Edward, Queen Mary destroyed the work of that monarch, and Cranmer breathed out his life in the flames. A great number of exiles had taken up their abode in the north of Germany, in Frankfort and Geneva. Calvin sighs over these troubles of the church in one of his letters to Bullinger. He suppresses his opinion of Cranmer. His remark on learning the death of Lady Jane Grey is worthy of quotation: "She has left," he said, "an image which deserves everlasting remembrance."

From the year 1554 we see frequently in Geneva, and in close intercourse with Calvin, a man of the most singular appearance; strongly built; with a bold, severe expression of countenance; of firm, but yet tender nature: this is the famous Scotchman, John Knox. It might have been imagined that two such powerful and ardent characters as these reformers could not have agreed well together; but they cherished for each other a genuine affection: the one could submit himself to the other. Knox's friendship with Calvin requires especial notice. He was a powerful instrument in diffusing the principles of Calvinism in England, Scotland, and even to a still wider extent; but we must carefully keep in view the circumstances by which they were distinguished. Knox was the founder of the Scotch presbyterian church, from which arose the rude, fierce spirits of a subsequent period. He it was who confounded the holy cause of truth with the interests of a political party; who impressed upon the Protestant church in England its peculiar outward character; and who, in this not apostolic, aroused a power which was afterwards to exercise so mighty and destructive an influence.

Calvin had no knowledge of this worldly spirit, nor can any one fairly impute to him the political tendency of the Protestants in France: he declared himself against it. All his principles and designs were opposed to such things; and this, though the French church had greater perils to encounter than that of Scotland, and had to combat with antagonists of a far more desperate character. Calvin, in this respect, stood by the side of Luther, who constantly advocated peace, desired to see the church developing itself through the power of the Spirit, and wished for no aid from worldly might or worldly policy. Both these great men were anxious to employ a theocratic, spiritual influence only, and to subject even the church itself, in other respects, to the civil government. At the most, Calvin could only be accused of giving too great a weight in the presbyterian form of church-polity to the popular, liberal element over the ministerial, or of neglecting to combine, when he might, the principle of episcopacy with that of presbyterianism.

The difference of character in Calvin and Knox was early displayed when the latter was in England, and interested himself in the revision of the Prayer-Book. Then, as subsequently, he exhibited the most decided hostility to the Anglican church, on account of its retaining some of the Catholic forms, and not adopting the severe rule of the Scotch. Calvin, who so energetically strove against superstition, was not in this case disposed to agree with Knox. He willingly suffered outward forms, in themselves indifferent, to remain, or at least did not assail them with fanatical violence, as if they had a real importance. It is possible, indeed, that he may have strengthened Knox in his admiration of apostolic simplicity; but the fundamental idea of the Scotch reformer, and his dislike to the principles of the English church, were of an earlier date; they may be traced back to the year 1547. He would allow no human interference, but desired to be guided solely by the plain rule of Scripture. Thus he refused to accept any appointment which would have imposed upon him the necessity of using the liturgy, and sharply reproved the English clergy, under Elizabeth, for having permitted the revival of many of the ancient forms. It is certain, however, that the first English reformers would gladly have adopted the same system of Protestant discipline, and church forms which Calvin had introduced into France; but they were resisted by too powerful a party. Calvin had addressed both Somerset and Cranmer with great earnestness in favour of these views. But Elizabeth subsequently confirmed the episcopal rule, which, in the form thus given it, petrified the church and deprived it of life; for it now ceased to enjoy any element of activity; it lost its synods; while, on the other side, the presbyterian church was destitute of the element of rest and durability.

Both Knox and Calvin became acquainted with each other when their characters were already formed. Mary ascended the throne of England in 1554; and Knox, with several other distinguished divines, immediately fled to the continent, and proceeded to Switzerland. This happened at the most splendid epoch of Calvin's life: his writings were now known throughout Europe, and people flocked to Geneva from all countries. He received the Scotchman in the most friendly manner. Their souls seemed, as it were, created for each other, through their communion in faith, hope, and works. Both were of the same age; but Knox venerated Calvin as a father, and looked to him for counsel and guidance. The church of Geneva corresponded to his ideal of a church. Although he was now fifty years of age, he devoted himself to study, under Calvin, with youthful ardour.

Indignant in the highest degree at the persecutions carried on by Queen Mary, Knox soon gave to the world one of his most violent writings, 'A Warning to the English Nation,' in which he described the wretched Gardiner and Bonner as the hangmen of Mary.

Several other English exiles arrived on the continent at this time, and formed churches at Strasburg, Basel, Zurich, Geneva, and other places. At Frankfort they were permitted to establish a congregation, under the condition that they should adopt the outward forms of the French reformed church, and renounce the English liturgy. The refugees chose Knox for their minister, and Calvin induced him to accept the call. But the churches of the exiles at Zurich and Strasburg now united to oppose that at Frankfort, and refused to communicate with it unless it agreed to retain the old English rites. Knox undertook the part of a mediator, and besought Calvin to settle the dispute: the latter stated his opinion, January 20, 1555. In the following year he went to Frankfort himself; but Knox, as an enemy to the English liturgy, was driven from his office: he returned to Geneva, and thence to Scotland. The church of that country was established in 1555. In the following year Knox formed the first combination against the Catholics, and this was the commencement of those political acts in which the reformer indulged; the example of which led to such important consequences; the justice of which has been so often doubted, and which, accordingly, form the most remarkable point in his history.

While the Scottish church was thus becoming established, the English exiles at Geneva elected Knox for their minister. He willingly accepted the call, and again returning to Calvin's city, he now took with him his wife and mother-in-law, from whom he had been so long separated (1556). This was the wife whom he early lost, and whom Calvin, in one of his letters, describes as "a most sweet woman," *suavissima*. Knox was sentenced by the catholics, in his absence, to the flames, and was burnt in effigy: he remained at Geneva two or three years, and this was the most tranquil period of his stormy life.

In 1557 Knox was recalled to his native country. Calvin advised him to obey the summons. He set out; but the Scotch were still unsettled, and he stopped at Frankfort. It was now that the persecution raged in France. An impious slander had been published against the reformed in Paris: they printed an Apology, and Knox translated it into English. But his countrymen had not the courage to receive him, and losing the satisfaction which he had looked for from the journey, he once more returned to Geneva. He now endeavoured to make his political ideas known by means of a work, in which he handled the difficult question, as to what circumstances may justify resistance to the chief magistrate. He arrived at the following conclusion: that sedition is altogether unlawful, but that an entire nation may rightly resist a tyrannical government. "The nobility formed," he said, "the defence of national freedom: the nobles must not let their brethren be murdered. They ought never, however, to rise from ambitious or mere political motives, but only for the cause of pure religion."

Nothing can show more clearly than this, that Knox was dependent upon himself for the development of his principles; and that Calvin, as his teacher, did not exercise an uncontrolled influence on his mind. Calvin never entertained the opinions above-stated: he exhorted the persecuted in France to contend only by prayer. Such indeed was the tenderness of his Christian conscience, that he advised those in prison not to attempt to escape, but to receive martyrdom as a grace from the hand of God.

Knox joined, at this time, with some friends in planning a new English translation of the Bible: this translation was known at a later period as the Geneva Bible, from the place where it was printed. But his political zeal drove him, at this time, to print his famous, but rudely written work, against the government of women, and in which he lays it down as a principle, that it is not lawful for a woman to ascend the throne. It was peculiarly a revolutionary writing, however much he protested against its being regarded in that light. His secret design was to prove the abuses of the government of the regent, and of that of Mary Stuart, which succeeded it. This violent production very uselessly excited the indignation of Mary, and made Elizabeth, the defender of the Protestant church, his enemy: she never forgave his rashness, and it was the cause of her equally disliking Calvin.

The nobles of Scotland now united in reality for the defence of the Protestant religion: they wrote to Calvin, begging him to use his influence with Knox, and to send him to their aid. Elizabeth was on the throne, and the members of the English congregation at Geneva returned to London in 1559. Knox however was so hated at the English court, on account of his political writings, that he dare not pass through England: this again roused his enmity to that country, and the old quarrel respecting the liturgy was renewed. But Elizabeth adopted a sound policy, and saved thereby both the church and the throne: she supported Scotland against France, which was striving to establish Mary Stuart on the throne of that country, with the design of subsequently placing her on that of England. Knox, in the mean time, was become a preacher in Edinburgh, and the head and soul of the evangelical party. Calvin however united with Cecil, Elizabeth's chancellor, in admonishing him of his duty, and subsequently endeavoured, as we shall see, to excuse himself to the queen.

At length war broke out: the French supported the queen of Scotland, and England the Protestants. A letter written at this time by Knox to Calvin, on the subject of discipline, is characteristically short. Calvin's answer is far more circumstantial, and his views are much milder and more moderate than those of Knox*: the latter was now become a political character. Elizabeth besieged Edinburgh and expelled the French. The queen-regent died. Francis II., the husband of Mary, ascended the French throne, on the death of Henry II., and thus the power of France fell into the hand of the Guises. The parliament in Scotland took advantage of this period to establish the Protestant religion by law (August 24, 1560). A confession of faith was drawn up: it was altogether Calvinistic, and proves that Knox was fully agreed with Calvin in belief. To God alone belongs all honour. Man has lost all by sin: he is delivered through Christ. He can of himself do nothing; but yet has involved himself in condemnation through his own choice. A book of discipline was also set forth by Knox: he shows his admiration of the rules followed at Geneva, and wrought out the system at full. Calvin had the delight to be made acquainted with this glorious progress of his plan, with this triumph of his doctrine and his discipline. The agreement thus existing between the systems established at Geneva and in Scotland, proves what M'Crie is unwilling to acknowledge, that Calvin exercised great influence in Scotland by means of Knox; but the latter indulged in excesses, and this first led the way to the corruption of the system. A letter which Calvin addressed to him, about this time, shows the desire of the writer to keep him within

* Ed. Laus. p. 283. Ed. Amst. p. 201.

the bounds of moderation*. Scotland was not fortunate in other respects. The possessions and revenues of the Catholic clergy were seized by the nobles, and not left for the support of the church, as in Switzerland (in Zurich, for example), and partly in several of the German states: hence the great poverty of the Scotch church and university.

It was at this time that Knox's wife died; at the period, that is, when she might have shared with him more prosperous circumstances. He received a letter from Calvin, containing only a few words on the subject; but so highly valued was the writer, that, according to M'Crie, Knox was filled with joy by these few†.

Queen Mary and Francis II. made another attempt to nullify the decree of the Scottish parliament; but Francis died, and Mary proceeded to Scotland to assume the government. Knox now stood opposed to the young queen; his situation was in the highest degree difficult; but impartial judges, who can rightly estimate his character as a great reformer, his iron strength, and his devotion to the truth, without however blinding themselves to his defects, or considering his fierceness and excesses deserving of praise, will acknowledge that, on the whole, he solved fairly the perplexing questions which he had to answer. He did not always support the dignity of a preacher of the gospel; and it is probable that Calvin would, in some things, have acted with greater moderation. Take, for example, Knox's public prayer for the queen, "Enlighten her heart, O Lord, if it be thy good will!" —as if the preacher was in doubt upon the subject. If he had the doctrine of election in view, he passed, by these words, the bitterest censure on his own belief; and gave occasion to the people to suppose that he, perhaps, did not even wish for the conver-

* Calvin had said in a letter which he wrote against ceremonies, "I know of nothing more important than your being cautious to employ as few ceremonies as possible. Consider carefully what is required of you." But always seeking the right medium, he says to Knox, "I hope that, in regard to ceremonies, you will moderate your zeal. We must take care to preserve the church free from all superstitious adornment, and must not suffer divine mysteries to be marred by childish additions; but holding this fast, do not forget that you must be ready to bear with some things which may not altogether please you."

† "Your loss," he says, "is a deep and bitter affliction to me. You had a wife, to whom few can be compared; but you know well where to find consolation, and I doubt not that you will bear this great sorrow with patience. Greet the pious brethren in my name." In a letter to Goodman, Ep. 306, he says, "I grieve not a little that our brother Knox has been deprived of his most sweet wife; but I rejoice that, afflicted as he has been, he has continued to labour strenuously for Christ and the church."

sion of the queen. In every case a malicious will was evident, although, on his death-bed, he declared that he had nothing of the kind in his heart. Calvin indeed discouraged praying for the papacy and the pope as such; but he cautiously added, "We must distinguish between the papal chair and the person*."

Knox was now settled as the head of the Protestant party: he acted in his character of citizen, as the champion of popular rights, and not as a minister only, as Calvin did, and as Beza, in the camp of Condé. A conversation which took place between Knox and secretary Maitland throws new light on the principles of this "son of thunder." Thus he defended his form of prayer, on the plea that Mary Stuart did not hear the gospel, but the mass, and that he therefore could not help doubting as to her conversion. Further, the minister desired to hear his views respecting the relation of rulers and subjects. Knox had made a distinction, in one of his sermons, between the persons to whom God has entrusted power and the ordinance of God; and had said, that people may resist the former without violating the latter, for that subjects are not bound to obey the unrighteous commands of their rulers. He now argued, that he made the above distinction according to the words of the apostle, who states, that God has established rulers for the upholding of peace, for the punishment of the wicked, and the protection of the good. If rulers therefore pervert this principle, and employ their power unjustly, this is not to be suffered: the madness of the tyrant must be resisted. He also added, that he could not allow Mary Stuart to hear the mass: thus he was intolerant against the catholics. He insisted not only that the mass should be abolished, but that the idolaters should be put to death by the people; for such was the law given by God to the Israelites. Maitland, on the other hand, remarked, that the people must not forestal the judgements of God: God would punish offenders by death, by wars, and other means. Knox was of opinion that the people might judge their princes.

These principles show that Knox formed the first link in the chain of those events which subsequently took place in England: he carried out the republican theory to its farthest extent, and united it in the closest manner with his views of the Gospel.

* MS. Bern, Sept. 27, 1552. "I know that we must distinguish between the person, and the abominable and cursed see. But it seems to me that they who pray by name for him who bears such a mark of reprobation, must have a great deal of leisure."

We cannot avoid therefore ascribing the overthrow of the English throne, in an after-age, effected as it was by the Presbyterian and Puritan party, in the name of God, to the influence of the spirit, which wrought so mightily through Knox, whose hatred to the English was no less conspicuous and powerful. The wretched principles which actually led to the events of which we are speaking, were but those of Knox carried to an extravagant excess, as the latter were themselves an exaggeration of Calvin's. It would be irrational however to make Calvin answerable for this; and no less unjust would it be, on the other hand, so to misrepresent Knox's lofty and, in many respects, even amiable character, as to place him in the light of a gloomy fanatic. He was a noble instrument in the hand of God; a benefactor of mankind, and a faithful champion of the truth.

The Scotch, as soon as they learnt that the Reformation was penetrating their country, prepared themselves for the necessary course of action. The French church in London began to assemble, and a pastor was sought from Geneva. Calvin sent it, towards the end of the year 1559, the well-known Gallars. Grindal, bishop of London, had done much to form this church. Calvin wrote to him, saying, "that he had with difficulty parted from Gallars; but that he had done so for the sake of God's kingdom. He was very much esteemed as a worthy servant of Christ." The next year the bishop sent his thanks, with a noble eulogy on Gallars*.

Calvin finished in 1559 his Commentary on Isaiah, and had dedicated it to the queen: we learn, however, that he was in no small perplexity on this account. The queen received the dedication angrily: Calvin had expressed himself as opposed to the government of women: he now endeavoured, as well as he could, to justify himself. In a letter to Cecil, he says, "that although a woman's being placed on the throne of a kingdom might generally be considered as a divine punishment, there were noble exceptions thereto†." Thus also, in writing to Bullinger, he says, that "Knox had asked him what he thought of the government of women. He freely answered, that there were some women possessed of extraordinary gifts, and who, through the peculiar blessing with which they were seen to be endowed, manifestly evinced that God had called them. Deborah was an instance of

* MS. Goth. ed. Bretschn. p. 220, Feb. 10, 1560.

† MS. Bern, Nov. 1559.

this truth; and Isaiah had not said untruly, that queens should be the protectors and nurses of the church*."

English churches had been formed at Zurich, Basel, Geneva, Aarau, Emden, Wesel, Duisburg, Frankfort, and Strasburg. They were by turns broken up and renewed, or others supplied their place, as was especially the case on the arrival of the refugees from France, at the repeal of the edict of Nantes. The churches of Emden and Frankfort then became established, and have continued flourishing to the present times. It has been already mentioned that Calvin dedicated his catechism to the reformed churches of East-Friesland: he wished to form a union with those communities. We must here give a brief account of the relation in which the reformer stood to the church at Frankfort. It exhibits him again in the character of a mediator; and affords a striking contrast to those other circumstances of his eventful life, which seemed to pass like meteors across his path.

When the refugees, who had been driven from Denmark, and the north of Germany, established a church at Frankfort, and were compelled to abandon the English liturgy, there was here a cause of strife, which was soon followed by another arising from the controversy on the sacrament. At the convention in 1555 it was formally resolved, that the Catholics and the communities holding the Augsburg Confession should alone enjoy the protection thus afforded; no other parties or sects were to be suffered on German ground. This last regulation was employed to excite the magistrates at Wesel and Frankfort against the English refugees. In the former of these places, the clergy assailed them as heretics; while the refugees on their part appealed to the judgement of Melancthon. A messenger was sent to Wittenberg, and a letter was written to Melancthon by Francis Perucell, the minister of the congregation. But respect for Melancthon availed them nothing. The council informed them that they must either shortly leave the city, or acknowledge that the true body of Christ is contained in the sacrament, and that He is eaten not only spiritually, but bodily with the mouth. The unhappy exiles prayed for time to consider; they were answered that they ought to thank the council for its moderation, for that it had the right to strip them of whatever they possessed, and even to punish them personally. Perucell acquainted Calvin with all these proceedings. But the Lutheran clergy continued furious against them; they even ex-

* Calvin to Bullinger, 3 Cal. Mai. 1554. Mosheim, Neue Nachr. Ketsergesch. p. 108.

pressed their rage in the pulpit. One Hermann described the exiles as wretches who disgraced the sacraments, and who had stolen like wolves into the sheep-fold, that they might diffuse the poison which they had themselves imbibed in England. The common people were greatly excited by these representations.

Somewhat more moderation was exercised by the council at Frankfort; but instead of cordially uniting together and exercising mutual forbearance, the English on the one side, and the French on the other, began to dispute on little differences in matters of ceremony, and on the various doctrines of the Lord's Supper. The quarrel thus excited between them was carried to such an extent, that they had almost proceeded to blows in the church. Calvin, who was informed of what was taking place, wrote to the council on the subject.

It has been stated that the refugees elected Knox their minister. The simple French liturgy gained the victory. When however the members of the English congregations at Zurich, and Strasburg, declared themselves against that at Frankfort, because it had not retained the Anglican ritual, Knox entreated Calvin to settle the dispute. Calvin had dedicated, in the August of 1555, his 'Harmony of the Gospels' to the Frankfort council; that body accepted the honour with thanks, and made the author a present of fifty gold pieces. In March 1556 Calvin wrote to them anew; he expressed his astonishment that they had suffered the work of Westphal to be printed at Frankfort, a work written especially against him, whereas he supposed his opinions to agree with those which they themselves professed. If, however, he added, there were any at Frankfort who differed from him, he should be glad to confer with them. This dissension was more particularly distressing to him on account of the refugees, who had left their native land for the sake of the Lord. If they had faults, still the council should treat them with moderation. The representatives of the Frankfort people quietly replied, that they owned they did not agree with him in opinion; that they were, notwithstanding, anxious for peace, and that they believed him to be a true servant of God.

But it was not long after this that they exhibited a very hostile attitude in regard both to Calvin and the refugees; accusing the former of church-tyranny. Calvin immediately wrote to the burgomaster Clauburg: he protested against the accusation of tyranny, and appealed to the testimony of his brethren, who often rather charged him with weakness. It is interesting to observe

Calvin's conduct in this whole affair. He spoke admirably to the unquiet spirits with whom he had to do, in favour of moderation. They wished to subject their minister, with whom they were discontented, to a fresh election, and even to further humiliations. Calvin expressed strongly his disapprobation of their proceedings. "Even Guelphs and Ghibellines," he said, "unite when they are subject to a common attack. You are attacked by those who are enemies to your sacrament. Valerand has repulsed them; and it is monstrous that he should now be exposed to violence from you." He afterwards adjured them to seek peace, and to submit themselves to the majority of the church-elders. Subsequently he appealed to them again. "If we were resolved to bear with nothing from others, everyone must have a world for himself alone. I love you all, and am as anxious to see your imperfections cured as I am my own." His indifference respecting useless ceremonies, in the sacrament especially, is well-deserving of remark. "There are some silly things to be tolerated in the English liturgy."

When Calvin found that he could accomplish nothing by letters, he resolved to visit Frankfort himself. He had but just returned from Bern, when he was attacked while preaching with such a severe fit of ague, that even his strong spirit could not overcome it; but after enduring the sickness for some time, he appeared again stronger than ever on the arena. Farel had offered to accompany him on his journey, but he would not allow him. He had heard that the plague had broken out at Frankfort; and he left without taking leave of Farel, intending thereby to spare his affectionate zeal.

The council of Geneva gave Calvin for his protector its principal herald, Eustachius Vinzens, who had formerly been sent to accompany him from Strasburg. Laski had already used his best efforts to inspire a friendly feeling at Frankfort. During his residence in that city, he was constantly occupied in endeavouring to unite the two Protestant churches. King Sigismund Augustus had encouraged him to undertake this work, the schism being as prejudicial to Poland as it was to Germany. Laski presented a memorial to the council at Frankfort, in which he showed, that no sufficient cause existed for the separation of the two Protestant churches. It was hoped that a conference appointed to take place on the 22nd of May, 1556, might lead to beneficial results; but Brentius ruined every prospect of reconciliation. He insisted that the reformed should sign the

Augsburg Confession; and the doctrine of ubiquity, so absurd in the eyes of Laski, was exalted by him above every other. Hence the schism was made wider.

We now see Calvin again sojourning in the city, where he some years before had met Melancthon. In a letter dated September 17, 1556, he complains of the vast amount of business which he had to do, and of the fury of the parties engaged in the controversy. "Certain it is that Satan has so befooled them, that there is no hope of restoring union*."

Some account of his residence at Frankfort is found in a letter to Melancthon†. "I have been led to this place through the quarrels which for the last two years have distracted the little churches here, speaking our language. The greatest danger may be apprehended, if very prudent measures be not adopted to avert it. Since my arrival in the city I have not had time to breathe; you must therefore pardon the shortness of this letter. I have however little need to be very anxious about your pardon on this account, for I see by your silence that you do not much wish for my letters; still, I am convinced not merely of your good feeling, but of your love towards me."

Calvin next states, that a certain Justus Welsius had employed him two days‡, and that he had openly disputed with him on the subject of free-will. Valerandus Pollanus was at strife with the burgomaster Clauburg. The subject of their dispute was the Consensus on the sacrament, which Bucer had set forth, and which the ministers of Frankfort, in accordance with Calvin's views, might subscribe. Among other proofs of his laboriousness, an old document exists at Gotha, a protocol, that is, written, in his own hand, and which he drew up as moderator of the presbytery in the controversy of the church with Pollanus§. He also preached at Frankfort, in the church of the White Nuns, which had been given to the refugees; and even administered baptism there, which was afterwards imputed to him as a great offence||. It appears that he did not visit the Lutheran ministers during his stay at Frankfort; but on the 23rd of September, the day be-

* MS. Bern. "Sane ita eos fascinavit Satan, ut nullam spem concordiæ reliquam faciat."

† Calvin to Melancthon, Sept. 17, 1556. In another letter addressed to Justus Jonas, he says, that he had scarcely an hour free.

‡ Salig, Geschich. der Augsburg. Confes. Bd. ii. s. 1140, gives an account of this man.

§ I have read the Consensus by Bucer, and with the exception of one or two heads, I should not hesitate, for the sake of peace, to accept it.

|| MS. Goth. ed. Bretschneider, p. 73.

fore his departure, he addressed the ministers assembled to commemorate the separation from Rome, and blessed them.

By the end of November Calvin was again at home. It is evident from certain expressions which we find him employing, that he had not fully accomplished the object of his journey. On the 21st of December, 1556, he complained to Clauburg, that the Frankfort senators had proved themselves wanting in resolution, and he wished him to take measures that the authors of the tumult might be bridled. In a letter to Holbrach, he calls the minister, Valerand, who was the chief fomenter, probably, of the quarrel, a devil*. He, in fact, at length accomplished the purpose to which his restlessness or ambition impelled him. The English and French were obliged, through his instrumentality, to subscribe the Augsburg Confession; the little word *substantially* being the only term omitted. Calvin however still remained in union with the church at Frankfort; it reposed confidence in him, and was glad to receive his advice. In a letter dated February 25, 1559, he expressed opinions of great importance†. Certain it is, that the magistrates treated the fugitives with no little harshness. They were required not only to subscribe, as forming the basis of a reunion, the Augsburg Confession, the Apology, and the Concordian formularies, which Bucer had drawn up at Frankfort, but to repudiate all the writings which were opposed to those documents, and to adopt the forms employed by their antagonists in the administration of the Lord's Supper. They consented to the first two articles; but after mutual recrimination it was resolved, on the part of those in power, that the church of the refugees should be closed till they consented to adopt altogether the ceremonies of the Lutherans, and their opinions on the subject of the Lord's Supper. They were, moreover, to elect a new preacher. The universities, and the princes on all sides, besought the Frankfort magistrates to treat the exiles with greater forbearance; they were, it was said, of the same faith with themselves. But in the year 1562 the intolerance of the Lutheran ministers proceeded to such an extent, that the refugees found themselves compelled to seek another asylum. Elizabeth invited them to England; some went to East Friesland. Those who travelled through Brabant were taken prisoners, thrown

* Dec. 22, 1556.

† MS. Tigur. Feb. 23, 1559. He again spoke of the anxiety and distress which he suffered. The ministers were quarrelling with each other. He exhorted them not to read either the German Théology (La Théologie Germanique), or a little work, entitled 'Der Neue Mensch.'

into dungeons, or committed to the flames. Many retired to Strasburg and Switzerland.

The history of the church, of which we have thus spoken, is worthy of attention. It gradually formed for itself a liturgy, which agreed neither with the Lutheran nor with the Reformed, especially in respect to ceremonies: it was a compound of these and of the English. The churches themselves were lost in distraction*.

CHAPTER X.

CALVIN'S RELATION TO THE NORTHERN CHURCHES.—HIS INFLUENCE IN POLAND. — CORRESPONDENCE WITH KING SIGISMUND AND WITH THE POLISH NOBLES.

CALVIN had already begun, in 1552, to place himself in communication with the Northern States, and had dedicated the French edition of his Commentary on the Acts of the Apostles to king Christian, who had introduced the Reformation into Denmark. He would fain have continued in friendly correspondence with the monarch, but the Lutheran clergy by their influence with the king prevented it. After the sacramental controversy with Westphal, Calvin altered the dedication to Christian, and dedicated the Commentary, in Latin, to prince Radzivill, the great promoter of the Reformation in Poland. He also about this time entered into correspondence with Gustavus Vasa, the enlightened king of Sweden. To this prince he dedicated his Commentary on the twelve minor prophets. He was induced to do this by the persuasion of one of his countrymen, who hoped thereby that some influence might be exercised on the mind of the king's son. We must here also mention his work against Menno Simon, well-known as the head of the anabaptists. It is comprehended in Calvin's collected correspondence. This Frieslander, who was originally a Catholic priest, published his doctrine at Emden. Laski had a conference with him, but it led to no result. Calvin subsequently attacked him, that is in 1559. Menno retired with several others to Poland, where tole-

* Salig, Bd. ii. s. 1135. The liturgy is given in Melchior Fronberger's account of the French and Netherland Churches, 1598.

rance and anarchy ruled together. Although Calvin could not introduce his doctrine into Denmark or Sweden, his animating, evangelical influence was thankfully recognized in Poland, independent of the war which he waged with the errors which there prevailed. Former church-historians have made little mention of his name in connection with Poland, and he is only incidentally alluded to by those of a later date. Evidences however still exist of his zeal and usefulness. The congregation at Posen, consisting partly of the descendants of the Bohemian brethren, may be referred to in proof of this. Greatly extended through the active devotion of George Israel, its chief elder, this community exhibited for a considerable time the very type and model of church order. The two monarchs, Sigismund and his son, were decidedly in favour of pure doctrine; they therefore treated the faithful with much kindness. Calvin seized the favourable opportunity, and placed himself in communication with all the great men of the kingdom.

The movement began between the years 1530 and 1540*. An early hostility was manifested to the doctrine of the Trinity. Cruciger preached the pure gospel in Poland in 1546; the doctrines of Calvin and Zwingli were always more favourably received there than those of Luther. The Taborites, who bore the name of Bohemian brethren, and had been driven in a body from their country, also exercised considerable influence in Poland. The Reformers became still more powerful under Sigismund Augustus. Nicolaus Olesnicki, urged on by Stancar, was the first to attack the Roman church. The monks of a convent in Pinczow were driven forth, the images were destroyed, and an experiment was made to introduce a public Protestant service after the example of that established at Geneva. We have no means of telling what influence the Genevese themselves had in this matter, but it is certain that Calvin corresponded at an early period with Tarnowski, stadtholder of Cracow, and with prince Radzivill, the grand marshal of Lithuania. Tarnowski was a remarkable character; although moderate, he was decidedly in favour of great changes; and he endeavoured to gain the pope's consent to the administration of the sacrament in both kinds, the performance of the service in the language of the country, the marriage of the clergy, and the abolition of fasts.

At the diet which assembled in the year 1550, the first of the

* Krasinsky, Gesch. d. Urspr. &c. d. Ref. in Polen, s. 55.

nobility, with Radzivill at their head, appeared as the advocates of the reformed faith, and as the accusers of the Romish clergy. The weakness of the papal party was manifest, but the truth did not prevail. At the diet of 1552*, evident indications existed of the decline of the Romish church. Orzechowski, a bold, rash man, who had been foremost in exciting agitation, vacillated to and fro, and at length became reconciled to the papal party. At this diet representatives were despatched to Trent, but with the declared hope that Rome might still accomplish her own thorough reform.

Calvin presented himself at this juncture. The Poles respected his doctrine and discipline; the free republican form of the synods agreeing far better with their national character than the consistorial form of the Lutherans. Thus he already enjoyed their confidence. But it was his design to bring his faith to the breach; and it is worthy of notice that he began his efforts, summoned, as he says, thereto, with the king himself. With sound policy, he admits the principle that great kingdoms may have patriarchates, and be placed under a primate. Thus we see how his powerful mind could discover its way through all forms, if free course was but secured for the gospel. Attentive to the strictest courtesy, he begins by showing that even kings must receive instruction from a servant of Christ; then follows an able eulogium on the liberal spirit of the monarch, with the remark, that rulers should be enlightened above all other men. "Remember," he says, "that in your person God has kindled a light for all Poland, and which cannot without great sin longer remain hidden. Let then that heroic energy at length break forth, which has already been too long slumbering." He next exhorts him not to allow himself to be held back by papistical principles: "The papists constantly object to us their hierarchy. They say, that although the position of the church is corrupt, it is not lawful, at least not for the laity, to point the finger at its errors, and that the papacy has inherited all power through Peter. But it is very strange, that Paul, when he admonishes us to cultivate unity, and speaks of one God, one faith, one baptism, and of one Spirit, one Lord, one body, should have forgotten what here would have been of such vast importance, namely, that there must be one great priest, by whose dignity and authority the whole church is to be held together in the bonds of unity. It

* Krasinsky, s. 120.

would have been a sad thing, had this been true, not to warn believers that it is God's intention that they should exist under such a head. Paul says, moreover, that the apostleship of the gentiles was given to him, as that of the Jews was to Peter. There is here indicated not only an equality between these two apostles, but such a division of their offices, that Peter would seem to have nothing whatever to do with us. In Ephesians iv. 11, it is not said that a vicar of Christ is appointed to represent him in his absence, but that there are apostles, preachers, doctors, who are to labour according to the measure of their ability. Certain it is, that if God had intended to set one above all the rest, he would have imparted to him, not a mere portion of the gifts of grace, but the whole fulness thereof."

He jests at the pretensions of the popes, in respect to their exclusive possession of the keys:—"What relation has the pope to Peter? Would not the seat of the primate have been at Jerusalem, if anywhere? There, where Christ beyond dispute exercised the great priestly office. In the Epistle to the Hebrews, the apostle does not establish a worldly priesthood, but he shows that Christ is the true high-priest, one who can have no successor, because he is after the order of Melchisedec. It is not for a mere man to govern the whole world. The avarice and pride of the Roman court fabricated this primacy. The ancient church founded patriarchates, and set primates over different provinces; and in the same manner it was lawful to appoint an archbishop for the renowned kingdom of Poland; not however that he might exercise lordship over the rest of the clergy, or repossess himself of the power which they had won for themselves, but that he might, for the sake of order, hold the first place in the synods, and preserve a holy union among his colleagues and the brethren. So also there might be bishops for the various provinces or cities, whose office it should be to keep order in all things, as circumstances required; and one might be chosen from every assembly of bishops, to whom the principal charge might be entrusted; for to endow a man with a fair portion of dignity, according to his state and occupation, is very different to subjecting the whole world to a single power. The Catholic theory is at strife with God's original appointment, and with the original plan of the church. For a bishop to be a bishop of bishops, he must himself be a bishop. Unworthy however is he of such a title who refuses to learn, but surrenders himself to idle pomp, and impiously destroys the doctrine of Christ."

Calvin, in the next place, protests against the immorality and impiety of the Roman court. His language becomes more and more vehement: he calls the whole Catholic church a sect. No reform, he says, could be expected from it; it could only exist by the ruin and misery of the church. To wait, therefore, for improvement, on the supposition that the pope would assent to it, was only to have recourse to an absurd subterfuge. "We now know," he says, "what the apostles meant when they proclaimed at the beginning, that the builders had rejected the chief corner-stone."

The king received this address graciously, and answered it: Calvin therefore continued his admonitions*. We see him, both in this and the following year, using every effort to excite the zeal of all the great and influential men in Poland. In one day he despatched four letters to that country†. That to the count of Tarnaw, general of the Polish army, is written in the most energetic language. Calvin spoke to him as a soldier to a soldier, exhorting him to place himself at the head of the soldiers of Christ. He seems to have understood his character, and to have endeavoured to work upon him, through his feelings both of duty and honour‡. Thus he represents to him the baseness of the papacy; the glory which God ascribes to the confession of the truth; and the rage of the enemies of Christ, which ought to stimulate more and more the noble zeal of his followers. "It is an honour to contend for God, and you must not be the last to do so." He further represented, that it was for the interest of the state to take this course. "Poland can never be quiet if the reformed religion be not established in the country."—"You may thus, therefore, evince also your fidelity to the king."—"God blesses those people only who accept the true faith."

The danger to the Catholic church increased every day. A protestant synod at Kosminek effected in 1555 a union between the Bohemian brethren and the Calvinists in Poland: this greatly strengthened the Protestant party. "God," says Calvin to a Polish knight, "always blesses this fellowship and communion of the members of Christ. The experience of the Waldenses, whom the Lord has so long proved, will be of very great use."

In the year 1555 the old disputes respecting the church were renewed at the diet of Piotrkow. It was announced to the king

* Ed. Laus. Ep. 218. Ed. Amst. p. 104.

† December 29, 1555.

‡ Ed. Laus. Ep. 220. Ed. Amst. p. 104.

that an immediate necessity existed to assemble a national synod, consisting of the representatives of all parties, who might take means for reforming the church, on the principles of Scripture; and that the meeting ought not to be formed of the Polish ministers only, but that the most distinguished reformers in various parts of Europe, and particularly Calvin, Beza, Melancthon, and the Italian Vergerio, who was then in Poland, should be invited to attend.

This proposal created a great sensation, but the Polish bishops had sufficient influence to nullify it. The Poles themselves however received Calvin's exhortations with profound attention. Two years subsequent to this they earnestly desired him to come to them alone, and to work there. This must have been the general wish, for he answered them in a letter addressed to all the nobility who had accepted the pure doctrine*. Excusing himself, he says, "I learn from a letter that my arrival among you would be acceptable, but I fear that my leaving this place might be attended with great injury to the church here." The council also would not allow his departure. These events occurred simultaneously with Laski's recal to Poland (1556), so that Calvin added: "Now that Heaven has granted you the privilege of enjoying the labours of that most excellent servant of Christ, a Lasco, I do not see why you should desire my presence so much; and if it be not really necessary, you cannot yourselves wish to take me from a station where I am usefully engaged." He promises however to seek the Lord for them in prayer.

The circumstance above-stated leads us to review briefly the life of a Lasco, and Calvin's relation to him. Calvin took advantage of every opportunity to praise this awakened man, and to express his esteem for him. There were few men indeed, even in these favoured times, so remarkable for vivacity, boldness and simplicity. He was descended from a noble family; was converted by Zwingli in the course of a journey through Germany, and lived some time with Erasmus, who entertained for him the most lively affection. When he found himself compelled to give up every hope of the reformation of the Catholic church, he went abroad (1537), married at Mainz, and was excommunicated by Rome. In 1554 he became superintendent of the East Frisian churches, where, after six years, but not till then, he was so happy as to see the Romish errors completely abolished. Albrecht

* MS Bern, 8 Mart. 1557.

of Prussia was now anxious to obtain his assistance in establishing the Reformation in his territories; but he declined the invitation, asserting the principle that the church should be wholly independent of the state. Thus also he separated entirely from the Lutherans, on publishing his Confession of Faith for East Friesland, which now pertained altogether to the Reformed communion. It was about this time, probably, that his more intimate acquaintance with Calvin began; and when the Lutherans acquired the upper hand in Friesland, he gladly accepted Cranmer's invitation to England (1548). Disguising himself, he ventured, according to his daring custom, to travel through Brabant. In the following year he became the head of the foreign Protestant churches in London, the admirable champion of their rights, and the overseer of their schools. It appears that he did not agree with Bucer on the subject of the Lord's Supper. Decided in character as he was, he had little in common with a man so ready to incline to many sides. Calvin mentioned this to his friend Farel*.

On his return to the continent, he was unwilling, on account of the Lutherans, to remain at Emden: he accordingly went to Frankfort. It was his object to reconcile the Lutherans and the Reformed in that city. We have already alluded to his writing on this subject: he also engaged in a colloquy for the same purpose, and went to Speier to regulate the proceedings. Calvin said to him†, "They will avoid a friendly colloquy as something odious; but if they be honest, they will find us ready for whatever is reasonable." He warned him earnestly to be cautious of Vergerius, and added, that he would himself hasten to be present, whenever the princes would actually hold a meeting. To this the Zurichers would never agree, and Calvin relates what Bullinger said to him against the colloquy.

Laski now engaged singly with Brentius: he disputed against the doctrine of ubiquity: it was founded neither on Scripture, nor on the church. The apology which he addressed to the council of Frankfort, and from which it appeared that he agreed with the Augsburg Confession, was written in obedience to the wish of the king of Poland. Calvin approved of it, but considered it heavy: he wrote to Laski August 28, 1556, saying,

* MS. Gen. Febr. 1551. He does not quite agree with Bucer, it seems, and he will not dissemble. But what wonder if he dissents from Bucer?

† MS, Bern, Mai. 15, 1556.

that "he was wholly of opinion that there was nothing in the Augsburg Confession which did not agree with his doctrine*."

Brentius had utterly destroyed the hope of a reunion. Laski proceeded to Wittenberg to confer with Melancthon: the latter gave him a letter to the king of Poland, exhorting him to promote the Reformation in that country. Laski, on his return, demonstrated, in a writing on the subject, the necessity of abolishing the Roman hierarchy† (December 1556). This was the time when Calvin exercised so much influence on the Poles, and the enterprising Laski was wholly devoted to accomplishing the work of reform. But nothing was left undone to make him an object of suspicion to the king: it was even reported that he was a determined enemy to his native land, and that he was engaged in collecting troops to effect a revolution. These reports made some impression on the monarch, till meeting with one of Laski's relations, who opened his eyes to the truth, he observed, "You know that such movements and disturbances frequently lead to the ruin of states. Say therefore to Laski, Carry on the work of religion among yourselves, and in a short time you will see that I look more to the help of God than to that of men‡."

But at the next diet the affair was again deferred, and put off by the machinations of Satan to another occasion. We see Laski, however, appointed chief superintendent of all the Protestant churches in Lesser Poland. The union of the Lutherans with the Reformed, for which preparation had been made by the junction of the latter with the Bohemian brethren, was the first object to engage his attention. He did not make a journey to the king, but he wrote to him. The Italian Lismanini now came to his aid: this person had already employed his influence to induce the king to promote the Reformation: he had expounded to him Calvin's Institutes twice a week, and had travelled into different Protestant countries for the purpose of affording the monarch a true account of their state. In the course of this journey he had visited Bern and Geneva, whence he travelled to Paris, on returning from which he came again to Geneva. There, in conformity with Calvin's exhortations, he publicly announced his conversion to Protestantism, and marked the event by marrying. This latter step was imprudent; it betrayed the views of the king, who now

* MS. Bern. "Mihi placet argumentum, nam et ita res habet et imprimis utile est cognosci, nihil esse in Confessione Augustana, quod non sit doctrinæ nostræ consentaneum."

† Krasinsky, s. 106.

‡ Ed. Laus. Ep. 234. Amst. 120. Utenhovius Calvino, Cracov. 1557.

forbad his return. The clergy pronounced him excommunicate, and the interest of Bullinger, Calvin and Beza was exerted for him in vain. It was not till 1555, when the synod at Pinczow was held, and when Calvin entreated the most influential of the Protestants to invite him to be present, that he dare venture to return. He lived for a long time concealed in the house of a Polish lady, Agnes Dluska, with whom Calvin also was in correspondence*. By means of Tarnow and Cruciger, he at last succeeded in placing Lismanini again in a sphere of activity; but the Italian, unfortunately, too readily inclined his ear to the despisers of the doctrine of the Trinity. He had entertained Lælius Socinus at his house in the year 1551, and it is probable that he then imbibed the doctrines of that teacher, though he concealed it while at Geneva. A synod at Cracow repeated the ban pronounced upon him. He subsequently went to Königsberg, where, in a fit of phrenzy, he deprived himself of life. Although now standing alone, Laski went boldly forward in the work of reform: his grand purpose was to effect a reformation after the example of that of England, and at the same time to accomplish the union of the two parties. By the efforts which he made, he laid the foundation for the settlement subsequently agreed upon at Sandomir.

At the diet held in 1556 the important law was passed, that it should be lawful for any nobleman to introduce the observance of the evangelical service into his house. Rome was called upon to correct the abuses with which it was charged. The pope had sent a legate, and he was present at the diet. Vergerio and Laski worked together: they introduced the reformation into Elbing and Danzig, and all seemed prepared for the separation of Poland from Rome.

It is remarkable that, worthy of praise as was Vergerio's conduct, Calvin constantly warned people against him, and manifested his own want of confidence in his character: he calls him a double-minded, ambitious, covetous, tricky, vain, unsettled man. Laski was of a character altogether different to this. In the year 1557 we again find Calvin praising this excellent man, in a letter respecting the Poles:—"If, after the war with Lievland, the reformation of the church be steadily carried forward, Laski will assuredly obtain that situation with the king which is due to piety, learning, experience and ability. The only danger

* MS. Gen. Calvin to Agnes Dluska, the mother of some young men studying at Zurich. 4 Cal. Jan. 1555.

is, that he may fail, in some degree, through too great an austerity*."

A synod was assembled by the Catholics at Lowicz, in which the abuses of the church were spoken of with great boldness. It had indulged of late in new excesses, and the whole people were enraged against it; but it was not till 1559 that an attempt was made to exclude the bishops from the senate: even this proved fruitless. The decrees however of the Council of Trent were utterly rejected by the diet. Thus the struggle between the two parties continued for years without any decisive event. Laski died in 1560, and saw no result of his faithful labours. This indecision on the part of the Poles greatly distressed Calvin: the volatile Antitrinitarians were mixed up with these proceedings. We learn from his letters to Tarnowsky the real state of affairs at this time: he had suggested to the timid mind of his correspondent the following noble thoughts: "Whatever dangers may threaten us, the overthrow of the perishable kingdom of this world can never appear a matter of so much consequence as to induce us, in order to uphold it, to neglect the service of God and the pure religion, on which depends our eternal salvation. But these fears are vain; for Christ, the prince of peace, would soon allay whatever storms Satan might excite." Tarnowski answered the simple minister of the Gospel in a haughty, jesting tone. Calvin's patient reply to his ironical objections was very admirable, and shows with what force and ability the reformer could act in such circumstances.

The Reformation could make no progress among minds so vacillating and capricious, and which did not feel the immediate tyranny of Rome, the people in general knowing nothing of the baptism of suffering, or of the penitence to which it leads, as in France, England and Germany. But Calvin performed his part: there was much that was noble in his correspondence with prince Radzivill, that ardent champion of the Reformation. The prince applied to him at an early period of the movement, and desired to be called his friend; but scarcely had he become confirmed in his faith, when the restless minds by which he was surrounded began to disturb the unity and purity of the doctrine which he had been led to embrace. Lælius Socinus was among the first to create this excitement. Calvin, as we have seen, commended him with affectionate earnestness to the Poles, and must have

* MS. Gen. 1557.

felt for him originally no slight regard. At a later period* he expressed strong doubts regarding him, and seems, after some few years, to have thoroughly understood both him and Ochinus†. Socinus however subsequently awakened new hopes, and was immediately received in the most friendly manner: he had deceived, in fact, both Calvin and Bullinger; the former observing, in writing to the latter, "that he willingly readmitted the now tranquillized Socinus to his friendship, seeing that he had renounced his errors‡."

But to understand the relation in which Calvin and Socinus stood to each other, the reader must refer to what has been said in an earlier part of this work. The injury which these seekers after something new inflicted on the church was greater even than the evils wrought by the papists. The works of Servetus were much read in Poland. Peter Gonesius was the first to reduce the errors of the Antitrinitarians of that country to a system: he publicly declared his opinions in 1556, and the progress of unbelief was so rapid and overwhelming, that the ruin of the reformed churches was generally expected. We have before spoken of Blandrata and Stancar: Calvin earnestly warned the Poles against them. At the synod of Pinczow, 1556, and subsequently to that, when Laski and Stanislaus Sarnicki resisted these false teachers, they failed to attain their end. Gregory Pauli, who took Blandrata's place when the latter was obliged to leave, and went to Siebenbürgen, professed, without secrecy, his opposition to the Trinity. Gentilis, Alciat, and Dudith, fulfilled their course there. The parties at length separated, and in the year 1563 the doctrines of the Antitrinitarians were formally condemned in an assembly of the Reformed. The Antitrinitarians now united with each other in one body, the foundation of the union being their common belief in the superiority of the Father to the Son: this took place in 1565, when they received their constitution.

But Calvin long continued to cherish hope, and he rejoiced that his system of discipline had, at least, been introduced into Poland. This was a triumph for the principles of the Reformation; but the Poles were too fond of unbridled liberty to be able to comprehend the worth of Calvinistic severity. In the letter last-cited Calvin admonished them to establish a seminary for

* MS. Gen. Calv. Bullingero, Aug. 7, 1554.
† MS. Bern. Calv. Vireto et Bezæ, April 10, 1556.
‡ MS. Gen. Calv. Bullingero.

ministers. About the same time he entered into correspondence with a learned and pious Pole, Doctor Andreas Tricesius, who had been requested to translate the Scriptures into the language of the country. He wrote also to Johannes Bonar, castellan of Viecz, to persuade him to become responsible for the expenses of this work*. Laski, some time before his death, united with several persons, some of whom even were inclined to Socinianism, in prosecuting this translation of the Bible into Polish: it was printed at Brzewsc, in Lithuania, in the year 1563.

But Calvin was often justly alarmed at the signs which he discovered of a restless character: the whole nation, in fact, seemed to him in a suspicious state, for few only proved themselves sincere†. In his care for the Poles he acted in a manner consistent with his general character. Thus to Stanislaus Sarnicki, who besought him, shortly before his death, again to address his people, he replied that it was useless for him now to write to them on the subject of the Trinity, for that his 'Admonition' to the Poles was already printed, and he appended it to his letter. This Admonition was not indeed the last, but it was one of Calvin's latest works, and his regard for the Poles was strikingly proved by his taking the pains to prepare it for the press, while he was daily sinking under his infirmities.

It is interesting for us to know, that in the midst of these theological struggles, the healthier portion of the congregations effected that which was not accomplished in any other church in Protestant countries; that is, the evangelical members of the community preserved unity, and yet retained distinct confessions. Poland rendered itself remarkable, from the first, by a noble tolerance. Punishment for heresy was wholly abolished; and although the Catholics constantly advised the persecution of those who fell away, and even Beza himself once wished strong measures to be taken against the Antitrinitarians, the government constantly answered, that the punishment of those who entertained different opinions was wholly forbidden. Hence the dissenters among the Protestants flocked to Poland as a place of refuge. This tolerance and mildness led to the union of the Swiss-reformed, the Bohemian brethren, or Waldenses, and the Lutherans‡. When the Bohemians here spoken of became known, by means of various reformers, in Germany and Swit-

* Both letters are in the MS. Paris.

† MS. Gen. Calv. Bullingero, Sept. 12, 1563.

‡ Krasinsky, s. 132, 142.

zerland, for their orthodoxy, the Lutherans evinced their readiness to own them as brethren, notwithstanding the efforts of Flacius Illyricus, who made a journey to Posen to hinder it. After many disputes and delays, and after the Wittenbergers had again declared themselves in favour of the measure, the union of the churches was proclaimed at Sandomir (1570) in a synod, from which the Antitrinitarians were excluded, on the condition that none of the three parties should force its particular confession upon the others, but that all should adopt a general Polish Confession.

But as no other means availed to uphold the Catholic church, an antagonist was now raised against the evangelical party far more formidable to it than even the vacillation and disbelief of some of its members: we allude to the Jesuits, who possessed themselves of all the resources of education. Bishop Hosius, on his return from Trent, prayed Lainez to send him some of his spiritual soldiers: this was in 1564. After the death of Sigismund Augustus in 1572, they had freer scope. The king, though irresolute in character, was of a noble and gentle disposition. There is little doubt that he would willingly have adopted the Protestant doctrine, and that form of it which was preached by the Swiss Calvinists. His plan, as recommended to him by Laski, was to let the reformation spring from the midst of the Polish church itself, whence a constitution would be secured for it similar to that of the church of England. But during the agitation which followed his reign, the Jesuits made great strides; a warning for the country, which can only regain legitimate freedom through the illuminating power of truth.

In France, to which we must now turn our attention, the evangelical church was destined to pursue a very different course, and to prepare for itself a future not allowed to Poland.

CHAPTER XI.

INFLUENCE OF CALVIN IN FRANCE.—RAPID DEVELOPMENT OF THE REFORMATION IN THE FIRE OF PERSECUTION.—MARTYRS IN THE REIGN OF HENRY II. AT LYONS, CHAMBERY, AND OTHER PLACES.—CALVIN'S DISTRESS.—HE EXHORTS THE GERMAN PRINCES TO INTERFERE.—BEGINNING OF THE CHURCH IN PARIS.—EMIGRATION OF THE REFORMED TO AMERICA.—HEROIC COURAGE OF THE CONFESSORS.—ANNE DU BOURG.—SKETCH OF EVENTS PRECEDING THE COLLOQUY OF POISSY.—BELIEF AND DISCIPLINE OF THE FRENCH CHURCH.—UNITY OF THE CHURCH UNDER CALVIN'S INFLUENCE.—HIS SUCCESS AT ITS HIGHEST POINT.—ANIMATING ADDRESS TO ALL THE GREAT PERSONAGES IN FRANCE BELONGING TO THE EVANGELICAL PARTY.

THE history of the Gospel in France is that of the heroism of its professors on the one side, and of a wrathful antichristianity, combined with the selfishness of the French princes, on the other. Far more anxious about their own authority, which seemed endangered by the new faith, than concerned respecting the defence of the Catholic church, the Romish, Spanish and French courts exhibit all those vices concentrated in one point which are usually spread over a wide space. The superstition of the priests, the intrigues of the Jesuits, the bloodthirsty cruelty of the regent, the violation of morality and justice, went hand in hand. Refreshing is it to contemplate the other side of the picture, where we see evangelical purity displaying its best influence. A wonderful phænomenon indeed it was, that Lutheranism, as it was then called, had spread to a wider extent in France than in any other country, except Germany, while it was in no other so fearfully oppressed.

We have already spoken of the beginning of the Reformation in France. The city of Meaux was the central point of the heroic conflict: it was there that the bishop, Briçonnet, and John Leclerc, defended their theses against the pope. It was at Meaux that the last persecution of the reformed took place previous to the French Reformation*. That great champion of the faith, who first preached the Gospel in Metz, died there soon after he had pro-

* Coquerel, Hist. des Églises du Désert, t. ii. towards the end.

claimed the truth. Pavans, L'Ermite de Livry, Denis de Rieux, Berquin, Renier, Caturce, were the first who, through their sufferings in the flames, kindled a holy fire, and proved anew that the blood of the martyrs is the seed of the true church. Wrought upon themselves by a mighty power, they wrought powerfully upon the people, so that a Catholic writer of that period, under the influence of strong emotion, observes, that "it was astonishing how men and women, nay, even young girls, went joyfully to die, and remained firm as rocks in their agony. Such examples, continually repeated, affected equally the hearts of the simple and the great; nor could they who were thus affected believe that the sufferers had not the truth on their side."

We have before described how that, towards the end of the reign of Francis I., the Waldensian villages were burnt, in the name of the king, while their unfortunate inhabitants were either massacred on the spot or sent to the gallies. It has also been stated that the king felt deeply the stings of conscience before his death, and how the city of Meaux suffered from persecution.

But Henry II. had now ascended the throne, and was surrounded by four advisers, who were in all respects the most determined enemies of the Gospel: they were, the Cardinal of Lorraine, Anne de Montmorency, the Marshal St. André, and the old mistress of the king, Diana of Poictiers, who controlled him, as Beza says, by a sort of magic. When the king solemnized his public entry into Paris, he expressed his wish to see one of the heretics. A poor Huguenot tailor was accordingly brought to him: the tailor was a man whose cowardice, it was supposed, might be safely reckoned upon; but, contrary to expectation, he proclaimed with energy the great truths of the Gospel; and when the king, hearing him address Diana of Poictiers somewhat rudely*, desired him to be burnt, he fixed his eyes so firmly on the monarch, that the latter could never forget his look. Many others were burnt in Paris at this festival, and the same spectacle presented itself on all sides. Beza gives a connected detail of the occurrences of the period†, extending to the year 1553.

On the 21st of June, 1551, the king issued the edict of Châteaubriant, which renewed all those previously published, and committed the trial and punishment of heretics, hitherto divided among several, to one tribunal exclusively, invested with the

* "Madame," he said, "be contented with having infected France, and do not mix your bad odour with things so sacred as the truth of God."

† Beza, l. c. i. p. 84.

power of life and death. The parliament was blamed for having been remiss in the prosecution of such offenders; and it was ordered that the possessions of all those who fled should be confiscated, and that no book printed in Geneva, or in any of the reformed states, should be admitted into the kingdom. The monarch, not contented with this, went a step further, and appointed Matthias Ori, of whom we have spoken in the trial of Servetus at Vienne, as chief inquisitor.

The year 1553 was rendered remarkable by the death of a great many holy martyrs, among whom were the five students at Lyons before alluded to. The Cardinal Tournon, who had gained great renown as a persecutor of heretics, had promised, on passing in his journey from Italy through Bern, to interest himself in behalf of the accused; but he was mocking the Bernese. As soon as he learnt that the king was inclined to yield in some degree, he employed his influence to the utmost to persuade him to stronger measures. The numerous letters however sent by the Bernese occasioned a delay in the execution of the five students, and they found time to carry on the work of evangelical conversion. Crespin's Martyrology has preserved several letters written by Calvin to the sufferers.

But if this period was rich in witnesses to the truth, how much more so was the year 1555! It was during this year that the bishops Hooper, Ridley, Latimer, and Cranmer, were condemned to the flames in England, the last-named suddenly evincing the Christian greatness which lay hid within him. France rivaled England in this conflict; and Calvin wrote to encourage the church there, especially afflicted by the death of five other confessors burnt at Chambery. The sufferings of the persons here spoken of were almost more edifying than those of the former martyrs. Three of them were ministers. Like the five students, they had all left Geneva singing psalms as they went forth with the grand design of spreading the Gospel in France, and winning souls for the Lord, although they beheld on all sides the smoke of burning piles, and had so many examples to deter them from their course. The fulness of joy inspired by the Holy Spirit was shown conspicuously in these martyrs. Having been speedily apprehended, they attained their end by leading many others, through the grandeur of their devotion, to a similar confession*.

One of these martyrs, Anton Laborie, was married. We quote some words of a letter which he wrote while in prison to his

* Hist. des Martyrs, p. 345, and Beza, Hist. Eccles. p. 97.

wife. They prove how high Calvin stood in the estimation and confidence of these believers, who must doubtless have known him better than his modern vilifiers. "Anna, my good sister! you know that you are still young, and are about to be separated from my society. If such be God's good will for us, comfort yourself in Him, and with the thought that Jesus Christ is your Father and your Husband. I am convinced that He will not forsake you. Pray to Him without ceasing for his holy word. Flee the society of the wicked; seek that of the pious. Follow not your own conceits, but the counsel of our right-minded friends, especially that of Mr. Calvin. He will not let you come to any harm, if you act according to his wish; and you know that he is led by the Holy Ghost. If you marry again, and I advise you to do so, I beg you to hearken to his opinion, and to do nothing without him."

Calvin's messengers fearlessly penetrated into the deepest dungeons. He wrote to the heroic confessors at the beginning of their imprisonment, and while they were not yet so fully confirmed in their resolution. Wishing to inspire them with a holy tranquillity against the approaching conflict, he says, "My brothers! as soon as we were informed of your imprisonment, I sent a messenger to you. It is not necessary to tell you what care we feel for you, and in what distress your bonds hold us. I doubt not that since so many believers are praying for you, our good God will grant you your wish, and hear your sighs. I can see indeed from your letters how he has already begun to work in you. If the weakness of the flesh show itself somewhat therein, and prove that you have to endure a hard struggle, I do not wonder thereat, but praise God for giving you the victory. Fulfil now what you have learnt; and since it has pleased the Master to employ you in his service, go forward therein as you have begun. Although the door is shut to you, and you can no longer edify those to whom you were sent by teaching, yet will the witness which you are about to give strengthen them from afar. God will add such force to this testimony, that it shall sound much farther than the human voice can reach. With regard to any earthly means for effecting your deliverance, I would that we possessed them, even though they afforded no hope of success. We will certainly do whatever in us lies, but God instructs us to take a higher view. Your main object must be so to collect your thoughts, that you may find rest in his fatherly goodness, not doubting but that He will guard both your body and spirit; and that if the blood of the faithful be precious to Him, He will manifestly show that it is so in your case, seeing that He has chosen you for his witnesses. If it be his good pleasure to make use of your lives as a seal to the truth,—(you know that this is a sacrifice of the highest worth to him)—let it be your consolation, that leaving all in his hands you can lose nothing; for if he keeps us under his guardianship even in this imperfect state, how much more will he not be the guardian of our souls when He has taken us back to Himself!"

No church had as yet been regularly formed. The martyrs were preachers. But in this season of confusion, a young man, De la Rivière, the son of the sieur de Launay, made the first attempt to found a church in Paris. This church continued to flourish till the reign of Louis XV., when it was destroyed, and did not revive till after the revolution. The father, a decided enemy of the Gospel, implored his son not to kill him with grief. Some friends however led the young man to Paris, where he held prayer-meetings in the house of De la Ferrière; the latter resolved not to let his infant child be baptized according to the Romish rites; and the community now formed elected Rivière for their minister, and also appointed elders and deacons. All this took place under the eyes of the parliament, which established a *chambre ardente* in the city, where the Sorbonne and the people gave full scope to their rage. The congregation of which we have spoken existed till 1557.

Calvin addressed the ministers, elders and deacons, for the first time, January 5, 1556. His language was strong and encouraging; he told them that he was anxious for their welfare, and sent them a minister from Geneva. They had asked for another, but he would have too much excited, says Calvin, the wrath of the enemy. Beza, Viret, or Farel, must have been the person alluded to. A letter written to Calvin from Paris, in 1557, by Thomas Querculus, who had been chosen the minister of the congregation then existing there, shows that it was well-established and flourishing. "Resting," he says, "upon the strong arm of the Lord, it becomes exalted more and more every day*." The writer also expresses his wish for a personal consultation with Calvin. Meaux, Angers, Poictiers, and many other cities, followed the example of the capital, and formed, amid numberless dangers, their several little communities.

In the year 1557 the persecutors became dissatisfied with the

* MS. Goth.

proceedings which they had hitherto instituted. The Cardinal Lorraine induced the king to establish a tribunal for the trial of heresy. The bull of the pope confirming the design was published on the 26th of April, but some difficulty still attended the execution of the plan. The battle of St. Quentin occurred: the evangelical church at Paris occupied itself in prayer, beseeching the Lord to turn away his wrath from the land. Great excitement prevailed. On the 4th of September, the faithful, to the number of four hundred, assembled in the night, that they might celebrate the Lord's Supper with greater solemnity. A sermon was preached on 1 Cor. chap. xi. But the priests had discovered the meeting and given the alarm. About midnight they rushed in with horrible clamours, and fell upon the congregation as it was preparing to depart. Some exclaimed that they were murderers, others Lutherans, and the people just awoke from sleep hastened to the spot armed with halberds. Many of the gentlemen of the congregation opened a way for themselves with their swords, but the others remained shut in, and guarded by the people till the arrival of the magistrates. The latter learnt on inquiry, that the congregation employed itself in reading the word of God, in prayer, and in partaking of the sacrament; that all disturbers of the peace, thieves and adulterers, were rigidly excluded from the society; that supplication was made for the king, as appeared by the liturgy; and that the service ended with singing of psalms. It appeared that many of the females, of whom there were about 140 in the congregation, were women of the first families. The multitude attacked them furiously as they were conveyed from the place of meeting.

The common voice was against the persecuted, and the king suffered himself to be led by the clergy. The misery of France was ascribed to the Protestants, as the misfortunes of the empire were to the Christians in the time of the primitive church. It was vulgarly reported that as soon as they extinguished the lights, the congregation gave itself up to every species of licentiousness.

All those who had been apprehended were cast into the most wretched dungeons. Their relatives despatched messengers to Germany and Switzerland to excite the princes of the Reformed states to intercede in their behalf. Twenty-one were condemned to die in the flames, and three were speedily led to execution. Beza describes the death of the youthful Gravelle, of the aged Clinet, and of the beautiful Philippa de Luns, in her 23rd year, widow of the sieur de Graveron, lately deceased. The 27th of September was the day of their death, and of their triumph; the day on which the Holy Ghost was to exhibit its power in the youth, the aged man, and the weak woman. Many similar spectacles were presented to the people in this Babel.

But in the meantime Geneva had turned its attention to these proceedings; and it is interesting to see how Calvin, while exhorting the sufferers boldly to encounter martyrdom, employed with fatherly anxiety all the earthly means in his power for their deliverance. The popular excitement was now somewhat abated, for no insurrection broke out, as the enemy had pretended would be the case; the slanders also which had been circulated were confuted. A mother, whose daughters it was said had been dishonoured, proved the falsehood of the charge before a judicial tribunal. Still greater benefit was conferred on the persecuted by the publication of a little book, spoken of in the *Livre des Martyrs*, and in which the testimony of the fathers is adduced in behalf of their doctrine. It was written by a minister of the church in Paris, named Chandieu. A Sorbonnist and inquisitor, De Mouchi, answered it with senseless fury.

While Calvin despatched Beza and Budé to the German cantons and to Germany itself, with all possible speed, in order to take measures for the liberation of the prisoners, he addressed the latter in a style of heroic earnestness. "We give you no other counsel but that which we should ourselves wish to adopt, were we in your case. It is better for us to hope for no safety here, but to expect a certain death, rather than fix a stain on the Gospel through our deceit or disbelief. Fruitful indeed are the ashes of the martyrs, whereas mere human designs bring with them sterility and a brand*." At the same time he wrote to a minister, imprisoned in Piedmont, exhorting him to a similar exercise of fortitude: this bold champion of the truth stood firm, was strangled and burnt. It was commonly reported that when the flames ascended, a white dove flew round about the fire,—an image of the purity of the martyr, whose soul was ascending to God.

Calvin expressed himself with great joy at the progress of the Gospel in France. "Wonderfully," he says, "does God protect the truth. The church in Paris has now four courageous ministers; and the number of the assemblies increases on all sides." We see from a great variety of letters, that Calvin was daily sending forth emissaries, who, although not always ministers,

* Ed. Laus. Ep. 243. Ed. Amstel. p. 172. MS. Gen. à Mlle. de Pantigny.

were sufficiently advanced in knowledge to instruct those who were disposed to learn; and probably carried evangelical books with them, as is done by the colporteurs of the modern evangelical societies.

An emigration to the states of Brazil took place about this time. It is an error to speak of a formal mission to that country; but it appears from a letter written by the minister of the emigrants, Richer, that they occasionally employed their thoughts about the conversion of the heathen. This experiment at colonization dates from the year 1557. A certain Maltese knight, Villegagnon, had represented to the Admiral Coligny, that he might form a secure establishment in America, take with him the persecuted believers, people the land, and convert the heathen. The scheme appeared so feasible, that the admiral was altogether inclined to adopt it. A little island belonging to Brazil was taken possession of by Villegagnon, and received the name of Coligny. Ministers and emigrants were now invited out. Geneva sent Richer and Chartier; but, contrary to the hope which he first held out to the community, Villegagnon opposed the Calvinists, persecuted them according to the French edict, and treated them as deceivers. Four of them, after making an excellent confession of their faith, were by his orders thrown into the sea; the others fled to France *.

We have already alluded to the journey undertaken by Farel, Beza and Budé, during the controversy on the Confession of Faith, for the purpose of interesting the German princes in behalf of the reformed. Frequent mention is made of these proceedings in Calvin's correspondence; he did whatever lay in his power to lessen the distress which prevailed, and set every engine at work which could be employed for that purpose. The state of political affairs seemed favourable to his efforts: Henry II. required the help of the German Protestants against Spain. But on the other hand, sad and discouraging were the dissensions which the Lutherans had introduced into Germany. The cantons sent a new embassy to the king: their petition was supported by the letters of the Elector Palatine; and the king seemed inclined to listen, the battle of St. Quentin having convinced him that it would be impolitic further to embitter the Germans. Calvin urged the elector Otto Heinrich to take a part in this work,

* Joh. v. Lery, an eye-witness, has given an account of the horrors attending the journey home. He was subsequently a reformed minister at Bern. See Dict. des Hommes Illust.

and earnestly entreated him to send an embassy to France*. From a letter to the court-preacher Diller, we find that the prince, deceived by false representations, would not follow the example of the other princes in sending ambassadors: he had been led to believe that the prisoners were already liberated.

The persecution in the meantime pursued its course. "In February 1558," says Calvin, in a letter to Farel†, "our very dear friends Beza and Budé travelled for the third time to visit the German princes. The king has besought three cardinals from Antichrist to superintend the inquisition. The Cardinal Lorraine has all the power in his own hands." Beza had journeyed to Frankfort, where an assembly of the electors was to be held: the Germans expended their time as usual in long debate, and approved the faith of the persecuted believers; but they did not arrive at the determination to interfere in their behalf, till many of them had already suffered in the flames. Several prisoners however were delivered through the intercession of the Protestant princes. The delay which occurred might be attributed to the unchristian influence of the Lutheran zealots.

It is well to observe how nobly Calvin laboured to cheer and uphold the oppressed churches in the midst of these dangers ‡. "The Lord," he says, "guards us with more care, than ever did a bird protect its young under the cover of its wings. As we see that the reins are given to the devil, and that he is suffered to trouble the poor church on all sides, place yourselves again under the banner of Jesus Christ; go into his school, that you may daily be instructed better; and pray your God that He may have mercy upon you as redeemed children."

When Calais, in 1558, was recovered by France, the king's courage revived, and the cardinal succeeded in establishing the tribunal of which we have before spoken; while Henry II. favoured the Guises, he promoted the growth of parties, and the misfortunes of the country. It is an error however to suppose, as some have done, that the movements which now took place were the result of political schemes formed under the mask of religion. A sufficient number indeed of political springs had been set in motion; but faith was also exercising its mighty influence, as, in Germany, the proceedings of Maurice of Saxony were not independent of religious impulses.

On the side of the Catholics, fanatical rage was not wanting;

* Ed. Laus. Ep. 257. Ed. Amst. p. 125.

† MS. Gen. Calv. Farello, Feb. 24, 1558. ‡ MS. Gen. Mai. 28, 1559.

but the evangelical party were desiring truth. It is confessed*, that inasmuch as the Calvinistic system had a moral tendency far stricter than the Lutheran, while the court of France was distinguished by its sensuality, a fiercer hostility was created between the two parties in France than in Germany, where the princes were more moral and temperate. The churches however grew and were strengthened in spirit; although, according to report, no fewer than fifty thousand Huguenots perished during the reigns of Francis I. and Henry II.† Calvin now, for the first time, called the evangelical "Protestants‡." Some excitement was created by the news which was brought, that many of the reformed wore the red cap, as a mark of distinction. Calvin expressed his dislike to this custom in a letter to the Admiral Coligny.

The affairs of the evangelical church now took another form. Its martyrs had hitherto been for the most part of the humbler classes; but the great men of the kingdom now began to declare themselves its champions, without however entering into formal union. The king of Navarre went to liberate Chandieu, one of the ministers of the church in Paris, with his own hand, from prison. Andelot Coligny took the minister Carmel to his estate in Brittany, and let him publicly preach there. Gaspar Coligny, the admiral, remained, after the taking of St. Quentin, a prisoner in the Netherlands. Calvin wrote to him in the elevated style in which he was accustomed to address the great, and exhorted him to read the Gospel. "You know," he said, "how depraved the world is; take heed then not to involve yourself in things which may pollute you: everything is now permitted except the confession of the true faith. Let us thèn so lay to our hearts the honour of God as not to hesitate to tread all things underfoot, when the extending of his kingdom is concerned, for the grace of the Lord shines infinitely higher than the favour of all mankind." Again: "This letter will show that I entertain a holy care for you, and brings its apology with it." Again exhorting him to give himself wholly to the Lord, he says: "Trust in the word of Christ, and all other things shall be added thereto." Another letter was written the same day addressed to the wife of the admiral, as if that already sent was not sufficiently impressive. Coligny was converted; and never had Calvin had a scholar like this distinguished man, who, still in the prime of

* A thought suggested by Leo's Weltgeschichte, s. 219.

† Ruchat, t. vi. p. 320.

‡ MS. Bern, Sept. 12, 1558. Calv. Farello.

life, became a mighty instrument in the diffusion of the truth. It was not till fourteen years after his conversion that he ended his glorious career*. Calvin again wrote to the Lady Coligny, expressed his sorrow at the captivity of her husband, and reminded her that it was "her duty to help him, by her example, to preserve his resolution." This was a grand period for Calvin: the minister of Geneva was the pastor of all the great men in France.

The ambassadors of the German princes now stood before Henry II.: he answered them graciously, but kept none of his promises. At this very time the members of the evangelical church had assembled in the *Pré des Clercs* at Paris, and were singing psalms in their customary strain of exalted devotion. The king of Navarre and his queen were present; multitudes thronged to the spot, and many climbed the trees in the neighbourhood that they might the better hear the sweet and sacred melody. Henry was in the camp at Amiens. It was told him that an insurrection had broken out. Andelot was accused, and after making a bold confession was thrown into prison. Calvin was ready with his encouraging exhortations. "He must strengthen himself," he said, "against all flattery, and against every fear. He must be as Moses was, who left the Egyptian court to take upon him the reproaches of Christ. We must confess the Lord, or the Lord will not confess us." The prisoner was treated severely. Calvin again addressed him: "God will strengthen you by his Spirit. We must bear the image of Christ, not in death only, but in burial; even though we faint, and lie as it were a long time under the earth.—The companions of Daniel would not pray to the idol; but they committed no crime against their king."

But so grievously was Andelot afflicted, that he once allowed himself to be conducted to hear mass. Calvin thus reproved him:—"The enemies of the truth have celebrated their victory: they have gained a triumph in your person, as they think, over our Lord Jesus Christ, and covered his doctrine with disgrace. Think on the martyrs, in the time of the Maccabees, who died rather than eat the flesh of an unclean animal, because to have done so would have been to testify against their belief. But I will not overwhelm you with sorrow."

The custom of singing psalms in the streets greatly increased in the South, and led to some disturbances. Claude, a minister

* His death took place in 1572.

at Lyons, relates that the faithful went singing through the streets in the evening. The edict of the king, now published, forbad this practice. This impelled a number of excitable minds so much the more to sing their psalms in the night. Claude prayed Calvin to employ his authority for the suppression of such proceedings.

The year 1559 was still more unquiet. A peace was concluded with Spain; and, according to one of the conditions, heresy was to be assailed and rooted out by every means that could be employed. In the month of August it was heard that Paul IV. had breathed his last, and had recommended the Inquisition, as the only sufficient means for the purpose, to employ itself against the Protestants. But just as he was expiring a popular tumult broke out; the palace of the Inquisition was torn down, and the prisoners were set free. The reformed churches of Switzerland were now in the greatest state of agitation: this was especially the case with Bern and Geneva; but they were narrowly watched. Geneva, as the central point of the light, was the most hated of all. It was the time when rich and poor laboured at the fortifications; and when we look at the court of France, and at the death-bed of the pope, it is interesting to turn round and behold the simple, energetic reformer rising from his study-table, spread over with his Commentary and his Institutions, and going forth to encourage by his example the erection of the city-walls. It was at the end of this year that he was admitted to the rights of a burgher*.

The Gospel was now extended throughout France. Beza speaks of a young man in Paris, named Jean Morel, who died with remarkable fortitude. The priests proclaimed aloud, "Death to all Lutherans;" and as soon as any one was so called, the people fell upon him with unbridled fury. Some of those who had been present on the night when the sacrament was administered, and who were still prisoners in Paris, besought consolation from Calvin, and he wrote to them in his usual comforting and animating strain†.

In the midst of these sanguinary persecutions, deputies from all the reformed churches in France secretly assembled in Paris.

* Régistres de 1559, 25 Dec. Many ministers and professors, it is said, having demanded and obtained the right of citizenship, M. Calvin was requested to accept it also; he expressed his thankfulness for the honour, and added, that he had not asked for it before, because he was anxious to avoid giving any colour to the suspicions which some had wickedly suggested, as to his wishing to gain political influence and power in Geneva.

† MS. Gen. Feb. 15, 1559.

The well-known Confession of Faith was drawn up, and, with the rule of discipline, reduced to forty articles: thus was established the unity of the French church. The plan on which this proceeding was founded had been formed after the administration of the Lord's Supper at Poictiers, where many ministers were assembled on the occasion. The first general synod met at Paris on the 26th of May, 1559, and through the influence of the minister Chandieu, the formulary was solemnly set forth in writing on the 28th of the same month. Thus the foundation-stone was laid, and herewith begins the life of the French reformed church*. The rule of discipline established for its guidance realized the theory which Calvin had fully exhibited in his 'Institutions,' but which he could only imperfectly execute at Geneva.

The Paris parliament was also assembled at this time, and employed itself in devising measures for the suppression of heresy. Some of the members spoke of a general council; others proposed to limit the punishment of heretics to banishment; and some desired to know definitely what was meant by heresy; every one being able to perceive clearly the grievous errors of the church itself. The truth conquered; and they would hear no more of the punishment of heretics. But the papists were filled with alarm, and so wrought upon the king, that he resolved to be present himself at one of the meetings of the parliament. The assembly was held in the monastery of the Augustins, the hall in which it usually met being adorned for the celebration of the marriage of Elizabeth, the daughter of the king, with Philip of Spain, and of Margaret, his sister, with the Duke of Savoy. The king entered the assembly accompanied by the Guises and all his courtiers. Every person was to be allowed to speak his sentiments freely; and the members of the council did so without hesitation.

Among these was Anne du Bourg, nephew of the chancellor of France, an excellent jurist, and distinguished for his legal knowledge above all others who attended the meetings of the reformed. Having given God thanks that the king had come to hear the

* This is the Confession which Beza presented to Charles IX. in 1561 at Poissy. It was subscribed in 1571, in a synod at La Rochelle, by Henry IV., the queen his mother, the Prince of Condé, Louis of Nassau, Coligny, Chatillon, and all the ministers. It was printed in Latin in 1566 and 1581. See Salig, ii. p. 273. A shorter confession, in eighteen articles, seen in Calvin's letters, was, as the superscription shows, addressed to Henry II. Ed. Amstel. p. 250.

things which concerned the Lord Jesus Christ, and which princes, before all men, were bound to defend, he spoke with the greatest freedom, as God prompted him, and at last exclaimed, "It is no light thing to condemn those who, in the midst of the flames, confess the name of Jesus Christ*."

The king arose, profoundly agitated, and conferred with his cardinals; then immediately leaving the chamber, he commanded Montgommery, the officer of the guard, to apprehend Du Bourg, with some others. They were thrown into the Bastile. Several of the councillors fled: the rest were obliged to submit. Thus was the parliament, for the first time, dishonoured, and the king swore that he wished with his own eyes to see Du Bourg burnt.

These proceedings took place in the month of June. An edict was published at Ecouen to root out the reformed, and similar orders were sent to all the provinces, with the threat, that if the magistrates were not diligent in the work they should themselves be punished. Du Bellay and Demochares were the judges of Du Bourg. The churches gave themselves to prayer. Their ruin seemed at hand; but the king was destined to fall in the midst of his triumph. It is well known that he was ambitious to shine in a tournament, preparations for which were made in the street St. Antoine, not far from the Bastile, where Du Bourg was confined. The king himself reached the lance to Montgommery: it broke against the breast of the monarch: a fragment flew into his eye and injured the brain. Catherine, moved by a species of presentiment, had entreated him in the morning not to go to the tournament. The circumstance was not forgotten, that he had expressed his desire to see with his own eyes the burning of Du Bourg and the others.

The king died on the 10th of July, and in the house which had been decorated for the nuptials. The festive-hall became his funereal chapel, and was covered with tapestry, which represented the conversion of St. Paul, with the words, "Saul, why persecutest thou me?"

Francis II., a youthful monarch, the husband of Mary Stuart, now ascended the throne. Catherine placed herself between the two parties. Six of the Guises were at the court. Whenever they became too powerful, she allowed the Protestants to gain strength. But the young king survived his accession only seventeen months. Catherine promised to put an end to the perse-

* Calvin gives a lively account of Du Bourg to Blaarer in 1560. Ed. Laus. Ep. 357. Ed. Amstel. p. 191.

cution. She was probably moved to express this determination through the representations of an aged protestant, who recalled to her recollection those better days when she herself was enraptured with the psalms of the Huguenots. Du Bourg had resolutely rejected all offers of deliverance. Calvin took his part in the business. Many of the great men of the kingdom were aroused, as the Duke de Longueville and the Marquis of Rottelin. The church in Paris addressed a petition to Catherine, couched in very strong language, for Du Bourg. Condé, the admiral, and Madame de Roye, exerted their influence with her daily in his behalf. She was once sufficiently excited to say, that the persecutions affected her, and that the reformed, who died with such exemplary fortitude, proved that they were inspired by a more than ordinary wisdom. She added, that she would learn what the doctrine was which could lead people to meet death as joyfully as if they were going to a marriage feast. This was the last indication of any sentiment in favour of the reformed. The Guises had all the power of the government in their hands (1560). Robbery and murder were still practised against the evangelical party. Houses suspected of harbouring them were forcibly entered. Nothing could be sadder than the appearance of the children of the persecuted believers, who wandered about helpless, from place to place, no one daring to shelter them, lest he might himself become exposed to suspicion. Calvin complained to Martyr and Bullinger respecting this sad condition of the church. The priests declared to the people that the reformed held their meetings in the dark, to eat children and commit other abominations. Catherine was informed that they had celebrated the festival of Easter (1560) with these shameful deeds. Induced by the Guises and the Chancellor Olivier, she gave the people of Paris permission to attack all these heretics. The tumultuous persecution which followed continued from August to March. But the reformed never omitted their customary service, and Beza gives a long list of those who died happily in the fire.

Du Bourg was kept a close prisoner in the Bastile: he was treated with every kind of severity, and frequently even put into an iron cage. His trial was suddenly determined upon; the Count-palatine Otto having sent ambassadors to require his presence in Heidelberg. The cardinal commanded that he should be put to death, before the request of the count could be formally made. When the church in Paris learnt that endeavours were being made to induce him to modify his confession, it besought him, by the minister Marlorat, to persevere, since, if he did so, his death would encourage many others to glorify God. He obeyed this counsel, and found means to address the church in an excellent epistle. Courage, wisdom, and a highly cultivated mind, were manifest in his whole conduct. Always free and mighty in spirit, he rejoiced in the Lord, and sang psalms, accompanying himself on a lute. When it was proposed to make an experiment for his liberation, he rejected the offer, and exhibited more and more cheerfulness as his end approached. His sentence was read to him: it purported that he should be burnt alive. "On hearing this," says Calvin, "he knelt down and thanked God that he had deemed him worthy of so great an honour as to allow him to die in the defence of eternal truth." For four hours he looked forward with joyful countenance expecting death. At the place of execution, which was surrounded by four hundred soldiers, he put off his clothes as tranquilly as if he were going to bed. When the executioner fixed the rope about his neck, he remarked that this was not necessary; for that he should be burnt slowly in the fire, according to the usual custom. He was however first strangled, and his body was then burnt to ashes.

The historian Mezeray relates, that the death of this member of the parliament made a greater impression on men's minds than a hundred ministers with their sermons. The fate of Du Bourg was that of many others after him. In order to detect the Lutherans, images of the saints were placed at the corner of the streets, and those who did not bow to them were immediately apprehended. Sometimes money was demanded for wax tapers, and a refusal was followed by committal to prison. The whole country was shaken. The Guises were masters of the government, and the young king and his mother were wholly in their power. Some of the better-disposed men in the kingdom met to consider measures for resisting this ruinous state of affairs; but their conscience was so tender, (a proof that they were led by the spirit of the Gospel,) that they inquired of many jurists and theologians in France and Germany, whether, in such a state of things, it was justifiable to oppose an existing government. It was decided, "That it was lawful to resist, if the princes of the house then reigning placed themselves at the head of the movement, and if the states, or the better part of them, called them thereto."

This decision was the beginning of the French civil and religious wars. Calvin's very strong expression on the subject shows plainly that he was altogether opposed to this drawing of the sword in France, however just the cause might appear. The conspiracy of Amboise now followed. The king was advised to destroy Geneva, as the one source of insurrections. But while all trembled, Calvin remained, according to the testimony of the chancellor Roset, altogether tranquil. This also appears from a letter which he wrote to Blaarer:—"They threaten us, and this city especially, from the notion that it is here that all insurrections have their birth; or they act as if they believed this, in order to have a pretence for abusing us. For almost the whole month our neighbours have supposed we were on the point of sinking. I have never however been able to believe that we had anything really to fear, nor do I believe that we now have; but should the greatest peril arrive, supported by the arm of God, we should await the issue undisturbed." So sharply were the movements of Geneva and Calvin watched, that the very words of the latter were repeated in the king's council*. An assembly of the nobles was called, August 21, 1560, to consider the evil tendency of the present agitation in the state. Calvin acquainted Bullinger with these proceedings†. "Before the discussion commenced, admiral Coligny suddenly rose, and desired of the king and the council that the believers in Normandy should be allowed the free exercise of their worship. He could bring 50,000 signatures to this petition." All present wondered at his boldness; but he was known as a knight without fear and without reproach. The king of Navarre had returned to his own territory. Beza was at present with him, and the queen was gained for the gospel; but no safe conduct could be procured for Beza on his return to Geneva, and Calvin reproached himself for having exposed him to so much danger‡. He had written in June to Sturm and Hottoman§, desiring them to persuade the German princes to address the king of France. "We will do all in our power," he added, "to excite the king of Navarre to demand the reins of government; for it is plain that the kingdom must be ruined by these agitations, this treachery and sloth. The pride of the Guises and their

* MS. Gen. Calv. Sulcero, Sept. 30, 1560.
† Ed. Laus. Ep. 309. Ed. Amstel. p. 143, Oct. 1, 1560.
‡ MS. Gen. Calv. Gallasio, 5 Non. Oct. 1560.
§ MS. Bern, 4 June, 1560.

avarice can no longer be endured. The consent of the queen-mother must be gained by the most earnest representations."

Those who were rightly disposed now anxiously urged the assembling of a general, or at least a national council. The admiral wished that in the meeting thus proposed, a decree might be passed allowing freedom of religion. He promised that this would be followed by the general tranquillity of the country. Guise skilfully overthrew these plans, and referred to the Council of Trent. All things were in disorder; but the church in Paris, wonderfully strengthened, had the boldness to hold its meetings even in the palace of justice; and Capel, one of the ministers present, openly displayed in the council-chamber the confession of the reformed church. It was now that the famous assembly took place at Orleans, where such important measures were to be adopted. The design of annihilating the Huguenots was frustrated by the sudden death of the king. The whole Protestant church had just held in silence a solemn day of penitence. Affairs might still take a prosperous turn. Calvin was opposed to the mention of war, and entertained the hope that everything might be brought to a happy conclusion without the shedding of one drop of blood. King Anton listened attentively to both him and Beza*. "When all trembled before the Guises, the hand of God helped us. The death of the young king must produce great changes†."

Calvin had soon reason to rejoice at the happy alteration in the state of affairs. "God," he says, "who pierced the eye of the father, has struck the ear of the son (Francis II. died of an ulcer in the ear). But many, alas! yield themselves to a foolish delight, as if the world could be changed in a moment; and because I do not sympathize with their folly, they accuse me of sloth. Should however the persecution cease, a wonderful conversion might be looked for in a short time."

Charles IX., only ten years old, was now king. Anton, to whom the regency properly pertained, magnanimously left the government to Catherine: the States said nothing, and the Guises were more prudent than all. Condé remained of his own accord in prison till he could justify himself: Calvin approved of his conduct. In the first assembly of the States, the chancellor L'Hopital delivered a long discourse for the purpose of tranquillizing all parties, and securing their obedience to the

* MS. Eccles. Bern, Calv. Sulcero, Dec. 11, 1561.

† MS. Bern, Calv. Sturmio, Dec. 16, 1560.

young king: he was devoted to the Huguenots. Many were dissatisfied. During these proceedings Pius IV. had made preparations for the opening of the Council of Trent. Monluc, bishop of Valence, jestingly remarked, that they were proposing to extinguish the fires in Paris with the water of the Tiber, instead of using the water of France itself. All the prelates of the kingdom were to assemble on the 20th of January, 1561. The pope was angry, and informed the queen that the sword must be drawn; that Spain and Italy would assist; and that if she did not wish to involve her own subjects in war, she must overthrow Geneva, whence all the evil proceeded*. He gave the same advice to the Duke of Savoy; but they could not agree to whom Geneva should afterwards belong.

The Waldenses were now assailed by a fresh persecution: their indignation was roused, and they seized their weapons†. This was the first example of the religious wars which were so soon to follow. Calvin again expressed his admiration to Coligny, and exhorted him to persevere in his onward course, however few might be found to imitate him‡:—"Be content with this, though the whole world should be blind and unthankful, that God and his angels are for you; and we must indeed satisfy ourselves with knowing, that the heavenly crown cannot be taken from us when we shall have virtuously finished here below the warfare of the Son of God, in whom standeth our eternal life."

The pope invited the German princes to be present at the Council of Trent§. Calvin wished that the king of France would unite with the queen of England, the German princes, and the Swiss, in a protest against the entire council||.

Although the regent soon found cause of dispute with Anton of Navarre, the position of the church daily improved. It was forbidden to employ the word Huguenot as a term of reproach: those who bore the name were to be undisturbed in their houses, and those who had been thrown into prison were to be liberated. The king went to Rheims to be crowned: there the cardinal of Lorraine declared that the Catholic church was on the point of ruin: he expressed his wish to hold an assembly of the clergy in Paris as a preparation for a larger meeting. The edict of July commanded peace, and heresy was to be punished with banish-

* Ruchat, t. vi. p. 371.
† MS. Bern, Calv. Leningo, Mart. 14, 1561.
‡ MS. Gen. Jan. 16, 1561.
§ Ep. 333 and 334 refer to this. Ed. Laus. Ed. Amstel. p. 178.
|| MS. Gen. 24 Sept. 1561.

ment only. The prelates were summoned to meet at Poissy, near St. Germain en Laye, where the court was held. Calvin had looked for this at the beginning of the year, and he hoped that the ministers of the new faith would obtain a safe conduct, so that they might be heard in the assembly, and see whether a union with the Catholic church might not still be possible. The king of Navarre wrote letters with his own hand to Peter Martyr, then at Zurich, and to Beza in Geneva.

Calvin's history becomes more and more intimately connected with that of France: he lived wholly for the church, and the church lived through him. Thus he daily sent out ministers to form new congregations, and he supported it by his consolatory addresses and his counsels: he was the soul of the whole. Owing to this his vast spiritual influence, and the view which the French took of the reformers as political malcontents, Calvin was supposed to exercise great political power, whereas to do so would have been a contradiction of his most fundamental principles. True it is that he was in union with all the great men of the party: even Coligny himself communicated to him his plans, and regarded him as the head of the Reformation.

Scarcely had Charles IX. ascended the throne, when a letter was addressed to the council at Geneva by the king, or rather by Catherine. "His council and the States," it is said, "had declared that all the disturbances in France had been occasioned by the preachers sent into the kingdom from Geneva: he therefore prayed that peace might be restored; that the ministers might be recalled; that no others like them should be sent; that God and the world were witnesses, that the king would be justified in taking vengeance on a city which was undermining his state."

An answer was desired to this epistle: the ministers were called before the council and replied through Calvin:—"They could not deny, that when men applied to them and desired to be admitted to the ministry, they admonished them to fulfil their duty, and to spread the knowledge of salvation as the Lord commanded; but they denied that they were guilty of creating disturbances in the kingdom of France. The Gospel was not preached for such an end, and they had used their utmost efforts to restrain those who had manifested a wish to go to Amboise, and were ready to justify themselves before the king himself if necessary."

This reply of the ministers was communicated to the king as

their defence; but it was added, that the council could not recal those whom it had not itself sent forth. The Catholics had indeed reason to think of these things; for in respect to the influence exerted by Calvin in promoting the diffusion of the new faith, it was estimated that, looking to France alone, there were five million professors of the reformed doctrines.

This intelligence created great delight in foreign countries. A minister named Beaulieu wrote to Farel from Geneva, October 3, 1561:—"I cannot tell you how much grace God is daily bestowing upon our church. There are men here from various places, as from Lyons, Nismes, Gap, and from the districts of Orleans and Poitiers, anxious to obtain labourers for these portions of the new harvest. From Tournon especially was the application made, and that in obedience to the urgent wish of the bishop. There were five hundred parishes in these parts which had discontinued the celebration of the mass, but were still without ministers. The poor people were famishing, but there was no one to furnish them with the bread of heaven. It is extraordinary how many hearers there are of Calvin's lectures: I believe there are more than a thousand daily. Viret is labouring for Nismes. I have heard men say, that if from four to six thousand preachers were sent forth, places would be found for them*."

Beza relates, that Catherine commissioned the admiral (1561, immediately after the conference at Poissy) to number the churches: there were 2150: the members of these petitioned for edifices, and offered their goods and their lives for the use of the state. Shortly after this, the whole of France seemed on the point of becoming Protestant†.

The best commentaries and other works of Calvin were now before the world, and had been placed in the hands of all classes by means of numerous editions: his influence was at the highest point. Peace was looked for in France; the reformed religion was triumphing; the church in Paris flourished; the numerous persons of distinction who belonged to it were anxious to increase its splendour; and Calvin was called to their aid; but the council of Geneva would not part with him. Calvin was not ungrateful, and he willingly remained in the little republic: he assured the Parisian community however of his esteem, and dedicated to it his 'Commentary on Daniel‡.'

* Ruchat, t. vi. p. 435. MS. Gen. Calv. to Bullinger, May 24, 1561.
† Aymon, Syn. t. i. pp. 21, 218.
‡ Ed. Laus. Ep. 308. Ed. Amstel. p. 151.

When the duchess of Ferrara expressed her wish to have a minister from Geneva, the council granted her request, with this exception only, that neither Calvin nor Beza should be sent*. Afterwards, when Beza was in France at the Colloquy of Poissy, Calvin again expressed himself to the purport, that it was vexatious to him to have it supposed that he wished to be called to France†.

To understand the real nature of Calvin's influence in France, we must read the extensive correspondence which he carried on with those who were seeking the Gospel in that country. I have already directed attention, in speaking of his pastoral labours, to the number of affecting letters in which he urges it as a duty on Protestants to leave Catholic France and seek a refuge in Geneva‡. The same sentiments are expressed in several of his letters to entire communities: but now persons of high rank submitted themselves humbly to his counsel, his warnings, and even to the reproofs of the minister, in the same way as the princes of Germany listened to Luther. And with what zeal did he labour for them! To show this the more completely, we must refer to what has been stated in the earlier part of this work, respecting his correspondence with the duchess of Ferrara. When an emissary from the king of France passed through Geneva, on his way to Ferrara, to compel the duchess to return to Catholicism, and there was reason to apprehend her fall, Calvin instantly despatched a messenger, named Colonge, to Ferrara with a letter, which has been preserved, and in which he encourages her to exercise resolution, and says that she ought to receive the messenger, not as coming from him, but from God§.

Some years after he again wrote to her for the purpose of strengthening her faith:—"Meditate carefully on the truth alluded to by Paul, namely, that if a perishable metal must be proved in the fire, much less can faith be spared the trial; but if you feel that you are weaker than you ought to be, turn yourself to Him who has promised that all who trust in Him shall be as the tree planted by the water-side, which, with its living root, shall never perish, whatever the storms which beat upon it. Give not the devil the opportunity of surprising you, and do not allow yourself to imagine, that by recanting you can avoid the conflict. Your fears will give the enemy the victory which he

* Régistres, Juill. 3, 1561. † MS. Bern, Oct. 1562.
‡ A' l'Abbesse de Thouars, &c. &c., 1553, 1554, 1558.
§ MS. Gen. 6 Août, 1554.

so greatly desires: we must be aware of his cunning to overcome it. For the rest, harden yourself, dear lady, against the frowns of the world. If you do good, this is the reward promised us from above."

Now, that is in the year 1560, after the death of her husband, her presence was required in France, to take part in the government. She was compelled to swear fidelity to the Catholics. Calvin appealed to her: "Since you have sinned in this, and offended God, you are not bound to keep this oath. You know that Herod is not praised for having observed the oath which he rashly took; but is known rather to have fallen into twofold condemnation." Calvin dissuaded the queen from taking a part in the government, suggesting that her counsels would not be received, and that it was only intended to make use of her name. He desired her to give herself wholly to the evangelical faith. "Jesus Christ," he says, "is well worth your forgetting, for his sake, France as well as Ferrara."

The duchess followed this counsel. In the persecutions, she devoted herself to the care of the unfortunate fugitives, and the old castle of Montargis, where she dwelt, obtained the name of an Hôtel Dieu. Calvin ceased not to exhort and encourage her with edifying words: "As the wanderer in the evening redoubles his steps, so ought advancing age to admonish you to leave a good witness on earth, as well as to bring one before God and the angels." His latest letters were addressed to her. In one of these he accuses her of too passionate a disposition, which was likely to produce much evil; but he praises her honest and pure confession, which she not only repeated with her lips, but made known by her noble actions, which nothing could surpass. The severity of the reformer is strikingly exhibited in that which he said to her respecting the consistory which she held in her castle, and in the proceedings of which she took part. He earnestly calls upon her to recollect, that as a woman she ought to respect the authority of the consistory, and that she must subject her people to the elders of the church. In conclusion, he sent her a medal which her father, Louis XII., had struck, and on which he was represented on horseback, with the inscription *Destruam Babylonem**. In reference to the question, who belonged to the elect? he compared the death of king Anton with that of the duke of Guise†.

This led to his correspondence with the king of Navarre: here

* MS. Gen. Jan. 8, 1564. † MS. Gen. April 1, 1564.

his words fell upon less fruitful ground; but he did not fail through want of energy, and what the king several times did in behalf of the reformed must be attributed to Calvin's influence*. In the early period of the movement the monarch rendered signal service to the evangelical cause; but he afterwards relapsed. During the persecution in 1558, Calvin exhorted him to do that which God expected of him. "You ought not to be ashamed to bear the reproach of Christ, which is more honourable than all the glory of the world†."

When king Anton, by the sorcery of Catherine, again proved unfaithful, Calvin described his character with great force, and related to Bullinger how severely he and Beza had chastised him in their addresses‡. He had been amused with the promise of Sardinia, and flattered with the expectation thus excited, he had delivered at Rome a declaration against the reformed doctrine. Calvin assailed him with the most indignant expressions: they show how he could deal with kings:—"The enemy has flung this dirt upon you that he might be able to sing a song of triumph at your disgrace. What would it help you, though the whole world were given you, if you had to do homage to the devil? §"

How great the confidence was which the king had formerly placed in Calvin, appears from the fact, that when he was in need of money he applied to the poor minister, whose yearly stipend amounted to only fifty dollars. Calvin obtained the required help, and involved himself thereby in the greatest perplexity, as he afterwards stated to the queen ||.

Things had now proceeded so far, that Calvin some months after wrote to Bullinger, saying, that "there was now nothing to hope from king Anton, for that he had given himself up to dissipation." Catherine had skilfully involved him in amours, and was so successful in her schemes, that he continued permanently her captive. This called forth a letter from Calvin, which, re-

* MS. Gen. Dec. 14, 1557. † MS. Gen. Juin 8, 1558.

‡ MS. Ecc. Bern. Calv. Bull. Mai 24, 1561.

§ MS. Gen. 1562.

|| MS. Gen. Juin 1563. Calvin, in his letter to the queen, states that he obtained the promise of a loan of 40,000 francs for the king; that the latter sent in great haste for 25,000; that he immediately got 10,000 for him, and that when the time came to pay this sum, he knew not on which side to turn himself. "I have never been," he said, "a financier, and I can assure you, that of the little which I had, and which was a mere nothing, I had exhausted the last shilling, even of that which I needed for daily use. But at length, God be praised, the payment was made." He spoke to the queen on the subject, not, he said, to ask for anything which he had given, but for the sake of those who had helped him in the difficulty.

ferring as it did to so delicate a matter, is characteristic of the writer:—"It is reported that you are hindered from doing your duty by some ridiculous love-affair, and that the devil has given you assistants, who seek neither your happiness nor your honour*."

Anton exhibited great repentance before his death, and vowed that if God spared his life he would serve the reformed church with entire devotion. Thus Calvin's words were not altogether useless.

But the correspondence which he had carried on with the queen had proved singularly edifying: he continued to the last to derive joy and consolation from this truly Christian woman: she it was who, in the season of distress which followed the Colloquy at Poissy, and when her husband had relapsed, uttered the well-known words, "If I held my kingdom and my son in my hand, I would rather cast them both into the sea than go to mass." She brought up Henry IV. in her own spirit, and thus Calvin's influence was not wanting in the formation of his character. While there was still any hope of delivering the king, he urged her, by the strongest arguments, to labour unceasingly to that end. The king had chosen an enemy of Calvin, Balduin, as tutor for his natural son. The reformer protested against this step, and even with threats†. When the king however had actually gone over to the Catholic party, Calvin sent Johanna many consolatory letters, as he did also during the religious wars. After the death of the king at Rouen he supported her by his counsel, advising her how to govern her dominions so as to secure the triumph of the truth; a necessary caution, near as she was to the king of Spain, whose dispositions were so little friendly towards her. He advised her to do all things with caution, and to entreat the German princes to further the cause of the Lord with their wonted affection‡.

It is interesting to hear Calvin's judgment on Henry IV., and in contrast therewith his opinion of Charles IX. and the terrible Catherine, who had not yet however wholly thrown off the mask. Of the young king, whose disposition was ruined by his mother, Calvin says§: "The king is only nominally of age; he is almost slavishly subservient to the will of others: were he permitted to think at all for himself, he would not be wholly opposed to us."

* MS. Paris. † MS. Gen. Dec. 24, 1561.
‡ MS. Paris, Jan. 20, 1563.
§ MS. Gen. Calv. Bullingero, 4 Non. Dec. 1563.

Calvin dedicated one of his latest works, the Commentary on the last four books of Moses, to Henry IV., then a boy of ten years*. He had alluded to him some time before, in a letter to La Gaucherie, his tutor, whom he requested to greet the son of the king for him†. The dedication abounds in noble and striking admonitions, as if he had had the boy before his eyes, and could guess the course of his future life. After bestowing distinguished praise upon the mother of Henry, he continues:—"Yours is the duty now to form yourself according to this pattern of all virtues. If you belie the heroic spirit which animates you, you will have so much the less excuse. Nothing can more delight the queen than your advancing in the ways of piety." He reminds him of the examples of Josiah and Hezekiah; warns him against courtiers and flatterers; against scoffers, who pretend that there can be no piety in such tender years; and against pleasure; as if, in short, he saw his future career spread out before him. In conclusion, he wishes for him, as Isaiah for Hezekiah, that the fear of the Lord might be his true treasure.

Let us contrast with this what Calvin said of the treacherous intrigues of Catherine. Although she took great pains to conceal her actual opinions, and pretended to pursue a middle path, her hatred to the Protestants was conspicuous over all. Her cunning had long been apparent to Calvin‡. Peter Martyr, her countryman, formed a similar opinion of her, many as were those whom she had deceived by her speciousness§. Another celebrated personage must also be mentioned, as exercising his influence on those remarkable times. The admonitions which Calvin and Beza could address to the prince of Condé, who sometimes forgot himself, like Anton, in the pleasures of the court, show the noble character of their apostolic earnestness‖:—"As soon as the world hears that you devote yourself to the love of women, your dignity and your fame will sink; the good will grieve, the wicked will laugh. Distractions exist there which cannot but hinder you in the fulfilment of your duty. Worldly vanity will necessarily exercise its power, and you must watch narrowly, or the light which God has given you will be extinguished. We hope, gracious sir, that this warning will be acceptable to you, when you consider how useful and necessary it is."

* Bern, 1553. The dedication was dated July 31, 1563.

† MS. Bern, Mai 26, 1559.

‡ MS. Tigur. Calv. Blaurero, 1561.

§ Ed. Laus. Ep. 288. Ed. Amst. p. 139.

‖ MS. Paris, Sept. 13, 1563.

We have not sufficient space to speak of the other great characters of the period; but we may briefly mention the duchess of Longueville, countess of Neuchatel, who came to Geneva, commended by Farel, to converse with Calvin on religious subjects*. On another occasion she hastened out of France with her son to Neuchatel, and prayed Calvin to attend a synod there, but which request the reformer could not fulfil: he frequently corresponded with her, and in speaking of her to others, praised her firmness and her faith. This was particularly the case in his letter to the marchioness de Rottelin.

We may also briefly mention the sieur de Soubize, whom Calvin advised as to his conduct in the case of some miserable man, who is described as having fallen from the faith†. He wrote to him on another occasion, urging in strong language the duty of laying aside weapons taken up against the commandment of the king.

Such was Calvin's reputation in the last period of his career, that all who stood high in the reformed party desired to have letters from him: these letters were themselves regarded as a great distinction.

From this summit of his influence and greatness, won by the energy of his spirit, we look back with pleasure to the commencement of his course; to his childhood; to God's way with him; to the time when, as a boy twelve years old, he went to Paris with the children of the Mommor family, and there, even at school, became the sedate censor of his companions. We follow him afterwards to the university, where he timidly kept himself retired, because from nature he was fond of quiet and solitude; while all, on the other hand, who had a taste for pure learning, came to him, a raw recruit, as he expresses it, for instruction; so that his solitary retreat was converted into a public school. And now we hear him praising with a loud voice the goodness of God, who, as he led David from the sheep-folds, and made him king of Israel, had also exalted him, so little at the beginning, to the high office of a herald and minister of the Gospel. "That which is to be great," said Mathesius of Luther, "must first be little."

The review which we have taken of Calvin's important correspondence with France will enable us the better to understand the influence which he exercised in the following events.

* Kirchhofer, t. ii. s. 149, 159.

† *D'un misérable, homme de rien* · perhaps king Anton.

CHAPTER XII.

BEZA AT THE COLLOQUY OF POISSY, 1561.—HIS ACCOUNT TO CALVIN.—OCCURRENCES SEPTEMBER 9, 1561.—THE REFORMED CHURCH RECOGNIZED BY THE EDICT OF JANUARY 1562.

We now enter upon the last period of Calvin's active career. The Colloquy at Poissy was, for the Reformed church, what the Diet of Augsburg was for the Lutheran; and Beza did in the one place what Melancthon did in the other. The former was sent by Calvin because "he could tread lighter than he could himself." To act, according to the meaning of this expression, was no more given to Calvin than to Luther, and they were both sensible of this point in their character. It is interesting to behold Luther at the period here referred to. We find him in the fortress of Ehrenburg, in Coburg. Guy Dietrich, who afterwards became intimate with Calvin, was witness of his faith, firm as a rock, and wrote to Melancthon:—"Dear Mr. Philip, I cannot sufficiently admire his noble fortitude, his joy, his faith and hope, in these lamentable times. Not a day passes in which he does not devote at least three hours to prayer, as most profitable to study. I was once so happy as to hear him pray. Help me God! what a spirit, what a faith, was in his words! . . . . 'I know that Thou art our dear Father, therefore am I assured that Thou wilt destroy the persecutors of thy children. But if Thou do it not, the danger is thine, as well as ours: the whole affair is thine. What we have done, we were obliged to do; therefore, dear Father, defend it!' When I heard him thus pray with a loud, clear voice, my heart burnt within me for great joy. Therefore doubt I not but that his prayer will afford mighty help in this, as men think, our ruined state."

Calvin, who bore, as Beza says, all the churches in his heart, exhibited a similar child-like trust during those perilous times of which we are speaking. The affair which was now in agitation was at first regarded as hopeless; but Calvin, in his preface to Daniel, exclaimed, addressing those who were engaged in the struggle, "That stone which has crushed the idolatrous kingdom to dust was not formed by the hands of man, and it is now grown to a great mountain. I warn you to be peaceable in the midst of the thunder of those threats by which you are assailed, till the vain tempest-cloud shall be dispersed by power from above, and disappear."

Beza states that Calvin not only employed himself in his own retirement at home in praying for the church, but aroused the people, by his sermons, to be diligent in supplicating God in this great necessity. The syndic, according to his advice, issued a public notice, in which the people were called upon to humble themselves, and earnestly seek the house of God. The season in which the Colloquy at Poissy occurred was marked by far greater troubles than those which distinguished the period of the German Diet. All depended upon a day. Luther was so happy as not to live to witness the religious war; but Calvin had to deal in France with the worst characters known to history. By the instrumentality of the Guises, and Catherine, the church was driven from its apostolic path, and assumed a warlike character, whereby it acquired a more definite position, till at length Henry IV. secured to the reformed a political existence. It was not till some time after that the church returned, according to Calvin's wish, into the path which it had left. Never however did it, of itself, give occasion to the civil wars in France. We may trace the whole of its subsequent trials to the events of which we have now to speak.

Catherine, after frequently flattering the Protestants, had issued the edict of St. Germain, which authorized the renewal of the persecutions. The admiral Coligny now came forward, and insisted that king Anton should take the place of Catherine as regent: this induced the latter to seek a reconciliation of the two parties, in order the better to secure for herself the support of both. The heads of the Protestant church rightly looked for much from these proceedings. It was now allowed them openly to proclaim the truth; and they were convinced, that if the gospel were but freely preached, and especially by such able men as Beza, or Calvin, they would obtain the victory. The king of Navarre, moreover, had allowed himself to be convinced by Balduin, that he might gain a great name were a union of parties once accomplished*.

The hopes of all were excited by the summoning of the prelates to Poissy. The heads of the Protestant party, anxious to see Calvin there, had written to him on the subject. He and Beza acquainted the council with the application, and prayed that the latter might be allowed to go to Zurich, to ask Peter Martyr of

* Schlosser, Leben Beza's, s. 98. Ruchat, t. vi. p. 407.

that canton for the important affair. He had received an invitation from France, and was ready to travel to the French court. The council would not suffer Calvin to join these two distinguished men in the journey unless hostages of the highest rank were given for his security: his colleague however was prepared to set off for Zurich and France. Zurich gave a friendly assent to the application made respecting Martyr, and France now invited both him and Beza in all proper form.

Beza gave good proof of his prudence in first consulting Bullinger on the manner in which he ought to express himself at Poissy. Bullinger had shown great indignation on account of the language used at Worms. Beza at length set out; and Calvin undertook to perform all his duties, in addition to his own, during his absence. This was a fresh instance of his activity, advanced now as he was in years, and oppressed by weakness *.

The opening of the celebrated assembly had been fixed for August 10th, 1561; it took place on the 9th of September. The states (*états généraux*) of the kingdom were assembled at the same time at Pontoise: it was there proposed that the queen-mother should resign the regency, but she skilfully avoided the danger. In an address to the king, the speaker said, that it was the duty of his majesty to follow the example of king Josiah, to read the Scriptures, to reform his kingdom, and allow the assemblies of the evangelical. The prelates met to prepare for the Colloquy, and the ministers of the reformed church arrived at the same time at Poissy; Marlorat, St. Pol, Merlin, Malot, Des Gallars, and Spina: Beza and Martyr arrived later. They were conveyed, for their security, to St. Germain en Laye, in the neighbourhood of the castle. Those who first arrived presented a petition to the king on the 17th of August. In this address they besought him to make their confession of faith known to his bishops, that they might learn their objections thereto; but they protested against the bishops being made their judges. They desired that he himself, his mother, the king of Navarre, and God's own word, should alone decide the cause. This petition they presented with their own hands to the king, who received it friendly. Beza reached St. Germain, and without any safe conduct, August 23, and Martyr still later.

* Among others, we may refer to the letter written August 27, 1561, MS. Gen. Speaking of the death of Varrenus, he says, "He is happy, I am miserable. We are unequal, in such paucity, to our burden." Some of the absent ministers had to be recalled; even Colonge from the duchess of Ferrara.

Beza now stood wholly exposed as a prey to the humours of the French court, and Catherine. But that court beheld in him a man of great accomplishments, of noble, elegant exterior; a Frenchman; mighty in speech; faithful; endowed with presence of mind, and ready at any moment to sacrifice his life for the Gospel. He first appeared before the regent one evening in the apartment of the king of Navarre, with many great personages: she had the courtesy to ask immediately after Calvin's health; and the conversation was carried on till far into the night*.

Amidst all the tumult of parties, the public preaching of the word was not interrupted. Sermons were delivered both in the castle of St. Germain and in other places, before large assemblies of the nobility. The freedom thus enjoyed was even increased by the arrival of the queen of Navarre. Beza received a short letter from Calvin, in which the latter warns him against allowing the Lotharingian to make him too secure, and adds jestingly, "I warn you that I am also a brother of the cardinal of Ferrara; for when he once embraced me here, thirteen years ago, he promised always to entertain for me the most brotherly affection: take care, therefore, not to oppose yourself too proudly to me, for I could return like with like." He desired that Des Gallars might be sent back to him as soon as possible.

As on the 8th of September the clergy had received no answer to their address presented on the 17th of August, they again applied to the king, and requested information to be given them in writing. Their petition was read in the presence of the whole court: the queen let them know that they must be content with her verbal assurance, that the bishops would not be their judges. Immediately after this, twelve Parisian priests, Sorbonnists, entered, and besought the queen not to allow heretics, who refused to recognize the bishops as judges, to dispute with them, which would occasion great scandal. They were answered, that it had been determined that the reformed should be heard. A royal secretary was directed to prepare the protocol: the Sorbonne protested against it.

Beza was permitted daily to proclaim the word of God before the king of Navarre; and so affected him, that he led him to mistrust the jurist Balduin, who had been invited to prepare the way for a union, and brought with him from Germany a double-meaning

* Beza gave an account of his interview and proceedings to Calvin, August 25, 1561. See also his Hist. Eccles. p. 494, and Ed. Laus. Ep. 309. Ed. Amst. p. 154.

treatise by Cassander, on the subject of religious communion. Beza was profoundly moved before the opening of the assembly. In a letter to Calvin* he says, "We in the meantime pray to God without ceasing, and are confident that the prayers of those at a distance will not be without fruit. If our friend Martyr hasten hither, his arrival will greatly strengthen our souls. We shall have to do with old sophists; and although we depend on this that the simple truth of the word will conquer, it is not for every one to solve their subtle falsehoods, and to meet their quotations from the fathers with others. When I consider these difficulties, I am full of anguish, and greatly lament the sin of which we are guilty, in tempting the goodness of God, by leaving the most excellent of his instruments unemployed. We have resolved however not to retreat a step, and we commit ourselves to Him whom the world cannot overcome. Lastly, dear brother, as you are unable to aid us by your presence, guide us like children by your counsel, and in all other ways, though from a distance. That we are nothing better than children, I see and feel daily; and I would that our Lord would glorify the praise of his wondrous wisdom by your mouth."

The next day, September 9, which was appointed for the conference, the assembly met about noon in the great refectory of the nunnery at Poissy. The king, only just twelve years old, sat upon a throne: on his right hand were his brother the duke of Orleans and the king of Navarre; on his left, the queen-mother and the queen of Navarre; and behind him numerous princes and nobles. On each side of the hall were three cardinals. Before them sat thirty-six bishops and archbishops; and behind these a crowd of doctors and clergymen of all ranks. Silence having been commanded, the king delivered a short address on the object of the assembly, and the means to be employed for restoring the peace of the kingdom. The chancellor then spoke: he stated that the nation stood exposed to ruin through the prevalence of religious discord; and he admonished the meeting, that if, perchance, corruptions had been introduced into the church, by avarice or sloth, they ought to oppose them with the whole weight of their authority; while the other party must rest assured, that it should no longer be said, that they were condemned unheard.

The ministers of the reformed church now approached, con-

* Ed. Laus. Ep. 310. Ed. Amst. p. 157. Beza Calvino, Aug. 30, 1561.

ducted by Francis Guise; they were twelve in number, and were habited in their usual simple style. Twenty-two deputies of the various congregations accompanied them; and the whole party now stood bareheaded, before the court. Beza, addressing himself to the king, began:—"The help of God is necessary to success, whatever be the undertaking:" saying this, he immediately knelt down and prayed. He commenced with a simple confession of sin, which to the present day serves as the introduction to every service in the reformed church. This being repeated, he said, "May the Lord render this important day profitable to his own honour, and to the salvation of France, and of all Christendom!" He then rose, and turning to the king, delivered a long discourse, in which he first endeavoured to confute the accusations brought against the reformed, and especially the error of the bishops, who sought to make it appear that the ministers of the new faith were anxious to set aside the higher offices of the Catholic church. "Do not believe," he said, "that in our poor estate we wish to liken ourselves to you; for rather do we desire to build the walls of Jerusalem, and to establish the spiritual Temple." He next showed, that, in the main doctrines, the reformed agreed with the Catholics; and then passing to the controverted points, he carefully enumerated them.

Beza was heard with profound attention. But when he began to touch upon the sacrament of the Lord's Supper, and yielding himself to the zeal imparted to him by the Zurichers, let fall the words, 'that the body of Christ is truly given us, but that, as to place, it is as far from the bread as heaven is from earth,' a sudden uproar arose among the cardinals and the bishops. Some seized upon the opportunity to exclaim, "He has blasphemed." Others stood up, and prepared to depart, without taking any notice of the presence of the king. The cardinal Tournon now rose, and prayed the king to command Beza to be silent, or to permit him and his party to withdraw; but neither was allowed. Beza then addressed the prelates, and said, "My lords, I beseech you to hear the end, which will content you:" and continuing his speech, he confuted the accusations brought by those who pretended that the reformed were engaged in exciting the people to rebellion. Having ended his argument, he again knelt down with all his companions, and presented to the king a copy of the confession of the reformed church*.

The cardinal Tournon now spoke: he prayed the king not to believe anything which had just been said, but to remain true to

* Hist. Eccles. p. 520.

the religion of his forefathers; he also desired that a day might be appointed, when he might answer Beza at length. The day after the conference, Beza apologized in writing for the rough expressions which he had used in regard to the sacrament of the Lord's Supper. It is easy to see however that the bishops only sought a pretence for breaking up the meeting. It is no less easy to discover, how deeply infected the queen and her courtiers were with error, and how far from conversion, when so noble a testimony to the faith could make no impression on their hearts. Sometimes indeed there was an appearance of assent, but they were employed solely in political intrigues.

In the meantime a letter arrived from Calvin: it affords evidence of his penetrating understanding, and speaks clearly of the issue of the conference. He had heard that a snare had been laid for the brethren; and that they had been required to subscribe the Augsburg Confession, in order to separate them from the Swiss*. "Let the others," he says, "think what they please, I am convinced that nothing good is intended, whatever they may promise. Believe me, the bishops will never allow it to come to an earnest disputation. They who are at the helm will rather be driven to extremities than be compelled to order: if it were left to them to prescribe conditions, they would probably engage in a little agreeable skirmish; but now they find that they must submit to certain laws, they will openly reject the proposal of a discussion. But if they pretend to arm themselves for the conflict, you have Peter Martyr, who, according to my reckoning, will have reached you at the right time. Although I have begged you so much not to speak of me, you cease not to oppose my wish: this in my judgment is not good. I have designedly barred the door against myself in my preface to Daniel. Not that this labour undertaken by you would be contrary to my inclinations, or that I should shrink from danger, but because I think that my presence is not required, where there are so many well-instructed and able persons. And certainly all, you and Merlin excepted, are sufficiently impetuous. The Augsburg Confession is, as you know, the torch of the Fury, who wishes to kindle a fire which would consume all France. But we must understand with what design this confession is pressed upon us: its lukewarmness has always been displeasing to the ardent: it was unsatisfactory to its author, and was chiefly intended for popular use;—not to mention, that its brevity has given rise to some obscurities, and

* Calvin to Beza, Sept. 10, 1561. Ed. Laus. Ep. 313. Ed. Amstel. p. 156.

that there are even deficiencies by which the truth appears mutilated. It would, moreover, be contrary to sense, to reject the French confession and adopt this. What materials for strife should we not thereby prepare for the future! since the greater part of the multitude will rarely give up a confession already received. I deny therefore that the cardinal and his creatures can have any honourable intentions, if they pretend to accept this confession; but they lay traps for you, hoping that thereby the present conference may be stopped, and all things thrown into confusion. I suspect, and indeed almost firmly believe, that a book was printed by Balduin, at Basel, for this purpose."

When Calvin however heard of the great day, he, like all others, was wonderfully inspirited, and exclaimed, "O happiest of all days, on which that freedom has been given to the church, which could not indeed fail to be given her, but which it has cost so much labour to win!" "Your speech," he says to Beza, "is here: God wonderfully guided both your spirit and your tongue. The word, which so greatly excited the wrath of the holy fathers, could not have been left unspoken, unless you had been willing shamefully to conceal the truth, and to expose yourself to the insults of these people, who, greatly to my wonder, made so much noise about this thing only, whereas they were struck no less heavily by other passages in your speech. It is ridiculous for them to pretend that the conference was broken up through your stumbling on this expression. They would have found out a hundred other causes of offence, though they now fasten so angrily on this one especially, as if they wished it to be believed that they were ready to subscribe to all the rest of our doctrine: we have therefore reason to rejoice that things have thus happened. I am anxious to see how the cardinal will contrive to repair his rags. If they have thus made an end, as I suspect they have, of the skirmish before the battle, they will never come, I believe, to a real fight. Although I have warned you not to be too hasty in requiring your dismissal, yet the legate, I must tell you, will be doing me a very acceptable service by allowing you a speedy departure."

The Catholic theologians had in the meantime assembled among themselves. The cardinal of Lorraine opened the meeting with these words: "Would that we had all been dumb or deaf!" It was resolved that the cardinal, aided by Claude d'Espence, should write a speech, the two main points of which should respect the church, and the sacrament of the Lord's Supper. It was also determined that they should draw up a counter-confession, which the reformed should be called upon to subscribe, and that if they refused, they should be condemned, and the conference broken up. The reformed, on being made acquainted with this proceeding, applied to the king, and the chancellor acknowledging the weight of their objections, the plan was frustrated.

On the 6th of September the second meeting was held. The cardinal, who had d'Espence at his back, delivered the speech which had been prepared, and which concluded with the words, "If the Protestants adhere to their belief, that Christ is in heaven only, and not on earth, then I confess that I am as far from their opinion as heaven is from earth." As soon as he had ended, Tournon rose to depart; but Beza said, and in the name of the ministers with him, to the king, "that he was ready immediately to answer the cardinal; and that if they would not hear him then, he desired them to appoint a day, on which the subject might be treated according to the Holy Scriptures." The bishops also turned to the king; and the latter informed the ministers, by the captain of the guard, that a time should be appointed for hearing them.

Beza and his companions were anxious to be heard immediately on the following day; but it was not till after a week that they obtained their wish. A third meeting was appointed for the 24th of September; it took place in a small apartment, in the presence of the queen-mother and the queen of Navarre. The princes, the council, five cardinals, with sixteen doctors and bishops, were also present. The Protestant church was to be represented by the ministers; among these was Peter Martyr, who had arrived three days before.

In this conference Beza spoke of the doctrine of the church, and occupied, as he states, an hour and a half in his speech: all heard him with the greatest attention, and he hoped that much good might follow his address. The cardinal, and a monk, De Xantes, answered him with the utmost vehemence; but the former passed suddenly to the doctrine of the sacrament: "See," he said, drawing a paper from his pocket, "what I have lately received from Germany: it is signed by forty-two ministers." This was the Würtemberg Confession, of the year 1559, and in which it was said, that the communicants receive the body of Christ truly, actually, and sacramentally. But the doctrine of transubstantiation was rejected. The passage in which this was stated, the cardinal omitted to read, but immediately demanded of the ministers whether they were willing to subscribe this document. "d'Espence," says Beza, "thought that we should not shrink from the word 'actually,' if the witness of a great man was cited to us: he therefore quoted three passages out of your own work against Hesshus. I interrupted him by observing, that I recognized the words of my teacher; but when I was preparing to answer, the purple autocrat would not allow me. I offered to prove to the queen not only the article on this point, but our whole confession; and I concluded by asking the cardinal, whether he would himself subscribe what he proposed to us. Caught in this net, he began to seek some subterfuge."

It was the object of the cardinal, as Calvin had shown, to perplex the reformed. By refusing to subscribe the Lutheran confession, they would become hated in Germany; while, by subscribing it, they would render themselves obnoxious to the Swiss. The design of the cardinal to break up the conference was obvious; and Calvin declared himself, from this time, opposed to the Augsburg Confession. It would have been inconsistent, he said to the king of Navarre, to receive this, and reject that to which they had solemnly pledged themselves. "If they had not so glorious a subscription as the blood of martyrs, yet was their confession drawn from the pure word of God, and had been already presented to the king*."

We return to the proceedings of the Colloquy. On the 26th of September the ministers presented a writing to the queen, in which they complained that they had been attacked, in the preceding conference, on their ministerial calling; that an effort had been made to induce them to sign a confession; whereas they were not there for themselves alone, but had the eyes of a million Protestants upon them and the conference: they desired a well-regulated discussion. Beza was answered by the cardinal, who exhibited no slight degree of warmth and excitement, that the Catholics had a right to complain of those who had forced themselves into their churches without a call; that the reformed did not desire peace, for that they were seeking to overthrow the two main supports of the kingdom of France, that is, the ecclesiastical and the royal authority; and he described them as enemies, who ought to be instantly carried before the magistrate.

Beza replied, that "If the Catholic party would first subscribe

* MS. Paris, 1561, au Roy de Navarre.

the Augsburg Confession, all might still be well." The doctrine of the Lord's Supper was now again brought forward. Peter Martyr spoke learnedly, in Italian, on the whole subject, and compelled all to enter into the very heart of the question. The queen-mother listened with attention; but the cardinal interrupted the speaker with the remark, "That he wished to have to do with those only who understood his language."

The Spaniard Laynez, the general of the Jesuits, now rose: he spoke for an hour; heaped abuse upon the Protestants; called their ministers "apes and foxes;" and asserted that they had submitted themselves to the Council of Trent. Beza answered him as he deserved, exposed him to ridicule, and continued the discussion with d'Espence.

But this conference proved fruitless. After much contention, Beza relates, night came on: all prepared to depart. The queen then called Beza and the cardinal into the midst of the assembly, and adjured them, in the name of God, to seek peace. All present rushed tumultuously around them: the strife was renewed: a confused murmur arose, and the increasing night alone put an end to the uproar. Overpowered with weariness, Beza, before retiring to rest, wrote to Calvin: "Here everything is disagreeable to me, compared with my very dear Geneva, the thought of which alone revives me."

The queen-mother now resolved that Monluc, a moderate catholic, d'Espence, and three others, should confer with Beza and Martyr, Des Gallars, Marlorat and L'Espine, respecting an agreement on the subject of the sacrament. In a second conference, held September 29, after these five had employed three days on each side in deliberation, a formulary was prepared which created general satisfaction*. All now believed, that as there was an agreement on the main point, every difficulty was removed. The queen ordered Monluc and Beza to be called into her presence; she expressed to them her entire approval. The cardinal, who also came, declared that he had never believed otherwise than what was now stated, and that the convention itself would doubtless be content with what had been done.

But the contrary to what was expected happened. When the formulary was presented to the whole assembly, though approved by many, it was rejected, after a debate of six days, on the 9th of October, by a majority of voices, as heretical. The cardinal was severely censured for his conduct: a counter-statement was

* See Schlosser, Leben Beza's, p. 142.

to be drawn up, showing the insufficiency and the defective character of the confession. The doctors and prelates declared that, if the reformed should refuse to subscribe the articles of belief, which it was now proposed to lay before them, they would separate from them for ever, and they must be banished as heretics from the kingdom. But notwithstanding this threat, a triumph was hereby prepared for the evangelical church. Calvin, oppressed with sickness, again cherished the hope that their affairs would prosper nobly.

"I can scarcely describe to you," he says, in a letter to Beza*, "how happy your letters make me; they place me in the midst of your proceedings: although our circumstances are not on all sides prosperous, we have more occasion for joy than for discontent and anger. Praised be our God, again and again, who intends to exalt us, as it seems, above the clouds, that we may embrace the feet of the victorious Christ, and look down triumphant from above upon our enemies, his as well as ours. I can give you nothing for thanks, unless you would be satisfied with brass instead of gold. That you may know however that while you are contending on the battle-field, in the sweat of your brow, and with all earnestness, I am here, in the shade, carrying on an easy conflict, I send you my answer to Balduin's libel. Be cautious not to object to anything therein, lest I should say that you belong to the faction which it will most displease."

Soon after this his hopes again declined, and in the same melancholy state of his health he wrote to Beza†: "I should have committed the task of writing to you to another, had I not feared that your distress and apprehensions might have been thereby increased. I should not be sorry to see the Colloquy broken up by our opponents under any circumstances: events are far from being sufficiently ripe to encourage the hope that pure religion can flourish with the consent of these men. To have been contented with only a part of what we asked, would have been nothing else than to interrupt the free course of truth. I could wish that in the present matter (the breaking-up of the Colloquy) you were ready to yield."

Now followed an intrigue with the German theologians, whom the cardinal had summoned with the design of increasing the confusion‡. Balduin appeared with the work written by Cas-

* Ed. Laus. Ep. 317. Ed. Amstel. p. 159, Oct. 7, 1561, to Beza.
† Ed. Laus. Ep. 323. Ed. Amstel. p. 162, Oct. 15, 1561.
‡ Beza, Hist. Eccles. p. 612–644.

sander, but too late to obtain applause, and already answered by Calvin. Jacob Andreä and his companions had an audience: they wished to compel a subscription to the Augsburg Confession, and, not succeeding, returned discontented home. The regent indeed said to the Tübingen theologians at their departure, that she was heartily attached to the Confession of Augsburg; but these words availed nothing. On the 13th of October the prelates retired from Poissy, but first made the king certain grants, so that it was commonly reported, that the convention had only been assembled in order to frighten the church, and to drag money from her*.

Such was the end of the celebrated Colloquy, which, through the sin of the clergy and of the queen, who were only anxious to avail themselves of the assistance of each party to oppress them both, remained apparently without result. But it was followed in reality by the most important consequences. The Protestants were now, for the first time, openly recognized, and their cause at once acquired unheard-of success. No one can justly accuse Calvin or Beza of extravagance in the views which they advocated at the Colloquy: they were in no wise enemies to episcopacy, and had never desired its abolition. Beza declared this distinctly in his first speech. But the cardinal of Lorraine had from twelve to fifteen benefices, bishoprics and archbishoprics; and was accused at the same time of corrupting all the fairest women at the court. How could men of this kind be made contented with one bishopric, one woman, and the severe Calvinistic moral code?

Beza was anxious, when Martyr left, to return to Geneva. On taking leave of the queen-mother, she said to him, "You are a Frenchman: we would fain avail ourselves of your aid to try whether we may not quiet the agitation of the kingdom." This compelled him to remain. The reformed began to preach publicly in all parts of the country; they even possessed themselves of some of the churches in various places, and experienced little resistance. Calvin was displeased at this, and expressed himself against it to Farel and Beza. When the command of the king was issued directing the immediate surrender of the churches, the reformed obeyed at once the direction of their ministers. Pastors were called for on all sides: the queen of Navarre desired to have three sent her. Calvin now exhorted Beza to remain in France for the sake of establishing the church.

* Beza, p. 665.

"You must remain," he wrote to him, "unless we would betray our own cause, and let the church, exposed now to the greatest danger, be altogether ruined." The prince of Condé, the queen of Navarre, and the admiral Coligny, addressed the council of Geneva that they might retain Beza in France: he was working beneficially on both parties.

It was at this time that the pope desired Philip of Spain to gain over Anton of Navarre for the Catholics. The Spaniards had deprived him of his territories, and it was proposed to him to separate from his present queen and marry Mary of Scotland. If he accepted this proposal, he was to be put in possession of Sardinia. He agreed to what was desired and rejoined the Catholics: the latter were therefore as little sincere in their wish for union as they had formerly been at Worms. Catherine however sent a plan of reformation to Rome, and the convention was dissolved. The so-called triumvirate, consisting of the duke of Guise, Montmorenci, and St. André, had now been formed. Catherine wished to employ the force of the evangelical party against this alliance, and she desired the admiral to give her the number of the reformed churches: she even inquired what number of troops they could bring her; and hence the Protestants in France were converted into a political party. Legitimate authority was employed in giving it this character. The queen ordered a manifesto to be read in all the churches; it stated, "That she was ready to employ the assistance of the Protestants against the foreigners, who, under the pretence of religion, were prepared to invade the kingdom." All the objections urged against the reformed fell to the ground when this was said.

Beza employed his time in Paris in labouring to spread the pure doctrine: he himself speaks forcibly in his letters to Calvin of his preaching in the Faubourg St. Antoine, and afterwards in the Medards-Kirche, and of the tumult and conflict there, when the priests rang all the bells to drown the voice of the preacher in the church-yard, and how thereupon the church was stormed. The reformers now preached for the first time under the protection of the magistrates, and they led ten priests bound through the streets of Paris. At length the edict of January 1562 was granted: by this the regent, as the rightful authority, secured to the evangelical church the free exercise of religion. The edict was published on the 6th of March. It was for Beza to manage the whole affair: his situation was one of great perplexity: Calvin constantly exhorted him to remain*; but the people of Geneva feared to lose him for ever†.

Preparations were made in February 1562 for another Colloquy. The regent thought that if she could bring the two parties to an agreement on the subject of images, all the rest might soon be arranged. A conference was accordingly held between the Sorbonnists and the Reformed in the great hall of the palace at St. Germain, and in the presence of the court. The first subject of discussion was the worship of images: this Beza treated with his customary skill. The Catholic bishops delivered their judgment on the other side: it was marked by moderation. The image of the Trinity was forbidden, and all superstitious observances were rejected; but Beza would yield nothing on this point. No dispute was to take place on this occasion respecting the sacrament. Calvin objected to Beza, that in his discussions with the Catholics, he depended too much on the testimony of the fathers.

Beza answered the Sorbonnists in a very eloquent treatise, which he presented to the regent upon his knees; and prayed her to remove images from the churches, particularizing those of the Trinity and of the Virgin, and those which were placed by the way-side, with the crucifixes, before which the people were accustomed to prostrate themselves. As the general of the Jesuits spoke much in allusion to the Council of Trent, the reformed declared, in an epistle to Catherine, that they themselves heartily desired a christian, a free, general council; one at which the churches of England, Scotland, Germany, Denmark, Poland, Sweden, and Switzerland, might be represented; protesting only against a repetition of the Council of Constance, and the appointment of the pope as judge of its proceedings, instead of submitting the whole to the rule of God's word. It seems that Calvin's opinion had been asked respecting the conditions of such a council. The ministers proposed it at the end of the meeting at St. Germain.

* Ed. Laus. Ep. 330. Ed. Amst. p. 165. He told him that he must on no account forsake his post, as long as he was permitted to remain, unless he was sure of leaving behind him some faithful successor. "If you suffer violence," he added, "you must bear it with patience. He who is compelled to depart does not forsake his post. If by the will or the permission of the church you are removed, there is nothing to say against it."

† MS. Gen. Calv. Bezæ, 19th Nov. 1561. The senate, Calvin says, was full of anxiety about him. Also, Jan. 1562, MS. Gen.:—The brethren were wonderfully rejoiced, he says, at receiving letters from him. Of himself he says, "I feel deprived of I know not what, while you are absent."

The reformed faith was, in the meanwhile, wonderfully successful: Calvin had the delight to see the Gospel established on a firm foundation*. The edict of January was the first victory of the evangelical church in France†: it was there declared, "That the king, by the edict of July, had strictly forbidden the holding of any assembly; but that this had not been observed: that he now therefore commanded the reformed immediately to vacate the churches which they had taken; to refrain from throwing down any cross or picture; to hold no meetings in any town; but it was added, they might, without being punished, assemble outside the towns for the purpose of religious worship: those who interfered with them in such cases should be severely punished: consistories and synods might also be held with the knowledge, and in the presence, of the proper authorities." Calvin remarked on this, that if the points here stated were properly observed, the papacy was overthrown‡; and this was also felt to be the case by the opposite party. The progress of the Reformation in France thus far resembled its course in Germany. The confession drawn up at Augsburg wrought with a distinct and quickening force; but it could not prevent the religious conflicts of after-years.

We have some interesting information respecting a conference which took place at this time, and which was held for the purpose of putting a blind before the eyes of the German princes. In the winter of the year 1562, we see the pious duke Christopher, with Brentius, Andreä, and other Lutheran theologians, setting off for Zabern in Alsace. Francis de Guise, and his brothers, the cardinal and the grand-prior, met them there. The cardinal appeared with a pious, benevolent countenance before the Germans: he wished it to be thought that he was a good Lutheran, and that he would willingly have signed the Augsburg Confession at Poissy. We have seen however that when Beza asked him to do so, he refused: now he declared that, as he valued his soul's salvation, he agreed with them. This took place on the 17th of February: but when it was believed that the princes had been lulled to sleep, an infamous and sanguinary scene was enacted on their return, at Vassy. The landgrave Philip wrote on the occasion to his deeply-afflicted cousin, saying, "It had often occurred that pious people were betrayed, but God would still find a way for the exposure of the Guises." This leads us to a review of the religious wars.

* MS. Bern. † Beza, p. 674. ‡ MS. Bern, Calv. Sturmio, 25 Mart. 1562.

CHAPTER XIII.

FIRST RELIGIOUS WAR.—THE PEACE.—1562–1563.

While the queen was employing her whole influence with the parliament to set all in motion, and thereby secure the publication of the edict of January, the duke of Guise arrived in Paris with a number of men prepared for controversy: his wife, a daughter of the duchess of Ferrara, accompanied him*. Enraged for a long time against the inhabitants of Vassy, who were Protestants, he sent thither his troops: it was the 1st of March. The reformed, to the number of a thousand or twelve hundred, were celebrating the Lord's Supper in a barn, with profound devotion. The duke sent word that they were not to disperse: he then surrounded the place with soldiers. Just as the preacher was beginning his sermon, the door was burst open; the murderers rushed, with horrid blasphemies, upon the unarmed multitude, and struck down whomever they found. Twenty-two persons were killed on the spot, and one hundred and sixteen wounded, many of whom died of the injuries they received. All were plundered; and the preacher was murdered while uttering the noble words of the psalmist, "Thou hast redeemed me, Thou God of truth!" Guise himself was present with drawn sword: he found a large bible and brought it to his brother, the cardinal, who stood in the neighbouring church-yard. "Read," said the duke, "the title of these writings of the Huguenots." The cardinal told him that the volume was the Holy Scriptures. "What," said the duke, confused, "has the Bible been written fifteen hundred years, and was only printed a year ago? *Par la mort de Dieu, tout n'en vaut rien.*"

Beza immediately demanded of the queen that judicial proceedings should be instituted against the murderers; but the duke of Guise laughed at the demand, and despised the orders of the queen, who being more skilled in intrigue than in government, was anxious to keep from offending either party. Guise was received in Paris with every mark of honour and rejoicing: the people shouted as he passed, "Long live the duke!" He was proud of his triumph, and king Anton and the queen entered into a strict confederacy with him. Beza stood exposed to the

* Beza, p. 722.

greatest danger, and was obliged to flee with all possible speed to Orleans; but it is easy to perceive by his letters how he, as well as Calvin, in the midst of all the threats and horrors by which the Protestants were assailed, still remained full of hope. The fire was now kindled throughout the kingdom: the Guises possessed themselves of the person of the king, and conveyed him to the castle of Melun: "Vassy" was the watch-word for massacre in many parts of the country, especially at Cahors, Toulouse, Tours, Amiens, and Sens.

But the whole body of French Protestants now arose; they besought Condé to come to their aid, and to insist on the rightful observance of the January edict. At the beginning of April this distinguished man took possession of the city of Orleans, and applied on all sides for troops and money. Beza called a general synod: it assembled, and letters were sent to all the congregations of the reformed in France. This was the first time that the synod of ministers acted in a political capacity; and this moment also impressed the church itself with its peculiar character. The reformed set themselves in motion, and seized several cities and churches, from which they banished the mass, and images. Even Lyons was taken by them, but more through the mild address of Viret than by the power of arms. Condé made it known by a manifesto, that he was resolved to defend the king and his edict by the sword. On the 11th of April he wrote to the Genevese, requesting them to offer up public prayers for him and for his cause: this was done through the whole of the war.

The most eminent men of the reformed party now hastened to Orleans, and bound themselves by an oath to oppose the Guises. Condé persuaded the whole of the nobility to subscribe an act of union, by which they pledged themselves to contend for the honour of God and the freedom of the king, and to punish blasphemy and blasphemers: hence it was ordered that the camp should always be attended by ministers.

During these proceedings Beza turned himself to the German princes, and even to the emperor Ferdinand, to ask for their cooperation.

From these turbulent scenes it is refreshing to direct our attention to Calvin, who had just at this time received a letter from Winterthur, where the aged Blaarer had, on the 4th of April, celebrated his seventieth birthday, and was now carrying on a correspondence by letter with the reformer at Geneva. Calvin spoke to him with piety and earnestness on the events of the period, and praised Beza as an instrument employed by God, in proclaiming his word to the people and to kings: he also showed how great were the evils with which France was threatened by the union of the Guises with some of the German princes*.

Beza was now the soul of the whole encampment, and had to employ his utmost efforts to restrain the passions of his party, in which however he was not always successful. Thus the treasury of St. Martin was plundered at Tours, and the tomb destroyed†. But Beza acted throughout consistently with his noble character, and was a preacher of peace in the midst of the storms of war: he everywhere raised his powerful voice against rapine and murder, and was often the deliverer of the Catholics. At Angers he presented himself before the parliament, and assured it that he and his party abhorred violence, and that it was only committed by the rabble which followed in their track. To his own associates he said, "God will never be the protector of robbers and murderers." Much bad conduct indeed must have been exhibited, when it required the whole influence of Coligny to prevent him from leaving the army altogether. He exhibited his moderation in the fairest light, when, after the siege of Rouen, his friend Marlorat and many others were murdered, and the reformed proposed to retaliate in their camp on the opposite party: he resisted this design with his whole power.

The general synod at Orleans opened its sittings on the 27th of April, in the presence of the prince of Condé, the admiral Chatillon, and several other men of distinction. Here too Calvin's enemy, the exiled Bolsec, appeared: he played the penitent, and promised to offer satisfaction to Bern and Geneva, but it was only, as soon as the churches there were threatened with danger, to return to his proper allies.

Calvin, deeply troubled at these warlike proceedings, said to Bullinger that grief and shame had prevented his writing to him‡. "The arrival of the English has greatly alarmed the enemy, and the Scotch will soon join them: the queen is again returned to the practice of her arts, and messengers have been sent to treat of peace. It is to be lamented that the rage of the parliament of Toulouse could not be bridled: it has slain by the

* Ed. Laus. Ep. 338. Ed. Amstel. p. 169.

† MS. Goth. to Carl Passelius, Schlosser, Leben Beza's, p. 165.

‡ June 9, Aug. 15, 1562. MS. Tur.

hand of the executioner above three hundred rich and worthy men, some of them nobles, and others the administrators of public functions. If you have any influence with the Bernese council, and can induce it to send troops to the support of the princes, I beseech you to do all you can to this end; for if the war be protracted, we and the entire kingdom are lost. The council of Geneva has borrowed 12,000 gold dollars to meet the expenses of the war."

Condé had entered into an alliance with the elector palatine; but, at the same time, he proposed to the court to abide by the edict of January, till a free council could be held; and he promised on these conditions to lay down his arms. But the triumvirate rejected his advances, and were resolved to have only one religion in the state. Condé complained aloud against them, and unmasked their plans. The religious war therefore now commenced in earnest. On the 3rd of July Condé prepared to give battle; but the enemy hesitated. The Guises spread a report through Germany, that they intended to introduce the Augsburg Confession into France; that the king and the court only opposed the design; and hence the assembly of so many troops for their defence. Condé hereupon sent a short confession to the German troops, and thus brought over a portion of them to his side. When this was found to be the case, the Catholics immediately sought the aid of the Spaniards and Italians.

In the midst of these events the plague broke out in Orleans, and the parliament proclaimed the reformed rebels. They protested against this act. On the 12th of October the Protestant army held a solemn day of penitence. About ten thousand persons died in Orleans, and eighteen thousand in Paris, before the pestilence ceased.

It may perhaps be asked, how could the reformed so suddenly commence this war, and that without any means of support? We have seen that, according to the discipline of the French reformed church, all the expenses of worship were to be borne by its members, even to the costs of the journeys undertaken by their ministers. That Calvin himself took great interest in these circumstances, appears from the fact, that he urged the several congregations to provide the money necessary for certain journeys, and that they obeyed his call*. Thus the churches in Languedoc were expected to raise money to pay the levies

* This appears from a letter to the church at Poitiers, August 1, 1558. MS. Gen.

for Andelot*. "God," he says, "again bowed us down; but when all was lost, He provided means, in a manner incomprehensible to us, for the uplifting of his church, as if awakening it from the dead."

The emperor Ferdinand was now at Frankfort (1562), whither he had gone for the purpose of holding a diet. Calvin seized the opportunity, probably in conformity with Beza's advice, to send him an excellent confession of the doctrines of the French reformed church. He hoped by these means to overcome the slanderous falsehoods of the Guises; and, as he relates, the way to Frankfort being closed, he afterwards made this writing public. It was in the same manner that, in the year 1535, one of his first works, the 'Institutions,' was written to support the faith of his brethren in France; and this, one of his last, was composed with the same definite purpose, and the same consistency of doctrine, as the former†.

That they might not be without a representative, the reformed had sent Jac. de Spifame to Frankfort: he was both a preacher and a man of business, and acted so skilfully at the diet, that all the intrigues of the Guises were discovered. Thus it was shown that Condé had begun this war, which in the course of a few months had cost the lives of 30,000 men, at the command of Catherine, so that he stood justified before the assembly, and the envoy was able to recommend the cause of France, by the most pressing arguments, to the consideration of the German princes.

Guise however besieged Rouen, which was taken by storm, and given up to the fury of the soldiers. The pillage continued eight days, and, among many other sacrifices, fell the worthy Marlorat. King Anton was wounded on the day when the city was taken, and died of the injuries which he had received, because in the fever with which they were attended, he refused to be separated from the sirens set around him by Catherine. This woman now kept a fair face with all parties and with all vices. It was now too late for Anton to turn his back on the Catholic clergy; but he ordered the book of Job to be read to him, and commanded his son to remain true to the king: he died in November. Condé was now the oldest prince of the house; he strove for his own personal interests, not for the church, which he plunged deeper and deeper into the stream of political life. During the year 1562 the war raged more fiercely than ever, but no decided blow was struck. Coligny and Beza with difficulty

* MS. Gen. Sept. 30, 1562.

† Senebier, t. i. p. 233.

prevented their allies from falling upon Paris, and exposing it to pillage.

At length, December 19, 1562, after many marches, the two stood opposite each other, near Dreux. Before the battle commenced, Beza preached a severe sermon against the covetousness, the love of slaughter, and the enmity, which were apparent both in the higher and lower ranks of the army. On the evening before the battle Condé had a dream, which he communicated to Coligny and Beza: he stated that he dreamt that he fought three battles; that in each, one of the triumvirs fell; but that in a fourth he himself was mortally wounded, and laid upon a funeral pile. Coligny regarded the whole as mere imagination, but Beza felt convinced that it was a presentiment of the battle which was just about to be fought. On the following morning the admiral led the troops to the first onset; he fell victoriously upon the enemy, and one of the generals, Montmorency, was taken prisoner. But the Swiss Catholics, animated by their fanaticism, restored the day: Condé was wounded, and taken prisoner. This dispirited the troops; but Coligny supplied the want of the prince, and Beza, having animated the soldiers by a speech* full of ardour, took his place in the foremost rank, as if he had been a standard-bearer. Coligny, after performing many heroic actions, drew off the remainder of the troops in good order, and retreated to Lyons. Among the slain on the opposite side was the marshal St. André.

We cannot pass over without mention a singular circumstance which occurred to Calvin at this time†. He was lying in bed on the Saturday evening, December 19, sick of the ague: the north wind, which rages violently at Geneva, and over the lake, had roared furiously for two days. Calvin uttered the remarkable words: "I know not what may be betokened, but it seemed to me last night as if I heard the blast of war-trumpets sounding fiercely in the air. I could not convince myself that it was not so. Let us pray, I beseech you; for assuredly there is something important going on." And on that very day the battle at Dreux took place. The news of the event soon arrived. Calvin, who felt a lively interest in all the occurrences of that year, wrote to Bullinger, "that the battle was not actually lost; that it was now for him to share in the Maccabean struggle."

Condé remained a prisoner; true indeed to his party, but more

* MS. Gen. Calv. Bullingero, Jan. 16, 1563.

† Beza, in Calvin's Life.

from hatred to the Guises than from regard to Beza's exhortations. Party fury was now at its height in France, and the duchess Renata, writing to Calvin, expressed herself in these melancholy words: "I am more afflicted than you can imagine, at beholding how half the people in this kingdom conduct themselves: the most pitiable deceits and enmities everywhere prevail. Such is the state of things, that little simple girls have been led to say, that they are ready to kill and slay with their own hands. This is not the rule which Christ and his apostles have given us; and I say it in the deepest distress of heart, because of the love which I bear for my faith, and for all who adhere to that which Christ has taught. I speak not of all, but of those whom I know."

After the battle at Dreux, the two parties were so enraged against each other that they even carried on the war in the winter, till the duke of Guise, at the siege of Orleans, was assassinated by a fanatic of the reformed party, a young nobleman, Jean de Merci, who also bore the name of Poltrot. Guise died of his wounds on the sixteenth day (February 24, 1563): shortly before his death he spoke with sorrow of the cruelties perpetrated at Vassy, entreated the queen to conclude a peace, and called those who should oppose it enemies of the state.

Peace was now generally spoken of: Montmorency, though a prisoner, resisted the idea; but Condé, also a prisoner, favoured it, for he loved the repose of a life at court: he was permitted to go to Orleans on his parole. The reformed ministers, seventy-two in number, held a meeting in that city; they all expressed their desire to have the edict of January established; to receive a promise of protection for their party; and an assurance that those who violated the guarantee should be punished. Condé complained of the severity of the ministers, while the latter accused him of indolence, and of being slow to take advantage of circumstances, which might secure the Reformation in France.

But the prince was under the influence of Catherine's courtly dames. We have seen what Calvin said on this matter. The queen now endeavoured, by means of Balduin, who advocated indifference, to induce Condé to conclude a peace with the Catholic party, and which should merely afford toleration to the reformed. Beza returned with the admiral to Orleans, in order to strengthen Condé's faith in the evangelical doctrines; but the latter prepared a treaty of peace, which received the immediate assent of the queen (March 19, 1563), without Coligny's being consulted on the subject. This peace was concluded at Amboise. The whole Protestant party was loud in the expression of its disgust and resentment*; but thus ended the first religious war. Calvin did not live to witness the second. Respecting the peace, he thus expressed himself to the prince of Condé†: "With regard to the conditions, I know well enough that it was not easy for you to obtain what you wished. If however you do not make use of your authority, that which has been concluded in behalf of the faithful will be like a body without a soul." He expressed a wish that the 'Confession' which he had sent to Frankfort, should be printed, so that the reformed faith might be made generally known, and that an effectual obstacle might be raised to the introduction of the Augsburg Confession into France. "By this measure," he said to the prince, "you will shut the door against all attempts to induce you to subscribe the Augsburg Confession." In conclusion, he commended Geneva to his care, and prayed him to use his influence as a mediator, and to effect a union with Switzerland. The Swiss had left the Genevese to themselves. Calvin spoke of this to Bullinger, and with eyes upraised to heaven: he again wrote to Condé respecting the 'Confession'; and to Bullinger he says, "It must be published with the signature of Condé, and of the other great personages. His word and reputation will thus bind him to us, and he will draw over the German princes to our side."

Beza, having fulfilled his mission in France, hastened back to Geneva, anxious to relieve Calvin of the vast load of occupations which had been imposed upon him by his absence, and hoping there to rest from his own toils in peace and friendship. Great gratitude was expressed towards him in France, and the thanks of the brethren were communicated to the council of Geneva‡. That body showed itself favourably disposed to the common cause, and shared in the general satisfaction. Thus it passed a resolution to give the clergy and professors, from time to time, a public entertainment, as is mentioned in the state-protocol§.

Calvin had the satisfaction to receive at this time a letter from the duchess of Ferrara, in answer to his own, already quoted. This was probably the most satisfactory period of his life. But we may see, from the letter alluded to, how little freedom resulted from the peace. The duchess had left Paris because a reformed

* MS. Gen. to Bullinger, April 8, 1563.

† MS. Gen. 10 Mai, 1563.

‡ Registres, 7 Mai, 1563.

§ Registres, 5 Mars, 1563.

minister was forbidden to preach in her house, even though it was situated in a village. She answered Calvin's exhortations with humility and respect, assuring him that she would follow his counsel, and not appear again in the consistory, although the queen of Navarre, the wife of the admiral, and the lady de Roye, did not fear being present. She thanked him for the gold medal which he had sent her, adding the remarkable words, important even to the present day, "I had never before seen such a one; and I have thanked God that the king, my father, chose the motto which it bears (*Destruam Babylonem*). Though God may not have given him the grace to fulfil the idea thus expressed, yet he may perhaps accomplish it by those who shall succeed to his place."

A few months before Calvin's death she complained to him, with the feelings of a mother, respecting the duchess of Guise, her eldest daughter, who supported the Catholics:—"I do not wish to distress you, but I am compelled to pour out my heart to you with the sorrow which is common to all the children of God. You know what the enemies of the truth design. The treaty of the pope with the king of Spain, with Venice, and the other Italian powers, among which is our neighbour—these imagine that they can root Christianity entirely out of the world; and the duchess of Guise resigns herself to a course which can only lead to ruin. Thankful should I be if she could be led by your influence to bridle her passions."

Calvin saw clearly the storm which impended over France, and to which the duchess alluded. He himself spoke more than once of the condition of the country, and urged the men who had power and influence to fulfil their duty*. "With regard," he said, "to the state of France, I see it so pressed on all sides with difficulties, that I almost fear everything must be begun anew; not that it would not be easy to find speedy means to improve its condition, if people had the goodwill to seek them; but you see to what a state we are come. I have written to the prince of Condé, but not in the style which you wished me to adopt, for it is very contrary to my nature to make him believe that white is black. I have also prayed the admiral to act more firmly in some respects; not as if it were absolutely necessary to urge him forward, but because he desired me to speak thus freely with him."

Calvin always stood in close relation to Coligny, who regarded

* MS. Gen. 8 Mai, 1563.

him as the head of the party, and carefully acquainted him therefore with whatever took place. Calvin says to Bullinger*, "I yesterday received letters, in which Coligny informs me, that he will send me and Beza a man as soon as possible who shall inform us of his plans. The admiral himself declares that he is prepared for the first attack."

Looking with a prophetic glance into the future, Calvin beheld the signs of a fearful storm, just ready to break out†. A few months before his end, and while the League was in process of formation, he received intelligence from Bullinger that the cardinal of Lorraine had effected an alliance between the papal powers. But notwithstanding this, never had the affairs of the Protestants been in a more prosperous condition. The admiral Coligny, summoned to Paris, had entered the capital with a retinue of five hundred horsemen, and was graciously received by the queen.

In Germany, affairs after Calvin's death wore a worse appearance than in France. A new conference was held at Mümpelgart between Beza, Fay, and Jac. Andreä, but it only afforded another proof of the unchristian spirit which was rapidly spreading through the whole Lutheran church. Westphal, Hesshus, Brentius, Flacius and Jac. Andreä were still the chief disputants; it was therefore no wonder that the Lutheran church continued to decline, as to its inner life, whilst the reformed church arose, in spite of all the pressure from without.

Calvin continued, though on a bed of sickness, to guide the churches with the spirit of a true reformer. Five months before his death he preached to the community of Chambery, formed as it had been among papists, on Christian decision, of which his whole life had been an example. "Build not," he said, "upon the sand: summon together all the force and resolution of which you are possessed, that you may be able to overcome all the obstacles which the servants of the devil cast in your way. Remember this, that it is not permitted you to serve both parties."

The share which Calvin took in these events obliges us to speak more particularly of his political influence.

Calvin has been accused, even up to the present times, of having caused all those civil wars which afflicted the period to which we are alluding. Roman Catholic historians, careless and uncritical, have laid this down as an axiom, and a host of pamphleteers have followed in their train. Catholics, like Bossuet,

* MS. Gen. Jul. 29, 1563. † MS. Tur. Calv. Stanis. Sarnicio.

pretend that he was involved in the conspiracy of Amboise; and this is repeated with the greatest rashness by all the ill-instructed minds of the party, to which truth is of little import. And further: Calvin, they say, laid the foundation-stone of the republic, without considering that the Gospel renews, but does not revolutionize. Even a protestant, in modern times, with more respect indeed, but with as much obscurity, has repeated the accusation. "That noble precept, 'The weapons of our warfare are spiritual,' vanishes by degrees from the standard of a religion which could not continue a religion or a church, but which sought to found a state." Thus the Protestants, it is insinuated, hoped to accomplish great things by means of a pretended impartiality, while the Catholics, on their side, resisted them with their wonted obstinacy.

The imperfect views of these writers may be traced to the errors which they commit in regard to Calvin's theocratic spirit. To many indeed the idea of a pure Christian theocracy is altogether strange. Calvin contended for the government of God, not for the government of the people. His political notions were framed in the spirit of the old prophets, but his designs were perpetually involved with civil affairs, through the interference of the council: it is not wonderful therefore that he should have been anxious to promote an alliance between France and Switzerland. The notion, that Protestantism sought the formation of a state, and not a church, is opposed both to reason and the Gospel. History shows, on the contrary, that it was in France only that the Protestant party acquired, through particular circumstances, a political character. The Guises trod both church and state under foot, and the temporal power was compelled, for its own security, to put weapons into the hands of the Protestants. It is false to assert that Calvin desired a republican form of government. The church-polity which he adopted was the polity of the primitive church. Where introduced into Germany, there it has continued without creating change or agitation. The German territories, in which the reformed system has prevailed, have never been more inclined than the Lutheran to revolution. The Protestant communities indeed have generally been opposed to change. Their religion renders them susceptible to reform, while Roman Catholic countries are necessarily exposed to a series of convulsions which must eventually lead to the downfall of the papacy, opposing itself as it does in its unyielding grossness to every species of improvement. Calvin's enemies ought, in common justice, to have listened to the enunciation of his principles, and to the expressions which he so distinctly uttered, proving as they do, that from the beginning to the end of his career he protested against every kind of warlike movement.

The reformers especially recognized the rights of the temporal power against the principle of the papacy. The state, with them, is a necessary moral institution*. Calvin however wished the church to have an existence proper to itself—an independent power; hence he subjected the state to the church, as the church to the state, which naturally introduces a theocracy. Each separate community forms a little republic, and from the whole springs a nobler and higher unity. But according to Calvin, every species of government was reconcileable with Christianity, even despotism. Where, however, representatives of the people exist, *populares magistratus*, it is their duty, if the people be oppressed, to resist any act of arbitrary power. Hence, under certain circumstances, Calvin could justify in France a rising against tyranny: he preferred the republican form only as it existed in ancient Israel, where the government was carried on in the name of God, not in the name of the people. The sovereignty of the people was altogether a novel idea to his mind: no particular form of government had, with him, a decided preference; each had its defects. He would have no war. In this he agreed with Luther; but the German reformer thought that if the elector of Saxony was attacked by those who persecuted his subjects, it would be the duty of that prince to defend his people by force of arms. Supposing however that some mistook the spirit of Calvin, and from the synodal form of church government in France, took occasion, in the struggle against Rome, to uphold republican principles; or that Henry IV. established a reformed state within a state, thus committing a great political error, Calvin was not answerable for the misuse which was thereby made of his doctrine. He observed to Sadolet, and to the count Tarnowsky, "that if the Christian religion gave occasion to disturbances, this must be attributed to applications of the system, not agreeable to the truth."

But Calvin has not been wanting of supporters. Thus, for example, the excellent Basnage readily undertook to prove that the conspiracy of Amboise was a political stratagem, which had no connection with the church. "The Catholics," said Mezeray,

* See the Institutes, t. iv. c. 20. s. 4, 26–31.

"feared for the freedom of the state." It was not the reformed who, as Bossuet wished to represent, were seeking to revenge their persecutions. This writer heaps falsehood upon falsehood, and sees not that it ill becomes one who delighted in violence to find fault with the reformers for venturing to defend themselves, as if, like an executioner appointed by the church, he had a right to their blood. But here is the truth. The plan of the conspirators, of whom the queen herself was the life, was laid with the design of securing the duke of Guise, and bringing him under the operation of the law. According to Basnage, the divines and jurists were desired to give their opinion, as to whether it were allowable to make a minister of state prisoner before his trial. No crime was committed in this case. All that was done was in obedience to the command of the queen, who was anxious to free herself from the tyranny of the Guises.

Bossuet adduces against Calvin one of his unpublished letters. The latter satisfied himself herein with simply condemning the violent proceedings of the baron von Adrets, who destroyed a number of images without any authority to do so: Calvin passed no censure on the war itself: but this letter in fact speaks greatly in his favour. The war carried on in France against the Guises, with the aid of legitimate authority, was a species of holy war. Calvin distinctly called the proceedings of Adrets, "a horrible scandal, calculated to bring disgrace on the Gospel;" and expressed a wish that whatever had been taken in the way of robbery should be restored. Numberless expressions indeed might be quoted, in which Calvin decidedly condemns the waging of war on account of the Gospel*.

With regard to the conspiracy of Amboise, Calvin expressed his disapprobation of the design as soon as it was communicated to him, and with such force, that he hoped he had prevented its execution. Applied to a second time, he still as resolutely declared his aversion to the plans of the conspirators. When however he was asked a third time, he assembled his colleagues and protested openly against the undertaking; and on finding that the parties concerned were resolved to proceed, he complained that his influence and advice were wholly neglected. He even preached against what was being done, and exclaimed, "Better were it a thousand times that we all perished, than that we should bring such infamy upon the name of Christians and the Gospel."

* MS. Paris, 16 Avril, 1561. He speaks in a similar manner in a letter to Bullinger, Mai 11, 1560. Ed. Laus. Ep. 293. Ed. Amstel. p. 142.

Beza, who was so rashly accused in the affair of Poltrot, was equally free from any guilt in this proceeding: he declared in the strongest manner, "that he never knew Poltrot; that he had had no intercourse with him, either directly or indirectly; nay, that he had never heard mention of the plan referred to." So also he said, that "when he prayed that Francis de Guise might be converted, or that the land might be freed from such an enemy, he had only done what the prophets and first Christians had done under similar circumstances,—'When wilt thou avenge the blood of the righteous?'"

The admiral Coligny was accused by the same party, the advocates of St. Bartholomew's night, as a wretch who had heard of Poltrot's design to murder the duke, and had taken no means to prevent it. But Coligny declared publicly, that he had warned the duchess of her husband's danger,—a service which would never have been rendered him on the part of the Guises*.

Calvin's oft-repeated sentiments show clearly how earnestly he endeavoured to calm the excited feelings of his associates. Thus he declared to them, that "if they wished to establish their rights by the sword, they would prevent God from helping them." —"One single drop of blood shed by you will overflow all France." He forbad their taking possession of the churches; and said, "that he should be not less indignant than the king against those who employed violence." In two of his letters to Soubize, the leader in the movement, he directed him to lay down his arms, as the king desired; and to submit himself to the legitimate authority of the state. He regarded it as something especially monstrous for a minister of religion to bear arms: "It is their duty to believe that the church will be extended by other and extraordinary means." He included the duke of Guise in the number of those for whom he prayed. It was not his fault that he could not, in that confused war of passions, bridle the spirit of political parties. Beza remained in Coligny's camp to lessen, as far as possible, the miseries occasioned by the strife, and Calvin addressed the troops in words of the mightiest import. Thus, notwithstanding the accusation of hostile polemics, there still remains inscribed on the standard which he raised, the apostolic motto, "The weapons of our warfare are not carnal, but spiritual."

* Beza, Hist. Eccles. l. vi. p. 297.

CHAPTER XIV.

CALVIN'S LATEST CONTROVERSIES.—THE FALSE REPORTS PUBLISHED BY HIS ENEMIES. — STRUGGLE AGAINST BALDUIN.

HAVING thus considered Calvin in his relation to France, and the important events of which it was the scene, we have now again, and in the concluding period of his career, to view him as a polemic. It was in fact the lot of this reformer, and of others like him, to have to contend with all the dark spirits of the age in which they lived. The last years of Calvin's life, as was the case with Melancthon, were troubled by a host of wranglers and calumniators, among whom Balduin, the jurist, might be regarded as the most hateful.

Calvin, after the death of his wife, when visited, as he so frequently was, by severe attacks of illness, assembled around his sick bed a number of young men, to whom he dictated his letters and his works. Among these young men there was one in whose conversation he greatly delighted, and whom he invited to his table, carefully instructing him, and allowing him the free use of his library, where his papers and manuscripts lay exposed. This was Francis Balduin, a native of Arras, and subsequently celebrated as a jurist at Heidelberg. It is gratifying to see how free from suspicion this great man was; how open he stood to the world, with nothing that he wished to hide; and how little he doubted men's honesty, though he had been so often employed in unmasking deceit and wickedness. Balduin however spoke of a journey to France, and at once disappeared: he took with him several of Calvin's papers, all of which he appears to have diligently perused, having possessed himself of those which he could employ most effectually in attacking the reformer. There were among them the letters from Bucer, in which he attacked Calvin with the strongest expressions of censure and reproof.

Balduin stood by the side of the cardinal at Poissy, when he planned the union which was to be the source of so many conflicts. He was sometimes a protestant; sometimes a papist. Cassander had printed a letter at Basel to promote his object. Calvin immediately ascribed it to Balduin, and at once wrote to

Beza, then at St. Germain, on the subject. Now began the strife. Calvin, in his preface to the Psalms, compared his case with that of David, who was also continually surrounded by enemies. But very different to Melancthon, he knew how to make his opponents sensible of his greatness and unyielding fortitude.

In this controversy the zeal of the reformer, advanced as he was in years, exhibited itself in all its strength; and many of his friends were of opinion that he, as well as Beza, ought to have reflected on the mildness proper to those who are saved. But it must be observed, that in the present instance, Calvin's personal feelings were concerned, and that they were excited to the highest degree by the treacherous ingratitude of the man towards whom he had behaved with so much unsuspecting kindness. Balduin moreover, although a skilful lawyer, proved himself, by the lax character of his plans of union, but an indifferent christian. This must have tended to increase the fervent zeal of both reformers, and it is impossible not to allow that they were in the right. Hence we also see why Senebier in his time, and Bayle, who looked down upon all religions, and Niceron, a catholic, passed no severe judgement upon Balduin. But both the last confessed that he must have been an extraordinarily unsettled man, for that he had changed his faith and his confession seven times. His conduct towards Calvin, which certainly merited severe punishment, they did not name.

The circumstance which gave occasion to the controversy with Calvin has been already stated. King Anton conferred with Balduin, and sent him back to Germany to form plans with Cassander. The ministers had already spoken twice at Poissy, in public debate, when Balduin appeared there with a copy of Cassander's project of union, as printed at Basel. Some discontent was expressed that he came so late. He now went to Paris, where he delivered his lectures; but he had lost much of his reputation through engaging in the late affair. Calvin, in his work against Cassander, without mentioning his name, alludes to Balduin as his guest, his former help and servant, and calls him a betrayer. This roused the anger of Balduin to the highest pitch, and gave him the long-wished-for opportunity of distinguishing himself in his church. Passing all bounds of moderation, he loaded his adversary with abuse, and proved himself to be neither Lutheran nor Calvinist, but simply a papist. Calvin, very embittered at finding himself so treated by a man whom he had brought up, soon proved to him that the ardour of youth was not yet extinguished in his spirit.

Some farther light is thrown on the cause of Calvin's anger by the report, that Balduin had been twice in Geneva before he was called to Bourges, and that he renewed his friendship with Calvin when no longer a youth. During the seven years that he dwelt at Bourges (1549–56) he professed outwardly the Catholic religion; but he carried on a close correspondence with Calvin, and assured him that he was inwardly a good protestant. If the statement therefore referred to be true, Calvin may have still cherished the hope that he would sooner or later return to the reformed church. But he must have come a third time to Geneva, on which occasion Calvin appears to have reproached him bitterly for his dissimulation in religion, and to have refused to forgive him till he exhibited sincere repentance. It may be mentioned, as a striking proof of his vacillating conduct, that after engaging in such a controversy with Calvin, he appeared in 1566 in the first assembly held by the malcontents in Breda, and drew up the paper in which they petitioned the duchess of Parma to admit the free exercise of the Protestant religion in her territories. He was a man in fact of all colours, while Cassander, on the contrary, appears to have been a genuine lover of peace. George Wicelius, who acted throughout his life in a similar manner, practised the same sort of vacillation in Germany.

Calvin assailed Cassander's writing in his well-known original style, sharp, caustic, and powerful*. It shows how impossible it is to unite both churches in their principles; for example, in the doctrines of scripture and tradition, a point which Cassander would leave for tradition to decide. Catholic tradition, as the unwritten truth, will alone suffice to allay religious strife. Heresies, says Cassander, were silenced from the first, not by the word of scripture, but by the right understanding thereof. Calvin, on the other hand, observes, "According to this, the Godhead of Christ rests on no other basis than the decree of a council." "And if," he justly adds, "we value the tradition or the interpretations of the first century as highly as the Bible, the main pillar of the faith is shattered; for original sin, justification,

* Calvin's paper against Balduin appeared at Geneva under the title of 'Io. Calvini Responsio ad versipellem quendam Mediatorem,' &c. &c.; and in French, 'Response à un certain moyenneur rusé,' &c. &c.

and the sufficiency of the sacrifice of Christ, are treated of but very obscurely in the writings of the oldest fathers. If there be a written and an unwritten word, by what signs shall we determine the truth of the latter, so as to distinguish it from what is false? The high antiquity of a tradition is no certain proof of its truth: otherwise we should be obliged to adopt all the horrible heresies which arose in the apostolic times. The clear light of the Gospel shines resplendent above all this darkness and confusion. A second characteristic of tradition consists in its universal reception; but by universal, the writer referred to means only the Roman Catholic church of the West."

On the one side indeed Cassander advocated the pure institution of Christ; for example, in regard to the sacrament; but on the other, he justified the use of the ceremonies which had been invented by the successors of the apostles. Thus a door was opened to all that was Romanistic. Calvin now assailed the unchristian character of the papacy itself, in which Cassander had sought the true church. Calvin acknowledged indeed that there were some remains of the true church in that of Rome; but he adds a review of the papacy, which proves the impossibility of a union between it and the Protestant churches.

The main obstacle however to such a union was the doctrine of justification: on this Calvin expresses himself as follows:—"The Catholics pronounce with great severity the condemnation of Arius, Sabellius, Nestorius, Eutyches, Marcion, and the Manichees. There is concord therefore among us, if it depend only on the doctrine of the divine and human nature, and their union. But when Paul teaches, that the church is established on Christ alone, he means thereby, that Christ is made unto us of the Father, wisdom, redemption, righteousness and sanctification. But has not Cassander rejected the wisdom here spoken of, when, like another Mahomet, he sets himself in its place, plays the Lord, and mars by his inventions the brightness of the Gospel? Let it be observed however that this reformer united with the doctrine of free-will, that of redemption as taught by Paul; and what is still more, that he spoke of good works as opposed to the righteousness which we receive through Christ. If, moreover, we must seek our holiness in Christ, as the result of a working-together of the human will with the grace of the Holy Spirit, which only comes to our aid,—if we look at the means, or the form of this grace, the whole theory must fall to the ground, if Christ be not our sole high-priest, our Mediator; and if we do not view the death of the Lord as our only and eternal offering to God."

Calvin speaks in a very christian spirit of the communion, which the reformed would so willingly have established with the Catholics; and this is important, as confuting the statements of those who impute to Calvin, especially in this controversy, so much gall and hatred. Of this I can find no trace in his works, with the exception of an occasional remark, expressed in the sarcastic tone common to his age. "With regard to the men themselves," he said, "we are not personally opposed to them; for we desire their salvation equally with our own. We do not indeed associate with the Catholics; but I ask, do we view them as swine, or dogs, because we avoid them? On the contrary, we truly pity their blindness, and would, as far as in us lies, put an end to their vices. We love them with christian goodwill: readily should we accept, yea, we are very anxious to receive them, if they will but join us in worshipping God with purity of heart. In short, we are prepared to make the first advances, and by all means to unite ourselves to them; but we would not that they should separate us from Christ; nor would we partake of their superstition, which would only harden and pollute us, and involve us in a common ruin and condemnation.—How irrational is the plan of union proposed! True religion is supposed to lie between us and the papists: both parties have their errors; so that in one respect both must be destroyed, and then the fragments must be sown together to form a new and a pure church."

Calvin had written this work, sorrowfully, in the absence of Beza, and while at the same time he had been deprived by death of the agreeable society of his young friend Varenius. He sent it to Beza, having before forwarded to him an abstract of its contents, that he might know what course to pursue. Balduin defended himself in a work for which he had obtained a privilegium in the year 1557, and which he now published, corrected, and with the addition of an appendix. This was soon followed by Calvin's rejoinder; in which, as he himself confesses, he came forth with a feeling of indignation. When Balduin again quickly answered him, Calvin briefly replied, that he would pursue the matter no further, for that his friend Beza would now take his place in the controversy. This declaration forms the introduction to Beza's answer, to which also Balduin still replied, determined to have the last word.

It is difficult to understand how Senebier and others could find fault with Calvin for his reply to Balduin, whose violence, unreasonable complaints, and abusive language, so richly deserved the treatment which they received. Calvin's work moreover is not uninteresting as illustrative of his character; resigning himself as he did, and according to his usual custom, so entirely to his present feeling. There is no mention indeed of doctrine in the answer; it is wholly personal. We quote the two following passages*:—"I allow that I am full of indignation. We remember the celebrated answer which Socrates gave to those who persuaded him to bring some people who abused him to trial. 'If an ass should kick at me,' he said, 'would you have me summon him before a court of justice?' Although I am very far from possessing such magnanimity as Socrates, yet long custom has hardened me against the barking of such dogs, and I have learnt in a better school, that God, in order to prove the patience of his servants, allows them to be assailed by slander and abuse.—True it is, that I am not elevated by the greatness of the revelations granted me, as if I were a Paul; still I acknowledge that I have this in common with the apostle, that a messenger of Satan has been sent by God to buffet me in the face, and that I am thus taught to humble myself. But as we must at all times pray to God to drive back the devil and his angels, it is our duty to oppose their revilings, lest the truth should be injured by the falsehoods which they thus promulgate."

The reformers were so situated, that they could not avoid replying to the foolish and wicked slanders with which they were assailed. If they had taken no notice of the barkings and lies of their enemies, they would have been regarded by the people as guilty. But it was for the people that they lived and laboured, and they were compelled therefore to adopt the rude language which the people could best understand. Calvin was sufficiently severe in his first reply to Cassander; but he was far more so in the second to Balduin. He is, in fact, throughout more vehement and passionate than in his earlier works. For example:—"Not only ought a brand and a sign to be set upon Balduin, to mark him as a slave, but he ought to be hung upon a gallows; for why should such a vile fellow be allowed to lift up his head from the dunghill, and darken the light of the sun with his wicked audacity?"

Referring to Servetus, Calvin says: "He tells a wretched false-

* Opusc. p. 2215. Ed. Amstel. viii. p. 316.

hood when he asserts, that I keep all others in bondage, and make them dependent on my will. Now I desire no other witnesses than those, who differing from me in opinion, yet continue to be my friends: but what follows is still more detestable. If any one opposes my plans, it is said, he is not only deprived of his rights, but loses his life. Such is the penalty of displeasing me. Castellio perhaps has requested him, as a mark of friendship, to defend the cause of Servetus. True it is that that unhappy man received the punishment due to his offences; but did this happen merely according to my will and pleasure? It is certain that his arrogance, no less than his impiety, was the cause of his ruin and death. But what of wrong did I commit, when the council of this city, encouraged indeed by me, but according to the decision of various churches, took just revenge of the horrible blasphemies of that wicked man? Melancthon approved of the proceeding, and commended the severity of the republic to imitation." The respect entertained for Melancthon was sufficient to silence all objections.

"It is surely not necessary to blind France in order to convince it of my faithfulness, my diligence, my honesty, discretion, patience, and daily labours for the church; things which have been evidenced from my youth by so many testimonies."—"This man accuses me of having called myself Lucanius in my letters, and out of this name he frames that of Lucianus, that he may abuse me as an enemy of the true God."—"Among other things laid to my charge is this, that I have no children. I answer, that the Lord did give me a child, but was pleased to deprive me of it. But thousands of children, in all parts of Christendom, have been given me in its place." In the conclusion, Calvin says of himself: "If I had Balduin's ambition, I could easily gain the honours after which he has so long and so vainly sought; but I willingly resign such things. Satisfied with my humble condition, I have ever delighted in a life of poverty, and am a burden to no one: I remain contented with the office which the Lord has given me. So far am I from seeking an increase of stipend, that I have given up a portion of that allowed me. I not only employ my best ability, my labour and study, to do good to the church to which I am more especially devoted; but I also endeavour, by every means in my power, to benefit all other churches: and so do I fulfil the duties of a teacher, that no one can discover in my earnest truth and diligence any trace of ambition. I bear with many annoyances; but I suffer neither the great nor the powerful to abridge my freedom of speech. Thus I give not the reins to the great by flattering them; nor fear I the displeasure of either one party or the other. Up to this hour, successful as I have been, I am free from pride; and though I have been assailed by many a storm and tempest, my courage and fortitude have never failed me, till God, by his especial goodness, has come to my deliverance. I live at peace with my associates, and endeavour with all sincerity to keep up the friendship which exists among us."

This public witness which the reformer gave of himself, in the place where he lived, before the eyes of all, and to the very end of his career, is well-deserving of attention. Such however was Balduin's confirmed hatred of Calvin, that he is reported to have said, "that he would rather live with Beza in hell than with Calvin in heaven." The mere presence of Calvin was a hell to him.

Some little polemical tracts have also to be mentioned as belonging to this period. The 'Congratulation to Gabriel de Saconay' is a very original paper, written against a priest of Lyons, who, although himself immoral, wished to defend good morals against the reformers, and therefore attacked the Genevese. Calvin draws a very comical and grotesque picture of this man, in the middle-age style, and makes him appear ridiculous from beginning to end. The writing has some worth, as affording a specimen of the wit and humour of the reformer. Saconay had reprinted a part of Henry the Eighth's work against Luther, with a very absurd preface of his own*. The work, which Calvin believed was written by a priest, but published by the wish of the king, under his name, had long been forgotten, and Saconay, a catholic priest of bad character, only employed it as a medium for accusing Calvin of intolerance, and Beza of sensuality.

Calvin took occasion from this circumstance to explain what ought to be understood by the word heresy: he shows that the determination of all questions must depend upon Scripture, and states the difference between the Romish and Reformed churches. From a critical examination of the papacy he passes to that of the doctrine of the sacrament, and confutes the several errors of the Catholics one by one.

This writing however contains much which is merely personal;

* "Il a cuydé estre demi-roy, si son nom estoit meslé à un nom royal," said Calvin.

for example, the answer to the accusation that Calvin would not suffer Luther's works to be printed at Geneva: but he shows that he thoroughly agreed with the German reformer, who, in treating of the unity of the church, prophesied the fall of the papacy*.

Another equally characteristic production, written in French, deserves also to be mentioned: it is an answer to Cathelin, formerly a Franciscan friar of Alby, who wrote fiercely against Calvin. The introduction is curious:—"So many foolish beasts are so detestably busy just now with paper and print, that respectable men of learning will be ashamed to have anything to do with printing." Cathelin surpassed all the rest in his rage against the reformed: he prayed the syndics to compel Calvin to clear himself. The latter added, that the papacy could not injure itself more than by countenancing such writers†.

A third work of a similar kind is supposed to have been written against a libertine from Holland: Ziegenbein quotes it by the title of 'Jean Calvin, de la vraye et fausse religion.' It is not found however either in the Latin edition of his works, or in the French 'Opuscules,' and was probably written by Viret‡.

* "Si tu t'enquerrois du pape, il te diroit que son royaume estant pourri comme de longue phthisie, est ainsi qu'une charogne qui n'a que le souffle. Je t'annonce que ce que tu crains le plus t'arrivera en bref, c'est que ta cuisine gelera; j'ai voulu achever mon propos par cette conjuration, parceque tu es de cette sorte de diable que l'on ne chasse que par le jeune."—Opus. p. 2128.

† Calvin says that this man came accompanied by a woman to Geneva, and was at first well-received:—"Puis ils ne purent tenir de diablier dans l'hostellerie et se prendre au poil pour essayer qui seroit le plus fort—et par leur propre bouche furent convaincus d'être un ruffien et une putaine." Calvin adds, that, "with regard to his preface, he understood only the high German, as they say" (that is, not at all). "It attacks the Reformation,—demands why I forbid giving alms to the papists,—asserts that I teach, that to vow chastity is to tempt God." Calvin makes some pointed remarks on the following subjects:—Vows, Auricular Confession, Absolution, Baptism, Regeneration, the Sacrament of the Eucharist, and thus concludes:—"If this rogue continues to annoy me with his babble, I shall easily learn to despise him, as I do so many others, a thousand times more formidable than he; for it is not my office to silence all the dogs that bark in the world."

‡ Senebier, Hist. Lit. de Genève, i. p. 518.

CHAPTER XV.

CALVIN TAKES LEAVE OF THE WORLD.—REVIEW OF THE CLOSE OF HIS LIFE.—HIS OUTWARD CIRCUMSTANCES AND INWARD STATE.—HIS LAST LABOURS.—FAREWELL ADDRESS TO THE MINISTERS, AND TO THE COUNCIL.—GENERAL MOURNING.—BEZA'S CHARACTER OF CALVIN.

CALVIN had frequently been on the point of leaving Geneva; but he felt himself to the last supported by the hand of God, as he was at the beginning, when Farel threatened him with the curse of God if he forsook Geneva, and when he listened to his words as to a distant storm. Among all the tempests however to which he stood exposed, he had ever the feeling that a great blessing was with him: he saw how magnificently his work prospered in France, and in the year 1560 he found his system of discipline adopted in the Palatinate. His Answer to Caspar Olevianus is well-known. The law in Geneva was administered with Roman strictness.

In the year 1563, a man named Villard, who had made mockery of a storm of thunder and lightning, while other people were praying in terror, and who had sinned in other respects against good morals, was seen led through the streets of Geneva, and afterwards whipped, by the public executioner. In the same year a book was thrown into the fire, amid a great concourse of people: this was the 'Discipline Ecclésiastique de Morelli de Villiers,' in which it was asserted, that the consistory was an institution of which nothing was known in the time of the apostles, and that the people alone had the right to judge of doctrine and morals. The synod of Orleans had condemned the book in 1562. Calvin conducted the process at Geneva, as is evident from the acts and remarks written in his own hand. The author was not allowed to partake of the Lord's Supper with the Genevese till he had confessed his error: he stood before the tribunal, August 26th, having promised to submit himself to the judgement of Calvin, Farel, and Viret. Calvin however declared very decidedly, that he would not place himself above the opinion of the synod. Certain questions were put to the author; but he refused to answer, except in writing. As no further reply was received from him, he was pronounced schismatic, excommunicated, and given over to the council; but he fled, and his wife pleaded his excuse. Such was the severe discipline, as shown by many examples, established at this period in Geneva.

Public affairs wore a very troubled appearance. Geneva was again (1563) threatened by Savoy*: all the representations made by the little republic to the Bernese were without avail. They had entered into a treaty of peace with Savoy. Thus Geneva at the end of the year was in danger, even during the celebration of the Christmas festival, and when all the people were assembled in the churches to partake of the Lord's Supper, of being attacked by the enemy. The city, visibly defended only by a wretched wall, was more than once surrounded and fortified, through the prayer of the faithful, by a wall of fire. Pius IV. closed this year the Council of Trent; and the cardinal of Lorraine there established, as before related, an alliance between the several Catholic powers of the South against the Gospel. We see Calvin shortly before his death resisting this confederacy with almost incredible energy: he adjured Bullinger, and all the brethren, in the name of God, to exert themselves to secure the renewal of the treaty between France and the Swiss, now coming to a close, that the Gospel might enjoy protection, peace, and a free course †.

In the last years of Calvin's life, during the most eventful times, and after his death, the plague raged with the most frightful violence, as if God had now mercifully designed to awaken men to more earnest reflection. Bullinger himself was attacked, but recovered, after losing his wife and two daughters ‡. "Wretched me!" he exclaimed, "that I should survive, to follow, half-dead, so many to the grave!" Multitudes died of the plague in Switzerland.

As in the case of Bullinger, with whom throughout his life he preserved the strictest friendship, Calvin remained faithfully attached to his other associates, and to the companions of his youth. Two letters still exist, written in the last years of his life, to Francis Daniel, whom he knew at the University, and to whom he, in 1533, dedicated one of his first works §. Thus also he manifested his friendship for Melancthon to the end: whether Melancthon himself valued it or not, it is equally estimable on the part of

* Ruchat, vii. p. 25. † MS. Eccles. Bern. Calv. Bullingero, Dec. 2, 1563.
‡ Ruchat, vii. p. 68. § Ed. Laus. Ep. 1. Ed. Amstel. p. i.

Calvin. The evening of their lives was troubled by numberless enemies. But Calvin remained free from mistrust, and never despaired of the human heart. In his iron breast he bore a warm and tender spirit: as long as Melancthon lived, it was his delight to pour out his heart to him from time to time. Thus he described to him in confidence his infirmities and his dangers, especially in the year 1558, rightly thinking that this might interest Melancthon. The letter here referred to is a genuine outpouring of the heart *.

Calvin still retained, in the four-and-fortieth year of his life, a youthful feeling: he says of himself, "What a young man I still am!" But in the year 1558 he was attacked by a violent fever, which bowed him down. It was now that he first began to feel old; and the sigh which occasionally escaped him shows that his thoughts were turned towards home. He let fall some words also, intimating that he hoped to see his friends again in eternal life. His patience and resignation, his hope in God, retained through those unbearable sufferings which frequently deprived him of sense, interest our profoundest sympathies on his side. His spirit, amid all his trials, never failed him. All his letters exhibit to the last, the same colour, freshness and simplicity. One last sigh, and the description of his sufferings, a month before his death, show that all his organs were invaded by disease †. His body was in fact broken up, and only his spirit lived in the wasted shell. The gentle and benevolent feeling which he displayed amid all these sufferings, uttering no complaints, but merely a sigh, presents him as an example to the afflicted, and a proof of the all-sufficient power of the Holy Spirit, even amid the tortures of the rack.

But never had Calvin been more oppressed with toil than, owing to Beza's absence, in the last few years of his life; hence the fire expended itself the more rapidly. People envied Calvin his high position; he was spoken of as if he had been a bishop, or lord of Geneva. We learn however from Beza, his successor, what were the burdens imposed upon him. If we enter his study, we shall see ample proofs of his diligence, even to the last.

* MS. Bern. Calv. Melancthoni, Nov. 19, 1558.

† MS. Gen. Calv. Bullingero, April 6, 1564. The pain of his side he said was abated, but his lungs were so affected that he could only breathe with great difficulty. He was afflicted with the stone, which had given him dreadful pain for the last twelve days. No medicine had availed to his relief. Riding on horseback might have helped him, but he was affected with another disorder which prevented his sitting on horseback; added to all this, he had the gout. Food was scarcely tolerable to him, and wine was bitter to his palate.

They are to be found in his controversial writings, and still more in his numerous commentaries, published at the close of his life. Beza states that Calvin's concluding labour was his Latin commentary on the last four books of Moses, which he translated into French. But the commentary on Joshua followed: this he finished while dying. The commentary on the first book of Moses was Luther's last work. Thus Mathesius relates, that Luther finished Genesis on the 17th of November, 1545, and uttered these last words: "There is now our dear Genesis; may the Lord grant that others after me may do better than I have! I can do no more. I am weak. Pray to the Lord for me, and beseech him to grant me a good, happy little hour."

Calvin's work against the Polish heretics belongs to this period; so also do his discourses addressed to the deputies of the Lyons synod. In a letter written towards the end of 1563, he himself speaks of the last literary labours in which he was engaged: this was only five months before his death. In July 1563 he wrote to the brethren in Dauphiné, anxious to inspire them, in those times of war and tumult, with a true feeling of the Gospel *. He also again, in writing to Bullinger, who had desired him to attack Brentius, expressed his feelings in respect to that violent and unsettled man, with that clear and deep conviction, (after the example of the gentle Peter Martyr) which attended him to the grave †.

With the peace of God in his heart, Calvin now laid himself down to rest. His life had been a constant struggle against the storm; and he felt that it had at length cast him upon the shore. Thus after so many toils and dangers, he was filled with inward joy. He had often said that he was never so happy as after completing numerous and difficult labours. His whole life lay, as it were, behind him, and the fruit of his exertions before his eyes. Let us hear what Beza says of this period:—"In the year 1562 it might be already seen, that Calvin was hastening with rapid strides to a better world. He ceased not however to comfort the afflicted, to exhort, to preach even, and to give lectures. The following year his sufferings so increased, that it was difficult to conceive how so weak a body, and exhausted as it had been by labour and sickness, could retain so strong and mighty a spirit. But even now he could not be induced to spare himself; for when he was obliged, against his will, to leave the duties of his public office unfulfilled, he was employed at

* Ed. Laus. Ep. 341. Ed. Amst. p. 171, Jul. 31, 1563.

† MS. Gen. Dec. 27, 1563.

home, giving advice to those who sought him, or wearing out his amanuenses by dictating to them his works and letters. The year 1564 was the first of his eternal rest, and the beginning, for us, of a long and justifiable grief. On the 6th of February he preached his last sermon, already much affected by a cough. He was now obliged wholly to discontinue his public duties, but, according to his wish, he was several times carried to the congregation: it was on the 31st of March that this occurred for the last time, and he could then utter only a few words."

But fearfully attacked as he was, and suffering so acutely as he did, not a word of complaint escaped him unworthy of a Christian, or indicative of weakness. We learn this from Beza, who was always at his side. His last letters, addressed to the physicians of Montpellier, and to Farel, show the most friendly disposition. The common opinion entertained at an early period, that there was something gloomy in his character, is strikingly confuted by the exemplary kindness which he exhibited in this season of suffering. When his agony was at the height, Beza relates, he only raised his eyes to heaven, and exclaimed, "How long, O Lord!" He had this expression frequently in his mouth, even while in health, when he heard of the sufferings of his persecuted brethren, whose afflictions distressed him day and night, far more than his own. "When we besought him," says Beza, "to refrain at least during his sickness from dictating and writing, he answered, 'Would you that the Lord should find me idle when He comes?'" The Holy Scriptures employed him to the last: they were to him as light in the darkness; for they announced to his soul the dawn of a new and eternal day. Such was the tenderness of his conscience that he would no longer receive his stipend, now that he was unable to perform the duties of his office *.

On the 10th of March, the council, deeply sensible of the greatness of the loss with which they were threatened, directed public prayers to be offered up, as in a season of the greatest afflictions †. Beza relates: "On the 10th of March, when several of the brethren came to him out of the city and from the country, we found him dressed, and sitting by the table at which he was accustomed to write or transact affairs. When he saw us enter, he rested his forehead on his hand, as he was wont to do when thinking deeply, and remained silent for some time. At length he spoke, and said, his voice frequently failing him, but

* Registres de Genève, 15 Mars, 1564. † Regist. 19 Mars, 1564.

with a serene and smiling countenance, 'My dear brothers! I thank you greatly for your tender care, and I hope a fortnight hence to assemble you all around me, yet once more; but it will be for the last time*. The Lord will then, I think, reveal what He has determined respecting me, and will probably take me to Himself.'"

On the day which he had mentioned, that is March 24, after he had censured the brethren according to the appointed order, and had been censured in turn, he said, that he felt that some alleviation of suffering was granted him by the Lord. He then asked for a New Testament in French, and read to us some of the marginal notes, requiring the opinion of the brethren respecting them, because he had undertaken, he said, to correct them.

The following day he was not so well, the labour which he had undergone having apparently exhausted his feeble frame. On the 27th, however, he desired to be carried to the door of the council-chamber. He ascended the steps leading to the hall, supported by two attendants; and there, having proposed to the senate a new rector for the school, he took off his scull-cap, and thanked the assembly for the kindness which he had experienced at its hands, and especially for the friendship which had been shown him during his last illness. "For I feel," he said, "that this is the last time that I shall stand here." These words were uttered in a voice scarcely audible; and he immediately took his leave of the council, the members of which were moved to tears.

"On the 2nd ot April," says Beza, "it being Easter-day, he was carried to church in a chair. He remained during the whole sermon, and received the sacrament from my hand. He even joined, though with a trembling voice, the congregation in the last hymn, 'Lord, let thy servant depart in peace:' and looking at the countenance of the departing one, easily might we discover the signs of Christian joyfulness."

On the 25th of the month he made his will: this instrument is strikingly illustrative of his character. It is as a full stream of the sentiments which filled his humble soul. He declares his belief, and commends himself to the mercy of God; he then disposes in the whole of 225 dollars. The strict observance of form in the will, and the severe but yet kind manner in which he

* The day alluded to was that appointed for the brotherly censureship of sermons, &c.

spoke in it of a thoughtless nephew, are very remarkable. Luther's peculiarities are also apparent in his last testament.

We quote the following passage from Calvin's :—"In the first place, I thank God that He has not only had mercy on his poor creature, having delivered me from the abyss of idolatry, but that He has brought me into the clear light of his Gospel, and made me a partaker of the doctrine of salvation, of which I was altogether unworthy; yea, that his mercy and goodness have borne so tenderly with my numerous sins and offences, for which I deserved to be cast from Him and destroyed. But especially is my soul filled with thankfulness for the grace and love of the Lord, in deigning to make use of my labour in proclaiming and extending his Gospel. I testify what I have in my soul, that I will live and die in this faith which He has given me; for I have no other hope but that which rests on his free election, the only foundation of my salvation; and with my whole heart do I embrace the mercy which Christ has prepared for me, that all my sins may be buried through the merits of his death and sufferings. I most humbly pray that I may be so purified and washed by the blood of this great Redeemer, shed for the sins of mankind, that I may be able to stand before his judgement-seat and bear his image on me. I testify also, that according to the measure of grace given me, I have taught his pure word, in preaching, in works, and in the exposition of Scripture: yea, in all the controversies which I have carried on against the enemies of the truth, I have employed no sophistry, but have fought the good fight in simplicity and truth. But, alas! the goodwill which I have had, and my zeal, if so it can be called, has been something so poor and cold, that I have failed in numberless ways in fulfilling my office; and but for the unbounded goodness of God, my goodwill would have been but smoke; yea, but for this, even the grace which He gave me would have only rendered me more guilty in his sight: therefore do I solemnly testify that I own no other power of salvation but this, that God, who is the God of mercy, is ready to manifest himself as the Father of so miserable a sinner."

His brother and Laurent de Normandie, who had come from Noyon with him, were appointed executors of his will. It was signed by the seven witnesses, who had been named by Calvin, and the notary, after it had been read with a loud and articulate voice.

It is instructive to compare with this of Calvin, Luther's characteristic opinion of himself, as given in the introduction to his will. Treating all legal forms with contempt, he says: "I am well enough known in heaven, upon earth, and in hell; and I am sufficiently respected to be trusted; for God, miserable sinner as I am, and deserving of condemnation, has out of his fatherly mercy entrusted me with the Gospel of his Son, and has made me true and faithful therein, so that many in the world have received it through me; and do, therefore, own me as a teacher of the truth; while I have been enabled to despise the ban of the pope, of the emperor, of kings, princes and priests; yea the hatred of all the devils. How then can my hand-writing fail to be a sufficient witness to a thing of such little importance; and if it can be said, 'Thus wrote Dr. Martin Luther, the steward of the things of God, and witness of his Gospel*!'"

Calvin now sent a message to the four syndics, and the several members of the council, stating that he wished, before leaving the world, to meet them once more in the senate-house; and that he would cause himself to be carried to the hall the following day: so at least he hoped to be able to do. The senators answered, that they should prefer to come to him, and besought him to have regard to his health. Accordingly, on the 30th of April, they proceeded from the council-chamber in solemn procession to his house. When they were assembled around him, he collected all his strength in order to repeat to them, without interruption, the address which he had prepared. His speech was noted down as he delivered it:—

"Most honourable Seigneurs! I cannot sufficiently thank you for the marks of respect which you have bestowed upon me, and which have been so wholly undeserved; or for the patience with which you have borne my manifold infirmities, always to me the greatest proof of your friendship and benevolence. And although I have had in my office here many struggles to endure, and have suffered many severe injuries, for thus must every righteous man in this world be proved, yet know I well that these things have not happened through any fault of yours. My earnest prayer now is, that if I have not been able to effect all that I should have done, you will not attribute this to my want of will, but to my want of means. This however I can with truth testify, that I have been devoted with my whole soul to your republic; and although I have not fulfilled my duty as I could have wished, I have

* Seckendorf, B. iii. p. 651, und De Wette, Briefsammlung, t. v. p. 422.

laboured with all my strength for the common good. It would be hypocrisy not to own that the Lord has been pleased to employ me, and that not unprofitably, in his service. But one thing more also must I earnestly entreat of you, and that is, to pardon me if I have done little in my public and private life in comparison with what I ought to have done. I own especially, that I am greatly indebted to your kindness, for bearing so patiently with my often unbridled impetuosity. I hope and trust that God will also forgive me the sins which I have thus committed. For the rest, and with regard to the doctrine which you have heard from me, I testify that I have taught it not lightly, or uncertainly, but purely and faithfully, according to the word of God which was entrusted to me. Were it otherwise, I know well that the wrath of God would certainly impend over me, whereas I am now convinced that my labours in teaching the word have not been unacceptable in his sight: and this I so much the rather state before God and before you, because I doubt not that the malicious and evil-minded will endeavour to pervert the weak, and corrupt the pure doctrine which you have heard from me."

After having spoken at large of the boundless mercy of God, of his goodness poured richly upon all, he exclaimed: "I myself am the best witness of the power of the Lord to deliver you out of the greatest dangers. You know well what position your state occupies; good or ill may befall you in these circumstances; I adjure you therefore before God, always to bear in mind that it is God alone who gives strength to states and cities, and that He demands of men the honour due to his omnipotence. Remember that David, that great king, testifies, that he fell the lowest while he was in the enjoyment of the profoundest peace; and that he would never have risen again, had not God in his infinite goodness stretched out his hand to him. How would it be then with us, poor, weak and wretched as we are, seeing that such was the case with so strong and mighty a man? The greatest possible humility of heart is necessary to you, that you may pursue your course with foresight and in the fear of God, ever hiding yourselves under his wings. Then will you be convinced that his help is a sufficient support, as you have before so often found it, even though the safety and prosperity of the state should seem to hang but on a little thread.

"And if it should be well with you, I beseech you do not follow the example of the unbelievers, but praise God with all humility. If misfortune should happen to you, and death should threaten you on all sides, then place your hope on Him who can even raise the dead. At such a time be especially convinced that you are visited by God, in order that you may learn to humble yourselves, and seek the covert of his wings. If you would preserve this republic in its present firm and happy condition, take care above all things not to suffer the holy institution which God has planted among you to be polluted with sin and blasphemy. He alone is the great God, the King of kings and Lord of lords, who puts honour upon those who honour Him, and casts down the scorners. Pray to Him according to his own law; and become more and more perfect in this knowledge, for we are always most distant from that in which we ought to be the most perfect. I know well enough the temper and manners of each one among you; and know also that you need admonition; not one of you, even the most excellent, is without many faults. Let every one, therefore, examine himself, and pray the Lord to bestow upon him that in which he is wanting.

"We see how many, and what great defects there are in most of the assemblies, in which the business of temporal states is carried on. One party is cold and negligent as to the public welfare, in order that it may secure its own advantage; another yields itself to its passions and prejudices; while a third abuses the glorious gifts of God, or becomes proud, and with a haughty trust in its own sufficiency, insists that that which seems good to itself, shall be accepted as such by all others. I exhort the aged, in the name of God, not to manifest envy towards the young who may be adorned with especial gifts. I exhort the younger to prove themselves free from all haughtiness of mind. Let not the one interrupt the course of the other: avoid personal enmities, and all those bitternesses which have turned so many in the government of republics from the right path. You will not fall into such errors if you severally confine yourselves to the duty which belongs to each, and execute faithfully the part entrusted to you by the state. In the execution of justice, I adjure you never to exhibit the slightest trace of favour or dislike. Let no one mar the right by subterfuge or art: let no one endeavour by his influence to contravene the strictness of the law: let no one swerve from what is just and honest.

"But should any one be tempted by a wrong feeling, let him be resisted with firmness; and let your looks be directed above to Him from whom all power is derived, and ask of Him the Holy Spirit. Lastly, I again beseech you to pardon my weaknesses, known as they are to God and the angels, and which, honourable sirs, I do not wish to conceal from you."

Having thus spoken, Calvin prayed to the great and good God, that he might furnish the members of the council with increased gifts of grace, and so lead them by his Holy Spirit, that they might labour effectually both for their own salvation, and for that of the people. He then offered his right hand to all present, and left them deeply affected and shedding floods of tears, as if taking their last leave of a father*.

On the 28th of April, when all the ministers of the Genevese territory were assembled at his house, according to his wish, he thus addressed them: "Do you, my brothers, when I am dead, persevere in this work, and your spirit will never faint; for the Lord will preserve this church and this republic against all the threats of their enemies. Let no strife exist among you, but exercise love one towards another. Never let the thought escape you of what you owe to this church, in which the Lord has placed you, and let nothing separate you from it. I know well enough that there are some, who when weary and disgusted with their duty, can easily invent excuses for forsaking it; but they will soon discover that the 'Lord is not mocked.' When I first came to this city, the Gospel was already preached here, but the greatest disorder prevailed on all sides, as if Christianity consisted wholly in the destruction of images. Nor were there wanting occasions of offence, which caused me endless distress. But the Lord, He is our God, so strengthened me, fearful and weak as I was by nature, that I never yielded to my adversaries: I returned hither from Strasburg, obeying the call, against my own will, because I thought that I could not be useful here; not knowing what the Lord had in store for me, and because the undertaking was involved in manifold and great difficulties.

"But as I continued to proceed in the work, I at length discovered, by the thing itself, that the Lord had blessed my labour. Do you, therefore, persevere in this calling: hold fast the established order, and exert yourselves to the end, that the people may be preserved in the love of pure doctrine. There are still among us some perverse and wicked spirits. But the whole, as you see, is not now evilly disposed; you would therefore be the more guilty in the sight of God, if by your negligence all were again to be thrown into confusion.—Further:

* They thanked him for all the services he had rendered them; and assured him, that they would always manifest their love to the surviving members of his family, for his sake.

My brothers, I testify to you, that a true and earnest affection has ever united me to you, and that I bid you farewell with the same feeling. If I have often during my sickness appeared less friendly, pardon me. I cannot thank you enough for having taken upon you, while I have been thus suffering, the burden of my duties." He then extended his right hand to each; "and we went from him," says Beza, "with very heavy hearts and wet eyes."

Having learnt on the 2nd of May, by a letter from Farel, that that now aged man, thinking more of his sick friend than of himself, proposed making a journey to Geneva, Calvin wrote to him the following letter in Latin*:—"Farewell, my best and most faithful brother: since it is God's will that you should survive me, live in the constant recollection of our union, which, in so far as it was useful to the church of God, will still bear for us abiding fruit in heaven. I wish you not to fatigue yourself on my account. My breath is weak, and I continually expect it to leave me. It is enough for me that I live and die in Christ, who is gain to his people both in life and in death. Once more farewell, with the brethren. Geneva, May 2, 1564." But notwithstanding this letter, the good old man came to Geneva, and having once more conversed with his friend and embraced him, he returned to Neuchatel.†

"The few remaining days of his life," says Beza, "Calvin spent in almost constant prayer. So weak, however, was his voice, through the shortness of his breath, that for the most part his sighs only were audible. But his eyes shone bright to the last, and he raised them to heaven, with such an expression, that it was easy to learn from them the fervour of his prayer. He frequently repeated in his agony, with profound sighs, the words of David, 'Lord, I opened not my mouth, for it was thy doing:' and from time to time those of Isaiah, 'I mourn as a dove.' I have also heard that he said, 'Thou dost sorely afflict me, O Lord: but it is consolation enough for me, and I suffer it willingly, since it is thine hand.'

"His doors must have stood open day and night, if all had

* Viret, it appears, was far distant. Kirchhofer says that Viret and Fabri laboured boldly in France, at Lyons, after Calvin's death (B. ii. p. 162). The letter here quoted is, Ep. 344. Ed. Laus., Ed. Amst. p. 172.

† Of Farel, we are told that he did not long survive his friend. His missionary zeal continued active to the last: unable to rest at home, he was continually seeking some new scene of action abroad. Thus in the spring of 1565, when he was 76 years old, he went to Metz, the sphere of his earliest labours. Arriving on the 12th of May, he preached and returned to Neuchatel, where he soon after died of exhaustion. He left behind him a son, and a little property of 120 livres. Ruchat, vii. pp. 75, 76.

been allowed to enter who came to manifest their sympathy with him; but as the weakness of his voice would not suffer him to speak with them, he desired that every one might be told that he would rather have his friends pray for him, than afflict themselves with the sight of his sufferings. He frequently said to me, whose presence, as I often heard, was never unacceptable to him, that it was a matter of conscience with him to disturb me as little as possible in the duties of my office. He was always so careful of time which belonged to the church, that, exercising almost too great a degree of strictness, he would not allow his friends to trouble themselves in the least about him, whereas they could have no greater joy in the world than to serve him.

"He thus continued to linger, consoling himself and his friends, till the 19th of May, on which day we were to hold our customary censure of the preachers, and to dine together in token of mutual friendship, seeing that two days afterwards we were to celebrate the Lord's Supper and the Easter-festival. He had given us permission to prepare our meal this day in his own house; and collecting all his strength, he desired to be carried from his bed into the next chamber. He then said, 'I come to you for the last time, my brothers, and shall no more sit at the table with you.' Such was the mournful beginning of this dinner: he however delivered the prayer, and took some food, his conversation being even cheerful, as far as it could be at such a time. The meal was not finished when he desired to be carried into the neighbouring room, where he addressed the company in the most joyous accents, and said, 'This wall of separation will not prevent me, though bodily absent, from being present at your meetings in spirit.' This was doubtless said in reference to his approaching death. What he had intimated took place. He continued from this day in a lying posture: his body, with the exception of his countenance, which always remained the same, was so emaciated, that it might have been especially said of him, that the spirit only was left."

Thus, those who saw Calvin on his death-bed might well recollect the case of Joshua the high-priest*, when Israel came out of captivity, and God spake to the prophet, "Is not this a brand plucked out of the fire?" So this man, adorned as he was with such various gifts, now lay there like a withered leaf.

"The day," continues Beza, "on which he died, namely May 27th, he seemed to suffer less, and even to speak with greater

* Zechariah iii. 1.

ease; but this was the last effort of nature. In the evening, about eight o'clock, the sure signs of death became suddenly apparent. As soon as this was made known to me, and to one of the brethren, by the servants, I hastened to the bed-side, and found him just as he quietly expired: neither feet nor hands were convulsed; he had not even breathed hard. He had retained his consciousness and reason to the end. Even his voice was preserved till his last breath, and he looked rather like one sleeping than one dead. Thus on this day, with the setting sun, the brightest light in the world, and he who had been the strength of the church, was taken back to heaven.

"During the night, and on the following day, great was the mourning throughout the city. The entire state wept for the prophet of the Lord; the church lamented the departure of its faithful pastor; the academy the loss of so great a teacher: all exclaimed in their grief, that they had lost a father, who, after God, was their truest friend and comforter. Many inhabitants of the city desired to see him after he was dead, and could hardly be induced to leave his remains.

"Some of those also, who had come from distant places to make his acquaintance and to hear him, among whom was a very distinguished man, the ambassador of the queen of England to France, were particularly anxious to behold his countenance, even in death. At first, all who wished were admitted; but as they were merely influenced by curiosity, it seemed advisable to his friends, in order to prevent the misrepresentations of adversaries, to put him early the next day, which was Sunday, in a shroud, and then inclose him as usual in a wooden coffin. At two o'clock in the afternoon, he was carried to the city church-yard, called the *Plain-Palais*. All the patricians of the city followed; they were accompanied by the clergy, the professors of the high-school, and by almost the whole city; not without many tears."

He was buried without the slightest pomp: this was according to his own expressed desire. Beza however wrote an epitaph on him. He had lived fifty-four years, ten months, seventeen days; and the half of this time he had consecrated to the service of the Gospel. Respecting his last will, the Genevese neither raised a monument to his memory, nor marked his grave with a stone. Thus, in the church-yard which is so decorated with the tombs of others, the grave of Calvin is unmarked and unknown. It will be shown at the last day. A beautiful brass medal has been lately cast in honour of his name. But his writings, and the example of his firm faith, have a durability greater than that of marble and brass; and certain it is, that wherever a church is praying, or a martyr is struggling for the faith, there Calvin is also present with his power of faith and prayer.

In proportion to the grief experienced in the reformed church, was the joy of the Roman Catholics. The pope expected that he might again win Geneva to his side, and even named seven missionaries for this especial work; but the council venerated the majesty of Calvin's character, and held firm to the truth, as if it had still the invisible before its eyes*.

Calvin died in Beza's arms: knowing that he deserved his entire confidence, he had charged him in his last hours with the duty of editing his correspondence for the use of the church†. Beza was Calvin's worthy successor, and was as free from ambition as Calvin himself.

We may here properly subjoin Beza's rapid sketch of Calvin's character. It forms the conclusion of his biography, and is a simple, fitting memorial, in harmony with the nature of the great man to whom it relates. The true spirit of olden times breathes in its language, and it may well be classed with the best compositions of the kind. The writer begins with the mention of Calvin's outward life, and then proceeds to that of his spiritual character.

"Calvin was not of large stature: his complexion was pale, and rather brown: even to his last moments his eyes were peculiarly bright, and indicative of his penetrating genius. He knew nothing of luxury in his outward life, but was fond of the greatest neatness, as became his thorough simplicity: his manner of living was so arranged, that he showed himself equally averse to extravagance and parsimony: he took so little nourishment, such being the weakness of his stomach, that for many years he contented himself with one meal a day. Of sleep he had almost none: his memory was incredible; he immediately recognized, after many years, those whom he had once seen; and when he had been interrupted for several hours, in some work about which he was employed, he could immediately resume and continue it, without reading again what he had before written. Of the nu-

* See Beza's Life of Calvin in French, p. 54.

† See Beza's Dedication of Calvin's correspondence to the Count Palatine Frederic.

merous details connected with the business of his office, he never forgot even the most trifling, and this notwithstanding the incredible multitude of his affairs. His judgement was so acute and correct in regard to the most opposite concerns about which his advice was asked, that he often seemed to possess the gift of looking into the future. I never remember to have heard that any one who followed his counsel went wrong. He despised fine speaking, and was rather abrupt in his language; but he wrote admirably, and no theologian of his time expressed himself so clearly, so impressively and acutely as he, and yet he laboured as much as any one of his contemporaries, or of the fathers. For this fluency he was indebted to the several studies of his youth, and to the natural acuteness of his genius, which had been still further increased by the practice of dictation, so that proper and dignified expressions never failed him, whether he was writing or speaking. He never, in any wise, altered the doctrine which he first adopted, but remained true to it to the last,—a thing which can be said of few theologians of this period.

"Although nature had endowed Calvin with a dignified seriousness, both in manner and character, no one was more agreeable than he in ordinary conversation. He could bear, in a wonderful manner, with the failings of others, when they sprung from mere weakness: thus he never shamed any one by ill-timed reproofs, or discouraged a weak brother; while, on the other hand, he never spared or overlooked wilful sin. An enemy to all flattery, he hated dissimulation, especially every dishonest sentiment in reference to religion: he was therefore as powerful and stormy an enemy to vices of this kind, as he was a devoted friend to truth, simplicity and uprightness. His temperament was naturally choleric, and his active public life had tended greatly to increase this failing; but the Spirit of God had taught him so to moderate his anger, that no word ever escaped him unworthy of a righteous man. Still less did he ever commit aught unjust towards others. It was then only, indeed, when the question concerned religion, and when he had to contend against hardened sinners, that he allowed himself to be moved and excited beyond the bounds of moderation.

"Let us take but a single glance at the history of those men who, in any part of the world, have been distinguished for their virtues, and no one will be surprised at finding, that the great and noble qualities which Calvin exhibited, both in his private and public life, excited against him a host of enemies. We ought not indeed to feel any wonder, that so powerful a champion of pure doctrine, and so stern a teacher of sound morals, as well at home as in the world, should be so fiercely assailed. Rather ought we to let our admiration dwell on the fact, that standing alone as he did, like the renowned hero of antiquity, he was sufficiently mighty among Christians to bridle so many monsters, availing himself only of that strongest of clubs, the Word of God. Thus, however numerous the adversaries which Satan excited against him (for he never had any but such as had declared war with piety and virtue), the Lord gave his servant sufficient strength to gain the victory over all.

"Having been for sixteen years a witness of his labours, I have pursued the history of his life and death with all fidelity; and I now unhesitatingly testify, that every Christian may find in this man the noble pattern of a truly Christian life and Christian death; a pattern, however, which it is as easy to counterfeit as it is difficult to imitate."

APPENDIX.

Vol. I. page 412.

The following is a copy of the Liturgical Prayer, which Calvin appointed to be repeated after the singing of the Psalms :—

"Nous invoquerons notre bon Dieu et pere, le suppliant que comme toute plenitude de sagesse et lumiere gist en lui, qu'il nous veuille illuminer par son St. esprit en la vraie intelligence de sa parole, nous faire grace que nous la recevions en vraie crainte et humilité, que nous soyons enseignés par icelle de mettre pleinement notre fiance en lui seul, le servir et honorer comme il appartient pour glorifier son St. nom en toute notre vie, et edifier nos prochains par nos bons exemples, lui rendant l'amour et la crainte que doivent fideles serviteurs à leurs maîtres et enfans à leurs peres, puisqu'il lui a plu nous faire cette grace de nous recevoir au nombre de ses serviteurs et enfans. Et le prierons ainsi que notre bon maître nous a enseigné, N. p."

Vol. II. page 194.

The following is the original of the curious document which the first accuser of Servetus presented to the Council :—

"Requête de Nicolas de la Fontaine.
(Rilliet, Rel. du proc. crim. p. 33.)

"Pardevant Vous, magnificques, puissans et tres-redoubtez Seigneurs, propose Nicolas de la Fontaine sestant constitué prisonnier en cause criminelle contre Michel Servet pour les graves scandales et troubles que le dict Servet a desja faict par lespace de vingt quattre ans ou envyron en la chrestienté, pour les blasphemes qu'il a prononcé et escript contre Dieu, pour les heresies dont il a infecté le monde, pour les meschantes calumnies et faulses diffamations quil a publié contre les vrais serviteurs de Dieu et notament contre Mr. Calvin duquel le dict proposant est tenu de maintenir l'honneur comme de son pasteur, sil veult estre tenu pour chrestien, et aussi à cause du blasme, et deshonneur qui pourroit avenir à l'eglise de Geneve pourceque le dict Servet condamne par especial la doctrine quon y presche.

"Daultant que du jour dhier le dict Servet fust examiné et ne respondit nullement à propos, ains, au lieu de respondre pertinement par oui ou non, dict ce que bon luy sembla comme vous pourrez voir que la pluspart de ses responses sont que chansons frivoles quil vous plaise le constraindre à respondre formellement sur chacun article sans extravaguer afin quil ne se mocque plus de Dieu ne de voz Seigneuries et aussi que le dict proposant ne soit frustré de son bon droict.

"Et quant le dict proposant aura verifié son intention, et que le dict Servet aura esté convaincu davoir escript et dogmatisé les heresies contenues aux interrogatoires, le dict proposant vous supplie humblement, que si vous congnoissez le dict Servet estre criminel et digne destre poursuyvy par vostre procureur fiscal, il vous plaise en faire declaration et le vouloir delivrer avec victoire de tous despens, dommaiges et interests, non pas quil fuye ou refuse de poursuivre une telle cause et querelle, laquelle tous chrestiens et enfans de Dieu doibvent maintenir jusques à la mort, mais pour ce quil entend que les us et coustumes de vostre ville portent cela, et que ce nest pas à luy dentreprendre sur la charge et office daultruy."

Vol. II. page 211.

"Requête de Michael Servet.

"Très-honorés Seigneurs!

"Je suis detenu en accusation criminelle de la part de Jehan Calvin, lequel ma faulsament accusé disant que javès escript 1. que les ames estiont mortelles et aussi que Jesu Christ navoyt prins de la Vierga Maria que la quatriesme partie de son corps. Ce sont choses horribles et execrables. En toutes les aultres heresies et en tous les aultres crimes ny en a poynt de si grand que de faire lame mortelle. Car à tous les aultres il y a sperance de salut et non point à cestui-ci. Qui dict cela ne croyt poynt quil y aie Dieu, ni justice, ni resurrection, ni Jesu Christ, ni sainte escriture, ni rien: sinon que tout è mort et que homme et beste soyt tout un. Si javès dict cela, non seulement dict, mais escript publicament pour enfecir le monde, je me condamnerès moy-mesme à mort.

"Pourquoy, Messeigneurs, je demande que mon faulx accusateur soit puni *pœna talionis*, et que soyt detenu prisonnier comme moy jusques à ce la cause soyt diffinie pour mort de luy ou de moy, ou aultre poine. Et pour ce faire, je me inscris contra luy à la dicte poine de talion. Et suys content de morir, si non est convaincu, tant de cecy que daultres choses que je luy mettré dessus. Je vous demande justice, Messeigneurs, justice, justice, justice.

"Faict en vos prisons de Geneve, le 22 de Septembre 1553.

"MICHEL SERVETUS
en sa cause propre."

The above was accompanied by another paper, in which Servetus enumerated six points in reference to the part which Calvin took in his apprehension at Vienne, and in regard to which he insisted that he ought to be judicially examined. Four other points also were stated upon which Servetus grounded his accusation of Calvin.

"Messeigneurs, il y a quatre raisons grandes et infaillibles, par les quieles Calvin doyt estre condamné.

"La premiere est, pour ce que la matiere de la doctrine nest poynt subjecte a accusation criminelle, comme vous ay monstré par mes requestes et monstrarè plus amplement par les anciens docteurs de leglise. Pour quoy il a grandament abussé de la criminalité et contre lestat dun ministre de levangile.

"La seconde raison est, pour ce quil est faulx accusateur, comme la presente inscription vous monstre et se prouvera facilement par la lecture de mon livre.

"La tierse est, que par frivoles et calumnieuses raisons veult opprimer la verité de Jesu Christ, comme par le rapport de nos escritures vous sera manifesté. Car il y a mis de grandes menteries et meschancetés.

"La quatrieme raison est, que en grande partie il ensuyt la doctrine de Simon Magus contre tous les docteurs qui furent jamays en leglise. Pourquoy comme magicien quil est, doyt non seulement estre condamné, mays doyt estre exterminé et dechacé de vostre ville. Et son bien doyt estre adjugé a moy en recompanse du mien, que luy ma faict perdre, la quiele chose, Messeigneurs, je vous demande. Faict le jour que dessus, etc.

"MICHEL SERVETUS
en sa cause propre."

Vol. II. page 215.

The sentence passed on Servetus was couched in the following terms. Whether Calvin had any share in its composition may be questioned.

"Le procès faict et formé par devant noz tres redoubtéz Seigneurs, scindiques, juges des causes criminelles de ceste Cité à la poursuitte et instance du Seigneur Lieutenant de ceste dicte Cité, ès dictes causes instant Contre Michel Servet, de Villeneufve au Royaume d'Aragon en Hespagne.

"Lequel premierement est esté atteint d'avoir, il y a environ vingt troys à vingt quatre ans faict imprimer ung Livre à Agnon en Alemagne contre la saincte et individue Trinité, contenant plusieurs et grans blasphemes contre icelle, grandement scandaleux ès Eglises des dictes Alemagnes: lequel livre il a spontanement confessé avoir faict imprimer, nonobstant les remonstrances et corrections à luy faictes de ses faulses opinions par les scavants docteurs evangelistes d'icelles Eglises des dictes Alemagnes.

"Item, et lequel livre est esté par les docteurs d'icelles Eglises d'Alemagne comme plein d'heresie reprouvé, et le dict *Servet* rendu fugitif des dictes Alemagnes à cause du dict livre.

"Item, et nonobstant cela le dict *Servet* a perseveré en ses faulses erreurs, infectant d'icelles plusieurs à son possible.

"Item, et non content de cela pour mieulx divulguer et espancher son dict venin et heresie dempuis peu de temps en ça il a faict imprimer un aultre livre à cachettes dans Vienne en Daulphiné, remply desdictes heresies, horribles et execrables blasphemes contre la saincte Trinité, contre le Filz de Dieu, contre le baptesme des petis enfans et aultres plusieurs saincts passages et fondemens de la religion chrestienne.

"Item, a spontanement confessé qu'en iceluy livre il appelle ceux qui croyent en la Trinité, trinitaires et atheistes.

"Item, et qu'il appelle icelle Trinité ung Diable et monstre à troys testes.

"Item, et contre le vray fondement de la religion chrestienne et blasphemant detestablement contre le filz de Dieu, a dict *Jesus Christ* nestre filz de Dieu de toute eternité, ains tant seulement dempuis son incarnation.

"Item, et contre ce que dit le scripture, *Jesus Christ* estre filz de David selon la chair, il le nye malheureusement, disant iceluy estre crée de la substance de Dieu le Pere, ayant receu troys elemens diceluy, et un tant seulement de la Vierge: En quoy meschamment il pretend abolir la vraye et entiere humanité de nostre Seigneur *Jesus Christ,* la souveraine consolation du pouvre genre humain.

"Item, et que le baptesme des petits enfans nest qu'une invention diabolique et sorcellerie.

"Item, et plusieurs aultres pointz et articles et execrables blasphemes desquelz ledict livre est tout farcy, grandement scandaleux et contre l'honneur et majesté de Dieu, du filz de Dieu et du Sainct Esprit: qu'est ung cruel et horrible murtrissement, perdition et ruine de plusieurs pouvres ames, estant par sa dessus dicte desloyable et detestable doctrine trahies. Chose epouvantable à reciter!

"Item, et lequel *Servet* remply de malice intitula iceluy son livre, ainsi dressé contre Dieu et sa saincte doctrine evangelique, *Christianismi Restitutio,* qu'est à dire restitution du christianisme; et ce pour mieulx seduyre et tromper les pouvres ignorans et pour plus commodement infecter de son malheureux et meschant venin les lecteurs de son dict livre, soubz l'umbre de bonne doctrine.

"Item, et oultre le dessus dict livre, assaillant par lettres mesmes nostre foy et mettant peine icelle infecter de sa poison, a voluntairement confessé et recogneu avoir escriptes lettres à ung des ministres de ceste cité, dans laquelle entre aultres plusieurs horribles et enormes blasphemes contre nostre saincte religion evangelique : il dit nostre evangile estre sans foy et sans Dieu et que pour ung Dieu nous avons ung Cerbere a troys testes.

"Item, et a davantage voluntairement confessé, qu'au dessus dict lieu de Vienne, à cause diceluy meschant et abominable livre et opinions, il fut faict prisonnier, lesquelles prisons perfidement il rompit et eschapa.

"Item, et n'est seulement dressé ledict *Servet* en sa doctrine contre la vraye religion chrestienne, mais comme arrogant innovateur dheresies, contre la papistique et aultres, si que à Vienne mesmes il est esté bruslé en effigie et de sesdictz livres cinq basles bruslées.

"Item, et nonobstant tout cela, estant icy ès prisons de ceste cité detenu, n'a laissé de persister malicieusement en ses dictes meschantes et detestables erreurs, les taschant soustenir avec injures et calumnies contre tous vrays chrestiens et fideles tenementiers de la pure immaculée religion chrestienne les appellant trinitaires, atheistes et sorciers, nonobstant les remonstrances à luy desia dès long temps en Alemagne, comment est dict, faictes et au mespris des reprehensions, emprisonnements ct corrections à luy tant ailleurs que icy faictes. Comme plus amplement et au long est contenu en son procès.

"Et Nous sindiques, juges des causes criminelles de ceste cité, ayans veu le procès faict et formé devant Nous, à linstance de nostre lieutenant ès dictes causes instant, contre Toy, *Michel Servet* de Villeneufve au royaume d'Arragon en Espagne, par lequel et tes voluntaires confessions en noz mains faictes, et par plusieurs foys reiterées et tez livres devant Nous produictz, nous consté et apart Toy *Servet* avoir dès longtemps mys en avant doctrine faulse et pleinement hereticale et icelle, mettant arrier toutes remonstrances et corrections, avoir d'une malicieuse et perverse obstination, perseveremment semée et divulguée jusques à impression de livres publiques, contre Dieu le Pere, le Filz et le Sainct Esprit : brefz contre les vrays fondemens de la religion chrestienne et pour cella tasché de faire schisme et troble en leglise de Dieu, dont meintes ames ont pu estre ruinées et perdues ; chose horrible et espouvantable, scandaleuse et infectante, et n'avoir heu honte ni horreur de te dresser toutallement contre la majesté divine et saincte Trinité : ains avoyr mys peyne et testre employé obstinement à infecter le monde de tez heresies et puante poyson hereticale, Cas et crime dheresie griefz et detestable et meritant grieve punition corporelle.

"A cez causes et aultres justes à ce Nous mouvantes, desirans de purger leglise de Dieu de tel infectement et retrancher dycelle tel membre pourry, ayans heu bonne participation de conseil avec noz citoyens et ayans invoqué le nom de Dieu, pour faire droit jugement, seans pour tribunal au lieu de nos majeurs, ayans Dieu et ses saintes escriptures devant noz yeux, disans au nom du Pere, du Filz et du Sainct Esprit, par iceste nostre diffinitive sentence, laquelle donnons ycy par escript, Toy *Michel Servet* condamnons à debvoir estre lié et mené au lieu de Champel, et là debvoir estre à un pilotis attaché, et buslé tout vifz avec ton livre, tant escript de ta main qu'imprimé, jusques à ce que ton corps soit reduict en cendre; et ainsin finiras tez jours, pour donner exemple aux aultres, qui tel cas vouldroient commettre. Et à Vous nostre lieutenant, commandons nostre presente sentence faictes mectre en execution."

Vol. II. page 11.

The following is the original Latin of Calvin's letter to Luther:—

"Excellentissimo Christianæ Ecclesiæ Pastori, D. M. Luthero, Patri mihi plurimum observando.

"S. Cum Gallos nostros viderem, quotquot a tenebris Papatus ad fidei sanitatem reducti erant, nihil tamen de confessione mutare, ac proinde se polluere sacrilegiis Papistarum, ac si nullum veræ doctrinæ gustum haberent, temperare mihi non potui, quin tantam sane socordiam, sicuti meo iudicio merebatur, acriter reprehenderem. Qualis enim hæc fides, quæ intus in animo sepulta, nullam in fidei confessionem erumpit? Qualis religio, quæ sub idololatriæ simulatione demersa iacet? Verum hic argumentum tractandum non suscipio, quod libellis duobus copiose sum prosequutus, unde si obiter eos adspicere molestum non erit, tum quid sentiam, tum quibus impulsus rationibus ita sentiam, melius perspicies. Horum vero lectione nonnulli ex nostris hominibus expergefacti, cum antea secure dormirent altum somnum, cogitare cœperunt, quidnam sibi agendum foret. Sed quia durum est vel omissa ratione sui vitam exponere periculo, vel, concitatis hominum offensionibus, mundi invidiam subire, vel, relictis fortunis et natali solo, voluntarium adire exilium, his difficultatibus retinentur, quo minus certi quidquam constituti habeant. Alias tamen rationes, et quidem speciosas obtendunt, sed quibus appareat prætextum ab illis qualemcunque quæri. Cæterum, quia suspensi quodammodo hæsitant, tuum iudicium audire desiderant, quod ut merito reverentur, ita illis magnæ confirmationis loco erit. Me ergo rogarunt, ut certum nuncium data opera ad te mitterem, qui responsum super hac re tuum ad nos referret: ego vero, quia et ipsorum magnopere interesse putabam, tua authoritate adiuvari, ne sic perpetuo fluctuentur, et mihi ipsi ultro expetendum id fuit, negare illis nolui, quod postulabant. Nunc ergo, Pater in Domino plurimum observande, per Christum te obtestor, hoc ut tædium meâ et ipsorum causâ devorare non graveris, primum, ut Epistolam eorum nomine scriptam et Libellos meos, tanquam per lusum, otiosis horis percurras, vel legendi negotium alicui demandes, qui tibi summam referat: deinde, ut sententiam tuam paucis verbis rescribas: invitus equidem facio, ut tibi inter tot tam graves et varias occupationes hanc molestiam exhibeam, sed, quæ tua est æquitas, cum non nisi necessitate coactus id faciam, veniam te mihi daturum confido. Utinam isthuc mihi, quo saltem ad paucas horas tuo congressu fruerer, liceret advolare! mallem enim et longe præstaret, non de hac quæstione modo, sed de aliis etiam tecum coram agere: verum, quod hic in terris non datur, brevi, spero, in regno Dei nobis continget. Vale, clarissime vir, præstantissime Christi Minister, ac Pater mihi semper honorande. Dominus te spiritu suo gubernare pergat usque in finem, in commune Ecclesiæ suæ bonum. 12 Calend. Febr. 1545.

"JOHANNES CALVINUS tuus."

Melancthon's Answer to the above.

"Clarissimo Viro, eruditione et virtute præstanti, D. Joanni Calvino, Pastori Ecclesiæ Genevensis, pio et fideli Amico suo, charissimo P. Melancthon S. 1545.

"Imo vero, Calvine charissime, mihi consilium de me ipso ostendas. Crescit enim hic certamen quod antea defugi. Cumque hactenus parcendum tranquillitati Ecclesiarum in his regionibus feris et horridis senserim, moderatissimeque loquutus sim, nunc duriora a me postulantur. Oro autem te ut me Deo piis votis commendes. D. Martino non exhibui tuam epistolam, multa enim suspiciose accipit: et non vult circumferri suas responsiones de talibus quæstionibus quas proposuisti. Ego utcunque respondi, nec meum judicium antefero tuæ et aliorum piorum virorum sententiæ. Scio me ἄνευ φιλονεικίας versatum esse in negotiis ecclesiasticis, et mediocriter dedisse operam ut multas res involutas evolverem et explicarem. Nunc exilia et alias ærumnas excepto. Bene vale, die quo ante annos 3846 Noë arcam ingressus est, quo exemplo Deus testatus est, se Ecclesiam suam, etiam cum ingentibus fluctibus quassatur, non deserere."

INDEX.

Albret, Johanna, mother of Henry IV., i. 19.
Amboise, the conspiracy of, ii. 369; Calvin's connection with, ii. 448.
Ameaux, prosecution and punishment of his wife, ii. 49; his attack on Calvin, ii. 57; Calvin's severity towards, ii. 58.
Anabaptists, in France and Germany, i. 40; the Reformation hindered by, *ib.*; Calvin's opposition to, and fundamental errors of some, *ib.*; Calvin's work 'Psychopannychia' directed against, i. 42; driven out of Geneva by Calvin, i. 114; Calvin writes against, ii. 42.
Angels, Calvin's doctrine respecting, i. 191.
Anton, king of Navarre, declares for the Reformation, ii. 362; falling away from the faith and Calvin's correspondence with, ii. 376.
Apocalypse, Calvin's opinion of, and reasons for not commenting on, i. 221, 225.
Art, as affected by the Reformation, i. 416.
Astrology, Calvin's work against, ii. 37.
Audin's life of Calvin, ii. 107.
Augustine's view of conversion, i. 205; of the church, i. 212.

Balduin, Francis, his changes in religion, ii. 410; his dispute with Calvin, ii. 411.
Baptism, the doctrine of, i. 82; Calvin's view of, i. 473; of infant, i. 83, 204; of the celebration of, i. 205.
Bayle, his opinion of Calvin, i. 221.
Belief, in the holy church, i. 372; harmony of Calvin's and Luther's, ii. 95.
Bern, progress of the Reformation in, i. 90; its hostility to Calvin, ii. 143; Calvin's discussion in the council of, ii. 30; quarrel with the Genevese, ii. 144; repudiates the practice of excommunication, ii. 325.
Bernhard, a preacher of Geneva, urges Calvin's return to that city, i. 250.
Berthelier, Philip, prosecution and acquittal of, ii. 307.
Beza, life and character of, i. 110, ii. 383; his friendship for Calvin, *ib.*; respecting Calvin's character, i. 276; answers Castellio's essay on toleration, ii. 36; characteristics of, ii. 85; Calvin's early friendship with, ii. 84, 112; his firm friendship for Calvin, ii. 151; his arrival in Geneva, ii. 84; at the colloquy at Poissy, ii. 380, 385; letters from Calvin to, ii. 383, 391; his influence in France, ii. 394; his conduct during the French religious war, ii. 398; at the battle of Dreux, ii. 401; returns to Geneva, ii. 403; appointed professor and minister of the school at Geneva, ii. 322; his death, ii. 112.
Bible, Olivetan's French, i. 226; Calvin edits, *ib.*; later editions of, i. 228; Castellio's translation of, *ib.*; Luther's German translation of, i. 229.
Bishops, Calvin respecting, i. 371; the Saxon divines respecting, i. 397.
Blandrata, ii. 246; Calvin's opinion of, and treatise against, ii. 265.
Bolsec, Jerome, his life and character, ii. 130; publicly attacks the doctrine of election, ii. 131; tenderness of the Swiss churches for, ii. 133; imprisoned, ii. 132; banished from Geneva, ii. 136; revival of his controversy with Calvin, ii. 150.
Bossuet, on Calvin's firmness of doctrine, i. 86.
Bourg Du, a martyr of the French church, ii. 368.
Bourgogne De, Calvin's correspondence with, i. 279; Calvin's friend-

ship with, ii. 140; his agreement with Bolsec, ii. 141.

Brazil, French emigration to, ii. 360.

Brentius, his controversy with Laski, ii. 346.

Bretschneider's opinion of Calvin, i. 304.

Bucer, seeks Calvin's friendship, i. 113; Calvin's opinion of, i. 114, ii. 112; respecting church property, i. 158; on pastoral visits, i. 445; his hostility to Servetus, ii. 172; his death, ii. 30, 112.

Bullinger, a favourer of religious persecution, ii. 210; letters from Calvin to Bullinger,—on his taking up his residence in Geneva, i. 106; on christian unity, i. 174; on the progress of the gospel in France, ii. 1; on his own consistency, ii. 77; on the doctrine of the Lord's Supper, ii. 78; on the hatred of the Bernese towards himself, ii. 144; respecting the religious wars, ii. 398.

Calvin, his characteristics as a man and a reformer,—compared with Farel and Viret, i. 108, 110; in comparison with Luther, i. 206, 227, 241, 271, 291, 297, 280, 303, 320, 321, 432, ii. 89; in comparison with Melancthon, i. 207, 238; in comparison with Zwingli, i. 208; in comparison with Augustine, i. 211; in comparison with Moses, i. 353, 359; in comparison with Servetus, ii. 161; in comparison with Vincentius of Paula, i. 421; his doctrine of the Lord's Supper, i. 83, 167, 235, 242, ii. 286; on church government, i. 84; constancy of his belief, i. 86, 304; his ability in argument, i. 122; his opinion of Luther, i. 123; his opinion on festivals and ceremonies, i. 134, 160, 418, ii. 116; on church discipline, i. 141, 383; on the punishment of heretics, *ib.*; his contempt of slander, i. 138; respecting the preparation for the Lord's Supper, i. 141, 142; on confession, i. 141, 417; on faith, i. 150, 198, 508, ii. 179; his feeling of responsibility as a minister, i. 154; respecting church property, i. 158; on the Reformation in England, i. 159; respecting the diet at Hagenau, i. 166; his conscientiousness, i. 167, 168; Luther's opinion of, i. 170; his love of unity and peace, i. 174, 180; respecting the controversy on the Lord's Supper, i. 178; his faithfulness as a christian, i. 183; energy of his faith, i. 188; on the Scriptures, i. 188, 210; his doctrine of the Trinity, i. 189; of angels, i. 191; of Satan, i. 192; of man's original state, *ib.*; of the human soul, i. 193; of free-will, i. 193, 497; of the omnipresence of God, *ib.*; of predestination, i. 193, 203; of original sin, i. 194; of the renewal of the Holy Ghost, i. 195; of the consequences of the fall, i. 196; of conversion, *ib.*; of salvation, i. 197; of good works, i. 199, 508; of election, i. 199, 201; of damnation, i. 199; of infant baptism, i. 204; his perfect reliance on the Scriptures, i. 210; his belief in the true God, *ib.*; respecting images, i. 207; respecting excommunication, *ib.*; Bayle's opinion of, i. 221; his knowledge of Hebrew and Greek, i. 222; his exegetical talent, i. 223, ii. 31; elegance and characteristics of his style, i. 223, 431; his confidence in Luther, i. 237; his disinterestedness, i. 240; considered as a poet, i. 241; as a comforter, i. 242; on submission to and reliance on God's will, i. 244; his inward life, i. 250; his love of poverty, i. 269; contrasts in his character, i. 275, 277; his pre-eminent conscientiousness, i. 275; his zeal in the cause of God, i. 276, 353; wrongly considered to be of a melancholy or surly disposition, i. 277; his sympathy for the sufferings of others, i. 274; his bodily ill-health, i. 280; his patience under affliction, i. 283; the "majesty of his character," i. 284; his hatred of the enemies of God, i. 286; an upholder of christian severity, *ib.*; his forgiveness of personal injuries, i. 287; the three distinguishing tendencies of his spirit, i. 289; his contempt of the world, i. 294; free from spiritual pride, i. 295; love of truth the fountain of his inner life, i. 297, 301; his view of martyrdom, i. 302; his feeling of the constant presence of God, i. 306; respecting exorcism and sorcery, i. 311; considered in his historical relation to the world, i. 319; his importance to the Reformation, i. 322; respecting church property, i. 336; confidence reposed in him as a politician, i. 338; on burials, i. 343, ii. 8; on theocracy, i. 349; as a legislator, i. 354, 358; his opinion of synods, i. 366; fundamental principles of his church polity, *ib.*; on bishops and presbyters, i. 371; on the ordination of the latter, *ib.*; on the election and office of doctors and preachers, i. 373; his view of the claims of the church, i. 374; his love of simplicity, i. 375; against the observance of outward forms, i. 376; on the relationship of church and state, i. 380, 388; an advocate for aristocratical government, i. 381; his spirit to be contemplated in his writings rather than in his doings, i. 390; his catechisms, i. 409; review of, and extracts from, i. 410; respecting congregational singing, i. 414; practical tendency of his mind, i. 423; his epistolary correspondence, i. 428; his acquaintance with Latin literature, i. 429; considered as a preacher, i. 431; against written sermons, i. 434; as a guide to salvation, i. 440; his rules for the conduct of ministers, i. 441; respecting the visitation of the sick, i. 442; on pastoral visits, i. 445; on attendance at public worship, *ib.*; his severity towards offenders, i. 448; his exhortation to the reading of the Scriptures, *ib.*; on repentance, i. 450; on steadfastness in the faith, *ib.*; against nominal christianity, i. 462; on public and private worship, i. 464; his praise of steadfastness under persecution, i. 465; his skill as a logician, i. 468; on usury, i. 469; on dissembling of faith, i. 470; on the lawfulness of resisting persecution, i. 471; on the marriage ceremony, i. 472; his opinion of theatres, i. 473; on the salvation of children dying before baptism, *ib.*; his general activity, i. 475; respecting the papal authority, i. 478; on free-will, i. 497; on regeneration by baptism, i. 507; his hatred of dissimulation, ii. 8; his opinion of Luther, ii. 16, 18; his magnanimity, ii. 20; his inward life, ii. 31; his methodical unity of thought, ii. 32; his resolution, ii. 69; his consolation in friendship, ii. 73; his desire of unity in the church, ii. 76, 294; his doctrine of predestination, ii. 94; Luther's opinion of, ii. 97; the world's opinion of, ii. 103; his various biographers, i. 300, ii. 107; his unfailing perseverance, ii. 306; his politics, ii. 406; his opposition to religious war, ii. 409; on justification, ii. 413; on heresy, ii. 417; his patience under affliction, ii. 422.

Calvin, his birth, i. 1; his parents and childhood, i. 21; his personal appearance, *ib.*; educated with the children of the noble family of Mommor, i. 22; obtains an appointment in his twelfth year in the Chapelle de la Gésine, i. 23; becomes a pupil in the high school of Paris, *ib.*; receives the living of Marteville, i. 24; changes the parish of Marteville for that of Pont l'Evêque, *ib.*; engages in the study of the law, *ib.*; loses his father in his youth, i. 25; becomes acquainted with Melchior Woolmar, i. 26; obtains the degree of doctor, i. 27; his conversion to the reformed faith, i. 29; compared with Luther's, *ib.*; its sincerity, i. 30; his own account of the same, i. 31; he publishes the two books of Seneca de Clementiâ, with a commentary, i. 33; peril attending the publication of this work, i. 35; contents of the commentary, *ib.*; flies from Paris, i. 37; protected by the queen of Navarre, *ib.*; returns to Paris, i. 38; publishes his work entitled 'Psychopannychia,' i. 39; visits Strasburg, i. 40; becomes acquainted with the German reformers, *ib.*; projects the conversion of Francis I., 48; his opposition to the Anabaptists, i. 40; publishes the 'Institutio,' i. 53; preface to the same, *ib.*; its origin and design, i. 69, 180; resides at Basel, i. 99; visits Ferrara, i. 100; returns to bid farewell to his country, *ib.*; becomes preacher and teacher of theology at Geneva, i. 105; his friendship with Farel and Viret, i. 106; translates into Latin the first Genevese catechism, i. 112; his disputes with Caroli, i. 114, 161; his works 'De fugiendâ Idolatriâ' and 'De Papisticis Sacerdotiis vel administrandis vel abjiciendis,' i. 118; contents of, and extracts from same, *ib.*; attempts to establish strict discipline in Geneva, i. 125; meets with much opposition, *ib.*; refuses the sacrament of the Lord's Supper to the Genevese, i. 127; banished from their city, i. 128; lives at Strasburg, i. 135; appointed lecturer and preacher there, i. 140; defends the Reformation against Sadolet, i. 148; present at the convention in Frankfort, i. 155; respecting the diet at Hagenau, i. 166; his work 'De Cœnâ,' i. 175; contents of, and extracts from same, i. 176; publishes a commentary on the Epistle to the Romans, i. 218; dedicated to Grynæus, *ib.*; edits Olivetan's French Bible, i. 226; his opinion of the Catholic disputants at the diet of Worms, i. 232; sent to Worms by the people of Strasburg, i. 234; forms an intimate friendship with Melancthon, *ib.*; confutes Robertus Moshamus, Dean of Passau, at Worms, *ib.*; obtains the title of "the Theologian," i. 235; temporary coldness between him and Melancthon, i. 239; his triumphal song (Epinicion), i. 241; the Genevese desire his return, i. 246; unwillingness of the people of Strasburg that he should leave them, i. 247; decides on returning to Geneva, i. 252; his reception there, i. 255; his domestic affairs, i. 257; his poverty, *ib.*; his marriage, i. 263; Luther's marriage compared with his, *ib.*; his opinion of his wife, i. 264; on the birth and death of his only son, i. 265; on the death of his wife, i. 266; his house at Geneva, i. 330; his first address to the Genevese after his recall, i. 331; establishes a court of morals in Geneva, i. 332; his position in Geneva, i. 346; universal worth of his church discipline, i. 365; the dedications of his works, i. 423; his pastoral labours, i. 425; his bodily ill-health, i. 280, 427; his lectures on the book of Job, i. 435; extracts from, i. 436; reproof given by him to a licentious community, i. 457; to a community under persecution, i. 453; to one suffering domestic persecution, i. 455; letters to persecuted converts, i. 467; writes against Pelagianism, i. 489; extracts from the work, i. 493; writes against the council of Trent, i. 501; extracts from the work, i. 502; his writings against the Nicodemites, ii. 8; his apology to same, ii. 9; letter from Melancthon to, ii. 13; writes against the Interim, ii. 27; his disputes with Castellio, ii. 34, 155; his works against relics and astrology, ii. 37; against the Anabaptists and libertines, ii. 42; his controversies with Perrini, ii. 62; respecting the proceedings of Gruet, ii. 68; insults heaped on him on account of Gruet's death, ii. 69; his friendship for Viret, ii. 74; signs the Consensus Tigurinus, ii. 81; publishes a commentary on the Epistles, ii. 109; dedicates it to Edward VI. of England, *ib.*; letter from Melancthon to, ii. 113; his work 'De Scandalis,' ii. 117; its contents, ii. 118; his controversy with George Siculus, ii. 129; holds a public disputation with Bolsec, ii. 32; his controversy with Troillet, ii. 138; his friendship for Farel and Jacques de Bourgogne, ii. 140; hostility of the Bernese towards, ii. 143; his appeal to the council of Bern, ii. 145; renewal of his dispute with Bolsec, ii. 150; his work 'Consensus Pastorum,' ii. 151; his correspondence with Servetus, ii. 179; his conduct towards Servetus at Geneva, ii. 193; his controversy with Servetus whilst a prisoner at Geneva, ii. 199; letter from Farel to, ii. 210; letter from Bullinger to, ii. 216; his part in the execution of Servetus, ii. 224, 228; his work against the latter, ii. 241; writes a treatise against Blandrata, ii. 265; his controversy with Gentilis, ii. 271; his controversy with Westphal on the doctrine of the sacrament, ii. 274; analysis of his work against Westphal, ii. 280; second and third works against Westphal, ii. 284; his correspondence with Melancthon, ii. 295; his controversy with Hesshus, ii. 296; his uneasiness respecting the church at Strasburg, ii. 304; publishes a commentary on St. John, ii. 306; his contest with Berthelier, ii. 307; personally insulted by his enemies at Geneva, ii. 312; visits Frankfort, ii. 337; disputes with Justus Welsius on free-will, ii. 338; his relation to the Northern churches, ii. 340; corresponds with Gustavus Vasa, king of Sweden, *ib.*; writes against Menno Simon, *ib.*; his influence in Poland, ii. 341; his letters to the Poles, ii. 342, 344; respecting the papal authority, ii. 343; his address to believers about to suffer martyrdom, ii. 356, 359; his influence in France, ii. 374; his correspondence with the king of Navarre, ii. 376; obtains money for the latter, *ib.*; dedication of his commentary on the four books of Moses to Henry IV. ii. 378; his opinion of the colloquy at Poissy, ii. 386; sends to the emperor Ferdinand a confession of the French reformed church, ii. 400; preaches at Chambery, ii. 405; opposes the conspiracy of Amboise, ii. 408; his dispute with Balduin, ii. 411; writes against Cassander's project of religious union, ii. 412; his last literary and controversial labours, ii. 422; his last illness, ii. 421; Beza's account of, ii. 422; his will, ii. 425; his dying address to the council of Geneva, ii. 426; to the ministers, ii. 429; his last hours and death, ii. 430, 432; his character by Beza, ii. 433.

Calvinism, its influence on England and Germany, i. 327, 328.

Caraccioli, Marquis of Vico, his life and character, ii. 129; his persecution, ii. 130.

Caroli, his life and dispute with Calvin, i. 114; his last appearance at Metz, i. 341; challenges Farel to a public disputation, i. 342.

Cassander projects a union of religious parties, ii. 411; Calvin writes against, ii. 412.

Castellio, resides with Calvin, i. 257; his character, life and writings, ii. 33, 36; disputes with Calvin, ii. 34, 155; Montaigne's opinion of, ii. 37; becomes a teacher in the school at Geneva, ii. 33; writes anonymously against the doctrine of election, ii. 36.

Catechism, the first Genevese, drawn up by Calvin and Farel, i. 112.

Catholic church, the constitution of, i. 417.

Chaponneau, Calvin's controversy with, ii. 33.

Charles, the Emperor, convokes the diets of Worms and Ratisbon, i. 230; seeks to unite religious parties, i. 232; admonition from Alexander Farnese to, i. 480; Calvin's counter-address to, i. 481; Luther's address on the triple defence of the papacy, i. 486.

Charles IX. ascends the throne of France, ii. 370; his letter to the council of Geneva, ii. 372.

Chemminus, letters from Calvin to, i. 25, 23.

Christ, Servetus on the humanity and eternity of, ii. 254, 256.

Church, the, Calvin on the government of, i. 84, 204; controversy respecting church property in Geneva, i. 335; on the jurisdiction of, i. 376; great simplicity of the service in the reformed, i. 375; its relation to the state, i. 380; the primitive, compared with the Calvinistic, i. 395; polity of the English, i. 400; the constitution of the Catholic, i. 417; Calvin's and Bullinger's wish for unity in, ii. 124, 125, 126.

Coligni, Admiral, heads the Reformation in France, ii. 369; letters from Calvin to, ii. 362; letters to the wife of, i. 283.

Commentaries by Calvin on the old and new Testaments, i. 218, 435, ii. 109, 306.

Confession, Calvin on, i. 141; Luther, Calvin and Wesley on, i. 417; confessions of the French church, i. 408; the Helvetic, i. 407.

Condé, forms an evangelical union at Orleans, ii. 397; taken prisoner at the battle of Dreux, ii. 401; concludes a peace with the Catholics, ii. 402; letter from Calvin to, ii. 403.

Conscience, liberty of, i. 405.

Consensus Tigurinus, the, discussion respecting, ii. 80; letters from Calvin respecting, ii. 80, 81; generally received by the reformed churches, ii. 83.

Consistory, the, its office and powers as established by Calvin, i. 385.

Contarini, Cardinal, at the diet of Ratisbon, i. 231.

Conversion, Calvin's doctrine of, i. 196; Augustine's doctrine of, i. 205.

Cop, Nicolas, rector of the Sorbonne in Paris, i. 37.

Coraud, Calvin's letters on the death of, i. 139.
Cordier, Maturinus, establishes a school in Geneva, i. 335.
Cranmer, letter from Calvin respecting the unity of the church to, ii. 125.
Creation, the, Servetus respecting, ii. 250.

Damnation, Calvin's and the reformers' doctrine of, i. 199, 201.
Daniel, Francis, letters from Calvin to, i. 17, 27, 34, 113.
Dedications of Calvin's works, i. 423, ii. 32.
Demoniacal possession, instance of, i. 310.
Denmark, the Reformation in, ii. 31.
Diets of Worms and Ratisbon, i. 230, 236.
Discipline, church, i. 360; Calvin's system of, i. 369, 383.
Dreux, the battle of, ii. 401; Beza's conduct at, *ib.*

Edward, king of England, dedications of Calvin's works to, ii. 30; his death, ii. 311.
Election, Calvin's doctrine of, i. 199, 201, 212; mystery of, i. 215; incompletely comprehended by Calvin, *ib.*; Bolsec's doctrine of, ii. 132; views at Basel and Bern respecting, ii. 133.
England, state of its church in 1509–1530, i. 3; influence of Calvinism on, i. 327; church polity of, i. 400; progress of the Reformation in, ii. 28; persecution in, ii. 355.
Eutychianism, the Lutherans accused of, i. 207.
Epistolary correspondence, Calvin's, i. 428; characteristics of, i. 429.
Excommunication, the doctrine of, i. 79; Calvin respecting, i. 377; Bern repudiates the practice of, ii. 325; moral effect of, i. 394.

Faber, Peter, letter from Calvin to, i. 292.
Faith, Calvin's doctrine of, i. 198; Servetus' doctrine of, ii. 245, 247.
Fall, the, Calvin on the consequences of, i. 196.
Farel, commences the Reformation in Geneva, i. 94; persecuted by the clergy of that place, *ib.*; holds a public disputation with Guy Fürbity, i. 96; narrowly escapes being poisoned, *ib.*; retains Calvin at Geneva, i. 105; his true friendship for Calvin, i. 107, 252; his strict discipline, i. 112; Calvin's reverence for, i. 252; commences the Reformation in Metz, i. 339; his desire of unity in the church, ii. 88; his favourable opinion of the Augsburg confession, *ib.*; Calvin's friendship for, ii. 140; a favourer of religious persecution, ii. 210; summoned before the council of Geneva, ii. 310; his marriage, ii. 321; letter from Beaulieu to, ii. 373; letters from Calvin to Farel, i. 107, 131; on church property, i. 158, 160; on his controversy with Caroli, i. 162, 165; respecting the Zurichers and Zwingli, i. 171; on the general affairs of Geneva, i. 173; on the theological discussion at Ratisbon, i. 236; on the conflicts of his own spirit, i. 251, 253; on his marriage, i. 264; on the death of his wife, i. 267; on the government of the Genevese church, i. 332; his projected reformation of Metz, i. 339; his dispute with Castellio, ii. 35; with Perrin, ii. 60; respecting Servetus, ii. 195; on the persecution in France, ii. 361.
Farnese, Alexander, his acts and character, i. 480; Calvin's writings against, i. 482.
Fathers, the primitive, clemency of, i. 379.
Ferrara, the duchess of, history of, i. 9, 11; Calvin at her court, i. 102; her regard for Calvin, *ib.*; letters from Calvin to,—on her steadfastness against temptation, i. 103, 313; on faithfulness to the truth, i. 450, ii. 374, 375; letters from the duchess to Calvin, ii. 402, 404.
Festivals of the church in Geneva, ii. 115.
France, characteristics of, i. 19; first reformed congregation at Meaux, i. 15; first martyrs of the Reformation in, i. 15; synodal form of government of the church of, i. 389; spiritual libertinism in, ii. 46; opinion respecting Calvin in, ii. 106; letters from Calvin to the martyrs of, ii. 356, 359; the Reformation and persecution in, ii. 353, 354; first French religious war, ii. 396; the synod at Orleans, ii. 398.
Francis I. of France, character of, i.

48; compared with Calvin, i. 53; Beza's opinion of, i. 7; a favourer of learning, i. 12; persecutes the Protestants, i. 50; Calvin dedicates his 'Institutes' to, i. 53.
Francis II. of France, short reign and death, ii. 366, 370; persecution of the Lutherans, ii. 367.
Freedom of conscience, favourers of, ii. 242.
Free-will, doctrine of, Calvin's, i. 193, 497; remarks on, i. 214.
Funeral service, the, Calvin's view of, ii. 8.

Galiffe's life of Calvin, ii. 107.
Gallars, is sent by Calvin to London, ii. 334.
Geneva, brief history of, i. 91; rise of the Reformation in, i. 94; the authority of the papacy set aside in, i. 97; blockaded by the duke of Saxony, *ib.*; bad state of morals in, i. 99, 125, ii. 48; disturbances in, i. 127, 134, ii. 311; Calvin's letters to the Genevese in his exile, i. 145; the Genevese earnestly desire Calvin's return to, i. 246; day of public penitence in, i. 331; establishment of a court of morals in, i. 332; its dispute with the Bernese, i. 338, ii. 144; the plague breaks out in, i. 344; Calvin's position in, i. 346; theocratic constitution of, i. 351; political constitution of, i. 353; the practice of torture retained in, i. 364; the Genevese confession of faith, i. 407; the libertines in, ii. 47; French refugees in, ii. 55; Infectionists in, ii. 50; festivals of the church abolished in, ii. 115; disputes respecting discipline, ii. 315; Calvin founds a school in, ii. 321.
Gentilis, Valentin, Calvin's opinion of, ii. 266; his doctrine of the Trinity, ii. 267; tried and condemned at Geneva, ii. 267, 268; retracts his opinions, ii. 269; set at liberty, *ib.*; persecuted at Bern, ii. 270; condemned and executed, ii. 271.
Georgii, David, intercedes for Servetus, ii. 212.
Germany, the Protestant princes of, intercede with the king of France in behalf of the reformers, i. 237; influence of Calvinism on, i. 328; its religious state considered, in a letter from Calvin to Myconius, i. 337; religious war in, ii. 19; opposition to the Interim, ii. 25, 26.
Grace, Calvin's doctrine of, i. 197.
Gribaldi, Matthæus, exiled from Geneva, ii. 263; from Bern, ii. 264.
Grotius's opinion of Calvin, i. 315.
Gruet, writes against Christianity, ii. 47; he libels Calvin, ii. 64; is prosecuted and condemned to death by the state of Geneva, ii. 66.
Grynæus, Simon, a friend of Calvin's, i. 40; Calvin dedicates to him his commentary on the Epistle to the Romans, i. 218; letter from Calvin to, i. 117.
Guise, the duke of, persecutes the Protestants, ii. 396; takes Rouen by storm, ii. 400; is assassinated at Orleans, ii. 402.

Hagenau, the diet at, i. 166.
Helvetic confession, the, i. 407.
Henry VIII. of England, defends the doctrine of the seven sacraments against Luther, i. 3; is divorced from queen Catherine and declared head and defender of the church of England in the place of the Pope, i. 4; Calvin's opinion of his divorce, i. 5; of his title of head of the church, i. 39.
Henry II. of France, persecutes the Protestants, ii. 358, 362; his death, ii. 366.
Henry IV. of France, departs from the truth, i. 67; assassinated, i. 68; Calvin's dedications to the same, ii. 378.
Heresy, Calvin's explanation of, ii. 417.
Heretics, on the punishment of, ii. 240.
Hesshus, Calvin's writings against, ii. 297.

Idelette de Bures, Calvin's marriage with, i. 263; character of, *ib.*
Images, Calvin respecting the use of, i. 207.
Infectionists in Geneva, ii. 50.
Innocency of man, Calvin on the original, i. 192.
Inquisition, the, its secret proceedings in Italy, i. 10.
'Institutes,' Calvin's, their origin, i. 69; contents, i. 72; design, i. 180, 187; analysis of, i. 186; their perspicuity, i. 209; usefulness, *ib.*; preface to the last edition, i. 85; the Strasburg edition, i. 182; the translations of, i. 185; opponents of, *ib.*

Interim in Germany, ii. 25, 26; Protestants and Catholics discontented with, ii. 27; Calvin writes against, *ib.*
Italy, at the time of the Reformation, i. 6; Protestant congregations in, i. 10.

Jesus as a mediator, i. 449.
Job, the book of, Calvin's lectures on, i. 436.
Julius III., Pope, character of, ii. 108.
Justification, Calvin's doctrine of, i. 510, ii. 413; Servetus's doctrine of, ii. 245, 257; difference of the views of the reformers and Servetus respecting, ii. 260; Stancarus and Osiander respecting, ii. 273.

Knox, John, characteristics of, ii. 327; becomes a preacher at Frankfort and Geneva, ii. 328; political writings of, ii. 330; brings Calvin's discipline into Scotland, ii. 331; opposes Queen Mary, ii. 332; letter to Locke on the affairs of Geneva from, ii. 318.
Krell, Nicolaus, trial and execution of, ii. 238.
Krummacher on Calvin's character, i. 184.

Labori, letter to his wife, ii. 356.
Laski, banished with his congregation from England, ii. 277; endeavours to unite the Protestant churches, ii. 337; appointed chief superintendent of the Protestant churches in Lesser Poland, ii. 347; Calvin's opinion of, ii. 348.
Lasmanini, ii. 347, 348.
Leclerc, John, the first martyr of the Reformation, i. 15.
Lefevre d'Etaples, life and acts of, i. 13.
Legrant, letter from Calvin to, i. 467.
Libertines, spiritual, Calvin writes against, ii. 42; pantheistic doctrines of, *ib.*; in France, ii. 46; in Geneva, ii. 47; political libertines, ii. 53; their opposition to Calvin and persecution of the exiles, ii. 53, 54; trials of Ameaux, Perrin and Gruet, ii. 57, 62, 65.
Liturgy, principles of Calvin's, i. 412.
Longueville, the duke of, letter from Calvin to, i. 466.
Lord's Supper, the, Calvin's doctrine of, i. 83, 141, 176, 342, ii. 78, 79, 80, 90, 285; Calvin on the preparation for, i. 142; the agreement of Calvin and Melancthon respecting, i. 155; Calvin in reference to the controversy on, i. 178; Calvin's and Luther's different views of, i. 207; the Calvinistic form of, i. 412; Calvin on the administration of, to the sick, i. 443; on the frequency of its celebration, i. 444; on its administration under both forms to the laity, i. 477; the opinions of the reformers respecting, i. 167; precepts for the celebration of, i. 385; the doctrine of the Lord's Supper set forth in the Consensus Tigurinus, ii. 82; history of the strife respecting, ii. 14, 89; Luther's doctrine of, ii. 90; Calvin's controversy with Westphal and Hesshus on, ii. 274–292; Calvin's correspondence with Melancthon on, ii. 295; Beza at the colloquy at Poissy respecting, ii. 385.
Lorrain, cardinal of, at the colloquy at Poissy, ii. 383, 392.
Louis XII. resists the papal pretensions, i. 11; refuses to persecute the Waldenses, i. 12.
Louis XIV. opposes the Reformation, i. 68.
Loyola founds the order of the Jesuits, i. 226.
Luther, condemned by the Sorbonne as a heretic, i. 14; the rapid spread of his writings, i. 10; his doctrine of the Lord's Supper, i. 173; compared with Calvin, i. 206, ii. 89; Calvin's confidence in, i. 237; compared with Calvin in respect to his marriage, i. 263; as a married pastor, *ib.*; his disinterestedness and contempt of wealth, i. 274; in conversation, i. 280; his weakness in the struggles of the faith, i. 304; his love of nature, i. 307; his view of the works of the devil, i. 308; his fear of the plague, i. 345; on church polity, i. 397; on congregational singing, i. 415; his address to Charles V. on the triple defence of the papacy, i. 486; defended by Calvin against Pighius, i. 493; letter from Calvin to, ii. 11; his dispute with the Swiss, ii. 14; Calvin's opinion of, ii. 16, 18; Zwingli's opinion of, ii. 18; his opinion of Calvin, ii. 97; his opinions on toleration, ii. 236; his will compared with Calvin's, ii. 426.

Macaire, letter from Calvin to, i. 278.
Man, the original nature of, i. 192.
Margaret, queen of Navarre, favours the Reformation, i. 13; her life and character, *ib.*; her strife with the Sorbonne, and Calvin's judgement thereon, ii. 16, 17.
Marriage-ceremony, Calvin on the celebration of the, i. 472.
Martyr, Peter, on the intellectual state of Italy at the time of the Reformation, i. 7; takes part in the Reformation of England, ii. 28; his character, ii. 86; Calvin's opinion of, *ib.*; his opinion of Servetus, ii. 234; respecting the church at Strasburg, ii. 304; at the colloquy at Poissy, ii. 390; letter from Calvin on the union of the faithful in Christ to, ii. 125; letter to Calvin on the state of England from, ii. 313.
Martyrs, of the French church, i. 50, ii. 6, 355, 361; Calvin respecting martyrdom, i. 302; martyrs of the church of Meaux, ii. 6; of the English church, ii. 355; letters from Calvin to, ii. 356, 359, 363.
Mathesius, on the state of the German church, i. 1; on Luther at the diet of Worms, i. 233; on Luther's struggles of faith, i. 303, 304; on Luther's love of nature, i. 307.
Maurice, Prince, establishes the Calvinistic church in Holland, i. 327; protests against the Tridentine synod, ii. 111; his manifesto, ii. 113.
Meaux, persecution of the church of, ii. 5.
Melancthon, converses with Calvin at Frankfort, i. 156; Calvin's opinion of, i. 160, 240, ii. 111; forms an intimate acquaintance with Calvin at Worms, i. 234; compared with Calvin and Luther, i. 238; his representation of the church, i. 396; his view of the doctrine of predestination, i. 499; on the Consensus Tigurinus, ii. 83; his doctrine of the Lord's Supper, ii. 90; favourable to the execution of Servetus, ii. 233; his correspondence with Calvin, ii. 295; his death, ii. 296.
Menno, Simon, Calvin writes against, ii. 240.
Metz, Farel invited by the Protestants to, i. 339.
Ministers of the gospel, respect to be shown to, i. 145.
Mompelgarten, church of, i. 342.
Morals, a court of, established in Geneva, i. 332.
More, Thomas, a promoter of the Reformation, i. 4.
Morus, his opinion of Calvin, i. 294.
Motte, De la, Alciat, accused of heresy and banished from Geneva, ii. 271.
Myconius, letters to, from Calvin on discipline, i. 333; on the affairs of Germany, i. 337.

Navarre, Calvin writes to the queen of, respecting the libertines, ii. 46; the king of Navarre favours the French Reformation, ii. 362.
Nestorianism, the Calvinists accused of, i. 207.
Netherlands, the, persecution in, i. 238.
Nicodemites, the, Calvin's 'Apology' to, ii. 9.
Normandie, Laurence de, Calvin dedicates the treatise 'de Scandalis' to, ii. 118.

Ochin, Bernardin, of Sienna, Calvin's favourable opinion of, ii. 88.
Œcolampadius holds a discussion with Servetus, ii. 171.
Olivetan's French translation of the Bible, i. 227.
Original sin, Calvin's doctrine of, i. 194; Servetus's, ii. 245; comparison of the views of the Protestant and Roman theologians respecting, i. 491; views of the council of Trent respecting, i. 506; Calvin's opposition to, i. 507.
Orleans, the synod at, ii. 398.
Osiander, heresies of, ii. 273.

Papal authority, Calvin's view of, i. 473.
Parental authority earnestly defended by the reformers, i. 361.
Pareus, Nicolaus, letter from Calvin to, i. 252.
Pastoral letters, Calvin's, to persecuted christians, i. 451, 453, 455, 467; to a waverer, i. 454; to an ill-disciplined community, i. 457; to an exile, i. 461; to reformed congregations, i. 463, 465; to the duke of Longueville, i. 466; to Legrant, i. 467; to the brethren at Aix, i. 471.
Paul III., character of, i. 480; his admonition to Charles V., *ib.*; Calvin's answer, i. 481; his death, ii. 108.

Pelagianism of the Romish church, i. 489.
Perrini, Ami, head of the libertines in Geneva, ii. 60; Calvin's friendship for, and subsequent disputes with, ii. 62; their reconciliation, ii. 63.
Persecution in France, i. 15, 238, ii. 353; in England, i. 238, ii. 355; in the Netherlands, i. 238; Calvin on the lawfulness of forcibly resisting, i. 471.
Philosophy, Servetus on, ii. 246.
Pighius, a defender of the Romish church, i. 89; Calvin's writings against, i. 492, ii. 95; letters from Calvin to, i. 138, 143.
Plague, the, in Geneva, i. 343; Calvin and Luther compared in respect to their fear of, i. 345.
Planck, his opinion of Calvin, i. 168; on the Consensus Tigurinus, ii. 181.
Poetry, in relation to the Reformation, i. 416.
Poissy, the colloquy at, ii. 380, 384; its results, ii. 392.
Poland, the Reformation in, ii. 341; Calvin in respect to, ii. 342; Calvin's letters to the Poles, *ib.*
Predestination, Calvin's doctrine of, i. 193, 203, ii. 94; Zwingli's doctrine of, i. 209; the controversy on, ii. 133; the Bernese theologians respecting, ii. 134; Calvin's dispute with Castellio respecting, ii. 156; Beza writes against Castellio in defence of, ii. 156; Wesley's opposition to the doctrine of, ii. 158.
Presbyters, Calvin respecting, i. 371.
Protestant church, the, accused by the Roman Catholics on account of the execution of Servetus, ii. 227.
Psalms, the, translations of, i. 414; old French version of, i. 415.
Psychopannychia, or, the sleep of the soul, Calvin's, i. 39; review of, and extracts from, i. 42.
Public worship, Calvin on attendance at, i. 445.
Purgatory, Calvin's doctrine of, i. 511; Servetus's notion of, ii. 261.

Ratisbon, the diet of, i. 231; inutility of, i. 236.
Redemption, Servetus on, ii. 245.
Reformation, the, first public acknowledgment of, in Geneva, i. 113; the development of art and poetry affected by, i. 416.
Reformed churches, the, desire that Servetus should be punished, ii. 213; intolerance of, ii. 237; the Calvinistic compared with the Lutheran, i. 222.
Reformers, the, unimaginativeness of, i. 306; their imperfect resignation, i. 307; extreme severity of, i. 360; their love of simplicity, i. 375; general review of the European, ii. 87.
Regeneration by baptism, Calvin's doctrine of, i. 507.
Relics, Calvin's work against, ii. 37.
Renata, *vide* Ferrara.
Richebourg, Louis, death of, i. 242; letter of condolence from Calvin to his father, *ib.*
Rivière, De la, founds a Protestant church in Paris, ii. 357.

Sacrament, *vide* Lord's Supper.
Sadolet, his character as a Catholic, i. 147; his address to the Genevese, *ib.*; Calvin's answer to, i. 148.
Saints, the worship of, i. 419.
Salvation, Calvin's doctrine of, i. 197.
Satan, Calvin respecting, i. 192.
Schools established by the reformers, i. 335.
Scriptures, the, internal evidence of their truth, i. 188; Calvin's idea of their inspiration, *ib.*; Calvin's perfect reliance on, i. 210; various expositors of, i. 219; Calvin's exposition of, i. 221.
Sermons, style of Calvin's, i. 433.
Servetus, his first conference with Calvin, i. 38; his doctrine of the Trinity, i. 190; wishes to form a league with Calvin, ii. 75; compared with Calvin, ii. 161; Mosheim's opinion of, ii. 164; his history, ii. 165; progress of his religious opinions, ii. 167; writes respecting the Trinity, ii. 169; Zwingli's opinion of, ii. 170; visits Basel, ii. 171; retracts his doctrine at that place, ii. 172; resides in France and Italy, ii. 173; favourable reception of his doctrines at Venice, *ib.*; his great talents, ii. 174; lectures at Paris, *ib.*; respecting the Holy Scriptures, ii. 176; his doctrine of justification by faith, ii. 178; his love of controversy, *ib.*; his correspondence with Calvin, ii. 179; his publications at Vienne, ii. 184; denounced by William Trie, *ib.*; summoned before the tribunal at Vienne, ii.

186; his trial, ii. 188; escapes from Vienne, ii. 190; condemned in his absence by the civil and ecclesiastical magistrates, ii. 191; resides at Geneva, ii. 192; arrested at that place, *ib.*; his trial, ii. 194; disputes with Calvin whilst a prisoner, ii. 199; appeals to an ecclesiastical tribunal, ii. 202; violence of his conduct, ii. 210; severity of the churches respecting, ii. 213; his liberality of opinion, ii. 230; condemned to death, ii. 215; his reception of his sentence, ii. 217; his last hours, *ib.*; becomes reconciled to Calvin, ii. 218; his character, ii. 229; as a theologian:—on faith, ii. 245, 247; on the Trinity, ii. 245–248; redemption and justification, ii. 257; original sin, *ib.*; infant baptism, ii. 246; rejects all the commonly received views of christianity, *ib.*; as a philosopher, *ib.*; on the omniscience of God, ii. 247; his favourable opinion of Irenæus, ii. 249; his doctrine of the Trinity Tritheism, *ib.*; respecting the creation of the universe, ii. 250; his platonic idea of God, ii. 251; his natural theology, ii. 253; superiority to Spinoza, *ib.*; on the fall of man, ii. 254; respecting Christ's humanity, *ib.*; on Christ's eternity, ii. 256; on the doctrine of the Holy Ghost, *ib.*; on free-will, ii. 258; his view of the means of grace, ii. 260; on the future state, ii. 261; his character in respect to his religious doctrines, ii. 262.

Siculus, George, Calvin's dispute with, ii. 128.

Sigismund, king of Poland, Calvin proposes a form of church government to, i. 401; dedicates his commentary on the Hebrews to, ii. 31.

Sin, *vide* Original sin.

Singing, Calvin's view of congregational, i. 414.

Smalclade, league of, ii. 20.

Socinus, Lælius, Calvin's opinion of, ii. 88; creates a disturbance amongst the reformed, ii. 349; recommended by Calvin to the Poles, *ib.*

Somerset, the duke of, letter from Calvin on church government to, i. 402; on written sermons, i. 434; on the fanatics in England, ii. 29.

Sorbonne, the, history of, i. 479; Calvin writes against, i. 477.

Soul, Calvin respecting the human, i. 193.

Spifame, Jac. de, sent to the diet at Frankfort by the Protestants, ii. 400.

Spina, Johannes von, a friend of Calvin's, i. 314.

Stancarus, Francis, life and heresies of, ii. 272.

State, the, union of the church with, i. 350.

Swiss, the, Luther's controversy with, ii. 14; disunion of the Swiss churches, ii. 145.

Synods, Calvin's opinion of, i. 366; office and authority of, i. 392.

Tauler on poverty in a christian's life, i. 269.

Theatres, Calvin's opinion of, i. 473.

Theocracy, i. 348; Calvin's idea of, i. 349; theocratic constitution of Geneva, i. 351; the theocratic ideal, i. 365.

Tholuck on Calvin's exegetical talent, i. 223.

Thourel, false judgement on Calvin by, i. 299.

Tournon, Cardinal, at the colloquy of Poissy, ii. 385.

Tradition, Calvin on scripture, ii. 412.

Transubstantiation, opinions of the reformers on, i. 236.

Trechsel's opinion of Calvin, ii. 107.

Trent, the council of, i. 300; history of, i. 501; Calvin's work against, *ib.*; the divines of Zurich refuse to attend, ii. 109; Calvin's opinion of, *ib.*

Tribunal, church, the Saxon divines on, i. 398.

Trie, William, denounces Servetus at Vienne, ii. 184, 187.

Trinity, Calvin's doctrine of, i. 189; Servetus's doctrine of, i. 190, ii. 169, 245, 248; Gentilis's doctrine of, ii. 267.

Troillet, one of Calvin's adversaries, i. 288, ii. 138; Calvin's discussion with, ii. 138; their reconciliation, ii. 139.

Unity in the church, ii. 123; Calvin's anxiety to establish, ii. 124, 126; Bullinger's wish for, ii. 125.

Vergerio, his activity in Poland, ii. 348.

Vico, Marquis of, Caraccioli, life and character of, ii. 129; persecution of, ii. 130.

Vincentius of Paula, character of, i. 420; compared with Calvin, i. 421; founds the order of the Sisters of Mercy and the House of Lazarus, i. 421.

Viret, Peter, life and character of, i. 109; Calvin respecting the marriage of, i. 261; Calvin's friendship for, ii. 74; letters from Calvin to:—in his banishment, i. 130; on his wife's sickness, i. 265; her death, i. 266; the state of the Genevese church, i. 335; respecting the plague, i. 345; his discipline, ii. 61; opinion of Servetus, ii. 76; of the Consensus Tigurinus, ii. 82.

Virgin Mary, the, worship of, i. 419.

Visitation of the sick, Calvin's view of, i. 442.

Waldenses in Provence and Piedmont; Calvin's opinion of, ii. 1; persecution of, ii. 3; Calvin assists and intercedes for, ii. 4; take up arms in their own defence, ii. 371.

Welsius, Justus, disputes with Calvin on free-will, ii. 338.

Wesley on confession, i. 417; on convents, i. 421.

Westphal, Calvin's controversy with, i. 290, ii. 275; Calvin's work against, ii. 280; his answer to the same, ii. 283; his doctrine of the sacrament, ii. 286.

Witchcraft, i. 308; punishment of, in Geneva, i. 363.

Wolmar, Calvin dedicates his commentary on the second Epistle to the Corinthians to, ii. 32.

Works, Calvin's doctrine respecting, i. 199.

Worms, the diet of, i. 230; theological disputes at, i. 235; unfortunate issue of, ii. 301.

Zurichers, the, urge Calvin to return to Geneva, i. 253.

Zwingli, life and character of, i. 87; his doctrine of the Lord's Supper, i. 167; Calvin's opinion of, i. 172, 208; compared with Calvin, i. 208, 369, ii. 90; his doctrine of predestination, i. 209; his sketch of church polity, i. 368; his opinion of Luther, ii. 18; compared with Luther, ii. 90; his opinion of Servetus, ii. 170.

THE END.

www.ingramcontent.com/pod-product-compliance
Lightning Source LLC
LaVergne TN
LVHW020518100826
845148LV00010B/1269
* 9 7 9 8 3 8 5 2 6 5 1 8 3 *